ADO 2.6
Programmer's Reference

David Sussman

Wrox Press Ltd.

About the Author

David Sussman is a developer, trainer and author, living in a quiet country village in Oxfordshire, surrounded by nothing but fields and trees. One day soon he intends to stop working so hard and get some form of social life.

ADO 2.6 Programmers Reference

Published by Wrox Press Ltd
Arden House, 1102 Warwick Road, Acock's Green, Birmingham B27 6BH, UK
Printed in USA
ISBN 1-861002-68-8

Trademark Acknowledgements

Wrox has endeavored to provide trademark information about all the companies and products mentioned in this book by the appropriate use of capitals. However, Wrox cannot guarantee the accuracy of this information.

Credits

Author
David Sussman

Category Manager
Dominic Lowe

Technical Architect
Adrian Young

Technical Editors
Paul Jeffcoat
Adrian Young

Project Administrator
Jake Manning

Index
Andrew Criddle
Martin Brooks

Cover
Shelley Frazier

Proof Readers
Chris Smith
Diana Skeldon

Technical Reviewers
Clive Browning
Robert Chang
James Conard
Mark Horner
Ron Landers
Kenneth Lo
Carl Prothman
Simon Robinson
John Timney
Khin Walker
Warren Wiltsie

Production Manager
Laurent Lafon

Production Coordinator
Mark Burdett

Design/Layout
Tom Bartlett
Mark Burdett
Laurent Lafon
Pippa Wonson

Illustrations
Shabnam Hussain

I thank God I am as honest as any man
living that is an old man and no honester th

Can counsel and speak comfort to the
which they themselves not feel

Much Ado About Nothing.

He wears his faith but as the fashion of

As merry as the day

He hath indeed better bettered expectation

(Act i. Sc. i.)

He wears his faith but as the fashion of his hat.
(Ibid)

As merry as the day is long.

th indeed better bettered expectation

(Act i. Sc. i.)

(Ibid)

Can counsel and speak comfort to that grief

Which they themselves not feel.

Much Ado About Nothing.

He wears his faith but as the fashion of his hat.
(Ibid)

(Ibid)

I was not born under

a rhyming planet

I was not born under a rhyming plan
sc.

For there was never yet
That could endure the t

merry as the day is long

Can counsel and speak comfort to that grie

Which they themselves not feel.

(Ibid)

He hath indeed better bettered expectation

I thank God I am as honest as any

living that is an old man and no hones

He wears his faith but as the fashion of his h

Much Ado About Nothing.

For there was never yet philospher
That could endure the toothache patiently.

(Ibid)

For there was never yet philospher
That could endure the toothache patiently.

I was not born u

Table of Contents

Table of Contents

Table of Contents

Table of Contents

Table of Contents

Table of Contents

Table of Contents

Table of Contents

Table of Contents

Table of Contents

I thank God I am as honest as any man

living that is an old man and no honester th

Can counsel and speak comfort to the

Much Ado About Nothing.

Which they themselves not feel

He wears his faith but as the fashion of

As merry as the day

He hath indeed better bettered expectation

(Act i. Sc. 1.).

He wears his faith but as the fashion of his hat.

(Ibid)

As merry as the day is long.

ch indeed better bettered expectation

(Act i. Sc. 1.).

(Ibid)

Can counsel and speak comfort to that grief

Much Ado About Nothing.

Which they themselves not feel.

He wears his faith but as the fashion of his hat.

(Ibid)

(Ibid)

I was not born under

I was not born under a rhyming plar

(sc.

For there was never yet

That could endure the t

a rhyming plane

merry as the day is long (sc. 2)

Can counsel and speak comfort to that grief

(Ibid)

Which they themselves not feel.

He hath indeed better bettered expectation

(Ibid)

I thank God I am as honest as any

living that is an old man and no hones

He wears his faith but as the fashion of his h

Much Ado About Nothing.   For there was never yet philospher

That could endure the toothache patiently.

(Ibid)

For there was never yet philospher

That could endure the toothache patiently.

Introduction

This book provides a comprehensive guide to the ways in which ADO 2.6 can be used in all kinds of applications. It demonstrates the use of ADO both in web applications written using ASP, and in compiled applications written using Visual Basic and other languages. It also includes a reference section for fast access to detailed lists of the properties, methods, and events available in ADO.

What Is ADO?

If you are new to data access programming with Microsoft technologies, you may not yet be aware of ADO, although it's hard not to have come across it if you've had anything at all to do with ASP programming. ADO stands for **ActiveX Data Objects** (although it's sometimes – mistakenly – called **Active Data Objects**).

ADO is a set of COM components that provide programmatic access to Microsoft's latest underlying data access technologies. You can use ADO through almost any programming or scripting language, as long as it can instantiate and use COM components.

ADO is based on an underlying data access technology called **OLE DB**. This is a defined set of COM interfaces that all data sources can implement through special drivers (or **providers**), and thereby expose their data content in a uniform way. OLE DB relies on a COM Interface (API), which is designed for use with languages like C++. ADO abstracts developers from the complex details of the OLE DB interfaces by providing a simplified set of COM-based components and interfaces that can be called from a far wider range of languages.

In other words, ADO gives us a standard way of managing data from all kinds of data stores, not just relational databases. In Chapter 1, we'll expand on these concepts to show you just how useful this whole approach is when building data access applications.

The design of ADO has also been driven by the ever-increasing role and importance of the Internet in application development. ADO provides a range of techniques with which remote data access can be achieved over the Internet, using a web browser or through custom applications written in a range of programming languages.

What Is This Book About?

This book covers the broad outlines and purpose of ADO as the Microsoft data access technology of the future. It also describes the new features that are included in ADO versions 2.5 and 2.6.

It covers advanced ADO topics, and acts as a vital reference on syntax and semantics for working with ADO. It also describes the ADO Extensions for Data Definition and Security (ADOX), as well as introducing ADO for Multi-Dimensional (OLAP) data and the Jet and Replication Objects.

In addition, this book explains how ADO fits into **Windows Distributed interNet Architecture** (DNA) – Microsoft's picture for distributed data-oriented applications – and describes the advantages of ADO over other existing Microsoft data access technologies.

Finally, it shows how ADO interfaces with the core OLE DB data access driver model to provide connectivity with a wide range of data stores. This can include messaging systems, text files, and specific non-standard data formats, as well as the more usual relational databases. In fact, anything can be considered a data store if there is an OLE DB Provider for it.

Who Is This Book For?

This book is a reference guide for the ADO programmer; it's primarily aimed at demonstrating and explaining the features of ADO 2.6 and the ways that they can be used. As such, it isn't a beginner's guide – though if you have programmed any data-access applications in the past, you'll be able to use it to get up-to-speed with ADO.

In particular, the book is aimed at application developers who already use Microsoft's data access methods in their applications, but want to take full advantage of the new features of ADO 2.5 and 2.6. It includes all the information required for any reasonably experienced developer to start using ADO within their web pages and distributed applications. Finally, it is ideal for existing ADO users, to bring them quickly up-to-date with version 2.6.

What Does It Cover?

In this book, we've avoided discussion of ASP and data handling programming in COM components – with the exception of the techniques directly connected with using ADO. As a result, the code examples are concise, and designed to demonstrate ADO techniques rather than to build entire applications. However, we do provide pointers to other sources of information to indicate the kind of things that can be achieved.

The book offers users an easy-to-follow tutorial and reference to ADO, by splitting the whole topic into neat and intuitive segments. This also makes it easier to find specific information later as you come to use ADO in real-world applications. To help out, a comprehensive quick reference section is also included. It lists the properties, methods and events of each of the objects found in ADO, ADOX, RDS, JRO, and ADOMB, together with other useful information.

The segmentation of the book looks like this:

❑ Introduction to ADO, and what's new in ADO 2.5 and 2.6

❑ Connecting to data stores, with or without the Connection object (including a discussion of driver technologies)

❑ The Command object, and techniques for executing queries against a data store

❑ Using the Recordset object to control recordsets and cursors, and how they are used to retrieve data from a data store

❑ A review of the Record and Stream objects introduced in ADO 2.5

❑ Collections of objects – including the Fields and Errors collections

❑ Remote data access, showing how ADO can be used in web-based and distributed applications

❑ Using ADOX for data definition and security

❑ Using ADOMD for multi-dimensional representation of data

❑ Using JRO for compaction, replication, and refreshing of data

❑ Data shaping, events, and offline usage

❑ Examination of ADO performance, comparing cursor and locking types

What Do I Need To Use This Book?

ADO has been available for some time, and it is installed with a whole range of other applications and development environments. The shipping of ADO has followed this path:

Version	Released with
1.5	Windows NT 4.0 Option Pack and IE 4.01
2.0	Visual Studio 6.0 Windows NT 4.0 Service Pack 4 (full install) Microsoft Data Access Components 2.0 (MDAC 2.0)
2.1	Office 2000 MDAC 2.1 SQL Server 7
2.5	Windows 2000 (all versions) MDAC 2.5
2.6	SQL Server 2000 MDAC 2.6

In the meantime, if you don't have version 2.6 of ADO, you can download it from the Microsoft Data Access site, at http://www.microsoft.com/data/. The Microsoft Data Access Components (MDAC) contains all of the components required for a particular version.

We provide the source code for the samples that you'll see in this book on our web site, and you can even run some of them directly from there – to save you the trouble of installing them on your own machine. You can get the code samples from the Support page of the Wrox Press web site, at http://www.wrox.com. This site also contains a range of other resources and reference material that you might find useful, including other books that demonstrate ADO applications.

To run the samples yourself, and build applications that use ADO 2.6, you will only require your usual preferred development tools – you should check your development tool for its compatibility with ADO 2.6. To build web-based or Intranet-based applications that use ASP, this will be just a web server that supports ASP 3.0, which means Windows 2000. For the remote data access examples in Chapter 9, the browser should be Internet Explorer 4.x or higher.

To build compiled applications that don't use the Internet or your own intranet, but rely on communication over a traditional LAN, you'll need just your own choice of programming language development tool. This will also be required if you want to build custom business components for Internet- or intranet-based applications.

Which Programming Language Do I Use?

Because ADO is COM based, it is language-neutral – in other words, it can be used in any programming language that supports the instantiation of ActiveX/COM objects. This includes Visual Basic, C++, Delphi, Java, and scripting languages such as JavaScript, JScript, and VBScript – as used in client-side browser and server-side ASP programming.

As such, we've provided some guidance as to how the ADO objects can be accessed in various languages in Chapter 1. We then use a Visual Basic-like syntax for each part of the ADO object model. We decided against including samples in each language because this really breaks up the flow of text. However, we've put together a package of samples that demonstrate ADO usage in a number of languages: Visual Basic, ASP/VBScript, ASP/JScript, and Visual C++. You'll find these samples, and supporting documentation, on our web site at http://www.wrox.com.

Conventions

We have used a number of different styles of text and layout in the book to help differentiate between the different kinds of information. Here are examples of the styles we use and an explanation of what they mean:

Bullets appear indented, with each new bullet marked as follows:

❑ **Important Words** are in a bold type font

❑ Words that appear on the screen in menus like the File or Window menus are in a similar font to the one that you see on screen

❑ Keys that you press on the keyboard, like *Ctrl* and *Enter*, are in italics

Code has several fonts. If it's a word that we're talking about in the text, for example, when discussing the For...Next loop, it's in this font. If it's a block of code that you can type in as a program and run, then it's also in a gray box:

```
objRec.Open "authors", objConn, adOpenKeyset, adLockOptimistic, _
            (adCmdTable OR adAsyncFetch)
```

Sometimes you'll see code in a mixture of styles, like this:

```
<OBJECT CLASSID="clsid:BD96C556-65A3-11D0-983A-00C04FC29E33"
        ID="dsoBookList" HEIGHT=0 WIDTH=0>
    <PARAM NAME="Server" VALUE="http://www.yourserver.com">
    <PARAM NAME="Connect" VALUE="SERVER="http://dataserver.com;
        DRIVER={SQL Server};DATABASE=yourdb;UID=anon;PWD=">
    <PARAM NAME="SQL" VALUE="SELECT * FROM BookList">
</OBJECT>
```

The code with a white background is code we've already looked at and that we don't wish to examine further.

Advice, hints, and background information come in an italicized, indented font like this.

> **Important pieces of information come in boxes like this.**

We demonstrate the syntactical usage of methods, properties (and so on) using the following format:

```
Recordset.Find(Criteria, [SkipRecords], [SearchDirection], [Start])
```

Here, the square braces indicate optional parameters.

Customer Support

We've tried to make this book as accurate and useful as possible, but what really matters is what the book actually does for you. Please let us know your views, either by returning the reply card at the back of the book, or by writing to us at feedback@wrox.com.

The **source code** for this book – including ADO samples in C++, Visual Basic, and scripting languages – is available for download at http://www.wrox.com.

We've made every effort to ensure there are no errors in this book. However, to err is human, and we recognize the need to keep you informed of errors as they're spotted and corrected. **Errata sheets** are available for all our books, at http://www.wrox.com. If you find an error that hasn't already been reported, please let us know. Appendix Q gives more information about how to submit errata.

Our web site acts as a focus for other information and support, including the code from all our books, sample chapters and previews of forthcoming titles.

I thank God I am as honest as any man living that is an old man and no honester than

Much Ado About Noihing.

Can counsel and speak comfort to the Which they themselves not feel

He wears his faith but as the fashion of

As merry as the day

He hath indeed better bettered expectation

(Act i. Sc. i.).

He wears his faith but as the fashion of his hat.
(Ibid)

As merry as the day is long.

th indeed better bettered expectation

(Act i. Sc. i.). (Ibid)

Much Ado About Nothing.

Can counsel and speak comfort to that grief
Which they themselves not feel.

He wears his faith but as the fashion of his hat.
(Ibid)

I was not born under

a rhyming plane

I was not born under a rhyming plan
(Sc.

For there was never yet
That could endure the

merry as the day is long (Sc. 2)

Can counsel and speak comfort to that grief

Which they themselves not feel.

(Ibid)

(Ibid)

He hath indeed better bettered expectation

I thank God I am as honest as any

(Act i. Sc. i.

living that is an old man and no hones

He wears his faith but as the fashion of his
(Ib

Much Ado About Nothing.

For there was never yet philospher
That could endure the toothache patiently.

(Ibid)

For there was never yet philospher
That could endure the toothache patiently.

I was not born u

1

What Is ADO?

ActiveX Data Objects (ADO) and OLE DB, its underlying technology, are going to play a big part in the future of data access. Microsoft has unequivocally committed its future to it, and quite rightly so. The paperless office has yet to appear, but the amount of data being stored on computer systems is increasing every day. This is shown quite clearly in the rate at which the Web is expanding – and that's just the public face of data. There's much more data that is hidden from general view, in corporate applications or intranets.

In this chapter we are going to look at the terms and technology behind ADO. If you need to start coding straight away then you could skip to the relevant chapters, but, like any form of learning, your understanding will be better if you have a good foundation.

So, to give you that good foundation, there are several important topics we will discuss in this chapter:

❑   What we mean by 'data'

❑   What we mean by a 'data store'

❑   How ADO fits with existing data access strategies

❑   Data access in the client-server world

ADO is central to Microsoft's data access strategy, so it's important to understand why it came about and what sort of a future it has. We'll be looking at these issues too.

What is Data?

If you've got a few spare minutes sometime, open up Windows Explorer and have a look around your hard drive. Make a mental note of how many separate pieces of information you've got: databases, documents, spreadsheets, e-mail messages, HTML and ASP documents, etc. Quite a lot, eh? They are all pockets of data, albeit stored in different forms. This might seem obvious, but traditionally data has really only been thought of as being stored in a database: to build a business application the data had to be in a database. While a large proportion of existing data may be contained in databases, why should the remaining data be excluded from our grasp? In fact, as computers get more powerful, the term 'data' is starting to include multimedia items such as music and video, as well as objects, and the more normal document-based data.

So, by 'data' we mean any piece of information whatever its contents. Whether it's your address book, your monthly expenses spreadsheet, or a pleading letter to the taxman, it's all data.

What are Data Stores?

Now we've established what we consider data to be, the definition of a Data Store might be fairly obvious – it's a place in which data is kept. However, there is much more to Data Stores than you might think. Instead of looking at your hard disk, let's look at mine this time, and see what I've got installed:

❑ **Databases**: We consider these the traditional store of data – I've got both SQL Server and Access databases, which I use to store everything from accounts and invoicing to sample databases for books.

❑ **Spreadsheets**: Financial data with year end figures for my tax returns and bills.

❑ **Mail and News**: I use Outlook and Outlook Express to handle my mail and Internet news.

❑ **Documents**: This is the largest proportion of data on my machine, containing all of my personal letters and documents, and chapters for books (including this one).

❑ **Graphics**: Screen dumps and pictures for books.

❑ **Internet**: HTML and ASP pages, containing samples and applications.

❑ **Reference Material**: Including MSDN and encyclopedias.

So that's the actual data, but how is it stored? Well, the databases are self-contained, so they are their own data store. The reference material is, by and large, stored in its own format, so that could also be considered a data store. The mail and news hold data on their own as well, so they are a data store. Everything else is stored as files – therefore the file system itself becomes a data store (OK, the data it stores is in a myriad of formats, but it's all stored in the same way – folders and documents).

You could even include my CD-ROM drive and tape backup unit. The CD-ROM uses the standard documents and folders format, so this could be considered part of the file system data store, but the tape backup has its own format, and could therefore be considered a data store too.

There are numerous other data stores, from mainframe file systems to databases and mail. As the enterprise gets bigger we also need to include user account databases, and other machines attached to the network, such as printers and scanners. They might not all be data stores themselves, but as items of data they'll be contained in a data store somewhere.

About Universal Data Access

Universal Data Access (UDA) is Microsoft's strategy for dealing with all of this data. It's aimed at providing high-performance access to a variety of data stores. The cynical amongst you might suspect this to be an attempt to shoehorn another Microsoft technology into the scene – but let's look at the modern business.

To be a successful business you have to be flexible, to adapt to change. How do you know when to change? There's no simple rule here, but most companies make decisions by asking a few questions. How much can we sell? How much *are* we selling? How much are our competitors selling? What's the profit margin? What does research show about what customers want? Questions like these can be answered using statistical analysis, but where do the statistics come from? That's right, data. But we've already seen that data is stored in many different ways, and there is no central way of accessing it all.

So with UDA we are looking at an easy-to-use methodology that allows access to multiple sources of data in a single way. Build in high performance and support for existing data access methods, and you're on your way to something that could make a real difference. It's important to remember that Universal Data Access is simply Microsoft's *strategy* for accessing data, not a technology. UDA is physically implemented as a collection of four technologies: ADO, OLE DB, RDS, and ODBC. Collectively these four technologies are known as the Microsoft Data Access Components (MDAC). This means that you don't have to bundle all of your data together into a single data store. Let's have a look at how this could work.

When building an application you can make sure it uses ADO for its data access, and ADO will talk to all of the data sources required. This means that programming is made easier, since only one programming syntax needs to be learned. Because ADO gives fast, transparent access to different types of data, there's no reason to use any other method.

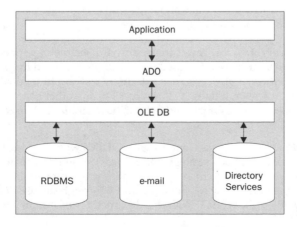

You can clearly see what Microsoft is intending when you look at the three main design goals for the Data Access Components:

❑ Meeting the key customer requirements, such as performance, reliability and broad industry support

❑ Giving access to the widest range of data sources, through a common interface

❑ Providing an easy migration path for existing data access technologies

So far they seem to be meeting these objectives admirably.

This method contrasts with Oracle who, naturally, are pushing Universal Server, in which all of the data will be stored under one central (proprietary) data store. The ultimate aim is the same – broader access to data. The Oracle approach involves a bigger initial investment in data conversion and translation as the data is imported to the store. But once that investment has been made, the data will be easy to access. Of course, ADO can be used to access Oracle databases.

In terms of superiority, it's difficult to choose between the two methods – the best method for you will be dependent upon your business needs and current computer systems. Bear in mind though, the following points:

❑ With UDA you can write code today to access most major data stores and develop your own OLE DB Provider to access those data stores that don't already provide support for UDA technologies.

❑ Data conversion is very costly and error prone. Additionally, it rarely results in a fully integrated solution – something much needed for the businesses of today to become the e-businesses of tomorrow.

❑ New data types and data stores are emerging all the time. Instead of waiting on Oracle or other vendors to write data migration tools, why not write data access code to retrieve and manipulate the data in its native data store and in its native format.

Existing Technologies

Before we explain why ADO came about, let's take a quick look at some existing technologies and see how they fit into the picture.

❑ **DB-Library (DBLib):** This is the underlying technology for connecting to SQL Server. It is primarily designed for C, but is often used in Visual Basic. Because it is specific to SQL Server, it is extremely fast and functional. For this very reason, however, it doesn't allow access to any other source of data. Other databases, such as Oracle and Sybase, have similar native communication libraries.

❑ **ODBC:** Open DataBase Connectivity (ODBC) was the first step on the road to a universal data access strategy. ODBC was designed (by Microsoft and other DBMS vendors) as a cross-platform, database-independent method for accessing data in any relational database through the use of an API, known as the ODBC API. While ODBC was designed for multi-database use, it is often only used on single, relational databases and, from a programmer's point of view, ODBC, like DBLib, is also complex to use because it was a low-level library. ODBC is also restricted to data sources that support SQL, and is therefore not suitable for non-SQL based data stores, although there are ODBC Drivers to allow access to text files.

❑   **DAO:** The Data Access Objects (DAO) were introduced with Microsoft Access, and provided a strictly hierarchical set of objects for manipulating data in Jet and other ISAM and SQL databases. These objects were first available with Visual Basic 3.0 and quickly became the most commonly used data access method for early Visual Basic programs. DAO also had the advantage of being able to sit on top of ODBC – this allowed it to communicate with many different databases.

❑   **RDO:** Aimed as the successor to DAO for Visual Basic programmers, Remote Data Objects (RDO) is a thin layer that sits on top ODBC, allowing better access to server databases, such as SQL Server. This brought the flexibility of ODBC with a much easier programming model than DBLib or the ODBC API, but like DAO it has a strictly hierarchical programming model. RDO also brought the world of remote database servers to the world of many programmers. RDO and ODBC share the same relationship as ADO and OLE DB – a thin layer on top of an underlying data access mechanism.

❑   **ODBCDirect:** An extension to DAO, ODBCDirect combined portions of DAO and RDO. It allows programmers to use the DAO programming model, and also allows access to ODBC data sources without having the Jet database engine loaded.

❑   **JDBC:** Java Database Connectivity (JDBC) was designed as another DBMS-neutral API, especially for use in Java applications.

The problems with these technologies are very simple. DBLib and ODBC are low-level APIs and therefore, for many programmers, are complex to use. DAO and RDO offer the user another interface to ODBC, but this introduces another layer of code to go through and performance can drop. Moreover, all of these technologies suffer from a very strict and hierarchical model, which adds extra overhead to both programming and execution.

They are also more or less constrained to providing access to relational databases, although Microsoft Excel and simple text documents could also be used as data sources when using ODBC. ODBC drivers have also been produced for object oriented and hierarchical databases, exposing the data in a relational form with rows and columns.

What is OLE DB?

OLE DB is designed to be the successor to ODBC. You might be asking, why do we need a successor? Well, there are three main trends at the moment. The first, fairly obviously, is the Internet. The second is an increasing amount of data being stored in a non-relational form, such as Exchange Server and file systems. The third is Microsoft's desire for a COM world, where all object usage is handled through their Component Object Model. In fact OLE DB encourages the use of componentization, allowing database functionality and data handling to be encapsulated into components.

The Internet brings a different aspect to standard data access because of its distributed nature. Applications are now being written on a truly global scale, and you can no longer guarantee that the data you are accessing is stored on your local network. This means that you need to give careful consideration to the *way* you access data, as well as the *type* of data you access. The new business opportunity of e-commerce has meant that selling becomes a whole new ball game – you can now have an application that shows pictures of your products, plays music, and even videos, all running over the Web. The Web is also more distributed (and often less reliable) than conventional networks, so your data access method has to take this into account. You can't, for example, assume that your client and server remain connected at all times during an application – in the stateless nature of the Web, this doesn't make sense.

OLE DB is a technology designed to solve some of these problems, and over time it will gradually replace ODBC as the central data access method. Even so, new versions of ODBC are supplied with ADO 2.6, and ODBC will continue to be developed and supported. OLE DB is the guts of the new data access strategy, but since it allows access to existing ODBC Data Sources, OLE DB provides an easy migration path.

Why ADO?

OLE DB is a COM-based set of object-oriented interfaces, and thus for a large proportion of the programming community it is too complex to use, or is not suitable because they use programming languages don't have access to custom COM interfaces. For example, C++ is required to access OLE DB directly because of the complexity of the OLE DB interface. ADO is the higher-level model that most people will use, because it allows access from dual-interface COM components that can be accessed from Visual Basic and scripting languages. It equates fairly well to the DAO level, where you create an object, and call its methods and properties. Being a COM component means it can be used from any language that supports COM – for example Visual Basic, VBA, scripting languages, and Visual C++.

So now our diagram looks even more enticing:

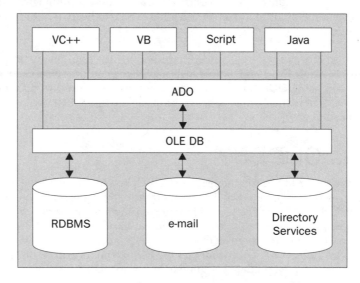

We have various languages, all with the ability to use a central data access strategy. Some languages (like Java and Visual C++) can talk directly to OLE DB, as well as talking to the easier ADO – although we'll only be looking at the ADO layer here.

ADO also improves speed and ease of development by providing an **object model** that allows data to be retrieved from a data source with as little as one line of code.

ADO addresses another pressing need, which is created by the increasing use of the Web as an application medium. Conventional applications are generally connected via a Local Area Network (LAN) to their data store. They can open a connection to the data, and keep that connection open throughout the life of the program. Consequently, the data store knows who is connecting. Many applications also process data on the client – perhaps a set of records that the user is browsing through or updating. Since the client is connected to the server, or source of the data, there's no trouble updating the data.

On the Web however, the underlying HTTP protocol is stateless. There's no permanent connection between client and server. If you think about the way the Web works for a second, you'll realize why this is a problem:

❑   You request a web page in your browser

❑   The web server receives the request, runs any server-side script, then sends the page back to you and the connection is closed

That's it. As soon as this is over the web server forgets about you. Admittedly, with ASP you can store some sort of session state, but it's not very sophisticated. How then, with this disconnected network, do you provide a system that allows data to be updated on the client and sent back to the server? This is where ADO comes in, with **disconnected recordsets**. This technology allows the recordset to be disassociated from the server, and then re-associated at a later date. Add this to the fact that you can update, insert, and delete records on the disconnected recordsets locally, and update the central set of records (the server) at a later date. In fact, disconnected recordsets don't have to be associated with a database at all – they can be manually created and used as a data store, in much the same way as collections. Manually created recordsets, however, cannot be used to update data stores.

The use of client-side data manipulation also allows you to sort data, find records, and generally manage recordsets without resorting to additional trips to the server. Although this idea primarily fits with the nature of web applications, it can work just as well for the standard type of applications running on a LAN, and can reduce network traffic.

Data Providers and Data Consumers

OLE DB introduces two new terms that help to explain how OLE DB and ADO fit together:

❑   A **Data Consumer** is something that uses (or consumes) data. Strictly speaking, ADO is actually a consumer, because it uses data provided by OLE DB.

❑ A **Data Provider** is (unsurprisingly) something that provides data. This isn't the physical source of the data, but the mechanism that connects us to the physical data store. The provider may get the data directly from the data store, or it may go through another layer (such as ODBC) to get to the data store. –

The initial set of OLE DB providers supplied with MDAC 2.6 consists of:

❑ **Jet 4.0**, for Microsoft Access databases. This allows access to standard Access databases, including linked tables. MDAC 2.0 shipped with the Jet 3.5 Provider.

❑ **Directory Services**, for stored resource data, such as Active Directory. With Windows 2000, the Directory Service allows access to user information, as well as network devices.

❑ **Index Server**, for Microsoft Index Server. This will be particularly useful as web sites grow because indexed data will be available.

❑ **Site Server Search**, for Microsoft Site Server. Again for use with web sites, especially large complex sites, where Site Server is used to maintain them.

❑ **ODBC**, for existing ODBC Drivers. This ensures that legacy data is not omitted as part of the drive forward.

❑ **Oracle**, for Oracle databases. Connecting to Oracle has never been particularly easy with Microsoft products in the past, but a native driver will simplify access to existing Oracle data stores.

❑ **SQL Server**, for Microsoft SQL Server, to allow access to data stored in SQL Server.

❑ **Data Shape**, for hierarchical recordsets. This allows creation of master/detail type recordsets, which allow drilling down into detailed data.

❑ **Persisted Recordset**, for locally saved recordsets, and recordset marshaling.

❑ **OLAP**, for accessing On Line Analytical Processing data stores.

❑ **Internet Publishing**, for accessing web resources that support Microsoft FrontPage Server Extensions or Distributed Authoring and Versioning (DAV).

❑ **Remoting Provider**, for connecting to data providers on remote machines.

This is just the list of standard providers supplied by Microsoft; other vendors are actively creating their own. For example, a company called ISG provides an OLE DB provider that allows connections to multiple data stores at the same time. Oracle provide an OLE DB provider, which it claims is better than Microsoft's Oracle provider, and most other database suppliers have OLE DB providers for their databases.

OLE DB also provides a few other services, such as a query processor and a cursor engine, so these can be used at the client. There are two reasons for this. First, it frees the actual provider from providing the service – thus the service can be smaller and faster. Second, it makes it available as a client service. This means that cursor handling can be provided locally, which is an important function of disconnected recordsets and Remote Data Services. Another advantage of the Cursor Service is that, as a client-based service, it can provide a more uniform set of features across all providers. Also, the persistence provider (MSPersist) – introduced in ADO 2.5 – has the ability to persist a recordset to a stream.

Providers and Drivers

It's important to understand how OLE DB Providers relate to ODBC Drivers, especially since there is an OLE DB Provider for ODBC, which seems somehow confusing. Take a look at the following diagram:

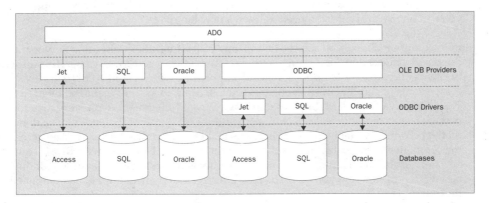

This distinctly shows the two layers. OLE DB Providers can be used to access data sources, including ODBC data sources. This allows OLE DB to access data for which there is an ODBC Driver, but no native OLE DB Provider, (such as DAV or Directory Services).

So, Providers are for OLE DB and Drivers are for ODBC.

Distributed Internet Architecture

Distributed interNet Architecture (DNA) is the strategy that Microsoft is defining as the ideal way to write distributed, n-tier, client-server applications. One of the interesting things about this strategy is that it's really just a set of ideas and suggestions, rather than a complex, locked-in solution. It's not a new idea, but there are now some really good tools that make creating this type of application relatively easy.

The basic premise is to partition your application into at least **three tiers**. The first tier is the **user interface tier** – this is what the user sees, and could be a web page or another type of application, written in any language. The second tier is where the **business rules** or processes lie – these determine where the data comes from, what rules apply to the data, and how it should be returned to the user interface. The third tier is the **data layer** – the actual source of the data:

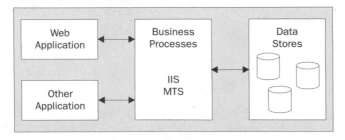

The great thing about DNA is that it aims to be language-independent, since it all hinges around COM (COM+ in Windows 2000). COM is the Component Object Model, which allows easy object creation and re-use. Any component that supports COM will fit into this picture, so you can write your application in ASP and JavaScript, Visual Basic, VC++, Delphi, or any language that supports COM. Likewise, your business components can be in any language, so you can program in whatever environment you feel happy in. There's no need to learn a new language.

In the diagram above, you can see that IIS and MTS (Internet Information Server and Microsoft Transaction Server) are mentioned in the Business Processes tier. IIS supplies the connection from web applications to components, which could be MTS components or stand-alone components (that is, components not managed by MTS). The great advantage of MTS is that it makes your middle tier suddenly very easy to manage – you can just create a component and install it into MTS. Once you've done that, it becomes available to all applications that can call components. You can access the components on remote machines using DCOM, MTS, or HTTP (with RDS). You also get the added advantage of transaction processing and easy scalability, without having to program it in yourself. The user interface can then be built in any language that supports COM.

> *If you want to learn more about MTS and its use in DNA applications, take a look at* Professional MTS MSMQ with Visual Basic and ASP *(Wrox Press, ISBN 1-861001-46-0), or* Professional Visual Basic 6 MTS Programming *(Wrox Press, ISBN 1-861002-44-0).*

ADO 2.6 Availability

The Microsoft Data Access Components (MDAC) are available as a separate download from the Microsoft web site, at http://www.microsoft.com/data. The file name is MDAC_TYPE.EXE.

If you're at all unsure of what version of ADO, or any of its components, you've got installed, then download the Component Checker from http://www.microsoft.com/data/download.htm. This utility will give you a complete list of ADO DLLs and their version numbers. You can also use the Version property of the Connection object (see Chapter 3).

New Features

ADO 2.5 and 2.6 have a host of new features that make programming easier and extend the goal of Universal Data Access. This section is not going to cover them thoroughly – we will deal with them in more detail in the later chapters – but serves to provide a summary.

ADO 2.5

The Record Object

The Record object is designed to deal with Document Source Providers – that is, those OLE DB Providers that don't access databases, but provide data from semi-structured data stores. Two examples of this are Microsoft Exchange Server 2000 and Internet Information Server 5.0. These are both sources of large amounts of data and the OLE DB Provider for Internet Publishing allows us to access both the structure of the data storage and the objects stored themselves.

The primary purpose of the Record object is to map a node in a tree-like structure of a document source. It works in conjunction with the Recordset, but is not directly applicable to relational data sources.

The Stream Object

The Stream object is a component that wraps the COM IStream interface, allowing easy access to streams of memory. This provides a way to transfer Recordsets directly to other components (such as the ASP 3.0 Request and Response objects) that support streams. The Stream is also used with Document Source Providers, to allow access to the contents of files.

ADO 2.6

Command Streams

Command streams allow a Stream object to be used as the source of a command. A good example of this is a Stream containing an XML command, to be executed against SQL Server 2000.

Results in Streams

Along with Command Streams, ADO 2.6 allows the results of a data query to be returned into a Stream object. This is particularly useful for obtaining XML data directly from SQL Server 2000.

Dialect Property

This identifies the syntax rules used by the provider when parsing strings or streams. Its main use is for XML-generated recordsets, where the dialect identifies what form of XML the recordset is stored in.

Single Row Resultsets

Because of the way ADO worked, singleton commands were always a performance hit, but ADO 2.6 has improved the performance of commands that only return a single row.

Field Status Values

The Status property of the Field object is now filled with information to help with the dreaded 'Errors Occurred' error.

SQL Variant Support for Cursor Service

Extended support for variant types has been added to the OLE DB Cursor Service.

ADOX Group and User Properties

The Properties collection has been added to the ADOX Group and User properties, to allow access to provider-specific properties.

ADO MD UniqueName support

The UniqueName property can now be used to access ADO MD objects. This means that parent collections no longer need to be populated to retrieve schema objects.

Examples

Since this is primarily a reference book, it seems sensible to give you a few documented samples of code, so that you can see what's possible and how some of the components fit together. You can use this as a sort of 'table of contents' to the rest of the book, where the various aspects are covered in more detail. A later section of this chapter goes into the language specifics in more detail, so we'll use Visual Basic here because it's easy to read and understand.

Example 1

The following section of Visual Basic code creates a connection to SQL Server, opens a recordset, and then adds some details from the recordset to a listbox:

```
' Define two object variables
' The object model is discussed in Chapter 2
Dim objConn     As ADODB.Connection
Dim objRs       As ADODB.Recordset

Set objConn = New ADODB.Connection
Set objRs  As New ADODB.Recordset

' Open a connection to the pubs database using the SQL Server OLE DB
' Provider
' Connection strings are discussed in Chapter 2
' The Connection object is discussed in Chapter 3
objConn.Open "Provider=SQLOLE DB; Data Source=Tigger; " & _
            "Initial Catalog=pubs; User Id=sa; Password="

' Open a recordset on the 'authors' table
' The Recordset is discussed in Chapter 5
   objRs.Open "authors", objConn, adOpenForwardOnly, adLockReadOnly,
            adCmdTable

' Loop while we haven't reached the end of the recordset
' The EOF property is set to True when we reach the end
While Not objRs.EOF
   ' Add the names to the listbox, using the default Fields collection
   ' The Fields collection is discussed in Chapter 6
   List1.AddItem objRs.Fields("au_fname") & " " & _
```

```
                    objRs.Fields("au_lname")
       ' Move to the next record
       objRs.MoveNext
Wend

' Close the objects
objRs.Close
objConn.Close

' Release the memory associated with the objects
Set objRs = Nothing
Set objConn = Nothing
```

Example 2

This example runs a SQL statement and doesn't expect a set of records to be returned. It also uses an ODBC Data Source Name called pubs, which has previously been set up.

```
' Define the object variable
Dim objConn      As ADODB.Connection

Set objConn = New ADODB.Connection

' Open a connection to the pubs database using the OLE DB Provider
' for ODBC
objConn.Open "DSN=pubs; UID=sa; PWD="

' Run a SQL UPDATE statement to update book prices by 10%
objConn.Execute "UPDATE titles SET price = price * 1.10" _
          , , adExecuteNoRecords + adCmdText

' Close the connection
objConn.Close

' Release the memory associated with the objects
Set objConn = Nothing
```

Example 3

This example runs a stored query in Access, passing in some parameters:

```
' Declare the object variables
' The Command object is discussed in Chapter 4
' The Parameter object is discussed in Chapter 4
Dim objConn      As ADODB.Connection
Dim objCmd       As ADODB.Command
Dim objRs        As ADODB.Recordset
Dim objParam     As ADODB.Parameter

Set objConn = New ADODB.Connection
Set objCmd = New ADODB.Command
```

```
' Open a connection to an Access pubs database,
' using the Access OLE DB provider
objConn.Open "Provider=Microsoft.Jet.OLE DB.4.0; " & _
                              "Data Source=C:\temp\pubs.mdb"

' Create a new Parameter, called RequiredState
Set objParam = objCmd.CreateParameter("RequiredState", adChar, _
                              adParamInput, 2, "CA")

' Add the Parameter to the Parameters collection of the Command object
objCmd.Parameters.Append objParam

' Set the active connection of the command to the open Connection object
Set objCmd.ActiveConnection = objConn

' Set the name of the stored query that is to be run
objCmd.CommandText = "qryAuthorsBooksByState"

' Set the type of command
objCmd.CommandType = adCmdStoredProc

' Run the stored query and set the recordset which it returns
Set objRs = objCmd.Execute

' Loop through the recordset, adding the items to a listbox
While Not objRs.EOF
    List1.AddItem objRs.Fields("au_fname") & " " & _
                  objRs.Fields("au_lname") & _
                  ": " & objRs.Fields("title")
    objRs.MoveNext
Wend

' Close the recordset and connection
objRs.Close
objConn.Close

' Reclaim the memory from the objects
Set objRs = Nothing
Set objCmd = Nothing
Set objParam = Nothing
Set objConn = Nothing
```

Example 4

This example uses the Fields collection of the recordset to loop through all of the fields in a recordset, printing out the details in the debug window:

```
' Declare the object variables
Dim objRs      As ADODB.Recordset
Dim objFld     As ADODB.Field

Set pbjRs = New ADODB.Recordset
```

```
' Open a recordset on the 'authors' table using the OLE DB Driver
' for ODBC
' without using a connection
objRs.Open "authors", "DSN=pubs", _
            adOpenForwardOnly, adLockReadOnly, adCmdTable

' Loop through the Fields collection printing the name of each Field
' The Fields collection is discussed in Chapter 6
For Each objFld In objRs.Fields
    Debug.Print objFld.Name; vbTab;
Next
Debug.Print

' Loop through the records in the recordset
While Not objRs.EOF
    ' Loop through the fields, this time printing out the Value
    ' of each field
    For Each objFld In objRs.Fields
        Debug.Print objFld.Value; vbTab;
    Next
    Debug.Print
    objRs.MoveNext
Wend

' Close the recordset and release the memory
objRs.Close
Set objRs = Nothing
Set objFld = Nothing
```

Example 5

This example is an ADOX example, and uses a Catalog and its associated Tables collection to list the tables in a data store:

```
' Declare the object variables
Dim objCat    As ADOX.Catalog
Dim objTable  As ADOX.Table
Dim strConn   As String

Set objCat = New ADOX.Catalog

' set the connection string
strConn="Provider=Microsoft.Jet.OLE DB.4.0; Data
Source=C:\temp\pubs.mdb"

' point the catalog at a data store
objCat.ActiveConnection = strConn

' loop through the tables collection
For Each objTable In objCat.Tables
    Debug.Print objTable.Name
Next

' clean up
Set objTable = Nothing
Set objCat = Nothing
```

Example 6

This example also shows ADOX, and uses a `Catalog`, its `Tables` collection, and the `Indexes` and `Columns` collections for a table, to print out a list of columns for the index:

```
Dim objCat     As ADOX.Catalog
Dim objTbl     As ADOX.Table
Dim objIdx     As ADOX.Index
Dim objCol     As ADOX.Column
Dim strConn    As String

Set objCat = New ADOX.Catalog

' set the connection string
strConn="Provider=Microsoft.Jet.OLE DB.4.0; Data
Source=C:\temp\pubs.mdb"
' point the catalog at a data store
objCat.ActiveConnection = strConn

' loop through the tables
For Each objTbl In objCat.Tables

    ' has the table got indexes
    If objTbl.Indexes.Count > 0 Then
       Debug.Print objTbl.Name

       ' loop through the indexes
       For Each objIdx In objTbl.Indexes
          Debug.Print vbTab; objIdx.Name; vbTab;
                       objIdx.PrimaryKey

          'loop through the columns in the index
          For Each objCol In objIdx.Columns
             Debug.Print vbTab; vbTab; objCol.Name
          Next
       Next
    End If
Next

' clean up
Set objCol = Nothing
Set objTbl = Nothing
Set objIdx = Nothing
Set objCat = Nothing
```

ADO in Visual Basic 6

Although this is an ADO book, it seems a good opportunity to take a quick look at two useful features in Visual Basic 6 which both rely on ADO. We're not going to look at these in detail, but just give you a little glimpse of what's possible.

Data Environment

The data environment makes database programming so much neater within Visual Basic, since you have a central place to keep all of your data store connection details:

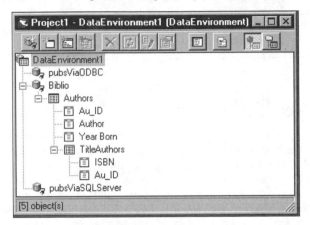

This diagram shows three connections – one to the SQL Server pubs database via the OLE DB Provider for ODBC, one to the Access database Biblio.mdb via the OLE DB Jet Provider, and one to the pubs database via the SQL Server OLE DB provider. The Biblio connection has two commands added to it – one to the Authors table, and a sub-command (mapping the one-to-many relationship), to the TitleAuthors table.

FlexGrid

This sub-command idea is one of the really cool things about the Data Environment, and it goes hand-in-hand with the new Hierarchical FlexGrid.

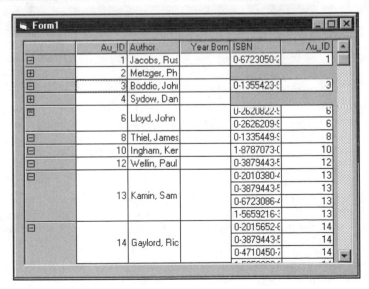

You can see that this grid shows the details from the AuthorTable and from the TitleAuthor table, and gives you the ability to expand items in the grid to show the sub-items. Achieving this took less than thirty seconds, as all you have to do is set the data environment, draw the grid on the form and set two properties. Hierarchical recordsets are examined in more detail in Chapter 11.

There are many other features in Visual Basic 6 that greatly increase productivity and make code easier to maintain, including a host of new data-bound controls aimed at use with ADO.

Language Differences

One of the things we've tried to do with this book is make it relatively language-independent. Since ADO can be used by any programming language that supports COM, the subject of which language to use for the samples in this book becomes quite a sticky one. Therefore, to help the widest possible audience, we've stuck with a pseudo-code type style. For example, in the examples that show something being printed we've just used `Print`. You can then substitute the command for your language of choice. The different methods for several common languages and environments are described below:

Language	Method	Notes
Visual Basic	`Debug.Print "message"`	Prints the text to the debug window
	`MsgBox "message"`	Pops up a window with the text
ASP & VBScript	`Response.Write "message"`	Returns the text to the browser
ASP & JavaScript	`Response.Write ("message");`	Returns the text to the browser
VBScript	`document.write "message"`	Inserts message into the HTML document
	`MsgBox "message"`	Pops up a window with the text
JavaScript	`document.write ("message");`	Inserts message into the HTML document
	`alert ("message");`	Pops up a window with the text

Although we've tried to make our samples as language-independent as possible, you'll notice that most of the samples in the book use a Visual Basic/VBScript style – because we see this to be the greatest market for ADO usage. However, the samples should be easy to translate into your favorite language.

If you want to use ADO in a variety of languages then have a look at the document entitled *Implementing ADO with Various Development Languages*. This can be found at http://msdn.microsoft.com/library/techart/msdn_adorosest.htm.

There is also a set of samples in a variety of languages available from the support page on the Wrox Press web site, at http://www.wrox.com.

Creating Objects

Creating the ADO objects is one area where pseudo-code doesn't really work too well. There are significant differences, even between such apparently similar languages as Visual Basic and VBScript. Therefore, this section is devoted to the act of creating objects – we'll look in some detail at how it's done in each of the five languages where we feel ADO is going to have most impact.

This isn't intended as a full explanation of all of the objects and how they are used in each language, but as a demonstration of the major differences between several of the most common languages.

Visual Basic

Before you can create an ADO object in Visual Basic you should ensure that you have a reference to the ADODB library set. From the Project menu, select References, and then choose Microsoft ActiveX Data Objects 2.6 Library. The ADO Extensions (ADOX) are in the library labeled Microsoft ADO Ext. 2.6 for DDL and Security. Once selected, there are three ways to create objects:

```
Dim objRs As New ADODB.Recordset
```

This creates the object reference immediately, but the object is not instantiated until the first property or method is called. This means that the object is not instantiated when declared, but later in the code – which can lead to debugging problems. A better solution is to use this method:

```
Dim objRs As ADODB.Recordset
Set objRs = New ADODB.Recordset
```

This creates a variable of the type Recordset, and then the Set line instantiates the object. The third method is the older style, using late binding, and is less used these days (and also doesn't require a reference to the ADODB library to be set):

```
Dim objRs As Object
Set objRs = CreateObject("ADODB.Recordset")
```

After an object has been created, invoking the methods and properties is extremely simple. For example:

```
objRs.Cursorlocation = adUseClient
objRs.Open "authors", objConn, adOpenStatic, _
                              adLockBatchOptimistic, adCmdTable
```

The ad constants are automatically available to you in Visual Basic once you have referenced the ADO library (as described above).

Looping through a recordset is just a question of using the MoveNext method and checking the EOF property:

```
While Not objRs.EOF
   Debug.Print objRs("field_name")
   objRs.MoveNext
Wend
```

ASP/VBScript

Creating the objects in VBScript is different from Visual Basic because VBScript doesn't have variable types (all variables are of Variant type) or support for adding references to type libraries (although it does use the Visual Basic syntax for assigning object variables using Set). Therefore there's no need to define the variables, although it's better to define them for ease of code maintenance and reliability:

```
Dim objRs
Set objRs = Server.CreateObject("ADODB.Recordset")
```

This creates a Recordset object in ASP script code.

You can also use the <% Option Explicit %> command to ensure that variables are required to be defined.

Using the object follows the same procedure as for Visual Basic:

```
objRs.CursorLocation = adUseClient
objRs.Open "authors", objConn, adOpenStatus, _
                               adLockBatchOptimistic, adCmdTable
```

The only difference here is that the constants are not automatically available – this is because scripting languages do not have access to the type library and its constants. There are two options available to you. The first is to use the integer values that these constants represent. The problem with this is that your code becomes sprinkled with various numbers whose meaning is not obvious to the reader. For example, without ADO's predefined constants the above statement would read:

```
objRs.CursorLocation = 3
objRs.Open "authors", objConn, 1, 3, 2
```

This makes your code harder to read, and therefore less maintainable.

The second option is to include the constants in your ASP script – this means that you can use the constant names instead of their values. You can include the ADO constants with the following line:

```
<!-- #INCLUDE FILE="adovbs.inc"-->
```

The include file, adovbs.inc, is installed in the default directory of Program Files\Common Files\System\ADO, and can be moved to your local ASP directory or referenced from a central virtual directory.

A better way to use the constants is to create a direct reference to the type library, using some meta data:

```
<!-- METADATA TYPE="typelib"
     FILE="C:\Program Files\Common Files\System\ADO\msado15.dll" -->
```

The advantage of this method is that you use the values from the ADO library itself, rather than those from the include file. This means that you don't have to worry that the location (or even the contents) of the include file might change. Note that the name of the DLL is always msado15.dll, whatever version of ADO you have.

> *To learn more about ASP, you could try* Beginning Active Server Pages 3.0 *(Wrox, ISBN 1-861003-38-2) or* Professional Active Server Pages 3.0 *(Wrox, ISBN 1-861002-61-0).*

Looping through recordsets in VBScript is exactly the same as in Visual Basic:

```
While Not objRs.EOF
   Response.Write objRs.Fields("field_name").Value
   objRs.MoveNext
Wend
```

JScript

JScript has a different syntax to VBScript, although much of the object usage is similar. The major thing to watch for is that JScript is case-sensitive. For example, to create a recordset in JScript you would use:

```
var objRs = Server.CreateObject("ADODB.Recordset");
```

Use of the methods and properties is also very similar:

```
objRs.CursorLocation = adUseClient;
objRs.Open ("authors", objConn, adOpenStatic, adLockBatchOptimistic,
         adCmdTable);
```

To loop through a recordset in JScript you would use:

```
while (!objRs.EOF)
{
   Response.Write (objRs("field_name"));
   objRs.MoveNext();
}
```

Visual C++

To use ADO within C++ you must import the ADO library:

```
#import "c:\program files\common files\system\ado\msado15.dll" \
    no_namespace \
    rename( "EOF", "adoEOF" )
```

You must make sure the filepath points to the location of your version of the ADO DLL. The `no_namespace` keyword is added so that you don't have to scope the ADO names. The `EOF` property has to be renamed due to an unfortunate name collision with the `EOF` constant defined in the Standard C library.

Creating an object follows this syntax:

```
_ConnectionPtr       pConnection;
pConnection.CreateInstance( __uuidof( Connection ) );
_RecordsetPtr        pRecordSet;
pRecordSet.CreateInstance( __uuidof( Recordset ) );
```

Summary

So far we've explored the principles of data access, and the range of problems created by the increasing variety and location of data and users. We've taken a bird's eye view of the significance of ADO and its advantages, and briefly looked at the other data access technologies it builds on, replaces or complements. We then moved on to take a closer look at the new features of MDAC 2.6. In particular, we've considered:

❑ Data and data stores

❑ The existing technologies for accessing data, and Microsoft's scheme to streamline data access, UDA

❑ What OLE DB and ADO 2.6 are, and how they tie in with each other

❑ The distinction between data providers and data consumers, and Microsoft's Distributed interNet Applications framework for client/server solutions

❑ The new features of ADO 2.5 and 2.6

❑ How to use the basics of ADO 2.6 in a variety of languages

In the next chapter we'll be moving on to discuss the ADO and ADOX object models

I thank God I am as honest as any man
living that is an old man and no honester th

Can counsel and speak comfort to th(

Much Ado About Nothing.

Which they themselves not feel

He wears his faith but as the fashion of !

As merry as the day

He hath indeed better bettered expectation

(Act i. Sc. 1.).

For there was never yet philospher
That could endure the toothache patiently.

He wears his faith but as the fashion of his hat.
(Ibid)

As merry as the day is long.

h indeed better bettered expectation

(Act i. Sc. 1.)
Much Ado About Nothing. (Ibid)

an counsel and speak comfort to that grief

Which they themselves not feel.

He wears his faith but as the fashion of his hat.
(Ibid)
(Ibid)

I was not born under

a rhyming planet

I was not born under a rhyming plan
(sc.
For there was never yet
That could endure the to

merry as the day is long

(sc. 2)

Can counsel and speak comfort to that grie

Which they themselves not feel.
(Ibid)

(Ibid)

He hath indeed better bettered expectation

I thank God I am as honest as any

living that is an old man and no honest

themselves not feel. (Ibid)

He wears his faith but as the fashion of his ha

Much Ado About Nothing. For there was never yet philospher
That could endure the toothache patiently.
(Ibid)

I was not born u

The ADO Object Model

Like all other data access technologies from Microsoft, ADO has a distinct object model, which defines the objects and interfaces, and how the objects relate to each other. If you've done any database programming before, you'll probably be familiar with the general layout of these objects, as they lean heavily on the lessons learned from DAO and RDO. ADO has a good object model, but it is not as strict as its ancestors, and thus it gives the programmer a great deal more flexibility, thereby reducing development time. For example, in ADO you can create a recordset of data using just a single line of code.

This has been achieved by flattening the object model. It's still shown in the documentation as a hierarchy (with a single object at the top), but some of the lower objects can exist in your code in their own right, without the need to create higher-level objects explicitly. This means that a programmer can use the object most suitable for a particular task, without having to create a lot of other objects that aren't really required in the program. If ADO requires these objects, then it creates them and uses them behind the scenes; and you need never know that they are there.

The ADO Object Model

In versions prior to 2.5, there are three main objects within ADO: the **Connection**, the **Command** and the **Recordset**. There is no hierarchy between the three main objects, and you can create them independently of each other. From version 2.5, two new objects are available: the **Record** and the **Stream**.

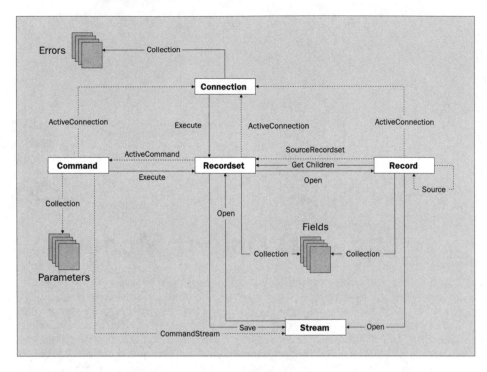

The objects shown as multiples are **collections**. Each collection can comprise zero-or-more instances of its associated object, as shown in the following table.

Collection	Associated Object
Errors	Error
Parameters	Parameter
Fields	Field
Properties	Property

Note that, while the main five objects can all exist independently in our code, the collections must be derived from their parent objects. So (for example) a `Recordset` contains a `Fields` collection, which in turn contains zero-or-more `Field` objects.

Enumerating the objects in a collection is the same for all collections – you just have to use a loop variable of the appropriate type. For example, in Visual Basic the following construct will step through each-and-every object in the `Errors` collection:

```
Dim objErr As ADODB.Error

For Each objErr In objConn.Errors
    Debug.Print objErr.Description
Next
```

The same method can be used in VBScript, although you don't give the object variable a specific type, because VBScript variables are `Variants`. For example in ASP you could use:

```
Dim objFld

For Each objFld In objRec.Fields
    Response.Write objFld.Name & "<BR>"
Next
```

In JScript you could use the `Enumerator` object. For example, in ASP you could use:

```
for(var objProp = new Enumerator(objConn.Properties);
        !objProp.atEnd();
    objProp.moveNext() )
{
  Response.Write (objProp.item().Name + '<BR>');
}
```

The Main ADO Objects

In this section we'll overview the roles of the three objects that make up the bulk of ADO functionality – `Connection`, `Command`, and `Recordset`.

The Connection Object

The `Connection` is actually the hub of ADO, because it provides the methods that allow us to connect to a data store. Note that when you create a `Recordset` or `Command` object, it is not necessary to create a connection first, because a `Connection` object is automatically created for you behind the scenes. What this means is that you can actually create a recordset or run a command with just a single line of code. For example:

```
rsAuthors.Open "authors","DSN=pubs",adOpenStatic,
        adLockReadOnly,adCmdTable
```

This creates a recordset on the `authors` table from the `pubs` database, based on the ODBC Data Source Name (DSN) `pubs`. Although this example is using a `Recordset` object, it actually creates a connection underneath. In fact, you can create a separate and explicit `Connection` object from the one that ADO created for you:

```
Set conPubs = objRec.ActiveConnection
```

This sort of mix-and-match approach to connection creation frees the programmer from a rigid structure and allows the code to be written in a way that is naturally easier.

Although this looks simple, you create a new connection every time you use a connection string to establish a connection to a data store (subject to connection pooling – see Chapter 3). If you are going to be running several commands or creating several recordsets, then it is recommended that you create a `Connection` object directly:

```
conPubs.Open "DSN=pubs; UID=sa; PWD="
```

or:

```
conPubs.Open "Provider=SQLOLEDB; Data Source=Piglet; " & _
           "Initial Catalog=pubs; User Id=sa; Password="
```

You can then use this `Connection` throughout your code, without worrying about the number of connections you are creating. Not only is this more efficient but it's faster too – because once a connection to a data store is established, it can be reused.

One area where you shouldn't try to use a single connection is in ASP pages, using the `Session` or `Application` scope. Creating an ADO object and storing it in a `Session` or `Application` variable has serious performance penalties if you want your ASP pages to scale. You can however, store the connection string in `Session` or `Application` scope.

Once you have decided upon the provider, the properties of the `Connection` object allow you to see what kinds of facilities are available from the data provider. For example, picking the SQL Server provider allows you to see some of the properties for that provider, even before the connection is opened:

```
conPubs.Provider = "SQLOLEDB"
For Each objProp in conPubs.Properties
     Print objProp.Name
Next
```

Since ADO is designed to run against different data stores, it's often worth checking that a particular function is supported, *before* you call it. You do this by examining the `Properties` collection of the `Connection` object. This is particularly useful when using ADO as part of a development or query tool that gives the user the ability to connect to different data stores. You could also, for example, use some of the properties to define a schema, if manually creating XML from the data.

The `Connection` object isn't just about connecting to, and holding information about, a data store. You can actually run commands and create recordsets with a `Connection` object too. For example:

```
conPubs.Execute "UPDATE titles SET price = price * 1.10", , _
              adCmdText + adExecuteNoRecords
```

This would run a SQL `UPDATE` query. Alternatively, to run a command and return a read-only recordset:

```
Set rsAuthors = objConn.Execute ("SELECT * FROM authors", , adCmdText)
```

So, not only can you use a `Recordset` object to connect to a data store, but you can also use a `Connection` object to create recordsets. It's all part of the 'code as you want' strategy.

An ADO operation may generate more than one error, and these are stored in the Connection object's Errors collection, which is discussed in more detail in Chapter 8. Although you might think this breaks the flexibility of the object model, it gives a central place to find error information. Since the Recordset and Command objects have a connection underneath, it is extremely simple to get access to this error information without creating a Connection object.

The Command Object

The Command object is designed to run SQL statements (assuming the provider supports the Command object), especially those that require parameters. This is an important point, because the use of stored queries and procedures is a great way to improve speed and segment your application, as well as fitting and that naturally with Windows DNA.

Like the Connection object, the Command object can be used to run action queries that don't return a recordset, as well as creating recordsets. Unlike the Connection, however, you'll need a couple more lines of code, because you cannot specify the command text in the same line as the line that specifies the command type:

```
objCmd.CommandText = "UPDATE titles SET price = price * 1.10"
objCmd.CommandType = adCmdText + adExecuteNoRecords
objCmd.Execute
```

To return a recordset you use a similar style:

```
Set rsAuthors = objCmd.Execute
```

The greatest difference in command execution comes when using the Parameters collection, because this allows you to use stored procedures, queries, and template and parameterized queries that are saved in the data store. This removes the SQL code from your program, making it faster and more maintainable. Using stored procedures, you can have SQL statements that are in a compiled form which perform a set of actions using the values you supply as parameters.

With a Command – if the data provider supports this facility – you can also save the command details for execution at a later date. This is known as a **prepared statement**, and allows the pre-compiled command to be run many times within the same connection. Once you've finished with your connection, the saved commands are automatically deleted. You can also use a command object more than once, and on different connections if you require (assuming that the command can be run on another connection). Just change the ActiveConnection property of the command to point to the new connection and re-run the command. If you wish to reuse the Command object, it's wise to close any active recordsets that were created as a result of the command's execution. This ensures that memory is deallocated correctly.

Another feature allows you to turn the command into a method of the Connection object, allowing you to build up a Connection object that contains many new methods. This is quite useful in client-server scenarios, because you could attach different commands to the connection depending upon the privilege of the user. This is explained in more detail in Chapter 4.

> Unlike the `Connection` and `Recordset` objects, which must be supported by every OLE DB provider, a provider's decision to support the `Command` object is entirely optional. Consequently, not all OLE DB Providers support the `Command` object.

The Recordset Object

The `Recordset` object is probably the most frequently used object in ADO, and consequently has more properties and methods than the other objects. Like the `Command` object, a `Recordset` can exist on its own or be attached to a `Connection`:

```
rsAuthors.Open "authors", "DSN=pubs", adOpenStatic, _
        adLockReadOnly, adCmdTable
```

This opens a recordset using a new connection. To use an existing connection, you simply substitute the connection string for the existing `Connection` object:

```
rsAuthors.Open "authors", conPubs, adOpenStatic, _
        adLockReadOnly, adCmdTable
```

This is the preferred method if you are creating several recordsets, because it means that the connection to the data store doesn't have to be established each time you create a recordset.

Another important point about the `Recordset` object is that it's the only way to specify the recordset's cursor type and lock type. If you use the `Execute` method of the `Connection` or `Command` object, it gives you the default cursor type, a read-only, forward-only cursor (often referred to as a **firehose cursor**, since the data is just 'squirted' to the recordset). If you need to use a `Command` and require a different cursor type, then you can specify the `Command` object as the source of the `Recordset`, instead of the table name or query text.

You use recordsets to examine and manipulate data from the data store. The `Recordset` object gives you facilities to move about through the records, find records, sort records in a particular order, and update records. You can do updating in two modes: either directly (where the changes are sent back to the data store as they are made) or in batches (where the changes are saved locally and then sent back to the data store in one go).

In client-server applications, you can also pass recordsets between the business logic tier and the user interface tier, where they can be manipulated locally. This saves database resources, which can be critical on large-scale applications, as well as minimizing network traffic. These recordsets are called **disconnected recordsets**.

The Record Object

The `Record` object was introduced in version 2.5, and is used in conjunction with a new type of OLE DB Provider, called Document Source Providers. Document Source Providers are designed to enable access to data stores of semi-structured data, such as file or mail systems. It was necessary to create a new object because of the way data is stored.

In relational data stores, such as SQL Server or Access, we work using set-based data, where every row is in a rowset and has the same structure as the other rows. Semi-structured data, on the other hand, doesn't follow this pattern as each row might have a different structure. If you think about the structure of a web site, then you'll start to understand how this works. A web site generally consists of directories and files. If you look at the top-level directory for a site, you might see something like this:

File Name	Type
default.htm	File
Images	Directory
menu.xml	File

All three items here have some common properties, such as a name, for example. However, they also have different properties – the directory doesn't have a size, but needs to indicate that it contains other files. These different properties are why we need a different object to cope with this sort of data. When dealing with semi-structured data, the `Record` object maps onto individual files, and the `Recordset` object is mapped onto a collection of files.

To access a directory through a `Record` object you use the following syntax:

```
Dim recRoot      As New ADODB.Record

recRoot.Open "", "URL=http://localhost"

recRoot.Close
```

Specifying `URL=` tells ADO to use the Internet Publishing Provider.

The Record object not only allows access to files, but gives management over them too. The `CopyRecord`, `MoveRecord`, and `DeleteRecord` methods give the ability to control files remotely.

> For more detailed information on the use of the `Record` object, consult *Professional Active Server Pages 3.0 (ISBN 1861002610)* or *Professional ADO 2.5 (ISBN 1861002750), both from Wrox Press.*

The Stream Object

The `Stream` object is a wrapper around a memory manager (in fact it's based around the COM `IStream` interface), and gives control over the contents of the memory used to store an object. This might sound rather complex, but it has wide-ranging uses and is simple to use.

There are several ways in which a `Stream` can be used. One of these is in conjunction with a Document Source Provider (such as the OLE DB Provider for Internet Publishing), giving access to the contents of a file on a web server. For example:

```
Dim stmFile      As New ADODB.Stream
Dim sContents    As String
```

```
stmFile.Open "URL=http://localhost/postinfo.html"

stmFile.Charset = "ascii"
sContents = stmFile.ReadText

stmFile.Close
```

This simply opens a file and reads the contents into a string. You also get the ability to write data out to the stream, where it is automatically saved to the file. This gives the ability to perform editing on remote files.

Stream objects have other roles – they can be used when saving and opening recordsets, as well as in conjunction with the Microsoft XML Parser.

For more detailed information on the use of the Stream object, consult Professional Active Server Pages 3.0 or Professional ADO 2.5, both from Wrox Press.

The Other ADO Objects

Now, let's take a look at the other objects that play a part in programming with ADO.

The Field Object and the Fields Collection

A Field object contains details about a single field (or column) in a recordset. Such information includes the data type of the field, its width, and so on.

The Fields collection contains a reference to an ADO Field object, for each field in a recordset, and there are two ways in which this can be used. The first is with existing recordsets, where you can examine each field, see its type, check its name, etc. This is quite useful when you are unsure of exactly what the recordset contains, and can be useful in scripting when showing tables dynamically. Using the Fields collection allows you to find the name of each field. For example, in ASP script you could do this:

```
Response.Write "<TABLE>"
For Each objFld In objRec.Fields
   Response.Write "<TR><TD>" & objFld.Name & "</TD></TR>"
Next
Response.Write "</TABLE>"
```

This creates an HTML table showing which fields are in the recordset objRec. In fact, using a similar method, you could easily create a simple script routine that accepts any recordset and builds an HTML table from it. You could use the Fields collection to supply the table header, showing the column names, and the recordset to fill in the details of the table.

Another use of the Fields collection is for creating programmatic, or fabricated, recordsets. In the past, arrays were often used when you needed to store several related items. The trouble with arrays is that you have to manage the array manually – you can't add data to a new array element without first creating room in the array.

Then came collections, to which you could add your own objects; but collections are also limited to objects and basic data types. So if you want to store some related items (records), with each item having different attributes (fields) then you can use a fabricated recordset.

For example, imagine that you need to store details from a questionnaire. You could create a recordset like so:

```
rsNew.CursorLocation = adUseClient
rsNew.Fields.Append "Name", adVarChar, 50, adFldFixed
rsNew.Fields.Append "Age", adInteger, , adFldFixed
rsNew.Fields.Append "Question1", adBoolean, , adFldFixed
. . .
rsNew.Fields.Append "Comments", adVarChar, 255, adFldFixed
```

The good thing about this method is that you can save the contents of this disconnected recordset to a file, as well as using it as a parameter for functions in business objects (just like recordsets obtained from OLE DB Providers).

The Error Object and the Errors Collection

An `Error` object contains details of a single error (or warning) returned from a data provider. Details include a description of the error, an error number and the source object that raised the error. When a provider encounters an error, or wishes to return information to the consumer, the details are placed in an `Error` object, and this is appended to the `Errors` collection.

The `Errors` collection holds all of the errors when a data provider generates an error or returns warnings in response to some failure. This is provided as a collection because a failure can generate more than one error. For example, the following statement generates two errors because X and Y are unknown columns:

```
objConn.Open "DSN=pubs"
Set objRec = objConn.Execute "SELECT X, Y FROM authors"
```

You could check the errors generated here by looping through the collection:

```
For Each objErr In conPubs.Errors
   Print objErr.Description
Next
```

If you don't have a predefined `Connection` object you can use the `ActiveConnection` property of the `Command` or `Recordset`:

```
rsAuthors.Open "SELECT X, Y FROM authors", "DSN=pubs", _
        adOpenStatic, adLockReadOnly, adCmdTable

For Each objErr In rsAuthors.ActiveConnection.Errors
   Print objErr.Description
Next
```

As with the `Fields` collection, you could easily build a simple routine that centralizes error handling.

There is always an `Errors` collection, but it will be empty if no errors have occurred. `Error` objects remain in the collection until the next data access error occurs, when they are cleared and replaced by the new error details.

The Parameter Object and the Parameters Collection

A `Parameter` object contains details of a single parameter for a `Command` object. Some of these details include the name, data type, direction, and value of the parameter. A parameter can be one of the following types:

❑   An input parameter, which supplies values to the statement represented by the `Command` object

❑   An output parameter, which supplies values from the statement represented by the `Command` object

❑   An input and output parameter

❑   A return value, which supplies the return value from the statement represented by the `Command` object

The usage of the various parameter types is discussed in more detail in Chapter 4.

The `Parameters` collection is unique to the `Command` object and is one way of allowing you to pass parameters into and out from stored queries and procedures. When using parameters you have two options. First, you can ask the data provider to fetch the parameters from the data source, and the `Parameters` collection will be filled in automatically for you:

```
objCmd.Parameters.Refresh
```

The downside of this is that it requires a trip to the server, which may cause your program to perform poorly – especially if you do this often. However, it's a great way of finding out what type and size the provider expects your parameters to be, and is very useful during development and debugging. You should note that not all OLE DB Providers (or ODBC Drivers) support the `Refresh` method.

The second option is to add the parameters to the collection manually, like so:

```
Set objParam = objCmd.CreateParameter ("ID",adInteger, _
                                    adParamInput, 8, 147)
```

This creates an input parameter called `ID`, which is an integer (length 8 bytes), with a value of 147. Once created, the parameter can be appended to the `Parameters` collection:

```
objCmd.Parameters.Append objParam
```

Another good use of the `Refresh` method is, when first connecting to the data store, to cache the parameters details locally, perhaps in an array or in a user collection. This sort of approach allows you to write generic routines that process stored procedures.

The Property Object and the Properties Collection

A `Property` object contains provider-specific information about an object. We know that objects have a fixed set of properties, but one of the fundamentals of OLE DB and ADO is that it can talk to a variety of data providers, and these providers often have different ways of working, or support different properties. If all providers had to support a fixed functionality, then OLE DB and ADO wouldn't really be very flexible – it would comprise the lowest common denominator of functionality. The solution is to provide a `Property` object for each provider-specific property, and a `Properties` collection to store all of the provider-specific properties.

For a `Connection`, the `Properties` collection contains a large amount of information about the facilities that the provider supports, such as the maximum number of columns in a `SELECT` statement, and what sort of outer join capabilities are supported. For a `Recordset`, there's just as much information, ranging from the current locking level to the asynchronous capabilities supported by the provider.

You can examine or set the value of an individual property by just using its name to index into the collection. For example:

```
Print conPubs.Properties("Max Columns in SELECT")
```

To examine all of the properties you can use a simple loop:

```
For Each objProp In conPubs.Properties
    Print objProp.Name
Next
```

You may well find that you never use this collection, unless you are writing an application that supports multiple data providers, in which case you may need to query the provider to examine what it supports.

The ADOX Object Model

The ADOX library contains extensions for Data Definition Language (DDL) and security, providing a way to access schema creation and modification, as well as accessing security credentials for the schema. Many data stores allow access to schema and security information, but they often differ in the command language used. ADOX abstracts these provider specific details into a common set of objects, allowing a single code set to be used regardless of provider-specific syntax.

The ADOX (ADO Extensions for DDL and Security) object model observes more of a hierarchy than the ADO object model, but that's because of the nature of the objects it contains. This means there is a parent object and several child objects:

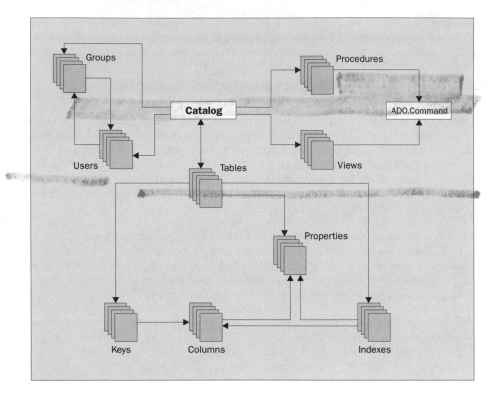

The Catalog Object

The `Catalog` object is a central repository, and is really just a container for all of the other objects. The `Catalog` object allows us to connect to a data store and examine the components that it comprises. With the `Catalog` object, we can use the `ActiveConnection` property to specify the data store that we want to connect to, and then use the collections to obtain more detailed information. It's also possible to obtain and set the owner of various objects without using the collections.

To use a catalog you just point to an existing `Connection` object, or a `Connection` string. For example:

```
Dim objCatalog As New ADOX.Catalog

Set objCatalog.ActiveConnection = objConn
```

or:

```
objCatalog.ActiveConnection = "Provider=SQLOLEDB; . . ."
```

The Table Object and the Tables Collection

A `Table` object represents a single table in a catalog, containing information such as the table name and the last change date. It is also a container for the `Columns`, `Indexes` and `Keys` collections (see below).

The `Tables` collection contains `Table` objects, one for each table in the catalog. An example of the `Tables` and `Columns` collections is shown in a moment (after we've introduced the `Columns` collection).

The Index Object and the Indexes Collection

An `Index` object contains the details for a single index on a table, identifying attributes such as the index name, whether the index is unique, whether the index allows nulls, etc. Using the `Index` object's `Columns` collection (see below), you can see which columns comprise the index.

The `Indexes` collection contains all of the `Index` objects for a particular `Table`. For example, the following code prints the indexes on a table, and the columns that make up each `index`:

```
Dim objIndex  As ADOX.Index
Dim objColumn As ADOX.Column

For Each objIndex In objTbl.Indexes
  Print objIndex.Name
  For Each objColumn In objIndex.Columns
    Print objColumn.Name
  Next
Next
```

The Key Object and the Keys Collection

A `Key` object contains information regarding a table key, identifying such items as its name, whether it is a primary or foreign key, the related table, etc. Like the `Index` object, the `Key` object contains a collection of `Column` objects, identifying the columns that make up the key.

The `Keys` collection contains a list of keys for a table. For example, the following prints all of the keys and columns for a table:

```
Dim objTbl    As ADOX.Key
Dim objColumn As ADOX.Column

For Each objTbl In objTbl.Indexes
  Print objTbl.Name
  For Each objColumn In objTbl.Columns
    Print objColumn.Name
  Next
Next
```

The Column Object and the Columns Collection

A `Column` object represents an individual column from a `Table`, `Index`, or `Key` object. In many respects it is similar to the ADO `Field` object; but rather than storing the details of a field, it holds the details of a stored column, such as its name, its data type, etc. For `Key` columns it contains details of the related columns, and for `Index` columns it contains details of the clustering and sorting. There is just one `Column` object, but what it contains differs depending upon its parent (`Table`, `Index`, or `Key`).

The Columns collection contains all of the columns for a particular Table, Key, or Index object. For example, to see all of the columns in a particular table you would use this:

```
Dim objTbl As New ADOX.Table
Dim objCol As ADOX.Column

Set objTbl = objCatalog.Tables(0)
For Each objCol In objTbl.Columns
  Print objCol.Name
Next
```

The syntax is very similar when looping through all of the Column objects associated with an Index or a Key object.

The Group Object and the Groups Collection

A Group object identifies a security group, containing a list of users in the catalog. Its main role is to allow the retrieval and setting of permission for a named group, or for allowing access to the Users collection, which contains a list of all users belonging to this group.

The Groups collection contains a list of Groups that belong to a particular catalog, or a list of Groups that a particular user belongs to. For example, the following enumerates the Groups in a Catalog, and then the Users in a Group:

```
Dim objGroup As ADOX.Group
Dim objUser  As ADOX.User

For Each objGroup In objCatalog.Groups
  Print objGroup.Name
  For Each objUser In objGroup.Users
    Print objUser.Name
  Next
Next
```

Not all providers support the Group object and Groups collection. At the moment the Jet provider gives the most comprehensive support.

The User Object and the Users Collection

A User object contains details of a single user of the data store and contains properties to retrieve or set the user name and the unique ID of the user, and methods to read and write permissions. The User object also contains a Groups collection, which is a list of groups to which the user belongs. You should be careful about writing recursive procedures that traverse the Users and Groups collections, because they point to each other.

The Users collection contains a list of all users in a catalog. An example of this is shown above, in the description of the Group object.

Not all providers support the User object and Users collection. At the moment the Jet provider gives the most comprehensive support.

The Procedure Object and the Procedures Collection

A `Procedure` object identifies a stored procedure in a catalog. The `Procedure` object has very few properties, mainly because one of these properties represents an ADO `Command` object. The `Procedure` object identifies the details about the stored procedure (such as its name and when it was last modified), while the `Command` object identifies the internal details of the procedure (such as the SQL text, etc.).

The `Procedures` collection contains a `Procedure` object for each stored procedure in the `Catalog`. For example, to access a stored procedure and its SQL text you could use the following code:

```
Dim objCmd As ADODB.Command

Set objCmd = objCat.Procedures("proc_name").Command
Print objCmd.CommandText
```

This uses the `Command` property of the `Procedure` object, to reference a standard ADO `Command` object and print the text (command string) of the `Command`.

The View Object and the Views Collection

A `View` object identifies a single view in a `Catalog`, which is a set of records or a virtual table. Like the `Procedure` object, the `View` contains a `Command` object, allowing access to the view command.

The `Views` collection contains a list of `View` objects, one for each view in the catalog.

For example, to obtain all views in a catalog you could do this:

```
Dim objView As ADOX.View

For Each objView In objCat.Views
    Print objView.Name
Next
```

Like the `Procedure` object, the `View` object also supports an ADO `Command` as a property. So, to access the details of the command you could use similar code:

```
Dim objCmd As ADODB.Command

Set objCmd = objCat.Views("view_name").Command
Print objCmd.CommandText
```

This object and collection is also provider-dependent.

The Property Object and the Properties Collection

The `Property` object and `Properties` collection are identical to their ADODB equivalents.

ADOX Supported Features

ADOX is not supported by all providers, even the Microsoft-supplied ones. Currently, only the OLE DB Provider for Microsoft Jet fully supports ADOX. For the other Microsoft OLE DB providers, all features are supported *except* for those listed below:

Microsoft OLE DB Provider for SQL Server

Object/Collection	Feature not supported
Catalog Object	Create method
Tables Collection	Properties for existing tables are read-only (properties for new tables can be read/write)
Views Collection	Not supported
Procedures Collection	Append method, Delete method, Command property
Keys Collection	Append method, Delete method
Users Collection	Not supported
Groups Collection	Not supported

Microsoft OLE DB Provider for ODBC

Object/Collection	Feature not supported
Catalog Object	Create method
Tables Collection	Append method, Delete method; Properties for existing tables are read-only (properties for new tables can be read/write)
Views Collection	Append method, Delete method, Command property
Procedures Collection	Append method, Delete method, Command property
Indexes Collection	Append method, Delete method
Keys Collection	Append method, Delete method
Users Collection	Not supported
Groups Collection	Not supported

Microsoft OLE DB Provider for Oracle

Object/Collection	Feature not supported
Catalog Object	Create method.
Tables Collection	Append method, Delete method; Properties for existing tables are read-only (properties for new tables can be read/write)

Microsoft OLE DB Provider for Oracle	
Object/Collection	**Feature not supported**
Views Collection	Append method, Delete method, Command property
Procedures Collection	Append method, Delete method, Command property
Indexes Collection	Append method, Delete method
Keys Collection	Append method, Delete method
Users Collection	Not supported
Groups Collection	Not supported

OLE DB Providers

We've already mentioned that ADO can connect to many different data providers, and this is due to OLE DB. Remember that ADO is just a layer that sits on top of OLE DB to hide the complexity. It seems sensible, though, to look at some of these OLE DB data providers in more detail. We need to see what differences there are between them, for although most of the ADO usage will be the same, OLE DB providers don't always support the same facilities. This is natural, because some of them are fundamentally very different. Most of the relational database providers, for example, will provide similar facilities, but other providers (such as the Provider for Internet Publishing) might not work in the same way.

When you install MDAC 2.6, you are supplied with the following OLE DB providers:

Provider	Description
MSDASQL	Microsoft OLE DB Provider for ODBC – allows connection to existing ODBC data sources, either via a System DSN or from dynamically provided connection details. See Chapter 1 for how ODBC Drivers relate to OLE DB.
Microsoft.Jet.OLE DB.4.0	Microsoft OLE DB Provider for Jet – allows connections to be directly established to Microsoft Access databases, including Access 97 and Access 2000.
SQLOLEDB	Microsoft OLE DB Provider for SQL Server – allows connections to be directly established to Microsoft SQL Server databases.
MSDAORA	Microsoft OLE DB Provider for Oracle – allows connections to be established to Oracle databases.

Table continued on following page

47

Provider	Description
MSIDXS	Microsoft OLE DB Provider for Index Server – allows connections to be established to Microsoft Index Server.
ADSDSOObject	OLE DB Provider for Microsoft Directory Services – allows connections to be established to Directory Services such as the Windows 2000 Active Directory and the Windows NT 4 Directory Services.
MSDataShape	Microsoft OLE DB Data Shape Provider – provides the ability to create hierarchical recordsets.
MSPersist	Microsoft OLE DB Persistence Provider – allows recordsets to be saved or persisted and later reconstructed.
MSDAOSP	Microsoft OLE DB Simple Provider – allows connections to be established to custom OLE DB Providers that expose simple (relational) data.
MSDAIPP.DSO.1	Microsoft OLE DB Provider for Internet Publishing – allows connections to be established to DAV compliant servers, to aid publishing data on the Internet.

These are just the defaults supplied, some of which may not appear, depending upon your installation options. For example, Index Server does not act as a remote provider, and you can only connect to local Index Servers. Therefore, if you do not have Index Server on your machine, the MSIDXS may not get installed.

You can find out which providers are available on your system by creating a new Data Link. This is similar to an ODBC DSN, but for OLE DB connections. You can create one in any directory using Windows Explorer, simply by right mouse clicking (or selecting the File menu), picking New, and selecting Microsoft Data Link.This creates a file with a .udl extension, and you can then view its properties. For Windows 2000 this option isn't available, but you can create a text file and then rename it so that its extension is .udl. You can then open the UDL file by double-clicking it. From the Provider tab you can see the available providers:

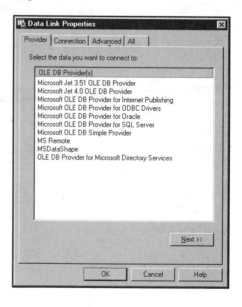

In fact, using the Data Link is a good way to create connection strings if you are unfamiliar with them – you can even use them instead of a DSN within connection strings (see the next section). You can create a Data Link file, filling in the details on screen, and then examine the resulting .udl file in Notepad.

Connection Strings

One of the major differences between the various OLE DB providers is found in the connection string: different providers require different information in order to make the connection to the data store.

ADO recognizes only four of the arguments in the connection string; the remaining arguments are passed on to the provider. The main argument you are interested in is Provider, which identifies the OLE DB provider to be used. The second argument is File Name, which can be used to point to an existing Data Link file. If you use a Data Link file then you can omit the Provider argument, because the Data Link file contains this information. The other two arguments (Remote Provider and Remote Server) relate to Remote Data Services, and are covered in detail in Chapter 9.

OLE DB Provider for the ODBC Drivers

The OLE DB Provider for ODBC is the default provider, so if you don't specify which one to use, this is what you'll get. If you *do* specify this provider explicitly in your connection string, you have to give the rather obscure name MSDASQL. When using the OLE DB Provider for ODBC, you have three choices: to use an existing ODBC System Data Source Name (DSN), a DSN-less connection string, or an ODBC File DSN.

For a DSN based connection, simply specify the data source name:

```
Provider=MSDASQL;DSN=data_source_name; UID=user_id;
PWD=user_password
```

For a DSN-less connection, the connection string varies with the database you are connecting to. It follows the same conventions as an ODBC connection string – you can see the parameters in the ODBC applet in the Control Panel. There is one important option that is the same for all ODBC connections, as it specifies the ODBC driver to use:

```
Provider=MSDASQL;Driver=
```

The name of the driver specified in the Driver attribute of the connection string will be one of those shown on the Drivers tab of the ODBC Control Panel applet. Your list of drivers may differ from those listed in the following screenshot:

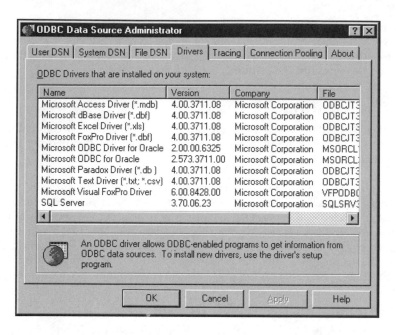

On Windows 2000 the ODBC Data Source Administrator, known as simply Data Sources (ODBC) on this platform, can be found under the Administrative Tools group. Regardless of platform, the list of ODBC Drivers installed on a given system can also be found in the system registry at HKEY_LOCAL_MACHINE\SOFTWARE\ODBC\ODBCINST.INI \ODBC Drivers.

You should enclose the driver name in curly braces. Let's look at some examples.

Microsoft Access

To connect to Microsoft Access, your connection string would start like this:

```
Provider=MSDASQL;Driver={Microsoft Access Driver (*.mdb)}
```

You then have to specify the full path and filename to the Access database, using the DBQ attribute:

```
Provider=MSDASQL;Driver={Microsoft Access Driver (*.mdb)};
DBQ=C:\mdb_name.mdb
```

Note: An interesting fact has recently come to light that causes the following error with the OLE DB Provider for ODBC:

Microsoft OLEDB Provider for ODBC Drivers error '80004005'
[Microsoft][ODBC Driver Manager] Data source name not found and no default driver specified

This seems to occur of you leave a space after the first semi-colon in the connection string shown above, just before the `Driver`. So, this works:

```
Provider=MSDASQL;Driver={Microsoft Access Driver (*.mdb)};
DBQ=C:\mdb_name.mdb
```

But this doesn't:

```
Provider=MSDASQL; Driver={Microsoft Access Driver (*.mdb)};
DBQ=C:\mdb_name.mdb
```

Notice the space – it's hard to spot.

Of course, since this is the default OLE DB Provider, you can use the following string (without specifying the `Provider`) perfectly well:

```
Driver={Microsoft Access Driver (*.mdb)}; DBQ=C:\mdb_name.mdb
```

Microsoft SQL Server

To connect to SQL Server using the OLE DB Provider for ODBC (MSDASQL) you need to supply a little more information:

❑ `Server` is the name of the SQL Server

❑ `Database` is the database name

❑ `UID` is the SQL Server user ID

❑ `PWD` is the password for the SQL Server user ID

For example:

```
Provider=MSDASQL;Driver={SQL Server}; Server=Tigger; Database=pubs;
UID=sa; PWD=
```

Microsoft Excel

There are three ways to connect to a Microsoft Excel (any version) spreadsheet. The first is by specifying the sheet name as the source of the `Recordset`:

```
objRs.Open "[Sheet1$]", objConn, adOpenDynamic, adOpenStatic,
adCmdTable
```

The second is by specifying the sheet name with a row and column area:

```
objRs.Open "Select * from `Sheet1$A2:C4`", oConn, adOpenStatic, _
                                adLockBatchOptimistic, adCmdText
```

The third is by specifying a range name:

```
objRs.Open "Select * from myRange1", oConn, adOpenStatic, _
                                  adLockBatchOptimistic, adCmdText
```

To use the range method, you must first make sure that a range has been specified in the spreadsheet. This range should enclose all of the data that you wish to select, and equates to the recordset. You can have any number of ranges in a spreadsheet. To create a range you select the cells in the spreadsheet and enter the name in the range box, like so:

You then specify the range as the Source parameter of the Recordset's Open method:

```
objRec.Open "Authors", objConn
```

In all three cases, the connection string needs to specify Microsoft Excel as the ODBC driver, and the speadsheet name as the data store name:

```
Provider=MSDASQL;Driver={Microsoft Excel Driver (*.xls)};
DBQ=C:\xls_name.xls
```

Text Files

Text files are slightly different from Excel files, in the following respect: in the connection string, you specify the directory where the text file resides, rather than the text file itself:

```
Provider=MSDASQL;Driver={Microsoft Text Driver (*.txt; *.csv)};
DBQ=C:\directory_name
```

You then specify the text file as the name of the recordset to open:

```
objRec.Open "TextFile.txt", objConn
```

OLE DB Provider for Jet

When using the provider for Jet you only need to specify the database name in the Data Source attribute of the connection string:

```
Provider=Microsoft.Jet.OLEDB.4.0; Data Source=C:\mdb_name.mdb
```

If you have a system database you can use the `Properties` collection to set this before opening the connection, but you must specify the provider first:

```
conDB.Provider = "Microsoft.Jet.OLEDB.4.0"
conDB.Properties("Jet OLEDB:System database") = "C:\system_db_name"
conDB.Open "Data Source-C:\pubs\pubs.mdb"
```

A database password is also set in this way:

```
objConn.Properties("Jet OLEDB:Database Password") = "LetMeIn"
```

OLE DB Provider for SQL Server

When establishing connections to SQL Server databases using the Microsoft OLE DB Provider for SQL Server (SQLOLEDB), the Data Source attribute is used to specify the name or address of the SQL Server. Consequently, an additional attribute named "Initial Catalog" is used to specify the name of the database for which the connection will be made:

```
Provider=SQLOLEDB; Data Source=server_name;
Initial Catalog=database_name; User Id=user id;
Password=user_password
```

For example:

```
Provider=SQLOLEDB; Data Source=Tigger; Initial Catalog=pubs;
User Id=sa; Password=
```

OLE DB Provider for Index Server

For Index Server you only need to specify the provider name, unless you have multiple catalogs in use under Index Server. In this case you use the `Data Source` to specify the required catalog:

```
Provider=MSIDXS; Data Source=catalog_name
```

OLE DB Provider for Internet Publishing

The Internet Publishing provider allows you to connect to Servers that support either the Microsoft FrontPage Server Extensions or the Distributed Authoring and Versioning (DAV, also known as WebDAV or HTTP-DAV) protocol. This allows you to use ADO to query the servers for directory contents, resources etc., as well as to update these resources. You use the `Data Source` attribute to specify the name of the web server:

```
Provider=MSDAIPP.DSO.1; Data Source=http://web.server.name
```

Alternatively you can add `URL=` to the front of the Data Source you are opening, which tells ADO that the Internet Publishing provider is being used. For example:

```
recRoot.Open "", "URL=http://web.server.name"
```

Data Link Files

A data link file can contain connection details for any OLE DB Provider. Data Link files have a suffix of `.udl`, and allow the connection details to be stored in a file, rather than being embedded within an application. Data link files can be created using Windows Explorer. Under Windows 2000 you should create a **Text File**, and then rename the suffix to `.udl`. Double clicking this file will open the Data Link Properties dialog. Under previous versions of Windows (and ADO) you can select **New Data Link File** from the Explorer context menu.

To use a Data Link file as a connection string you simple set the `File Name` option to point to the `.udl` file:

```
objConn.Open "File Name=C:\temp\pubs.UDL"
```

Asynchronous Processing

Asynchronous processing was one of the new features in ADO 2.0, and allows commands to be executed at the same time as other commands. This is particularly useful when creating very large recordsets, or running a query that may take a long time, as you can continue with another task and allow ADO to tell you when the command has finished via an event. You can also cancel a long running command if you wish. Events can also be used to perform pre-processing and post-processing around certain ADO operations such as opening a `Recordset` or establishing a `Connection`.

> Note that ASP scripting languages do not support events on the server. Client-side script does support events.

Events

2

For ADO, only the `Recordset` and `Connection` objects support events. There are generally two types of events:

- ❏ `Will...` events – those that are called before an operation starts
- ❏ `...Complete` events – those that are called after it has completed

There are a few other events that are called after an event has completed, but they are not part of the `Will...` and `...Complete` event pairs.

A `Will...` event is called just before the action starts. It gives you the chance to examine the details of the action, and to cancel the action if you decide that you do not want it to run. The `...Complete` event is called just after the action completes, even if the operation was cancelled. If it was cancelled then the `Errors` collection is filled with details of why it was cancelled.

The `Will...` events generally have an argument, `adStatus`, indicating the status of the event. You can set this argument to `adStatusCancel` before the method ends, to cancel the action that caused the event. For example, suppose a connection generated a `WillConnect` event; setting `adStatus` to `adStatusCancel` will cancel the connection. The `ConnectComplete` event will then be called, with a status indicating that the connection failed.

The nature of events means that there can be several `Will...` events that could result from a single action. Although all of these will be called, there is no guaranteed order in which this will happen.

Event Pairings

The way the `Will...` and `...Complete` events are generated can often be confusing, especially in terms of what happens when you wish to cancel the operation that raised the event. The action triggers the `Will...` event, which has its own event procedure. This code runs, and then the action itself is run. After the action is finished, the `...Complete` event is triggered, which runs its event procedure. Once that has completed, execution will continue at the line after the action. The following diagram shows this using `Connection` events, when opening a connection·

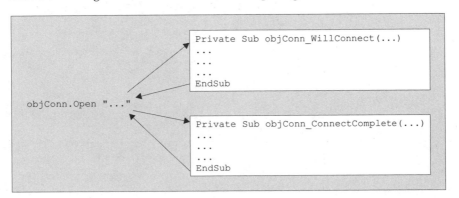

In the `WillConnect` event procedure we can decide whether we want this action (that is, the `objConn.Open`) to take place or not. The event procedure has a parameter called `adStatus`, which we can use. If we set this to `adStatusCancel` before the event procedure finishes, then the action is cancelled. The `ConnectComplete` event will still run, but its parameters will indicate that an error has occurred. For example:

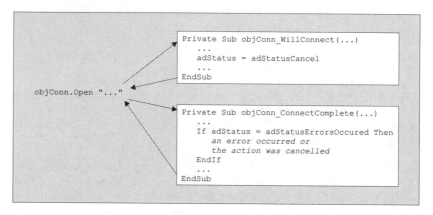

The important thing to note is that the `ConnectComplete` event is still generated, but the connection does not actually take place.

Some actions may generate more than one event, so what happens here? Well, the `Will...` event is always generated before its associated `...Complete` event; but when there are two `Will...` events, the order in which they are generated is not guaranteed. If you cancel the action from within an event procedure, and this happens to run as the first event procedure, then the second set of event procedures (both the `Will...` and the `...Complete`) are never generated. For example, imagine a recordset where you have events to detect when fields and records change:

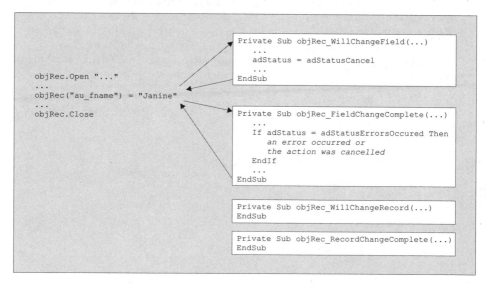

Here the action has been canceled in the `WillChangeField` event procedure. The `FieldChangeComplete` event procedure runs, but indicates that an error occurred, and the actual action, that of setting the field value is not executed. The `WillChangeRecord` and `RecordChangeComplete` event procedures are not run.

While these diagrams use Visual Basic, the choice of language is not crucial: it's the order of events that's important.

Events in Visual Basic

To use events within Visual Basic you declare a variable using the `WithEvents` keyword. This must be a module/form/class/control level, or global variable, as `WithEvents` is invalid within procedures:

```
Private WithEvents m_rsAuthors As ADODB.Recordset
```

Note that the `New` keyword is omitted when using this syntax, because you can't instantiate objects at the same time as declaring the variable with events. You have to do this separately:

```
Set m_rsAuthors = New ADODB.Recordset
```

Once you have declared the variable, the object will appear in the objects list in the code combo, and a list of events in the event drop-down list:

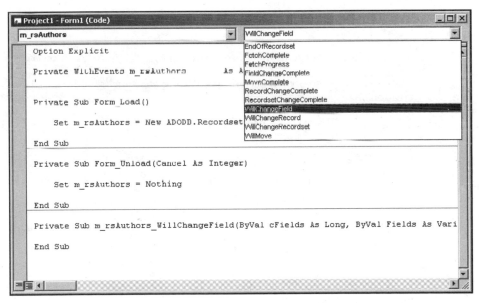

Connection Events

There are nine Connection events:

❑ BeginTransComplete is called after a BeginTrans method has completed.

❑ CommitTransComplete is called after a CommitTrans method has completed.

❑ RollbackTransComplete is called after a RollbackTrans method has completed.

❑ WillConnect is called just before a connection is established.

❑ ConnectComplete is called after a connection is established.

❑ Disconnect is called after a connection has disconnected.

❑ WillExecute is called before an Execute method is run.

❑ ExecuteComplete is called after an Execute method has completed.

❑ InfoMessage is called when the provider returns information messages.

An example of the ...Complete events could be to indicate to the user the status of their connection. The individual events for a Connection are discussed in more detail in Chapter 3.

Recordset Events

The Recordset has more events than the Connection:

❑ FetchProgress is called periodically during an asynchronous recordset creation.

❑ FetchComplete is called when the recordset has been fully populated with its records.

❑ WillChangeField is called before an action causes a field to change.

❑ FieldChangeComplete is called after an action caused a field to change.

❑ WillMove is called before an action causes the current record to change.

❑ MoveComplete is called after an action caused the current record to change.

❑ EndOfRecordset is called when there is an attempt to move beyond the end of the recordset.

❑ WillChangeRecord is called before an action causes the data in the current record to change.

❑ RecordChangeComplete is called after an action caused the data in the current record to change.

❑ WillChangeRecordset is called before an action causes a change to an aspect of the recordset (such as a filter).

❑ RecordsetChangeComplete is called after an action caused the recordset to change.

The Will... events can be used to notify the user that an action may change data, or may change the underlying records in the recordset.

A word of caution when using the new ADO Data Control in Visual Basic 6: this automatically updates records when using the video style buttons to move around the records. This differs from the standard Data Control. If you change a field, then the WillChangeField event is called, and if the value is not correct you can cancel the action. However, what gets cancelled is the Update, not the move. It's not a major problem, but something to bear in mind.

The individual events for a Recordset are discussed in more detail in Chapter 5.

Object Usage

One thing that confuses some people is when to use which object. After all, the Connection, Command, and Recordset objects are all capable of returning a recordset of data. There are only a few hard and fast rules, but in general here's what you should do:

❑ If you only ever need to run queries that don't return a recordset, and those queries are not parameterized statements (such as stored procedures) with output parameters, then use the Connection object and the Execute method.

❑ If you need to use stored procedures with output parameters then you must use the Command object. If you need to specify the cursor type or lock type, then you must use a Recordset object.

❑ If you are creating only one or two recordsets of data, then you can use the Recordset to implicitly establish a connection to a data store by passing in a connection string in the ActiveConnection parameter of a Recordset object's Open method.

❑ If you are creating two or more recordsets, then explicitly create a Connection object first, then reuse the Connection object when opening the Recordset objects. Remember that each time you connect to a data store with a connection string, a new connection is opened, or retrieved from the connection pool.

Summary

This chapter has introduced the ADO object model, examined how you go about connecting to data stores, and looked at the connection strings for a variety of OLE DB providers. It has also briefly introduced asynchronous processing and the use of events, the details of which are covered in the Chapters 3 and 5, where the `Connection` and `Recordset` objects are looked at in more detail.

Most of the rest of the book is concerned with the properties, methods and events of the various ADO objects and related libraries, such as the Extensions for DDL and Security (ADOX), Multi-dimensional Queries (ADOMD), and Jet Replication (JRO).

I thank God I am as honest as any man
living that is an old man and no honester th

Can counsel and speak comfort to th
Which they themselves not feel

Much Ado About Nothing.

He wears his faith but as the fashion of

As merry as the day

He hath indeed better bettered expectation

(Act i. Sc. i.).

He wears his faith but as the fashion of his hat.
(Ibid)

As merry as the day is long.

indeed better bettered expectation

(Act i. Sc. i.).

(Ibid)

Much Ado About Nothing.

Can counsel and speak comfort to that grief

Which they themselves not feel.

He wears his faith but as the fashion of his hat.
(Ibid)

(Ibid)

I was not born under
a rhyming planet

I was not born under a rhyming plan

For there was never yet
That could endure the t

merry as the day is long

Can counsel and speak comfort to that grief

Which they themselves not feel.

(Ibid)

He hath indeed better bettered expectation

I thank God I am as honest as an

living that is an old man and no hon

He wears his faith but as the fashion of his h

Much Ado About Nothing.

For there was never yet philospher
That could endure the toothache patiently.

(Ibid)

For there was never yet philospher
That could endure the toothache patiently

I was not born u

3

The Connection Object

The Connection object is what connects the consumer to the provider, that is, it's the link between the program and the data. As you've already seen, the flat model of ADO means that Connection objects don't need to be created explicitly. Instead, you can pass a connection string directly to a Command or Recordset object, and ADO will create the Connection object for you. However, explicitly creating a Connection object is worthwhile if you are planning to retrieve data from the data source more than once, because you won't have to establish a fresh connection each time.

Connection Pooling

Following the newsgroups in the early days of ADO, there was a lot of talk about connection pooling, and whether the benefits really are worthwhile. One of the most time-consuming operations you can perform is the act of connecting to a data store, so anything that can speed this up is defined as 'a good thing'.

Connection pooling means that ADO will not actually destroy connection objects unless it really needs to. The signal for destroying a Connection object is dictated by a timeout value: if the connection hasn't been reused within the allotted time, it is destroyed. Here's how it works. Suppose you open a connection, perform some data access, and then close the connection. From your point of view, the connection is closed. But underneath, OLE DB keeps the connection in a pool, ready for it to be used again. If you then decide that you need to open a connection to the same data store again, you will be given a Connection object from the pool of connections, and ADO *doesn't* have to perform all of the expensive data store stuff again. You may not necessarily get the exact same connection object back, but you'll get one that matches the same connection details that you previously used. In fact, existing objects will be given to anyone who requests them, so connection pooling is even more effective in a multi-user system.

One important point to note about connection pooling is that connections will only be reused if they match the exact connection details. So on multi-user systems, if you specify the same data store but use different user names and passwords, then you will create a new connection, rather than having one reused from the pool. This may seem like a disadvantage, but pooling must be done this way to avoid breaking security – it just wouldn't be right to reuse a connection if the user details differed. You could, of course, create a generic user and perform all of your data access through this user, thus maximizing the use of pooling.

You should also realize that connection pooling is *not* the same as connection sharing. An individual connection is not shared among multiple connection requests. Pooling means that *closed* connections are re-used, and not open ones.

You can test to see whether connection pooling really is working by using a tool to monitor the active connections to a data store. For example, with Microsoft SQL Server you can use SQL Trace. Executing the following code shows only one connection being opened:

```
For iLoop = 1 To 5
    objConn.Open strConn
    objConn.Close
Next
```

However, if you turn off connection pooling, you'll find that the five connections are opened and then immediately closed, one after another.

Although you probably wouldn't want to, you can turn off connection pooling by adding the attribute OLE DB Services = -2 to the end of the connection string:

```
strConn = " . . .; OLE DB Services = -2"
```

Alternatively, you can achieve the same result by setting the Connection object's Properties entry equal to -2 as in this example:

```
objConn.Properties("OLE DB Services") = -2
```

This property takes values from the DBPROPVAL_OS constants (see Appendix B). If you've already flicked to the back to find the constant with a value of -2, you'll notice there isn't one. There is, however, a constant to turn connection pooling on, so to turn it off you have to use some binary arithmetic. Take the value for turning on connection pooling and perform a logical NOT operation on it.

DBPROPVAL_OS_RESOURCEPOOLING has a value of 1, so:

```
DBPROPVAL_OS_RESOURCEPOOLING = 00000001
NOT DBPROPVAL_OS_RESOURCEPOOLING = 11111110
```

and this equals -2.

If you're using an include file that contains these constants then you can use this format:

```
objConn.Properties("OLE DB Services") = DBPROPVAL_OS_ENABLEALL AND _
                        (NOT DBPROPVAL_OS_RESOURCEPOOLING)
```

This says we want all services enabled, apart from resource pooling.

The Properties collection is discussed in more detail in Chapter 8.

For ODBC connections, the **ODBC Control Panel** applet controls connection pooling.

Connection State

One important point to note about connection pooling is that the state of the connection is reset when the connection is returned to the pool. This means that if you have set any properties for the connection, the values of these properties will return to their default values. So, even though pooling returns the same connection to you, you cannot rely upon the connection's previous state.

Methods of the Connection Object

Now let's take a look at how we work with the Connection object. We'll spend the remainder of this chapter looking at the methods, properties, collections, and events that it makes available to us. Let's begin with the methods.

The BeginTrans Method

The BeginTrans method begins a new transaction.

```
Level = Connection.BeginTrans()
```

A transaction provides atomicity to a series of data changes to a recordset (or recordsets) within a connection, allowing all of the changes to take place at once, or not at all. Once a transaction has been started, any changes to a recordset attached to the Connection are cached until the transaction is either completed or abandoned. At that stage, all of the changes will be either written to the underlying data store (if the transaction is committed) or discarded (if the transaction is aborted).

The return value indicates the level of nested transactions. This will be 1 for a top-level transaction, and will be incremented by 1 for each subsequent contained transaction. You can ignore this value if you don't need to keep track of transaction levels.

Not all providers support transactions, and calling this method against a provider that does not support transactions will generate an error. To check that transactions are supported you can check the Transaction DDL dynamic property of the connection's Properties collection. For example:

```
intSupported = objConn.Properties("Transaction DDL")
If intSupported = DBPROPVAL_TC_ALL Then
    ' transactions are fully supported
    objConn.BeginTrans
End If
```

DBPROPVAL_TC_ALL has a value of 8. The constants are explained in more detail in Appendix B, and the `Properties` collection in Appendix C.

For a good description of transactions, check out the MSDN article titled *Microsoft SQL Server: An Overview of Transaction Processing Concepts and the MS DTC*, available at http://msdn.microsoft.com/library/backgrnd/html/msdn_dtcwp.htm.

Nested Transactions

Nested transactions allow you to have transactions within transactions, and allow you to segment your work in a more controlled manner. For example, consider the situation shown here:

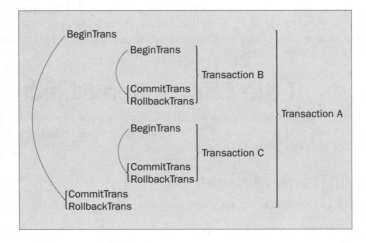

Transaction A starts – this is the first transaction, and no changes made within this transaction will be visible outside of the transaction (unless dirty reads are being used, which allow you to read values before a transaction is committed). Then Transaction B starts, and the nesting level is now 2. While B is running, the changes in B are not visible to Transaction A. When Transaction B finishes it either commits or rolls back – at this stage, A can see the changes made in B, but processes outside of Transaction A cannot. The same happens with C – its changes will not be visible to A until C commits or rolls back. Once A commits, all of the changes (that is, those in A, B, and C) are visible to other processes. Note that if A rolls back its changes, it rolls back transactions B and C, irrespective of whether they have committed or not.

It's possible to use connection attributes (set the `Attributes` property to include `adXactCommitRetaining`) to force transactions to start automatically on commit and rollback – and this can have serious consequences when nesting transactions. This is because every time you commit or rollback a transaction, a new one is automatically started. Imagine some code like this:

```
objConn.BeginTrans              ' start first transaction
  objConn.BeginTrans            ' start nested transaction
    ' do some processing
  objConn.CommitTrans           ' commit nested transaction
```

If auto-transaction mode is in place, then as soon as this nested transaction is committed, another nested transaction is started. You don't have a way to commit a transaction without it starting another, so you can never get back to the level 1 transaction.

You might never use nested transactions (or be able to for that matter – as some providers, including the Provider for ODBC, don't support them), but it's good to be aware that this problem can arise.

> The best way to build transactional systems is to utilize the facilities of MTS, where you don't need to write any code to start or end transactions. MTS also allows for distributed transactions, allowing applications to be distributed across machines.

See also the CommitTrans method and the RollbackTrans method.

The Cancel Method

Cancels the execution of a pending, asynchronous Execute or Open operation.

```
Connection.Cancel
```

This is particularly useful when writing applications that allow a user to specify connection details, or when users explicitly log on to a connection. If, after a certain delay, the connection has not been established, you can inform the user and offer the option of canceling the connection attempt. For example, in Visual Basic you could open the connection asynchronously, and offer the user a Cancel button, which would call this method.

The Close Method

Closes an open connection and any dependent objects.

```
Connection.Close
```

Closing a connection does not remove it from memory, and you can change its settings and reopen it. In order to free the object from memory (assuming no one else is using the object), you must set the object variable to Nothing. For example:

```
objConn.Close
Set objConn = Nothing
```

If you want to ensure you don't get an error when trying to close a connection that is not open, you can check the Connection object's State property:

```
If objConn.State = adStateOpen Then
  objConn.Close
End If
Set objConn = Nothing
```

When the connection's `Close` method is called, associated recordsets and commands behave differently. Any `Recordset` objects associated with the connection are closed. Any `Command` objects associated with the connection will persist, but the `ActiveConnection` parameter will be cleared, thus disassociating the command from any connection.

When the `Close` method is called, any pending changes in `Recordset` objects associated with the connection will be cancelled. If you call the `Close` method while there is a transaction in progress, an error will be generated. This is a run time error, number 3246, saying that the `Connection` object cannot be explicitly closed while in a transaction. In comparison, if a `Connection` object falls out of scope then any incomplete transactions will be rolled back, and in this case *no* error is generated.

The CommitTrans Method

Saves any pending changes and ends the current transaction.

```
Connection.CommitTrans
```

All changes made since the previous `BeginTrans` will be written to the data store. This only affects the most recently opened transaction, and you must resolve lower-level transactions before resolving higher-level ones. So, if you are nesting transactions, you cannot start two transactions and then `Commit` or `Abort` the outer transaction without first `Committing` or `Aborting` the inner transaction, since they refer to the same connection.

If the `Connection` object's `Attributes` property is set to `adXactCommitRetaining` then the provider automatically starts a new transaction after a `CommitTrans` call.

See also the `BeginTrans` method and the `RollbackTrans` method.

The Execute Method

Executes the query, SQL statement, stored procedure, or provider-specific text.

```
Set Recordset = Connection.Execute(CommandText, [RecordsAffected],
                                   [Options])
```

Parameter	Type	Description	Default
`CommandText`	`String`	Contains the SQL statement, table name, stored procedure name, or provider-specific text to execute.	
`RecordsAffected` (Optional)	`Long`	For action commands, a variable into which the provider returns the number of records that the operation affected.	

Parameter	Type	Description	Default
Options (Optional)	Long	A value that indicates how the provider should interpret the CommandText argument.	adCmdUnspecified

Options can be one or more of the CommandTypeEnum constants:

❑ adCmdText, for a SQL string.

❑ adCmdTable, for a table name, whose columns are returned via a SQL command.

❑ adCmdTableDirect, for a table name, whose columns are all returned.

❑ adCmdStoredProc, for a stored procedure name.

❑ adCmdFile, for a saved recordset.

❑ adCmdUnknown, for an unknown command type.

❑ adCmdUnspecified, to indicate the command type is unspecified. ADO will work out the command type itself, but this will lead to poorer performance, so you should always explicitly set the command type.

You can also add the following ExecuteOptionEnum modifiers to Options:

❑ adAsyncExecute, for asynchronous execution.

❑ adAsyncFetch, for asynchronous fetching.

❑ adAsyncFetchNonBlocking, for asynchronous fetching that does not block.

❑ adExecuteNoRecords, for a non-row returning command.

More details of these options can be found under the CommandType property (see Chapter 4).

The Execute method returns a new Recordset object, even if it is not used. If the command did not return any rows then the recordset will be empty. If you specify the adExecuteNoRecords option, then a null recordset is returned. The Recordset object returned is always a forward-only, read-only cursor (often called a firehose cursor). However, you can specify different cursor types by using the Open method of the Recordset object, instead of the Connection's Execute method.

You can use this method with or without some arguments, and with or without it returning a recordset. For example, to return a recordset you could use this syntax:

```
strCommandText = "SELECT * FROM authors"
Set rsAuthors = objConn.Execute (strCommandText, , adCmdText)
```

If the statement specified in the `strCommandText` parameter does not return any rows, then you should include the `adCmdExecuteNoRecords` option, as this can improve performance, because the null recordset is not automatically returned:

```
strCommandText = "UPDATE titles SET price = price * 1.10"
objConn.Execute strCommandText, , adCmdText + adExecuteNoRecords
```

To supply multiple values you add them together.

If you want to find out how many records were affected by the command then you can use the `RecordsAffected` argument, passing in a variable. This is especially useful for action queries, where a recordset is not returned:

```
strCommandText = "UPDATE titles SET Price = Price * 1.10"
objConn.Execute strCommandText, lngRecsAffected, adCmdText
Print lngRecsAffected & " were updated."
```

If you are using `RecordsAffected` and you find that it always returns -1 when you are expecting a different value, then check that there are no data store options that stop the returning of this information. SQL Server, for example, has a `SET NOCOUNT ON` statement, which stops the number of rows affected by a command from being returned. Check that this option is not set anywhere in your command (you might not realize it's there if you are using a stored procedure), and check that it's not set as a global database variable.

To have the command executed asynchronously you can also add one of the asynchronous flags to the `Options` argument. For example:

```
objConn.Execute strCommandText, lngRecsAffected, adCmdText + _
                           adAsyncExecute
```

An `ExecuteComplete` event will be raised when this operation finishes. This happens even if the command is executed synchronously, but is more useful when asynchronous operations are in use.

The Open Method

Opens a connection to a data source, so that commands can be executed against it.

```
Connection.Open([ConnectionString], [UserID], [Password],
[Options])
```

Parameter	Type	Description	Default
Connection String (optional)	String	The connection information	
UserID (optional)	String	The user name to use when connecting	

Parameter	Type	Description	Default
Password (optional)	String	The user password to use when connecting	
Options (optional)	Long	Extra connection options	adConnect Unspecified

Options can be one of the ConnectOptionEnum constants. At the moment the only supported constants are adAsyncConnect (which indicates the connection should be made asynchronously) and adConnectUnspecified (the default, which indicates a synchronous connection is to be made).

The ConnectionString property takes its value from the ConnectionString argument if used.

Values passed in the UserID and Password arguments override similar values passed in the ConnectionString argument – unless the Password you supply in the argument is blank, in which case the ConnectionString password still seems to take effect.

Some typical connections strings are shown below. For the ODBC Provider connecting to an Access database, you would use:

```
Driver={Microsoft Access Driver (*.mdb)}; DBQ=database_file
```

The DBQ argument points to the physical path name of the Access database. To connect to SQL Server, again using ODBC, you would use:

```
Driver={SQL Server}; Server=server_name; Database=database_name;
        UID=user_name, PWD=user_password
```

Switching over to the native OLE DB drivers, connecting to Access would be like this:

```
Provider=Micrsoft.Jet.OLEDB.4.0; Data Source=database_file
```

For SQL Server, using the native driver, it would be:

```
Provider=SQLOLEDB; Data Source=server_name; Initial
        Catalog=database_name; User Id=user_name;
Password=user_password
```

More details of the different connection strings that can be used for the more common OLE DB Providers can be found under the ConnectionString property, as well as in Chapter 2.

The OpenSchema Method

Obtains database schema information from the provider.

```
Set Recordset = Connection.OpenSchema(Schema, [Criteria],
[SchemaID])
```

Parameter	Type	Description	Default
Schema	SchemaEnum (Long)	The type of schema query to run.	
Criteria (Optional)	Variant	An array of query constraints for each Schema option. This is generally the column names and values to filter on.	
SchemaID (Optional)	Variant	The GUID for a provider specific schema query not defined by the OLE DB specification.	

Each value of SchemaEnum has a specific set of criteria values. This list is large and is included in Appendix B.

This method is most useful for obtaining table and procedure names from a data store. For example:

```
Set rsTables = objConn.OpenSchema(adSchemaTables)
While Not rsTables.EOF
   Debug.Print rsTables("TABLE_NAME")
   Debug.Print rsTables("TABLE_TYPE")
   rsTables.MoveNext
Wend
```

The various schemas are examined in detail in Appendix D.

For multi-dimensional (OLAP) providers using adSchemaMembers, the restrictions can either be the columns in the members schema, or one of the MDTREEOP constants, as defined in Appendix L.

An alternative method of obtaining schema information is to use the ADOX library, as discussed in Chapter 10.

The RollbackTrans Method

Cancels any changes made during the current transaction and ends the transaction.

```
Connection.RollbackTrans
```

All changes made since the previous BeginTrans will be cancelled. This only affects the most recently opened transaction, and like CommitTrans, you must resolve lower-level transactions before resolving higher-level ones.

Also, if the Connection object's Attributes property is set to adXactCommitAbort then the provider automatically starts a new transaction after a RollbackTrans call.

See also the BeginTrans method and the CommitTrans method.

Properties of the Connection Object

The Attributes Property

Indicates the transactional facilities of a `Connection` object.

```
Long = Connection.Attributes
Connection.Attributes = Long
```

Its value can be one or more of the `adXactAttributeEnum` constants:

- ❏ `adXactCommitRetaining`, to ensure that a new transaction is started automatically after a `CommitTrans`

- ❏ `adXactAbortRetaining`, to ensure that a new transaction is started automatically after a `RollbackTrans`

- ❏ A combination of both, to indicate that a new transaction is started automatically after an existing transaction is finished

Note that not all providers support this property.

In Visual Basic you can combine two or more values by ORing them together:

```
objConn.Attributes = adXactCommitRetaining OR adXactAbortRetaining
```

Beware of automatic transaction enlistment when using nested transactions, as this can lead to problems committing the higher-level transactions. For more details of this see the *Nested Transactions* subsection of the discussion of the `BeginTrans` method, earlier in this chapter.

The CommandTimeout Property

Indicates how long, in seconds, to wait while executing a command before terminating the command and generating an error. The default is 30.

```
Long = Connection.CommandTimeout
Connection.CommandTimeout = Long
```

If the timeout period is reached before the command completes execution, then an error is generated and the command cancelled. Setting this property to 0 will force the provider to wait indefinitely.

For example, the following will ensure that an error is generated if the command doesn't complete within 10 seconds:

```
objConn.CommandTimeout = 10
```

Note that the `Command` object's `CommandTimeout` property does *not* inherit the value set here. So the `CommandTimeout` property of a `Connection` object only applies to statements executed through the use of the `Execute` method.

The ConnectionString Property

Contains the details used to create a connection to a data source.

```
String = Connection.ConnectionString
Connection.ConnectionString = String
```

ADO only supports the following five arguments in the connection string (and all other arguments are ignored by ADO and passed directly to the provider):

❑ `Provider=` identifies the name of the provider

❑ `File Name=` identifies the name of the provider-specific file containing connection information (for example, a UDL file)

❑ `Remote Provider=` is the name of a provider that should be used when opening a client-side connection (this only applies to RDS)

❑ `Remote Server=` is the path name of the server that should be used when opening a client-side connection (this only applies to RDS)

❑ `URL=` is the absolute URL identifying a resource, such as a file or directory

The provider can change the connection string while the connection is being established, as it fills in some of its own details.

You cannot pass both the `Provider` and `File Name` arguments. Specifying a `File Name` will cause ADO to load the specified Data Link (`.udl`) file which contains all of the necessary connection information. For more information about Data Link files see Chapter 2.

Some examples of various connection strings are shown here. For the ODBC provider connecting to Microsoft Access:

```
Driver={Microsoft Access Driver (*.mdb)}; DBQ= database_name
```

For the ODBC provider connecting to Microsoft SQL Server:

```
Driver={SQL Server}; Server=server_name; Database=database_name;
          UID=user_name; PWD=password
```

You can also use an existing DSN. To use a DSN called `pubs`, you would specify this connection string:

```
DSN=pubs; UID=sa; PWD=
```

The pros and cons of using a DSN versus a full ODBC connect string are discussed in Chapter 14.

When using the OLE DB provider for ODBC, notice that you can omit the `Provider` option (because it is the default).

For the OLE DB provider connecting to Microsoft Access:

```
Provider=Microsoft.Jet.OLEDB.4.0; Data Source=database_name
```

For the OLE DB provider connecting to Microsoft SQL Server:

```
Provider=SQLOLEDB; Data Source=server_name;
        Initial Catalog=database_name; User Id=user_name;
        Password=user_password
```

For example, to connect to a SQL Server using the OLE DB provider you would do something like this:

```
objConn.ConnectionString = "Provider=SQLOLEDB; " & _
                           "Data Source=TIGGER;" & _
                           "Initial Catalog-pubs; " & _
                           "User Id=davids; Password=letmein"
objConn.Open
```

If, when you open a connection, you pass the connection details into the ConnectionString argument, then the ConnectionString property will be filled in with these details.

For more information on connection strings, refer to Chapter 2.

The ConnectionTimeout Property

Indicates how long, in seconds, to wait while trying to establish a connection before aborting the attempt and generating an error. The default is 15 seconds.

```
Long = Connection.ConnectionTimeout
Connection.ConnectionTimeout = Long
```

If the timeout period is reached before the connection opens, then an error is generated and the connection cancelled. Setting this property to 0 will force the provider to wait indefinitely.

You cannot set this property once the connection has been established.

The CursorLocation Property

Sets or returns the location of the cursor engine.

```
CursorLocationEnum = Connection.CursorLocation
Connection.CursorLocation = CursorLocationEnum
```

This can be set to one of the following CursorLocationEnum values:

❑ adUseClient, to use a client-side cursor.

❑ adUseClientBatch, to use a client-side cursor.

❑ adUseServer, to use a server-side cursor.

❑ adUseNone, to indicate no cursor services are used. This is included for backward compatibility and should not be used.

A disconnected recordset can only be achieved by setting the `CursorLocation` property to `adUseClient`.

A `Recordset` created against the `Connection` object will inherit the value set here.

Changing the `CursorLocation` property has no effect on existing `Recordsets` associated with a `Connection`.

The performance issues surrounding various cursor types are discussed in Chapter 14.

The DefaultDatabase Property

Indicates the default database for a `Connection` object.

```
String = Connection.DefaultDatabase
Connection.DefaultDatabase = String
```

You can access objects in other databases by fully qualifying the objects, if the data source or provider supports this.

For example, using Microsoft SQL Server, you can create two recordsets on different databases:

```
objConn.DefaultDatabase="pubs"

rsOne.Open "authors", objConn, _
                adOpenKeyset, adLockReadOnly, adCmdTable

rsTwo.Open "Sales.dbo.Orders", objConn, _
                adOpenKeyset, adLockReadOnly, adCmdTable
```

The first uses the `authors` table from the default `pubs` database, and the second uses the `Orders` table in the `Sales` database. Note that this option is not available when using the RDS client-side `Connection` objects.

The IsolationLevel Property

Indicates the level of transaction isolation for a `Connection` object.

```
IsolationLevelEnum = Connection.IsolationLevel
Connection.IsolationLevel = IsolationLevelEnum
```

The isolation level allows you to define how other transactions interact with yours, and whether they can see your changes and vice versa.

This value only comes into effect when you call the `BeginTrans` method. The provider may return the next greater level of isolation if the requested level is not available.

The value can be one of the `IsolationLevelEnum` constants:

❑ `adXactUnspecified`, which indicates that the provider is using a different isolation level to the one you specified, but that it cannot determine what this isolation level is.

❑ `adXactChaos`, which indicates that a higher-level transaction has control over the records. This means that you cannot overwrite any pending changes from another user.

❑ `adXactBrowse` or `adXactReadUncommitted`, which allows you to view uncommitted changes in another transaction. You should be careful when using either of these values, as the changes in another transaction have not been committed. They could therefore be rolled back, leaving you with invalid values.

❑ `adXactCursorStability` or `adXactReadCommitted` (the default), which indicates that you can only view changes in other transactions once they have been committed. This guarantees the state of the data. However, new records and deleted records will be reflected in your recordset.

❑ `adXactRepeatableRead`, which doesn't allow you to see changes made from other transactions unless you re-query the recordset. Once you have re-queried the recordset, you can see new records that might have been added by other users to the records that compose your recordset.

❑ `adXactIsolated` or `adXactSerializable`, which indicates that transactions are completely isolated from each other. This means that all concurrent transactions will produce the same effect as if each transaction was executed one after the other.

The Mode Property

Indicates the available permissions for modifying data in a `Connection`.

```
ConnectModeEnum = Connection.Mode
Connection.Mode = ConnectModeEnum
```

The value can be one of the `ConnectModeEnum` constants:

❑ `adModeUnknown`, which is the default, to say that permissions cannot be determined, or haven't been set yet

❑ `adModeRead`, for read-only permissions

❑ `adModeWrite`, for write-only permissions

❑ `adModeReadWrite`, for read/write permissions

❑ `adModeRecursive`, to indicate that the `adShare` permissions should be applied recursively

❑ `adModeShareDenyRead`, for preventing other users from opening a connection with read permissions

❑ `adModeShareDenyWrite`, for preventing other users from opening a connection with write permissions

❑ `adModeShareExclusive`, for preventing other users from opening a connection

❑ `adModeShareDenyNone`, for allowing users to open a connection with any permissions, and ensures that neither read nor write permissions can be denied to other users

You can use this to set or return the provider access permission for the ⦁current connection.

You cannot set this property on open connections, and not all providers support all options.

The Provider Property

Indicates the name of the provider for a `Connection` object.

```
String = Connection.Provider
Connection.Provider = String
```

This property can also be set by the contents of the `ConnectionString` property.

Note that specifying the provider in more than one place can have unpredictable results. Microsoft doesn't actually specify what 'unpredictable' means in this case, but it's probably best to only set this in one place. The `Provider` property must be set before trying to access any provider-specific dynamic properties, otherwise the default OLE DB Provider for ODBC is assumed.

If no provider is specified then the default is MSDASQL, the Microsoft OLE DB Provider for ODBC. The providers supplied with MDAC 2.6 are:

❑ **MSDASQL**, for ODBC

❑ **MSIDXS**, for Index Server

❑ **ADSDSOObject**, for Active Directory Services

❑ **Microsoft.Jet.OLEDB.4.0**, for Microsoft Jet databases, both Access 2000 and earlier version.

❑ **SQLOLEDB**, for SQL Server

❑ **MSDAORA**, for Oracle

❑ **MSDataShape**, for the Microsoft Data Shape with hierarchical recordsets. This provider is discussed in more detail in Chapter 11

❑ **MSDAIPP.DSO.1**, for Internet Publishing

❑ **MSDAOSP**, for developing simple OLE DB providers that expose data in simple tabular (row/column) format

❑ **MSPersist**, for persisting or saving a `Recordset` to a file or object that supports the standard COM `IStream` interface (such as ASP's `Request` or `Response` objects or ADO's `Stream` object)

The various `Provider` and `ConnectionString` options are discussed in more detail under the `ConnectionString` property, as well as in Chapter 2.

The State Property

Describes whether the `Connection` object is open or closed. For asynchronous connections it also indicates whether the state is connecting, opening, or retrieving.

```
Long = Connection.State
```

This will be one of the following `ObjectStateEnum` constants:

❑ `adStateOpen` for an open connection

❑ `adStateClosed` for a closed connection

❑ `adStateConnecting`, for an asynchronous connection that is still connecting to a provider

❑ `adStateExecuting`, for an asynchronous connection that is executing a command

❑ `adStateFetching`, for an asynchronous connection that is fetching data

You can use the `State` property to ensure that you don't generate errors when closing a connection. For example, to ensure that a transaction is commited:

```
If objConn.State = adStateOpen Then
   objConn.CommitTrans
   objConn.Close
End If
```

The Version Property

Indicates the version number of the MDAC components.

```
String = Connection.Version
```

Note that the version number of the provider can be obtained from the `Connection` object's `Properties` collection.

This property is read only.

Events of the Connection Object

Connection events can be quickly summarized as follows:

❑ `BeginTransComplete` is raised after a transaction has begun

❑ `CommitTransComplete` is raised after a transaction has been committed

❑ `ConnectComplete` is raised after the connection has been established

❑ `Disconnect` is raised after a connection has been closed

❑   ExecuteComplete is raised after an Execute method call has completed

❑   InfoMessage is raised when the provider returns extra information

❑   RollbackTransComplete is raised after a transaction has been rolled back

❑   WillConnect is raised just before the connection is established

❑   WillExecute is raised just before a statement is executed

These events work in both synchronous and asynchronous modes.

All events will have a bi-directional parameter, adStatus, to indicate the status of the event. This is of type EventStatusEnum and on entry to the procedure can be one of the following constants:

❑   adStatusOK, to indicate that the action that caused the event was successful.

❑   adStatusErrorsOccured, to indicate that errors or warnings occurred, in which case the Errors collection should be checked.

❑   adStatusCantDeny. On a Will… event this indicates that you cannot cancel the action that generated the event; on a …Complete event it indicates that the action was cancelled.

❑   adStatusUnwantedEvent, which indicates that the action that generated the event should no longer generate events.

On a Will… event (and assuming adStatusCantDeny is not set), before the procedure exits you can set adStatus to adStatusCancel to cancel the action that caused this event. This also generates an error indicating the event has been cancelled. For example, assume that you have moved from one record to the next – this will raise a WillMove event on the recordset. If you decide that you do not wish to move to another record, you can set adStatus to adStatusCancel, and the Move action will be cancelled. This allows you to perhaps cancel actions where the data is incorrect.

When using Will… events, one thing to watch for is implicit method calls. Taking the above Move as an example, if the current record has been edited, then ADO implicitly calls Update. In this case you might get more than one Will… event. We discuss this in more detail in Chapter 5.

If you no longer wish to receive events for a particular action, then before the procedure exits you can set adStatus to adStatusUnwantedEvent, and they will no longer be generated.

The BeginTransComplete Event

Fires after a BeginTrans method call finishes executing.

```
BeginTransComplete(TransactionLevel, pError, adStatus, pConnection)
```

Parameter	Type	Description
TransactionLevel	Long	Contains the new transaction level of the BeginTrans that caused the event.
pError	Error	If adStatus is adStatusErrorsOccurred, this is an Error object that describes the error that occurred. Otherwise it is not set.
adStatus	EventStatus Enum (Long)	Identifies the status of the message.
pConnection	Connection	The Connection object upon which the BeginTrans was executed.

You can use this to trigger other operations that are dependent upon the transaction having been started. For example, you might like to build a transaction monitoring system, and you could log the start of the transaction in this event.

The CommitTransComplete Event

Fires after a CommitTrans method call finishes executing.

```
CommitTransComplete(pError, adStatus, pConnection)
```

Parameter	Type	Description
pError	Error	If adStatus is adStatusErrorsOccurred, this is an Error object that describes the error that occurred. Otherwise it is not set.
adStatus	EventStatus Enum (Long)	Identifies the status of the message.
pConnection	Connection	The Connection object upon which the CommitTrans was executed.

You can use this to trigger other operations that are dependent upon the transaction having been completed successfully, such as updating log files or an audit trail.

The ConnectComplete Event

Fires after a connection is established.

```
ConnectComplete(pError, adStatus, pConnection)
```

3

ADO: Connection Object

Parameter	Type	Description
pError	Error	If adStatus is adStatusErrorsOccurred, this is an Error object that describes the error that occurred. Otherwise it is not set.
adStatus	EventStatus Enum (Long)	Identifies the status of the event.
pConnection	Connection	The Connection object for which this event applies.

You can use the ConnectComplete event to examine the details of the connection and whether it completed successfully. For example, the following Visual Basic example shows how you could use the ConnectComplete event:

```
Private Sub objConn_ConnectComplete(ByVal pError As ADODB.Error,
                   adStatus As ADODB.EventStatusEnum,
                   ByVal pConnection As ADODB.Connection)
    Select Case adStatus
    Case adStatusErrorsOccurred
        Print "Errors occurred whilst attempting to connect."
        Print "Connection String is: " & pConnection.ConnectionString
        Print "Error description: " & pError.Description
    Case adStatusOK
        Print "Connection successful."
    End Select
End Sub
```

The section of code that is not highlighted is the definition of the event procedure and is automatically created by Visual Basic. (For more on using events with Visual Basic, see Chapter 2.)

The Disconnect Event

Fires after a connection is closed.

```
Disconnect(adStatus, pConnection)
```

Parameter	Type	Description
adStatus	EventStatus Enum (Long)	Identifies the status of the event.
pConnection	Connection	The Connection object for which this event applies.

You can use this to examine whether the disconnection was successful. You can also use it to track users as they log onto and off from data sources. It can also be useful to alert users when a connection drops unexpectedly.

The ExecuteComplete Event

Fired after a statement has finished executing.

```
ExecuteComplete(RecordsAffected, pError, adStatus, pCommand,
                pRecordset, pConnection)
```

Parameter	Type	Description
Records Affected	Long	A Long variable into which the provider returns the number of records that the operation affected.
pError	Error	If adStatus is adStatusErrorsOccurred, then this is an Error object that describes the error that occurred. Otherwise it is not set.
adStatus	EventStatus Enum (Long)	Identifies the status of the event.
pCommand	Command	The Command object for which this event applies. This may not be set if a Command object was not used.
pRecordset	Recordset	The Recordset object upon which the Execute was run. This may be empty if a non-recordset-returning command was run, such as an action query.
pConnection	Connection	The Connection object upon which the Execute method was called.

This allows you to examine whether the command completed successfully, and how many records it affected. You can use this instead of the RecordsAffected argument of the Execute method. The following Visual Basic code shows the use of this event.

```
Private Sub objConn_ExecuteComplete(ByVal RecordsAffected As_Long, _
    ByVal pError As ADODB.Error, _
    ByVal adStatus As ADODB.EventStatusEnum, _
    ByVal pCommand As ADODB.Command, ByVal pRecordset As _
    ADODB.Recordset, ByVal pConnection As ADODB.Connection)

    If adStatus = adStatusOK Then
        Print RecordsAffected & " records were affected by this command."
    End If

End Sub
```

The code that has not been highlighted is the Visual Basic generated event procedure.

The InfoMessage Event

Fires whenever a connection event operation completes successfully and the provider returns additional information, such as a warning.

```
InfoMessage(pError, adStatus, pConnection)
```

Parameter	Type	Description
pError	Error	If adStatus is adStatusErrorsOccurred, then this is an Error object that describes the error that occurred. Otherwise it is not set.
adStatus	EventStatus Enum (Long)	Identifies the status of the event.
pConnection	Connection	The Connection object upon which the statement was executed.

The parameters define what type of information message this is. This is particularly useful when dealing with ODBC data sources, especially to SQL Server, as it returns informational messages that could be logged in an audit trail.

For example, you could connect to the pubs database on SQL server with this connect string:

```
Driver={SQL Server}; Server=Tigger; Database=pubs; UID=sa; PWD=
```

and then put this code into the InfoMessage event procedure:

```
Private Sub oConn_InfoMessage(ByVal pError As ADODB.Error, _
        adStatus As ADODB.EventStatusEnum, _
        ByVal pConnection As ADODB.Connection)

    Dim objError As ADODB.Error

    Debug.Print pError.Description

    For Each objError In pConnection.Errors
        Debug.Print vbtab; objError.Description
    Next

End Sub
```

On my server, the above code generates the following warnings when connecting to the pubs database in SQL Server, using the OLE DB Provider for ODBC:

```
[Microsoft] [ODBC SQL Server Driver] [SQL Server] Changed database
         context to 'master'.
[Microsoft] [ODBC SQL Server Driver] [SQL Server] Changed database
         context to 'master'.
[Microsoft] [ODBC SQL Server Driver] [SQL Server] Changed language
         setting to 'us_english'.
[Microsoft] [ODBC SQL Server Driver] [SQL Server] Changed database
         context to 'pubs'.
```

In general this event can be used to track connection messages, or actions on the connection that return the ODBC `SQL_SUCCESS_WITH_INFO` result.

The RollbackTransComplete Event

Fires after a `RollbackTrans` method call has finished executing.

```
RollbackTransComplete(pError, adStatus, pConnection)
```

Parameter	Type	Description
pError	Error	If adStatus is adStatusErrorsOccurred, then this is an Error object that describes the error that occurred. Otherwise it is not set.
adStatus	EventStatus Enum (Long)	Identifies the status of the event.
pConnection	Connection	The Connection object upon which the RollbackTrans method was called.

You can use this event to trigger other operations that depend upon the transaction having failed, such as writing to log files. For example:

```
Private Sub objConn_RollbackTransComplete(ByVal pError As
                  ADODB.Error, adStatus As
ADODB.EventStatusEnum, _
                  ByVal pConnection As ADODB.Connection)
Print "Transaction was rolled back. Changes have not been saved "
End Sub
```

This could be extremely useful in nightly batch jobs.

The WillConnect Event

Fires before a connection is opened, indicating that the connection is about to be established.

```
WillConnect(ConnectionString, UserID, Password, Options, adStatus,
         pConnection)
```

Parameter	Type	Description
Connection String	String	The connection information.
UserID	String	The user name to use when connecting.
Password	String	The user password to use when connecting.
Options	Long	Extra connection options, as passed into the Options parameter of the Connection object's Open method.
adStatus	EventStatus Enum (Long)	Identifies the status of the event.
pConnection	Connection	The Connection object for which this event applies.

The parameters supplied can be changed before the method returns – for instance if the user has specified certain connection attributes, but you wish to change them. As an example, imagine an application that allowed the user to specify connection details. You could prevent them from connecting as a certain user, but allow the connection to be established as another:

```
Private Sub objConn_WillConnect(ConnectionString As String, _
       UserID As String, Password As String, Options As Long, _
       adStatus As ADODB.EventStatusEnum, _
       ByVal pConnection As ADODB.Connection)

    If adStatus = adStatusOK Then
       Select Case UserID
       Case "sa"
          Print "Connection as system administrator not allowed."
          adStatus = adStatusCancel
       Case "Guest"
          UserID = "GuestUser"
          Password = "GuestPassword"
       End Select
    End If

End Sub
```

This stops the user trying to connect as sa and cancels the connection attempt. If a user tries to connect as Guest then the user ID is changed to GuestUser and connection proceeds. This allows you to have a set of real user details that are hidden, whilst exposing a viewable set of user details.

The WillExecute Event

Fires before a pending command executes on the connection.

```
WillExecute(Source, CursorType, LockType, Options, adStatus, pCommand,
            pRecordset, pConnection)
```

Name	Type	Description
Source	String	The SQL command or stored procedure name.
CursorType	CursorTypeEnum (Long)	The type of cursor for the recordset that will be opened. If set to adOpenUnspecified the cursor type cannot be changed.
LockType	LockTypeEnum (Long)	The lock type for the recordset that will be opened. If set to adLockUnspecified the lock type cannot be changed.
Options	Long	The options that can be used to execute the command or open the recordset, as passed into the Options argument.
adStatus	EventStatusEnum (Long)	Identifies the status of the event.
pCommand	Command	The Command object for which this event applies. This may be empty if a Command object was not being used.
pRecordset	Recordset	The Recordset object for which this event applies. If the Execute method call didn't return a recordset, then this will be an empty Recordset object.
pConnection	Connection	The Connection object for which this event applies.

The execution parameters can be modified in this procedure, as it is called before the command executes.

This is particularly useful when building user-query type applications where the user has the ability to set details of the connection, since it allows you to examine the parameters and modify them if necessary. For example:

```
Private Sub objConn_WillExecute(Source As String, _
    CursorType As ADODB.CursorTypeEnum, LockType As _
    ADODB.LockTypeEnum, _
    Options As Long, adStatus As ADODB.EventStatusEnum, _
    ByVal pCommand As ADODB.Command, ByVal pRecordset As _
    ADODB.Recordset, ByVal pConnection As ADODB.Connection)

    If Source = "SalaryDetails" Then
        Print " Nice try, but you're not allowed to look at these"
        adStatus = adStatusCancel
    End If

End Sub
```

The above code cancels the event if someone tries to connect to the
SalaryDetails table.

You can also use this technique to protect against *ad hoc* insertions and deletions, and
it is an easy way to build business logic into the connection. A better way to protect
against this sort of amendment to data or tables is to implement proper security,
and to use a 3-tier business model, where data access is only possible through
controlled operations.

Collections of the Connection Object

The collections are discussed in depth in Chapter 8.

The Errors Collection

Contains all of the Error objects created in response to a single failure involving
the provider.

```
Connection.Errors
```

The Errors collection is only cleared by ADO when another ADO operation
generates an error.

Note that the Errors collection often contains warnings and other informational
messages from the provider, as well as errors. For this reason, it's a good idea to use
the Clear method of the Errors collection before certain operations, to ensure that
the warnings are relevant to the most recent operation. In particular, you should use
the technique for the Resync, UpdateBatch, and CancelBatch methods or the
Filter property on a Recordset object, and for the Open method on a
Connection object. Explicitly clearing the errors allows you to use the Count
property of the collection to quickly identify whether errors have occurred.

The Properties Collection

Contains all of the Property objects for a Connection object.

```
Properties = Connection.Properties
```

The Properties collection is discussed in more detail in Chapter 8 and a full list of
the properties available is in Appendix C.

I thank God I am as honest as any man

living that is an old man and no honester th

For there was never yet philospher
That could endure the toothache patiently.

Can counsel and speak comfort to th

Which they themselves not feel.

Much Ado About Nothing.

He wears his faith but as the fashion of h

As merry as the day

He hath indeed better bettered expectation

(Act i. Sc. i.).

He wears his faith but as the fashion of his hat.

(Ibid)

As merry as the day is long.

h indeed better bettered expectation

(Act i. Sc. i.).

(Ibid)

Can counsel and speak comfort to that grief

Much Ado About Nothing.

Which they themselves not feel.

He wears his faith but as the fashion of his hat.

(Ibid)

(Ibid)

I was not born under

a rhyming plane

I was not born under a rhyming plane

(Sc. 2

For there was never yet

That could endure the to

merry as the day is long

(Sc. 2)

Can counsel and speak comfort to that grief

(Ibid)

Which they themselves not feel.

He hath indeed better bettered expectation

(Ibid)

I thank God I am as honest as any

living that is an old man and no honest

He wears his faith but as the fashion of his ha

(Ibi

Much Ado About Nothing.

For there was never yet philospher
That could endure the toothache patiently.

(Ibid)

themselves not feel.

(Ibid)

I was not born u

The Command Object

Although the Connection object allows the execution of commands (such as SQL statements or stored procedures) against a data store, the Command object has greater functionality and flexibility, especially when stored procedures are being used. It's not actually a requirement that data providers support the Command object, although all of the major providers do.

You might be required to pass parameters into stored procedures or stored queries and, as you'll see in this chapter, there's more than one way to do this. One method involves the use of the Parameters collection, which allows complete control over the individual parameters passed to a procedure or query. It's for this reason that the Parameters collection is covered in this chapter (rather than with the other collections in Chapter 8).

> When using stored procedures that have output parameters, you have to use a Command object. The Command object's Parameters collection allows the passing of parameters into and out of stored procedures, as well as allowing a recordset to be passed back to the application.

Methods of the Command Object

The Cancel Method

Cancels execution of a pending asynchronous Execute method call.

```
Command.Cancel
```

The Cancel method is particularly useful when allowing users to submit their own asynchronous queries, as these can often have long execution times, and you may wish to provide them with a Cancel button on the screen.

The CreateParameter Method

Creates and returns a reference to a new `Parameter` object.

```
Set Parameter = Command.CreateParameter([Name], [Type],
                                        [Direction],
                                        [Size], [Value])
```

The method's arguments are all optional:

Parameter	Type	Description	Default
Name	String	The name of the parameter.	
Type	DataTypeEnum (Long)	The data type of the parameter.	adEmpty
Direction	ParameterDirection Enum (Long)	The direction of the parameter.	adParam Input
Size	Long	The maximum length of the parameter value in characters or bytes.	0
Value	Variant	The value for the parameter.	

The `ParameterDirectionEnum` constants list is as follows:

❑ `adParamUnknown`, to indicate that the direction of the parameter is unknown

❑ `adParamInput`, to indicate that the parameter is an input parameter to the command

❑ `adParamOutput`, to indicate that the parameter is an output parameter from the command

❑ `adParamInputOutput`, to indicate that the parameter is both an input to and an output from the command

❑ `adParamReturnValue`, to indicate that the parameter is a return value from the command

The `DataTypeEnum` list is quite large, and is included in Appendix B.

`CreateParameter` is used to create the parameters that are to be passed to stored procedures and stored queries. There are two ways of using `CreateParameter`: the first is with all of its arguments, and the second is without any arguments. For example, the following two sets of code are logically equivalent ways of assigning specific values to a `Parameter` object's properties:

```
Set objParam = objCmd.CreateParameter("ID", adInteger,
                                      adParamInput, 8,
                                      123 )
```

and:

```
Set objParam = objCmd.CreateParameter
objParam.Name = "ID"
objParam.Type = adInteger
objParam.Direction = adParamInput
objParam.Size = 8
objParam.Value = 123
```

Note that the code above does not add the parameter to the `Parameters` collection of the `Command` object concerned. For this, you must call the `Append` method of the `Command` object, and pass a reference to the `Parameter` object that is to be added to the `Parameters` collection. For example:

```
objCmd.Parameters.Append objParam
```

Multiple parameter objects can be appended to the `Parameters` collection of a `Command` object. However, if you attempt to append a `Parameter` object that does not have a specific value assigned to at least one of its properties, an error will be generated. We'll take a look at the `Parameter` object itself later in this chapter.

If the `NamedParameters` property is `True`, the names of the `Parameter` objects in the `Parameters` collection are used to match the parameters to the parameters in the underlying command. If the `NamedParamters` property is set to `False` (the default), then the parameters in the `Parameters` collection are matched to those in the stored procedure or query by the order in which they're listed. In particular, this means that the name you assign to a `Parameter` in the collection (via the `CreateParameter` method or the `Name` property) need not be the same as the corresponding parameter name within the procedure or query. It's the *order* of parameters that's important, not the names – although it's best to use similar (or the same) names both in the collection and in the procedure or query.

The Execute Method

Executes the query, SQL statement, or stored procedure specified in the `CommandText` property, or the command specified in the `CommandStream` property.

```
[Set Recordset = ]Command.Execute([RecordsAffected], [Parameters],
                                   [Options])
```

Parameter	Type	Description	Default
RecordsAffected	Long	A Long variable into which the provider returns the number of records that the operation affected.	
Parameters	Variant	An array of parameter values passed to the statement specified in the Command's CommandText property. Output parameters will not return correct values if passed here.	

Parameter	Type	Description	Default
Options	Long	A value that indicates how the provider should interpret the CommandText or CommandStream properties of the Command object.	-1

RecordsAffected can be used to determine how many records were affected by the command executed. For example:

```
objCmd.CommandText = "UPDATE titles SET royalty = royalty * 1.10"
objCmd.Execute lngRecs
Print "Number of records affected by command: "
Print lngRecs
```

Parameter values passed in the Parameters argument will override any values in a Command's Parameters collection. For example:

```
objCmd.Parameters.Refresh
objCmd.Parameters("@FirstParam") = "abc"
objCmd.Execute , Array("def")
```

This command will use def as the value for the @FirstParam parameter, instead of the value abc supplied in the Parameters collection.

Options can be one of the following CommandTypeEnum constants:

❑   adCmdText, to indicate that the command text is to be interpreted as a text command, such as a SQL statement.

❑   adCmdTable, to indicate that the command text is to be interpreted as the name of a table.

❑   adCmdTableDirect, to indicate that the command text is to be interpreted directly as a table name. This allows ADO to switch some internal options in order to provide more efficient processing. (See the section on the CommandType property.)

❑   adCmdStoredProc, to indicate that the command text should be interpreted as the name of a stored procedure or stored query.

❑   adCmdUnknown, to indicate that the nature of the command text is unknown.

Additionally, you can add one or more of the ExecuteOptionEnum constants:

❑   adAsyncExecute, to indicate that the command should be executed asynchronously.

❑   adAsyncFetch, to indicate that after the initial batch of rows is fetched, remaining rows are fetched asynchronously.

❑ adAsyncFetchNonBlocking, indicates that asynchronous fetching is used. However, if the requested row has not yet been fetched, the last row fetched is supplied instead.

❑ adExecuteNoRecords, to indicate that the command does not return any records. Any rows that are returned are discarded.

❑ adExecuteRecord, to indicate that the result of the command is a single row and should be returned as a Record object.

❑ adExecuteStream, to indicate that the results of the command should be returned as a Stream object.

For asynchronous operations you can add adAsyncExecute to the Options argument to make the command execute asynchronously, and adAsyncFetch or adAsyncFetchNonBlocking to force the recordset to be returned asynchronously:

```
objCmd.Execute  , , adCmdTable OR adAsyncExecute OR adAsyncFetch
```

Using streams as command input and output is a new feature of ADO 2.6. The difference is that you use the CommandStream property to specify the stream containing the command to be executed. You can also use the dynamic property "Output Stream" to specify a stream into which the output of the command should be placed. For example:

```
' construct the SQL query
sSQL = "<ROOT xmlns:sql='urn:schemas-microsoft.com:xml-sql'>" & _
       "<sql:query>SELECT * FROM authors FOR XML AUTO" & _
       "</sql:query>" & _
       "</ROOT>"

' place the query in the stream
stmQuery.WriteText sSQL, adWriteChar
stmQuery.Position = 0

objCmd.CommandStream = stmQuery
objCmd.Dialect = "{5D531CB2-E6Ed-11D2-B252-00C04F681B71}"
objCmd.Properties("Output Stream") = stmOutput
objCmd.Execute
```

At this stage the stream stmOutput contains the results of the command. In ASP you could use the Response object here:

```
objCmd.Properties("Output Stream") = Response
```

This would stream the command output directly to the browser. If using the XPATH Dialect then you can also set the following dynamic properties:

Dynamic Property	Description
Mapping Schema	The XML schema that maps XML elements and attributes to tables and columns.
Base Path	The directory containing the mapping schema.

Properties of the Command Object

The ActiveConnection Property

Indicates the Connection object to which the Command object currently belongs.

```
Set Connection = Command.ActiveConnection
Set Command.ActiveConnection = Connection
Command.ActiveConnection = String
String = Command.ActiveConnection
```

This can be a valid Connection object or a connection string, and must be set before the Execute method is called, otherwise an error will occur.

There is a subtle difference between using an existing Connection object and a connection string when setting the ActiveConnection. For example, consider the following lines of code:

```
objConn.Open "Provider=Microsoft.Jet.OLEDB.4.0; " & _
                   "Data Source=C:\ADO\ADOTest.mdb"
Set objCmd.ActiveConnection = objConn

objCmd.ActiveConnection="Provider=Microsoft.Jet.OLEDB.4.0; " & _
                   "Data Source=C:\ADO\ADOTest.mdb"
```

These code fragments both appear to do the same thing; however, the first uses an existing Connection object, whereas the second will implicitly create a new connection. Connection pooling, however, may reuse an existing connection if it can speed up the connection in this second case.

In Visual Basic, if you set the value of ActiveConnection to Nothing then the Command object is disassociated from the connection, but remains active. However, note what happens to the parameters. If the provider supplied the parameters (i.e. via the Refresh method of the Parameters collection) then the Parameters collection will be cleared. On the other hand, if the parameters were created and appended manually then they are left intact. This could be useful if you have several commands with parameters that are the same.

The CommandStream Property

Identifies the Stream object containing the command details.

```
Variant = Command.CommandStream
Command.CommandStream = Variant
```

The CommandStream can be any valid Stream, or object that supports the IStream interface. For example, in an ASP page the input stream (Request) might contain the command details. Since the ASP Request object supports the standard COM IStream interface in ASP version 3.0, the following code allows us to assign the contents of the Request object to the CommandStream property:

```
<%
  Set cmdC = Server.CreateObject("ADODB.Command")

  Set objCmd.CommandStream = Request

objCmd.ActiveConnection = ". . ."
objCmd.Dialect = ". . ."
objCmd.Execute , , adExecuteStream
%>
```

The dynamic property "Output Stream" allows the output of a command to be placed into a stream. For example, the above code could be modified to output the results of the command to the Response object:

```
<%
  Set objCmd = Server.CreateObject("ADODB.Command")

  Set objCmd.CommandStream = Request

objCmd.ActiveConnection = ". . ."
objCmd.Dialect = ". . ."
objCmd.Properties("Output Stream") = Response
objCmd.Execute , , adExecuteStream
%>
```

The CommandStream and CommandText properties are mutually exclusive. Setting one will clear the other.

This property is new to ADO 2.6.

The CommandText Property

Contains the text of a command to be issued against a data provider.

```
String = Command.CommandText
Command.CommandText = String
```

This can be a SQL statement, a table name, a stored procedure name, or a provider-specific command, and the default is an empty string.

For example, to set the command text to a SQL string, you can do the following:

```
objCmd.CommandText = "SELECT * FROM authors WHERE state = 'CA'"
```

There are a number of ways to pass parameters into a stored procedure in SQL Server. One way is to use the parameters contained in the Parameters collection. Another way is to pass the stored procedure and its arguments as a text command:

```
objCmd.CommandText = "usp_MyProcedure ('abc', 123)"
objCmd.CommandType = adCmdStoredProc
Set objRs = objCmd.Execute()
```

This method is sometimes quicker to code than using the Parameters collection, although you obviously have no way to use output parameters with this method. Alternatively, you could use the Parameters argument of the Execute method:

```
objCmd.CommandText = "usp_MyProcedure"
objCmd.CommandType = adCmdStoredProc
Set objRs = objCmd.Execute (, Array("abc", 123))
```

If you set the Command object's Prepared property to True, then the command will be compiled and stored by the provider (if it supports prepared statements) before executing. This prepared statement is retained by the provider for the duration of the connection. If you are using the SQL Server provider, this may create a temporary stored procedure for you (if you have the "Use Procedure for Prepare" dynamic property in the Connection object's Properties collection, as discussed in Appendix C). This is particularly useful when the same command is to be executed several times, but with different parameters.

The Parameters collection is explained in more detail later in this chapter.

The CommandStream and CommandText properties are mutually exclusive. Setting one will clear the other.

The CommandTimeout Property

Indicates how long, in seconds, to wait while executing a command before terminating the command and generating an error. The default is 30 seconds.

```
Long = Command.CommandTimeout
Command.CommandTimeout = Long
```

An error will be generated if the timeout value is reached before the command completes execution, and the command will be cancelled. If you are using Visual Basic and ADO events, then the ExecuteComplete event will be fired when the error is generated, and you can check the pError argument to detect the error. You can also trap the error and examine the error details.

This property bears no relation to the Connection object's CommandTimeout property, that is to say, it is not inherited from the connection.

The CommandType Property

Indicates the type of the Command object.

```
CommandTypeEnum = Command.CommandType
Command.CommandType = CommandTypeEnum
```

The CommandTypeEnum constants are defined under the Execute method, as well as in Appendix B.

You should use this property to optimize the processing of the command. The reason for doing this is that it informs the provider what sort of command you will be executing, before the command is actually performed. This allows the provider to decide what to do in advance, and this often gives an increase in performance because ADO doesn't have to figure out the type of command.

The distinction between adCmdTable and adCmdTableDirect is quite subtle. Consider the following:

```
objCmd.CommandText = "authors"
objCmd.CommandType = adCmdTable
```

This actually sends SELECT * FROM authors to the provider. In contrast, consider this code:

```
objCmd.CommandText = "authors"
objCmd.CommandType = adCmdTableDirect
```

This only sends the statement authors to the provider. Some providers may not support direct table names, and may require explicit SQL statements.

The performance implications of these options are discussed in more detail in Chapter 14.

The Dialect Property

Identifies the dialect to be used for the CommandStream or CommandText properties.

```
String = Command.Dialect
Command.Dialect = String
```

The Dialect property is a GUID (Globally Unique IDentifier) and is provider dependent, allowing the provider to support multiple dialects. The default dialect is standard SQL, identified by the following GUID:

```
{C8B521FB-5CF3-11CE-ADE5-00AA0044773D}
```

For the SQL XML format supported by SQL Server 2000, you would use the following GUID:

```
{5D531CB2-E6Ed-11D2-B252-00C04F681B71}
```

For XPATH support you should use:

```
{EC2A4293-E898-11D2-B1B7-00C04F680C56}
```

You should consult your provider documentation to find out any provider specific dialects.

More details about XML interaction can be found in the ADO help files.

ADO: Command Object

4

The Name Property

Indicates the name of the Command object.

```
String = Command.Name
Command.Name = String
```

In many cases you probably won't use this property, but it could be used to uniquely identify a Command object in a collection of commands. For example, imagine an application that allows users to build up a number of commands. You could store these in a collection and use the Name property of the commands to identify them. Think about the query window in SQL Server – you could build quite a good emulation of this using ADO to connect to multiple data sources, and using a collection to store various command objects.

Commands as Connection Methods

There is a rarely-noted feature that goes like this: if you name a Command object and then associate the command with a Connection object, the Connection object inherits a method corresponding to the name of the Command. This is a dynamic method, which doesn't show up as part of the object's methods or properties within code editors such as Visual Basic.

Let's consider an example. Suppose you have two types of user – a Clerk and a Manager – and both types need to look at employee details. Managers are allowed to see the salary details, while the humble clerks are not. You have decided to use stored procedures to encapsulate all of your SQL logic, so you have two possibilities. The first is to build a single SQL statement to return the employee details, and have it check whether the user is a manager or a clerk. Your user then calls a business object, which fetches the data:

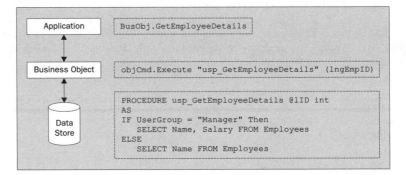

Note that you now have a business rule built into the SQL. In many cases this is not a problem (and indeed could be deemed good practice), but this doesn't always fit everyone's needs. You may find that you'd rather not put business rules into your SQL code. For instance, in this example, you also have to work out details such as how to establish which group the user belongs to. That's not a particularly complex problem, but here's an alternative situation that keeps all the business logic in the same place:

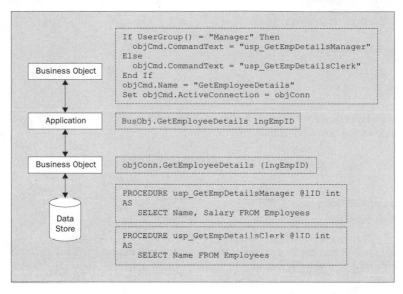

In this situation, the application first calls a business object, perhaps when it starts, and the business object establishes the role: clerk or manager. This sets the appropriate stored procedure and attaches the command as a method of the connection. Later on, the application can simply call the business object that calls this new method. Since the method is one of two stored procedures, the correct stored procedure is run. Although this seems like more code, it actually simplifies some of the programming. It puts the business logic in a component where it is easily reused, and it also makes the stored procedures simpler – these will now run faster because there is no run-time decision to make.

> Using this method you must set the Name property before setting the ActiveConnection, otherwise an error occurs.

One thing that's not documented very clearly – or very often – is that when using this method, the newly named procedure accepts the parameters of the stored procedure, as well as an extra argument – a recordset. For example, imagine the following stored procedure:

```
CREATE PROCEDURE usp_TestProcOne
    @sAuLName varchar(40)
AS
    SELECT * FROM authors
    WHERE   au_lname = @sAuLName
```

You could call this using the following code:

```
strConn = "Provider=SQLOLEDB; Data Source=SQL7Server; " & _
          "Initial Catalog=TestData; User Id=sa; Password="
objConn.Open strConn
```

```
objCmd.CommandText = "usp_TestProcOne"
objCmd.CommandType = adCmdStoredProc
objCmd.Name = "TestProc"
Set objCmd.ActiveConnection = objConn

objConn.TestProc "Ringer", objRec
```

This passes `Ringer` into the stored procedure as the parameter, and the results are returned in the recordset `objRec`.

Another shortcut is to just call the stored procedure name directly against the connection:

```
objConn.Open " . . ."
objConn.usp_TestProcOne "Ringer", objRec
```

If ADO doesn't recognize the command, then it passes the command and parameters to the provider to see if it can handle it. If the provider recognizes the command, the command is executed; otherwise an error is generated. Note that this, of course, will result in poorer performance.

One particularly interesting feature of named commands is that a variation on this allows you to retrieve output parameters of a stored procedure, even when the provider doesn't support it. This is covered in more detail in the section at the end of the chapter.

The NamedParameters Property

Indicates whether or not parameter names should be passed to the provider.

```
Boolean = Command.NamedParameters
Command.NamedParameters = Boolean
```

Setting this property to `True` means that ADO will pass the name of each parameter to the provider, where the name will be used to match up the parameters. If the value is `False` (the default), then parameters are interpreted in the order they are created. It is more efficient to add parameters by position because, when adding by name, ADO has to match the parameters to their underlying counterparts.

The Prepared Property

Indicates whether or not to save a compiled version of a command before execution.

```
Boolean = Command.Prepared
Command.Prepared = Boolean
```

The default value of the property is `False`. It should be set to `True` when the command is to be repeated several times. Although the compilation process will slow for the first execution of the command, subsequent executions will be quicker since the command text does not have to be parsed and the execution plan can be reused.

If you're using the SQL Server provider, and you set the "Use Procedure for Prepare" dynamic property of the Connection object to True, then a temporary stored procedure will be created for prepared commands. If you find that you need to prepare a lot of statements, you might want to consider moving the SQL into a stored procedure, since this will be more efficient than preparing statements.

> Use Procedure for Prepare *is one of the provider-specific dynamic properties of the ADO* Connection *object. For more on ADO's dynamic properties, and how to use them see Appendix C.*

If you are creating prepared commands against SQL Server and not disconnecting, then you should ensure that the temporary database (tempdb) has enough space to accommodate the stored procedures.

The State Property

Describes whether the Command object is open, closed, or currently processing a command.

```
Command.State = ObjectStateEnum
```

State can be one of the following ObjectStateEnum constants:

- ❑ adStateClosed indicates that the command is closed
- ❑ adStateOpen indicates that the command is open
- ❑ adStateExecuting indicates that the command is currently executing
- ❑ adStateFetching indicates that the command is currently fetching records
- ❑ adStateConnecting indicates that the command is currently connecting to the provider

Using the State property allows you to detect the current state of the command. For example, to detect if the Command is still executing an asynchronous query you could use this line:

```
If objCmd.State = adStateExecuting Then
    Print "Command is still executing"
End If
```

Collections of the Command Object

The Parameters Collection

Contains all of the Parameter objects for a Command object.

```
Parameters = Command.Parameters
```

The Parameters collection is most often used when passing arguments to stored procedures or queries. Parameter objects are appended to this collection by use of the Append method:

```
Set objParam = objCmd.CreateParameter("ID", adInteger, _
                                      adParamInput, 8, 123)
objCmd.Append objParam
```

You can iterate through the objects in this collection in Visual Basic or VBScript by using the For Each...Next command. For example:

```
For Each objParam In objCmd.Parameters
    Print objParam.Name
Next
```

If your provider is capable of describing the parameters of a stored procedure or query, then you can use the Refresh method to get the provider to fill in the Parameters collection for you:

```
objCmd.Parameters.Refresh
```

The Parameters collection is discussed more fully later in this chapter.

Other collections, and their methods and properties, are covered in more detail in Chapter 8.

The Properties Collection

Contains all of the provider-specific, dynamic Property objects for a Command object:

```
Properties = Command.Properties
```

The Parameter Object

The Parameter object comprises all of the information for a single parameter to be used in a stored procedure or query, and is only really used in conjunction with the Command object and its associated Parameters collection.

Methods of the Parameter Object

The AppendChunk Method

Appends data to a large or binary Parameter object.

```
Parameter.AppendChunk Data
```

Parameter	Type	Description	Default
Data	Variant	The data to be appended to the parameter.	

The first `AppendChunk` call after editing the parameter details writes data to the parameter, overwriting any existing data. Subsequent calls add to existing data. Although the documentation states that a parameter must support long data for this method to work, this doesn't appear to be compulsory for SQL Server. You can check the `Attributes` property (see below) to see if it contains `adParamLong`, which will indicate if it supports long data.

This method is most often used when storing images in tables. There's a full discussion of using images with `AppendChunk` at the end of Chapter 8.

The `Parameter` object's `AppendChunk` method is functionally equivalent to the `AppendChunk` method of the `Field` object, and it works in the same way. The only difference is that you are dealing with a different base object.

Properties of the Parameter Object

The Attributes Property

Indicates one or more characteristics of a `Parameter` object.

```
ParameterAttributesEnum = Parameter.Attributes
Parameter.Attributes = ParameterAttributesEnum
```

This can be one or more of these `ParameterAttributesEnum` values:

- ❏ `adParamSigned`, to indicate that the parameter will accept signed values. This is the default.
- ❏ `adParamNullable`, to indicate that the parameter will accept null values.
- ❏ `adParamLong`, to indicate that the parameter accepts long data, such as binary data.

You can combine these values by using a logical OR statement:

```
objParam.Attributes = adParamNullable OR adParamLong
```

Setting `adParamLong` doesn't appear to be compulsory for binary data. A SQL Server stored procedure with a parameter of type image will accept long data without this set.

The Direction Property

Indicates whether the `Parameter` object represents an input parameter, an output parameter, or an input/output parameter, or if the parameter is a return value from a stored procedure.

```
ParameterDirectionEnum = Parameter.Direction
Parameter.Direction = ParameterDirectionEnum
```

ParameterDirectionEnum can be one of the following values:

- ❑ adParamUnknown, to indicate that the direction of the parameter is not known

- ❑ adParamInput, to indicate that the parameter is to pass information to the stored procedure or query

- ❑ adParamOutput, to indicate that the parameter is to receive information from the stored procedure or query

- ❑ adParamInputOutput, to indicate that the parameter can be used to pass information to, and return information from, a stored procedure or query

- ❑ adParamReturnValue, to indicate that the parameter will contain the return value of the stored procedure or query

In a SQL Server stored procedure, you would declare an output parameter by appending OUTPUT to the parameter declaration. For example, the following SQL code creates a stored procedure with input and output parameters, and return values:

```
CREATE PROCEDURE usp_GetValues
     @PubID     char(4),          -- indicates an input parameter
     @Value     integer   OUTPUT  -- indicates an output parameter
AS
BEGIN
     . . . .
RETURN 123                        -- indicates the return value
```

The return value is always the first parameter (index position 0) in the Parameters collection, and is named RETURN_VALUE. If you're creating parameters, you'll need to create the return value first:

```
objCmd.CreateParameter   "RETURN_VALUE", adVarInteger, _
                          adParamReturnValue, 8, lngRetVal
```

The return value should be declared as a long integer. If you use Refresh, then a return value parameter is always created, irrespective of whether the stored procedure returns a value with the RETURN statement.

You can also set this property by using the Direction argument of the Command object's CreateParameter method.

> **Microsoft Access does not support output parameters or return values.**

The Name Property

Indicates the name of the Parameter object.

```
String = Parameter.Name
Parameter.Name = String
```

This just identifies the parameter name within the `Parameters` collection, and doesn't have to be the same as the name of the parameter as defined in the stored procedure or query – but it makes sense to keep these the same. This makes the code more readable and easier to maintain.

You can also set this property by using the `Name` argument of the `Command` object's `CreateParameter` method.

Once the `Parameter` object has been appended to the `Parameters` collection, this property becomes read-only, because its name becomes its key in the `Parameters` collection.

The NumericScale Property

Indicates the scale of numeric values for the `Parameter` object.

```
Byte = Parameter.NumericScale
Parameter.NumericScale = Byte
```

The numeric scale indicates how many digits are to the right of the decimal point.

Both the `NumericScale` and `Precision` properties are required in order to process SQL data of numeric type correctly. Both Oracle and SQL Server 7.0 support numeric types, using both native OLE DB Providers and the OLE DB Provider for ODBC.

Furthermore, note that the `NumericScale` and `Precision` properties cannot be set via the `Command` object's `CreateParameter` method. If you need to set these properties (for example, in the scenario described in the previous paragraph) you must create an explicit `Parameter` object – and set its properties before appending it to the `Parameters` collection.

The Precision Property

Indicates the degree of precision for numeric values in the `Parameter` object.

```
Byte = Parameter.Precision
Parameter.Precision = Byte
```

The precision indicates the maximum number of digits that are used to represent a numeric value.

The `Precision` property, like the `NumericScale` property, is required for the correct processing of SQL data of numeric type – as supported by both Oracle and SQL Server 7.0, using both native OLE DB Providers and the OLE DB Provider for ODBC. There's more about this in the previous section on the `NumericScale` property.

The Size Property

Indicates the maximum size, in bytes or characters, of a `Parameter` object.

```
Long = Parameter.Size
Parameter.Size = Long
```

4

ADO: Command Object

There are a few things to watch out for when using the `Size` property:

❑ For variable-length parameters (such as character strings or binary data), you must always set the `Size`, so that the provider knows how much space to allocate for the parameter. If you don't specify the size an error will be generated.

❑ If you use the `Parameters` collection's `Refresh` method to force the provider to fill in the parameter details, the `Size` for variable-length parameters may be their maximum potential size, and memory may be allocated for these parameters accordingly.

❑ For binary data you have to be quite specific about the size of the parameter. For example, if a SQL Server stored procedure has a parameter of type `image`, and you `Refresh` the parameters, the size of this parameter is returned as `2147483647`. If you create the parameters yourself and use this size, and then use `AppendChunk` to add the data to the parameter, there are no problems – but creating the parameter with the actual size of the binary data doesn't work. That's because `Size` is the *maximum* size of the parameter, not its actual size.

The Type Property

Indicates the data type of the `Parameter` object.

```
DataTypeEnum = Parameter.Type
Parameter.Type = DataTypeEnum
```

A full list of the `DataTypeEnum` values is shown in Appendix B, but the following table lists the data types used by the SQL Server and Jet providers and shows how the underlying data store's data types map to those of ADO. The empty table cells indicate that there is no direct mapping between the two database types.

SQL Server 6.5	SQL Server 7.0	SQL Server 2000	Access 97	Access 2000	Enum Value
binary	binary	binary	Binary		adBinary
varbinary	varbinary	varbinary			adVarBinary
char			Text		adVarChar
	char	char			adChar
varchar	varchar	varchar			adVarChar
datetime	datetime	datetime			adDBTimeStamp
smalldatetime	smalldatetime	smalldatetime			adDBTimeStamp
float			Single	Single	adSingle
real	real	real			adSingle
int	int	int	Long Integer	Long Integer	adInteger
smallint	smallint	smallint	Integer	Integer	adSmallInt
tinyint	tinyint	tinyint	Byte	Byte	adUnsignedTinyInt

SQL Server 6.5	SQL Server 7.0	SQL Server 2000	Access 97	Access 2000	Enum Value
money small money	money small money	money small money	Currency	Currency	adCurrency
bit	bit	bit	Yes/No	Yes/No	adBoolean
timestamp					adVarBinary
text			Memo		adVarChar
image			OLE Object		adVarBinary
	float	float	Double	Double	adDouble
			Date/ Time	Date/ Time	adDate
	unique identifier	unique identifier	Replication ID	Replication ID	adGUID
			Value		adEmpty
	nvarchar	nvarchar		Text	adVarWChar
				Memo	adLongVar WChar
	ntext	ntext		Hyper link	adLongVar WChar
	decimal	decimal		Decimal	adNumeric
	numeric	numeric			adNumeric
	image	image		OLE Object	adLongVar Binary
	nchar	nchar			adWChar
	text	text			adLongVar Char
	timestamp	timestamp			adBinary
		bigint			adBigInt
		sql_ variant			adVariant

There are a few interesting (and often confusing) things to note. For example, date parameters in SQL Server don't map to the obvious adDate datatype, but rather to the adDBTimeStamp data type; and the timestamp maps to adVarBinary for SQL Server 6.5 and adBinary for SQL Server 7.0. You should also note that adInteger maps to Visual Basic's Long data type – it doesn't fit VB's Integer type. If the parameters are of the wrong type, they can cause your commands to fail.

If you wish to create your parameters using the CreateParameter method, but you're having trouble matching datatypes or sizes, then the simplest fix is to temporarily call the Refresh method and examine the Parameters collection. You can do this in VBScript by looping through the collection, or by using the Locals window in Visual Basic. You can then copy the values that ADO has used and amend your code accordingly. Don't forget to remove the Refresh once you've sorted out your parameters – leaving it in will cause a performance penalty.

You'll find more on data types in Appendix E.

The Value Property

Indicates the value assigned to the Parameter object.

```
Variant = Parameter.Value
Parameter.Value = Variant
```

This is the default property and can be omitted if desired.

The value of a parameter can only be read once, and the recordset should be closed before you read the value (depending upon the "Output Parameter Availability" dynamic property of the Connection). Reading a value more than once returns an empty value. For more details on this, see the section on parameter values at the end of this chapter.

For a parameter holding binary data, you can use the Value property to set it's value instead of using the AppendChunk method. For example:

```
objRec.Parameters("@Logo").Value = varChunk
```

There's a full description of using binary data at the end of Chapter 8.

The Parameters Collection

When dealing with stored procedures or queries that accept arguments, you have three options:

1. Use the Command object's Execute method, passing in the parameters as an array of values into the second argument of this method. Not all providers support this.

2. Use the Command object's Execute method, passing the parameters in the Command's Parameters collection.

3. Use the Command object's Execute method, passing the parameter values as part of the command text.

In many cases the first is acceptable (and is in fact easier to code), but the one restriction of this is that you can't return any values from your stored procedure. For example, suppose you have a stored procedure like this:

```
CREATE PROCEDURE usp_AuthorsByState
    @RequiredState    char(2),
    @ID               integer    OUTPUT
AS
BEGIN
    SELECT *
    FROM    authors
    WHERE   state = @RequiredState

    SELECT @ID=123

    RETURN 456
END
```

This procedure does three things:

1. It returns a recordset using one of the parameters to restrict the rows that are returned.

2. It sets the output parameter to an arbitrary value (123 in this case).

3. It returns another arbitrary value (456 in this case).

Although the output value and return value are falsely constructed, it illustrates two common techniques for returning information from a stored procedure.

If you wished to call this stored procedure *without* using the Parameters collection, you could do so using code like this:

```
objCmd.CommandText = "usp_AuthorsByState"
objCmd.CommandType = adCmdStoredProc
Set objRec = objCmd.Execute (, Array("CA", lngID))
```

This simply calls the procedure, passing in two arguments – CA to filter the recordset, and lngID (a long integer) to be used as the output parameter. This works fine, as ADO builds a Parameters collection from the values you supply. However, note that the output parameter (lngID) is never populated with the output value, and there's also no way to access the return value. So while this method is extremely easy to use, it doesn't give you the functionality that the Parameters collection does.

There's a caveat to this approach: if you reference the Parameters collection before calling the Execute method, the Parameters collection is then Refreshed automatically for you. For example:

```
objCmd.CommandText = "usp_AuthorsByState"
objCmd.CommandType - adCmdStoredProc
Print "Parameter Count - " & objCmd.Parameters.Count
```

During the Print statement, ADO automatically calls a Refresh and populates the Parameters collection. The key point is that there are *three* parameters, not two: the return value, the input parameter (the required state), and the output parameter (the ID value). This means that the next line might fail, because it doesn't use enough parameters:

```
Set objRec = objCmd.Execute (, Array("CA", lngID))
```

However, this line works:

```
Set objRec = objCmd.Execute (, Array(lngRV, "CA", lngID))
```

This shows that if you populate the Parameters collection yourself, or use the Array method, then you don't need to worry about the return parameter. However, if you Refresh the Parameters collection (or if it is refreshed implicitly for you) then you'll find that the return value becomes the first parameter in the collection.

Note that not all providers or versions of SQL Server may support this automatic refresh (or indeed the Refresh method itself). If you are using SQL Server 6.5 you should ensure that you have installed the latest Catalog Procedures – see the SQL Books online for more details on this.

4

ADO: Command Object

Differences from ADO 2.0

The automatic refreshing of parameters in ADO 2.1 onwards is different from what occurred in ADO 2.0. Using an explicit `Refresh` works for both the OLE DB Provider for ODBC and the OLE DB Provider for SQL, in both versions of ADO. However, using the implicit refresh gives different results.

I've used the following code to test the automatic refresh facility in ADO 2.0 and ADO 2.1 onwards:

```
objCmd.CommandText = "usp_AuthorsByState"
objCmd.CommandType = adCmdStoredProc
Print "Parameter Count = " & objCmd.Parameters.Count
```

If you are using SQL Server 6.5 (and you haven't updated your Catalogs) then only the OLE DB Provider for ODBC will return the correct parameter information to the `Parameters` collection. If you *have* updated your catalogs, or if you're using SQL Server 7, then there are differences between the ways that the two versions of ADO handle the parameters. The list below shows which combinations of ADO, providers, and data stores support automatic refreshing of parameters:

ADO Version	Provider	SQL Server	Supported
2.0	OLE DB for ODBC	6.5	Yes
		7.0	Yes
	OLE DB for SQL	6.5	Yes
		7.0	No
2.1 onwards	OLE DB for ODBC	6.5	Yes
		7.0	No
		2000	No
	OLE DB for SQL	6.5	No
		7.0	No
		2000	No

Don't think that this removal of functionality is a detrimental step. In this case it is a deliberate (and documented) move to improve performance and reduce network traffic.

Parameter Types in ASP

When using the array method in ASP scripting languages you have to make sure that any variables used for output parameters have the correct data type. When you declare variables in scripting languages, they are **variants**, and this may not match the correct parameter type. The output parameter has to have the correct type, even though you can't actually use it. For example, in VBScript:

```
Dim lngID
Set objRec = objCmd.Execute (, Array(lngRV, "CA", lngID))
```

This produces an error, which indicates that a parameter object has not been supplied. That's because `lngID` is a variant and doesn't have a default type or value. However, this section of code works:

```
Dim lngID
lngID = 1
Set objRec = objCmd.Execute (, Array(lngRV, "CA", lngID))
```

This forces the variant to hold the correct data type – it gives `lngID` a sub-type of `Integer`, which is compatible with the integer type declared in the stored procedure (SQL Server integers map to `Longs` in Visual Basic and in Scripting languages).

The `Parameters` collection contains a `Parameter` object for each parameter in a stored procedure, including the return value if the procedure has one. It only has two properties and three methods.

Methods of the Parameters Collection

The Append Method

Appends a `Parameter` object to the `Parameters` collection.

```
Parameters.Append(Object)
```

Parameter	Type	Description	Default
Object	Parameter	The Parameter object to be appended to the collection.	

Parameters are created using the `CreateParameter` method, and you must set the `Type` property before calling this method. For example:

```
Set objParam = objCmd.CreateParameter
objParam.Name = "Name"
objParam.Type = adVarChar
objParam.Direction = adParamInput
objParam.Size = 25
objParam.Value = "Janine"
objCmd.Parameters.Append objParam
```

Although more cumbersome to use than the `Refresh` method to build a parameter list, this method is much more efficient, as it minimizes the total number of calls made to the provider.

You can create a parameter with just one line, using the following:

```
Set objParam =
objCmd.CreateParameter("State",adChar,adParamInput,2,"CA")
```

You can combine the `Append` and `CreateParameter` methods into a single statement:

```
objCmd.Parameters.Append _
        objCmd.CreateParameter("State",adChar,adParamInput,2,"CA")
```

The Delete Method

Deletes a `Parameter` object from the `Parameters` collection.

```
Parameters.Delete(Index)
```

Parameter	Type	Description	Default
Index	Variant	The number or name of the Parameter object to be removed from the collection.	

You must use the `Parameter` object's index or its `Name` when deleting a parameter. You cannot use an object variable. For example, we can delete the parameter called `ID` using this line:

```
objCmd.Parameters.Delete ("ID")
```

Here's another example. The following line deletes the first parameter in the collection:

```
objCmd.Parameters.Delete (0)
```

The Refresh Method

Updates the `Parameter` objects in the `Parameters` collection.

```
Parameters.Refresh
```

This has the impact of querying the data provider for details of the parameters, such as the name, size, direction, and so on. You can then access the parameters by name or ordinal number by indexing into the collection. For example:

```
objCmd.Parameters.Refresh
objCmd.Parameters(0).Value = 1
objCmd.Parameters("@FirstName") = "Janine"
```

You should use this method only when you are willing to accept the performance hit of the provider re-querying the data source for the parameter details. This is especially important if the same set of parameters is used frequently.

You can use this method quite effectively by querying the provider for the parameters once – for example, at the start of the program. You could then copy the parameter details into a global variable (perhaps an array or a collection, or even a local, fabricated recordset), where it can be used many times during the program. The advantage with this method is that you don't have to keep repeating `CreateParameter` calls, and you can create a generic piece of code to run a command. In addition, you can change the stored procedure without having to change the code that runs the command. The disadvantage is, of course, the delay as the program starts whilst the parameters are read in. However, you may consider this delay worthwhile, as it gives you a good chance to display that fancy splash screen you've always wanted!

If you do not create your own `Parameters` for a command and access the `Parameters` collection (for example, setting the value of a parameter), then ADO will call `Refresh` automatically, to fill the collection. Not all providers support the `Refresh` method.

The performance issues regarding `Refresh` are discussed in Chapter 14.

Properties of the Parameters Collection

The Count Property

Indicates the number of `Parameter` objects in the `Parameters` collection.

```
Long = Parameters.Count
```

You can use the Visual Basic or VBScript `For Each...Next` command to iterate through the parameters collection without using the `Count` property. For languages that do not support enumeration of collections, you can use this property in a loop.

The Item Property

Allows indexing into the `Parameters` collection to reference a specific `Parameter` object.

```
Parameter = Parameters.Item(Index)
```

Name	Type	Description	Default
Index	Variant	The number or name of the parameter within the collection.	

This is the default property and can be omitted. For example, the following lines are identical:

```
objCmd.Parameters.Item(1)
```

```
objCmd.Parameters(1)
```

```
objCmd.Parameters("@FirstName")
```

Retrieving Output Parameters

The ability to return information from stored procedures in parameters is extremely useful, but there are some points you should be aware of. The first is whether output parameters are supported at all by the provider – Access doesn't support them. The second is at what stage the output parameters are available, and for this there are two choices:

1. The parameter is available as soon as the command has been executed.

2. The parameter is available only after the recordset has been closed.

This latter option is the one you have to watch for, because in that case, ADO will only read the parameter values from the provider once. This means that if you read the parameter before closing the recordset, then close it, and then try to read the parameter value again, the value may not be available.

You can check to see which of the modes your provider supports, by examining the "Output Parameter Availability"dynamic property for the connection. This will return one of the three DBPROPVAL_OA constant values:

❑ DBPROPVAL_OA_ATEXECUTE, which indicates that the parameters are available after the command has been executed. This has a value of 2.

❑ DBPROPVAL_OA_ATROWRELEASE, which indicates that the parameters are available after the recordset has been closed. This has a value of 4, and is the option supported by SQL Server.

❑ DBPROPVAL_OA_NOTSUPPORTED, which indicates that output parameters are not supported. This has a value of 1.

You could check these values with code like this:

```
Set objCmd.ActiveConnection = objConn

objCmd.CommandText = "usp_ProcedureWithOutputParam"
objCmd.CommandType = adCmdStoredProc
objCmd.Parameters.Append objCmd.CreateParameter("RETURN_VALUE", _
                            adInteger, adParamReturnValue)
Set objRec = objCmd.Execute

intParamAvail = objConn.Properties("Output Parameter Availability")
If intParamAvail = DBPROPVAL_OA_ATROWRELEASE Then
    ' parameter not available until recordset is closed
    objRec.Close
End If
intRV = objCmd.Parameters("ReturnValue")
```

This isn't a problem with commands that do not return recordsets, as there is no recordset to close.

Output Parameters Without Closing Recordsets

There are two solutions to the problem of parameters not being available until the recordset is closed. The first is simply a matter of using client-side cursors, which allows the parameters to be immediately available.

The second method involves the naming of stored procedures using the Command object's Name property. You've already seen that code similar to this is allowed:

```
strConn = "Provider=SQLOLEDB; Data Source=SQL7Server; " & _
          "Initial Catalog=TestData; User Id=sa; Password="
objConn.Open strConn

objCmd.CommandText = "usp_AStoredProcedure"
objCmd.CommandType = adCmdStoredProc
Set objParam = objCmd.CreateParameter("ID", adInteger, _
                                  adParamInput, 8, 123)
objCmd.Parameters.Append objParam
Set objParam = _
       objCmd.CreateParameter("Name", adVarChar, _
                              adParamInput, 25, "Janine")
objCmd.Parameters.Append objParam
objCmd.Name = "StoredProcedureName"
Set objCmd.ActiveConnection = objConn


objConn.StoredProcedureName
```

This was never well documented, but what's even less well documented is that you can pass the arguments to the stored procedure and a recordset object like so:

```
objConn.StoredProcedureName Argument1, Argument2, objRec
```

The arguments are accepted by the stored procedure in the normal way, and the recordset object is filled accordingly. As soon as this command is executed, you can access the return and output parameters, even though the recordset is still open.

As a word of warning, you shouldn't really rely on this procedure – because it's not documented, there's no way of telling whether this will continue to work in future versions of ADO.

I thank God I am as honest as any man

living that is an old man and no honester th

Can counsel and speak comfort to th

Much Ado About Nothing.

Which they themselves not feel

He wears his faith but as the fashion of

As merry as the day

He hath indeed better bettered expectation

(Act i. Sc. 1.).

He wears his faith but as the fashion of his hat.
(Ibid)

As merry as the day is long.

ch indeed better bettered expectation

(Act i. Sc. 1).

(Ibid)

Much Ado About Nothing.

Can counsel and speak comfort to that grief

Which they themselves not feel.

He wears his faith but as the fashion of his hat.
(Ibid)

I was not born under

I was not born under a rhyming plan
(Sc.

a rhyming planet

For there was never yet

That could endure the to

merry as the day is long (sc. 2)

Can counsel and speak comfort to that grief

Which they themselves not feel.

(Ibid)

He hath indeed better bettered expectation

(Ibid)

I thank God I am as honest as an

living that is an old man and no honest

He wears his faith but as the fashion of his ha

Much Ado About Nothing.

For there was never yet philospher
That could endure the toothache patiently.

(Ibid)

For there was never yet philospher
That could endure the toothache patiently

I was not born u

The Recordset Object

The recordset is really all about data, so it's at the very heart of ADO. A recordset contains all of the columns and rows returned from a specific action.

Methods of the Recordset Object

The AddNew Method

Creates a new row for an updateable `Recordset` object.

```
Recordset.AddNew([FieldList], [Values])
```

Parameter	Type	Description	Default
FieldList	Variant	A single name or an array of names or ordinal positions of the fields in the new row.	
Values	Variant	A single value or an array of values for the fields in the new row. If FieldList is an array then Values must also be an array with the same number of elements.	

You can only use `AddNew` when the recordset supports addition of new rows. You can check this by examining the `Supports` method:

```
If objRs.Supports(adAddNew) Then
    ' recordset supports additions
End If
```

You can use `AddNew` in two ways. The first is without any arguments, which places the current row pointer on the new row. You can then set values to the fields for the new row and save the changes with Update if using immediate update mode, or UpdateBatch if using batch update mode (LockType = adLockBatchOptimistic). When you are adding a new row, and have set the various fields for the row, you can also save the changes by moving off the row. Calling MoveFirst or MoveLast will move to the beginning or end of the recordset respectively. Calling MoveNext will place you at EOF, and calling MovePrevious will move you to the row before the new row.

The second method uses the arguments, allowing you to pass in an array of fields and values. For example, the following line adds a new row filling in one field:

```
objRs.AddNew "author", "Jan Lloyd"
```

The following line adds one row, but fills in two fields:

```
objRs.AddNew Array("author", "year born"), Array("Jan Lloyd", 1969)
```

If you are using arguments to supply both the field names and values, and batch update mode is not being used, then the changes are effective immediately – that is, there is no need to perform the Update method. ADO will automatically call the Update method if you use AddNew while editing the current row, or adding a new row. You can check the EditMode property for the value of adEditAdd to determine if this is so.

However, if you are using batch update mode, you must still call the UpdateBatch method to update the data source.

If you're using the array method to add rows (as demonstrated above), you must ensure that both arrays contain the same number of arguments, and that the details of the arrays are in the correct order. The array method is also particularly good when you are creating (fabricating) your own recordsets.

AutoNumber and Identity Fields

The following question is probably one of the most frequently asked questions about ADO, and it's of particular interest to people converting from DAO:

> *When using AutoNumber and Identity fields, how do you add a new row, and then get the key value for the newly added row?*

Unfortunately there's not always a simple answer; it depends on the provider you are using, as well as items like the cursor location, cursor type, locking method, and indexes on the table.

ADO states that after adding a new row, when you then Update that row, the cursor is placed on the newly added row. This is exactly what you need, but the Identity or AutoNumber value may not be available. For example, code such as this may not produce the desired result:

```
objRs.AddNew
objRs("field_name") = "field_value"
```

```
objRs.Update

Print objRs("ID")
```

This assumes that ID is an automatically incrementing field.

The table below indicates which combinations of providers and target databases support retrieval of auto-incrementing fields:

Provider	Target	Indexed	Cursor Location	Cursor Type	Lock Type
ODBC	Access 97 Access 2000	Yes	Server	Keyset	Pessimistic Optimistic
		No	Server	Keyset	Pessimistic Optimistic
	SQL Server 6.5	Yes	Server	Keyset	Pessimistic Optimistic
	SQL Server 7.0	Yes	Server	Keyset	Pessimistic Optimistic
		Yes	Client	All	Pessimistic Optimistic
		No	Client	All	Pessimistic Optimistic
	SQL Server 2000	Yes	Server	Keyset	Pessimistic Optimistic
			Client	Forward Only	Pessimistic
Jet 4.0	Access 97	Yes	Server	All	All
		No	Server	All	All
	Access 2000	Yes	Server	All	All
		Yes	Client	All	Pessimistic Optimistic
		No	Server	All	All
		No	Client	All	Pessimistic Optimistic
SQL OLEDB	SQL Server 6.5	Yes	Server	Keyset	Pessimistic Optimistic
	SQL Server 7.0	Yes	Client	All	Pessimistic Optimistic
	SQL Server 2000	No	Client	All	Pessimistic Optimistic

Any combination not shown in the list does not support the availability of the auto-number field.

Obtaining the identity value directly only works when adding rows directly using AddNew, and will not work if using commands and SQL INSERT statements.

Using @@IDENTITY

If you are using SQL Server and you need to use a combination that does not support the auto-number field, then you can use the global value that represents the latest IDENTITY value added. Using this, you can obtain the value you need. For example, in a stored procedure you could do this:

```
CREATE PROCEDURE usp_AddAuthor
    @sAuLName       varchar(25),
    @sAuFName       varchar(25)
AS
BEGIN
    INSERT INTO authors (au_lname, au_fname)
    VALUES (@sAuLName, @sAUFName)

    RETURN @@IDENTITY
END
```

This adds a new row and then returns the IDENTITY field just used. You can then run this stored procedure using a Command object, and access the return value through the first member (index 0) in the Parameters collection. Alternatively, you can return the identity value as an output parameter. You can also use this technique when running straight SQL queries.

One thing to watch when using this technique – @@IDENTITY is a global variable and represents the last IDENTITY value updated, irrespective of the table. So if you have an INSERT trigger on a table, and the table the trigger inserts into has an identity field, then @@IDENTITY will reflect this value, rather than the one you intended.

Because the server handles this facility, you can use this with any type of cursor and location.

The Cancel Method

Cancels execution of a pending asynchronous Open operation.

```
Recordset.Cancel
```

This is particularly useful when allowing users to submit queries, as it can be used to give them an opportunity to cancel the query if they feel it is taking too long.

If you call the Cancel method on a recordset that was not opened asynchronously then an error will be generated.

The CancelBatch Method

Cancels a pending batch update when in batch update mode.

```
Recordset.CancelBatch([AffectRecords])
```

Name	Type	Description	Default
AffectRecords	AffectEnum	Determines which rows will be affected by the batch cancel.	adAffectAll

The AffectEnum value can be one of the following constants:

❑ adAffectCurrent, to only cancel updates for the current row

❑ adAffectGroup, to only cancel updates for rows that match the current Filter, which must be set before using this option

❑ adAffectAll, to cancel all pending updates, even those not shown due to a Filter

❑ adAffectAllChapters, to cancel all pending updates in child (chapter) recordsets, when using shaped data

You should be careful when using adAffectGroup. With this setting, rows that do not match the current filter are *not* cancelled: so if your Filter is not set as you intend, it's possible you'll fail to cancel all of the pending changes that you wanted to cancel.

You should always check the Errors collection after performing this method. It's a good way to catch underlying conflicts, such as a row having been deleted. Conflict resolution is discussed in more detail later in this chapter.

It's always sensible to set the current row position to a known row after this call, as the current row can be left in an unknown position after a CancelBatch method call.

The CancelUpdate Method

Cancels any changes made to the current row or to a new row prior to calling the Update method.

```
Recordset.CancelUpdate
```

This is used when in normal update mode, and cancels changes to the current row only.

You can use this to cancel the addition of a new row, in which case the current row becomes the row you were on before adding the new row.

5

ADO: Recordset Object

The Clone Method

Creates a duplicate `Recordset` object from an existing `Recordset` object.

```
Set Recordset_Clone = Recordset.Clone([LockType])
```

Name	Type	Description	Default
LockType	LockTypeEnum	The lock type to create the new recordset with.	adLockUnspecified

In this case `LockTypeEnum` is a subset of the full list of constants, and should be one of:

❑ `adLockUnspecified`, to indicate that the cloned recordset should have the same lock type as the original recordset

❑ `adLockReadOnly`, to indicate that the cloned recordset should be read-only

It's important to note that this doesn't create two independent recordsets. Rather, it creates two pointers (which are `Recordset` objects), both pointing to the same recordset. This allows you to have two separate cursors open on the same set of rows, allowing you to move the row pointers independently. There is only one set of data, so changes made through either the original recordset pointer or through the clone pointer appear in the other. The important thing to remember is that a `Recordset` object is just a pointer to a set of data. Therefore a `Clone` is just another pointer to the same set of data.

Cloning recordsets is often more efficient than creating a new recordset with the same request criteria, because it avoids a trip to the server.

Cloning is only allowed on bookmarkable recordsets (for more on bookmarkable recordsets see section on the `Bookmark` property, later in this chapter). Bookmarks are valid in all clones. You can use the `Supports` method to determine if bookmarks are supported in the recordset:

```
If objRs.Supports(adBookmark) Then
    Set objRsClone = objRs.Clone
End If
```

If you make any changes to a recordset, then those changes will be visible in all clones until the time you `Requery` the original recordset. At that stage the cloned recordset will no longer be synchronized with the original recordset (you effectively have two recordsets), and will contain the set of rows before the `Requery` took place.

The Close Method

Closes the `Recordset` object and any dependent objects.

```
Recordset.Close
```

You should beware of closing the recordset when changes are in place, as the following will occur:

❑ When in batch update mode, changes will be lost.

❑ When in immediate update mode, an error will be generated.

Closing a recordset does not free all of its resources from memory, and you should set its object variable to Nothing in VB (or to null in JScript) to achieve this:

```
Set objRs = Nothing
```

> **The best method of using recordsets is to open the recordset as late as possible, and close it (and free any associated resources) as early as possible, thus minimizing the amount of time the recordset is opened. This can aid in conserving database resources.**

To be absolutely sure that you protect against errors, you can also check to see whether the recordset is open before closing it:

```
If objRs.State = adStateOpen Then
     objRs.Close
End If
Set objRs = Nothing
```

The CompareBookmarks Method

Compares two bookmarks and returns an indication of the relative values.

```
CompareEnum = Recordset.CompareBookmarks(Bookmark1, Bookmark2)
```

Parameter	Type	Description	Default
Bookmark1	Variant	The bookmark for the first row to be compared.	
Bookmark2	Variant	The bookmark for the second row to be compared.	

CompareEnum will be one of the following constants:

❑ adCompareLessThan, to indicate that the first bookmark is before the second

❑ adCompareEqual, to indicate that the bookmarks are equal

❑ adCompareGreaterThan, to indicate that the first bookmark is after the second

❑ adCompareNotEqual, to indicate that the bookmarks are not equal, and not ordered

❑ adCompareNotComparable, to indicate that it is not possible to compare the two bookmarks

5

ADO: Recordset Object

For more on setting bookmarks, see the section on the Bookmark property (later in this chapter). The CompareBookmarks method is only applicable for comparing bookmarks from the same recordset or its clones. Even if two recordsets were created in exactly the same way, their bookmarks are not guaranteed to be the same.

Bookmarks are comparable across Sort and Filter method calls since these do not change the rowset.

Note that this compares the actual bookmarks, not the values in the rows that the bookmarks point to.

The Delete Method

Deletes the current row or group of rows.

```
Recordset.Delete([AffectRecords])
```

Parameter	Type	Description	Default
AffectRecords	AffectEnum	A value that determines how many rows this method will affect.	adAffectCurrent

The AffectEnum type can be one of the following constants:

- ❏ adAffectAllChapters, to delete all chapters (child recordsets) associated with the row or group of rows. For more details on chapters, see Chapter 13
- ❏ adAffectCurrent, to delete only the current row
- ❏ adAffectGroup, to delete only rows that match the current Filter
- ❏ adAffectAll, to delete all rows

Remember that when in batch update mode, the rows are only *marked* for deletion, and are not removed from the data store itself until UpdateBatch is called.

Once a row has been deleted, the current deleted row remains active until you move away from it. Attempting to access values from a deleted row will result in an error.

If the Recordset contains multiple tables, and the "Unique Table" dynamic property is set, then only rows from this unique table are deleted.

An error will be generated if the recordset does not support deletions. You can use the Supports method to determine if the recordset support deletions:

```
If objRs.Supports(adDelete) Then
    objRs.Delete
End If
```

You should also check the Errors collection, as the provider may return errors due to conflicts with the underlying data.

The Find Method

Searches the `Recordset` for a row that matches the specified criteria.

```
Recordset.Find(Criteria, [SkipRecords], [SearchDirection], [Start])
```

Parameter	Type	Description	Default
Criteria	String	The statement that specifies the column name, comparison operator, and value to use for the search. Only one criterion is supported, and multiple values by use of OR or AND will generate an error.	
SkipRecords	Long	The offset (from the current row, or from the bookmark specified by the Start parameter) from which point the search should begin.	0
Search Direction	Search Direction Enum	Indicates the direction of the search.	adSearch Forward
Start	Variant	The bookmark for the row from which the operation should begin.	

`SearchDirection` can be one of the following `SearchDirectionEnum` constants:

- ❑ `adSearchForward`, to search forward in the recordset
- ❑ `adSearchBackward`, to search backward in the recordset

`Start` can be a valid bookmark, or one of the `BookmarkEnum` constants:

- ❑ `adBookmarkCurrent`, to start the search on the current row
- ❑ `adBookmarkFirst`, to start the search from the first row
- ❑ `adBookmarkLast`, to start the search from the last row

`Criteria` follows the basic form of a SQL `WHERE` clause. For example:

```
state = 'CA'
```

```
age = 13
```

```
au_lname LIKE 'S*'
```

*Both * and % are acceptable as wildcard characters, although they can only be used at the end of the search string.*

If `Criteria` is met, then the current row is positioned on the found row. If `Criteria` is not met, then:

❑ If you're searching forwards, the current row is set to be the end of the recordset (and `EOF` is set)

❑ If you're searching backwards, the current row is set to be the beginning of the recordset (and `BOF` is set)

For example:

```
objRs.Find "au_lname = 'Lloyd'"
If objRs.EOF Then
    Print "Record was not found"
End If
```

You can use `Criteria` to search for values that are less than, equal to, greater than, or like a particular value. For example:

```
objRs.Find "Price < 14.99"
objRs.Find "Price > 14.99"
objRs.Find "au_lname LIKE 'L*'"
```

The latter will find all values of `au_lname` that start with `L`.

Only single search values are allowed with `Find`. Using multiple search values with `AND` or `OR` generates an error. For example:

```
objRs.Find "au_lname = 'Lloyd' AND au_fname = 'Janine'"
```

This is invalid and will generate an error. This is one area where the direct migration from DAO to ADO will cause problems.

If you do need to use multiple criteria values, then your only choice is to create a new recordset, or use a `Filter`, which does accept multiple values.

Not all providers support the `Find` method, so you can use the `Supports` method to identify whether this is supported by the recordset:

```
If objRs.Supports(adFind) Then
    objRs.Find "au_lname = 'Lloyd'"
End If
```

The GetRows Method

Retrieves multiple rows of a `Recordset` object into a multi-dimensional array.

```
Variant = Recordset.GetRows([Rows], [Start], [Fields])
```

Parameter	Type	Description	Default
Rows	Long	Indicates how many rows to retrieve. The default indicates that all remaining rows in the recordset should be fetched.	adGetRowsRest
Start	Variant	The bookmark for the row from which the operation should begin.	The current row
Fields	Variant	A single field name, an ordinal position, an array of field names, or an array of ordinal values representing the fields that should be fetched.	All columns

`Start` can be a valid bookmark, or one of the `BookmarkEnum` constants:

❑ `adBookmarkCurrent`, to start the search on the current row

❑ `adBookmarkFirst`, to start the search from the first row

❑ `adBookmarkLast`, to start the search from the last row

The array returned by the `GetRows` call is automatically sized to fit the requested columns and rows. The columns are placed into the first dimension of the array, and the rows placed into the second. For example:

```
varRec = objRs.GetRows
intCols = UBound(varRec, 1)
intRows = UBound(varRec, 2)

For intRow = 0 To intRows
    For intCol = 0 To intCols
        Print varRec(intCol, intRow)
    Next
Next
```

Although this is not the obvious way around, this column/row order has been used to allow backward compatibility with DAO and RDO. In fact, the main reason for this is that it's easy to modify the second dimension of an array, to add more data, but it's much harder to modify the first dimension once data is in the array. Any values that do not make sense to store in an array, such as chapters or images, are given empty values.

For `Fields`, you can specify either a single field name, or an array of fields to be returned. Here are a couple of examples:

```
varRec = objRs.GetRows (, , "au_lname")
```

```
varRec = objRs.GetRows (, , Array("au_lname", "au_fname"))
```

If using the latter method, then the order in which the columns are placed in the array dictates the order in which they are returned.

After you call `GetRows`, the next unread row becomes the current row. If there are no more rows, `EOF` is set.

When dealing with a large recordset you may find that calling `GetRows` several times with a smaller number of rows is more efficient than calling it once to retrieve all rows. For example, if calling `GetRows` on a table with 1,000 rows, it might be quicker to call it 10 times using 100 as the number of rows to retrieve (depending upon the cursor type and location), rather than retrieving all rows at once. This is examined in more detail in Chapter 14.

The GetString Method

Returns a `Recordset` as a string.

```
String = Recordset.GetString([StringFormat], [NumRows],
                             [ColumnDelimiter], [RowDelimiter],
                             [NullExpr])
```

Parameter	Type	Description	Default
StringFormat	StringFormat Enum	The format in which the recordset should be returned.	adClipString
NumRows	Long	The number of rows to be returned from the recordset. If this is not specified, or if it is greater than the number of rows in the recordset, then all rows will be returned.	-1
Column Delimiter	String	The delimiter to use between columns.	TAB character

Parameter	Type	Description	Default
RowDelimiter	String	The delimiter to use between rows.	CARRIAGE RETURN character
NullExpr	String	Expression to use in place of NULL value.	Empty string

The only valid value for StringFormatEnum is adClipString. You can use this method quite effectively to populate text boxes in Visual Basic, or to quickly create HTML tables in ASP. For example, the code below shows how to fill a text box (named Text1, with its MultiLine property set to True):

```
Dim objConn As New ADODB.Connection
Dim objRs  As New ADODB.Recordset

objConn.Open "Provider=SQLOLEDB; Data Source=Tigger; " & _
             "Initial Catalog=pubs; User ID=sa; Password="

objRs.Open "select au_lname from authors", objConn, _
           adOpenForwardOnly, adLockReadOnly, adCmdText

Text1.Text = objRs.GetString (,,,vbCrLf)

objRs.Close
objConn.Close
Set objRs = Nothing
Set objConn = Nothing
```

The next example shows how to quickly create an HTML table:

```
NBSPACE = chr(160)
Set objConn = Server.CreateObject("ADODB.Connection")
Set objRs = Server.CreateObject("ADODB.Recordset")

objConn.Open "Provider=SQLOLEDB; Data Source=Tigger; " & _
             "Initial Catalog=pubs; User ID=sa; Password="

objRs.Open "authors", objConn, _
           adOpenForwardOnly, adLockReadOnly, adCmdTable

Response.Write "<TABLE BORDER=1><TR><TD>"
Response.Write objRs.GetString (adClipString, -1, _
                   "</TD><TD>", _
                   "</TD></TR><TR><TD>", _
                   NBSPACE)
Response.Write "</TD></TR></TABLE>"

objRs.Close
objConn.Close
Set objRs = Nothing
Set objConn = Nothing
```

5

ADO: Recordset Object

131

This saves having to loop through the `Fields` collection to manually build the table.

Only row data is saved to the string, not schema data. You cannot, therefore, reopen a recordset from this string.

The Move Method

Moves the position of the current row pointer in a `Recordset`.

```
Recordset.Move(NumRecords, [Start])
```

Parameter	Type	Description	Default
NumRecords	Long	The number of rows the current row position moves.	
Start	Variant	The bookmark for the row from which the operation should begin.	AdBookmark Current

`Start` can be a valid bookmark, or one of the `BookmarkEnum` constants:

- ❏ `adBookmarkCurrent`, to start the search on the current row
- ❏ `adBookmarkFirst`, to start the search from the first row
- ❏ `adBookmarkLast`, to start the search from the last row

You can supply a negative number for `NumRecords` to move backwards in the recordset. For example, to move backwards three rows you could do this:

```
objRs.Move -3
```

You should be aware that forward-only recordsets will not allow moving backwards, and may not allow moving forwards by any number other than 1. You can use the `Supports` method to check for this:

```
If objRs.Supports(adMovePrevious) Then
    objRs.Move -3
End If
```

If your recordset has a `CacheSize` other than 1, then you are allowed to move within the rows in the cache, but not to rows outside the cache.

If you move past the beginning or end of the recordset, then you will be positioned on `BOF` or `EOF`, and the properties set accordingly. A subsequent call to `Move` beyond the start or end of the recordset will generate an error, as will trying to `Move` in an empty recordset.

If the current row has been changed, and `Update` not called, then a move will implicitly call `Update`. You should call `CancelUpdate` before calling `Move` if you do not wish to keep the changes.

The MoveFirst Method

Moves the position of the current row pointer to the first row in the `Recordset`.

```
Recordset.MoveFirst
```

This moves to the first non-deleted row in the recordset, and sets `BOF` if all rows are deleted or if there are no rows in the recordset.

You should check to see whether the recordset supports moving to the first row, before issuing a `MoveFirst`. For example:

```
If objRs.Supports(adMoveFirst) Then
    objRs.MoveFirst
End If
```

> You should be aware that some providers (for example SQL Server 6.5 and 7.0), implement the `MoveFirst` by resubmitting the query to the database server, having the effect of re-opening the recordset, thus placing you back on the first row. This only happens with server-side cursors. This could have serious consequences on performance if the command you are running takes a long time. SQL Server 2000 has a smarter cursor engine, and does not resubmit the query.

If the current row has been changed, but you haven't yet called `Update`, then a `MoveFirst` will implicitly call `Update`. If you do not wish to keep such changes, then you should call `CancelUpdate` before calling `MoveFirst`.

The MoveLast Method

Moves the position of the current row to the last row in the `Recordset`.

```
Recordset.MoveLast
```

This moves to the last non-deleted row in the recordset, and sets `EOF` if all rows are deleted, or if the recordset is empty.

You should check to see whether the recordset supports moving to the last row, before issuing a `MoveLast`. For example:

```
If objRs.Supports(adMoveLast) Then
    objRs.MoveLast
End If
```

One odd problem you may encounter is when using server-based cursors for read-only, forward-only recordsets. Your provider may say that `MoveLast` is supported, and yet moving to the last row generates the following message:

The rowset does not support fetching backwards.

5

ADO: Recordset Object

This seems a misleading error, and may be due to the way `MoveLast` is implemented – by using a built-in bookmark on the last row. So this error could result from the fact that forward-only, read-only cursors don't support bookmarks, even though the error message doesn't imply this. I've no confirmation of this, but it seems a sensible reason.

If the current row has been changed, and `Update` not called, then a `MoveLast` will implicitly call `Update`. You should call `CancelUpdate` before calling `MoveLast` if you do not wish to keep the changes.

The MoveNext Method

Moves the position of the current row to the next row in the `Recordset`.

```
Recordset.MoveNext
```

If you try to move past the last row in a recordset, then the `EOF` property is set. Subsequent calls to `MoveNext` will generate an error.

If the current row has been changed, and `Update` not called, then a `MoveNext` will implicitly call `Update`. You should call `CancelUpdate` before calling `MoveNext` if you do not wish to keep the changes.

The MovePrevious Method

Moves the position of the current row to the previous row in the `Recordset`.

```
Recordset.MovePrevious
```

If you try to move past the first row in a recordset, then the `BOF` property is set. Subsequent calls to `MovePrevious` will generate an error.

You can use the `Supports` method to check whether `MovePrevious` can be used on the recordset:

```
If objRs.Supports(adMovePrevious) Then
    objRs.MovePrevious
End If
```

If the current row has been changed, and `Update` not called, then a `MovePrevious` will implicitly call `Update`. You should call `CancelUpdate` before calling `MovePrevious` if you do not wish to keep the changes.

The NextRecordset Method

Clears the current `Recordset` object and returns the next `Recordset` by advancing through a series of commands specified as the source of the recordset.

```
Set Recordset = Recordset.NextRecordset([RecordsAffected])
```

Parameter	Type	Description	Default
Records Affected	Long	A variable into which the provider returns the number of rows that the operation affected.	

`RecordsAffected` is only meaningful for a recordset that does not return any rows.

This can be useful if you wish to build up a set of SQL statements and send them all to the provider in one go. However, not all of the data may be returned to the client in a single batch, and this may require a trip to the server for each recordset. Each SQL command will be executed when the `NextRecordset` command is issued. Issuing a `Close` on the recordset will close the recordset without executing any outstanding commands.

You could use this for returning separate lists to be used in combo boxes. For example, imagine the following code that creates a stored procedure:

```
CREATE PROCEDURE usp_ListBoxes
AS
BEGIN
    SELECT * FROM authors
    SELECT * FROM titles
END
```

Opening a recordset on this stored procedure would return the first command in the series. Once you've finished with the data from that recordset, you could issue a `NextRecordset` command to execute the next command. For example:

```
objRs.Open "usp_ListBoxes", objConn, adOpenForwardOnly, _
                      , adLockReadOnly, adCmdStoredProc

Set objRsTitles = objRs.NextRecordset
```

Notice that the above example returns the next recordset into a new recordset variable. You can also use the same variable:

```
Set objRs = objRs.NextRecordset
```

The next recordset can be returned in several states:

❑ As a closed recordset, but with rows; you can open the recordset and proceed as normal

❑ As a closed recordset (with no rows), for a recordset that does not return rows

❑ As an empty recordset (with no rows), where both `BOF` and `EOF` will be set

5

ADO: Recordset Object

You should therefore check the `State` property and the `BOF` and `EOF` properties to determine the status of the recordset. When there are no more recordsets, the recordset object will be set to `Nothing`.

There is one problem with this in Visual Basic, though, if you declare your variables in a particular format. For many years I have used the following format:

```
Dim objRs As New ADODB.Recordset
```

This causes the variable to be created if it is set to `Nothing`, which means that testing the recordset object variable for `Nothing` doesn't work. For example:

```
objConn.Open "Provider=SQLOLEDB; Data Source=Tigger;" & _
             " Initial Catalog=pubs; User Id=sa; Password="
objRs.Open "usp_ListBoxes", objConn, adOpenStatic, _
                            adLockOptimistic, adCmdStoredProc

Do
    ' do something with recordset
    Set objRs = objRs.NextRecordset
Loop While Not (objRs Is Nothing)
```

If you step through this routine in Visual Basic and look at the **Locals Window** when there are no more recordsets, you'll see that `objRs` is indeed `Nothing`. However, the test fails, and sets the `objRs` from `Nothing` back to a variable with a value. The way around this is to check for the `ActiveCommand` property of the `Recordset`. So, change the end of the loop to:

```
Loop While Not (objRs.ActiveCommand Is Nothing)
```

This just seems to be a quirk of Visual Basic, and there's a sample on the web site showing this in action.

Alternatively, if you code according to the currently recommended style, you'll avoid this problem. Declare and set your variables in two stages:

```
Dim objRs As ADODB.Recordset
Set objRs = New ADODB.Recordset
```

When using immediate update mode, a call to `NextRecordset` will generate an error if editing is in progress, so you should ensure that you have updated or cancelled the changes.

Closing the recordset will terminate any further pending commands.

Not all providers support multiple recordsets, so you should consult your provider documentation. Additionally, note that they are not applicable to client side-cursors.

The Open Method

Opens a recordset.

```
Recordset.Open([Source], [ActiveConnection], [CursorType],
               [LockType], [Options])
```

Parameter	Type	Description	Default
Source	Variant	A valid Command object, a SQL statement, a table name, a stored procedure, a URL, a Stream object, or the file name of a persisted recordset.	
Active Connection	Variant	A valid Connection object or a connection string, which identifies the connection to be used.	
CursorType	CursorType Enum	The type of cursor that the provider should use when opening the recordset. If the provider doesn't support the requested cursor type then it may use a different type.	adOpen Forward Only
LockType	LockType Enum	The type of locking (concurrency) that the provider should use when opening the recordset.	adLock ReadOnly
Options	Long	If the Source argument represents something other than a Command object or a persisted recordset, then Options indicates how the provider should interpret the Source argument.	adCmdText

CursorTypeEnum can be one of the following constants (these are covered in more detail under the CursorType property):

❑ adOpenForwardOnly, for a recordset that allows forward movement only.

❑ adOpenKeyset, for a keyset-type cursor

❑ adOpenDynamic, for a dynamic-type cursor

❑ adOpenStatic, for a static-type cursor

`LockTypeEnum` can be one of the following constants (these are covered in more detail under the `LockType` property):

❏ `adLockReadOnly`, for a read-only recordset

❏ `adLockPessimistic`, for pessimistic locking

❏ `adLockOptimisitic`, for optimistic locking

❏ `adLockBatchOptimistic`, for batch optimistic locking

`Options` can be one or more of the following `CommandTypeEnum` or `ExecuteOptionEnum` constants:

❏ `adCmdText`, to indicate that the command is a textual command

❏ `adCmdTable`, to indicate that the command is a table name

❏ `adCmdStoredProc`, to indicate that the command is a stored procedure

❏ `adCmdUnknown`, to indicate that the command type is unknown

❏ `adCmdTableDirect`, to indicate that the command is a table

❏ `adCmdFile`, to indicate that the command is a saved recordset

❏ `adAsyncFetch`, to fetch the records asynchronously

❏ `adAsyncFetchNonBlocking`, to fetch the rows asynchronously, but without blocking the return

❏ `adAsyncExecute`, to execute the command asynchronously

The first five of these are discussed in more detail in Chapter 4, under the `CommandType` property. The constant `adAsyncFetchNonBlocking` is ignored if the recordset is opening a persisted recordset from a stream.

You can deal with persisted files in two ways. This first is by setting the `Provider` to `MSPersist`:

```
objRs.Open "c:\temp\authors.xml", "Provider=MSPersist"
```

The second is to use the `adCmdFile` argument:

```
objRs.Open "c:\temp\authors.xml", , , , adCmdFile
```

For URL usages, you should specify the file or directory as the `Source`, and the absolute URL (or scope) as the `ActiveConnection`:

```
objRs.Open "images", "URL=http://localhost/testsite"
```

For `Stream` usage, you can just specify the stream name:

```
objRs.Open stmData
```

In ASP pages you can use this to open recordsets persisted into the `Request` object from the browser:

```
objRS.Open Request, , , , adCmdFile
```

For asynchronous usage, you use a logical `OR` to add the asynchronous option. For example:

```
objRs.Open "authors", objConn, adOpenKeyset, adLockOptimistic, _
          (adCmdTable OR adAsyncFetch)
```

You can then use the `State` property or the `FetchComplete` event to determine when the recordset has been fully populated.

The difference between `adAsyncFetch` and `adAsyncFetchNonBlocking` is what happens when you request a row that has not yet been fetched. If the recordset has been opened using `adAsyncFetch` and you request a row that hasn't been fetched yet, then the operation will wait until the requested row is available. If the recordset has been opened using `adAsyncFetchNonBlocking` and you request a row that hasn't been fetched yet, you are placed at the end of the recordset.

Note that this is the end of the recordset as it currently exists – because the recordset is being populated asynchronously there may still be more rows to be fetched. So in this mode, `EOF` is the last row that has been fetched, not the physical end of the set of rows.

Opening a recordset does not guarantee that there are any rows available. If you open a recordset with rows then you are automatically placed on the first row. If the recordset doesn't contain any rows then both `BOF` and `EOF` will be `True`. Ideally you should check for this before accessing the rows:

```
objRs.Open "select * from some_table", objConn
If Not objRs.EOF Then
    ' it is safe to access rows
End If
```

The Requery Method

Updates the data in a `Recordset` object by re-executing the query on which the object is based.

```
Recordset.Requery([Options])
```

Name	Type	Description	Default
Options	Long	Indicates the options to use when requerying the recordset.	adOptionUnspecified (-1)

This is equivalent to issuing a `Close` and `Open`. Since you cannot change the settings of the recordset, setting `Options` is merely an optimization issue to help ADO. The exception to this is if you add either of the asynchronous flags, `adAsyncFetch` or `adAsyncFetchNonBlocking`, which cause the Requery to be executed asynchronously.

If you `Requery` a recordset while editing an existing row, or adding a new one, you will generate an error.

When using client-side cursors, you can only issue `Resync` (and not a `Requery`) against a non-read-only recordset.

The Resync Method

Refreshes the data in the current `Recordset` object from the underlying database.

```
Recordset.Resync([AffectRecords], [ResyncValues])
```

Name	Type	Description	Default
AffectRecords	AffectEnum	Determines how many rows will be affected.	adAffectAll
ResyncValues	ResyncEnum	Specifies whether underlying values are overwritten.	AdResyncAll Values

`AffectRecords` can be one of the following `AffectEnum` constants:

❑ `adAffectCurrent`, to refresh just the current row

❑ `adAffectGroup`, to refresh all rows in the current `Filter`

❑ `adAffectAll` to refresh all rows in the recordset

`ResyncValues` can be one of the following `ResyncEnum` constants:

❑ `adResyncAllValues`, to refresh all of the value properties, effectively overwriting any pending updates

❑ `adResyncUnderlyingValues`, to refresh only the `UnderlyingValue` property

Using `adResyncUnderlyingValues` allows you to repopulate the `UnderlyingValue` property without discarding any changes or the `OriginalValue` property. This is particularly useful for investigating optimistic update conflicts, and is discussed in more detail later in this chapter.

If the recordset contains multiple tables, and the "`Unique Table`" and "`Resync Command`" dynamic properties are set, then only rows from this unique table are resynchronized, using the command specified.

Not all providers support resynchronization, so you should use the `Supports` method before issuing a `Resync`:

```
If objRs.Supports(adResync) Then
    objRs.Resync
End If
```

Unlike the `Requery` method the `Resync` method does not re-execute the underlying command.

The Save Method

Saves the `Recordset` to a file.

```
Recordset.Save([Destination], [PersistFormat])
```

Name	Type	Description	Default
Destination	Variant	The complete path name of the file where the recordset should be saved, or a Stream object.	
PersistFormat	PersistFormat Enum	The format in which the recordset should be saved.	adPersist ADTG

`PersistFormat` can be one of:

- ❑ adPersistADTG, to save the recordset in a proprietary binary format
- ❑ adPersistXML, to save the recordset as an XML file

Using `Save` means the following actions will apply:

- ❑ Only rows in the current `Filter` are saved
- ❑ If the recordset is being fetched asynchronously then the `Save` will be blocked until all rows are fetched
- ❑ The first row becomes the current row once the save is complete

`Destination` should only be used for the initial save. Subsequent saves on the same recordset will automatically save to the same file, unless another filename is specified. Attempting to save over an existing file will generate an error. If `Destination` is omitted, then the `Source` property will be used as the name of the file.

For streams, the `Destination` should be a valid `Stream` object, or an object that supports the `IStream` interface. For example:

```
Dim stmData As New Stream
objRs.Save stmData, adPersistXML
```

5

ADO: Recordset Object

or:

```
Dim domXML As New MSXML.Document
objRs.Save domXML, adPersistXML
```

In ASP this can be the `Response` object:

```
objRs.Save Response, adPersistXML
```

Saving in XML format cannot be done from hierarchical recordsets that are based on parameterized queries (for example, a stored procedure with parameters), since the child recordsets are only fetched upon each row access of the parent. Pending updates in a hierarchical recordset also mean that you cannot save to XML.

You can only use the `Save` method from a script executed by Microsoft Internet Explorer when the Internet Explorer security settings are low or custom. For more details on this see the article entitled *ADO and RDS Security Issues in Microsoft Internet Explorer*, available at http://msdn.microsoft.com/library/sdkdoc/dasdk/mdse3wj3.htm.

Recordset Persistence

The `Save` method of recordsets allows data to be saved to a local file, and then re-opened with the `Open` method. The great point about this is that it suddenly opens up the world of roving users. You now have the opportunity to provide the same application to both connected and disconnected users, and an easy way for them to switch states.

Imagine a sales situation where sales people occasionally take their laptops on the road with them. You could provide a Work Offline option that saves their data locally. On the road the application can open these persisted recordsets, and work on them as normal. When the user connects back online, the master copy of the data can be updated with the offline data.

Here's some Visual Basic code that can do this:

```
objRs.CursorLocation = adUseClient
objRs.Save "c:\temp\OfflineData.dat"

' disconnect from connection and close connection
Set objRs.ActiveConnection = Nothing
objRs.Close
objConn.Close

' now re open in offline mode
objRs.Open "c:\temp\OfflineData.dat"
```

This could be executed when the user wishes to work offline. The recordset is saved locally, the connection and recordset closed, and then the local recordset opened. The user would be disconnected from the server and could continue as normal, although only the saved data would be available. Any new information, or information not saved, would only become available once the connection to the server was re-established.

To get back online, you would do this:

```
' reconnect to the data source
strConn = "Provider=SQLOLEDB; Data Source=Tigger; " & _
          " Initial Catalog=pubs; User Id=sa; Password="
objRs.ActiveConnection = strConn

' update the master table with the offline changes
objRs.UpdateBatch
```

This connects the recordset to a connection and then uses `UpdateBatch` to update the master copy of the rows with the local copy. See the section on Conflict Resolution below for more details on this.

You can see that this makes writing offline applications no different from writing an online application. You could have a simple flag that is set when the application is offline to indicate that the saved copies of the recordset are opened when the application starts.

This method also works in browser situations, as you can use the XMLHTTP object in IE to persist RDS client recordsets from the browser back to ASP pages. The web site has a sample that shows how this is done.

Conflict Resolution

Using client-side cursors and disconnected recordsets is great, especially since we have the ability to amend rows and send them back to the server to update the master copy of the database. One thing you have to consider, however, is how to resolve conflicts between changes to the data you've made, and any changes that might have happened due to other users.

If you think back to the offline code, we used `UpdateBatch` to update the master rows, and this will generate errors if any of the rows conflicted with underlying recordset changes. There are two ways to investigate this problem:

1. Have error trapping in the routine that calls `UpdateBatch`. You can then filter the recordset using `adFilterConflictingRecords` to see which rows caused the problem.

2. Use the recordset events, and place some code in the `RecordChangeComplete` event. If errors are generated by conflicts, then the recordset will already be filtered for you in the `RecordChangeComplete` event procedure.

If you choose the latter approach, then your code could look like this:

```
Private Sub objRs_RecordChangeComplete( _
        ByVal adReason As ADODB.EventReasonEnum, _
        ByVal cRecords As Long, _
        ByVal pError As ADODB.Error, _
        adStatus As ADODB.EventStatusEnum, _
        ByVal pRecordset As ADODB.Recordset)
```

```
        Dim objFld       As ADODB.Field

        If adStatus = adStatusErrorsOccurred Then
            Print cRecords & " caused errors.:"
            For Each objFld In pRecordset.Fields
                Debug.Print "Name"; vbTab; objFld.Name
                Debug.Print "Value"; vbTab; objFld.Value
                Debug.Print "UV"; vbTab; objFld.UnderlyingValue
                Debug.Print "OV"; vbTab; objFld.OriginalValue
            Next
        End If

    End Sub
```

Of the event procedure arguments, adStatus indicates that an error occurred, and cRecords identifies the number of rows that failed. pRecordset is the recordset filtered to show only those conflicting rows.

You can also use the Status property of the Field object to determine the reason why a particular field caused the conflict. This is covered in more detail in Chapter 8.

For more details on the arguments for this event see the RecordChangeComplete event procedure later in this chapter.

A small sample application showing these techniques is available from the Wrox Press web site (http://www.wrox.com).

The Seek Method

Uses an Index to perform searches to locate specific rows.

```
    Recordset.Seek KeyValues, SeekOption
```

Parameter	Type	Description	Default
KeyValues	Variant Array	The column values to search for.	
SeekOption	SeekEnum	The type of comparison to be made.	adSeekFirstEQ

SeekOption takes its value from one of the following SeekEnum constants:

- ❑ adSeekAfter, to find the key just after the match
- ❑ adSeekAfterEQ, to find the key equal to or just after the match
- ❑ adSeekBefore, to find the key just before the match
- ❑ adSeekBeforeEQ, to find the key equal to or just before the match
- ❑ adSeekFirstEQ, to find the first key equal to the match
- ❑ adSeekLastEQ, to find the last key equal to the match

`KeyValues` is a variant array to allow for indexes that contain multiple columns.

If the row being sought is not found, no error is returned, and the current row is placed at `EOF`.

You use the `Seek` method in conjunction with the `Index` property. For example:

```
objRs.Index = "FullName"
objRs.Seek Array("Janine", "Lloyd"), adSeekFirstEQ
If objRs.EOF Then
    Print "Row not found"
End If
```

Not all providers support the `Seek` operation. To check this you should use `adSeek` with the `Supports` method.

The `Seek` operation is only supported by server-based cursors (`CursorLocation = adUseServer`). This is because it uses the cursor service and indexes on the provider, rather than facilities of ADO.

The Supports Method

Determines whether a specified `Recordset` object supports a particular functionality.

```
Boolean = Recordset.Supports(CursorOptions)
```

Parameter	Type	Description	Default
CursorOptions	CursorOption Enum	One or more values to identify what functionality is supported.	

`CursorOptions` can take one or more of the following `CursorOptionEnum` constants:

- ❑ `adAddNew`, to indicate that the recordset supports addition of new rows, via the `AddNew` method

- ❑ `adApproxPosition`, to indicate that the recordset supports absolute position, via the `AbsolutePosition` and `AbsolutePage` properties

- ❑ `adBookmark`, to indicate that the recordset supports bookmarks, via the `Bookmark` properties

- ❑ `adDelete`, to indicate that the recordset supports row deletion, via the `Delete` method

- ❑ `adFind`, to indicate that the recordset supports the finding of rows, via the `Find` method

- ❑ `adHoldRecords`, to indicate that changes to the recordset will remain if you fetch more rows

- ❑ `adIndex`, to indicate that you can use the `Index` property to set the current Index

5

ADO: Recordset Object

❑ `adMovePrevious`, to indicate that the recordset supports movement backwards, via the `MoveFirst`, `MovePrevious`, `Move`, or `GetRows` methods

❑ `adNotify`, to indicate that the recordset supports notifications, and will return events

❑ `adResync`, to indicate that the recordset allows the underlying data to be refreshed with the `Resync` method

❑ `adSeek`, to indicate that you can use the `Seek` method to find rows by an Index

❑ `adUpdate`, to indicate that the recordset allows records to be updated with the `Update` method

❑ `adUpdateBatch`, to indicate that the recordset allows rows to be updated with the `UpdateBatch` method

You can use the `Supports` method to find out which features a recordset makes available. For example, the following lines establish whether the recordset is updateable:

```
If objRs.Supports(adUpdate) Then
  ' recordset supports updates
End If
```

You can use Boolean logic to check for multiple values:

```
If objRs.Supports(adDelete Or adAddNew) Then
  ' recordset supports both Delete and AddNew
End If
```

Note that, even if the recordset supports a particular feature, the underlying data may make the feature unavailable – and this may result in errors from the provider. For example, you may have a recordset based on a view where only certain columns are updateable; the recordset will support `adUpdate`, but certain columns may not allow updating. This means that you should really check the `Errors` collection after each operation.

The Update Method

Saves any changes made to the current `Recordset` object.

```
Recordset.Update([Fields], [Values])
```

Parameter	Type	Description	Default
`Fields`	`Variant`	A single name or `Variant` array representing the names or ordinal positions of the fields to be modified.	

Parameter	Type	Description	Default
Values	Variant	A single name or Variant array representing the values for the fields in the new or updated row.	

You can update fields in three ways. First, by assigning values to fields and then calling the Update method:

```
objRs("au_lname").Value = "Lloyd"
objRs("au_fname").Value = "Janine"
objRs.Update
```

Second, you can pass a single field name with a single value:

```
objRs.Update "au_lname", "Lloyd"
```

Third, you can pass multiple field names and multiple values:

```
objRs.Update Array("au_lname", "au_fname"),
             Array("Lloyd", "Janine")
```

The three methods are interchangeable. There's little difference between the methods unless updating multiple fields, in which case you should use the first or third methods. Each Update issues a command to the server, so you can make your code more efficient by issuing fewer updates.

Using any of the Move methods when editing a row will implicitly call Update.

If the recordset contains multiple tables, and the "Unique Table" dynamic property is set, then only rows from this unique table can be updated. This is discussed in more detail in the Dynamic Properties section, at the end of the chapter.

The UpdateBatch Method

Writes all pending batch updates to disk.

```
Recordset.UpdateBatch([AffectRecords])
```

Name	Type	Description	Default
AffectRecords	AffectEnum	Determines how many rows will be affected.	adAffectAll

AffectRecords can take any of the following AffectEnum constants:

❑ adAffectCurrent, to refresh just the current row

❑ adAffectGroup, to refresh all rows in the current Filter

❑ adAffectAll to refresh all rows in the recordset

Using `UpdateBatch` allows changes to be cached until such time as you request the underlying data store to be updated. Caching starts when opening a recordset with `adLockBatchOptimistic`.

A failure to update will cause the `Errors` collection to be populated, and you can use the `Filter` property to see which rows failed. The failure could be caused by a conflict between a change made by you and a change made by another user. There's more on conflicts earlier in this chapter.

If the recordset contains multiple tables, the "`Unique Table`" dynamic property is set, and the "`Update Resync`" dynamic property is set to `True`, then a `Resync` is performed directly after the update.

The order in which updates occur on the provider is not guaranteed to be the same as the order in which they were performed on the client.

Properties of the Recordset Object

The AbsolutePage Property

Specifies in which page the current row resides.

```
PositionEnum = Recordset.AbsolutePage
Long = Recordset.AbsolutePage
Recordset.AbsolutePage = PositionEnum
Recordset.AbsolutePage = Long
```

`PositionEnum` can be a valid page number, or one of the following constants:

❑ `adPosBOF`, to indicate or position the current row pointer at the beginning of the recordset.

❑ `adPosEOF`, to indicate or position the current row pointer at the end of the recordset.

❑ `adPosUnknown`, to indicate that the current page is unknown. This could be because the recordset is empty, or because the provider does not support this property, or because the provider cannot identify the current page.

When setting the value of the `AbsolutePage` property, the row pointer is set to the first row in the specified page. Thus, if you set the `AbsolutePage` property to 1, this moves to the first page of the recordset, and thus sets the row pointer to the first row in the recordset. This is used in conjunction with the `PageSize` property, described later in this chapter.

The AbsolutePosition Property

Specifies the ordinal position of a `Recordset` object's current cursor position.

```
PositionEnum = Recordset.AbsolutePosition
Recordset.AbsolutePosition = PositionEnum
```

`PositionEnum` can be a valid row number, or one of the following constants:

❑ `adPosBOF`, to indicate or position the current row pointer at the beginning of the recordset.

❑ `adPosEOF`, to indicate or position the current row pointer at the end of the recordset.

❑ `adPosUnknown`, to indicate that the current position is unknown. This could be because the recordset is empty, the provider does not support this property, or it cannot identify the current position.

You cannot use the absolute position to identify a row uniquely, because this value changes as rows are added and deleted. Of course, you could use `AbsolutePosition` to point to a row through the life of the recordset if your recordset does not allow additions or deletions. However, the `AbsolutePosition` is affected by the use of `Sort` and `Index`, as it points to a row at a particular position in the recordset, and not to an individual row, irrespective of its position. If you need to identify a row throughout sorts and filters, you should use a bookmark.

The ActiveCommand Property

Indicates the `Command` object that created the associated `Recordset` object.

```
Set Command = Recordset.ActiveCommand
```

When the recordset was created from a command, you can use this property to access the `Command` object's properties and parameters. For example:

```
objCmd.CommandText = "usp_foo"

Print objRs.ActiveCommand.CommandText
```

This is particularly useful when you have only been supplied with the recordset, such as in the Visual Basic 6 Data Environment, which provides details of commands used to create recordsets. Since these can be created at design time, this property allows you to extract the details at run time.

If the recordset was not created from a command, then this property will be `Null`.

The ActiveConnection Property

Indicates to which `Connection` object the specified `Recordset` object currently belongs.

```
Set Variant = Recordset.ActiveConnection
Set Recordset.ActiveConnection = Variant
Recordset.ActiveConnection = String
String = Recordset.ActiveConnection
```

The `ActiveConnection` can be set to a pre-existing `Connection` object, in which case you use the `Set` form:

```
Set objRs.ActiveConnection = objConn
```

Alternatively, you can set the `ActiveConnection` by using a connection string, in which case an implicit `Connection` object is created for you:

```
objRs.ActiveConnection = "DSN=pubs"
```

This property will inherit the value from the `ActiveConnection` argument of an `Open` command, or from the `Source` property of a `Command`. The `ActiveConnection` property may also be modified by the provider, to allow access to provider-specific connection information.

You can disassociate a client-side recordset from a connection by setting this property to `Nothing`. The recordset remains valid, and can be reconnected to any `Connection` object at a later date.

The BOF Property

Indicates whether the current row pointer is before the first row in a `Recordset` object.

```
Boolean = Recordset.BOF
```

If your recordset is empty, then the `BOF` and `EOF` properties will both be `True`.

The Bookmark Property

Can be used to return a bookmark that uniquely identifies the current row in a `Recordset` object, or to set the current row pointer to the row identified by a valid bookmark.

```
Variant = Recordset.Bookmark
Recordset.Bookmark = Variant
```

Using the `Clone` method on a recordset gives two recordsets with interchangeable bookmarks. This means that bookmarks between cloned recordsets are identical. However, bookmarks from different recordsets (that is, non cloned, or cloned after the `Requery` method has been called) are not interchangeable, even if the recordsets were created from the same source or command.

You can use this property to store the position in the recordset temporarily, allowing you to return to that position at a later date. For example:

```
varBkmk = objRs.Bookmark
' ... some processing that changes the current row ...
objRs.Bookmark = varBkmk
```

For example, this is quite useful when using the Find method (which positions you at EOF if the row you are searching for was not found):

```
varBkmk = objRs.Bookmark

objRs.Find "au_lname = 'Lloyd'"
If objRs.EOF Then
   Print "Row not found - now moving cursor from EOF to bookmarked
         row"
   objRs.Bookmark = varBkmk
End If
```

Bookmarks are generally only supported on keyset and static cursors and client-side cursors. Server based dynamic cursors do not support bookmarks because their membership is not fixed. You should check the adBookmark value (using the recordset's Supports method) to verify this.

The CacheSize Property

Indicates the number of rows from a Recordset object that are cached locally in memory. This defaults to 1.

```
Long = Recordset.CacheSize
Recordset.CacheSize = Long
```

The cache size affects how many rows from the recordset are fetched from the server in one go and held locally, and this can have an effect on performance and memory usage. When a recordset is first opened, only a certain number of rows (the number stored in CacheSize) are fetched locally – and the remaining rows are not fetched until required. If you move to a row that's not in the current cache, the provider will fetch another cache of rows. So, a cache larger than 1 is generally more efficient. Chapter 14 shows the difference in speed between a cache of 1 and a larger value. Changing the size of the cache can have an effect on both client and server-based cursors.

An important point to note is that rows in the cache do not reflect underlying changes made by other users, until Resync is issued, or until recordset navigation options cause those rows to be re-read.

You can change the cache size during the life of a recordset, but the new size only becomes effective when the next cache of data is retrieved. A cache size of 0 is not allowed and generates an error.

An undocumented feature, which is not officially supported, is that a negative cache size causes rows to be fetched backwards from the current row, rather than forwards.

The CursorLocation Property

Sets or returns the location of the cursor engine.

```
CursorLocationEnum = Recordset.CursorLocation
Recordset.CursorLocation = CursorLocationEnum
```

CursorLocationEnum can be one of the following constants:

- ❑ adUseClient, to specify the Microsoft Client cursor

- ❑ adUseServer, to specify the cursor support supplied by the data provider, assuming it supports server-based cursors

Server-side cursors often support better concurrency than client-side cursors, because it's the actual provider that is handling the concurrency control.

Client-side cursors must be used when creating disconnected recordsets.

The CursorType Property

Indicates the type of cursor used in a Recordset object.

```
CursorTypeEnum = Recordset.CursorType
Recordset.CursorType = CursorTypeEnum
```

CursorTypeEnum can be one of the following constants:

- ❑ adOpenForwardOnly, for a recordset that only allows forward movement, one row at a time. It is therefore not possible to use anything other than MoveNext or Move with a value of 1, unless the CacheSize is greater than 1. Bookmarks are not supported on this cursor type, since absolute position is not a requirement.

- ❑ adOpenKeyset, for a keyset-type cursor. This gives you a set of rows for which the data is up-to-date with the underlying data, but the number of rows may not be, as additions and deletions may not be visible to the cursor. Keyset cursors work by storing the keys to the row of data, and only fetching the data when it is required. Therefore the set of rows is fixed, but the data is not fixed. Deleted rows still remain in the recordset, but as a hole. Insertions by other users are not visible (since they weren't part of the original set of keys), but insertions by you may be visible (if they match the rowset criteria). Movement is supported both forwards and backwards.

- ❑ adOpenDynamic, for a dynamic type cursor. The membership of rows in the recordset is not fixed. New rows added by any user will be visible, deleted rows will not be visible, and any data changes will be visible. Movement is supported both forwards and backwards.

- ❑ adOpenStatic, for a static type cursor, where the data is fixed at the time the cursor is created. Movement is supported both forwards and backwards.

For keyset cursors you can control the visibility of inserted and deleted rows by use of the following dynamic properties:

- ❑ Remove Deleted Records, will remove deleted rows from the keyset

- ❑ Own Inserts Visible, will ensure that your own inserts into the keyset are visible

- ❑ Other Inserts Visible, will ensure that inserts by other people are visible in the keyset

Not all providers support all cursor types, and the actual cursor type used may depend on the cursor location. For this reason you should query the `CursorType` property after the recordset has been opened, to see what type the provider has used. The cursor types requested and supported by the main providers are included in Chapter 14.

The DataMember Property

Specifies the name of the data member to be retrieved from the object referenced by the `DataSource` property.

```
String = Recordset.DataMember
Recordset.DataMember = String
```

Used to create data-bound controls in Visual Basic using the Data Environment.

The `DataMember` identifies the object in the `DataSource` that will supply the recordset.

The DataSource Property

Specifies an object containing data to be represented as a `Recordset` object.

```
Set Object = Recordset.DataSource
Set Recordset.DataSource = Object
```

It is used to create data-bound controls in Visual Basic 6 using the Data Environment.

The `DataSource` identifies the object in the Data Environment to which the `DataMember` belongs.

The EditMode Property

Indicates the editing status of the current row.

```
EditModeEnum = Recordset.EditMode
```

`EditModeEnum` will be one of the following constants:

❑ `adEditNone`, to indicate that the current row has no edits in progress

❑ `adEditInProgress`, to indicate that the current row is being edited

❑ `adEditAdd` to indicate that the current row is being added – that is, it's a new row

❑ `adEditDelete`, to indicate the current row has been deleted

You could use this in an interactive application that allows users to edit and move around rows. Since moving around rows intrinsically calls `Update`, you may want to offer the user the option of canceling or saving changes before moving to another row. For example, imagine a section of Visual Basic code that runs when a **Next Row** button is pressed:

5

ADO: Recordset Object

```
If objRs.EditMode = adEditInProgress Then
    strMsg = "The current row has changed. " & _
            "Would you like to save the changes?"
    If MsgBox (strMsg, vbYesNo) = vbNo Then
        objRs.CancelUpdate
    End If
End If
objRs.MoveNext
```

This simply checks the edit mode before moving to another row.

The EOF Property

Indicates whether the current row pointer is after the last row in a `Recordset` object.

```
Boolean = Recordset.EOF
```

The Filter Property

Indicates a filter for data in the `Recordset`.

```
Variant = Recordset.Filter
Recordset.Filter = Variant
```

The `Filter` property can be set to a valid filter string, an array of bookmarks, or one of the following `FilterGroupEnum` constants:

- ❑ `adFilterNone`, which removes any current filter and shows all rows

- ❑ `adFilterPendingRecords`, for batch update mode, which shows only rows that have been changed but not yet sent to the server

- ❑ `adFilterAffectedRecords`, which shows only rows affected by the last `Delete`, `Resync`, `UpdateBatch`, or `CancelBatch`

- ❑ `adFilterFetchedRecords`, which shows rows in the current cache

- ❑ `adFilterPredicate`, which shows deleted rows

- ❑ `adFilterConflictingRecords`, which shows rows that caused a conflict during the last batch update attempt

You can filter with an array of `Bookmarks`. This small section of Visual Basic code shows an example of this:

```
Dim avarBkmk (5)
avarBkmk(0) = objRs.Bookmark
' ...some more processing...
avarBkmk(1) = objRs.Bookmark
objRs.Filter = Array(avarBkmk(0), avarBkmk(1))
```

This can be quite useful when allowing users to select multiple rows from a list.

Using a normal string as a filter follows much the same syntax as a SQL WHERE clause, as the following examples show:

```
objRs.Filter = "au_lname = 'Lloyd'""
objRs.Filter = "au_lname LIKE 'L*'"
objRs.Filter = "Price > 10.99 AND Price < 15.99"
objRs.Filter = "InvoiceDate > #04/04/98#"
```

You'll notice that multiple conditions are allowed here, unlike the Find command. When using date fields, you have to use the VBA syntax, surrounding the date with # symbols.

Once the Filter has been set, the cursor is placed on the first row in the newly filtered recordset.

To cancel a filter, call the Filter method again – this time, either use adFilterNone or specify an empty string (" "):

```
objRs.Filter ""
```

The Index Property

Indicates the name of the index currently in effect.

```
String = Recordset.Index
Recordset.Index = String
```

The Index property refers to a previously defined table index. This can be either an index that was created on the base table, or an ADOX Index object.

Changing an Index may change the current row position, which may therefore update the current row.

You cannot set the Index if a Filter has been set on the recordset, if the recordset is still processing an asynchronous operation, or from within a WillChangeRecordset or RecordsetChangeComplete event handler.

The Index property is not related to the indexing used by the dynamic Optimize property.

Not all providers support the Index property. To check this you should use adIndex with the Supports method.

The LockType Property

Indicates the type of locks placed on rows during editing.

```
LockTypeEnum = Recordset.LockType
Recordset.LockType = LockTypeEnum
```

LockTypeEnum can be one of the following constants:

❑ adLockReadOnly, for a read-only recordset, where the provider does no locking and the data cannot be changed

❑ adLockPessimistic, for pessimistic locking, where the provider attempts to lock edited rows at the data source

❑ adLockOptimistic, for optimistic locking, where the provider locks rows on a row-by-row or page-by-page basis, when Update is called

❑ adLockBatchOptimistic, for batch update mode, where locking occurs when UpdateBatch is called

Only adLockBatchOptimistic or adLockReadOnly are supported by client-side cursors. If you attempt to use any other lock type you'll get adLockBatchOptimistic.

The locking method you choose is really going to depend upon the application. Since pessimistic locking locks the row at the data source as you start editing, you don't have to worry about a conflict with another user's changes, unless the row is already locked when you try to lock it. However, this implies a permanent connection to the data store, which may be either impractical or impossible.

Optimistic locking gives you better resource management, but you then have to cater for conflicts, as the lock doesn't actually occur until you try to Update the row. This means that someone else might have changed the row between the time that you started editing it and the time that you went to Update it. Since ADO doesn't know which copy is correct, it deals with this by generating an error, which can be trapped. This error number is -2147217885, however not all providers report error information correctly. To get the best error information you'll need to use the OLE DB Provider for ODBC.

Although batch locking can be used with server-based cursors, it's more useful with client cursors. This allows changes to multiple rows before committing them to the data store in a single batch.

The MarshalOptions Property

Indicates which rows are to be marshaled back to the server.

```
MarshalOptionsEnum = Recordset.MarshalOptions
Recordset.MarshalOptions = MarshalOptionsEnum
```

MarshalOptionsEnum can be one of the following constants:

❑ adMarshalAll, to send all rows back to the server, which is the default

❑ adMarshalModifiedOnly, to send back to the server only those rows that have changed

Marshaling is the term given to transferring a recordset between two processes. This could be between the client and the server in a two-tier system or between the client and a middle-tier in an n-tier system.

This property is only applicable when using disconnected, client-side recordsets. By marshaling only the changed rows (as opposed to all rows), you can greatly improve performance. If only a few rows are modified locally, less data needs to be sent back to the server process.

You can use this quite effectively when using n-tier client-server architecture, using a business object on the server to supply recordsets. These can be modified locally, and only the changed rows are sent back to the business processes for updating.

The MaxRecords Property

Indicates the maximum number of rows that may be returned to a `Recordset` object as the result of a query.

```
Long = Recordset.MaxRecords
Recordset.MaxRecords = Long
```

You can only set this property while the recordset is closed. The `MaxRecords` property defaults to 0, which indicates that all rows should be returned.

This is quite useful for applications that allow users to submit queries, since you can limit the set of rows if it is too big.

While this property is supported, not all providers may implement it.

The PageCount Property

Indicates how many pages of data are contained in the `Recordset` object.

```
Long = Recordset.PageCount
```

The recordset will consist of a number of pages – each page contains a number of rows equal to `PageSize`, except for the last page, which may contain fewer rows. If the `PageSize` is not set then PageCount will be -1.

The `PageCount` property allows you to move quickly to the last page in a recordset:

```
objRs.AbsolutePage = objRs.RecordCount/objRs.PageCount
```

This positions your row pointer on the first row of the last page. Note that not all providers support the `PageCount` property.

The PageSize Property

Indicates how many rows constitute one page in the `Recordset`.

```
Long = Recordset.PageSize
Recordset.PageSize = Long
```

You can use this to change the number of rows in a page. For example, imagine a web application that shows search results from Microsoft Index Server. You could allow the user to page through these rows, and to specify how many rows should be seen in each page.

The page size doesn't correspond to the cache size. The cache is a way of managing the transfer of a number of rows from the server to the client. In comparison, the page size is merely a logical structure that can be used for display purposes. The page size allows you an easy way to access a group of rows that are next to each other in the recordset.

Not all providers support PageSize.

The RecordCount Property

Indicates the current number of rows in the Recordset object.

```
Long = Recordset.RecordCount
```

The RecordCount will only be accurate for recordsets that support approximate positioning or bookmarks. In practice this is generally all cursor types except server-side, forward-only cursors and server-side, dynamic cursors. If the row count cannot be accurately determined, it is set to -1. You can test to see if the recordset supports approximate positioning or bookmarks by using the Supports method:

```
If objRs.Supports(adBookmark Or adApproxPosition) Then
    ' RecordCount will be accurate
End If
```

If the Recordset does not support approximate positioning or bookmarks, it must be fully populated before an accurate RecordCount value can be returned. One way to achieve this is by using MoveLast to move to the last row in the recordset, assuming the recordset supports MoveLast. If MoveLast is not supported, then all rows will have to be read before an accurate count can be determined. In general, static and keyset cursors return the correct count, as do dynamic cursors under certain providers, but forward-only cursors return -1.

If the recordset is being fetched asynchronously, the same rules apply. The RecordCount will be accurate if approximate position or bookmarks are supported, even if the asynchronous command is still running and the recordset has not been fully populated with rows. In this case the number of rows is the number returned so far.

The Sort Property

Specifies one or more field names on which to sort the Recordset, and the direction of the sort.

```
String = Recordset.Sort
Recordset.Sort = String
```

The sort string should be a comma-separated list of columns to dictate the hierarchy of the sort order, each optionally followed by the sort direction. The default sort direction is ASC.

For example:

```
objRs.Sort = "au_lname ASC, au_fname DESC"
```

You must use a client-side cursor (`CursorLocation = adUseClient`). Once the sort is set, then a temporary index will be created for each field in the `Sort`. You can also force the creation of local indexes by setting the `Optimize` property (of the `Field` object's `Properties` collection) to be `True`. For example:

```
objRs("au_lname").Properties("Optimize") = True
```

This will create a local index, which will speed up sorting and searching.

The Source Property

Indicates the command or SQL command for the data in a `Recordset` object.

```
String = Recordset.Source
Recordset.Source = String
Set Recordset.Source = Variant
```

This is useful for identifying the actual command text used to create the recordset, especially if it was created from a Command object.

The State Property

Gives the state of the recordset in both synchronous and asynchronous mode. Indicates whether the recordset is open, closed, or whether it is executing an asynchronous operation.

```
ObjectStateEnum = Recordset.State
```

`ObjectStateEnum` can be one or more of the following constants:

- ❑ `adStateClosed`, indicating that the recordset is closed
- ❑ `adStateOpen`, indicating that the recordset is open
- ❑ `adStateConnecting`, indicating that the recordset is currently connecting to the data store
- ❑ `adStateExecuting`, indicating that the recordset is currently executing a command
- ❑ `adStateFetching`, indicating that the recordset is currently fetching rows

When the recordset is opened asynchronously, you should use logical operations to test these values. For example:

```
If (objRs.State And adStateFetching) = adStateFetching Then
   Print "Recordset is still fetching rows"
End If
```

A positive test for `adStateExecuting` or `adStateFetching` implies `adStateOpen`, but you cannot test for this alone.

5

ADO: Recordset Object

159

The Status Property

Indicates the status of the current row with respect to batch updates or other bulk operations.

```
RecordStatusEnum = Recordset.Status
```

`RecordStatusEnum` can be one or more of the `RecordStatusEnum` constants shown in Appendix B.

The StayInSync Property

Indicates, in a hierarchical `Recordset` object, whether a reference to the child row should change when the parent row changes.

```
Boolean = Recordset.StayInSync
Recordset.StayInSync = Boolean
```

The default for this is `True`; if set to `False`, a reference to a child recordset will remain pointing to the old recordset, even though the parent row may have changed.

Hierarchical recordsets are covered in more detail in Chapter 13, in the discussion on Data Shaping.

Events of the Recordset Object

ADO 2.6 supports notifications, which allow providers to notify the application when certain events occur. Event ordering is covered in Chapter 2, and examples of event usage are available on the supporting web site.

Event Status

All events will have a bi-directional parameter, `adStatus`, to indicate the status of the event. This is of type `EventStatusEnum`, and can be one of the following constants:

- ❏ `adStatusOK`, to indicate that the action that caused the event was successful

- ❏ `adStatusErrorsOccured`, to indicate that errors or warnings occurred, in which case the `Errors` collection should be checked

- ❏ `adStatusCantDeny`; on a `Will...` event this indicates that you cannot cancel the action that generated the event; on a `...Complete` event it indicates that the action was cancelled

- ❏ `adStatusUnwantedEvent`, which indicates that the action that generated the event should no longer generate events

On a `Will...` event (and assuming `adStatusCantDeny` is not set), before the procedure exits, you can set `adStatus` to `adStatusCancel` to cancel the action that caused this event. This also generates an error indicating that the event has been cancelled. For example, assume that you have moved from one row to the next – this will raise a `WillMove` event on the recordset. If you decide that you do not wish to move to another row, you can set `adStatus` to `adStatusCancel`, and the `Move` action will be cancelled. This allows you to perhaps cancel actions where the data is incorrect.

When using `Will...` events, one thing to watch for is implicit method calls. Taking the above `Move` as an example; if the current row has been edited, then ADO implicitly calls `Update`. In this case you might get more than one `Will...` event.

If you no longer wish to receive events for a particular action, then before the procedure exits you can set `adStatus` to `adStatusUnwantedEvent`, and they will no longer be generated for the current object instance.

The EndOfRecordset Event

Fires when there is an attempt to move to a row past the end of the `Recordset`.

```
EndOfRecordset(fMoreData, adStatus, pRecordset)
```

Parameter	Type	Description
fMoreData	Boolean	Set to True if it is possible to append more data to pRecordset while processing this event.
adStatus	EventStatus Enum	Identifies the status of the message.
pRecordset	Recordset	A reference to the Recordset object for which this event applies.

While in this event procedure, more rows can be retrieved from the data store and appended to the end of the recordset. If you wish to do this, you should set the parameter `fMoreData` to `True`. After returning from this procedure, a subsequent `MoveNext` will allow access to the newly added rows. This can be useful if you wish to provide your own paging scheme, as you can read in the next batch of rows when the user attempts to move past the end of the current page of rows.

The FetchComplete Event

Fires after all the rows in an asynchronous operation have been retrieved into the `Recordset`.

```
FetchComplete(pError, adStatus, pRecordset)
```

Parameter	Type	Description
pError	Error	If adStatus is adStatusErrorsOccurred, this is an Error object that describes the error that occurred. Otherwise it is not set.

Parameter	Type	Description
adStatus	EventStatus Enum	Identifies the status of the message.
pRecordset	Recordset	A reference to the Recordset object for which the rows were retrieved.

This is most useful when the recordset is being fetched asynchronously, as it avoids having to check the state of the recordset periodically.

The FetchProgress Event

Is fired periodically by the provider during an asynchronous operation, to report how many rows have been retrieved so far.

```
FetchProgress(Progress, MaxProgress, adStatus, pRecordset)
```

Parameter	Type	Description
Progress	Long	The number of rows that have currently been retrieved.
MaxProgress	Long	The maximum number of rows expected to be retrieved.
adStatus	EventStatus Enum	Identifies the status of the message.
pRecordset	Recordset	A reference to the Recordset object for which the rows are being retrieved.

MaxProgess may not contain the total number of rows to be fetched, if the recordset type does not support this.

This would be used for updating status indicators on user screens.

The provider determines when, and why this event is raised.

The FieldChangeComplete Event

Fires after the values of one or more Field objects have been changed.

```
FieldChangeComplete(cFields, Fields, pError, adStatus, pRecordset)
```

Parameter	Type	Description
cFields	Long	The number of Field objects within Fields.
Fields	Variant	An array of Field objects with completed changes.

Parameter	Type	Description
pError	Error	If adStatus is adStatusErrorsOccurred, this describes the error that occurred. Otherwise it is not set.
adStatus	EventStatus Enum	Identifies the status of the message.
pRecordset	Recordset	A reference to the Recordset object for which this event applies.

You can use this to update status indicators, or to trigger other actions that are dependent upon some fields being changed.

The MoveComplete Event

Fires after the current position in the Recordset changes.

```
MoveComplete(adReason, pError, adStatus, pRecordset)
```

Parameter	Type	Description
adReason	EventReason Enum	The reason for the event.
pError	Error	If adStatus is adStatusErrorsOccurred, this is an Error object that describes the error that occurred. Otherwise it is not set.
adStatus	EventStatus Enum	Identifies the status of the message.
pRecordset	Recordset	The Recordset object for which this event applies.

adReason will be one of a subset of the EventReasonEnum constants:

❑ adRsnMoveFirst, when a MoveFirst is issued

❑ adRsnMoveLast, when a MoveLast is issued

❑ adRsnMoveNext, when a MoveNext is issued

❑ adRsnMovePrevious, when a MovePrevious is issued

❑ adRsnMove, when a Move is issued

❑ adRsnRequery, when a Requery is issued, or a Filter is set

adReason might also assume the value of adRsnMove when the AbsolutePage or AbsolutePosition property is set, or a Bookmark is set, or a new row is added with AddNew. In addition, this value is generated when the recordset is opened.

These could also be generated when a child recordset has events and the parent recordset moves.

5

ADC: Recordset Object

The RecordChangeComplete Event

Fires after one or more rows change in the local recordset.

```
RecordChangeComplete(adReason, cRecords, pError, adStatus,
                     pRecordset)
```

Parameter	Type	Description
adReason	EventReason Enum	Specifies the reason for the event.
cRecords	Long	The number of rows changing.
pError	Error	If adStatus is adStatusErrorsOccurred, this is an Error object that describes the error that occurred. Otherwise it is not set.
adStatus	EventStatus Enum	Identifies the status of the message.
pRecordset	Recordset	The Recordset object for which this event applies, containing only the changed rows.

adReason will be one of a subset of the EventReasonEnum constants:

- ❑ adRsnAddNew, when an AddNew is issued

- ❑ adRsnDelete, when a Delete is issued

- ❑ adRsnUpdate, when an Update is issued

- ❑ adRsnUndoUpdate, when an Update is cancelled, with CancelUpdate or CancelBatch

- ❑ adRsnUndoAddNew, when an AddNew is cancelled, with CancelUpdate or CancelBatch

- ❑ dRsnUndoDelete, when a Delete is cancelled, with CancelUpdate or CancelBatch

- ❑ adRsnFirstChange, when the row is changed for the first time

You could use this event for creation of an audit trail, or triggering other actions that are dependent upon the data having changed.

The RecordsetChangeComplete Event

Fires after the Recordset has changed.

```
RecordsetChangeComplete(adReason, pError, adStatus, pRecordset)
```

Parameter	Type	Description
adReason	EventReason Enum	Specifies the reason for the event.
pError	Error	If adStatus is adStatusErrorsOccurred, this is an Error object that describes the error that occurred. Otherwise it is not set.
adStatus	EventStatus Enum	Identifies the status of the message.
pRecordset	Recordset	The Recordset object for which this event applies.

adReason will be one of a subset of the EventReasonEnum constants:

- ❑ adRsnRequery, when a Requery is issued
- ❑ adRsnReSynch, when a Resync is issued
- ❑ adRsnClose, when a Close is issued

The WillChangeField Event

Fires before a pending operation changes the value of one or more Field objects.

```
WillChangeField(cFields, Fields, adStatus, pRecordset)
```

Parameter	Type	Description
cFields	Long	The number of Field objects within Fields.
Fields	Variant	An array of Field objects with pending changes.
adStatus	EventStatus Enum	Identifies the status of the message.
pRecordset	Recordset	The Recordset object for which this event applies.

This can be useful for validating user input.

This can occur due to the following Recordset operations: setting the Value property, and calling the Update method with field and value array parameters.

The WillChangeRecord Event

Fires before one or more rows in the Recordset change.

```
WillChangeRecord(adReason, cRecords, adStatus, pRecordset)
```

Parameter	Type	Description
adReason	EventReason Enum	Specifies the reason for the event.
cRecords	Long	The number of rows changing.
adStatus	EventStatus Enum	Identifies the status of the message.
pRecordset	Recordset	The Recordset object for which this event applies.

adReason will be one of a subset of the EventReasonEnum constants:

- ❑ adRsnAddNew, when an AddNew is issued
- ❑ adRsnDelete, when a Delete is issued
- ❑ adRsnUpdate, when an Update is issued
- ❑ adRsnUndoUpdate, when an Update is cancelled, with CancelUpdate or CancelBatch
- ❑ adRsnUndoAddNew, when an AddNew is cancelled, with CancelUpdate or CancelBatch
- ❑ dRsnUndoDelete, when a Delete is cancelled, with CancelUpdate or CancelBatch
- ❑ adRsnFirstChange, when the row is changed for the first time

You could use this when actions might change the record, and this can be used in parallel with WillChangeField.

The WillChangeRecordset Event

Fired before a pending operation changes the Recordset.

```
WillChangeRecordset(adReason, adStatus, pRecordset)
```

Parameter	Type	Description
adReason	EventReason Enum	Specifies the reason for the event.
adStatus	EventStatus Enum	Identifies the status of the message.
pRecordset	Recordset	The Recordset object for which this event applies.

adReason will be one of a subset of the EventReasonEnum constants:

- ❑ adRsnRequery, when a Requery is issued
- ❑ adRsnReSynch, when a Resync is issued
- ❑ adRsnClose, when a Close is issued

You can use this to identify when an action would cause the underlying set of rows to change.

The WillMove Event

Fires before a pending operation changes the current position in the `Recordset`.

```
WillMove(adReason, adStatus, pRecordset)
```

Parameter	Type	Description
adReason	EventReason Enum	The reason for the event.
adStatus	EventStatus Enum	Identifies the status of the message.
pRecordset	Recordset	The `Recordset` object for which this event applies.

`adReason` will be one of a subset of the `EventReasonEnum` constants:

❑ `adRsnMoveFirst`, when a `MoveFirst` is issued

❑ `adRsnMoveLast`, when a `MoveLast` is issued

❑ `adRsnMoveNext`, when a `MoveNext` is issued

❑ `adRsnMovePrevious`, when a `MovePrevious` is issued

❑ `adRsnMove`, when a `Move` or `AddNew` is issued, or `AbsolutePage` or `AbsolutePosition` is set, or the current row is moved by setting the `Bookmark`, or the recordset is opened

❑ `adRsnRequery`, when a `Requery` is issued, or a `Filter` is set

This allows you to identify when an action will cause the current row to change.

Collections of the Recordset Object

The Fields Collection

The `Fields` collection contains zero or more `Field` objects, each representing a field in the recordset, and is the default collection for a `Recordset`.

```
Recordset.Fields
```

You can iterate though the `Fields` collection to access each `Field` object individually:

```
For Each objField in objRs.Fields
    Print "Field name is " & objField.Name
Next
```

The `Fields` collection and `Field` object are discussed in more detail in Chapter 8.

The Properties Collection

The Properties collection contains Property objects, each representing an extended property supplied by the provider for the recordset.

```
Recordset.Properties
```

You can iterate through the Properties collection to access each Property object individually:

```
For Each objProp in objRs.Properties
    Print "property name is " & objProp.Name
Next
```

The Properties collection is discussed in more detail in Chapter 8 and Appendix C.

Dynamic Properties

There are a few dynamic properties that are worth covering in a little detail here, rather than in Appendix C, where you might miss them.

The Resync Command Property

The Resync Command property specifies a command string that the recordset's Resync method will use to refresh data in the Unique Table. This allows you to customize what happens when data in the Unique Table is resynchronized. For example, imagine that a recordset is created by the following query:

```
SELECT *
FROM    publishers JOIN titles
ON      publishers.pub_id = titles.pub_id
```

Here, the Unique Table property should be set to titles, and its primary key, title_id, is the key that uniquely identifies rows in this recordset. You can specify that only rows from the Unique Table that match the non-unique table are resynchronized. This allows you to resynchronize the data for just the Unique Table, rather than data for the whole query.

The Resync Command would therefore be:

```
SELECT *
FROM    publishers JOIN titles
ON      publishers.pub_id = titles.pub_id
WHERE   titles.title_id = ?
```

The Resync Command should generally be the same as the recordset definition, but with the addition of a WHERE clause parameterizing the primary key of the Unique Table. You add a question mark as the parameter, and ADO handles the matching of this to the non-unique table. In the example above, the result is that only the rows that matched the original query are returned.

The rows affected by the `Resync` are dependent upon the `Update Resync` property, described below.

The Unique Catalog Property

The `Unique Catalog` property specifies the catalog (or database name, depending upon your database server terminology) containing the table named in the `Unique Table` property.

The Unique Schema Property

The `Unique Schema` property specifies the schema (or owner, depending upon your database server terminology) of the table named in the `Unique Table` property.

The Unique Table Property

The `Unique Table` property specifies the name of the base table upon which edits are allowed. This is required when recordsets are created from `JOIN` statements. For example, consider the following SQL statement:

```
SELECT *
FROM    publishers JOIN titles
ON      publishers.pub_id = titles.pub_id
```

In this example you could set `Unique Table` to `titles`, to indicate that `titles` is the table that contains the unique information. For many-to-one queries, you generally set `Unique Table` to point to the many table, since this is the table that will contain unique keys for the recordset.

When `Unique Table` is set, the `AddNew`, `Delete`, `Resync`, `Update`, and `UpdateBatch` methods of the recordset only affect the table named in this property.

You should generally set the `Unique Schema` or `Unique Catalog` properties before setting the `Unique Table` property, as the table, schema, and catalog names uniquely identify the base table.

The `Unique Table` is directly related to the `Resync Command` property.

The Update Resync Property

The `Update Resync` property specifies whether an implicit `Resync` method is called directly after an `UpdateBatch` method. This gives you the choice as to which rows (if any) are resynchronized. One of the main reasons for the inclusion of these `Resync` properties is the need for client-cursor based applications to have a better way of handling data changes, especially the insertion of new rows.

The values for this property can be one or more of the `CEResyncEnum` constants:

❑   `adResyncNone`, to indicate that no `Resync` is performed.

❑   `adResyncAutoIncrement`, to indicate that a `Resync` is performed for all successfully inserted rows, including values of any auto-incremental columns. This is the default.

- ❑   adResyncConflicts, to indicate that a Resync is performed for updated or deleted rows that failed because of concurrency conflicts.

- ❑   adResyncUpdates, to indicate that a Resync is performed for all rows that were updated successfully.

- ❑   adResyncInserts, to indicate that a Resync is performed for all rows that were successfully inserted, including values of any auto-incremental columns.

- ❑   adResyncAll, to indicate that a Resync is performed for all rows that have pending changes.

These constants are part of the standard ADO type library.

To set more than one value you should join them together:

```
objRs.Properties("Update Resync") = adResyncUpdates OR
adResyncInserts
```

I thank God I am as honest as any man

living that is an old man and no honester th

Can counsel and speak comfort to th

Which they themselves not feel

For there was never yet philospher
That could endure the toothache patiently.

Much Ado About Nothing.

He wears his faith but as the fashion of !

As merry as the day

He hath indeed better bettered expectation

(Act i. Sc. i.).

He wears his faith but as the fashion of his hat.
(Ibid)

As merry as the day is long.

ch indeed better bettered expectation

(Act i. Sc. i.).

(Ibid)

Much Ado About Nothing.

Can counsel and speak comfort to that grief

Which they themselves not feel.

He wears his faith but as the fashion of his hat.
(Ibid)

I was not born under

a rhyming planet

I was not born under a rhyming plan
(Sc.

For there was never yet
That could endure the to

merry as the day is long (Sc. 2)

Can counsel and speak comfort to that grief

Which they themselves not feel.
(Ibid)

He hath indeed better bettered expectation
(A

I thank God I am as honest as any

living that is an old man and no hones

He wears his faith but as the fashion of his ha
(Ibi

Much Ado About Nothing.   *For there was never yet philospher*
That could endure the toothache patiently.
(Ibid)

I was not born u

The Record Object

The Record object is designed for use with Document Source Providers – the OLE DB Provider for Internet Publishing is the first to enable its use. Although this provider shipped with ADO 2.1, its functionality was severely limited, and it was only with the release of ADO 2.5 that all of its features were made available. The only change with version 2.6 is that the Command object can now return results into a Record.

> The OLE DB Provider for Internet Publishing is a Web Distributed
> Authoring and Versioning (WebDAV) client, and will work against any
> WebDAV-enabled web server. WebDAV is a W3C standard for document
> authoring over the Web. For more information on WebDAV see
> **www.webdav.org**.

Document Source Providers are those providers that allow access to stores of data that are document-based (such as file systems), rather than stores that are relational in nature (such as databases). With relational data stores, there is an easy mapping between a set of data (such as a table or the results of a SQL statement) and a Recordset object. However, with document providers this mapping becomes more difficult, because not every document contains the same properties. For example, in relational data, each row has the same structure as the previous row. There is the same number of columns, and each of the columns is the same. Non-relational data doesn't follow this pattern, so it wouldn't be easy to try and use a Recordset. The general term for this type of data is semi-structured data.

This is best explained by looking at the Internet Publishing Provider, and using it to connect to a web server (in this case Microsoft Internet Information Server 5.0). For example, consider the following web site:

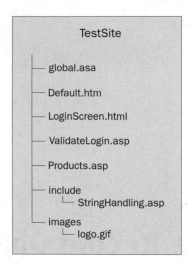

There are three directories, and a number of files of differing types. Although these files have some common properties (such as a name), there are properties only applicable to certain types. For example, documents have a size, whereas a directory doesn't. Note, that to obtain this sort of information from an IIS 5.0 web site, directory browsing must be enabled.

In ADO terms, you would use both the Record and the Recordset objects – the Record object would map onto individual items, and the Recordset would contain collections of items. So a Record would hold the top-level directory, TestSite, and a Recordset would hold the files contained within that directory, including sub-directories. The Recordset only contains information about the common properties, such as name, last access time, and so on. Since these are common across all files (whether documents or directories), each row in the Recordset will have the same structure as the previous row. However, each item (each row in the recordset) individually may have extra properties, and to access these you use a Record object, using the source of the Record as the current row in the Recordset.

The following pseudo-code should make this clearer:

```
Open directory as a Record.
Extract Recordset of children
Loop through rows in Recordset
    If the row points to a directory
        Open the sub-directory as a new Record
        Extract Recordset of children
        Loop . . .
    Else
        Print out details of file from Recordset
    End If
End Loop
```

*There's a full set of samples on the supporting web site (**www.wrox.com**) to show how this works in more detail. The Record and Stream objects are covered in depth in Professional ADO 2.5 Programming(ISBN 1861002750, also by Wrox Press.*

Methods of the Record Object

The Cancel Method

Cancels the execution of an asynchronous method call.

```
Record.Cancel
```

This method will cancel an `Open`, `CopyRecord`, `DeleteRecord`, or `MoveRecord` method call.

The Close Method

Closes an open `Record` object.

```
Record.Close
```

The CopyRecord Method

Copies a file or directory from one location to another.

```
String = Record.CopyRecord([Source], [Destination], [UserName],
                           [Password], [Options], [Async])
```

Name	Type	Description	Default
Source	String	The URL of the file or directory to be copied.	
Destination	String	The URL of the location where the Source is to be copied to.	
UserName	String	The user ID, if required, to authorize access to the Destination.	
Password	String	The user password, if required, to authorize access to the Destination.	
Options	CopyRecord Options Enum	Options to specify the behavior of the copy.	adCopy Unspecified
Async	Boolean	Indicates whether or not the copy should be performed asynchronously.	False

The Options can be one of the following:

❑ adCopyAllowEmulation, to use a download/upload method if the copy fails.

❑ adCopyNonRecursive, to copy only the current directory, but no children.

❑ adCopyOverWrite, to overwrite an existing file or directory. If Destination is a directory, all children of that directory will be lost.

❑ adCopyUnspecified, to indicate the default copy operation is performed.

By default, the copy operation is recursive, so if Source indicates a directory, all files and directories under Source will be copied. For example:

```
recRoot.CopyRecord "http://localhost/TestSite/", _
                   "http://localhost/LiveSite", _
                   "davids", "SneakYpAssword"
```

However, to copy only the files under the top level directory, you would do this:

```
recRoot.CopyRecord "http://localhost/TestSite/", _
                   "http://localhost/LiveSite", _
                   "davids", "SneakYpAssword", _
                   adCopyNonRecursive
```

The values of Source and Destination must be different otherwise an error is generated. If no Source is provided, then the current Record object is taken as the source.

The return value is provider dependent, but is typically the value of the Destination.

The DeleteRecord Method

Deletes a file or directory and sub-directories.

```
Record.DeleteRecord([Source], [Async])
```

Name	Type	Description	Default
Source	String	The URL of the file or directory to be deleted.	
Async	Boolean	Indicates whether or not the delete should be performed asynchronously.	False

If Source is empty, then the file or directory specified by the Record object is deleted; in which case you should close the Record object after performing the delete, since subsequent behavior of the object is provider dependent.

If a Recordset was used as a source for the Record, then the Recordset will need to be refreshed to reflect the deleted record. For example:

```
' open the root directory
recRoot.Open "http://localhost/TestSite"

' get a recordset of the files in that directory
rsChildren = recRoot.GetChildren

' open a new Record, using the current row as the source.
' this gives us a Record pointing directly at the file
recFile.Open rsChildren

' delete the file
recFile.DeleteRecord
```

At this stage the file has been deleted, but it still exists as a row in the `Recordset`. To correct this you should do the following:

```
rsChildre.Requery
```

The `Recordset` now accurately reflects the files in the directory.

The GetChildren Method

Returns a `Recordset` containing the files and directories of the current `Record`.

```
Set Recordset = Record.GetChildren
```

The provider determines the fields that make up the `Recordset`, for example:

```
recRoot.Open "", "URL=http://localhost/TestSite"

Set rsChildren = recRoot.GetChildren

While Not rsChildren.EOF
    . . .
Wend
```

The properties of files are available through the `Fields` collection of the `Recordset`. For example:

```
Debug.Print rsChildren.Fields("RESOURCE_ABSOLUTEPARSENAME")
```

The `Fields` accessible through the OLE DB Provider for Internet Publishing are discussed at the end of this chapter. How to navigate down through a directory tree is also covered there.

The MoveRecord Method

Moves a file or directory from one location to another.

```
String = Record.MoveRecord([Source], [Destination], [UserName],
                          [Password], [Options], [Async])
```

Name	Type	Description	Default
Source	String	The URL of the file or directory to be moved.	
Destination	String	The URL of the location where the Source is to be moved to.	
UserName	String	The user ID, if required, to authorize access to the Destination.	
Password	String	The user password, if required, to authorize access to the Destination.	
Options	MoveRecord Options Enum	Options to specify the behavior of the move.	adMove Unspecified
Async	Boolean	Indicates whether or not the move should be performed asynchronously.	False

Options can be one of the following:

❑ adMoveAllowEmulation, to use download, upload, delete operations to simulate the move operation.

❑ adMoveDontUpdateLinks, to ensure that hypertext links of the source Record are not updated. Updating of links is provider specific.

❑ adMoveOverWrite, to overwrite the destination file or directory, if it exists.

❑ adMoveUnspecified, to perform the default move operation.

If Destination already exists then an error will be generated, unless adMoveOverWrite is specified. For example:

```
recRoot.MoveRecord "http://localhost/TestSite/", _
                   "http://localhost/LiveSite", _
                   "davids", "SneakYpAssword", adMoveOverWrite
```

The values of Source and Destination must be different otherwise an error is generated.

Some changes to the current Record (or Recordset if that's where the Record originated – see the Open method for more details) will not be updated immediately. The ParentURL property is one example, and the Record will need to be closed (or requeried) for this to reflect its new value, similar to the code shown under the DeleteRecord method.

The return value is provider dependent, but is typically the value of the `Destination`.

The Open Method

Opens a file or directory, or creates a new file or directory.

```
Record.Open([Source], [ActiveConnection], [Mode], [CreateOptions],
            [Options], [UserName], [Password])
```

Name	Type	Description	Default
Source	Variant	The URI of the file or directory, a Command object, an Open Recordset object, or a string containing a table name or SQL statement.	
ActiveConnection	Variant	A connection string or open Connection object.	
Mode	ConnectMode Enum	The access mode for the Record.	adMode Unknown
CreateOptions	RecordCreate OptionsEnum	Indicates whether a file should be opened or created. Ignored when Source is not a URL.	adFail IfNotExists
Options	RecordOpen OptionsEnum	Specific options for the open command.	adOpenRecord Unspecified
UserName	String	The user ID, if required, to authorize access to the Source.	
Password	String	The user password, if required, to authorize access to the Source.	

The `ConnectModeEnum` constants are discussed under the `Mode` property, and they specify what permissions are to be applied to the resource being opened.

`CreateOptions` can be one of the following `RecordCreateOptionsEnum` constants:

❑ adCreateCollection, to create a new collection resource (for example a directory).

❑ adCreateNonCollection, to create a new simple resource (for example a file).

❑ adCreateOverwrite, to force an existing file or directory to be overwritten.

❏ adCreateStructDoc, to create a new structured document.

❏ adFailIfNotExists, to ensure an error is generated if the Source does not exist.

❏ adOpenIfExists, to force any existing file or directory to be opened (when added to the other adCreate options, apart from adCreateOverwrite).

Options can be one of the following RecordOpenOptionsEnum constants:

❏ adDelayFetchFields, to ensure that fields are not fetched until their first access.

❏ adDelayFetchStream, to ensure that the default stream is not fetched until requested.

❏ adOpenAsync, to open the Record asynchronously.

❏ adOpenRecordUnspecified, to indicate no specific open options are specified.

❏ adOpenSource, to open the source of the resource, rather than its processed output (for example an ASP file).

The Source argument can be one of the following:

❏ A URL pointing to the file or directory to be opened. This can be an absolute or relative URL. If a relative URL is used, then ActiveConnection defines the scope (root) of the relative URL.

❏ An open Recordset object, whose current row identifies the URL to open.

❏ A Command object that will return a single row. If more than one row is returned, the first row is used as the Source, and the Errors collection will have a warning added to it.

❏ A SQL SELECT statement that returns a single row. If more than one row is returned, the first row is used as the Source, and the Errors collection will have a warning added to it.

❏ The name of a table.

For example, the following all use URLs to open the Record:

```
rec.Open "http://localhost/testsite"
rec.Open "images", "URL=http://localhost/testsite"
rec.Open "default.htm", "URL=http://localhost/testsite"
```

The following uses an open Connection object:

```
conSite.Open "URL=http://localhost/testsite"
rec.Open "default.htm", conSite
```

The following opens a recordset, containing files in the images folder, and then opens a record using the recordset as the source. Since the recordset contains more than one row, the first row in the recordset (the first file in the images directory) is the file the Record opens:

```
rs.Open "images", "URL=http://localhost/testsite", , ,
adCmdTableDirect
rec.Open rs
```

This technique is also useful when traversing through directory structures, since the GetChildren method of the Record returns a Recordset of the child files:

```
recParent.Open "http://localhost/testsite"
Set rsChildren = rec.GetChildren
recChild.Open rsChilren
```

The following uses a SQL statement, where only a single row (in this case the first row) is returned into the Record:

```
strCon = "Provider=SQLOLEDB; Data Source=Eeyore; " & _
         "Initial Catalog=pubs; User ID=sa; Password="
rec.Open "SELECT * FROM authors", strCon, , , adOpenExecuteCommand
```

The following uses a Command object as the source:

```
strCon = "Provider=SQLOLEDB; Data Source=Eeyore; " & _
         "Initial Catalog=pubs; User ID=sa; Password="
cmd.CommandText = "usp_AuthorByID"
cmd.CommandType= adCmdStoredProc
cmd.Parameters.Append cmd.CreateParameter("@au_id", adVarChar, _
                                   adParamInput, 22, "172-32-
1176"

rec.Open cmd, strCon, , , adOpenExecuteCommand
```

Or, if the Command already has the connection defined:

```
rec.Open cmd, , , , adOpenExecuteCommand
```

Properties of the Record Object

The ActiveConnection Property

Identifies the connection string or Connection object to which the Record belongs.

```
String = Record.ActiveConnection
Record.ActiveConnection = String
Set Variant = Record.ActiveConnection
Set Record.ActiveConnection = Variant
```

Once the Record is open this property is read-only.

The Mode Property

Indicates the permissions used when opening the resource.

```
Record.Mode = ConnectModeEnum
ConnectModeEnum = Record.Mode
```

`ConnectModeEnum` can be one or more of the following constants:

- ❑ `adModeRead`, to indicate read-only permissions. This is the default value.

- ❑ `adModeReadWrite`, to indicate both read and write permissions.

- ❑ `adModeRecursive`, to indicate that permission should be applied recursively.

- ❑ `adModeShareDenyNone`, to allow other users to open this resource with any permissions.

- ❑ `adModeShareDenyRead`, to prevent other users opening the resource with read permissions.

- ❑ `adModeShareDenyWrite`, to prevent other users opening the resource with write permissions.

- ❑ `adModeShareExclusive`, to prevent other users from opening the resource.

- ❑ `adModeUnknown`, indicates that either the permissions have yet to be set, or that they cannot be identified.

- ❑ `adModeWrite`, to indicate write permissions.

When using the `adModeShare...` constants, you can add `adModeRecursive` to indicate that permissions should be applied recursively. This would apply the permissions to all children and sub-children of the resource when the record is opened.

For example, to apply read and write permissions recursively to a directory and its children:

```
recWeb.Mode = adModeReadWrite + adModeRecursiverecWeb.Open
"URL=http://localhost/testsite"
```

This property cannot be changed once the `Record` is open.

When using a client-side (RDS) Connection the `Mode` property can only be set to `adModeUnknown`.

The ParentURL Property

Indicates the absolute URL of the parent of this `Record`.

```
String = Record.ParentURL
```

If the Record is the root URL of a web site, then this property will have a null value. If a SQL statement is used as the source of the Record, then a run-time error will be generated when accessing this property.

This property is read-only.

The RecordType Property

Identifies the type of the Record.

```
RecordTypeEnum = Record.RecordType
```

RecordTypeEnum can be one of the following constants:

- ❑ adSimpleRecord, to indicate a simple resource that does not contain children (a file)
- ❑ adCollectionRecord, to indicate a resource that contains children (a folder)
- ❑ adStructDoc, to indicate a COM structured document

This property is read-only.

The Source Property

Indicates the item represented by the Record.

```
Set Variant = Record.Source
Set Record.Source = Variant
```

This property returns the value of the Source argument of the Open method, and therefore contains one of the following:

- ❑ An absolute or relative URL
- ❑ A reference to a Recordset object
- ❑ A reference to a Connection object

The State Property

Indicates whether the Record is open or closed:

```
ObjectStateEnum = Record.State
```

ObjectStateEnum will be one or more of:

- ❑ adStateClosed, to indicate the Record is closed
- ❑ adStateOpen, to indicate the Record is open
- ❑ adStateConnecting, to indicate that the Record is currently connecting
- ❑ adStateExecuting, to indicate that the Record is executing a command
- ❑ adStateFetching, to indicate that the Record is fetching rows of data

ADO: The Record Object

6

183

A combination of values is possible if asynchronous operations are being used. For example, if an asynchronous command is being executed, both `adStateOpen` and `adStateExecuting` would be set. This could be tested by:

```
If (rec.State And adStateOpen) = adStateOpen Then
    ' The record is open
    If (rec.State And adStateExecuting) = adStateExecuting Then
        ' . . . but it's still executing a command
```

This property is read-only.

Collections of the Record Object

The Fields Collection

Contains a `Field` object for each field in the record.

```
Fields = Record.Fields
```

For URL-based `Records`, the `Field` objects are mapped from the properties of the files and directories of the URL, such as the MIME type, the URL, and so on (the full list is shown a little later). For non URL-based `Records`, then the `Field` objects are mapped from the underlying provider. For example, a `Record` opened from a SQL query would have the `Fields` mapped from the database columns that were returned in the query.

When indexing into the `Fields` collection you can use a field number, a field name, or for the `Record` object, one of the `FieldEnum` constants:

❑   `adDefaultStream` to return the default stream of the Record

❑   `adRecordURL` to return the absolute URL of the Record

The `Field` object is discussed in more detail in Chapter 8.

The Properties Collection

Contains a `Property` object for each provider specific property.

```
Properties = Record.Properties
```

This is discussed in more detail in Chapter 8.

Fields of a Record

This section details the fields supplied by the OLE DB Provider for Internet Publishing, when `Record` objects are opened from URLs.

Field	Type	Description
CHAPTERED_CHILDREN	advarWChar	Indicates the rowset chapter containing the children of the resource. Not used by the OLE DB Provider for Internet Publishing.
DEFAULT_DOCUMENT	adVarWChar	The URL of the default document for a folder.
RESOURCE_ABSOLUTEPARSENAME	adVarWChar	The absolute URL, including path.
RESOURCE_CONTENTCLASS	adVarWChar	The likely use of the resource.
RESOURCE_CONTENTLANGUAGE	adVarWChar	The resource language.
RESOURCE_CONTENTTYPE	adVarWChar	The MIME type of the resource.
RESOURCE_CREATIONTIME	adFileTime	The time the resource was created.
RESOURCE_DISPLAYNAME	adVarWChar	Display name of the resource.
RESOURCE_ISCOLLECTION	adBoolean	Indicates whether or not the resource is a collection (has children).
RESOURCE_ISHIDDEN	adBoolean	Indicates whether or not the resource is hidden.
RESOURCE_ISMARKEDFOROFFLINE	adBoolean	Indicates whether or not the resource is marked for offline usage.
RESOURCE_ISREADONLY	adBoolean	Indicates whether or not the resource is read-only.
RESOURCE_ISROOT	adBoolean	Indicates whether or not the resource is the root of a collection.
RESOURCE_ISSTRUCTURED DOCUMENT	adBoolean	Indicates whether or not the resource is a structured document such as a Word document.
RESOURCE_LASTACCESSTIME	adFileTime	The time the resource was last accessed.
RESOURCE_LASTWRITETIME	adFileTime	The time the resource was updated.
RESOURCE_PARENTNAME	adVarWChar	The URL of the parent resource.
RESOURCE_PARSENAME	adVarWChar	The URL of the resource.
RESOURCE_STREAMSIZE	adUnsigned BigInt	The size of the default stream.

6

ADO: The Record Object

> You should note that RESOURCE_CONTENTTYPE and
> RESOURCE_CONTENTCLASS might have their values reversed. At the
> time of writing this was the case, but this may have been corrected for
> the release.

DAV Fields

There are some Fields that begin with DAV. These are for Distributed Authoring and
Versioning, and they map onto the existing Fields in the following way:

Field	DAV Field
RESOURCE_PARSENAME	DAV:lastpathsegment
RESOURCE_PARENTNAME	DAV:parentname
RESOURCE_ABSOLUTEPARSENAME	DAV:href
RESOURCE_ISHIDDEN	DAV:ishidden
RESOURCE_ISREADONLY	DAV:isreadonly
RESOURCE_CONTENTTYPE	DAV:getcontenttype
RESOURCE_CONTENTCLASS	DAV:getcontentclass
RESOURCE_CONTENTLANGUAGE	DAV:getcontentlanguage
RESOURCE_CREATIONTIME	DAV:creationtime
RESOURCE_LASTACCESSTIME	DAV:lastaccessed
RESOURCE_LASTWRITETIME	DAV:getlastmodified
RESOURCE_STREAMSIZE	DAV:getcontentlength
RESOURCE_ISCOLLECTION	DAV:iscollection
RESOURCE_ISSTRUCTUREDDOCUMENT	DAV:isstructureddocument
DEFAULT_DOCUMENT	DAV:defaultdocument
RESOURCE_DISPLAYNAME	DAV:displayname
RESOURCE_ISROOT	DAV:isroot

The reason why there are two sets of properties is that Internet Publishing is built on
top of a protocol called WebDAV, and IIS 5.0 is a WebDAV server. It's therefore
possible to use any WebDAV client to access IIS 5.0, so it must support the official set
of DAV properties.

I thank God I am as honest as any man
living that is an old man and no honester th

Can counsel and speak comfort to th
Which they themselves not feel

Much Ado About Nothing.

He wears his faith but as the fashion of

As merry as the day

He hath indeed better bettered expectation

(Act i. Sc. i.).

He wears his faith but as the fashion of his hat.
(Ibid)

As merry as the day is long.

indeed better bettered expectation

(Act i. Sc. i).

(Ibid)

Can counsel and speak comfort to that grief

Much Ado About Nothing.

Which they themselves not feel.

He wears his faith but as the fashion of his hat.
(Ibid)

I was not born under

a rhyming plane

I was not born under a rhyming plane

For there was never yet
That could endure the to

merry as the day is long (Sc. 2)

Can counsel and speak comfort to that grief

Which they themselves not feel.
(Ibid)

He hath indeed better bettered expectation

(Ibid)

I thank God I am as honest as an

living that is an old man and no honest

He wears his faith but as the fashion of his ha
(Ibi

Much Ado About Nothing.   For there was never yet philospher
That could endure the toothache patiently.

(Ibid)

For there was never yet philospher
That could endure the toothache patiently.

I was not born u

The Stream Object

The `Stream` object is designed for much the same purpose as the COM `IStream` interface, and provides a way to read and write the contents of files, or streams of data. Support for streams is not only available in this separate object, but has been built into the `Command` and `Recordset` objects, allowing greater flexibility when using ADO with other technologies, such as XML and ASP.

There are several places where `Stream` objects can be used:

❑   To store data internally within applications. Since the `Stream` is a simple memory manager, you can create `Stream` objects to store arbitrary amounts of data, such as XML, text, and so on.

❑   In conjunction with the OLE DB Provider for Internet Publishing (discussed in more detail in the previous chapter) and the `Record` object. Since the `Record` object allows access to and manipulation of remote files, the `Stream` adds the ability to access the contents of these files. Together the two give full support for remote editing of files over HTTP.

❑   As a way of transferring data to other applications that support `Stream`s, such as ASP 3.0, where the `Request` and `Response` objects both have stream support.

There's also nothing to stop you using streams in your own applications to provide other applications or developers easy data access. The supporting web site (www.wrox.com) has an application that uses the `Stream` objects – this application is discussed fully in the Wrox Press book Professional ADO 2.5 Programming (ISBN 1861002750).

> Streams do not perform caching of data, and are intrinsically linked to their underlying objects. This means that it's not necessary to flush the contents, either periodically or before closing a stream. Data written to a stream is automatically flushed to the underlying object.

Methods of the Stream Object

The Cancel Method

Cancels the execution of an asynchronous Open method call.

```
Stream.Cancel
```

If the adOpenStreamAsync flag was specified on the Open method call, then using Cancel allows the open to be aborted before it has completed.

The Close Method

Closes an open Stream object.

```
Stream.Close
```

You can use the State property to determine if the stream is open before attempting to close it.

```
If stmData.State = adStateOpen Then
    stmData.Close
End If
```

It's not necessary to flush the stream before closing, as the close automatically performs a Flush.

The CopyTo Method

Copies a specified number of characters or bytes from one stream to another.

```
Stream.CopyTo(DestStream, [CharNumber])
```

Name	Type	Description
DestStream	Stream	The destination Stream object into which characters are to be copied.
CharNumber	Long	The number of bytes or characters to copy. The default is -1, which indicates that all characters or bytes from the current stream position to the end of the stream should be copied.

The start position of the copy for both the source and destination streams is determined by the current position in the stream, as specified in the Position property. After the copy the Position is immediately after the last byte copied. Data in the destination stream is overwritten.

For the destination stream, the end of the stream is either:

❑ Left where it is, if the number of bytes copied is less than were remaining. That is, copying does not truncate the destination stream – to do this you would use the SetEOS method.

❑ Extended, if the number of bytes copied is greater than were remaining. That is, the destination stream increases in size, and ends immediately after the copied data.

For example:

```
Dim stmSource    As New ADODB.Stream
Dim stmTarget    As New ADODB.Stream

stmTarget.Open

stmSource.Open "URL=http://localhost/testsite/default.htm"

stmSource.CopyTo stmTarget
```

You cannot copy from a binary stream to a text stream, although you can copy from a text stream to a binary stream.

The Flush Method

Forces the contents of the stream into its underlying object.

```
Stream.Flush
```

The buffer is continuously flushed by ADO, so it's only necessary to use this method call when you want to force the changes to be written to the underlying object. For example, use this method if you change the contents of a stream opened from a file, and you want those changes to be immediately available.

The LoadFromFile Method

Loads the contents of a file into the stream.

```
Stream.LoadFromFile(FileName)
```

Name	Type	Description
FileName	String	A UNC format string containing the file to be loaded.

You must open the Stream before loading contents into it, at which time the current contents are overwritten, and the end of the stream (EOS) is set to the end of the loaded contents. The beginning of the stream becomes the current position. For example:

```
stmSource.Open "URL=http://localhost/testsite/default.htm"
stmSource.LoadFromFile "D:\temp\NewDefault.htm"
```

ADO: The Stream Object

7

If the Stream object is associated with a URL, this association still exists. Only the contents of the stream change. In the above example the stream is still attached to the default.htm file, but now the contents of that file are the contents that were originally in NewDefault.htm.

The Open Method

Opens a Stream object.

```
Stream.Open([Source], [Mode], [Options], [UserName], [Password])
```

Name	Type	Description
Source	Variant	The URL of the resource to be opened, or a Record object, whose default stream is used as the source.
Mode	ConnectModeEnum	The access mode used when opening the stream. The default is adModeUnknown.
Options	StreamOpenOptionsEnum	Additional options identifying how the stream should be opened.
UserName	String	The user ID if security credentials are required to access to the resource.
Password	String	Password for the user ID.

The Mode argument can be one of the ConnectModeEnum constants, as detailed under the Mode property.

The Options argument can be one or more of the StreamOpenOptionsEnum constants:

❑ adOpenStreamAsync, to open the stream asynchronously.

❑ adOpenStreamFromRecord, to indicate that the Source argument specifies a Record object, whose default stream should be used.

❑ adOpenStreamUnspecified, to indicate that the default options should be used. This is the default value and means that synchronous operation is performed, with the source being supplied by a URL.

If a Record object is used as the source, then the security credentials and mode are ignored, and are taken from the Record object.

For example, to open a stream from a URL:

```
Dim stmSource   As New ADODB.Stream

stmSource.Open "URL=http://localhost/testsite/default.htm"
```

To use a `Record` as the source (which is why the source is a `Variant`):

```
Dim stmSource    As New ADODB.Stream
Dim recRoot      As New ADODB.Record

recRoot.Open "default.htm", "URL=http://localhost/testsite"

stmSource.Open recRoot
```

The Read Method

Reads a number of bytes from a binary stream.

```
Variant = Stream.Read([NumBytes])
```

Name	Type	Description
NumBytes	Long	The number of bytes to read from the stream. The default is -1.

The `NumBytes` argument can be the actual number of bytes, or one of the `StreamReadEnum` constants:

❑ `adReadAll`, to read all characters from the current position to the end of the stream. This is the default value, and is the same as omitting this argument.

❑ `adReadLine`, to read only the next line. The `LineSeparator` identifies the character that separates lines.

Only the remaining bytes are read from the stream if the number requested is larger than the number left. A `Null` value is returned if there are no more bytes remaining.

If the number of bytes is not specified, then all remaining bytes are returned.

After reading, the current position in the stream is the byte after the last one read, or the end of the stream if all bytes are read (in which case the `EOS` property is set to `True`).

The ReadText Method

Reads a number of characters from a text stream.

```
String = Stream.ReadText(NumChars)
```

Name	Type	Description
NumChars	Long	The number of characters to read from the Stream. The default is -1.

7

ADO: The Stream Object

The `NumChars` argument can be the actual number of characters, or one of the `StreamReadEnum` constants:

- ❑ `adReadAll`, to read all characters from the current position to the end of the stream. This is the default value, and is the same as omitting this argument.

- ❑ `adReadLine`, to read only the next line. The `LineSeparator` identifies the character that separates lines.

Only the remaining characters are read from the stream if the number requested is larger than the number left. A `Null` value is returned if there are no more characters remaining.

For example:

```
strContents = stmData.ReadText
```

You may have to set the `Charset` property of the stream before reading data from it, since the default character set is Unicode.

If the number of characters is not specified, then all remaining characters are returned.

The SaveToFile Method

Saves the contents of a binary stream to a file.

```
Stream.SaveToFile(FileName, Options)
```

Name	Type	Description
FileName	String	The fully qualified name of the file, in UNC format.
Options	SaveOptionsEnum	Indicates whether a new file should be created, or existing files overwritten.

The `Options` argument can be one of the `SaveOptionsEnum` constants:

- ❑ `adSaveCreateNotExist`, to create a new file only if the file doesn't already exist. This is the default value.

- ❑ `adSaveCreateOverWrite`, to overwrite an existing file.

After saving, the position of the stream is placed at the beginning.

If the `Stream` object is associated with a URL, this association still exists. For example:

```
stmSource.Open "URL=http://localhost/testsite/default.htm"
stmSource.SaveToFile "D:\temp\OldDefault.htm"
```

Here `stmSource` is still associated with the `default.htm` file. The `SaveToFile` method simply copies the contents of a stream to a local file, and doesn't re-associate the stream with that new file.

The SetEOS Method

Sets the current position to be the end of the stream.

```
Stream.SetEOS
```

Any bytes or characters after the current position are truncated.

This is useful when used after `Write`, `WriteText`, or `CopyTo` method calls, which do not set the end of the stream. For example:

```
stmData.WriteText "Some new text"
stmData.SetEOS
```

The SkipLine Method

When reading text streams, skips a line, including the line separator character.

```
Stream.SkipLine
```

The `LineSeparator` property is used to identify the character that separates lines.

For example, imagine processing a text configuration file where, if the first character is a #, the line is a comment and should be skipped:

```
Dim stmFile As ADODB.Stream
Dim sChar   As String

Set stmFile = New ADOD.Stream

stmFile.Type = adTypeTxt
stmFile.Charset = "ascii"
stmFile.LineSeparator = adCRLF
stmFile.ReadFromFile "c:\temp\config.txt"

While Not stmFile.EOS
    ' read the first character to check for the comment
    sChar = stmFile.ReadText(1)
    If sChar = "#" Then
        stmFile.SkipLine
    Else
        Debug.Print s & stmFile.ReadText(adReadLine)
    End If
Wend
stmFile.Close
```

You cannot skip beyond the end of a stream – you will just remain at `EOS` if you attempt this, and no error will be generated.

The Write Method

Writes data to a binary stream.

```
Stream.Write(Buffer)
```

Name	Type	Description
Buffer	Variant	The array of bytes to be written to the stream.

After the write, the current stream position is the byte after the last one just written. The end of the stream is not set when you use this method, unless you write beyond the end of the existing contents.

The WriteText Method

Writes characters to a text stream.

```
Stream.WriteText(Data, [Options])
```

Name	Type	Description
Data	String	The string containing the characters to be written to the stream.
Options	StreamWriteEnum	Identifies whether line separators are written after the specified string.

Options can be one of the StreamWriteEnum constants:

- ❏ adWriteChar, to just write the supplied string characters.
- ❏ adWriteLine, to write the supplied string characters, and then the LineSeparator character.

For example:

```
stmData.WriteText "This is the new stream contents."
```

After the write, the current stream position is the character after the last one just written. The end of the stream is not set when you use this method, unless you write beyond the end of the existing contents.

Properties of the Stream Object

The Charset Property

Identifies the character set into which the text stream contents should be translated.

```
Stream.Charset = String
String = Stream.Charset
```

The default value is Unicode, but other values can include ascii, windows-1252, and so on. The full range of supported character sets is held under the following registry key:

```
HKEY_CLASSES_ROOT\MIME\Database\Charset
```

If the stream is open, then you must be at the start of the stream before setting this property. It is ignored for binary streams, since these are handled by way of bytes rather than characters.

The EOS Property

Indicates whether or not the current position is at the end of the stream.

```
Boolean = Stream.EOS
```

Similar in use to the EOF property of Recordsets, this can be used to identify when the end of the stream has been reached:

```
While Not stmData.EOS
    Debug.Print stmData.ReadText(adReadLine)
Wend
```

The LineSeparator Property

Identifies the character used to separate lines in the stream,

```
Stream.LineSeparator = LineSeparatorEnum
LineSeparatorEnum = Stream.LineSeparator
```

This value is used when specifying adReadLine in the Read or ReadText methods, and is also used by the SkipLine method.

The default value is adCRLF. Other values are adCR and adLF.

The Mode Property

Identifies the mode used to open the stream.

```
Stream.Mode = ConnectModeEnum
ConnectModeEnum = Stream.Mode
```

ConnectModeEnum can be one or more of the following constants:

❑ adModeRead, to indicate read-only permissions. This is the default value.

❑ adModeReadWrite, to indicate both read and write permissions.

❑ adModeShareDenyNone, to allow other users to open this resource with any permissions.

❏ adModeShareDenyRead, to prevent other users opening the resource with read permissions.

❏ adModeShareDenyWrite, to prevent other users opening the resource with write permissions.

❏ adModeShareExclusive, to prevent other users from opening the resource.

❏ adModeUnknown, indicates that either the permissions have yet to be set, or that they cannot be identified.

❏ adModeWrite, to indicate write permissions.

When using the adModeShare options you can also specify adModeRecursive to make the permissions be set recursively.

The Position Property

Identifies the current position within the stream.

```
Stream.Position = Long
Long = Stream.Position
```

The position of the first byte or character in the stream is 0, and all other positions are an offset from this. You cannot use a negative value to move backwards through the stream – to do this you can specify the current position and subtract the number of bytes you wish to move backward.

Specifying a Position beyond the end of the stream will increase the size of the stream, and any new bytes will be null, unless the stream is read-only. In which case Position is set to the supplied (but meaningless) number, and no error is generated.

Position is always the number of bytes, so for multi-byte character sets you may have to divide the position by the number of bytes in each character to get the actual character number.

The Size Property

Identifies the size, in bytes, of the stream.

```
Long = Stream.Size
```

If the size of the stream is unknown, -1 is returned.

The size of the stream is only limited by system resources, although the value returned by the Size property will never exceed the value of a Long.

The State Property

Indicates whether the stream is open or closed.

```
ObjectStateEnum = Stream.State
```

This can be one of the `ObjectStateEnum` constants:

❏ `adStateClose`, to indicate the stream is closed.

❏ `adStateOpen` to indicate the stream is open.

The Type Property

Identifies the type of stream.

```
Stream.Type = StreamTypeEnum
StreamTypeEnum = Stream.Type
```

`StreamTypeEnum` can be one of:

❏ `adTypeBinary`, to indicate a binary stream.

❏ `adTypeText`, to indicate a text stream. This is the default value.

If you set the type of an empty stream to be text and then write binary data to it, the type is changed to binary. Writing text to a binary stream does not change the type, since the text data is just accepted as a string of bytes. You can only set the type when at the beginning of the stream.

Collections of the Stream Object

The Stream object has no collections.

ADO: The Stream Object

7

I thank God I am as honest as any man
living that is an old man and no honester than

Can counsel and speak comfort to that
Which they themselves not feel

Much Ado About Nothing.

He wears his faith but as the fashion of

As merry as the day

He hath indeed better bettered expectation

(Act i. Sc. 1.).

He wears his faith but as the fashion of his hat.
(Ibid)

As merry as the day is long.

th indeed better bettered expectation

(Act i. Sc. 1.).

(Ibid)

Much Ado About Nothing.

Can counsel and speak comfort to that grief

Which they themselves not feel.

He wears his faith but as the fashion of his hat.
(Ibid)
(Ibid)

I was not born under

a rhyming planet

I was not born under a rhyming pla
sc
For there was never yet
That could endure the

merry as the day is long
(Sc. 2)

Can counsel and speak comfort to that grief

Which they themselves not feel,
(Ibid)

He hath indeed better bettered expectation

I thank God I am as honest as any

living that is an old man and no honest

He wears his faith but as the fashion of his h
(Ib

Much Ado About Nothing.   For there was never yet philospher
That could endure the toothache patiently.
(Ibid)

For there was never yet philospher
That could endure the toothache patiently.

I was not born u

Collections

Nearly everything you do in ADO uses a collection of some sort. Even the simple task of opening a `Recordset` gives you a collection of fields. When looking at collections you need to look at two things:

❑   The collection itself

❑   The objects in the collection

You'll find that the ADO collections and objects are named sensibly, where the collection is the plural and the object the singular:

Object	Collection
Error	Errors
Field	Fields
Parameter	Parameters
Property	Properties

This chapter is divided into three main sections covering the `Error` object and the `Errors` collection, the `Field` object and the `Fields` collection, and the `Property` object and the `Properties` collection. The `Parameter` object and `Parameters` collection were discussed in Chapter 4. At the end of this chapter, there are shorter sections covering indexing and the retrieval and storage of images.

The Error Object

An `Error` object is used to hold all of the details pertaining to a single error, warning, or informational message from an OLE DB provider, and therefore contains only data access errors. For example, consider the following two sections of code:

```
strConn = "Provider=SQLOLEDB; Data Source=(local); " & _
                          "Initial Catalog=pubs; User ID=sa"
objRs.Open "select foo from authors", strConn
```

```
strConn = "Provider=SQLSERVER; Data Source=(local); " & _
                          "Initial Catalog=pubs; User ID=sa"
objRs.Open "select * from authors", strConn
```

The first example generates errors from the provider (since `foo` is a not a valid column in the authors table), and the second example generates an exception (since the `Provider` attribute in the connection string is incorrect).

`Error` objects are stored together in the `Errors` collection, which in turn belongs to the `Connection` object. This means that if you want to access the errors, you have to refer to the `Errors` collection of the connection on which they were generated. For example, if you have an explicit connection object called `objConn`, the first error in the collection can be accessed as follows:

```
objConn.Errors(0).Description
```

Here's another example. If you had a `Recordset` object without an explicit connection, then you can use the recordset's `ActiveConnection` property to get access to the errors:

```
objRec.ActiveConnection.Errors(0).Description
```

Since each `Error` object contains a single error, and the provider can return multiple errors, you should really iterate through the entire `Errors` collection to see all of the possible errors. In Visual Basic, for example, you would do this:

```
Dim objErr As ADODB.Error

For Each objErr in objConn.Errors
    Print "Error: " & objErr.Description
Next
```

Methods of the Error Object

The `Error` object has no methods.

Properties of the Error Object

The Description Property

A description string associated with the error.

```
String = Error.Description
```

This is the default property of the Error object, so it can be omitted if required. The following two lines of code, for example, are equivalent in action (although not readability):

```
Print objConn.Errors(0).Description
```

```
Print objConn.Errors(0)
```

The HelpContext Property

Indicates the ContextID in the help file for the associated error, if one exists.

```
Long = Error.HelpContext
```

You can use this property if you wish to integrate your application with the standard Windows help system. You can do this by calling the Windows help functions, then using the HelpContext to identify the ID number of the help description.

If no further help is available, this property will have the value 0.

The HelpFile Property

Indicates the name of the help file, if one exists.

```
String = Error.HelpFile
```

Use this in conjunction with the HelpContext property when interacting with the Windows help system. If no help file exists, this will be an empty string.

The NativeError Property

Indicates provider-specific error code for the associated error.

```
Long = Error.NativeError
```

This is useful for identifying errors produced, say, in stored procedures. The native error will be the *underlying* error code. So, if an error is generated in the data store, it's this error that is returned via the NativeError property. This is useful for tracking down the error in the provider documentation, since the NativeError is the error code returned by the data provider.

8

ADO: Collections

The Number Property

Indicates the number that uniquely identifies an `Error` object.

```
Long = Error.Number
```

This is a unique ADO number (equivalent to the Windows API HRESULT) that corresponds to the error condition. For example, many database-related errors will generate their own error number, which gets stored in the `NativeError` property, and the ADO `Number` property will probably get set to one of the following non-specific errors:

❑   `-2147217900` (hex `80040E14`) – 'The command contained one or more errors'

❑   `-2147467259` (hex `80004005`) – 'Unspecified error'

In either case, we can deduce that it was an underlying object that caused the error.

If an `Error` object represents a warning (rather than an error) then its `Number` property will be `0`. A full list of the error numbers is included in Appendix P.

The Source Property

Indicates the name of the object or application that originally generated the error.

```
String = Error.Source
```

This could come from the class name of an object, the provider, or ADO. For example, ADO errors will be in the form:

```
ADODB.ObjectName
```

where `ObjectName` is the ADO object that generated the error. You'll notice that, in the errors shown in the section on Error Examples later in this chapter, the `Source` doesn't follow this form: this is because those errors were generated by the provider.

The SQLState Property

Indicates the SQL state for a given `Error` object.

```
String = Error.SQLState
```

This will contain the 5-character SQL error code if the error occurred during a SQL command. If the error doesn't have a specific SQL error code then this may be blank. You should consult your provider's SQL documentation for a list of these error codes.

The SQL state error codes are defined by the SQL Access Group and the X/Open group, and are a standard for SQL error messages. Most database documentation will contain a list of SQL error messages.

The Errors Collection

The Errors collection contains zero or more Error objects, each representing a single error from the provider. Certain error events may produce more than one error event, so each is placed in its own error object, but the collection of errors relates to a single provider error.

Methods of the Errors Collection

The Clear Method

Removes all of the Error objects from the Errors collection.

```
Errors.Clear
```

This is called automatically when an error occurs, so the new error information can be entered. It is ADO (rather than the provider) that performs this clearing – this enables the provider to supply multiple error details in response to a single error condition. There's no way to stop this happening; if you need to keep error information you can store it in a custom data store, such as a collection or recordset.

You might think that this method is a bit superfluous if the Errors collection is cleared automatically, but there are some actions that cause the Errors collection to be filled with warning information. This specifically affects the Resync, UpdateBatch, and CancelBatch methods of the recordset, where records may have been deleted at the source while you were editing them.

Another case of this is miscellaneous warnings from the provider. For example, look at the following lines of Visual Basic code:

```
Dim objRs As New ADODB.Recordset
objRs.Open "authors", "DSN=pubs", _
            adOpenDynamic, adLockOptimistic, adCmdTable
```

This may appear fairly innocuous, but running this may fill in an Error in the Errors collection of the ActiveConnection property of the recordset. For SQL Server you get the following:

```
Description:   [Microsoft][ODBC SQL Server Driver]Cursor concurrency
               changed
HelpContext:   0
HelpFile:
NativeError:   0
Number:   0
Source:   Microsoft OLE DB Provider for ODBC Drivers
SQLState:   01S02
```

There's nothing wrong here; it's just that when you create a `Recordset` object, the cursor type is initially `adForwardOnly`. But here we have requested a different type, so the provider kindly tells us that it has changed the cursor type. These warnings are dependent upon the provider and data store. You can differentiate between errors and warnings in your `Errors` collection by checking for an error number of 0 (signifying a warning) in your error routines.

Clearing the `Errors` collection before an operation allows you to easily see if that operation generated errors (or warnings), since you can easily check the `Count` property after the operation.

The Refresh Method

Updates the `Error` objects with information from the provider.

```
Errors.Refresh
```

You can use this to ensure that the `Errors` collection contains the latest set of error information from the provider. Having said that, I've yet to come across a situation where the collection isn't populated and needs refreshing.

Properties of the Errors Collection

The Count Property

Indicates the number of `Error` objects in the `Errors` collection.

```
Long = Errors.Count
```

You should use the Visual Basic or VBScript `For Each...Next` command to iterate through the `Errors` collection without using the `Count` property. For example:

```
If Errors.Count > 0 Then
    For Each objErr In objConn.Errors
        Print objErr.Number & " " & objErr.Description
    Next
End If
```

The Item Property

Allows indexing into the `Errors` collection to reference a specific `Error` object.

```
Error = Errors.Item(Index)
```

Name	Type	Description	Default
Index	Variant	The number of the error in the collection. Zero based.	

This is the default property of the `Errors` collection and can be omitted. For example, both of the following lines are logically identical:

```
objConn.Errors.Item(0)
```

```
objConn.Errors(0)
```

If you're coding in a scripting language then you should specify the `Item` property – omitting `Item` causes a small performance penalty, because an extra internal call to `IDispatch` is required to query the interface. In fact, using the `Item` property in every language increases readability.

Error Examples

The following piece of Visual Basic code shows a good way to list all of the errors in the `Errors` collection:

```
Public Sub ErrorTest()
    ' set the error handling on
    On Error GoTo ShowErrors

    Dim objConn    As ADODB.Connection
    Dim strConn    As String
    Set objConn = New ADODB.Connection

    ' set the connection string
    strConn = "put your connection string here"

    objConn.Open strConn
    objConn.Execute "UPDATE pub_info Set pub_id='1111' " & _
                    "WHERE pub_id='9999'"

    objConn.Close
    Set objConn = Nothing

    Exit Sub

ShowErrors:

    ' check for the connection failing
    If objConn.State = adStateClosed Then
        Debug.Print "Connection could not be opened: " & _
                                        Err.Description

        Set objConn = Nothing
        Exit Sub
    End If

    ' is it really an ado error?
    If objConn.Errors.Count = 0 Then
        Debug.Print "Error: " & Err.Description
    Else
        Dim objErr As ADODB.Error
```

```
        For Each objErr In objConn.Errors
            Debug.Print "Description:"; vbTab; objErr.Description
            Debug.Print "HelpContext:"; vbTab; objErr.HelpContext
            Debug.Print "HelpFile:"; vbTab; objErr.HelpFile
            Debug.Print "NativeError:"; vbTab; objErr.NativeError
            Debug.Print "Number:"; vbTab; objErr.Number
            Debug.Print "Source:"; vbTab; objErr.Source
            Debug.Print "SQLState:"; vbTab; objErr.SQLState
        Next
    End If


    objConn.Close
    Set objConn = Nothing
End Sub
```

This uses the pubs database, and tries to run a SQL statement that violates referential integrity.

If you run this command using different OLE DB providers and data stores, you'll get similar (but not quite the same) results – as the following subsections show. The descriptions have been wrapped to make it easier to read – it's normally one long string.

OLE DB Provider for ODBC to SQL Server

Using the OLE DB provider for ODBC connected to SQL Server, you will notice that you get two errors generated. The first is an error indicating the exact nature of the error, and the second indicates that the command has been aborted. You can clearly see the SQL Server error numbers and descriptions:

```
Description: [Microsoft][ODBC SQL Server Driver][SQL Server]UPDATE
statement conflicted with COLUMN FOREIGN KEY constraint
'FK__pub_info__pub_id__2AEA69DC'. The conflict occurred in database
'pubs', table 'publishers', column 'pub_id'
HelpContext:    0
HelpFile:
NativeError:    547
Number:   -2147217900
Source:   Microsoft OLE DB Provider for ODBC Drivers
SQLState:   23000


Description: [Microsoft][ODBC SQL Server Driver][SQL Server]Command
has been terminated.
HelpContext:    0
HelpFile:
NativeError:    3621
Number:   -2147217900
Source:   Microsoft OLE DB Provider for ODBC Drivers
SQLState:   01000
```

You can also see that the ADO error number is the same – this corresponds to 'The command contained one or more errors', so it's important that you use the NativeError property to identify the exact problem.

A full list of ADO error numbers and descriptions is included in Appendix P.

OLE DB Provider for ODBC to Access

Using the OLE DB provider for ODBC to connect to an Access database with the same structure, you only get one error – the actual error that occurred. The Access ODBC driver doesn't send an extra error back.

```
Description:    [Microsoft][ODBC Microsoft Access Driver] You can't add
or change a record because a related record is required in table
'publishers'.
HelpContext:    0
HelpFile:
NativeError:    -1613
Number:    -2147217900
Source:    Microsoft OLE DB Provider for ODBC Drivers
SQLState:    23000
```

SQL Server Provider

Using the native OLE DB provider for SQL Server we get two errors – almost identical to the ODBC details:

```
Description:    UPDATE statement conflicted with COLUMN FOREIGN KEY
constraint 'FK_pub_info_publishers'. The conflict occurred in
database
'pubs', table 'publishers', column 'pub id'.
HelpContext:    0
HepFile:
NativeError:    547
Number:    -2147217900
Source:    Microsoft OLE DB Provider for SQL Server
SQLState:    23000
```

```
Description:    The statement has been aborted.
HelpContext:    0
HepFile:
NativeError:    3621
Number:    -2147217900
Source:    Microsoft OLE DB Provider for SQL Server
SQLState:    01000
```

Jet Provider

For the OLE DB provider for Jet we only get one error, but we do get a full description of it:

8

ADO: Collections

```
Description:   You can't add or change a record because a related record
is required in table 'publishers'.
HelpContext:     5003000
HelpFile:
NativeError:    -535037517
Number:    -2147467259
Source:    Microsoft JET Database Engine
SQLState:    3201
```

Notice that the ADO error number is slightly different – this corresponds to 'Unspecified error'. Also notice that the `NativeError` property returns a different error number than for the ODBC case, although both of these error numbers correspond to 'Application-defined or object-defined error'.

The Field Object

A `Field` object represents a single field (or column) in a `Recordset` object or `Record` object. When you open a recordset, you'll find a `Fields` collection that contains zero or more `Field` objects. This `Fields` collection will contain a `Field` object for each column in the recordset and, as you move through the rows, the `Fields` collection changes its contents to represent the fields of the chosen record.

Although `Field` objects can exist on their own, they are really only useful when used in conjunction with a `Recordset` object. Unless you are creating your own recordsets (with the `Recordset` object's `Append` method), where you create fields, you'll generally be dealing with existing `Field` objects. You can reference these in several ways. The first is by accessing the `Field` directly through the `Fields` collection, as shown in the following examples, where we print the data types of some `Field` objects:

```
Print objRs.Fields(0).Type
```

```
Print objRs.Fields("FirstName").Type
```

The `Fields` collection is the default collection of a recordset and can therefore be omitted, if desired:

```
Print objRs("FirstName").Type
```

Second, you can use a `Field` object explicitly in your code:

```
Dim objFld As ADODB.Field

Set objFld = objRs.Fields("FirstName")
Print objFld.Type
```

The advantage of doing this is in situations where you are referencing the field several times. Using a reference to a `Field` object in a separate variable, as opposed to referencing the field in the collection, is more efficient.

Third, you can use the `Item` property of the `Fields` collection:

```
Print objRs.Fields.Item("FirstName")
```

All of these methods are functionally equivalent, although there may be performance differences. Using the `Item` property is faster in scripting languages, and using a `Field` object will be faster if you plan to reference several properties or methods of a single field.

Methods of the Field Object

The AppendChunk Method

Appends data to a large or binary `Field` object.

```
Field.AppendChunk(Data)
```

Name	Type	Description	Default
Data	Variant	The data to be appended to the object.	

The first call to `AppendChunk` (after you start editing a field) writes data to the field, overwriting any existing data in the buffer. Subsequent calls add to existing data.

You can only use `AppendChunk` if the `Attributes` property includes `adFldLong`.

This is most often used when dealing with images, large text fields, or BLOBs (Binary Large OBjects) stored in databases. A full discussion of this is included at the end of this chapter.

The GetChunk Method

Returns all or a portion of the contents of a large or binary `Field` object.

```
Variant = Field.GetChunk(Length)
```

Name	Type	Description	Default
Length	Long	The number of bytes or characters to be retrieved.	

The first call returns data beginning at the start of the field. Subsequent calls start where the last call left off, unless you read the value of another field, in which case a call to `GetChunk` for the current field starts at the beginning of the field again.

You can only use `GetChunk` if the `Attributes` property includes `adFldLong`.

Like `AppendChunk`, this is most often used with images, and a full discussion is included at the end of the chapter.

8

ADC: Collections

Properties of the Field Object

The ActualSize Property

Indicates the actual length, in bytes, of a field's value.

```
Long = Field.ActualSize
Field.ActualSize = Long
```

You should use this property when you need to set or find out how long a field actually is (rather than how long it can be – for that, use the DefinedSize property). For fixed length data types, these two properties will be the same, but they may be different for variable length data.

The Attributes Property

Indicates characteristics of a Field object.

```
Long = Field.Attributes
```

This will be one or more of the following FieldAttributeEnum values:

❑ adFldMayDefer, to indicate that the contents of the field are not retrieved from the provider along with the rest of the data, but are only retrieved when they are referenced. This is particularly useful for recordsets that contain large BLOBs (Binary Large OBjects), where the BLOB may not be referenced.

❑ adFldUpdatable, to indicate that the field can be updated.

❑ adFldUnknownUpdatable, to indicate that the provider doesn't know whether the field can be updated.

❑ adFldFixed, to indicate that the field contains fixed length data.

❑ adFldIsNullable, to indicate that Null values can be used when writing to the field.

❑ adFldMayBeNull, to indicate that the field may contain a Null value when you read from the field.

❑ adFldLong, to indicate that AppendChunk and GetChunk can be used on the field, since it contains long binary data.

❑ adFldRowID, to indicate that the field contains a row ID that cannot be updated. This doesn't indicate the Access **AutoNumber** or SQL Server **IDENTITY** fields, but rather an internal row number field, which is unique across the database. Oracle has these natively but many other data stores don't.

❑ adFldRowVersion, to indicate a field that uniquely identifies the version of the row, such as a SQL **Timestamp** field.

❑ adFldCacheDeferred to indicate that the values for this field will be cached once it has been read for the first time, and reading the value again will read from the cache.

- ❏ `adNegativeScale` to indicate that the values for this field have a negative scale.

- ❏ `adKeyColumn` to indicate that this field is part of a key.

- ❏ `adFldIsChapter` to indicate that this field is a chaptered recordset.

- ❏ `adFldIsCollection` to indicate that this field is a collection object (when used with the Internet Publishing Provider).

- ❏ `adFldIsDefaultStream` to indicate that this field points to the default stream for the object.

- ❏ `adFldIsRowURL` to indicate that the field contains the URL of the underlying resource (when used with the Internet Publishing Provider).

- ❏ `adFldUnspecified`, to indicate that the provider cannot specify the attributes.

Since this property can be a combination of values, it may not directly match one of the above constants. To check that a value is set you should use a procedure like this:

```
If (Field.Attributes AND ad_constant) = ad_constant Then
    Print "field supports that attribute"
End If
```

For example, to check to see if a field might contain Null values:

```
Set objField = objRs.Fields("field_that_might_be_null")
If (objField.Attributes And adFldMayBeNull) = adFldMayBeNull Then
    Print "Field may contain a null"
End If
```

Note that this property is read/write when fabricating your own recordsets, and becomes read-only once this fabricated recordset is opened. For new `Field` objects added to a `Record` object, you can only set the `Attributes` once the `Value` has been set and the `Fields` collection's `Update` method called to force the provider to append the field.

The DataFormat Property

Identifies the format the data should be displayed in.

```
Set DataFormatObject = Field.DataFormat
Set Field.DataFormat = DataFormatObject
```

This is only useful when used in conjunction with Visual Basic 6 or Visual J++ 6, which include the `DataFormat` object. This object contains several properties to identify the type of data the object holds, and the way in which it should be displayed. For example, in Visual Basic 6 you could do this:

```
Set txtDate.DataFormat = objRs.Fields("InvoiceDate").DataFormat
```

For more information on this you should consult the Visual Basic 6 or Visual J++ 6 documentation.

The DefinedSize Property

Indicates the defined size (in bytes) of the `Field` object.

```
Long = Field.DefinedSize
```

For variable width fields this indicates the maximum width of the field – as opposed to the `ActualSize` property that identifies the actual size. For example, a SQL Server column declared as `varchar(20)` would have a `DefinedSize` of 20, irrespective of the actual size of the text it contains.

Note that this field is read/write when creating your own recordsets, and becomes read-only once the fabricated recordset is opened.

The Name Property

Indicates the name of the `Field` object.

```
String = Field.Name
```

This is a necessary field when creating your own `Field` objects to add to the existing `Fields` collection, or when creating a new recordset.

It is also useful when dynamically creating tables in ASP Script code, or filling grids manually in Visual Basic. For example, in ASP, you could create a table header using the `Name` property:

```
Response.Write "<TABLE><THEAD><TR>"
For Each objField In objRs.Fields
    Response.Write "<TH>" & objField.Name & "</TH>"
Next
Response.Write "</TR></THEAD>"
```

You could then go on to create the rest of the table using the values from the recordset. You can see examples of this in the Wrox Press ASP books, such as *Beginning ASP 3.0 (ISBN 1-861003-38-2)* and *Professional ASP 3.0 (ISBN 1-861002-61-0)*.

Note that this field is read/write when creating your own recordsets, and becomes read-only once the fabricated recordset is opened. For new `Field` objects added to a `Record` object, you can only set the `Name` once the `Value` has been set and the `Fields` collection's `Update` method called to force the provider to append the field.

The NumericScale Property

Indicates the scale of numeric values for the `Field` object.

```
Byte = Field.NumericScale
```

This identifies how many digits are stored to the right of the decimal place for numeric data. For non-numeric data, this will be 0 or 255, depending upon the provider and field type.

Note that this field is read/write when creating your own recordsets, and becomes read-only once the fabricated recordset is opened.

The OriginalValue Property

Indicates the value of a `Field` object that existed in the record before any changes were made.

```
Variant = Field.OriginalValue
```

The original value is the value stored in the field before any changes were saved to the provider. This allows the provider to simply return to the original value when you do a `CancelBatch` or `CancelUpdate` method call. For example:

```
' Assume when read that the field contains a value of 10.99
Set objField = objRs.Fields("Price")
objField.Value = 15.99
Print objField.OriginalValue    ' Prints 10.99
Print objField.Value            ' Prints 15.99
objRs.CancelUpdate
Print objField.Value            ' Prints 10.99
```

For related information see the `UnderlyingValue` and `Value` properties.

This property is read-only.

The Precision Property

Indicates the degree of precision for numeric values in the `Field` object.

```
Byte = Field.Precision
```

The precision is the maximum number of digits that will be used. For non-numeric fields, this is 255.
Note that this field is read/write when creating your own recordsets, and becomes read-only once the fabricated recordset is opened.

The Status Property

Indicates the status of the `Field` after it has been appended to the `Fields` collection.

```
FieldStatusEnum = Field.Status
```

The set of constants in `FieldStatusEnum` is quite large, and is included in Appendix B.

You can use this value to determine whether `Field` objects have been successfully appended to the `Fields` collection of a `Record` object. Changes to the collection are cached until the `Update` is called, at which point the `Status` is set to one or more of the `FieldStatusEnum` values. For example, if you don't have permission to insert or delete fields you can check the `Status` in the following way:

```
If (fld.Status And adFieldPermissionDenied) = _
                        adFieldPermissionDenied Then
    Debug.Print "Permission denied while ";

    If (fld.Status And adFieldPendingInsert) = _
                        adFieldPendingInsert Then
        Debug.Print "adding a field"
    End If

    If (fld.Status And adFieldPendingDelete) = _
                        adFieldPendingDelete Then
        Debug.Print "deleting a field"
    End If
End If
```

For `Field` objects belonging to a `Recordset`, this always returns `adFieldOK`.

The Type Property

Indicates the data type of the `Field` object.

```
DataTypeEnum = Field.Type
```

The data type will be one of the `DataTypeEnum` values, such as `adInteger` or `adVarChar`. Since this list is quite long, we've included it in Appendix B. Not all providers support all data types, but when creating recordsets you should be able to use all types, and the provider will compensate for any types it doesn't support by converting them into an equivalent supported type. When creating your own recordsets, you should use the data type most appropriate to the type of data you wish to store.

Note that this field is read/write when creating your own recordsets, and becomes read-only once the fabricated recordset is opened.

The UnderlyingValue Property

Indicates a `Field` object's current value in the database.

```
Variant = Field.UnderlyingValue
```

The underlying value differs from the original value, as this property holds the current value of the field as stored in the cursor. This would, for example, hold the value if another user changed the value of a field. So if you call the `Resync` method, your fields will get repopulated with values from the `UnderlyingValue` property.

The `UnderlyingValue` is really only useful for those situations where your cursor will not see data changes made by other users, such as in batch operations. In particular this will be:

❑ All client-side updateable cursors

❑ Server-based keyset cursors, except for the OLE DB Provider for Jet

Interestingly, there is a difference between server-side keysets and static cursors for the OLE DB Provider for SQL Server – despite the fact they both actually use keyset cursors. When requesting a keyset cursor you get a keyset cursor, and it supports UnderlyingValue. *However, when requesting a static cursor, you are returned a keyset cursor, but it doesn't support* UnderlyingValue. *If you examine the dynamic properties of the recordset under these two conditions you'll see that the properties are not the same, which seems to indicate that the properties are not updated when the server changes the cursor type.*

This property is particularly useful when dealing with conflicts between values that you have changed and values that other users have changed. We examine conflict resolution in more detail in Chapter 5.

For related information see the OriginalValue and Value properties.

The Value Property

Indicates the value assigned to the Field object.

```
Variant = Field.Value
Field.Value = Variant
```

This indicates the current value of the field, and may not reflect the value stored in the database. This is noticeable in situations where client-cursors or server-based static cursors are used, where the data you have in your recordset, doesn't reflect the current state of records in the database (that is to say, another user might have changed the values). The difference between the three value fields is quite simple:

❑ Value contains the current value of the field in your current recordset. So if you've made any changes to the field, they will be reflected in the Value.

❑ OriginalValue contains the value of the field as it was before you made any changes.

❑ UnderlyingValue contains the value of the field, as stored in the database, which might include changes made by other users.

This is the default property of a field and can be omitted if required. For example, the following lines of code are functionally equivalent:

```
Print objRs("FirstName").Value
```

```
Print objRs("FirstName")
```

```
Print objRs.Fields("FirstName")
```

If you are appending fields to the Fields collection of a Record, then the Value property must be set and the Update method called before any other properties of the Field.

You might need to specify the `Value` property when using collections. For example, consider the following Visual Basic code:

```
Dim colNames As New Collection

colNames.Add objRs.("FirstName"), "Name1"
Debug.Print colNames("Name1")
objRs.MoveNext
Debug.Print colNames("Name1")
```

You might expect the same name to be printed twice, since you probably assume that the name was the only thing to be stored in the collection. However, it's actually the `Field` object that gets stored in the collection, and the `Field` object just points to a particular field in the recordset. So, when you move to the next row, the `Field` reflects those changes. If you want to store the actual field contents in the collection you need to do this:

```
Dim colNames As New Collection

colNames.Add objRs.("FirstName").Value, "Name1"
```

For related information see the `UnderlyingValue` and `OriginalValue` properties.

Collections of the Field Object

The Properties Collection

Contains all of the `Property` objects for a `Field` object.

```
Field.Properties
```

The `Properties` collection contains all of the properties that are associated with a particular field. This is discussed in more detail in Appendix C.

The Fields Collection

The `Fields` collection contains zero or more `Field` objects. In existing recordsets there will be one `Field` object for each column in the recordset. When creating new recordsets, you append `Field` objects to the `Fields` collection.

The `Fields` collection is the default collection of the `Recordset` object, which means that you don't need to specify its name. For example, the following two lines are functionally equivalent:

```
objRs.Fields("FirstName")
```

```
objRs("FirstName")
```

For `Fields` of the `Record` object you can also use the `FieldEnum` constants to index into the collection:

```
objRs.Fields(adDefaultStream)
```

```
objRs.Fields(adRecordURL)
```

These constants return the default stream and the URL of the underlying object.

Scripting languages will suffer a slight performance penalty when omitting the default collection name.

Methods of the Fields Collection

The Append Method

Appends a `Field` object to the `Fields` collection.

```
Fields.Append(Name, Type, [DefinedSize], [Attrib])
```

Name	Type	Description	Default
Name	String	The name of a new field object.	
Type	DataTypeEnum	The data type of the new field.	adEmpty
Defined Size	Long	The defined size in characters or bytes of the new field. The default value is derived from Type.	0
Attrib	FieldAttribute Enum	The attributes for the new field.	adFld Unspecified

You should set the `CursorLocation` property to `adUseClient` before calling this method because you cannot append fields to an existing recordset created from a data store.

You cannot append fields of the following types: `adArray`, `adChapter`, `adEmpty`, `adPropVariant`, and `adUserDefined`. Also, although `adIDispatch`, `adIUnknown`, and `adIVariant` can be appended, the results could be unpredictable. These data types will have no use for the majority of ADO programmers, and have been included for completeness.

If you are appending fields to the `Fields` collection of a `Record`, remember that the `Value` property must be set and the `Update` method called before any other properties of the `Field`.

This is quite useful for those situations where you would like some data to be processed as a recordset, but it is not so useful in a data store, and there is no provider for accessing it. You could create a recordset and append your own fields to it. For example:

```
Dim objRs    As New ADODB.Recordset

objRs.CursorLocation = adUseClient
objRs.Fields.Append "Name", adVarChar, 25, adFldMayBeNull
objRs.Fields.Append "Age", adInteger, 8, adFldFixed
```

Calling this method for an open recordset, or a recordset in which the `ActiveConnection` property has been set, will generate a run-time error. This applies even if the recordset has been disconnected from a data store.

Creating Recordsets

Creating recordsets actually has some very interesting uses, some of which have nothing to do with databases or large stores of data. Consider the following:

❑   You have a source of data for which there is no OLE DB provider, but you want to provide a consistent access to this data for your programmers. You could create a component that reads this data in, and then creates a recordset that is exposed to the caller of the component.

❑   You are creating a multi-tier client-server application that needs to pass data around from tier to tier, but you don't want it to be bound up creating arrays and odd structures. You could create a recordset that contains the data, and have the recordset passed around. This does, however, rely on having ADO installed on the client.

❑   You are using Microsoft Message Queue Server, and need to pass data in the messages. The body of an MSMQ message must be a string of data, or an object that can persist its data, and ADO 2.6 can do this. It's not actually the object itself that is passed, but its data and state. Suppose you have a group of traveling sales staff, who regularly need to send sales reports back to base. Instead of having to connect back to the server to update the data, they could pass their data back and forth as a message, which means that the data is available to be processed whenever the server is free.

Creating a recordset is simply a matter of appending fields to an empty recordset that is not connected to a data source. For example, in Visual Basic this could be done with the following code:

```
Dim objRs      As New ADODB.Recordset

objRs.Fields.Append "OrderNumber", adVarChar, 10
objRs.Fields.Append "OrderDate", adVarChar, 20
```

This just creates a recordset with two fields, both holding text data, which can be `Null`. At this stage you have a closed recordset, so you can open it, and then add data as though it were a recordset created from a data source. For example:

```
objRs.Open
objRs.AddNew
objRs.Fields("OrderNumber").Value = 1
objRs.Fields("OrderDate") = Now()
objRs.Update
```

The CancelUpdate Method

Cancels pending changes made to the `Fields` collection when adding fields to a `Record` object.

```
Fields.CancelUpdate
```

Any pending field inserts, deletions, or changes are cancelled and the fields are returned to their previous values. The `Status` property is set to `adFieldOK` after this method call.

The Delete Method

Deletes a `Field` object from the `Fields` collection.

```
Fields.Delete(Index)
```

Name	Type	Description	Default
Index	Variant	The name or index number of the `Field` object to delete.	

You can use this to delete fields that you have added to your own recordset. For example:

```
objRs.Fields.Delete("Age")
```

Note that there is no way to check if a field exists in the collection without referring to the field. In that case, a run-time error will be generated (error 3265), which you must trap.

You cannot use this method on an open recordset.

The Refresh Method

Updates the `Field` objects in the `Fields` collection.

```
Fields.Refresh
```

Using this method has no visible effect. You should use the `Recordset` object's `Requery` method to retrieve changes.

The Resync Method

Refreshes the data in the `Fields` collection of a `Record` object.

```
Fields.Resync ResyncValues
```

221

ResyncValues can be one of the ResyncEnum constants:

❑ adResyncAllValues, to resynchronize all values

❑ adResyncUnderlyingValues, to resynchronize only the UnderlyingValue property

If the Status of a Field is adFieldPendingUnknown or adFieldPendingInsert, then Resync has no effect.

The Status value of a Field is only modified if there is an error during synchronization.

The Update Method

Saves (to the underlying data store) any pending changes made to the Fields collection of a Record object.

```
Fields.Update
```

Changes made to the Fields collection of a Record object are not made permanent until this method is called.

Properties of the Fields Collection

The Count Property

Indicates the number of Field objects in the Fields collection.

```
Long = Fields.Count
```

In Visual Basic or VBScript you can use the For Each.Next command to iterate through the Fields collection without referring to the Count property.

This property is read-only.

The Item Property

Allows indexing into the Fields collection to reference a specific Field object.

```
Field = Fields.Item(Index)
```

Name	Type	Description	Default
Index	Variant	The name or index number of the item in the collection.	

This is the default property of the `Fields` collection and can be omitted. For example, the following lines are equivalent:

```
objRs.Fields.Item(1)
```

```
objRs.Fields(1)
```

```
objRs.Fields("FirstName")
```

```
objRs.Fields.Item("FirstName")
```

Since `Fields` is the default collection, you don't need to specify it in your code:

```
objRs("FirstName")
```

The Property Object

A `Property` object contains the attributes of a single property, for any of the following objects:

❑ `Connection`

❑ `Command`

❑ `Record`

❑ `Recordset`

❑ `Field`

Each of these objects contains a `Properties` collection, which, in turn, contains zero or more `Property` objects. It's important to realize that these do not contain the standard properties for an object, but rather the extended, or provider-specific properties. In use, this generally means provider-specific characteristics, such as Jet-specific features for the Access provider. The documentation for the Provider should detail these properties.

A detailed list of properties is included in Appendix C.

Methods of the Property Object

The `Property` object has no methods.

Properties of the Property Object

The Attributes Property

Indicates characteristics of a `Property` object.

```
Long = Property.Attributes
```

The Attributes can be one or more of the PropertyAttributesEnum values:

- ❏ adPropNotSupported, to indicate that the provider does not support the property.

- ❏ adPropRequired, to indicate that this property must be specified before the data source is initialized.

- ❏ adPropOptional, to indicate that this property does not have to be specified before the data source is initialized.

- ❏ adPropRead, to indicate that the property can be read by the user.

- ❏ adPropWrite, to indicate that the property can be set by the user.

For example, before you connect to SQL Server you can examine the Attributes of the User ID property in the Properties collection:

```
Print objConn.Properties("User ID").Attributes
```

This gives a value of **1537**, which is a combination of some of the above constants:

Attribute	Binary Value	Decimal Value
adPropRequired adPropRead adPropWrite	00000000001 01000000000 10000000000	1 512 1024
Total:	11000000001	1537

You don't have to worry about the numbers because you can test the attributes using the constants:

```
intAttr = objConn.Properties("User ID").Attributes
If (intAttr AND adPropRequired) = adPropRequired Then
    ' Property is required
End If
```

The Name Property

Indicates the name of the Property object.

```
String = Property.Name
```

This is the name by which the provider knows the property.

The Type Property

Indicates the data type of the Property object.

```
DataTypeEnum = Property.Type
```

For example, the User ID property of a connection has a value of adBStr, which indicates a string.

The list of constants for DataTypeEnum is quite large, and is included in Appendix B.

The Value Property

Indicates the value assigned to the Property object.

```
Variant = Property.Value
Property.Value = Variant
```

Some properties may be read-only, and do not allow you to set the Value, so you should check the Attributes beforehand:

```
intAttr = objConn.Properties("property_name").Attributes
If (intAttr AND adPropWrite) = adPropWrite Then
  objConn.Properties("property_name").Value = some_value
End If
```

This is the default property of the Property object and can be omitted if desired.

The Properties Collection

The Properties collection contains zero or more Property objects, to indicate the extended properties of the applicable object. You can examine all of the properties by enumerating through the collection. For example:

```
For Each objProp In objConn.Properties
    Print objProp.Name
Next
```

This is a particularly good way to find out which extended properties are supported by a provider.

Methods of the Properties Collection

The Refresh Method

Updates the Property objects in the Properties collection with the details from the provider.

```
Properties.Refresh
```

The Refresh method is useful for the Properties collection because the default provider is the OLE DB Provider for ODBC: if you have set the Provider property to point to a different provider, you will need to Refresh the properties to ensure that they are applicable to the changed provider.

8

ADO: Collections

Properties of the Properties Collection

The Count Property

Indicates the number of `Property` objects in the `Properties` collection.

```
Long = Properties.Count
```

You can use the Visual Basic or VBScript `For Each..Next` command to iterate through the properties collection without using the `Count` property. For languages that do not support enumeration of collections you can use this property in a loop.

The Item Property

Allows indexing into the `Properties` collection to reference a specific `Property` object.

```
Property = Properties.Item(Index)
```

Name	Type	Description	Default
Index	Variant	The number or name of the property in the collection. Zero-based.	

This is the default property of the `Properties` collection and can be omitted. For example, the following lines are equivalent:

```
object.Properties.Item(1)
```

```
object.Properties(1)
```

```
object.Properties("property_name")
```

Indexing

ADO 2.0 introduced the concept of **local indexing**, for client cursors, and this has remained unchanged with version 2.6. This is achieved using one of the `Field` object's dynamic properties, called `Optimize`. The way it works is that you decide which field you want to index, and then set the `Optimize` property to `True`. For example:

```
Set objField = objRs("au_lname")
objField.Properties("Optimize") = True
```

You don't have to use a `Field` object, as you can just access the properties directly from the recordset's field:

```
objRs("au_lname").Properties("Optimize") = True
```

This creates a local index, which will improve sorting and finding records. Setting the property to `False` will delete the index.

Future versions of ADO are expected to provide an `Indexes` collection and `Index` objects to help us manage local indexes, and give us greater control over them. Microsoft has yet to finalize plans for this.

Using Images with ADO

This can be one of the most confusing aspects of using databases, as it never seems quite as intuitive as it should be. Many people say that storing images in databases isn't the most efficient use of the database, and that it can be slow. However, there are times when you need to do this, such as when you have legacy data or if a third party supplies your data to you.

I think a preferable solution is to store the images on disc as files, and just store the file name in the database. There are several reasons why I think this:

1. As a rule, databases aren't designed to store large binary data, and therefore the storage and handling of them can be slower than it is for other fields.

2. Keeping images separate allows them to be updated more easily. For example, where you have different people designing your images, it's easier to just provide them with a directory, rather than having to get them back into the database.

3. There's currently no easy way to stream images directly from a database into another location in an application. For example, in HTML an image must come from an HTTP address, and in Visual Basic applications images or icons can only be loaded from files or resource files.

These are just my opinions, and shouldn't deter you from storing images in a database if you want to.

Images and Parameters

There are a few simple rules to follow when using images with parameters:

❑ If reading and writing images from disc, then you should read into, and write from, a `Byte` array.

❑ The ADO `Parameter` object's `Type` should be `adVarBinary`.

❑ The ADO `Parameter` object's `Length` should be the maximum size of the binary data. For a SQL Server `image` or an Access OLE Object parameter this is 2,147,483,647.

❑ Either set the `Value` property directly, or use `GetChunk` and `AppendChunk` to get the image data into your ADO `Parameter`.

One thing to watch out for when dealing with images using stored procedures in SQL Server is that your procedure cache might not be big enough to allow the use of large images. In this case you'll get error 701, and you should consult the SQL Server documentation for details of how to increase this cache.

Here are a few examples to show how this works.

Storing Images using Parameters

The following shows how you could read an image from a file and store it in a SQL Server database. We'll use Visual Basic to grab the image file, and a stored procedure to place it in the database. Here's the stored procedure:

```
CREATE PROCEDURE usp_UpdateLogo
      @PubID      char(4),
      @Logo       image
AS
      UPDATE    pub_info
      SET       logo = @Logo
      WHERE     pub_id = @PubID
```

This simply updates the logo field for the publisher ID supplied.

The code to call this procedure from Visual Basic could look like this:

```
Dim objConn     As New ADODB.Connection
Dim objCmd      As New ADODB.Command
Dim bytChunk()  As Byte
Dim varChunk    As Variant


' open bitmap file
Open "c:\temp\wrox.bmp" For Binary As #1

' resize the byte array, read in the data space, and close it.
ReDim bytChunk(LOF(1))
Get #1, , bytChunk()
varChunk = StrConv(bytChunk, vbUnicode)
Erase bytChunk
Close #1


' connect to data store
objConn.Open "Provider=SQLOLEDB; Data Source=Tigger; " & _
             "Initial Catalog=pubs; User ID=sa; Password="

' set up command
With objCmd
     Set .ActiveConnection = objConn
     .CommandText = "usp_UpdateLogo"
     .CommandType = adCmdStoredProc

     ' create the parameters
     .Parameters.Append .CreateParameter("@PubID", adVarChar, _
                                  adParamInput, 4, "0736")
     .Parameters.Append .CreateParameter("@Logo", adVarBinary, _
                                  adParamInput, 2147483647)

     ' set the parameter value
     ' use either this command, which is commented out
     ' .Parameters("@Logo").Value = varChunk
```

```
            ' or this one
            .Parameters("@Logo").AppendChunk varChunk

            ' now run the command
            .Execute
End With

objConn.Close

Set objCmd = Nothing
Set objConn = Nothing
```

Passing the Image in Smaller Chunks

You may find that reading the whole image file into memory at once is wasteful of resources, especially considering how large images can be. You can break this down into smaller chunks, and use AppendChunk to append chunks of the image into the parameter. The Visual Basic code from above would be modified like this:

```
Dim objConn            As New ADODB.Connection
Dim objCmd             As New ADODB.Command
Dim bytChunk(512)      As Byte                    ' Note the size
Dim varChunk           As Variant

' open bitmap file
Open "c:\temp\wrox.bmp" For Binary As #1

' don't read the image file yet

' connect to data store
objConn.Open "Provider=SQLOLEDB; Data Source=Tigger; " & _
             "Initial Catalog=pubs; User ID=sa; Password="

' set up command
With objCmd
    .ActiveConnection = objConn
    .CommandText = "usp_UpdateLogo"
    .CommandType = adCmdStoredProc

    ' create the parameters
    .Parameters.Append .CreateParameter("@PubID", adVarChar, _
                                adParamInput, 4, "0736")
    .Parameters.Append .CreateParameter("@Logo", adVarBinary, _
                                adParamInput, 2147483647)

    ' continue reading from file whilst we haven't hit EOF
    While Not EOF(1)
        ' Read in a small chunk. The amount read is determined
        ' by the size of the byte array we are reading into
        Get #1, , bytChunk()

        ' Append the smaller array to the parameter
        .Parameters("@Logo").AppendChunk bytChunk()
    Wend
```

```
      ' run the command
      .Execute
End With

objConn.Close
Close #1

Set objCmd = Nothing
Set objConn = Nothing
```

This performs exactly the same action, only using a small chunk of memory to repeatedly read in from the image file. You may find this marginally slower, but it is more efficient on memory and network resources.

Retrieving Images using Parameters

If you want to retrieve images from a database via a stored procedure, the first thing to note is that it's *not* possible to assign an image to a variable (at least, not with SQL Server). This means that you cannot have a stored procedure like this:

```
CREATE PROCEDURE usp_FetchLogo
     @PubID    char(4),
     @Logo     image OUTPUT
AS
     SELECT  @Logo = logo
     FROM    pub_info
     WHERE   pub_id = @PubID
```

Instead, if you need to extract images using a stored procedure, then you must return a recordset, even if that recordset only contains one row and one field.

Images and Fields

Using images with `Recordset` fields is very similar to using `Parameters`.

Storing Images in Fields

To store images directly into fields quite simply requires a call to the `AppendChunk` method. The following Visual Basic code shows this:

```
Dim objConn      As New ADODB.Connection
Dim objCmd       As New ADODB.Command
Dim objRs        As ADODB.Recordset
Dim bytChunk()   As Byte

' open bitmap file
Open "c:\temp\single.bmp" For Binary As #1

' resize the byte array, read in the data, and close it.
ReDim bytChunk(LOF(1))
Get #1, , bytChunk()
Close #1
```

```
' open the connection
objConn.Open "Provider=SQLOLEDB; Data Source=Tigger; " & _
            "Initial Catalog=pubs; User ID=sa; Password="

With objCmd
    ' set the commmand properties
    .ActiveConnection = objConn
    .CommandText = "usp_FetchLogo"
    .CommandType = adCmdStoredProc
    ' create the parameters
    .Parameters.Append .CreateParameter("@PubID", adVarChar, _
                                    adParamInput, 4, "0736")

    ' create and open a new recordset
    Set objRs = New ADODB.Recordset
    objRs.Open objCmd, , adOpenDynamic, adLockOptimistic, _
                                    adCmdStoredProc
End With

' update the logo field, passing in the image
objRs("logo").AppendChunk (bytChunk)
objRs.Update

objRs.Close
objConn.Close

Set objRs = Nothing
set objCmd = Nothing
Set objConn = Nothing
```

In this case, we've used a stored procedure called usp_FetchLogo *to fetch
the image from the database. The SQL code for* usp_FetchLogo *is shown
later in this chapter.*

Smaller Chunks

To use a smaller chunk size to conserve the memory resources on the client is quite
simple too.

```
Dim objConn         As New ADODB.Connection
Dim objCmd          As New ADODB.Command
Dim objRs           As ADODB.Recordset
Dim bytChunk(512)   As Byte                         ' note the size

' don't read the bitmap file yet

' open the connection
objConn.Open "Provider=SQLOLEDB; Data Source=Tigger; " & _
            "Initial Catalog=pubs; User ID=sa; Password="

With objCmd
    ' set the command properties
    .ActiveConnection = objConn
    .CommandText = "usp_FetchLogo"
    .CommandType = adCmdStoredProc
```

```
            ' create the parameters
            .Parameters.Append .CreateParameter("@PubID", adVarChar, _
                                         adParamInput, 4, "0736")

            ' create and open the recordset
            Set objRs = New ADODB.Recordset
            objRs.Open objCmd, , adOpenDynamic, adLockOptimistic, _
                                         adCmdStoredProc
        End With
```

```
' open bitmap file
Open "c:\temp\chunks.bmp" For Binary As #1

' whilst we haven't reached the end of the image file
While Not EOF(1)
    ' Read in a small chunk. The amount read is determined
    ' by the size of the byte array we are reading into
    Get #1, , bytChunk()

    ' append this small array to the field
    objRs("logo").AppendChunk (bytChunk)
Wend
Close #1
```

```
' update the field
objRs.Update

objRs.Close
objConn.Close

Set objRs = Nothing
Set objCmd = Nothing
Set objConn = Nothing
```

Retrieving Images from Fields

Retrieving images from fields is extremely simple, using the Value of the field, or the
GetChunk method. This Visual Basic code shows how it can be done:

```
Dim objConn     As New ADODB.Connection
Dim objCmd      As New ADODB.Command
Dim objRs       As ADODB.Recordset
Dim bytChunk()  As Byte

' open the connection
objConn.Open "Provider=SQLOLEDB; Data Source=Tigger; " & _
            "Initial Catalog=pubs; User ID=sa; Password="

With objCmd
    ' set up the command
    .ActiveConnection = objConn
    .CommandText = "usp_FetchLogo"
    .CommandType = adCmdStoredProc
```

```
      ' create the parameters
      .Parameters.Append .CreateParameter("@PubID", adVarChar, _
                                     adParamInput, 4, "0736")

      ' now run the command
      Set objRs = objCmd.Execute
End With

' extract the logo into a variable
bytChunk = objRs("logo")

' store the image to a file and load it into a picture box
' Note: Visual Basic has no method to accept the image directly
'       from the variable so you have to save it to disk first
Open "c:\temp\image.bmp" For Binary As #1
Put #1, , bytChunk()
Close #1
Picture1.Picture = LoadPicture("c:\temp\image.bmp")

objRs.Close
objConn.Close

Set objRs = Nothing
Set objCmd = Nothing
Set objConn = Nothing
```

This used a Command object and parameters, but you could equally use just a recordset and return a whole set of records with images.

Smaller Chunks

One of the disadvantages of using the above method is that, for a large image (such as a 24-bit full color picture), it requires a large amount of memory on the client, and is not particularly efficient. If you think about how large images can get, then there seems little point in clogging up the user machine with a large amount of dynamic storage.

To alleviate this problem you can use GetChunks and limit the amount it reads. For example, the above Visual Basic code could be rewritten like this:

```
Dim objConn     As New ADODB.Connection
Dim objCmd      As New ADODB.Command
Dim objRs       As ADODB.Recordset
Dim bytChunk()  As Byte
Dim varChunk    As Variant

' open the connection
objConn.Open "Provider=SQLOLEDB; Data Source=Tigger; " & _
             "Initial Catalog=pubs; User ID=sa; Password="

With objCmd
    ' set up the command
    .ActiveConnection = objConn
    .CommandText = "usp_FetchLogo"
    .CommandType = adCmdStoredProc
```

```
    ' create the parameters
    .Parameters.Append .CreateParameter("@PubID", adVarChar, _
                                          adParamInput, 4, "0736")

    ' now run the command
    Set objRs = objCmd.Execute
End With
```

```
' open the output file
Open "c:\temp\barf.bmp" For Binary As #1

' read in the first chunk
varChunk = objRs("logo").GetChunk(512)

' GetChunk returns Null if there is no more data
While Not IsNull(varChunk)
    ' convert the data to a byte array and write it to the file
    bytChunk = varChunk
    Put #1, , bytChunk()

    ' read in the next chunk
    varChunk = objRs("logo").GetChunk(512)
Wend
```

```
' close the file and load the picture
Close #1
Picture1.Picture = LoadPicture("c:\temp\barf.bmp")

objRs.Close
objConn.Close

Set objRs = Nothing
Set objCmd = Nothing
Set objConn = Nothing
```

You might think that this is much slower, but the delay is hardly noticeable.

Retrieving Images into a Stream

The new feature of allowing the results of a `Command` to be stored in a `Stream` is particularly suited to images, as it avoids the need to have code to handle the file. For example, the following code creates and opens a new `Stream` object, into which the results of our `usp_FetchLogo` stored procedure are stored. The contents of the `Stream` are then written directly to a file:

```
Dim objConn     As New ADODB.Connection
Dim objCmd      As New ADODB.Command
Dim objStm      As New Stream

' open the connection
objConn.Open "Provider=SQLOLEDB; Data Source=Tigger; " & _
             "Initial Catalog=pubs; User ID=sa; Password="
```

```
' open the stream
objStm.Open

With objCmd
    ' set up the command
    .ActiveConnection = objConn
    .CommandText = "usp_FetchLogo"
    .CommandType = adCmdStoredProc

    ' create the parameters
    .Parameters.Append .CreateParameter("@PubID", adVarChar, _
                                    adParamInput, 4, "0736")

    ' set the output stream
    .Properties("Output Stream") = objStm

    ' now run the command
    objCmd.Execute , , adExecuteStream
End With

' save the file
objStm.SaveToFile "c:\temp\image.bmp"

objConn.Close

Set objCmd = Nothing
Set objConn = Nothing
```

Images Using ASP

The same sort of procedure to push an image to the browser is just as simple in ASP.
We'll start with a stored procedure to fetch the image:

```
CREATE PROCEDURE usp_FetchLogo
    @lPubID  int
AS
    SELECT   logo
    FROM     pub_info
    WHERE    pub_id = @lPubId
```

Now imagine an ASP page called GetLogo.asp:

```
<!--METADATA TYPE="TypeLib" FILE="C:\Program Files\Common
                Files\SYSTEM\ADO\MSADO15.DLL"-->
<%
    ' turn on buffering and set the mime type
    Response.Buffer = True
    Response.ContentType = "image/bmp"

    Dim objConn
    Dim objCmd
    Dim objRs
    Dim bytChunk
    Dim sID
```

```
' get the required id
sID = Request.QueryString("pub_id")

Set objConn = Server.CreateObject("ADODB.Connection")
Set objCmd = Server.CreateObject("ADODB.Command")
Set objRs = Server.CreateObject("ADODB.Recordset")

' open the connection
objConn.Open "Provider=SQLOLEDB; Data Source=Tigger; " & _
             "Initial Catalog=pubs; User ID=sa; Password="

' set the command details
objCmd.ActiveConnection = objConn
objCmd.CommandText = "usp_FetchLogo"
objCmd.CommandType = adCmdStoredProc

objCmd.Parameters.Append objCmd.CreateParameter("@PubID", _
                         adVarChar, adParamInput, 4, sID)

' run the command and extract the logo
Set objRs = objCmd.Execute
bytChunk = objRs("logo")

' write image to the browser
Response.BinaryWrite bytChunk
Response.End
%>
```

You could use this from another ASP page as the source of the image tag. For example:

```
<IMG SRC="GetLogo.asp?pub_id=0736">
```

I thank God I am as honest as any man
living that is an old man and no honester th

Can counsel and speak comfort to th
which they themselves not feel

Much Ado About Nothing.

He wears his faith but as the fashion of h

As merry as the day

He hath indeed better bettered expectation

(Act i. Sc. 1).

He wears his faith but as the fashion of his hat.
(Ibid)

As merry as the day is long.

h indeed better bettered expectation

(Act i. Sc. 1).

(Ibid)

an counsel and speak comfort to that grief

Much Ado About Nothing.

Which they themselves not feel.

He wears his faith but as the fashion of his hat.

(Ibid)

(Ibid)

I was not born under

a rhyming plane

I was not born under a rhyming plane
Sc. 2

For there was never yet
That could endure the to

merry as the day is long

(Sc. 2)

Can counsel and speak comfort to that grief

(Ibid)

Which they themselves not feel.

(Ibid)

He hath indeed better bettered expectation

(Ibid)

I thank God I am as honest as any

(Act i. Sc. 1).

living that is an old man and no honest

He wears his faith but as the fashion of his ha

(Ibi

Much Ado About Nothing.

For there was never yet philospher
That could endure the toothache patiently.

(Ibid)

I was not born u

For there was never yet philospher
That could endure the toothache patiently.

Remote Data Services

Remote Data Services (RDS) differs from ADO, in that RDS is a set of objects designed to work in the browser, and provide client-side data facilities. It sits on top of ADO, and works in Internet Explorer, providing a way to handle data within DHTML, and to easily allow data to be displayed in HTML elements. RDS not only allows data to be displayed, but also allows data updates, and provides methods for updating the original data store. In effect, RDS provides an offline copy of the data.

This chapter will cover the RDS objects, such as the Data Space Objects, Data Source Objects, and so on, but doesn't give an exhaustive tutorial into their workings. For that you should consult the Wrox Press book *Professional ADO 2.5 RDS Programming with ASP 3.0 (ISBN 1-861003-24-2)*.

RDS Support

The use of RDS is browser-dependent, and only the Microsoft Internet Explorer browser (version 4 and above) fully supports RDS. If you'd like to use RDS but need to support other browsers, then the MSDN site has a good article describing this – you can find it at http://msdn.microsoft.com/workshop/dbdwnlvl.asp.

You should also be aware that applications using RDS might have to contend with different versions of RDS on the client. Internet Explorer 4 shipped with RDS version 1.5, while Internet Explorer 5, Office 2000, and Visual Studio 6 shipped with version 2.0. ADO 2.5 shipped with Windows 2000, as well as being available as a download. For general compatibility issues you should read the following knowledge-base articles, available from http://support.microsoft.com:

- ❑ Q216389 – Maintaining Binary Compatibility in Components with ADOR
- ❑ Q195049 – Maintain Binary Compatibility in Components Exposing ADO
- ❑ Q201580 – ADO 2.0 and ADO 2.1 Binary Compatibility

At the time of writing there were no other issues concerning compatibility.

You can obtain the latest versions of ADO and RDS at http://www.microsoft.com/data.

RDS Objects

Since RDS uses both client and server-side components, they are best described in conjunction with a diagram:

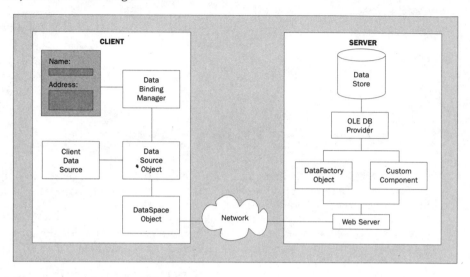

At the server we have the following:

❑ **Data Store**, which is the source of the data.

❑ **Data Factory Object** or **Custom Component**, which supply only the requested data. The custom component can be any COM-compliant component.

❑ **Web Server**, which provides the interface from the server to the client.

This means that you must have certain facilities installed on your web server. The NT 4.0 Option Pack supplies RDS version 1.5, and versions 2.0 and 2.1 are available for download. Windows 2000 comes with ADO 2.5, and both 2.5 and 2.6 are available for download at http://www.Microsoft.com/data. See the section entitled 'RDS Support' later in this chapter for more details.

On the client side we have the following:

❑ **Data Space Object**, which takes the data from the web server and makes it available to a Data Source object.

❑ **Data Source Object**, which along with the client data cache holds the data on the client.

❑ **Data Binding Manager**, which connects the Data Source Object to HTML Tags. See the Data Binding section later in the chapter for more details.

❑ **Client HTML tags**, which display the data.

In the diagram we've just seen, the use of Client and Server is a *logical* separation, and does not have to represent a physical separation of the two items. The web server, for example, can exist on the same machine as the client, which means that RDS based applications can be created and tested on a single machine. Also certain Data Source Objects (such as the Tabular Data Control and the XML Data Control) can work with local data files, and do not always require a server to supply the data.

In essence, RDS is just a way of handling data remotely. It provides a way for HTML pages to access data from a remote data source, allowing data changes, and providing a way for data to be sent back to the original data store. Its use is simplified by the fact that underneath each Data Source Object is a standard ADO recordset. Because it is a disconnected recordset (that is, not permanently connected to the data store) it uses the client cursor engine.

Data Source Objects

The simplest way to use RDS is through the use of a Data Source Object (DSO). A DSO provides the data to the client interface, allowing it to be bound to HTML elements as well as manipulated directly by way of an ADO `Recordset`.

There are several Data Source Objects available as part of the standard IE 4 or IE 5 installation, or as a separate download. They are generally created by use of the HTML `OBJECT` tag, for which an ActiveX control has the general form:

```
<OBJECT CLASSID="clsid:class id of object"
        ID="id of HTML tag" HEIGHT="0" WIDTH="0">
  <PARAM NAME="parameter name" VALUE="parameter value">
  <PARAM NAME="parameter name" VALUE="parameter value">
</OBJECT>
```

Setting a unique `ID` allows data binding to take place, and using a `Height` and `Width` of zero ensures that the control doesn't take up any space on the page. You can give a height and width, but since the control doesn't have a visible interface, there's not much to see.

The parameter names correspond to the properties of the object, and are listed below with each object. For example:

```
<OBJECT CLASSID="clsid:BD96C556-65A3-11D0-983A-00C04FC29E33"
        ID="dsoAuthors" HEIGHT="0" WIDTH="0">
  <PARAM NAME="Server" VALUE="http://www.yourserver.com">
  <PARAM NAME="Connect" VALUE="DSN=pubs">
  <PARAM NAME="SQL" VALUE="SELECT * FROM authors">
</OBJECT>
```

You can also set the parameters (as well as calling methods) from within script, by referencing the properties:

```
<SCRIPT Language="JScript">
    dsoAuthors.Server = "http://www.yourserver.com";
    dsoAuthors.Connect = "DSN=pubs";
```

9

Remote Data Services

```
        dsoAuthors.SQL = "SELECT * FROM authors"
        dsoAuthors.Refresh;
    </SCRIPT>
```

There are various security implications when using RDS. See the Security Issues section at the end of this chapter for more details.

We will be covering the following Data Source Objects:

❑ Remote Data Service (RDS) Control, which is designed to handle data from SQL databases.

❑ The Tabular Data Control (TDC), which is designed for data stored in text files.

❑ Java Database Control (JDBC), which is a DSO written in Java, and therefore available for use in other browsers.

❑ Microsoft HTML Control, which is designed for data that is formatted in HTML.

❑ XML Java Applet, which is another Java written applet, this time for XML data. It only provides read-only access to the data.

❑ The XML Control, which is designed for data in XML form. The XML DSO is more commonly known as an XML Data Island.

Remote Data Service Data Control

In older versions of RDS, the RDS Data Control was known as the Advanced Data Control (ADC). It is automatically installed with Internet Explorer 4.0 or higher.

Class ID	BD96C556-65A3-11D0-983A-00C04FC29E33
Source	C:\Program Files\Common Files\System\MSADC\msadco.dll
Prog ID	RDS.DataControl

Instantiating the RDS Data Control

You instantiate the RDS Data Control with the use of an OBJECT tag, taking the following form:

```
<OBJECT CLASSID="clsid:BD96C556-65A3-11D0-983A-00C04FC29E33"
        ID="DataControl" WIDTH="0" HEIGHT="0">
    <PARAM NAME="Connect" VALUE="ConnectString">
    <PARAM NAME="Server" VALUE="ServerURL">
    <PARAM NAME="SQL" VALUE="SQLQueryString">
    <PARAM NAME="URL" VALUE="URLpath">
</OBJECT>
```

Methods of the RDS Data Control

The Cancel Method

Cancels an asynchronous action.

```
datacontrol.Cancel
```

If data is being fetched asynchronously, for example when the FetchOptions property is set to adcFetchAsync or adcFetchBackground, then calling the Cancel method will cancel the fetching operation.

After this call, the ReadyState property is set to adcReadyStateLoaded and the Recordset will be empty.

The CancelUpdate Method

Cancels changes made to the source recordset.

```
datacontrol.CancelUpdate
```

Because an RDS recordset is disconnected from the original data store, CancelUpdate ensures that any changes made to the recordset since the last Refresh or SubmitChanges method call will be discarded. The cache of changes is reset to empty, and any bound controls are refreshed with the original data.

The CreateRecordSet Method

Creates an empty, disconnected recordset on the client.

```
Object = datacontrol.CreateRecordSet(varColumnInfos)
```

Parameter	Type	Description
varColumnInfos	Variant	An array of arrays defining the columns for the recordset.

varColumnInfos should be a variant array, with each column of the inner array being defined by one of the following four elements:

- ❑ Name, for the name of the column
- ❑ Type, for the data type of the column
- ❑ Size, for the size of the column; for fixed length types this must be -1
- ❑ Nullability, to indicate if the column can contain a null value

For the data type you should use one of the ADO DataTypeEnum values (except for adChapter, adDBFileTime, adEmpty, adFileTime, adIDispatch, adIUnknown, adLongVarChar, adPropVariant, adUserDefined, adVariant, and adVarNumeric, which are not supported). For a full list of these data types and their associated values you should consult Appendix B.

The data type may be converted into an equivalent type, but you won't see this until the recordset is populated. The possible substitutions are:

Original Type	Substituted Type
adDBTimeStamp	adDate
adBSTR adVarwChar adLongVarWChar	adWChar
adChar adLongVarChar	adVarChar
adLongVarBinary	adVarBinary

The column arrays should be appended to another array, which becomes the method argument. For example:

```
<SCRIPT LANGUAGE=" JScript">

function cmdCreateNew.onclick()
{
    var aField1 = Array(4);
    var aField2 = Array(4);
    var aField3 = Array(4);
    var aField4 = Array(4);
    var aCols = Array(4);

    // create the individual columns
    aField1[0] = "ID";              // name
    aField1[1] = 3;                 // type - adInteger
    aField1[2] = -1;                // size
    aField1[3] = false;             // nullability

    aField2[0] = "FirstName";       // name
    aField2[1] = 202;               // type - adVarWChar
    aField2[2] = -1;                // size
    aField2[3] = false;             // nullability

    aField3[0] = "LastName";        // name
    aField3[1] = 202;               // type - adVarWChar
    aField3[2] = -1;                // size
    aField3[3] = false;             // nullability

    aField4[0] = "DateOfBirth";     // name
    aField4[1] = 7;                 // type - adDate
    aField4[2] = -1;                // size
    aField4[3] = false;             // nullability

    // add the columns to an array
    aCols[0] = aField1;
    aCols[1] = aField2;
    aCols[2] = aField3;
    aCols[3] = aField4;
```

```
        // create a new recordset
        // dsoNew and dsoTest are data controls on the
        // page as OBJECT tags or created in code
        dsoNew.SourceRecordset = dsoTest.CreateRecordset (aCols);

        // add some data
        dsoNew.AddNew;
        dsoNew.Fields(0) = 1;
        dsoNew.Fields(1) = "Rob";
        dsoNew.Fields(2) = "Smith";
        dsoNew.Fields(3) = 68/03/05;
        dsoNew.Update;
    }
</SCRIPT>
```

The recordset created is a standard ADO disconnected recordset.

The Move... Methods

Move to the appropriate row in the recordset.

```
datacontrol.MoveFirst
datacontrol.MoveNext
datacontrol.MovePrevious
datacontrol.MoveLast
```

These methods are the same as the `Recordset` methods of the same name, and move to the first, next, previous, and last row in a recordset.

The Refresh Method

Refreshes the data from the data source.

```
datacontrol.Refresh
```

Since RDS works in a disconnected environment, it's possible for the data it's using to become out of sync with the data in the original data source. Calling `Refresh` will update the current data.

The `Refresh` method will discard any unsaved changes, and will position the recordset at the first record. Bound HTML elements will reflect the new data.

The Reset Method

Resets the client-side recordset based on filter and sort criteria.

```
datacontrol.Reset(fRefilter)
```

Parameter	Type	Description
fRefilter	Boolean	Setting this to `True` will apply the reset to any records already filtered, whereas setting this to `False` applies the `Filter` to the original set of data. Default is `True`

9

Remote Data Services

You should use this method after setting the `FilterColumn`, `FilterCriterion`, `FilterValue`, `SortColumn`, or `SortDirection` properties to ensure that the filter is applied. For example:

```
datacontrol.FilterColumn = "au_fname"
datacontrol.FilterCriterion = "="
datacontrol.FilterValue = "Alex"
datacontrol.Reset(false)
```

This method will fail if there are unsaved changes in the data.

The SubmitChanges Method

Sends pending changes to the data source.

```
datacontrol.SubmitChanges
```

When sending changes back to the data source, only the changes are sent and one of two actions can occur. Either the changes will *all* succeed, or *all* will fail – it is not possible for some changes to succeed while others fail. For more information on failed changes, see the Conflict Resolution section in Chapter 5.

Properties of the RDS Data Control

The Connect Property

Indicates an ADO connection string to connect to the data source.

```
datacontrol.Connect = String
String = datacontrol.Connect
```

For locally, persisted files, the connection string can simply be:

```
Provider=MSPersist
```

The ExecuteOptions Property

Indicates whether or not to use asynchronous execution.

```
datacontrol.ExecuteOptions = adcExecuteOptionEnum
adcExecuteOptionEnum = datacontrol.ExecuteOptions
```

The value can be one of the `adcExecuteOptionEnum` constants:

Constant	Value	Description
`adcExecSync`	1	Indicates that the command should be executed synchronously. This is the default.
`adcExecAsync`	2	Indicates that the command should be executed asynchronously.

Synchronous operations mean that control is not returned to the calling program until the data fetching action has been completed. This means that when a data control on a page is running a command to fetch data from a data source, the data control waits until the command has been processed before to continuing. Asynchronous operations return control as soon as the command has been sent to the data server.

The FetchOptions Property

Indicates the type of fetching being used.

```
datacontrol.FetchOptions = adcFetchOptionEnum
adcFetchOptionEnum = datacontrol.FetchOptions
```

The value can be one of the following adcFetchOptionEnum constants:

Constant	Value	Description
adcFetchUpFront	1	Indicates that all records are fetched before control is given back to the application. This is the default.
adcFetchBackground	2	Indicates that control is given back to the application as soon as the first batch of records has been fetched.
adcFetchAsync	3	Indicates that control is given back to the application immediately, and that fetching of records continues in the background.

If you are using adcFetchBackground and you try to access a record that has not yet been retrieved, the application will not receive control back until the record has been fetched. So, your application blocks until the required record is available.

If you are using adcFetchAsync and you try to access a record that has already been fetched, then you will be placed on that record. If the record has not yet been fetched, control is given back to the application immediately – you will be placed on the closest record and EOF will be set for the recordset. This means that when using adcFetchAsync you should really check the ReadyState property before attempting to move to the end of the recordset, because otherwise you will just be moved to the last fetched record, while other records are still being fetched.

The FilterColumn Property

Indicates the column upon which filtering should take place.

```
datacontrol.FilterColumn = String
String = datacontrol.FilterColumn
```

Setting the FilterColumn property does not activate the filter. For this you need to use the Reset method, which applies the filter and changes the recordset to contain only the directed rows. The full recordset is maintained by RDS.

The FilterCriterion Property

Indicates the criteria to be used for filtering.

```
datacontrol.FilterCriterion = String
String = datacontrol.FilterCriterion
```

The value for `FilterCriterion` can be one of the following:

- ❑ < for less than
- ❑ <= for less than or equal to
- ❑ = for equal to
- ❑ >= for greater than or equal to
- ❑ > for greater than
- ❑ <> for not equal to

Setting the `FilterCriterion` property does not activate the filter. For this you need to use the `Reset` method.

The FilterValue Property

Indicates the value to filter for.

```
datacontrol.FilterValue = String
String = datacontrol.FilterValue
```

Setting the `FilterValue` property alone does not activate the filter. To activate the filter, use the `Reset` method.

The Handler Property

Indicates what handler to use.

```
datacontrol.Handler = String
String = datacontrol.Handler
```

The `Handler` enables custom logic to be executed on the server when RDS is used to work directly with remote OLE DB providers. This allows you to build your own custom server-side data handlers, instead of using the default one. One reason for doing this is to provide more control over requests and access rights.

The handler is a COM objects that implements the `IDataFactoryHandler` interface, and it only has two methods; `GetRecordset` and `Reconnect`.
There's a detailed explanation of this feature inthe MSDN Online article entitled *Using the Customization Handler Feature in RDS 2.0* – available at
http://msdn.microsoft.com/library/sdkdoc/dasdk/usin1x68.htm.

The InternetTimeout Property

Indicates the time in milliseconds to wait for HTTP requests.

```
datacontrol.InternetTimeout = Long
Long = datacontrol.InternetTimeout
```

This property allows you to customize how long to wait before an error is generated. The default value is 300000, which is 5 minutes.

This doesn't override the server timeout facility. Whichever timeout is reached first is used.

The ReadyState Property

Indicates the state of the control.

```
adcReadStateEnum = datacontrol.ReadyState
```

This property can be one of the adcReadStateEnum values:

Constant	Value	Description
adcReadyStateLoaded	2	To indicate that the recordset is open, but no data has been received from the source.
adcReadyStateInteractive	3	To indicate that the recordset is currently receiving data from the source.
adcReadyStateComplete	4	To indicate that the recordset is fully populated, and has received all of its data from the source.

The Recordset Property

Returns the ADO Recordset object underlying this data control.

```
Recordset = datacontrol.Recordset
```

The underlying recordset is a standard ADO Recordset object, so you can therefore use the recordset methods to manipulate the records in the data control. For example, if using single table binding you could have several buttons to perform the navigation:

```
<INPUT ID="cmdFirst" TYPE="BUTTON" VALUE="<<"
   onclick="dsoAuthors.Recordset.MoveFirst();">

<INPUT ID="cmdPrevious" TYPE="BUTTON" VALUE="<"
   onclick="dsoAuthors.Recordset.MovePrevious();">

<INPUT ID="cmdNext" TYPE="BUTTON" VALUE=">"
   onclick="dsoAuthors.Recordset.MoveNext();">

<INPUT ID="cmdLast" TYPE="BUTTON" VALUE=">>"
   onclick="dsoAuthors.Recordset.MoveLast();">
```

9

Remote Data Services

The Server Property

Indicates the web server URL.

```
datacontrol.Server = String
String = datacontrol.Server
```

The Server property can be a standard HTTP or HTTPS URL, the name of a machine (without the leading //) for DCOM use, or empty for local in-process use. For example:

```
dtacontrol.Server = "http://www.wrox.com"
```

> *If using HTTP, the name of the server must be the same as the name of the machine that the HTML or ASP has been downloaded from. This is a deliberate security restriction – to ensure that only data from data stores on the same server are allowed.*

The SortColumn Property

Indicates the column upon which to perform sorting.

```
datacontrol.SortColumn = String
String = datacontrol.SortColumn
```

Once the SortColumn is set, the SortDirection should be set, and the Reset method called.

The SortDirection Property

Indicates the direction in which to sort.

```
datacontrol.SortDirection = Boolean
Boolean = datacontrol.SortDirection
```

This value is True for ascending sorts, and False for descending sorts. The Reset method applies the sort.

The SourceRecordset Property

Sets the ADO Recordset to be used for the data control.

```
Set Recordset = datacontrol.SourceRecordset
Set datacontrol.SourceRecordset = Recordset
```

This property allows you to set the source data of a data control to an existing ADO Recordset.

The SQL Property

Indicates the SQL query string used to generate the data.

```
datacontrol.SQL = String
String = datacontrol.SQL
```

The SQL string uses the SQL dialect of the server.

Events of the RDS Data Control

The onerror Event

Raised if an event is generated whenever an error occurs during a data operation.

```
onerror(SCode, Description, Source, CancelDisplay)
```

Parameter	Type	Description
SCode	Integer	The status code of the error.
Description	String	The error description.
Source	String	The query or command that caused the error.
CancelDisplay	Boolean	Allows you to prevent an error dialog being shown.

If you set the CancelDisplay parameter to True in the onerror event procedure, then no error dialog box is displayed. For example:

```
<SCRIPT LANGUAGE="JScript" FOR="dsoAuthors"
                        EVENT="onerror">

    // code to handle the error

    CancelDisplay = true;
</SCRIPT>
```

The onreadystatechange Event

Raised when the state of the Data Source Object changes, for example when a new set of data is loaded.

```
onreadystatechange
```

The event has no parameters with which to identify the state, but the this object refers to the active object. You can then examine the readyState property to see what the state is. For example, in JScript:

```
<SCRIPT LANGUAGE="JScript" FOR="dsoAuthors"
                        EVENT="onreadystatechange">

    if (this.readyState == 'complete')
        // data has been completely read in
</SCRIPT>
```

In VBScript you use the Me object (which is equivalent to the this object in JScript and refers to the active object):

```
<SCRIPT LANGUAGE="VBScript" FOR="dsoAuthors"
                        EVENT="onreadystatechange">
```

```
        If Me.readyState == 'complete' Then
            ' data has been completely read in
        End If
   </SCRIPT>
```

Values for the `readyState` are:

- ❑ `uninitialized`, to indicate the object is not initialized with data.
- ❑ `loading`, to indicate the object is currently loading data.
- ❑ `interactive`, to indicate the object has not fully loaded its data, although it can be interacted with.
- ❑ `complete`, to indicate the control is completely loaded.

The Tabular Data Control

The Tabular Data Control is automatically installed with Internet Explorer 4.0 or higher, and is designed to handle data from text files.

Class ID	`333C7BC4-460F-11D0-BC04-0080C7055A83`
Source	`C:\WINNT\System32\tdc.ocx`
Prog ID	`TDCCtl.TDCCtl`

By default, the TDC will only allow data to be loaded from the same domain as the web page, and any other domain will silently fail. This is a deliberate security restriction to protect against unauthorized access to private data. If you need to allow access to data files on other domains, then you can add the following domain details to the beginning of the data file.

```
        domain_string: header_string "=" domain_list
        header_string: "@!allow_domains"
        domain_list: domain_spec [; domain_list ]
        domain_spec: * | [*.] domain | ipaddr
```

Wildcards are in domain names (*.wrox.com), but they are not supported in IP addresses. For example, if Wrox wanted to expose a text file, but only allow access from the `tigger` server on `ipona.co.uk` and all servers on `stonebroom.co.uk`, the domain details would be:

```
   @!allow_domains=tigger.ipona.co.uk;*.stonebroom.co.uk
```

These servers are not part of the Wrox domain, but it's the data that controls where it can be seen.

Instantiating the TDC

```
   <OBJECT CLASSID="clsid:333C7BC4-460F-11D0-BC04-0080C7055A83"
                       ID="DataControl" WIDTH="0" HEIGHT="0">
      <PARAM NAME="DataURL" VALUE="composer.csv">
   </OBJECT>
```

Methods of the Tabular Data Control

The Reset Method

Updates the local recordset to reflect current filter and sort criteria.

```
datacontrol.Reset
```

Properties of the Tabular Data Control

The AppendData Property

Identifies whether or not the new data replaces the existing recordset or is appended to the existing recordset.

```
datacontrol.AppendData = Boolean
Boolean = datacontrol.AppendData
```

If this is set to True, the new data is appended to the end of the existing recordset when the Reset method is called.

The default value is False.

The CaseSensitive Property

Indicates whether string comparisons will be case sensitive.

```
datacontrol.CaseSensitive = Boolean
Boolean = datacontrol.CaseSensitive
```

The default value is True.

The CharSet Property

Identifies the character set of the data.

```
datacontrol.CharSet = String
String = datacontrol.CharSet
```

The default value is windows-1252. For more information on the available character sets, search on http://msdn.microsoft.com.

Character sets are particularly important when dealing with data containing non-English characters, such as umlauts, cedillas, and so forth. Identifying the character set of the data correctly ensures that you won't receive errors when the data control tries to load the data. This is particularly important with XML data, as you may receive XML parsing errors if your data contains characters that are not included in your character set.

9

Remote Data Services

The DataURL Property

Indicates the URL of the data file.

```
datacontrol.DataURL = String
String = datacontrol.DataURL
```

The EscapeChar Property

The escape character used in the source data file.

```
datacontrol.EscapeChar = String
String = datacontrol.EscapeChar
```

The Tabular Data Control is designed to take textual data in a tabular form, with columns and rows being separated by special characters, and a special character to distinguish text data. These characters are defined by the FieldDelim, RowDelim, and TextQualifier properties. If your data needs to have one of these characters in it, then the character should be escaped, by placing the EscapeChar in front of it. For example, suppose you have some data in the following form:

```
ID,FirstName,LastName,Address
1,Jan,Lloyd,14 Coniston Close, Borden, Hants
2,Nigel,Futter,23a Lemington Road, Risely, Beds
```

There are only four columns, separated by commas, but the fourth column has commas in it. Since the comma is the column delimiter any commas within columns need to be escaped, like so:

```
ID,FirstName,LastName,Address
1,Jan,Lloyd,14 Coniston Close\, Borden\, Hants
2,Nigel,Futter,23a Lemington Road\, Risely\, Beds
```

In this instance we could set the properties of the TDC as follows:

```
dataControl.FieldDelim = ","
dataControl.EscapeChar = "\"
```

The FieldDelim Property

Identifies the character that delimits columns in the data file.

```
datacontrol.FieldDelim = String
String = datacontrol.FieldDelim
```

Only a single character can be used, and it defaults to a comma. For example, to change this to a colon:

```
datacontrol.FieldDelim = ":"
```

The Filter Property

Indicates the filter that will be applied to data.

```
datacontrol.Filter = String
String = datacontrol.Filter
```

The `Filter` property is similar to a SQL WHERE clause without the WHERE.
For example:

```
dataControl.Filter = "LastName=Lloyd"
```

To filter on wildcards you can use the asterisk:

```
dataControl.Filter = "LastName=L*"
```

The Language Property

Specifies the language of the data file.

```
datacontrol.Language = String
String = datacontrol.Language
```

The default language is eng-us.

The ReadyState Property

Indicates the state of the control as data is received.

```
datacontrol.ReadyState = Long
Long = datacontrol.ReadyState
```

`ReadyState` can be one of the following ADCReadyStateEnum constants:

Constant	Value	Description
adcReadyStateComplete	4	All the available rows have arrived, or an error occurred preventing (more) data arriving.
adcReadyStateInteractive	3	Rows are still arriving from the server.
adcReadyStateLoaded	2	The control is loaded and waiting to fetch rows from the server.

The RowDelim Property

Specifies the character that delimits each row in the data file.

```
datacontrol.RowDelim = String
String = datacontrol.RowDelim
```

Remote Data Services

Only a single character can be used, and it defaults to carriage return. For example, to use the ~ character as a row delimiter:

```
dataControl.RowDelim = "~"
```

The Sort Property

Specifies the sort order for the data file.

```
datacontrol.Sort = String
String = datacontrol.Sort
```

For the sort order, you specify the column names as a comma-delimited list. The default order is ascending, but you can insert a minus sign (-) before each column to sort in a descending order. For example:

```
dataControl.Sort = "LastName,FirstName,-Age"
```

The TextQualifier Property

Indicates the character that is used to enclose text fields.

```
datacontrol.TextQualifier = String
String = datacontrol.TextQualifier
```

If some of your columns contain characters that might be column delimiters you can either escape the delimiters (see discussion of the EscapeChar property, above in this chapter), or use a text qualifier around the column. For example:

```
ID,FirstName,LastName,Address
1,Jan,Lloyd,14 Coniston Close, Borden, Hants
2,Nigel,Futter,23a Lemington Road, Risely, Beds
```

There are only four columns, separated by commas, but the fourth column has commas in it. Using a text qualifier ensures that the commas are not seen as column delimiters:

```
ID,FirstName,LastName,Address
1,Jan,Lloyd,"14 Coniston Close, Borden, Hants"
2,Nigel,Futter,"23a Lemington Road, Risely, Beds"
```

The default is the double quote mark ("). Naturally your fields cannot include characters the same as the qualifier, otherwise the end of the text field is assumed, and any additional data is taken as part of the next field.

The UseHeader Property

Indicates whether or not the first row of the data file contains heading information, for example column names and data types.

```
datacontrol.UseHeader = Boolean
Boolean = datacontrol.UseHeader
```

The simplest form just shows column names:

```
ID,FirstName,LastName,Address
1,Jan,Lloyd,"14 Coniston Close, Borden, Hants"
2,Nigel,Futter,"23a Lemington Road, Risely, Beds"
```

The heading row can optionally contain data types for the columns. For example:

```
ID:Int,FirstName:String,LastName:String,Address:String
1,Jan,Lloyd,"14 Coniston Close, Borden, Hants"
2,Nigel,Futter,"23a Lemington Road, Risely, Beds"
```

The data type can be one of the following:

- ❑ String, for textual data; this is the default
- ❑ Date, for dates
- ❑ Boolean, for Yes/No or True/False
- ❑ Int, for whole numbers
- ❑ Float, for floating point numbers

For Date fields, you can add a space and then D, M, or Y to indicate the date style. The TDC assumes dates are numbers separated by characters, so any character date separator will work. For example:

```
Name:String, DateOfBirth:Date YMD
Dave,66/06/11
Rob,68.03.05
```

For Boolean values, the following applies:

- ❑ A value of Yes, True, 1, -1, or any *non-zero number* is interpreted as True. This is case insensitive.
- ❑ A value of No, False, or 0 is interpreted as False.

Events of the Tabular Data Control

The onreadystatechange Event

This event is triggered when the ReadyState property changes. You can use this to detect when the TDC has fully loaded the data into the Data Source Object.

The event has no parameters with which to identify the state, but the this object refers to the active object (that is, the data control). For example:

```
<SCRIPT LANGUAGE="JScript" FOR="dsoAuthors"
                  EVENT="onreadystatechange">
```

```
         if (this.readyState == 'complete')
            // data has been completely read in
</SCRIPT>
```

The Java Data Base Control (JDBC)

The Java Data Base Control (also known as the Java DSO) is a Data Source Object written entirely in Java, and is therefore available for browsers other than Microsoft Internet Explorer, such as Netscape Navigator or Opera. All other DSOs use the HTML OBJECT tag, but the Java DSO is created with an APPLET tag.

The Java DSO is available as either compiled class files or as source, so you can extend it if required. You can get the Java DSO from http://msdn.microsoft.com/downloads/samples/internet/author/datasrc/jdbcapplet.

If you want to learn more about JDBC, you should consult a specialist book. There's a good discussion of JDBC in Ivor Horton's *Beginning Java 2 (Wrox, ISBN 1-861002-23-8)*.

Instantiating the JDBC Object

```
<APPLET CODE="JDC.class" ID="dsoAuthors" WIDTH=0 HEIGHT=0>
  <PARAM NAME=cabbase VALUE= "jdc.cab">
  <PARAM NAME="dbURL" VALUE="jdbc:odbc:pubs">
  <PARAM NAME="showUI" VALUE="false">
  <PARAM NAME="sqlStatement" VALUE="select * from authors">
  <PARAM NAME="allowInsert" VALUE="true">
  <PARAM NAME="allowDelete" VALUE="true">
  <PARAM NAME="allowUpdate" VALUE="false">
  <PARAM NAME="user" VALUE="">
  <PARAM NAME="password" VALUE="">
  <PARAM NAME="filterColumn" VALUE="">
  <PARAM NAME="filterCriterion " VALUE="">
  <PARAM NAME="filterValue " VALUE="">
  <PARAM NAME="driver" VALUE="">
</APPLET>
```

You can obtain the JDC CAB file from MSDN, at http://msdn.microsoft.com/downloads/c-frame.htm?928521190764#/downloads/samples/internet/default.asp.

Methods of the Java DSO

The apply Method

Applies a sort or a filter to the recordset of the DSO.

```
datacontrol.apply()
```

For example:

```
dataControl.filterColumn = "au_lname";
dataControl.filterCriterion = "=";
dataControl.filterValue = "Homer";
dataControl.apply();
```

The commitChanges Method

The commitChanges method is implemented as a stub and will raise an error if called. Since this method cannot be implemented in a generic way, Microsoft has left this to be implemented by the user if required. In other words, it exists, but doesn't work.

Properties of the Java DSO

The allowInsert Property

Indicates whether or not inserts (that is, new rows) are allowed against the DSO.

```
datacontrol.allowInsert = Boolean
Boolean= datacontrol.allowInsert
```

Inserts only affect the local data and are not sent to the server.The current Java DSO doesn't allow updates to the data source – see the CommitChanges method for more details.

The allowDelete Property

Indicates whether or not deletes are allowed against the DSO.

```
datacontrol.allowDelete = Boolean
Boolean= datacontrol.allowDelete
```

Deletes only affect the local data and are not sent to the server.

The allowUpdate Property

Indicates whether or not updates are allowed against the DSO.

```
datacontrol.allowUpdate = Boolean
Boolean = datacontrol.allowUpdate
```

Updates only affect the local data and are not sent to the server.

The cabbase Property

Specifies the code location of the data control

```
datacontrol.cabbase = String
String = datacontrol.cabbase
```

This is a general APPLET property that identifies the location of the applet code. The applet will be downloaded if it is not already installed on the client. For example:

```
dataControl.cabbase = "http:/www.wrox.com/cabs/jdso.cab"
```

The dbURL Property

Identifies the ODBC Data Source Name (DSN) that supplies the data.

```
datacontrol.dbURL = String
String = datacontrol.dbURL
```

9

Remote Data Services

259

The connect string takes the following form:

```
jdbc:subprotocol:subname
```

The driver Property

Indicates the JDBC Bridge driver to use.

```
datacontrol.driver = String
String = datacontrol.driver
```

The JDBC Bridge is what interfaces the JDBC calls to a data source. The Java SDK ships with an ODBC bridge, allowing you to use JDBC to access ODBC data sources.

The filterColumn Property

Indicates the column index or name to filter on.

```
datacontrol.filterColumn = String
String = datacontrol.filterColumn
```

The filterCriterion Property

Indicates the filter criteria.

```
datacontrol.filterCriterion = String
String = datacontrol.filterCriterion
```

The value for `FilterCriterion` can be one of:

- ❑ < for less than
- ❑ <= for less than or equal to
- ❑ = for equal to
- ❑ >= for greater than or equal to
- ❑ > for greater than
- ❑ <> for not equal to

The filterValue Property

Indicates the value to filter on.

```
datacontrol.filterValue = String
String = datacontrol.filterValue
```

The password Property

Indicates the user password needed to connect to the data store.

```
datacontrol.password = String
String= datacontrol.password
```

The preloadRows Property

Indicates the number of rows to preload before loading asynchronously.

```
datacontrol.preloadRows = Long
Long = datacontrol.preloadRows
```

When loading data synchronously, this property indicates the number of rows that are initially loaded before the rest of the rows are loaded asynchronously.

The showUI Property

Indicates whether or not a user interface for the applet should be displayed.

```
datacontrol.showUI = Boolean
Boolean = datacontrol.showUI
```

The Java DSO does not have a User Interface.

The sortColumn Property

Indicates the column number or name upon which to sort.

```
datacontrol.sortColumn = String
String = datacontrol.sortColumn
```

The sortDirection Property

Indicates the direction in which to sort.

```
datacontrol.sortDirection = String
String = datacontrol.sortDirection
```

The sqlStatement Property

Indicates the SQL statement used to return the data.

```
datacontrol.sqlStatement = String
String = datacontrol.sqlStatement
```

The user Property

Indicates the user name needed to connect to the data source.

```
datacontrol.user = String
String = datacontrol.user
```

Events of the Java DSO

The Java DSO does not implement any events directly, although some DSO events are available through the APPLET. See the section later in this chapter on Events for more details.

Remote Data Services

The MSHTML DSO

The MSHTML DSO is part of Internet Explorer and allows a DSO to be created based upon HTML tags. To be included in the data, the HTML tags must include an ID attribute. When parsing an HTML page, unique ID attributes become the columns, and the values within the tags become the column values. Separate rows are created by having tags with the same ID attribute. The parser ignores the actual HTML tag type – only the ID and the data are important.

An example of an HTML data file is shown below:

```
<DIV ID="PersonID">101</DIV>
<SPAN ID="FirstName">Jan</SPAN>
<H1 ID="LastName">Lloyd</H1>
<PRE ID="PersonID">104</PRE>
<SPAN ID="FirstName">Rob</SPAN>
<H2 ID="LastName">Smith</H1>
```

Each unique ID field would translate to a column, giving us three columns: PersonID, FirstName, and LastName. There would be two rows in the data set because there are two sets of tags with the same ID fields. The actual HTML tag is ignored, as are HTML tags without an ID attribute.

The data is taken sequentially from the top down.

Class ID	25336921-03F9-11CF-8FD0-00AA00686F13
DLL	%SystemRoot%\System32\mshtml.dll
Prog ID	htmlfile_FullWindowEmbed

Instantiating the MSHTML DSO

```
<OBJECT ID="dsoAuthors" DATA="HTMLFile.html" HEIGHT="0" WIDTH="0">
</OBJECT>
```

The DATA attribute points to the HTML file containing the data.

Methods of the MSHTML DSO

The MSHTML DSO does not have any methods.

Properties of the MSHTML DSO

The Recordset Property

Returns the ADO Recordset object underlying this data control.

```
Recordset = datacontrol.Recordset
```

The underlying recordset is a standard ADO Recordset object, so you can therefore use the Recordset methods to manipulate the records in the data control. For example, if using single table binding you could have several buttons to perform the navigation:

```
<INPUT ID="cmdFirst" TYPE="BUTTON" VALUE="<<"
    onclick="dsoAuthors.Recordset.MoveFirst();">

<INPUT ID="cmdPrevious" TYPE="BUTTON" VALUE="<"
    onclick="dsoAuthors.Recordset.MovePrevious();">

<INPUT ID="cmdNext" TYPE="BUTTON" VALUE=">"
    onclick="dsoAuthors.Recordset.MoveNext();">

<INPUT ID="cmdLast" TYPE="BUTTON" VALUE=">>"
    onclick="dsoAuthors.Recordset.MoveLast();">
```

Events of the MSHTML DSO

The MSHTML DSO does not have any distinct events, although it responds to the standard data binding events which are discussed in the Events section of this chapter.

The XML Java Applet in IE 4

The XML DSO Java Applet ships with IE 4 and provides read-only access to XML data. It's particularly useful for hierarchical data.

A known problem with the XML DSO is that, when binding hierarchical data to HTML tables in a situation where you have a parent record with different child records, the second child record does not get bound correctly. A way around this is to use the C++ XML DSO, which can be instantiated either in an OBJECT tag or from within code. The C++ XML DSO is covered under the IE 5 section.

Instantiating the Java Applet

```
<APPLET CODE="com.ms.xml.dso.XMLDSO.class" ID="dsoAuthors"
                       HEIGHT="0" WIDTH="0" MAYSCRIPT="True">
    <PARAM NAME="URL" VALUE="XMLDataFile.xml">
    <PARAM NAME="SCHEMA" VALUE="SchemaFile.xml">
</APPLET>
```

The Java Applet has a visible interface, so you can give it a height and width (60 and 100 perhaps). The interface shows trace messages showing successful loading of the XML data or error messages. Rather conveniently, the interface is green when successful and red for errors.

You can also embed XML directly between the APPLET tags:

```
<APPLET CODE="com.ms.xml.dso.XMLDSO.class" ID="dsoAuthors"
        HEIGHT="0" WIDTH="0" MAYSCRIPT="True">
<?xml version="1.0"?>
<AUTHORS>
  <AUTHOR>
    <au_id>101</au_id>
    <au_fname>Jan</au_fname>
    <au_lname>Lloyd</au_lname>
  </AUTHOR>
  <AUTHOR>
    <au_id>104</au_id>
```

9

Remote Data Services

```
        <au_fname>Rob</au_fname>
        <au_lname>Smith</au_lname>
    </AUTHOR>
  </AUTHORS>
  </APPLET>
```

Essentially, the Java DSO is a forerunner of the XML Data Island in IE 5.

Methods of the IE 4 XML DSO

The clear Method
Clears the data from the DSO

```
datacontrol.clear
```

After this control the data control is empty.

The getDocument Method
Returns the loaded document.

```
datacontrol.getDocument
```

This is synonymous with the `Document` property.

The getError Method
Returns the most recent error encountered by the DSO.

```
datacontrol.getError
```

This is synonymous with the `Error` property.

The getSchema Method
Returns the XML schema of the DSO.

```
datacontrol.getSchema (Format)
```

Parameter	Type	Description
Format	Boolean	`True` to format the schema, `False` to return the schema without formatting.

Formatting the schema simply adds whitespace, to allow it to be displayed in a more readable form.

The getXML Method
Returns the XML data.

```
datacontrol.getXML (Format)
```

Parameter	Type	Description
Format	Boolean	True to format the XML data, False to return the XML data without formatting.

Formatted data appears neatly embedded (just like IE 5 does when you view an XML file), whereas unformatted means that the XML is just returned as is, with no formatting.

The init Method

Reloads the XML Data.

```
datacontrol.init
```

If the URL PARAM exists, then the VALUE is used to reload the XML data. If no URL PARAM exists, the XML data is taken to be inline, between the APPLET tags. If no XML exists, then no action is taken.

The load Method

Loads the XML specified in the supplied file.

```
datacontrol.load (File)
```

Parameter	Type	Description
File	String	The URL of the XML Data document.

For local URLs, the load method is dependent upon the security settings of your browser, which may not allow access to the local drives.

This differs from the init method since you can specify the source of the XML data, whereas the init method only reloads existing data.

The save Method

Saves the XML to a file.

```
datacontrol.save (File)
```

Parameter	Type	Description
File	String	The name of the file to save the XML into.

For local URLs, the save method is dependent upon the security settings of your browser, which may not allow access to the local drives.

The setRoot Method

Sets the root of the document for the DSO.

```
datacontrol.setRoot (elem)
```

Remote Data Services

9

Parameter	Type	Description
elem	Element	The element to set as the root node of the DSO.

The updateSchema Method

Updates the SCHEMA whenever the document is changed.

```
datacontrol.updateSchema
```

This method is automatically called by the clear, load, and setRoot methods.

Properties of the IE 4 XML DSO

The Document Property

Returns a DOM document object containing the DSO document.

```
Object = datacontrol.Document
```

This is synonymous with the getDocument method.

The Error Property

Returns the most recent error description encountered by the DSO.

```
String = datacontrol.Error
```

This is synonymous with the getError method.

The URL Property

Identifies the URL of the source of the data.

```
datacontrol.URL = String
String = datacontrol.URL
```

Events of the XML DSO

The Java XML DSO does not implement any events directly, although DSO events are available through the APPLET. See the section on Events later in this chapter for more details.

The XML Tag in IE 5

Internet Explorer 5 natively supports XML by way of an XML tag. Embedding XML Data into HTML is called using XML Data Islands, and there are two ways to specify the data. The first way is to use the SRC attribute to specify the name of the XML data file:

```
<XML ID="dsoAuthors" SRC="authors.xml"></XML>
```

Alternatively, you can embed the XML data between the XML tags:

```
<XML ID="dsoAuthors"
<?xml version="1.0"?>
<AUTHORS>
  <AUTHOR>
    <au_id>101</au_id>
    <au_fname>Jan</au_fname>
    <au_lname>Lloyd</au_lname>
  </AUTHOR>
  <AUTHOR>
    <au_id>104</au_id>
    <au_fname>Rob</au_fname>
    <au_lname>Smith</au_lname>
  </AUTHOR>
</AUTHORS>
</XML>
```

Class ID	550dda30-0541-11d2-9ca9-0060b0ec3d39
DLL	%SystemRoot%\System32\msxml.dll
Prog ID	Microsoft.XMLDSO

Instantiating the XML DSO as an Object

Since XML is handled by MSXML, which is a COM object, it can be also created using an HTML OBJECT tag.

```
<OBJECT CLASSID="clsid:550dda30-0541-11d2-9ca9-0060b0ec3d39"
                             ID="dsoAuthors" HEIGHT="0"
WIDTH="0">
</OBJECT>
```

This method also works for the XML DSO in IE 4.

Code

You can also create and load the XML DSO from code:

```
<SCRIPT LANGUAGE="JavaScript">
function window.onload()
{
  var docAuthors = XMLDSO.XMLDocument;
  docAuthors.loadXML("authors.xml")
}
</SCRIPT>
```

or:

```
<SCRIPT LANGUAGE="JavaScript">
function window.onload()
{
  var docAuthors = new ActiveXDocument("Microsoft.xmldom");
  docAuthors.loadXML("authors.xml")
}
</SCRIPT>
```

Remote Data Services

9

Methods of the IE 5 XML DSO

The XML DSO does not implement any methods directly, although the DSO does expose the XML Document object, which allows loading and parsing of XML.

> For more details on this you should consult an XML DOM reference book, such as *XML IE 5 Programmer's Reference* (Wrox, ISBN 1-861001-57-6), and for more details on XML you should consult *Professional XML* (Wrox, ISBN 1-861003-11-0). If you don't know anything about XML, then the *Beginning XML* book (ISBN 1-861004-41-2) is a good place to start.

Properties of the IE 5 XML DSO

The JavaDSOCompatible Property

Indicates whether or not the DSO behaves in a way that is compatible with the Java XML DSO supplied with IE 4.

```
datacontrol.JavaDSOCompatible = Boolean
Boolean = datacontrol.JavaDSOCompatible
```

A value of True indicates that the same behavior as the IE 4 Java DSO is applied when parsing XML. The default value is False, which uses the new parsing mode. See the Parsing Rules section for more details on how the XML is parsed into rows and columns.

The readyState Property

Indicates the state of the DSO with regard to its data.

```
String = datacontrol.readyState
```

Values for the readyState are:

❑ uninitialized, to indicate the object is not initialized with data

❑ loading, to indicate the object is currently loading data

❑ interactive, to indicate the object has not fully loaded its data, although it can be interacted with

❑ complete, to indicate the data is completely loaded

The XMLDocument Property

Returns or sets the XML DOM Document for the data control.

```
datacontrol.XMLDocument = XMLDOMDocument
XMLDOMDocument = datacontrol.XMLDocument
```

This allows you access to the DOMDocument object, allowing manipulation of the XML through the DOM. For example:

```
var doc = dsoXMLBooklist.XMLDocument;
var el = doc.getElementsByTagName("CATEGORY").item(0);
alert(el.xml);
```

This searches for XML tags by name and retrieves the first tag that matches.

Events of the XML DSO

The XML DSO does not implement any events directly, although DSO events are available through the OBJECT. See the section on Events later in this chapter for more details.

Parsing Rules

There are set rules for how the XML data is parsed into rows and columns:

❑ Each sub-element and attribute becomes a column in the same row.

❑ The column name is the sub-element or attribute name, unless the parent element has an attribute and sub-element of the same name. In this case an exclamation mark (!) is added to the beginning of the column name.

❑ A column based on an attribute is always a simple column, that is, one containing normal string or number data.

❑ If an element has sub-elements or attributes then the column becomes a row column. This corresponds to a chapter column in a hierarchical recordset.

❑ Multiple instances of sub-elements under different parents use different rules. If any instance implies a row, then all instances become rows. If all instances imply a column, then the element becomes a column.

❑ Each row has an extra column called $Text. This contains the sub-elements of the row concatenated together. This is particularly useful when your XML elements have attributes and you wish to bind data to HTML elements. This is explained in more detail in the Data Binding section.

When in Java Compatibility mode, the rules are simpler:

❑ Any element that contains another element is a row

❑ Text-only elements are columns

❑ Attributes are ignored

If you want to define your own rules as to how the XML elements are converted into rows or columns then you need to add a Document Type Definition (DTD) to the XML data:

```
<XML ID="dsoAuthors"
<?xml version="1.0" ?>
<!DOCTYPE AUTHORS [
    <!ELEMENT AUTHORS (AUTHOR+)>
    <!ELEMENT AUTHOR (au_id, au_fname, au_lname)>
```

Remote Data Services

```
        <!ELEMENT au_id (#PCDATA)>
        <!ELEMENT au_fname (#PCDATA)>
        <!ELEMENT au_lname (#PCDATA)>
]>

<AUTHORS>
  <AUTHOR>
    <au_id>101</au_id>
    <au_fname>Jan</au_fname>
    <au_lname>Lloyd</au_lname>
  </AUTHOR>
  <AUTHOR>
    . . .
</AUTHORS>
```

RDS DataSpace

The DataSpace object is responsible for creating a client-side proxy to communicate with the server, and often goes hand-in-hand with the DataFactory object. When you use a DSO, a DataSpace object is created on the client behind the scenes, connecting to the web server automatically (a bit like a proxy/stub). The DataSpace performs the marshaling, facilitates the packaging, unpackaging, and transport of the data from the client to the server, and vice-versa.

Class ID	BD96C556-65A3-11D0-983A-00C04FC29E36
Source	C:\Program Files\Common Files\System\MSADC\msadco.dll
Prog ID	RDS.DataSpace

Instantiating the RDS DataSpace Object

```
<OBJECT CLASSID="clsid:BD96C556-65A3-11D0-983A-00C04FC29E36"
        ID="dspDataSpace" HEIGHT="0" WIDTH="0">
</OBJECT>
```

Methods of the DataSpace Object

The CreateObject Method

Creates a server-side object.

```
variant = dataspace.CreateObject (ProgID, Connection)
```

Name	Type	Description
ProgID	String	The Program ID (ProgID or class string) of the object to create.
Connection	String	Connection details of the web server or machine name.

The connection details can be a URL for a web server, a UNC name for a machine, or an empty string for a local, in-process business object. For example:

```
dfFactory = dspSpace.CreateObject ("RDSServer.DataFactory",
                               "http://servername.com");
```

This creates an instance of the `DataFactory` component, which is explained shortly, on the web server **servername.com**. If you use an ASP file instead of an HTML file you can use the `ServerVariables` method of the `Request` object to extract the name of the web server:

```
dfFactory = dspSpace.CreateObject ("RDSServer.DataFactory",
                http://<%=Request.ServerVariables("SERVER_NAME")%>");
```

You are not limited to creating the `DataFactory` with this method – you can create any COM object. This is discussed in more detail in the DataSpace and DataFactory Usage section, later in this chapter.

Properties of the DataSpace Object

The InternetTimeout Property

Indicates the HTTP timeout in milliseconds.

```
dataspace.InternetTimeout = Long
Long = dataspace.InternetTimeout
```

When creating proxy objects, the `DataSpace` will wait for the amount of time specified in this property. If no response is received from the server, then an error is generated. The default value is 300000, that is, 5 minutes.

Events of the DataSpace Object

The `DataSpace` object has no events.

RDSServer DataFactory

The `DataFactory` is the server-side part of the proxy process, being used to marshal data from the server to the client. You can use the `DataFactory` to execute SQL queries on the server, and return the data to the client.

Although the `DataFactory` is a server-side object, you can instantiate it with a command in the HTML in the client page:

```
dfFactory = dspSpace.CreateObject ("RDSServer.DataFactory",
                               "http://servername.com");
```

Class ID	9381D8F5-0288-11d0-9501-00AA00B911A5
Source	C:\Program Files\Common Files\System\MSADC\msadcf.dll
Prog ID	RDSServer.DataFactory

Methods of the DataFactory Object

The ConvertToString Method

Converts a recordset into a MIME64 string that represents the recordset data.

```
String = DataFactory.ConvertToString(Recordset)
```

Parameter	Type	Description
Recordset	Recordset	An ADO Recordset to convert to a string.

This method was useful in early versions of ADO (pre 2.0) when you needed to transfer a recordset between server and client. Recordsets from ADO 2.0 onwards can now marshal themselves across HTTP, so this method is less used.

The CreateRecordSet Method

Creates and returns an empty disconnected recordset.

```
Object = DataFactory.CreateRecordSet(ColumnInfos)
```

Parameter	Type	Description
ColumnInfos	Variant	An array of arrays containing the column details.

ColumnInfos should be a variant array, with each column being defined by four array elements:

- ❑ Name, for the name of the column
- ❑ Type, for the data type of the column
- ❑ Size, for the size of the column; for fixed length types this must be -1
- ❑ Nullability, to indicate if the column can contain a null value

For the data type you should use one of the ADO DataTypeEnum values (except for adChapter, adDBFileTime, adEmpty, adFileTime, adIDispatch, adIUnknown, adLongVarChar, adPropVariant, adUserDefined, adVariant, and adVarNumeric, which are not supported). For a full list of these data types and their associated values you should consult Appendix B.

The column arrays should be appended to another array, which becomes the method argument. For example:

```
<SCRIPT LANGUAGE="JavaScript">

function cmdCreateNew.onclick()
{
    var aField1 = Array(4);
    var aField2 = Array(4);
    var aField3 = Array(4);
    var aField4 = Array(4);
    var aCols = Array(4);

    // create the individual columns
    aField1[0] = "ID";              // name
    aField1[1] = 3;                 // type - adInteger
    aField1[2] = -1;                // size
    aField1[3] = false;             // nullability

    aField2[0] = "FirstName";       // name
    aField2[1] = 202;               // type - adVarWChar
    aField2[2] = -1;                // size
    aField2[3] = false;             // nullability

    aField3[0] = "LastName";        // name
    aField3[1] = 202;               // type - adVarWChar
    aField3[2] = -1;                // size
    aField3[3] = false;             // nullability

    aField4[0] = "DateOfBirth";     // name
    aField4[1] = 7;                 // type - adDate
    aField4[2] = -1;                // size
    aField4[3] = false;             // nullability

    // add the columns to an array
    aCols[0] = aField1;
    aCols[1] = aField2;
    aCols[2] = aField3;
    aCols[3] = aField4;

    // create a new recordset
    recNew = DataFactory.CreateRecordset (aCols);
}
</SCRIPT>
```

The Query Method

Executes a SQL query and creates a `Recordset`.

```
Recordset = DataFactory.Query(Connection, Query)
```

Parameter	Type	Description
Connection	String	The connection details of the data store.
Query	String	The SQL query to run.

9

Remote Data Services

The `Query` string should be in the native database format. For example:

```
dfFactory = dspSpace.CreateObject ("RDSServer.DataFactory",
                                    "http://servername.com");
recAuthors = dfDataFactory.Query ("DSN=pubs",
                                   "SELECT * FROM authors");
```

The SubmitChanges Method

Given a recordset with pending changes, this method submits them to the database identified in the connection string

```
DataFactory.SubmitChanges(Connection, Recordset)
```

Parameter	Type	Description
Connection	String	The connection details of the data store.
Recordset	Recordset	The `Recordset` containing the changes.

When sending changes back to the data source, only the changes are sent, and one of two actions can occur. All of the changes succeed, or all of them fail. It is not possible for some changes to succeed whilst others fail. Handling of errors is covered in chapter 5, in the discussion on Conflict Resolution.

Properties of the DataFactory Object

The `DataFactory` has no properties.

Events of the DataFactory Object

The `DataFactory` has no events.

DataSpace and DataFactory Usage

The `DataSpace` and `DataFactory` perform the client and server ends of the data marshaling. Using the two together with a data control, it's easy to get data from a server, allow the user to modify it, and then send those changes back to the server. All this can be performed over HTTP, and therefore allows the creation of genuine web applications.

In its simplest form you can use the `DataFactory` on the server to perform your data access:

```
<!-- normal RDS DataControl object, no parameters set -->
<OBJECT ID="dsoDataControl"
        CLASSID="clsid:BD96C556-65A3-11D0-983A-00C04FC29E33">
</OBJECT>

<!-- client-side RDS DataSpace object -->
<OBJECT ID="dspSpace"
        CLASSID="CLSID:BD96C556-65A3-11D0-983A-00C04FC29E36">
```

```
</OBJECT>

<SCRIPT LANGUAGE="JavaScript">

  // create a DataFactory object
  dfFactory = dspSpace.CreateObject("RDSServer.DataFactory",
                                     "http://servername.com");

  // create a recordset using the DataFactory
  recAuthors = dfFactory.Query("DSN=pubs",
                                "SELECT * FROM authors");

  // assign the recordset to the DataControl
  dsoDataControl.SourceRecordset = recAuthors;

</SCRIPT>
```

This does expose one flaw – that of the connection details being visible at the client. A way around this is to use a custom business component. This will be a COM-compliant object (and therefore only available in IE), or perhaps an ActiveX DLL written in Visual Basic and hosted on the server.

```
<!-- normal RDS DataControl object, no parameters set -->
<OBJECT ID="dsoDataControl"
         CLASSID="clsid:BD96C556-65A3-11D0-983A-00C04FC29E33">
</OBJECT>

<!-- client-side RDS DataSpace object -->
<OBJECT ID="dspSpace"
         CLASSID="CLSID:BD96C556-65A3-11D0-983A-00C04FC29E36">
</OBJECT>

<SCRIPT LANGUAGE="JavaScript">

  // create a custom business object
  objWroxBooks = dspSpace.CreateObject("Wrox.Books",
                                        "http://servername.com");

  // create a recordset using the business object
  recAuthors = objWroxBooks.GetAuthors();

  // assign the recordset to the DataControl
  dsoDataControl.SourceRecordset = recAuthors;

</SCRIPT>
```

The business object should return a disconnected, client-side recordset.

DHTML Events

When using Data Source Objects in HTML pages, the DSO extends the DHTML event model with events of its own. Although these appear as part of the DSO they are in fact implemented by DHTML, and therefore appear on all HTML Elements that can be sources of data.

The following table lists the events that are generated by the DSO:

Event	Cancelable	Applies to
onbeforeupdate	True	bound elements
onafterupdate	False	bound elements
onrowenter	False	DSO
onrowexit	True	DSO
onbeforeunload	False	window
ondataavailable	False	DSO
ondatasetcomplete	False	DSO
ondatasetchanged	False	DSO
onerrorupdate	True	bound elements
onreadystatechange	False	DSO
oncellchange	False	DSO
onrowsinserted	False	DSO
onrowsdelete	False	DSO

All events are raised (that is bubble) to parent objects, apart from onbeforeunload, which applies to the window object, and therefore has no parent.

The oncellchange, onrowsinserted, onrowsdelete events are new for IE 5.

Events that are marked as cancelable allow cancellation of the event, and thus can be used to prevent certain actions taking place. For example, canceling the onbeforeupdate event can prevent data changes taking place.

The onbeforeupdate Event

This event is fired when an element is about to lose focus and the data in that element has been changed.

This event is not fired if the data is changed from within scripting code.

Returning False from the event procedure will cancel the event, and stop the user leaving a data bound field. For example:

```
<SCRIPT FOR=txtDateOfBirth EVENT=onbeforeupdate>

    if ( some test on the date here)
        bRV = false;
    else
        bRV = true;

    event.cancelBubble = true;

    return bRV;

</SCRIPT>
```

In this example, the `onbeforeupdate` of the `txtDateOfBirth` field is used, which performs some validation upon the entered date, before the update takes place. The validation sets a variable to be `true` if the date is valid, and `false` if invalid. This value is used as the return value for the procedure, which prevents the update from taking place, and prevents the user from leaving the field. The `cancelBubble` method is set to `true` to prevent this event from being raised to parent objects.

The onafterupdate Event

This event fires after the data has been transferred to the data provider. If the `onbeforeupdate` event is canceled, this event does not fire.

The onrowenter Event

This event fires when a new row of data becomes the current row. You can use this to process the data before it is shown (perhaps to format it), or to update other elements on the page.

The onrowexit Event

This event fires before the current record pointer moves to a new row. This could happen if you use recordset navigation, if you delete the current record, or if you leave the page.

You can use this event to perform validation at the record level. In a similar way to the example in the `onbeforeupdate` event, you could perform validation for the fields in an entire row, rather than validating each field.

The onbeforeunload Event

This event fires before the current page becomes unloaded. This could be caused by navigating to another page, using the browser's Back or Forward buttons, Refreshing the page, submitting a request from a FORM element, or selecting from the Favorites folder.

This event cannot be cancelled.

The ondataavailable Event

This event is fired by the DSO when records are available for use. This does not guarantee that all of the records are available (in asynchronous operations), rather that some are available.

This event may fire several times, or may not fire at all. This depends upon the DSO.

The ondatasetcomplete Event

This event fires when all of the data is loaded into the DSO.

This `event` object has a property, `reason`, which identifies the download state. The values for this are:

- ❏ 0, to indicate a successful download of data.
- ❏ 1, to indicate the download of data was aborted.
- ❏ 2, to indicate a failure in downloading the data.

Remote Data Services

9

For example:

```
function dsoAuthors.ondatasetcomplete()
{
  if (event.reason = 2)
    alert ("Failed to load data");
}
```

The ondatasetchanged Event

This event is fired after a new data set is requested, or when the current set of data is filtered or sorted.

The data might not be available when this event fires, but the meta data (fields, data types, etc.) will be available.

You could use this event to dynamically populate other controls.

The onerrorupdate Event

This event fires when there is an error transferring the data from the server to the client.

If this event is cancelled, system dialog boxes describing the error are not shown.

The onreadystatechange Event

This event fires when the state of the DSO changes. You can examine the readyState property of the this object (or the Me object in VBScript) to identify the state, which will be one of:

❑ uninitialized, to indicate that the object is not initialized with data

❑ loading, to indicate that the object is currently loading its data

❑ interactive, to indicate that the object can be interacted with even though it is not fully loaded

❑ complete, to indicate that the data is completely loaded

The oncellchange Event

This event is fired when data changes in any element. You can use the dataFld property to indicate which field changed.

The onrowsdelete Event

This event is fired before rows are deleted. While the event is not cancelable, you can use the bookmarks collection to examine the deleted records.

The onrowsinserted Event

This event is fired after rows are added. While the event is not cancelable, you can use the bookmarks collection to examine the new records.

Data Binding

There are many HTML fields that can be bound to DSOs. There are four attributes that affect data binding:

❑ DATASRC, which indicates the DSO that is supplying the data. You should use the ID of the DSO, with a hash (#) symbol in front of the ID value.

❑ DATAFLD, which indicates the field in the DSO to bind to.

❑ DATAFORMATAS, which indicates how the bound data is to be formatted.

❑ DATAPAGESIZE, which indicates the number of rows to show when using tabular data binding.

The table below shows which elements support data binding:

HTML Element	Bound Property	Update Data?	Tabular binding?	Display as HTML?
A	href	No	No	No
APPLET	PARAM	Yes	No	No
BUTTON	innerText and innerHTML	No	No	Yes
DIV	innerText and innerHTML	No	No	Yes
FRAME	src	No	No	No
IFRAME	src	No	No	No
IMG	src	No	No	No
INPUT TYPE=CHECKBOX	checked	Yes	No	No
INPUT TYPE=HIDDEN	value	Yes	No	No
INPUT TYPE=LABEL	value	Yes	No	No
INPUT TYPE=PASSWORD	value	Yes	No	No
INPUT TYPE=RADIO	checked	Yes	No	No
INPUT TYPE=TEXT	value	Yes	No	No
LABEL	innerText and innerHTML	No	No	Yes
LEGEND	innerText and innerHTML	No	No	No

9

Remote Data Services

HTML Element	Bound property	Update data?	Tabular binding?	Display as HTML?
MARQUEE	innerText and innerHTML	No	No	Yes
OBJECT	param	Yes	No	No
SELECT	text of selected option	Yes	No	No
SPAN	innerText and innerHTML	No	No	Yes
TABLE	none	No	Yes	No
TEXTAREA	value	Yes	No	No

Tabular Binding

Tabular data binding involves the use of TABLE elements. The table is bound to a DSO and the table cells are bound to individual columns. For example:

```
<TABLE DATASRC="#dsoAuthors">
 <THEAD>
  <TR>
    <TH>ID</TH>
    <TH>First Name</TH>
    <TH>Last Name</TH>
  </TR>
 </THEAD>
 <TBODY>
  <TR>
    <TD><SPAN DATAFLD="au_id"></SPAN></TD>
    <TD><SPAN DATAFLD="au_fname"></SPAN></TD>
    <TD><SPAN DATAFLD="au_lname"></SPAN></TD>
  </TR>
 </TBODY>
 </TABLE>
```

The table is automatically created, with the number of rows being determined by the number of rows in the recordset. To limit the number of rows you can use the DATAPAGESIZE attribute:

```
<TABLE ID="tblAuthors" DATASRC="#dsoAuthors" DATAPAGESIZE="10">
 <THEAD>
   <TR>
     <TH>ID</TH>
     <TH>First Name</TH>
     <TH>Last Name</TH>
   </TR>
 </THEAD>
 <TBODY>   <TR>
     <TD><SPAN DATAFLD="au_id"></SPAN></TD>
     <TD><SPAN DATAFLD="au_fname"></SPAN></TD>
     <TD><SPAN DATAFLD="au_lname"></SPAN></TD>
   </TR>
 </TBODY>
 </TABLE>
```

You can then add buttons to move through the pages:

```
<INPUT TYPE="BUTTON" ID="cmdNextPage" VALUE=">P"
                     onclick="tblAuthors.nextPage();">
<INPUT TYPE="BUTTON" ID="cmdPreviousPage" VALUE="<P"
                     onclick="tblAuthors.previousPage();">
```

Single Record Binding

Single record binding involves displaying a single record at a time. Each HTML element that is to bind to data specifies both the DATASRC and the DATAFLD attributes. For example:

```
ID: <INPUT TYPE="TEXT" DATASRC="#dsoAuthors"
                       DATAFLD="au_id" SIZE=6><P>
First Name: <INPUT TYPE="TEXT" DATASRC="#dsoAuthors"
                       DATAFLD="au_fname" SIZE=20><P>
Last Name: <INPUT TYPE="TEXT" DATASRC="#dsoAuthors"
                       DATAFLD="au_lname" SIZE=20><P>
Title: <SELECT DATASRC="#dsoAuthors" DATAFLD="au_title" SIZE=4>
       <OPTION>Mr
       <OPTION>Mrs
       <OPTION>Miss
       </SELECT><P>
```

To navigate through the recordset you can add a series of buttons:

```
<INPUT TYPE="BUTTON" ID="cmdFirst" VALUE="<<"
                   onclick="dsoAuthors.recordset.MoveFirst();">
<INPUT TYPE="BUTTON" ID="cmdPrevious" VALUE="<"
                   onclick="dsoAuthors.recordset.MovePrevious();">
<INPUT TYPE="BUTTON" ID="cmdNext" VALUE=">"
                   onclick="dsoAuthors.recordset.MoveNext();">
<INPUT TYPE="BUTTON" ID="cmdLast" VALUE=">>"
                   onclick="dsoAuthors.recordset.MoveLast();">
```

Since the HTML elements are bound to the data source, moving through the data source refreshes the UI.

Formatting Data

You can use the DATAFORMATAS property to specify how the data from the DSO is to be formatted. A value of HTML means that any HTML elements in the data are applied, and a value of TEXT means that any HTML elements are shown as plain text.

For example:

```
<TABLE DATASRC="#dsoAuthors" DATAPAGESIZE="10">
 <TR>
  <TD><SPAN DATAFLD="au_id"></SPAN></TD>
  <TD><SPAN DATAFLD="au_fname" DATAFORMATAS="HTML"></SPAN></TD>
  <TD><SPAN DATAFLD="au_lname"></SPAN></TD>
 </TR>
</TABLE>
```

This allows formatting, such as <B> or <I> tags to emphasize or italicize text, to be embedded within the data.

Updating Data

Many DSOs can update the server with any changes made to the data. This is simply a matter of calling the submitChanges method of the DSO. For example:

```
<INPUT TYPE="BUTTON" ID="cmdSubmit" VALUE="Submit"
                    onclick="dsoAuthors.submitChanges();">
```

When using the DataFactory directly, you also use the submitChanges method, but you must also specify the connection information and the recordset as arguments:

```
<SCRIPT LANGAUGE="JavaScript">
function cmdSubmit.onclick()
{
   dfFactory.SubmitChanges("DSN=pubs", dsoAuthors.recordset);
}
</SCRIPT>
```

If you are using a custom business object, then you have to provide a custom method to accept the changed recordset. For example, a Visual Basic component could implement a method like this:

```
Public Sub UpdateRecords (oRec As ADODB.Recordset)
    ' set the connection to the data store
    ' assumes g_sConnect is a global string previously set
    oRec.ActiveConnection = m_sConnect

    ' now update the source data
    oRec.UpdateBatch
End Sub
```

This could be called from the same page that created the custom object:

```
<SCRIPT LANGUAGE="JavaScript">
function cmdUpdate.onclick()
{
  ' get the recordset
  oRec = dsoAuthors.Recordset

  ' marshal only changed records
  oRec.MarshalOptions = 1;   // adMarshalModifiedOnly

  ' call custom component method
  objWroxBooks.UpdateRecords (oRec)
}
</SCRIPT>
```

Security Issues

If you are using MTS as part of your data application then you need to read the article *BUG: MTS Impersonation Returns Incorrect Caller When Using RDS* at http://support.microsoft.com/support/kb/articles/q184/7/02.asp. This details a large security hole in RDS. There is a patch available, for which you must call Microsoft Support.

From version 2.0 of RDS, a new set of security features was added, based around a configuration file. When RDS is installed an INI file called `msdfmap.ini` is placed in your `Windows` (or `WINNT`) folder. This file allows you to completely customize the settings for the `DataFactory` when it is instantiated by a client. You should consult the RDS documentation for full details of this, as well as a series of MSDN articles:

❑ Using the Customization Handler Feature in RDS 2.0

❑ Remote Data Service in MDAC 2.0

❑ Security and Your Web Server

❑ ADO and RDS Security Issues in Microsoft Internet Explorer

Custom Business Objects

Microsoft's Internet Information Server has security settings that restrict which objects can be instantiated by the `CreateObject` method of the `DataSpace` object. If you are using custom business objects then you need to add the details of these objects to the registry.

> **Remember to back up the Registry first before making any changes to it.**

The simplest way is to create a `.reg` file:

```
REGEDIT4
[HKEY_CLASSES_ROOT\CLSID\{your_component_guid}\Implemented
Categories\{7DD95801-9882-11CF-9FA9-00AA006C42C4}]
[HKEY_CLASSES_ROOT\CLSID\{your_component_guid}\Implemented
Categories\{7DD95802-9882-11CF-9FA9-00AA006C42C4}]
[HKEY_LOCAL_MACHINE\System\CurrentControlSet\Services\W3SVC\
Parameters\ADCLaunch\your_component_class_string]
```

The first line tells `regedit` that this is a valid `.reg` file. The next two entries enable the **Safe for Scripting** setting, and the third allows IIS to instantiate the component on the server. Note that each entry should be on one line, not wrapped like the code shown here. Place the file on the server machine, then double-click it to merge the values into the registry.

I thank God I am as honest as any man

living that is an old man and no honester th

Can counsel and speak comfort to the

Which they themselves not feel.

He wears his faith but as the fashion of

As merry as the day

He hath indeed better bettered expectation

(Act i. Sc. i.).

Much Ado About Nothing.

He wears his faith but as the fashion of his hat.
(Ibid)

As merry as the day is long.

h indeed better bettered expectation

(Act i. Sc. i.)

(Ibid)

Much Ado About Nothing.

Can counsel and speak comfort to that grief

Which they themselves not feel.

He wears his faith but as the fashion of his hat.
(Ibid)

I was not born under

a rhyming plane

I was not born under a rhyming plane
(Sc. 2

For there was never yet

That could endure the to

merry as the day is long

(Sc. 2)

Can counsel and speak comfort to that grief

Which they themselves not feel.

(Ibid)

He hath indeed better bettered expectation

(Act i. Sc.

I thank God I am as honest as any

living that is an old man and no honest

He wears his faith but as the fashion of his ha

(Ibi

Much Ado About Nothing.

For there was never yet philospher
That could endure the toothache patiently.

(Ibid)

For there was never yet philospher
That could endure the toothache patiently

I was not born u

themselves not feel.

(Ibid)

10

ADOX Objects and Collections

This chapter deals with the ADO Extensions for Data Definition and Security, ADOX. This is the big new feature of ADO 2.1, and allows the manipulation of the metadata of the data store, through ADO objects and methods; thus removing the necessity to learn the explicit syntax of the data provider.

This is made possible because the ADOX objects abstract the data store's objects into an easily workable form. For example; most databases have users and groups to deal with security issues – to allow these to be easily accessed by developers, ADOX has `User` and `Group` objects.

Here's a look at the object model again:

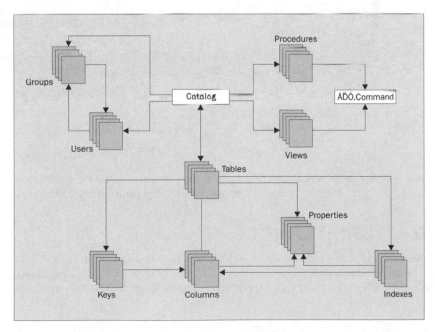

The ADOX objects are described individually. As the handling of collections is the same for each collection, they have been included as a single section at the end of the chapter.

> **For ADOX 2.6, the only new feature has been the addition of a Properties collection to the User and Group objects.**

Of the OLE DB providers currently available, the Jet provider has the fullest support for ADOX. Other providers may not support all properties and methods. The table below shows which features are *not* supported for the SQL Server and Oracle providers:

Provider	Object/ Collection	Feature *not* supported
SQL Server	Catalog Object	Create method.
	Tables Collection	Properties are read only for existing tables.
	Views Collection	Not supported.
	Procedures Collection	Append method, Delete method, Command property.
	Users Collection	Not supported.
	Groups Collection	Not supported.
Oracle	Catalog Object	Create method.
	Tables Collection	Append method, Delete method, Properties are read only for existing tables.
	Views Collection	Append method, Delete method, Command property.
	Procedures Collection	Append method, Delete method, Command property.
	Indexes Collection	Append method, Delete method.
	Keys Collection	Append method, Delete method.
	Users Collection	Not supported.
	Groups Collection	Not supported.

If you wish to use ADOX against a different provider, you should consult the provider-specific documentation, for more details on supported properties for ADOX.

The Catalog Object

The Catalog object is the parent for all objects as it deals with catalog or data store information. The Catalog can be equated to a single connection to a data store, and, the objects underneath the Catalog are the objects (metadata) within that data store.

Methods of the Catalog Object

The Create Method

Creates a new catalog. In most cases this means the creation of a new database.

```
String = Catalog.Create(ConnectString)
Set Connection = Catalog.Create(ConnectString)
```

Name	Type	Description
ConnectString	String	The connection string for the catalog to be created.

The return value is either a connection string or an ADO Connection object, depending upon how you call the method. For example, the following line of code sets strConn to the connection string of the new database:

```
Dim objCat    As New ADOX.Catalog
Dim strConn   As String

strConn = objCat.Create("Provider=Microsoft.Jet.OLEDB.4.0;" & _
                        "Data Source=C:\temp\newdb.mdb")
```

The following code, however, sets objConn to a Connection object:

```
Dim objCat    As New ADOX.Catalog
Dim objConn   As ADODB.Connection

Set objConn = objCat.Create("Provider=Microsoft.Jet.OLEDB.4.0;" & _
                        "Data Source=C:\temp\newdb.mdb")
```

If you use a scripting language (such as VBScript), where variables are all Variants, then the Set keyword determines what type of variable you receive back from the Create method. Without using Set, you get a string (the connection string), and with Set you get a pointer to a Connection object.

The GetObjectOwner Method

Retrieves the user or group name of the owner of the specified object.

```
String = Catalog.GetObjectOwner(ObjectName, ObjectType,
[ObjectTypeId])
```

Name	Type	Description
ObjectName	String	The name of the object.
ObjectType	Object TypeEnum	The type of the object
ObjectTypeId	Variant	A GUID. If the object type is provider-specific and not a standard OLE DB object type, ObjectType must be set to adPermObjProviderSpecific.

`ObjectType` can be one of the following:

- ❑ `adPermObjColumn`, to specify that the object is a column.

- ❑ `adPermObjDatabase`, to specify that the object is a database.

- ❑ `adPermObjProcedure`, to specify that the object is a procedure.

- ❑ `adPermObjProviderSpecific`, to specify that the object is of a provider-specific type.

- ❑ `adPermObjTable`, to specify that the object is a table.

- ❑ `adPermObjView`, to specify that the object is a view.

> **For scripting languages, these constants are not in the include files supplied with ADO. They are available in Appendix I, as well as an include file from the supporting web site.**

Note that to use this method with the Jet provider you must explicitly set a security database. For example:

```
strConn = "Provider=Microsoft.Jet.OLEDB.4.0; " & _
          "Data Source=C:\temp\pubs.mdb; " & _
          "Jet.OLEDB:System Database=" & _
          "c:\Program Files\Microsoft Office\Office\System.mdw"

objCat.ActiveConnection = strConn
Print objCat.GetObjectOwner ("authors", adPermObjTable)
```

The SQL Server provider does not support this method.

The SetObjectOwner Method

Sets the user or group as the owner of the specified object.

```
Catalog.SetObjectOwner(ObjectName, ObjectType, UserName,
[ObjectTypeId])
```

Name	Type	Description
ObjectName	String	The name of the object.
ObjectType	ObjectTypeEnum	The type of the object.
OwnerName	String	The name of the User or Group who will be the new owner of the object.
ObjectTypeId	Variant	A GUID. If the object type is provider-specific and not a standard OLE DB object type, `ObjectType` must be set to `adPermObjProviderSpecific`.

ObjectType can be one of the following:

- ❏ adPermObjColumn, to specify that the object is a column.
- ❏ adPermObjDatabase, to specify that the object is a database.
- ❏ adPermObjProcedure, to specify that the object is a procedure.
- ❏ adPermObjProviderSpecific, to specify that the object is of a provider-specific type.
- ❏ adPermObjTable, to specify that the object is a table.
- ❏ adPermObjView, to specify that the object is a view.

To set the new owner of a table you would use this method like this:

```
objCat.SetObjectOwner "authors", adPermObjTable, "Jan"
```

Note that to use this method with the Jet Provider you must explicitly set a security database.

Properties of the Catalog Object

The ActiveConnection Property

Sets or retrieves the information detailing the connection to the data store.

```
String = Catalog.ActiveConnection
Catalog.ActiveConnection = String
Set Connection = Catalog.ActiveConnection
Set Catalog.ActiveConnection = Connection
```

The connection details can either be a valid ADO connection string, or an ADO Connection object. For example, either of the two following constructs is valid:

```
strConn = "Provider=Microsoft.Jet.OLEDB.4.0; Data
Source=c:\temp\pubs.mdb"
objConn.Open strConn
Set objCat.ActiveConnection = objConn
```

```
strConn = "Provider=Microsoft.Jet.OLEDB.4.0; Data
Source=c:\temp\pubs.mdb"
objCat.ActiveConnection strConn
```

Setting the ActiveConnection property to Nothing will close the catalog.

Collections of the Catalog Object

The objects that make up the Collections are briefly mentioned here, but are covered in more detail under each object heading.

10

ADOX: Object & Collections

The Tables Collection

Returns a collection of the tables that are contained in this catalog.

```
Set Tables = Catalog.Tables
```

This is the default collection.

The Groups Collection

Returns a collection of the user group accounts that are contained in this catalog.

```
Set Groups = Catalog.Groups
```

The Users Collection

Returns a collection of the user accounts that are contained in this catalog.

```
Set Users = Catalog.Users
```

The Procedures Collection

Returns a collection of the stored procedures that are contained in this catalog.

```
Set Procedures = Catalog.Procedures
```

The Views Collection

Returns a collection of the views that are contained in this catalog.

```
Set Views = Catalog.Views
```

The Table Object

The Table object contains all of the details (such as columns, keys, and so on) for a single table. It's equivalent to looking at the table in design view in the database and seeing the properties.

Methods of the Table Object

The Table object has no methods.

Properties of the Table Object

The DateCreated Property

Identifies the date upon which the table was created.

```
Variant = Table.DateCreated
```

The DateModified Property

Identifies the date when the table was last modified.

```
Variant = Table.DateModified
```

The Name Property

The name of the table.

```
Table.Name = String
String = Table.Name
```

The ParentCatalog Property

Identifies the parent catalog for the table.

```
Set Catalog = Table.ParentCatalog
Set Table.ParentCatalog = Catalog
```

You can use the `ParentCatalog` property to set provider-specific properties before the table is added to the catalog. For example:

```
Dim objCat As New ADOX.Catalog
Dim objTbl As New ADOX.Table

objCat.ActiveConnection = "Provider=Microsoft.Jet.OLEDB.4.0; " & _
                          "Data Source=c:\temp\pubs.mdb"

objTbl.Name = "tblNewTable"
objTbl.Columns.Append "FirstName", adVarWChar, 25
objTbl.Columns.Append "LastName", adVarWChar, 25
objTbl.Columns.Append "Age", adInteger

Set objTbl.ParentCatalog = objCat
objTbl.Properties("Jet.OLEDB:Table Validation Rule") = "[Age]>18"
objTbl.Properties("Jet.OLEDB:Table Validation Text") = "Age must be
over 18"

objCat.Tables.Append objTbl

Set objTbl = Nothing
Set objCat = Nothing
```

The Type Property

Identifies the type of table.

```
String = Table.Type
```

This can be one of the following strings:

❑ `TABLE`, for a normal table.

❑ `SYSTEM TABLE`, for a provider system table.

❑ `GLOBAL TEMPORARY`, for a temporary table.

10

ADOX: Object & Collections

Collections of the Table Object

The Columns Collection

Contains a `Column` object for each column in the table.

```
Set Columns = Table.Columns
```

You can use the `Columns` collection to find the details for each `Column`:

This is the default collection.

The Indexes Collection

Contains an `Index` object for each index associated with the table.

```
Set Indexes = Table.Indexes
```

The Keys Collection

Contains a `Key` object for each key associated with the table.

```
Set Keys = Table.Keys
```

The Properties Collection

Contains a `Property` object for each provider-specific property of the table.

```
Set Properties = Table.Properties
```

The `Properties` collection is covered in more detail in Chapter 8, and a full list of ADOX properties is in Appendix J.

The Index Object

The `Index` object contains all of the details for a single index on a table.

Methods of the Index Object

The `Index` object has no methods.

Properties of the Index Object

The Clustered Property

Indicates whether or not the `Index` is clustered.

```
Index.Clustered = Boolean
Boolean = Index.Clustered
```

By default, indexes are not clustered.

You can only set this property before appending an Index to the Indexes collection.

Clustered indexes mean that the data is stored in the same physical order as the index, which speeds up access to the data. Not all databases support clustered indexes. For more information on this, consult *Inside SQL Server 7.0*, by Ron Soukup and Kalen Delaney (MS Press).

The IndexNulls Property

Indicates what happens to index entries that contain Null values.

```
Index.IndexNulls = AllowNullsEnum
AllowNullsEnum = Index.IndexNulls
```

AllowNullsEnum can be one of the following constants:

- ❑ adIndexNullsAllow, ensures that key columns with Null values have index values. The index entry will itself be Null.
- ❑ adIndexNullsDisallow, ensures that if the key columns are Null, index entries are not allowed. Attempting to insert a record with Null values in a key column will generate an error. This is the default value.
- ❑ adIndexNullsIgnore, allows Null values in key columns, but they are ignored, and an index entry is not created.
- ❑ adIndexNullsIgnoreAny, allows Null values in any part of the key (for multiple columns), but they are ignored, and an index entry is not created.

You cannot change this property on Index objects that already exist in the Indexes collection.

The Name Property

Sets or retrieves the name of the Index

```
Index.Name = String
String = Index.Name
```

This is the default property.

The PrimaryKey Property

Indicates whether or not the Index is the primary key of the table.

```
Index.PrimaryKey = Boolean
Boolean = Index.PrimaryKey
```

The default value is False, and you can only set this value for Index objects that have not yet been added to the Indexes collection.

The Unique Property

Indicates whether or not the keys in the Index must be unique.

```
Index.Unique = Boolean
Boolean = Index.Unique
```

10

ADOX: Object & Collections

The default value is `False`, and you can only set this value for `Index` objects that have not yet been added to the `Indexes` collection.

Collections of the Index Object

The Columns Collection

Contains a `Column` object for each column that exists in the `Index`.

```
Set Columns = Index.Columns
```

Although many indexes comprise only a single column, it's important to remember that multiple columns are supported by (probably) all databases.

The Properties Collection

Contains a `Property` object for each provider-specific property that exists in the index.

```
Set Properties = Index.Properties
```

The Key Object

The `Key` object represents a table key, which may be primary, foreign, or unique.

Methods of the Key Object

The `Key` object has no methods.

Properties of the Key Object

The DeleteRule Property

Indicates what happens when a primary key is deleted.

```
Key.DeleteRule = RuleEnum
RuleEnum = Key.DeleteRule
```

`RuleEnum` can be one of the following constants:

❑ `adRICascade`, to indicate that deletes are cascaded, meaning that sub-tables (that is the 'many' table in a 'one-to-many' join) are also deleted. This avoids the problem of orphaned records.

❑ `adRINone`, to indicate that deletes are not cascaded. This is the default value, and will result in orphaned records.

❑ `adRISetDefault`, to indicate that the foreign key should be set to its default value for deletes, and will result in orphaned records.

❑ `adRISetNull`, to indicate that the foreign key should be set to null for deletes, and will result in orphaned records.

You can only set this value on keys before you add them to the `Keys` collection.

The Name Property

Indicates the name of the `Key`.

```
Key.Name = String
String = Key.Name
```

The RelatedTable Property

If the key is a foreign key, then this represents the name of the foreign table.

```
Key.RelatedTable = String
String = Key.RelatedTable
```

To identify the column in the related table, you use the `RelatedColumn` property of the `Column` object. For example:

```
objKey.RelatedTable = "sales"
objKey.Columns("store_id").RelatedColumn = "store_id"
```

The Type Property

Indicates the type of the key.

```
Key.Type = KeyTypeEnum
KeyTypeEnum = Key.Type
```

`KeyTypeEnum` can be one of the following constants:

- ❑ `adKeyForeign`, to indicate that the key is a foreign key.
- ❑ `adKeyPrimary`, to indicate that the key is a primary key.
- ❑ `adKeyUnique`, to indicate that the key is unique.

The UpdateRule Property

Indicates what should happen when primary keys are updated.

```
Key.UpdateRule = RuleEnum
RuleEnum = Key.UpdateRule
```

`RuleEnum` can be one of the following constants:

- ❑ `adRICascade`, to indicate that updates are cascaded.
- ❑ `adRINone`, to indicate that updates are not cascaded. This is the default value.
- ❑ `adRISetDefault`, to indicate that the foreign key should be set to its default value for updates.
- ❑ `adRISetNull`, to indicate that the foreign key should be set to null for updates.

You can only set this value on keys before you add them to the `Keys` collection.

10

ADOX: Object & Collections

Collections of the Key Object

The Columns Collection

Contains a `Column` object for each column in the key.

```
Columns = Key.Columns
```

The Column Object

The `Column` object relates to an individual column, or field, in a `Key`, `Table`, or `Index`.

Methods of the Column Object

The `Column` object has no methods.

Properties of the Column Object

The Attributes Property

Retrieves or sets the individual characteristics of a `Column`.

```
Column.Attributes = ColumnAttributesEnum
ColumnAttributesEnum = Column.Attributes
```

`ColumnAttributesEnum` can be one or both of the following values:

❑   `adColFixed`, to indicate that the column is of a fixed length.

❑   `adColNullable`, to indicate that the column may contain `Null` values.

The default value of `ColumnAttributesEnum` has neither of these attributes set. You should use bitwise operations to set multiple values, or to retrieve individual attributes. For example, to set both attributes:

```
Set objCol = objTable.Columns("state")
objCol.Attributes = adColFixed Or adColNullable
```

And to check for a single attribute:

```
If (objCol.Attributes And adColFixed) = adColFixed Then
    Print "The column is of a fixed width"
End If
```

The DefinedSize Property

Sets or retrieves the maximum size (in characters) of a column.

```
Column.DefinedSize = Long
Long = Column.DefinedSize
```

For variable length columns, this indicates the maximum amount of data that the column may contain. It defaults to 0, and a value is not explicitly required for fixed length data types. For example:

```
objCol.Type = adInteger
```

```
objCol.Type = adVarChar
objCol.DefinedSize = 10
```

In the latter case the DefinedSize must be set, because a variable character type must have a specified length.

You can only set this value on Column objects before they are appended to the Columns collection.

The Name Property

Sets or retrieves the name of a column.

```
Column.Name = String
String = Column.Name
```

For example:

```
objCol.Name = "Age"
objCol.Type = adInteger
```

This is the default property.

The NumericScale Property

Sets or retrieves the scale for a numeric column.

```
Column.NumericScale = Byte
Byte = Column.NumericScale
```

This is only applicable to columns of type adNumeric or adDecimal, and any value in this property will be ignored for all other column types.

The NumericScale defines how many digits are stored to the right of the decimal place, and is used in conjunction with the Precision property.

The default value is 0.

The ParentCatalog Property

Sets or retrieves the `Catalog` to which this column belongs.

```
Set Catalog = Column.ParentCatalog
Set Column.ParentCatalog = Catalog
```

The `ParentCatalog` property allows you to set provider-specific properties before the column is appended to the `Columns` collection. For example:

```
strConn = "Provider= Microsoft.Jet.OLEDB.4.0; Data
Source=c:\temp\pubs.mdb"
objCat.ActiveConnection = strConn

objTbl.Columns.Append "Name", adVarWChar
objCol.Name = "Age"
objCol.Type = adInteger

Set objCol.ParentCatalog = objCat
objCol.Properties("Jet.OLEDB:Column Validation Rule") = ">18"
objCol.Properties("Jet.OLEDB:Column Validation Text") = _
                                    "Age must be over 18"
objTbl.Columns.Append objCol

objCat.Tables.Append objTbl
```

You can only set this value on `Column` objects before they are appended to the `Columns` collection.

The Precision Property

Sets or retrieves the maximum precision of data in the column.

```
Column.Precision = Long
Long = Column.Precision
```

This is only applicable to columns that are numeric, and is ignored for other column types.

The default value is 0.

The RelatedColumn Property

For foreign key columns, this sets or retrieves the name of the column in the related table.

```
Column.RelatedColumn = String
String = Column.RelatedColumn
```

You can only set this value on `Column` objects before they are appended to the `Columns` collection.

An error will be generated if you try to read this value for columns that are not part of keys. The only way to tell if a `Column` is part of a key is to check the `Columns` collection for a `Key`.

The SortOrder Property

For a `Column` in an `Index`, this indicates the order in which the `Column` is sorted.

```
Column.SortOrder = SortOrderEnum
SortOrderEnum = Column.SortOrder
```

`SortOrderEnum` can be one of the following:

❏ `adSortAscending`, to sort in ascending order.

❏ `adSortDescending`, to sort in descending order.

The default sort order is ascending.

Accessing this property on a column that is not part of an index will generate an error.

The Type Property

Sets or retrieves the data type for the values that will be held in the column.

```
Column.Type = DataTypeEnum
DataTypeEnum = Column.Type
```

Because of its size, the listing for `DataTypeEnum` is not shown here, but can be seen in Appendix B.

The default value is `adVarWChar`. Not all providers support all data types, and you should use Appendix E as a guide for picking the correct type for your provider.

You can only set this value on `Column` objects before they are appended to the `Columns` collection.

> *The difference between* `adVarChar` *and* `adVarWChar` *(and, indeed, other types with a W in them) is that the W types support Unicode, allowing for extended character sets. Jet 4 fully supports Unicode, therefore these W types are now the default over their non-Unicode equivalents.*

Collections of the Column Object

The Properties Collection

Contains all of the `Property` objects for the `Column`.

```
Set Properties = Column.Properties
```

The `Properties` collection contains provider-specific properties, and behaves exactly the same as the `Properties` collection of ADO that is discussed in Chapter 8. A full list of ADOX properties available is in Appendix J.

10

ADOX: Object & Collections

The Group Object

The group object identifies a security group account. As a general rule, most databases support the symmetrical nature of groups and users, where a Group can contain many users, and each User can belong to many groups. This allows you to set permission for a group as a whole, rather than for individual users.

Methods of the Group Object

The GetPermissions Method

Retrieves the group permissions for an object, or for a class of object.

```
RightsEnum = Group.GetPermissions(Name, ObjectType, [ObjectTypeId])
```

Name	Type	Description
Name	Variant	The object name for which the permissions are to be retrieved.
ObjectType	ObjectTypeEnum	The type of object .
ObjectTypeId	Variant	A GUID. If the object type is provider-specific, and not a standard OLE DB object type, ObjectType must be set to adPermObjProviderSpecific.

ObjectType can be one of the following ObjectTypeEnum constants:

- ❑ adPermObjColumn, to specify that the object is a column.
- ❑ adPermObjDatabase, to specify that the object is a database.
- ❑ adPermObjProcedure, to specify that the object is a procedure.
- ❑ adPermObjProviderSpecific, to specify that the object is of a provider-specific type.
- ❑ adPermObjTable, to specify that the object is a table.
- ❑ adPermObjView, to specify that the object is a view.

The return value is a combination of one or more of the RightsEnum constants; a list of which is shown in Appendix I. You can test for individual permissions by using bitwise operations:

```
lngPerms = objGroup.GetPermissions ("authors", adPermObjTable)
If (lngPerms And adRightReadDesign)= adRightReadDesign Then
    Print "You have permissions to read the table design"
End If
```

You can also test for multiple permissions:

```
lngPerms = objGroup.GetPermissions ("authors", adPermObjTable)
If (lngPerms And adRightReadDescign = adRightReadDesign) Or
    (lngPerms And adRightWriteDesign = adRightWriteDesign) Then
        Print "You can read from and write to the table design"
End If
```

Substituting Null for the Name parameter allows you to examine the permissions on the container. For example, the following shows the permissions on the Tables container, identifying what permissions the group has for new tables:

```
lngPerms = objGroup.GetPermissions (Null, adPermObjTable)
```

The SetPermissions Method

Sets the group permissions for an object, or for a class of object.

```
Group.SetPermissions(Name, ObjectType, Action, Rights, [Inherit],
                [ObjectTypeId])
```

Name	Type	Description
Name	Variant	The name of the object for which to set permissions.
ObjectType	ObjectTypeEnum	The object type.
Action	ActionEnum	The type of permission action to set.
Rights	RightsEnum	The individual permissions to set.
Inherit	InheritTypeEnum	Indicates the type of permissions inheritance for containers and objects. Default is adInheritNone.
ObjectTypeId	Variant	A GUID. If the object type is provider specific and not a standard OLE DB object type, ObjectType must be set to adPermObjProviderSpecific.

ObjectType can be one of the following ObjectTypeEnum constants:

❑   adPermObjColumn, to specify that the object is a column.

❑   adPermObjDatabase, to specify that the object is a database.

❑   adPermObjProcedure, to specify that the object is a procedure.

❑   adPermObjProviderSpecific, to specify that the object is of a provider-specific type.

❑   adPermObjTable, to specify that the object is a table.

❑   adPermObjView, to specify that the object is a view.

Action can be one of the following ActionEnum constants:

- ❑ adAccessDeny, to deny the specific permissions to the Group or User.

- ❑ adAccessGrant, to grant the specific permissions to the Group or User. This grants an individual permission, and will leave other permissions in effect.

- ❑ adAccessRevoke, to revoke any specific access rights to the Group or User.

- ❑ adAccessSet, to set the exact permissions for the Group or User. Any existing permissions will be replaced by the new set of permissions.

Rights can be one or more of the RightsEnum constants, a list of which is shown in Appendix I, and indicates the permissions to be set on the object for the group.

Inherit can be one of the InheritTypeEnum constants, and allows you to specify whether containers inherit permissions from the contained object:

- ❑ adInheritBoth, to indicate that both objects and other containers inherit permissions for the object.

- ❑ adInheritContainers, to indicate that other containers inherit permissions for the object.

- ❑ adInheritNone, to indicate that no permissions are inherited.

- ❑ adInheritNoPropogate, to indicate that the adInheritObjects and adInheritContainers permissions are not propagated to child objects.

- ❑ adInheritObjects, to indicate that permissions are only inherited by objects that are not containers.

To set more than one right, you should combine them together:

```
lngRights = adRightInsert Or adRightUpdate
objGroup.SetPermissions "authors", adPermObjTable, adAccessGrant,
lngRights
```

If you wish to set the permissions for the container, you can supply Null for the name:

```
lngRights = adRightInsert Or adRightUpdate
objGroup.SetPermissions Null, adPermObjTable, adAccessGrant,
lngRights
```

This sets the rights on the Tables container, to allow inserts and updates.

Properties of the Group Object

The Name Property

Sets or retrieves the name of the group account.

```
Group.Name = String
String = Group.Name
```

This is the default property.

The ParentCatalog Property

Identifies the parent catalog to which this group belongs.

```
Set Catalog = Group.Name
```

Collections of the Group Object

The Users Collection

Contains all of the user accounts that belong to this group.

```
Set Users = Group.Users
```

To list all of the users in a particular group, you can use the For..Each construct.

The Properties Collection

Contains a Property object for each provider-specific property of the group.

```
Set Properties = Group.Properties
```

The Properties collection is covered in more detail in Chapter 8, and a full list of ADOX properties is in Appendix J.

The User Object

The User object contains the details of a single user account.

Methods of the User Object

The ChangePassword Method

Allows the user password to be changed.

```
User.ChangePassword(OldPassword, NewPassword)
```

Name	Type	Description
OldPassword	String	The existing user password.
NewPassword	String	The new user password.

To clear a password, or to represent a blank password, you should use an empty string. For example, to clear the password for a user:

```
objUser.ChangePassword "abc123", ""
```

The GetPermissions Method

Retrieves the user permissions on an object.

```
RightsEnum = User.GetPermissions(Name, ObjectType, [ObjectTypeId])
```

Usage of the GetPermission method for a User object is exactly the same as the GetPermissions method for the Group object.

The SetPermissions Method

Sets the user permissions for an object, or for a class of object.

```
User.SetPermissions(Name, ObjectType, Action, Rights, [Inherit],
[ObjectTypeId])
```

Usage of the SetPermissions method for a User object is exactly the same as the SetPermissions method for the Group object.

Properties of the User Object

The Name Property

Identifies the name of the user.

```
User.Name = String
String = User.Name
```

This is the default property.

The ParentCatalog Property

Identifies the parent catalog to which this user belongs.

```
Set Catalog = User.Name
```

Collections of the User Object

The Groups Collection

Contains a Group object for each group to which the user belongs.

```
Set Groups = User.Groups
```

The Properties Collection

Contains a Property object for each provider-specific property of the user.

```
Set Properties = User.Properties
```

The `Properties` collection is covered in more detail in Chapter 8, and a full list of ADOX properties is in Appendix J.

The Procedure Object

The `Procedure` object contains the details of a stored procedure. It does not directly contain the SQL text associated with the stored procedure, but just identifies the procedure in the catalog – that is the meta data. To access the SQL that makes up the procedure, you use the `Command` property of the `Procedure` object.

Methods of the Procedure Object

The `Procedure` object has no methods.

Properties of the Procedure Object

The Command Property

Indicates an ADO `Command` object that contains the procedure details.

```
Set Command = Procedure.Command
Set Procedure.Command = Command
```

The following providers do *not* support the `Command` property, and will return an error if you try to reference it:

❑ OLE DB Provider for SQL Server.

❑ OLE DB Provider for ODBC.

❑ OLE DB Provider for Oracle.

For providers that support the `Command` interface, you can set, and retrieve the command details, using the ADO `Command` properties:

```
Set objCmd = objCat.Procedures("qryPriceDetails")
Print objCmd.CommandText
```

Or you can update the procedure:

```
objCmd.CommandText = "UPDATE Products SET Price = Price * 1.05"
Set objCat.Procedures("qryUpdatePrices") = objCmd
```

This is the default property.

The DateCreated Property

Indicates the date the procedure was created.

```
Variant = Procedure.DateCreated
```

You will need to `Refresh` the collection to see this value for newly appended procedures.

10

ADOX: Object & Collections

305

The DateModified Property

Indicates the date the procedure was last modified.

```
Variant = Procedure.DateModified
```

You will need to Refresh the collection to see this value for newly appended procedures.

The Name Property

Indicates the name of the procedure.

```
String = Procedure.Name
```

The View Object

The View object contains details of views in the catalog. For Microsoft Access, this includes standard select queries.

Methods of the View Object

The View object has no methods.

Properties of the View Object

The Command Property

Indicates an ADO Command object that contains the view details.

```
Set Command = View.Command
Set View.Command = Command
```

The following providers do *not* support the Command property and will return an error if you try to reference it:

❑   OLE DB Provider for SQL Server.

❑   OLE DB Provider for ODBC.

❑   OLE DB Provider for Oracle.

For providers that support the Command interface, you can set, and retrieve the command details, using the ADO Command properties:

```
Set objCmd = objCat.Views("vwTradePriceList")
Print objCmd.CommandText
```

Or you can set the command text:

```
objCmd.CommandText = "SELECT Product, TradePrice From Products"
Set objCat.Views("vwTradePriceList").Command = objCmd
```

This is the default property.

The DateCreated Property

Identifies the date the view was created.

```
Variant = View.DateCreated
```

The DateModified Property

Identifies the date the view was last modified.

```
Variant = View.DateModified
```

The Name Property

Identifies the name of the view.

```
String = View.Name
```

Collections

The handling of ADOX collections is similar to that of ADOX objects, so they have been included here as a single section.

The table below details the objects and their collections.

ADOX Object	Collections
Catalog	Tables, Groups, Users, Procedures, Views.
Table	Columns, Indexes, Keys, Properties.
Index	Columns, Properties.
Key	Columns.
Column	Properties.
Group	Users, Properties.
User	Groups, Properties.
Procedure	
View	

The differences between the collections are that:

❑ The `Properties` collection is a read-only collection, and therefore does not have an `Append` or `Delete` method. The `Properties` collection is the same as the ADO `Properties` collection, and is detailed in Chapter 8.

❑ The remaining collections have different `Append` methods. These are detailed below.

Enumerating collections can be achieved with the `For Each` statement in Visual Basic or VBScript, or the `Enumerator` object in JScript. C++ users should use standard enumerators to access each element in the collection.

10

ADOX: Object & Collections

Methods of a Collection

The Append Method

The Columns Collection

Adds a new `Column` to the collection.

```
Columns.Append(Item, [Type], [DefinedSize])
```

Name	Type	Description
Item	Variant	A `Column` object to append; or the name of the new column to append.
Type	DataTypeEnum	The data type of the column. Default is `adVarWChar`.
DefinedSize	Long	The maximum column size. Default is `0`.

Because of its size, the listing for `DataTypeEnum` is not shown here, but can be seen in Appendix B.

The `Append` method can take one of two forms. The first is to append an existing `Column` object to the collection:

```
objColumn.Name = "FirstName"
objColumn.Type = adVarWChar
objColumn.DefinedSize = 25
objTable.Columns.Append objColumn
```

The second method is to define the column name:

```
objTable.Columns.Append "FirstName", adVarWChar, 25
```

The Groups Collection

Adds a new group to the collection.

```
Groups.Append(Item)
```

Name	Type	Description
Item	Variant	A `Group` object, or the name of the group to be added.

You can specify either a valid `Group` object, or just the name of a group in this method. For example, the following are equivalent:

```
objGroup.Name = "Finance"
objCat.Groups.Append objGroup
```

```
objCat.Groups.Append "Finance"
```

The Indexes Collection

Adds a new Index to the collection.

```
Indexes.Append(Item, [Columns])
```

Name	Type	Description
Item	Variant	An Index object, or the name of the index to append.
Columns	Variant	A variant array listing the column names contained in the Index.

You can specify either an existing Index object or the name that the new index is to have:

```
objIndex.Name = "NameIndex"
objIndex.Columns.Append "FirstName", adVarWChar, 10
objIndex.Columns.Append "LastName", adVarWChar, 10
objTable.Indexes.Append objIndex
```

```
objTable.Indexes.Append "NameIndex", Array("FirstName", "LastName")
```

If your index consists of only a single column, then you can omit the Array usage:

```
objTable.Indexes.Append "FirstNameIndex", "FirstName"
```

The Keys Collection

Adds a new key to the collection.

```
Keys.Append(Item, [Type], [Column], [RelatedTable],
[RelatedColumn])
```

Name	Type	Description
Item	Variant	A Key object or the name of the key to append.
Type	KeyTypeEnum	The type of the key. Default is adKeyPrimary.
Column	Variant	The column that the key applies to.
RelatedTable	String	For a foreign key, the Table that the key points to.
RelatedColumn	String	For a foreign key, the Column in the RelatedTable that the key points to.

The key Type can be one of the KeyTypeEnum constants:

- ❏ adKeyForeign, to indicate the key is a foreign key.

- ❏ adKeyPrimary, to indicate the key is a primary key.

- ❏ adKeyUnique, to indicate the key is unique.

The item being appended can either be a valid `Key` object, or the name of the key:

```
objKey.Name = "PKau_id"
objKey.Columns.Append "au_id", adKeyPrimary
objTable("authors").Keys.Append objKey
```

```
objTable("authors").Keys.Append "PKau_id", adKeyPrimary, "au_id"
```

When dealing with foreign keys you should set the `RelatedTable` and `RelatedColumn` arguments accordingly, to point to the primary key:

```
objTable("authors").Keys.Append "FKpub_id", adKeyForeign, _
                    "pub_id", "publishers", "pub_id"
```

The Procedures Collection

Adds a new procedure to the collection.

```
Procedures.Append(Name, Command)
```

Name	Type	Description
Name	String	The name of the new procedure.
Command	Object	An ADO Command object containing the procedure details.

As with the `Command` property, this method is not supported by all providers. In such cases, you can easily create new stored procedures:

```
objCmd.Name.CommandText = "UPDATE . . ."
objCat.Procedures.Append "UpdateValues", objCmd
```

The Tables Collection

Adds a new `Table` to the collection.

```
Tables.Append(Item)
```

Name	Type	Description
Item	Variant	A Table object, or the name of the table to add.

The `Item` can be either a valid `Table` object, or the name of the table to be added:

```
objTable.Name = "Contacts"
objCat.Tables.Append objTable
```

```
objCat.Tables.Append "Contacts"
```

The Users Collection

Adds a new user to a group or to a catalog.

```
Users.Append(Item, [Password])
```

Name	Type	Description
Item	Variant	A user object or the name of the user to add.
Password	String	The user password.

The `Item` can be either a valid `User` object or the name of a user:

```
objUser.Name = "Jan"
objCat.Users.Append objUser
```

```
objCat.Users.Append "Jan", "Vouvray"
```

You must ensure that a `User` is added to the `Catalog` before adding the `User` to a `Group`. This is because the `User` must have a valid user account before it can be added to a `Group`.

The Views Collection

Adds a new view to the catalog.

```
Views.Append(Name, Command)
```

Name	Type	Description
Name	String	The name of the new procedure.
Command	Object	An ADO Command object containing the procedure details.

As with the `Command` property, this method is not supported by all providers. In these cases, you can easily create new views:

```
objCmd.Name.CommandText = "SELECT . . ."
objCat.Views.Append "GetValues", objCmd
```

The Delete Method

Deletes an object from the collection.

```
Collection.Delete(Item)
```

Name	Type	Description
Item	Variant	The number or name of the object to be deleted.

10

ADOX: Object & Collections

`Item` can either be the number; that is, its position in the collection; or the name of the object to delete. For example, to delete a `View` from the `Views` collection you could use either of these lines:

```
objCat.Views.Delete(0)
```

```
objCat.Views.Delete("qrySalesByQuarter")
```

The Refresh Method

Refreshes the collection from the provider, ensuring that any deleted objects are no longer shown, and that new objects are available.

```
Collection.Refresh
```

Using `Refresh` ensures that any changes taking place by other users of the `Catalog` are reflected in your collection objects.

Properties of a Collection

The Count Property

Identifies the number of objects within the collection.

```
Long = Collection.Count
```

For example, to determine the number of tables within a `Catalog` you could use this code:

```
Print objCatalog.Tables.Count
```

The Item Property

Allows indexing into the collection, by either name or number.

```
Set Object = Collection.Item(Item)
```

Name	Type	Description
Item	Variant	The name of the object, or its number.

This is the default method and can be omitted. For example, in indexing into the `Columns` collection, both of the following are equivalent:

```
Set objColumn = objTable.Columns ("Name")
```

```
Set objColumn = objTable.Columns.Item("Name")
```

I thank God I am as honest as any man
living that is an old man and no honester th

Can counsel and speak comfort to th

Much Ado About Nothing.

He wears his faith but as the fashion of h

As merry as the day

He hath indeed better bettered expectation

(Act i. Sc. 1).

He wears his faith but as the fashion of his hat.
(Ibid)

As merry as the day is long.

h indeed better bettered expectation

(Act i. Sc. 1).

Much Ado About Nothing.

(Ibid)

Can counsel and speak comfort to that grief
Which they themselves not feel.

He wears his faith but as the fashion of his hat.
(Ibid)

I was not born under

a rhyming plane

I was not born under a rhyming plane
(Sc. 2

For there was never yet p
That could endure the to

merry as the day is long

(Sc. 2)

Can counsel and speak comfort to that grief

Which they themselves not feel.

(Ibid)

He hath indeed better bettered expectation

I thank God I am as honest as an

living that is an old man and no honest

He wears his faith but as the fashion of his ha
(Ibi

Much Ado About Nothing.

For there was never yet philospher
That could endure the toothache patiently.

(Ibid)

I was not born u

ADO Multi-Dimensional

The ADOMD library is a companion to the standard ADO library, and is specially developed to integrate with On Line Analytical Processing (OLAP) servers. The best way to think about OLAP is to think of spreadsheets. You could compare a normal spreadsheet to a standard database table – you have rows and columns in both. OLAP data also has rows and columns, but is more like the Pivot Table in Microsoft Excel. OLAP is designed for performing complex analysis, such as calculations, summaries, etc. more easily than can be done with SQL. Some of the analysis you can perform with OLAP is perfectly easy with a spreadsheet (in fact the Pivot Table in Excel is very similar to OLAP analysis), but when the data starts getting large, the handling of the spreadsheet becomes more complex.

This chapter doesn't give an exhaustive look into how ADOMD should be used. For that you should consult Professional ADO 2.5 Programming (Wrox Press, ISBN 1-861002-75-0).

To understand OLAP you really need an example, so let's take one of the SQL Server default database: pubs. Suppose you want to see the book sales for each Publisher, grouped by State and City, and sub-grouped by the period of sale (Year, Quarter, Month, Day). What you are aiming for is something like this:

+ State	- Year	- Quarter	+ Month	All Publishers	Algodata Infosystems	Binnet & Hardley
All Geography	- 1994	- Quarter 3	Quarter 3 Total	163	15	40
			+ September	163	15	40
+ CA	All Dates	All Dates Total		275	65	90
	- 1992	1992 Total		80		80
		- Quarter 2	Quarter 2 Total	80		80
			+ June	80		80
	+ 1993	1993 Total		110	65	10
	- 1994	1994 Total		85		
		- Quarter 3	Quarter 3 Total	85		
			+ September	85		
+ OR	All Dates	All Dates Total		80	65	15
	- 1992	1992 Total				
		- Quarter 2	Quarter 2 Total			
			+ June			
	+ 1993	1993 Total		55	55	
	- 1994	1994 Total		25	10	15
		- Quarter 3	Quarter 3 Total	25	10	15
			+ September	25	10	15

This sort of data analysis is possible with standard SQL queries, or even using the Pivot Table in Excel, but there's a better way – use an OLAP server that can take raw data (from any data source) and transform it into easily accessible structures. That transformation is one of the key points of OLAP. It makes it very easy and efficient to produce this type of analysis – both by providing a language similar to SQL which is more powerful for this kind of procedure, and by internally storing selected data in different structures that make such analyses more efficient to perform.

These OLAP structures come in two sets and map onto the ADOMD objects. The first set represents how the OLAP server stores the data, and consists of the following objects:

❑   Catalog, which is the container for all OLAP objects. This identifies the OLAP server, and the actual data server that supplies the original data. Although this chapter uses Microsoft SQL Server and Microsoft's OLAP Server, there is no reason why they have to be from the same supplier – the ADOMD objects don't require a specific OLAP server.

❑   CubeDef, which is a container for a set of data. The CubeDef used in producing the previous screenshot is called AllSales and contains the structures that identify the States, Dates (Years, Quarters and Months) and Publishers. A CubeDef doesn't represent how the data is shown – it just represents what the structures are and what they contain. The name CubeDef suggests only 3 axes of data, but that's not the case – there can be more than three.

❑   Dimension, which is a distinct set of items, giving you a way to break down data. The diagram above shows several distinct Dimension objects: Geography (to identify the States and Cities), Dates (to identify the date of the book sales) and Publishers (to identify the book publishers). The Dimensions give us the headings on both axes of the diagram. Moreover, as you can see, Dimensions can be nested, which gives a hierarchy.

❑   Hierarchy, which identifies the relationship of the items within a Dimension. So, for the Dates dimension we have three Hierarchy objects: Year, Quarter, and Month. The hierarchies give us sub-headings.

❑   Level, which identifies the elements in an individual Hierarchy. For the Dates dimension we have a Hierarchy called Year – each year in the Dimension is a Level. Likewise, there is a Level for each Publisher.

❑   Member, which represents a unique item in a Level. This is equivalent to the cells in the diagram. A Member is unique in an OLAP structure since it represents the intersection of the Levels.

The second set of OLAP structures represent the data as it is actually being displayed. So if you run a query against an OLAP server you get a set of data, which comprises:

❑   CellSet, which represents the whole set of data. This would be equivalent to the entire diagram above.

❑   Axis, which represents one of the physical axes of the CellSet. For example, the diagram above would require an Axis for the rows (the y-axis) and another Axis for the columns (the x-axis).

❏ Cell, which is a single cell. In the diagram above, a Cell would represent the quantity sold.

❏ Position, which is an individual row or column.

❏ Measure, which is a quantitative, numerical column, and is usually the name of the item that is shown in each cell. It's the *actual data to be shown*. In the diagram above the Measure is the quantity of books sold.

The object model diagram below illustrates how these objects relate to each other. As you can see, many (although not all) of the objects listed above are contained within collections:

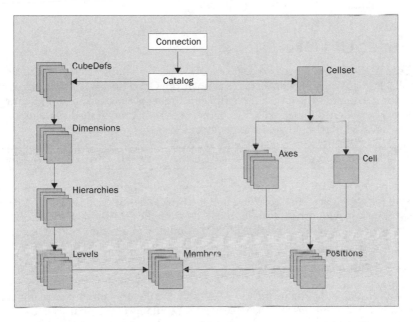

This might all seem to be just another confusing way to represent data. However, OLAP servers give you the ability to manipulate data much more easily than most relational databases. Abstracting the data into known terms (Geography, Sales, Publishers) makes the data more accessible for users – because they are less reliant upon knowing the physical structure of the data in the database.

Multi-Dimension Extensions

SQL Server 7.0 and newer versions implement Multi-Dimension Extensions (MDX), which is a set of SQL extensions that allow processing of OLAP queries. For example, the above set of data could be generated with the following:

```
SELECT     Publishers.Members ON COLUMNS,
CROSSJOIN (Geography.Members, Dates.Members) ON ROWS
FROM       AllSales
```

Although different from standard SQL, it's not hard to understand. The first line indicates that the `Publishers` are to be shown on the columns (that's the x-axis). The second line indicates that we are doing a cross-join – so for each Publisher we want to show something on the rows (the y-axis). In this case we want to see the `Geography` (that is States) and the `Dates` (that is Years and Quarters). This is what makes OLAP so powerful, as it's easy to say 'for each one of these, show me this and that'. It allows you to join related sets of data together in an easily viewable form. The third line just identifies where the data is coming from.

The MDX extensions allow the use of OLAP names (Members, Levels, and so on) in SQL queries. For more information on MDX you should consults the SQL 7 documentation.

OLAP Servers

To use ADOMD you'll need access to an OLAP server – there are several OLAP servers available but Microsoft SQL Server comes with an OLAP server as standard, so check out the documentation. The OLAP server for SQL Server is extremely easy to set up and use, and can be obtained (along with SQL Server itself) as a time-limited evaluation. The limit is 120 days, which should give you plenty of time to get to know it.

> **For SQL Server 2000, the OLAP Services are called Analysis Services.**

To use ADO with OLAP you will need to install the **Client components** when you install the OLAP Services, ensuring that the **PivotTable Service** is installed. This is the service that provides the interface from ADO into the OLAP Service. The SQL Server installation CD contains a set of ADOMD examples, in a variety of languages.

The Catalog Object

A `Catalog` object contains the `CubeDefs` that make up a multi-dimensional query. The `Catalog` identifies the OLAP server that contains the structures to be used for OLAP queries.

Methods of the Catalog Object

The `Catalog` object has no methods

Properties of the Catalog Object

The Name Property

Identifies the name of the catalog.

```
String = Catalog.Name
```

This property is defined by the OLAP server, and cannot be changed.

The ActiveConnection Property

Identifies the ADO `Connection` to the OLAP data provider.

```
Set Connection = Catalog.ActiveConnection
Set Catalog.ActiveConnection = Connection
String = Catalog.ActiveConnection
Catalog.ActiveConnection = String
```

This can be an existing ADO `Connection` object or an ADO connection string. For example:

```
Provider=MSOlap; Data Source=Eeyore; Initial Catalog=Pubs; User
ID=sa; Password=
```

Collections of the Catalog Object

The CubeDefs Collection

Contains a `CubeDef` for each multi-dimensional query in the catalog.

```
CubeDefs = Catalog.CubeDefs
```

You can use the `CubeDefs` collection to access individual `CubeDef` objects:

```
Set objCubeDef = objCatalog.CubeDefs("AllSales")
```

The Microsoft OLAP Server/Analysis Services installs the FoodMart sample, which has six CubeDefs.

The CubeDef Object

A `CubeDef` object contains the related dimensions from a cube of multi-dimensional data.

Methods of the CubeDef Object

11

ADOMD: Objects & Collections

The GetSchemaObject Method

Returns the schema object from the CubeDef.

```
Object = CubeDef.GetSchemaObject(eObjType, bsUniqueName)
```

Name	Type	Description
eObjType	adObjectTypeEnum	The type of object to retrieve.
bsUniqueName	String	The UniqueName of the object to retrieve.

eObjType can be one of the adObjectTypeEnum constants:

- ❑ adObjectTypeDimension, to retrieve a Dimension object
- ❑ adObjectTypeHierarchy, to retrieve a Hierarchy object
- ❑ adObjectTypeLevel, to retrieve a Level object
- ❑ adObjectTypeMember, to retrieve a Member object

The Schema object will be a Dimension, Hierarchy, Level, or Member object. The GetSchemaObject method allows you to retrieve it directly, without knowing where it is in the hierarchy of objects.

This method is new to ADO 2.6 and allows direct access to the object by way of its unique name.

Properties of the CubeDef Object

The Name Property

Identifies the name of the CubeDef.

```
String = CubeDef.Name
```

You can use the Name property to index into the Catalog object's CubeDefs collection:

```
Set objCubeDef = objCatalog.objCubeDefs("AllSales")
```

The Description Property

Contains descriptive text for the CubeDef.

```
String = CubeDef.Description
```

Collections of the CubeDef Object

The Dimensions Collection

Contains a Dimension object for each dimension in the CubeDef.

```
Dimensions = CubeDef.Dimensions
```

For example, the AllSales CubeDef in the example diagram has three dimensions: Geography, Publishers, and Dates.

The Properties Collection

Contains a Property object for each provider-specific property.

```
Properties = CubeDef.Properties
```

This works in the same way as the `Properties` collection for the ADO objects, where the provider implements specific functionality that cannot be covered by the ADOMD objects.

The Dimension Object

A `Dimension` object represents a single dimension from a cube in a multi-dimensional query.

Methods of the Dimension Object

The `Dimension` object has no methods.

Properties of the Dimension Object

The Name Property

Identifies the name of the `Dimension`.

```
String = Dimension.Name
```

You can use the `Name` property to index into the `Dimensions` collection of the `CubeDef` object:

```
Set objDimension = objCubeDef.Dimensions("Geography")
```

The Description Property

Contains descriptive text for the `Dimension`.

```
String = Dimension.Description
```

The UniqueName Property

Indicates the unique name for the `Dimension`.

```
String = Dimension.UniqueName
```

Because of the complexity of dimensions, it's possible that you may find yourself using two (or more) `Dimension` objects with the same `Name` property. In such cases, `UniqueName` can be used to provide an unambiguous name for each `Dimension` object.

The need for a `UniqueName` is unlikely to arise with dimensions, since they are the highest objects in the hierarchy, but it may be necessary in other circumstances. You'll get a better understanding of this by looking up the `UniqueName` property of the `Level` object, later on.

ADOMD: Objects & Collections

Collections of the Dimension Object

The Hierarchies Collection

Contains a `Hierarchy` object for each hierarchy in the dimension.

```
Hierarchies = Dimension.Hierarchies
```

For instance, in our pubs database example, the `Dates` dimension has a `Dates` hierarchy.

The Properties Collection

Contains a `Property` object for each provider-specific property.

```
Properties = Dimension.Properties
```

This works in the same way as the `Properties` collection for the ADO objects, where the provider implements specific functionality that cannot be covered by the ADOMD objects.

The Hierarchy Object

A `Hierarchy` object identifies a single way in which data from a `Dimension` can be represented. This is often called an aggregation or a roll-up.

Methods of the Hierarchy Object

The `Hierarchy` object has no methods.

Properties of the Hierarchy Object

The Name Property

Identifies the `Hierarchy` object within the `Hierarchies` collection of a `Dimension`.

```
String = Hierarchy.Name
```

The Description Property

Descriptive text for the `Hierarchy`.

```
String = Hierarchy.Description
```

The UniqueName Property

Provides a unique name with which to identify the `Hierarchy` in the collection.

```
String = Hierarchy.UniqueName
```

The UniqueName property allows us to uniquely identify a Hierarchy object, and is particularly useful when we have multiple Hierarchy objects possessing the same Name. Thus, it allows us to have multiple Hierarchy objects with the same name, if the situation demands. Look up the UniqueName property of the Level object.

Collections of the Hierarchy Object

The Levels Collection

Contains a Level object for each level in the hierarchy.

```
Levels = Hierarchy.Levels
```

For example, the Dates hierarchy has the following Levels: All, Year, Quarter, Month, and Day. When this hierarchy was created (using the wizard in the Analysis Services Manager), it was identified as a time dimension using the order date (ord_date) as the date field. The wizard knows this is a date, and automatically creates the necessary levels that belong to a date. This allows analysis on any part of the date.

The Properties Collection

Contains a Property object for each provider-specific property.

```
Properties = Hierarchy.Properties
```

This works in the same way as the Properties collection for the ADO objects, where the provider implements specific functionality that cannot be covered by the ADOMD objects.

The Level Object

A Level object identifies a single step (or layer of aggregation) in a Hierarchy.

Methods of the Level Object

The Level object has no methods.

Properties of the Level Object

The Name Property

Identifies the name of the Level.

```
String = Level.Name
```

The Description Property

A textual description of the Level.

```
String = Level.Description
```

The Caption Property

Identifies the text to that is written on the screen when the Level is displayed.

```
String = Level.Caption
```

The Depth Property

Identifies how deep in the hierarchy this Level is.

```
Integer = Level.Depth
```

The Level object's Depth property is the number of levels between the root of the hierarchy and the Level object. For example, in the diagram at the beginning of this chapter, we have a Hierarchy object called Dates. The levels of this hierarchy (and their depths) are as follows:

Level Name	Depth
(All)	0
Year	1
Quarter	2
Month	3
Day	4

The UniqueName Property

Provides a unique name for the Level.

```
String = Level.UniqueName
```

The UniqueName allows for multiple Level objects that have the same Name.

For example, let's assume we have two Levels that are date-based – perhaps order date and restocking date. Each Level has a hierarchy of date information like so:

OrderDate	RestockDate
All	All
Year	Year
Quarter	Quarter
Month	Month
Day	Day

If you have just the hierarchy name (the Name property) you won't know which Level it belongs to. The UniqueName property combines the name of the current object, with the names of all parent objects. So, if we shown the table again, this time with the UniqueName, you will get this:

OrderDate	RestockDate
[OrderDate].[All]	[RestockDate].[All]
[OrderDate].[Year]	[RestockDate].[Year]

OrderDate	RestockDate
[OrderDate].[Quarter]	[RestockDate].[Quarter]
[OrderDate].[Month]	[RestockDate].[Month]
[OrderDate].[Day]	[RestockDate].[Day]

Each part of the hierarchy is surrounded by square brackets, and separated from other parts of the hierarchy by a period. It is this naming convention that allows each object to be uniquely named.

Collections of the Level Object

The Members Collection

Contains a Member object for each unique row or column in the Level object.

```
Members = Level.Members
```

For example, let's consider the Month Level. The initial thought is that this should contain 12 Members, one for each month, but that's not the case. In fact, it only contains a month if there is data for that month. So, in actual fact, we have:

❏   June, from 1992

❏   February, from 1993

❏   March, from 1993

❏   May, from 1993

❏   October, from 1993

❏   December, from 1993

❏   September, from 1994

This illustrates that you cannot make assumptions about what levels will be available just from the object name. It's the data that defines what's available.

The Properties Collection

Contains a Property object for each provider-specific property.

```
Properties = Level.Properties
```

This works in the same way as the Properties collection for the ADO objects, where the provider implements specific functionality that cannot be covered by the ADOMD objects.

The Member Object

A Member object represents the data in a Dimension.

Methods of the Member Object

The Member object has no methods.

Properties of the Member Object

The Name Property

Indicates the name of the Member.

```
String = Member.Name
```

The Type Property

Identifies the type of the Member.

```
MemberTypeEnum = Member.Type
```

MemberTypeEnum can be one of the following constants:

- ❑ adMemberRegular, to indicate that the member is data that has come directly from the data source

- ❑ adMemberMeasure, to indicate that the member is a Measure, and represents a quantitative attribute

- ❑ adMemberFormula, to indicate the member is calculated from a formula

- ❑ adMemberAll, to indicate that the member represents all members for a given level

- ❑ adMemberUnknown, to indicate the type is unknown

The default is adMemberRegular.

The Caption Property

Identifies the text to that is written to the screen when the Member is used in a hierarchical query.

```
String = Member.Caption
```

The ChildCount Property

Identifies how many child members the Member object contains.

```
Long = Member.ChildCount
```

The child members can be reached via the Children property.

The Children Property

Identifies the child members of which this `Member` is the parent.

```
Members = Member.Children
```

To make this clearer, look again at the diagram at the beginning of this chapter, and consider the `Dates` hierarchy. This has levels for the different types of date measurement (all dates, years, quarters, months, and days). OLAP allows you to look at data in a variety of different ways because each `Member` (in the `Members` collection of each `Level`) has a collection of sub-`Member` objects, which are the children of the current `Member`. You can see this more clearly in the table below:

Level Name	Member	Child Member
(All)	All Dates	1992
		1993
		1994
Year	1992	Quarter 2
	1993	Quarter 1
		Quarter 2
		Quarter 4
	1994	Quarter 3
Quarter	Quarter 2	June
	Quarter 1	February
		March
	Quarter 2	May
Month	June	15
	May	22
		24

The Description Property

The descriptive text for the member.

```
String = Member.Description
```

The DrilledDown Property

Indicates whether or not the `Level` has been drilled down.

```
Boolean = Member.DrilledDown
```

This property shows whether the `Member` is contained in the deepest level of the hierarchy, that is whether we have *drilled down* as far as possible. If so, this property returns `True`. Otherwise, the `Member` possesses child members and this property returns `False`.

11

ADOMD: Objects & Collections

The LevelDepth Property

Identifies how deep this Member is within the Level's hierarchy.

```
Long = Member.LevelDepth
```

The LevelDepth property is the same as the Depth property for the Level, and it is included for a Member because you can access Member objects from their positions in a CellSet, and not just from the Levels collection.

The LevelName Property

Indicates the name of the Level to which the Member belongs.

```
String = Member.LevelName
```

The Parent Property

Indicates the parent object of this Member.

```
Member = Member.Parent
```

In the discussion of the Children property above, the table illustrates the concept of the parent/child relationship among Member objects.

The ParentSameAsPrev Property

Identifies whether the parent of this member is the same as the parent of the preceding Member in the Members collection.

```
Boolean = Member.ParentSameAsPrev
```

You can use this property to identify siblings, or Member objects that are on the same level.

The UniqueName Property

Indicates the unique name for the Member.

```
String = Member.UniqueName
```

Following on from the list of Levels shown in the Levels collection, you can see how the list of unique names shows the complete hierarchy of objects, and ensures that no duplicate names ever exist:

```
[Dates].[All Dates].[1992].[Quarter 2].[June]
[Dates].[All Dates].[1993].[Quarter 1].[February]
[Dates].[All Dates].[1993].[Quarter 1].[March]
[Dates].[All Dates].[1993].[Quarter 2].[May]
[Dates].[All Dates].[1993].[Quarter 4].[October]
[Dates].[All Dates].[1993].[Quarter 4].[December]
[Dates].[All Dates].[1994].[Quarter 3].[September]
```

Collections of the Member Object

The Properties Collection

Contains a `Property` object for each provider-specific property.

```
Properties = Member.Properties
```

This works in the same way as the `Properties` collection for the ADO objects, where the provider implements specific functionality that cannot be covered by the ADOMD objects.

The Cell Object

A cell represents a single item of data, at the intersection of a number of `Axes` in a `CellSet`. This is much like a cell in a spreadsheet, and is uniquely identified by the `Positions` along the `Axes`.

Methods of the Cell Object

The `Cell` object has no methods.

Properties of the Cell Object

The Value Property

Indicates the value contained within the cell.

```
Cell.Value = Variant
Variant = Cell.Value
```

The FormattedValue Property

Indicates the formatted value of the cell.

```
Cell.FormattedValue = String
String = Cell.FormattedValue
```

The value from this property is the `Value` property formatted according to its type.

The Ordinal Property

The `Ordinal` property uniquely identifies a cell within a `CellSet`.

```
Long = Cell.Ordinal
```

The cellset notionally identifies each cell as though the cellset is a multi-dimensional array, and each array element has a unique number. Cells are numbered starting from 0, and the `Ordinal` can be used in the `Item` property of the `CellSet` to quickly locate a cell.

For the exact formula used to calculate the cell `Ordinal` you should consult the ADOMD documentation.

Collections of the Cell Object

The Positions Collection

Contains a collection of Position objects.

```
Positions = Cell.Positions
```

Each Cell comprises a number of Axes, and each Axis contains a number of Position objects. Each Position object uniquely identifies a row or column in the Axis.

You can use the Positions collection to iterate through each Position:

```
For Each objPos In objCell.Positions
    Print objPos.Name
Next
```

The Properties Collection

Contains an ADO Property object for each provider-specific property.

```
Properties = Cell.Properties
```

This works in the same way as the Properties collection for the ADO objects, where the provider implements specific functionality that cannot be covered by the ADOMD objects.

The CellSet Object

A CellSet object contains the results of a multi-dimensional query against an OLAP server. It contains collections of Cell objects, a collection of Axis objects, and details of the connection and query.

Methods of the CellSet Object

The Open Method

Opens a new CellSet based upon a multi-dimensional query.

```
CellSet.Open([DataSource], [ActiveConnection])
```

Parameter	Type	Description
DataSource	Variant	The multi-dimensional query that will retrieve the data.
ActiveConnection	Variant	Either an ADO Connection object or an ADO connection string.

The `DataSource` argument corresponds to the `Source` property of the `CellSet`. Multi-dimensional queries use their own variant of the SQL language (which is a standard). For example:

```
strQuery = "SELECT [Books].MEMBERS ON ROWS," & _
                " [Stores].MEMBERS ON COLUMNS" & _
            " FROM [PubsOLAP]"

objCellSet.Open strQuery, objConn
```

For more information on multi-dimensional queries you should consult the appropriate documentation, such as the SQL Server OLAP documentation, the MDX documentation in the Data Access SDK, or the MDAC web site, at http://www.microsoft.com/data.

The `ActiveConnection` argument corresponds to the `ActiveConnection` property.

The Close Method

Closes an open `CellSet`.

```
CellSet.Close
```

Closing a `CellSet` will release any child collections associated with the `CellSet`.

Properties of the CellSet Object

The ActiveConnection Property

Identifies the connection to which the `CellSet` or `Catalog` belongs.

```
Set Connection = CellSet.ActiveConnection
Set CellSet.ActiveConnection = Connection
String = CellSet.ActiveConnection
CellSet.ActiveConnection = String
```

This can be a valid ADO `Connection` object or an ADO connection string. Like ADO, if the string method is used then a new connection is made.

If the `ActiveConnection` argument of the `Open` method was used to specify the connection, then the `ActiveConnection` property inherits the value from the argument.

The Source Property

Identifies the multi-dimensional query used to return the data.

```
Variant = CellSet.Source
CellSet.Source = Variant
```

If the `DataSource` argument of the `Open` method was used to specify the query, then the `Source` property inherits its value from the argument.

The State Property

Identifies the current state of the CellSet.

```
Long = CellSet.State
```

The State can be one of the following ADO ObjectStateEnum constants:

❑   adStateOpen, to indicate the CellSet is open

❑   adStateClosed, to indicate the CellSet is closed

The FilterAxis Property

Indicates the filtering information for the CellSet.

```
Axis = CellSet.FilterAxis
```

If filtering has been used to restrict the data returned during the query, then the FilterAxis property will return an Axis object, usually containing one row, with the filter information.

The Item Property

Allows indexing into the Cellset to reference a specific Cell object.

```
Set Cell = CellSet.Item(Index)
```

Parameter	Type	Description	Default
Index	Variant	The number of the Cell in the collection. Zero-based.	

This is the default property, which means that its name can be omitted when called. For example, the following lines are equivalent:

```
Set objCell = objCellSet.Item(1)
```

```
Set objCell = objCellSet(1)
```

Collections of the CellSet Object

The Axes Collection

Contains an Axis object for each axis in the CellSet.

```
Axes = CellSet.Axes
```

This collection will always contain at least one Axis object. You can iterate through the Axes collection to examine the data in the CellSet. For example, consider the following OLAP query:

```
SELECT  Publishers.Members  ON COLUMNS,
        Geography.Members   ON ROWS,
        Dates.Members       ON PAGES
FROM    AllSales
```

This creates three `Axis` objects in the collection, for `Publishers`, `Geography`, and `Dates`.

The Properties Collection

Contains an ADO `Property` object for each provider-specific property.

```
Properties = CellSet.Properties
```

This works in the same way as the `Properties` collection for the ADO objects, where the provider implements specific functionality that cannot be covered by the ADOMD objects.

The Axis Object

An `Axis` object is an axis from the `Axes` collection of a `CellSet`. It represents the rows and columns of data in a query.

Methods of the Axis Object

The `Axis` object has no methods.

Properties of the Axis Object

The Name Property

Returns the name of the `Axis`.

```
String = Axis.Name
```

The DimensionCount Property

Returns the number of `Dimensions` on this `Axis`.

```
Long = Axis.DimensionCount
```

Collections of the Axis Object

The Positions Collection

Contains a collection of `Position` objects.

```
Positions = Axis.Positions
```

Using the `Positions` collection allows you to iterate through the unique rows and columns in a query.

11

ADOMD: Objects & Collections

The Properties Collection

Contains an ADO `Property` object for each provider-specific property.

```
Properties = Axis.Properties
```

This works in the same way as the `Properties` collection for the ADO objects, where the provider implements specific functionality that cannot be covered by the ADOMD objects.

The Position Object

A `Position` object contains the members of those dimensions that identify a point along a specific axis. For example, consider the following OLAP query:

```
SELECT  Publishers.Members  ON COLUMNS,
        Geography.Members   ON ROWS,
        Dates.Members       ON PAGES
FROM    AllSales
```

Let's suppose you examine just one set of members – Geography, for example. In this case, the `Positions` collection will contain an entry for each unique column:

```
[Geography].[All Geography]
[Geography].[All Geography].[CA]
[Geography].[All Geography].[CA].[Fremont]
[Geography].[All Geography].[CA].[Los Gatos]
[Geography].[All Geography].[CA].[Tustin]
[Geography].[All Geography].[OR]
[Geography].[All Geography].[OR].[Portland]
[Geography].[All Geography].[WA]
[Geography].[All Geography].[WA].[Remulade]
[Geography].[All Geography].[WA].[Seattle]
```

A `Position` contains the members and levels that allow a row or column to be uniquely identified.

Methods of the Position Object

The `Position` object has no methods.

Properties of the Position Object

The Ordinal Property

Identifies a position along an axis.

```
Long = Position.Ordinal
```

The `Ordinal` is a unique identifier for a position and corresponds to the `Index` of the position in the `Positions` collection.

Collections of the Position Object

The Members Collection

Contains a `Member` object for each member in the `Position` object.

```
Members = Position.Members
```

The ADOMD Collections

All collections in ADOMD have the same properties and work in the same way. The objects and collections are shown below:

Object	Contains collections:
Catalog	CubeDefs
CubeDef	Dimensions, Properties
Dimension	Hierarchies, Properties
Hierarchy	Levels, Properties
Level	Members, Properties
Member	Children, Properties
CellSet	Axes, Properties
Axis	Positions, Properties
Cell	Positions, Properties
Position	Members

Note that these collections do not offer any events or collections of their own.

Collection Methods

The Refresh Method

Updates the collection from the provider to ensure that it contains the latest objects.

```
Collection.Refresh
```

Collection Properties

The Count Property

Indicates the number of objects in the collection.

```
Long = Collection.Count
```

The Item Property

Allows indexing into the collection to reference a specific object.

```
Set Object = Collection.Item(Index)
```

Parameter	Type	Description
Index	Variant	The number or name of the object in the collection. Zero-based.

This is the default property, which means that its name may be omitted when called. For example, the following lines (which use the Positions collection) are equivalent:

```
Set objPosition = objPositions.Item(1)
```

```
Set objPosition = objPositions(1)
```

I thank God I am as honest as any man
living that is an old man and no honester th

Can counsel and speak comfort to the
Which they themselves not feel

Much Ado About Nothing.

He wears his faith but as the fashion of !

As merry as the day

He hath indeed better bettered expectation

(Act i. Sc. 1.).

He wears his faith but as the fashion of his hat.
(Ibid)

As merry as the day is long.

h indeed better bettered expectation

(Act i. Sc. 1.)

Much Ado About Nothing.

(Ibid)

an counsel and speak comfort to that grief
Which they themselves not feel.

He wears his faith but as the fashion of his hat.
(Ibid)

(Ibid)

I was not born under
a rhyming plane

I was not born under a rhyming plane
(Sc. 2)

For there was never yet
That could endure the to

merry as the day is long (Sc. 2)

Can counsel and speak comfort to that grief
Which they themselves not feel.

(Ibid)

He hath indeed better bettered expectation

I thank God I am as honest as any

living that is an old man and no honest

He wears his faith but as the fashion of his ha
(Ibi

Much Ado About Nothing.

For there was never yet philospher
That could endure the toothache patiently.

(Ibid)

I was not born u

12

Jet and Replication Objects

The Jet and Replication Objects (JRO, in msjro.dll) allow you to manipulate the replication features of a database through a simple set of objects. Although JRO is part of ADO, it only applies when replicating Access databases (to and from other Access databases, as well as to and from SQL Server). Replication allows you to have a number of copies of the same database, with the ability to synchronize changes between them. This is particularly useful in situations where the database user might be absent from the office but still requires database access. Users leaving the office can take a copy with them on a laptop computer, and synchronize changes on returning. Replication doesn't take place in real-time, but has to be initiated by the user, so there is no performance hit.

With the JRO you can:

❑   Compact databases

❑   Set passwords and encryption on databases

❑   Create replica databases

❑   Synchronize replica sets

❑   Control the memory cache

Replication allows you to create any number of copies of a database in which changes may be shared and synchronized between the copies. These copies are called the **replica set,** and you can replicate between any members in a replica set.

One of the replicated databases in a replica set database is designated the **design master**. Changes to objects (tables, queries, and so on) can only be made in the **design master**. Any replica in the replica set can be the design master (by default it's the first replica created), but you can only have one design master at any time.

A database may be defined as replicable, but not actually be replicated. This just means that the database *can* be replicated if desired, but it isn't at the moment.

If replication is used with Access 2000 and SQL Server 7.0 onwards, then you can get full, bi-directional data replication between the Access and SQL Server databases. For more details on this, and other areas of replication, you should consult the documentation of Microsoft Office 2000, Microsoft SQL Server, and Microsoft Office Developer Edition. The object model looks like this:

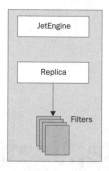

If you'd like to learn more about Access replication then the Microsoft Jet Database Engine Programmer's Guide (Second Edition), Microsoft Press, has a chapter devoted to it. It doesn't discuss JRO at all, but covers what happens to Access databases during the replication process, and how you can best use replication. In fact, if you're an Access programmer, it's worth getting the book anyway, since there's lots of useful information in there.

Creating Replica Databases

Creating a replica database is extremely simple, and only involves selecting the **Create Replica...** option from the **Tools** menu:

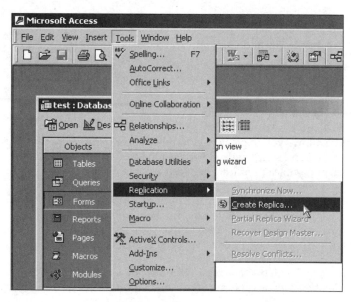

Creating a replica can only be done on a closed database, so Access will ask you if it's OK to do this. You are then asked if you'd like a backup copy of the database made. It's always wise to say "yes" to this question, since creating the replica results in changes to the database, and you cannot change a replicated database back into a non-replicated database.

You are then asked for the name and location of the replica database, and Access goes ahead and creates it. The current copy then becomes the design master.

The Replica Object

The Replica object represents a copy of a replicated database. Using a replica database is simply a matter of instantiating the Replica object:

```
Dim objRep As JRO.Replica
Set objRep = New JRO.Replica
```

Once the object is created, you can the set the ActiveConnection property, and call the methods.

Methods of the Replica Object

The CreateReplica Method

Creates a replica of any database that is replicable (that allows replicas of itself to be created).

```
Replica.CreateReplica(replicaName, description, [ReplicaType], _
                       [Visibility], [Priority], [updatability])
```

Parameter	Type	Description
replicaName	String	The name and path of the replica to be created.
description	String	A description of the newly replicated database.
ReplicaType	ReplicaTypeEnum	Indicates the type of the replica database to create. Default is jrRepTypeFull.
Visibility	VisibilityEnum	Indicates the visibility of the new replica database. For more details see the Visibility property. Default is jrRepVisibilityGlobal.
Priority	Long	The priority of the database for use in conflict resolution. For more details see the Priority property. Default is −1.

Parameter	Type	Description
updatability	UpdatabilityEnum	Indicates the type of updates allowed in the new replica database. Default is jrRepUpdFull.

ReplicaType can be one of the following ReplicaTypeEnum constants:

❑   jrRepTypeFull, to indicate a full replica; this is the default

❑   jrRepTypePartial, to indicate a partial replica

Visibility can be one of the following VisibilityEnum constants:

❑   jrRepVisibilityGlobal, to indicate a global replica

❑   jrRepVisibilityLocal, to indicate a local replica

❑   jrRepVisibilityAnon, to indicate an anonymous replica

For more information on these options refer to section on the Visibility property.

Updatability can be one of the following UpdatabilityEnum constants:

❑   jrRepUpdFull, to indicate that the new replica allows changes to the schema and records

❑   jrRepUpdReadOnly, to indicate that the new replica does not allow changes to the schema and records

For example:

```
Dim objDB As JRO.Replica
Set objDB = New JRO.Replica

objDB.ActiveConnection = _
    "Provider=Microsoft.Jet.OLEDB.4.0; Data
Source=C:\Temp\pubs.mdb"
objDB.CreateReplica _
    "C:\Temp\NewReplica.mdb", "A new replica", jrRepTypePartial
```

You can only create a replica of the source database if the source database is replicable – that is, its ReplicaType property must not be jrRepTypeNotReplicable.

The GetObjectReplicability Method

Identifies whether or not the object is replicated, or has been marked so as to be replicated the next time synchronization between replicas takes place.

```
Boolean = Replica.GetObjectReplicability(objectName, objectType)
```

Parameter	Type	Description
objectName	String	The name of the object.
objectType	String	The type of the object.

objectName identifies the object that is to be tested for replicability. The objectType is the container name in Access, so this will be Tables, Queries, Forms, Reports, Macros, or Modules.

If objectName is contained in a non-replicable database, then the GetObjectReplicability method will return True – because the object will be replicable if the database is made replicable. This method doesn't actually take account of the replicability of the database itself – just the requested object.

A value of False indicates that the database is replicable, but that the object itself is not replicable.

For example:

```
If objDB.GetObjectReplicability("authors", "tables") = True Then
    Print "The authors table may be replicated in the future"
End If
```

The MakeReplicable Method

Adjusts the properties of the database to allow it to be replicated.

```
Replica.MakeReplicable([connectionString], [columnTracking])
```

Parameter	Type	Description
connectionString	String	The full path of the database that is to be made replicable.
columnTracking	Boolean	Indicates whether changes are tracked by row or column. Default is True, indicating column tracking.

The source database must be opened exclusively before it can be made replicable.

The PopulatePartial Method

Populates a partial replica.

```
Replica.PopulatePartial(FullReplica)
```

Parameter	Type	Description
FullReplica	String	The full path of the replica database to be populated with data.

You can only replicate a database if it is replicable – that is, its ReplicaType property must not be jrRepTypeNotReplicable.

12

For full details on the implications of replication, including conflict resolution and orphaned records, you should consult the Jet documentation.

The SetObjectReplicability Method

Sets whether or not an object will be replicated (in the event of a call to the `CreateReplica` method).

```
Replica.SetObjectReplicability(objectName, objectType, _
                               replicability)
```

Parameter	Type	Description
objectName	String	The name of the object to replicate.
objectType	String	The type of the object.
replicability	Boolean	Set to True to make this a replicable object, and False to keep the object local.

Note that, if the database has not been marked for replication, then all of its objects are replicable by default – unless `SetObjectReplicability` is used to mark them otherwise. This is to allow all objects to be automatically replicated, once the database is made replicable.

For example:

```
objDB.SetObjectReplicability "authors", "tables", False
```

The object type is the container name in Access, so this will be `Tables`, `Queries`, `Forms`, `Reports`, `Macros`, or `Modules`.

The Synchronize Method

Synchronizes two replica databases from the same replica set.

```
Replica.Synchronize(target, [syncType], [syncMode])
```

Parameter	Type	Description
target	String	The full path of the target replica database with which the current database will synchronize, or the name of a Synchronizer to manage the target replica database, or the Internet server on which the target replica is located.
syncType	SyncTypeEnum	The type of synchronization to be performed. Default is jrSyncTypeImpExp.
syncMode	SyncModeEnum	The synchronization method to be used. Default is jrSyncModeIndirect.

syncType can be one of the following `SyncTypeEnum` constants:

- ❑ `jrSyncTypeExport`, to export changes from the current database to the target database

- ❑ `jrSyncTypeImport`, to import changes from the target database into the current database

- ❑ `jrSyncTypeImpExp`, to exchange changes between the current database and the target database

syncMode can be one of the following `SyncModeEnum` constants:

- ❑ `jrSyncModeIndirect`, to indicate that indirect synchronization is to take place. This is where the *target* parameter contains the name of the synchronizer that will perform the remote synchronization, and is best used over poor or inconsistent lines, such as WANs or modem lines.

- ❑ `jrSyncModeDirect`, to indicate that direct synchronization is to take place. Here, both databases are opened together and the appropriate changes made.

- ❑ `jrSyncModeInternet`, to indicate that synchronization will take place over the Internet. Here, the *target* parameter will contain the URL of the Internet server on which the target database is located.

Synchronization is simply a matter of exchanging records that have changed between databases. Direct is the most common method, where you have the two Access replicas available on the local network. In this case, Access checks each replicable object to see whether it needs to be copied to the other database. The Internet mode performs a similar operation, but allows the target database to be located on an Internet server. The Indirect mode allows synchronization to take place even when the target database is unavailable, perhaps through a known poor connection, a slow WAN link or modem. In this case, the changes aren't directly made to the target database, but placed in a 'drop-box' (such as a shared folder), where they can be picked up at a later date by the target database.

If the synchronization process detects conflicts it will create a table containing the conflicting records. This will be the same name of the original table, but with `_Conflict` added. See the `ConflictTables` property for more information.

Properties of the Replica Object

The ActiveConnection Property

Indicates the ADO `Connection` string or object.

```
Set Object = Replica.ActiveConnection
Set Replica.ActiveConnection = Object
String = Replica.ActiveConnection
Replica.ActiveConnection = String
```

You can use the standard ADO formats for this. Here are a couple of examples:

```
objDB.ActiveConnection = "Provider=Microsoft.Jet.OLEDB.4.0; " & _
                         "Data Source=C:\temp\pubs.mdb"
```

```
Set objDB.ActiveConnection = objConn
```

The ConflictFunction Property

This points to the name of a function that will be used to perform conflict resolution.

```
Replica.ConflictFunction = String
String = Replica.ConflictFunction
```

This function allows you to specify your own method for resolving conflicts. The default action is for Access to call its built-in conflict resolver. This is a fairly simple routine, and is based on the version number of the record (stored in a field added to the table when the replica is created). Every time a change is made to a record this field is incremented, and Access uses the difference in version numbers to determine which record contains the data that wins the update. The assumption used is that the record whose version number has changed the most is the correct record. If both records contain the same version number, then the `ReplicaID` property of the replica set is used, and the lowest one wins.

If you wish to use your own conflict resolution function, use something like:

```
objDB.ConflictFunction = "MyConflictResolver()"
```

Your function should be a public function (not a sub) in the database, and its job is to look through the replica tables and work out which record is the correct one. If you intend to do this, you'll need to think very carefully about what determines the correct record. The Access method is simplistic, but is logical. You can't rely on things such as the date the record was changed, because dates on different machines might be different (especially if they are in different time zones).

The function you build will have to open both tables and check each field in each record, seeing whether any changes have been made. If so, then you'll need some form of business logic to pick the correct record, or you will need to provide a user interface, to display both records and let the user decide which is the correct record.

The ConflictTables Property

Identifies the list of tables that contain conflict information.

```
Recordset = Replica.ConflictTables
```

If conflict errors are generated during synchronization, a table is created containing the conflicting rows, and the `ConflictTables` property will contain a recordset made up of two columns. The first column, `TABLE_NAME`, indicates the first table which contains the original data; the second column, `CONFLICT_TABLE_NAME`, indicates the table containing the conflicting rows. You can then open the conflicting table, fetch a conflicting row of data, and compare it with the original row from the original table.

For example, imagine synchronizing a database with a table called 'authors'. If there were any conflicts, table called 'authors_Conflict' would be created containing the conflicting rows. In this case, the ConflictTables would contain:

TABLE_NAME	CONFLICT_TABLE_NAME
authors	authors_Conflict

The DesignMasterId Property

The unique ID of the design master database.

```
Replica.DesignMasterId = Variant
Variant = Replica.DesignMasterId
```

This property is created automatically at the time a database is set to be the design master. The DesignMasterId is a GUID value.

Each replica in a replica set has a Globally Unique ID (GUID), which is used to uniquely identify it. The only values for DesignMasterId are GUIDs from other replicas in the replica set.

The Priority Property

Identifies the relative priority of a replica during conflict resolution.

```
Long = Replica.Priority
```

During conflict resolution the following applies:

❑ The replica with the highest Priority value wins. Priorities range from 0 to 100.

❑ If the Priority values are equal, the replica with the highest ReplicaID wins.

The default priority for global replicas is 90% of the priority of the parent replica. The value for local and anonymous replicas is 0.

The ReplicaId Property

A unique identifier for a replica database.

```
Variant = Replica.ReplicaId
```

This value is a GUID, which is automatically generated at the time the replica is created.

The ReplicaType Property

Identifies the type of the replica database.

```
ReplicaTypeEnum = Replica.ReplicaType
```

ReplicaTypeEnum can be one of the following constants:

- ❑ jrRepTypeNotReplicable, to identify that the database is not replicable; this is the default

- ❑ jrRepTypeDesignMaster, to indicate that the database is the design master

- ❑ jrRepTypeFull, to indicate that the database is a full replica

- ❑ jrRepTypePartial, to indicate that the database is a partial replica

A value of jrRepTypeNotReplicable does not mean that the database can never be replicated, but that it has not yet been made replicable. You can use the MakeReplicable method to make the database replicable at run-time.

The RetentionPeriod Property

Identifies the number of days for which replica histories should be kept.

```
Replica.RetentionPeriod = Long
Long = Replica.RetentionPeriod
```

A replica set retains details of changes for the number of days (from 5 to 32,000) specified in this property.

The default value is dependent on how the database was made replicable. If the database was made replicable with the Replication Manager, RDO or ADO, the RetentionPeriod value defaults to 60. If the database was made replicable with Access, the RetentionPeriod value defaults to 1000.

You can set this property at any time, but only on a design master database.

The Visibility Property

Indicates the visibility of the database.

```
VisibilityEnum = Replica.Visibility
```

VisibilityEnum can be one of the following constants:

- ❑ jrRepVisibilityGlobal, to indicate a global replica

- ❑ jrRepVisibilityLocal, to indicate a local replica

- ❑ jrRepVisibilityAnon, to indicate an anonymous replica

A global replica is typically the design master, and is allowed to synchronize with any replicas in the replica set. A local or anonymous replica can only synchronize with a global replica, and not other replicas in the set. The difference between a local and an anonymous replica is that the global replica can see local replicas, but not anonymous ones. This is useful in situations where you have a central hub that is the global replica, which, perhaps automatically, performs the replication process with other replicas in the set, but not anonymous ones because it cannot see them. The user of the anonymous replica can then synchronize at his or her will. This allows databases to be part of a replica set, but not to take part in the standard synchronization process, thereby allowing them to be synchronized when required.

For more information on replica schemes you should consult the Access documentation.

Collections of the Replica Object

The Filters Collection

Contains a `Filter` object for each filter specifying replication information.

```
Set Filters = Replica.Filters
```

There's more on the `Filters` collection later in this chapter. Before we look at that, we'll take a look at what an individual `Filter` object can do.

The Filter Object

A `Filter` object specifies the details of a filter that limits the records transferred during replication. This allows you to create partial replicas containing a subset of the main database. A partial replica is still a bi-directional one, but with less data.

Don't confuse the `Filter` object with the `Filter` method of the ADO `Recordset` object – the two are not related. `Filter` objects are created by adding them to the `Filters` collection of the `Replica` object.

Methods of the Filter Object

There are no methods for the `Filter` object.

Properties of the Filter Object

The FilterCriteria Property

Sets or returns the string that controls the filter.

```
String = Filter.FilterCriteria
```

The filter string is a standard SQL WHERE clause, without the WHERE keyword. The filter only determines which records in a table are replicated, but not which tables. For this, you must set the table so that it isn't replicable.

The filter criteria are set in the Append method of the `Filters` collection.

The FilterType Property

Indicates the type of the filter.

```
FilterTypeEnum = Filter.FilterType
```

`FilterTypeEnum` can be one of the following constants:

- ❑ `jrFilterTypeRelationship`, to indicate that the filter is based on a relationship

- ❑ `jrFilterTypeTable`, to indicate that the filter is based on a table

The filter type is set in the `Append` method of the `Filters` collection.

The TableName Property

Identifies the table to which the `Filter` applies.

```
String = Filter.TableName
```

When the filter is based on a one-to-many relationship, the table name is the table on the many side of a join.

The filter table name is set in the `Append` method of the `Filters` collection.

The Filters Collection

The `Filters` collection contains a `Filter` object for each filter applicable to the replication process. You cannot create more than one filter of the same type on a table.

Methods of the Filters Collection

The Append Method

Adds a new filter to the collection.

```
Filters.Append(TableName, FilterType, FilterCriteria)
```

Parameter	Type	Description
TableName	String	The name of the table to which the filter applies, or (if the filter is based on a relationship) the name of the table on the many side of a join.
FilterType	FilterType Enum	The type of filter.
FilterCriteria	String	The SQL clause that makes up the filter.

The `FilterType` can be one of the following constants:

❑ `jrFilterTypeRelationship`, to indicate that the filter is based on a relationship

❑ `jrFilterTypeTable`, to indicate that the filter is based on a table

Using the filter types specified above, you can create filters that apply either to tables or to relationships. For example, the following creates a filter based upon a table:

```
objDB.Filters.Append "authors", jrFilterTypeTable, "state='CA'"
```

The second example creates a filter based upon a join:

```
objDB.Filters.Append "authors", _
                jrFilterTypeRelationship, "qryPublishersAuthors"
```

For the `FilterCriteria` you specify the query that makes up the relationship, and for the `TableName` you specify the table that is on the many side of the relationship.

The Delete Method

Deletes a `Filter` object from the collection.

```
Filters.Delete(Item)
```

Parameter	Type	Description
Item	Variant	The index number or table name of the `Filter` object to be deleted.

The Refresh Method

Refreshes the collection so that changes are visible.

```
Filters.Refresh
```

Properties of the Filters Collection

The Count Property

Returns the number of `Filter` objects in the collection.

```
Long = Filters.Count
```

The Item Property

Allows indexing into the collection, by either name or number.

```
Filter = Filters.Item(Item)
```

Parameter	Type	Description
Item	Variant	The name of the Filter, or its index number.

This is the default method, which means that the method name can be omitted when the method is called. For example, the following expressions are equivalent:

```
objReplica.Filters("Name")
```

```
objReplica.Filters.Item("Name")
```

The JetEngine Object

The JetEngine object gives you control of the Jet Database Engine.

Methods of the JetEngine Object

The CompactDatabase Method

Copies and compacts a database into a new database.

```
JetEngine.CompactDatabase(SourceConnection, DestConnection)
```

Parameter	Type	Description
SourceConnection	String	An ADO Connection string identifying the database that is to be compacted.
DestConnection	String	An ADO Connection string identifying the new database that is to be created from the compaction.

Using this method you cannot compact in-place, that is, you cannot compact a database into itself. You must specify the database name and location of the new database to be created, or an error will be generated. For example:

```
objJE.CompactDatabase "Provider=Microsoft.Jet.OLEDB.4.0; " & _
                      "Data Source=C:\temp\pubs.mdb", _
               "Provider=Microsoft.Jet.OLEDB.4.0; " & _
                      "Data Source=C:\temp\newpubs.mdb"
```

The connection string only allows a limited set of provider-specific properties – all other properties are ignored. The allowed properties are:

Property	Source	Destination
Provider	✓	✓
Data Source	✓	✓

Property	Source	Destination
User Id	✓	
Password	✓	
Locale Identifier		✓
Jet OLEDB:Database Password	✓	✓
Jet OLEDB:Engine Type	✓	✓
Jet OLEDB:Registry Path	✓	
Jet OLEDB:System Database	✓	
Jet OLEDB:Encrypt Database		✓
Jet OLEDB:Don't Copy Locale on Compact		✓
Jet OLEDB:Compact Without Relationships		✓
Jet OLEDB:Compact Without Replica Repair		✓

These properties are added to the connection string in the usual way. For example:

```
objJE.CompactDatabase "Provider=Microsoft.Jet.OLEDB.4.0; " & _
                      "Data Source=C:\temp\pubs.mdb; " & _
                      "User Id=davids; Password=abc123", _
            "Provider=Microsoft.Jet.OLEDB.4.0; " & _
                      "Data Source=C:\temp\newpubs.mdb;" & _
                      "Jet OLEDB:Encrypt Database=True"
```

For more details on these properties consult the ADO Properties collection in Appendix C.

The RefreshCache Method

RefreshCache allows you to force any pending writes to the database, and refresh the memory with the latest data from the database.

```
JetEngine.RefreshCache(Connection)
```

Parameter	Type	Description
Connection	Connection	An open ADO Connection object for which the cache should be refreshed.

In high multi-user applications you can use this method to free memory locks.

I thank God I am as honest as any man

iving that is an old man and no honester th

Much Ado About Nothing.

Can counsel and speak comfort to the

Which they themselves not feel

He wears his faith but as the fashion of

As merry as the day

He hath indeed better bettered expectation

(Act i. Sc. i.).

He wears his faith but as the fashion of his hat.

(Ibid)

As merry as the day is long.

h indeed better bettered expectation

(Ibid)

(Act i. Sc. i.).

Much Ado About Nothing.

an counsel and speak comfort to that grief

Which they themselves not feel.

He wears his faith but as the fashion of his hat.

(Ibid)

(Ibid)

I was not born under

a rhyming plane

I was not born under a rhyming plan

(Sc.

For there was never yet

That could endure the to

merry as the day is long

(Sc.

Can counsel and speak comfort to that grief

Which they themselves not feel.

(Ibid)

(Ibid)

He hath indeed better bettere(Ibid)xpectation

(Ibid)

I thank God I am as honest as any

(Act i Sc. i.

living that is an old man and no honest

He wears his faith but as the fashion of his ha

(Ibi

Much Ado About Nothing.

themselves not feel.

(Ibid)

I was not born u

13

Data Shaping

In this chapter, we'll take a comprehensive look at Data Shaping. The Data Shape provider originally shipped with ADO 2.0. It provides a way to arrange sets of related data hierarchically; it also provides an efficient way to transfer related sets of data from the server to a client. ADO 2.1 added some new features to the Data Shape Provider and, although ADO 2.6 hasn't introduced anything new, it's still worth covering in detail. If you've only ever looked at ADO 2.0, then ADO 2.1 introduced the following:

- ❑ **Hierarchy Reshaping**, to allow the creation of new hierarchies based upon existing data

- ❑ **Grandchild Aggregates and Grouping**, to allow aggregation of the values of specific grandchildren in a hierarchy into a higher aggregation level

- ❑ **Parameterized Computed Children**, to allow an aggregate level to be inserted between a parent and parameterized child

Examples of these are shown later in the chapter.

The easiest way to understand data shaping is to use another term that is often employed – **hierarchical recordsets**. Think about all of those times that you've had master and detail recordsets – publishers and books are a good example. The easiest way to imagine this is to think of the Windows file system, where you have folders and sub-folders. In data shaping terms you have recordsets and sub-recordsets. Take a look at the following diagram, which shows a shape we want to achieve (not it's actual structure) involving `publishers`, `titles`, and `sales` from the SQL Server default pubs database:

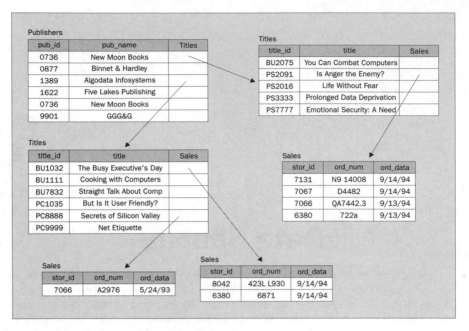

This could be created with the following `SHAPE` command:

```
SHAPE {SELECT * FROM publishers}
APPEND ((SHAPE {SELECT * FROM titles}
    APPEND ({SELECT * FROM sales}
    RELATE title_id TO title_id))
RELATE pub_id TO pub_id)
```

What this produces is a recordset for the publishers, with an extra column containing another recordset for titles. The `Titles` recordset also has an extra column for the `Sales` recordset. These child recordsets are often called **chapters** – and the data type of the column would be `adChapter`. In the above example only three recordsets are created – one each for `Sales`, `Titles`, and `Publishers`. What the shaping service does is provide a way to map the relational structure of primary and foreign keys in a table, with a parent-child relationship.

The child column actually contains the details that relate the parent to the child, and when you access the child column, the child recordset is filtered so only the correct rows are shown. So, creating the above hierarchy against SQL Server, you can see (using SQL Trace in SQL 6.5 or SQL Profiler in SQL 7) three statements sent to the server:

```
select * from publishers
select * from titles
select * from sales
```

These are all sent in one command, and returned as multiple recordsets. All of the data is sent back at once. The client only has three recordsets, so resource usage is kept to a minimum, although the amount of data could still be substantial.

The data shape provider performs no optimization on the SQL statements sent to the server. For example, consider the following SHAPE command:

```
SHAPE {select * from publishers where state = 'ca'}
APPEND ({select * from titles}
RELATE pub_id TO pub_id)
```

This returns two recordsets – the first containing details of all publishers where the state is ca, and the second containing all titles. This isn't a joined query, so the titles query returns all titles, not just those for publishers in ca. The data shaping actually takes place on the client, and the Data Provider is just the supplier of data.

Child Data Caching

You can force the Data Shape provider to query the data source for the child data each time a parent row is accessed. To do this, set the "Cache Child Rows" dynamic property to False:

```
objRs.Properties("Cache Child Rows") = False
```

Normally this property is True – this tells the local cursor service to cache the child data. By setting it to False, you ensure that the cursor service requeries the data provider for new information each time a parent row is accessed. This ensures that the data for the child is up-to-date, but it does impose a performance penalty, although the initial load might be quicker.

Child Recordsets

When you access a row in the parent recordset, the child recordset automatically reflects the values related to the parent – in fact the child recordset is closed and then reopened with the new values.

You can change this behavior so that when you move to a new record the child recordset does not change. This behavior is controlled by the StayInSync property of the Recordset. Setting this to True (the default) keeps the child recordset synchronized with its parent. Setting it to False ensures that no synchronization takes place. For example:

```
objRs.StayInSync = False
```

One use of this is if you want to move around the parent recordset without the overhead of the child recordset being available.

Using Data Shaping

There are two important things to know if you want to use data shaping:

- ❏ You have to use the MSDataShape provider. Your provider that supplies the data becomes the Data Provider.
- ❏ You have to use a special Data Shape language, which is a superset of SQL.

13

Data Shaping

If you've got Visual Basic 6 then there's a really quick way to produce your shape commands using the Data Environment Designer (select the **Project** menu and **Add Data Environment**). The Data Environment Designer can write your SHAPE commands for you, saving you from having to worry about the syntax, but it's worth while learning it anyway, especially if you are working in ASP and may not have Visual Basic installed. You'll see examples of the designer later in the chapter.

The Shape Language

The SHAPE command has its own formal grammar, which we won't list here (it's included in the ADO documentation which is installed when you install the Microsoft Data Access Components), but we will go through the way you use this command. In general, your shape command will look something like this:

```
SHAPE {parent_command} [[AS] table_alias]
APPEND ({child_command} [[AS] child_table_alias]
        RELATE parent_column TO child_column) [[AS] column_name]
```

This defines the parent and the child, and how they relate. The parent_command and child_command are the statements that define the parent and child recordsets. In most cases these will be SQL statements, but they can be any command appropriate to the OLE DB Provider in use. You can happily omit the table_alias, but the column_name is extremely useful as it defines the name of the column containing the child recordset. Take the pubs database and show an example using publishers and titles:

```
SHAPE {SELECT * FROM publishers}
APPEND ({SELECT * FROM titles}
        RELATE pub_id TO pub_id) AS recTitles
```

So, the first line is the parent – this will be a list of publishers:

```
SHAPE {SELECT * FROM publishers}
```

For each publisher we want a list of titles, so we APPEND a query that lists the titles:

```
APPEND ({SELECT * FROM titles}
```

Now we identify how the two commands are linked together. This is the primary key in the parent table and the foreign key in the child table:

```
        RELATE pub_id TO pub_id) AS recTitles
```

The alias used here is what the new column will be called. The data shape provider creates this new column on the parent, and for each entry, this column contains a recordset of its own.

Here's a simple piece of VB code that creates a shape and navigates through the records in both the parent and the child – you'll need to change the connect string to point to your server for this:

```
Dim objConn      As ADODB.Connection
Dim objRs        As ADODB.Recordset
Dim objRsTitle   As ADODB.Recordset
Dim strShape     As String

Set objConn = New ADODB.Connection
Set objRs = New ADODB.Recordset

' use the data shape provider,
' with SQL Server as the source of the data
objConn.Provider = "MSDataShape"
objConn.Open "Data Provider=SQLOLEDB; Data Source=Tigger; " & _
             "Initial Catalog=pubs; User Id=sa; Password="

' define our shape string and open the recordset
strShape = "SHAPE {SELECT * FROM publishers}" & _
           " APPEND ({SELECT * FROM titles}" & _
           " RELATE pub_id TO pub_id) AS recTitles"
objRs.Open strShape, objConn

' loop through the parent records
While Not objRs.EOF
    Debug.Print objRs("pub_name")

    ' set the recordset for the child
    ' records and loop through them
    Set objRsTitle = objRs("recTitles").Value
    While Not objRsTitle.EOF
        Debug.Print vbTab; objRsTitle("title")
        objRsTitle.MoveNext
    Wend
    objRs.MoveNext
Wend

objRs.Close
objConn.Close
Set objRs = Nothing
Set objConn = Nothing
Set objRsTitle = Nothing
```

The first thing to notice about this is that we set the Data Provider to point to the OLE DB provider that actually supplies the data, and we set the Provider property to MSDataShape. So the actual OLE DB Provider is MSDataShape – its job is to get the data from somewhere else and shape it. This means we have to tell the Data Shape provider where we want the actual data to come from – we've done that here through the Data Provider part of the connection string. This means that the Data Shape provider can take data from any OLE DB provider.

The SHAPE command becomes the source of our recordset, and we can loop through this as normal. Notice that we use a second recordset to point to the child recordset, which is stored as a column in the first recordset. The Value of this column is the child recordset. This produces the following output:

13

Data Shaping

359

New Moon Books
   You Can Combat Computer Stress!
   Is Anger the Enemy?
   Life Without Fear
   Prolonged Data Deprivation: Four Case Studies
   Emotional Security: A New Algorithm
Binnet & Hardley
   Silicon Valley Gastronomic Treats
   The Gourmet Microwave
   The Psychology of Computer Cooking
   Computer Phobic AND Non-Phobic Individuals: Behavior Variations
   Onions, Leeks, and Garlic: Cooking Secrets of the Mediterranean
   Fifty Years in Buckingham Palace Kitchens
   Sushi, Anyone?
Algodata Infosystems
   The Busy Executive's Database Guide
   Cooking with Computers: Surreptitious Balance Sheets
   Straight Talk About Computers
   But Is It User Friendly?
   Secrets of Silicon Valley
   Net Etiquette
Five Lakes Publishing
Ramona Publishers
GGG&G
Scootney Books
Lucerne Publishing

Notice that some records don't have child records. In this case, an empty recordset is created.

You don't have to assign a different variable to hold the child recordset to a `Recordset` object if you don't want to. Instead, you can access the child recordset directly:

```
objRs("recTitles").Value.Fields("title")
```

Multiple Children

In the above example we saw publishers and titles, but a parent recordset is not restricted to only one child recordset. For example, the publishers also have employees, and we may wish to include this information in our data schema:

```
SHAPE {SELECT * FROM publishers}
APPEND ({SELECT * FROM titles}
        RELATE pub_id TO pub_id) AS rsTitles,
       ({SELECT * FROM employee}
        RELATE pub_id TO pub_id) AS rsEmployees
```

This follows the same rules as the above example, but we are appending two commands. The parent is `publishers`, to which we `APPEND` two select queries (separated by a comma), giving them the names `rsTitles` and `rsEmployees`. The syntax for these is the same, indicating the relationship of the parent to the child:

```
SHAPE {parent_command} [[AS] table_alias]
APPEND ({child_command_1} [[AS] child_table_1_alias]
       RELATE parent_column TO child_column_1) [[AS] column_name_1],
       {child_command_2} [[AS] child_table_2_alias]
       RELATE parent_column TO child_column_2) [[AS] column_name_2]
```

The recordset would now have two extra columns, which you could use in the same way as above:

```
Set objRsTitles = objRs("rsTitles").Value
Set objRsEmps = objRs("rsEmployees").Value
```

Grandchildren

Data shaping doesn't have to be limited to sets of data one level deep. Each of the child records can have its own children, thus allowing you to nest to arbitrary depths. For example, suppose we wanted to add the sales for each title, showing the date purchased and the number sold. The SHAPE command now becomes:

```
SHAPE {SELECT * FROM publishers}
APPEND (( SHAPE {SELECT * FROM titles}
    APPEND ({SELECT * FROM sales}
    RELATE title_id TO title_id) AS rsSales)
RELATE pub_id TO pub_id) AS rsTitles
```

This just adds another APPEND and RELATE command to relate the new child table to its parent. So now you could change your code accordingly. Add a new variable declaration:

```
Dim objRsSales As ADODB.Recordset
```

And then add the loop to print the sales:

```
Set objRsTitle = objRs("rsTitles").Value
While Not objRsTitle.EOF
    Debug.Print vbTab; objRsTitle("title")
    Set objRsSales = objRsTitle("rsSales").Value
    While Not objRsSales.EOF
        Debug.Print vbTab; vbTab; objRsSales("ord_date");
                           vbTab; objRsSales("qty")
        objRsSales.MoveNext
    Wend

    objRsTitle.MoveNext
Wend
```

What you now see is this:

Binnet & Hardley
  Silicon Valley Gastronomic Treats
    12/12/93 10
  The Gourmet Microwave
    14/09/94 25
    14/09/94 15

>The Psychology of Computer Cooking
>Computer Phobic AND Non-Phobic Individuals: Behavior Variations
>   29/05/93 20
>Onions, Leeks, and Garlic: Cooking Secrets of the Mediterranean
>   15/06/92 40

The SQL statement is not limited to just SELECT *, and you can use almost any SQL statement you like. The only restriction is that you must have matching columns in the parent and child SELECTs, but this is not different from a normal SQL join or sub-query.

Summarizing with Shapes

The data shape language also has a way to produce summary information, allowing your parent to hold summary details, while the children hold the individual details. This is really useful for those drill-down situations in management information systems where you show a total and then can drill down into the details. For example, imagine that you wanted to find out the total sales of each book subject area, as well as being able to see the sales for individual titles.

For this type of data shape, you need to use a different form of the shaping language:

```
SHAPE {child_command} [[AS] table_alias]
COMPUTE aggregate_field_list
BY group_field_list
```

For example, you could construct a shape command like this:

```
SHAPE {SELECT * FROM titles}  AS rsTitlesSales
COMPUTE TitlesSales, SUM(TitlesSales.ytd_sales) AS NumberSold
BY type
```

The first line is familiar – you are creating a shape, and it is to be called rsTitlesSales. You want to sum the ytd_sales column of this shape, grouping on the type column. Your parent recordset will contain three columns:

❑   type, which is the column we grouped on

❑   NumberSold, which is the column we summed

❑   rsTitlesSales, which is the child recordset

The child recordset contains the SQL statement from the first line and, as a result of this, everything in the titles table.

You could access the result with code like this:

```
While Not objRs.EOF
    Debug.Print objRs("type"); vbTab; objRs("NumberSold")

    Set objRsSales = objRs("rsTitlesSales").Value
    While Not objRsSales.EOF
        Debug.Print vbTab; objRsSales("title"); _
```

```
                        vbTab; objRsSales("ytd_sales")
            objRsSales.MoveNext
      Wend
      objRs.MoveNext
  Wend
```

And the results it produces would be like this:

```
business    30788
   The Busy Executive's Database Guide   4095
   Cooking with Computers: Surreptitious Balance Sheets   3876
   You Can Combat Computer Stress!   18722
   Straight Talk About Computers   4095
mod_cook    24278
   Silicon Valley Gastronomic Treats   2032
   The Gourmet Microwave   22246
```

Stored Procedures

In addition to using SELECT queries in your shape commands, you can also use stored procedures. For example, imagine two stored procedures:

```
CREATE PROCEDURE usp_AllPublishers
AS
     SELECT *
     FROM   publishers
```

and:

```
CREATE PROCEDURE usp_TitlesByPubID
     @PubID char(4)
AS
     SELECT *
     FROM   titles
     WHERE  pub_id = @PubID
```

The first just returns all publishers, and the second returns all titles for a given publisher. You could create a shape command to use these two as follows:

```
SHAPE {{CALL dbo.usp_AllPublishers }}
APPEND ({{CALL dbo.usp_TitlesByPubID( ?) }}
RELATE pub_id TO  PARAMETER 0) AS rsTitlesByPubID
```

Notice that instead of the SELECT commands we previously had, there is now a call to the stored procedures – the statement is passed directly through to the OLE DB Provider (SQL Server in this case), and therefore uses the appropriate provider syntax. The stored procedure for the child takes a parameter – since the parameter is to be filled in by the parent, we RELATE the pub_id field to the parameter – the foreign key of the child. The shape command processor automatically takes care of filling in this parameter for each child recordset. While this might look cool, you should be aware that this can have a detrimental effect on performance, as the child stored procedure is executed each time it is referenced. If you have stored procedures that are children, then all parameters must participate in the relationship.

13

Data Shaping

If you wanted the parent stored procedure to accept an argument, such as the country, then it could be written like this:

```
CREATE PROCEDURE usp_PublishersByCountry
    @Country varchar(30)
AS
    SELECT *
    FROM    publishers
    WHERE   country = @Country
```

The shape command would now become:

```
SHAPE {{CALL dbo.usp_PublishersByCountry( ?) }}
APPEND ({{CALL dbo.usp_TitlesByPubID( ?) }}
RELATE pub_id TO  PARAMETER 0) AS rsTitlesByPubID
```

You can pass a parameter into this command in three ways. The first is to add it in manually:

```
SHAPE {{CALL dbo.usp_PublishersByCountry('USA') }}
APPEND ({{CALL dbo.usp_TitlesByPubID( ?) }}
RELATE pub_id TO  PARAMETER 0) AS rsTitlesByPubID
```

The second is to create a Command object and use the Parameters collection:

```
strShape = "SHAPE {{CALL dbo.usp_PublishersByCountry(?) }}" & _
           "APPEND ({{CALL dbo.usp_TitlesByPubID(?) }}" & _
           "RELATE pub_id TO PARAMETER 0) AS rsTitlesByPubID "

objCmd.CommandText = strShape
objCmd.Parameters.Append objCmd.CreateParameter("@Country", _
                              adVarChar, adParamInput, 30, "USA")
Set objCmd.ActiveConnection = objConn
Set objRs = objCmd.Execute
```

The third is again to use a Command object, but this time, pass the parameter into the Execute method:

```
objCmd.CommandText = strShape
Set objRs = objCmd.Execute  (, Array("USA"))
```

You can pass in multiple parameters using any of these methods.

Parameter Based Shapes

When using a parameter-based hierarchy, the data is not fetched all at once when the command is executed. When the parent row is accessed, the parameter query is executed with the parameter details from the parent. This data is then cached locally. This means that there will be a trip back to the server to fetch data the first time a new row is accessed. However, this approach can be a lot more efficient if the user is only interested in a subset of parent rows, since only the required child rows will be fetched. This contrasts with a non-parameter based shape where all of the child rows are fetched.

You can change this behavior by setting the "Cache Child Rows" dynamic property, as discussed earlier.

Updating Shaped Recordsets

Using data shaping doesn't mean that your recordsets behave any differently from normal recordsets. Assuming that your recordset allows updating, then you can treat shaped recordsets as you would normally: adding, updating, and deleting records. For example:

```
Set objRsTitles = objRs("titles").Value
objRsTitles("qty") = objRsTitles("qty") + 1
objRsTitles.Update
```

This sets a variable, objRsTitles, to point to the child recordset, and then updates a value. Changing the relating field in the parent recordset means that the child recordset will become orphaned. Likewise, changing the relating field in the child recordset will stop it being related to its previous parent, and it may end up being related to a different parent.

Data Shaping in Visual Basic 6

Having shown you the hard way to create shape commands, you won't be surprised to find that Visual Basic 6 has a quick (and rather cool) way to do this, as part of its Data Environment. To create a data shape command you first add a command to the Data Environment. I created a connection to the pubs database, and then added a command, pointing to the publishers table. You can do this by selecting the connection, right-clicking the mouse, selecting Add Command, and then adding the command details. You'll have to enter SQL query details, via the General tab of the Properties... of the command.

Then you add a child command (right-click on the existing publishers command). In this case we'll write a command to query the titles table. With child commands you have to specify the relationship (after adding the SQL query details into the General tab's SQL Statement box):

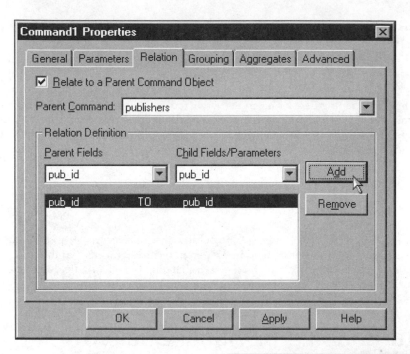

Once the child command has been added, you'll see it appear under its parent:

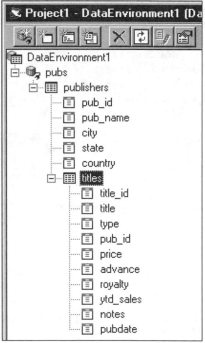

If you then right-mouse click on the parent, you can pick Hierarchy Info... from the menu to see the shape command:

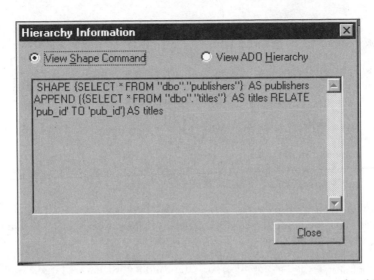

Another great thing about Visual Basic 6 is that it has a grid, the Hierarchical FlexGrid, which binds directly to hierarchical recordsets, allowing you to drill-down to the child data:

	pub_id	pub_name	city	state	country	title_id	title	type
⊟						BU2075	You Can Co	business
						PS2091	Is Anger the	psychology
	0736	New Moon I	Boston	MA	USA	PS2106	Life Without	psychology
						PS3333	Prolonged D	psychology
						PS7777	Emotional S	psychology
⊟						MC2222	Silicon Valle	mod_cook
						MC3021	The Gourme	mod_cook
						MC3026	The Psycho	UNDECIDE
	0877	Binnet & Har	Washington	DC	USA	PS1372	Computer Ph	psychology
						TC3218	Onions, Lee	trad_cook
						TC4203	Fifty Years ir	trad_cook
						TC7777	Sushi, Anyor	trad_cook
⊟						BU1032	The Busy Ex	business
						BU1111	Cooking with	business
	1389	Algodata Inf	Berkeley	CA	USA	BU7832	Straight Talk	business
						PC1035	But Is It Use	popular_con
						PC8888	Secrets of S	popular_con
						PC9999	Net Etiquett	popular_con
	1622	Five Lakes F	Chicago	IL	USA			
	1756	Ramona Pul	Dallas	TX	USA			
	9901	GGG&G	München		Germany			
	9952	Scootney Bo	New York	NY	USA			

Of course, if you haven't got Visual Basic 6 you'll have to do it manually.

Why Data Shaping?

All of this might seem very smart, but what's the real use, especially when you can achieve the same result by joining the tables together? Well, imagine a parent recordset that has a hundred rows and ten columns. It has a child recordset containing ten rows per parent row. Now look at a normal SQL join:

13

Data Shaping

```
SELECT * FROM parent INNER JOIN child
ON parent.id = child.id
```

For each row on the *many* side, there will also be a row from the *one* side containing ten columns. Those ten columns from the *one* side will be the same for each of the ten rows on the *many* side. That's an awful lot of wasted network traffic and data handling.

If you use data shaping, then the parent row is only included once, so instead of 1000 rows containing the parent data we only have 100. You still have 1000 rows of child data, but the parent data is not repeated. Overall, it's smaller, easier to manage, and produces less network traffic when marshaled as a disconnected recordset. However, you should be aware of the way that data shaping actually works.

When you create a simple relation (for example, the relation between `publishers` and `titles`), then both tables will be fetched before the hierarchy is created. A new field (a pointer to the child recordset) is added to the parent recordset – and when the child is referenced, a filter is applied to the child recordset. This means that all child recordsets are fetched in advance, so, if the child recordsets are large, you might find that this is slower than a normally joined recordset, and may lead to more network congestion. The only way around this is to use a parameterized child recordset, where the child rows are only fetched when accessed.

Reshaping Hierarchies

Reshaping allows you to reuse existing recordsets held by the shape provider, allowing them to become children of new `SHAPE` commands. If the new `SHAPE` command doesn't require new data from the original data provider, then the shaping is performed entirely within the shape provider on the client; otherwise the data is fetched from the provider. This reshaping allows you write applications that allow users to manipulate data, without the necessity of re-fetching it.

The easiest way to understand this is via a few examples. Consider the following shape command:

```
SHAPE {SELECT * FROM titles} AS rsTitles
    APPEND ({SELECT * FROM sales} AS rsSales
        RELATE title_id TO title_id)
```

This will give the following:

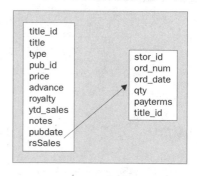

Here we have a recordset containing the details from the `titles` table. The last column, `rsSales`, is a chapter column containing the recordset of the `sales` table.

A new recordset can be created using a new shape command:

```
SHAPE rsSales
       COMPUTE rsSales, SUM(rsSales.qty) AS Sum_qty1 BY stor_id
```

This creates the following structure:

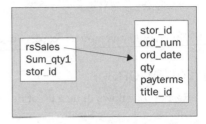

The existing `rsSales` recordset is reshaped, with a new parent being added, which contains summary details of the sales quantity. The original recordset is unchanged by this new shape.

Another parent addition could be:

```
SHAPE {SELECT * FROM publishers}
       APPEND (rsTitles RELATE pub_id TO pub_id)
```

This creates a new shape using the publishers as the top level, and appending the already existing shape `rsTitles` to it:

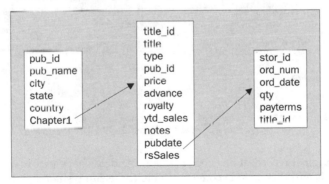

Notice that the APPENDed chapter has been given the default name of `Chapter1` – this is because in the code fragment above we didn't use the AS clause to assign a specific name to `rsTitles`.

You can also use reshaping to gain access to all of the records in a child recordset. For example, consider this shape command:

```
SHAPE {SELECT * FROM titles} as rsTitles
       APPEND ({SELECT * FROM sales} AS rsSales
                RELATE title_id TO title_id)
```

13

Data Shaping

When you access the child recordset you only ever see the records related to the parent. However, we know that there are actually two recordsets in existence – one for the parent and one for the child – and that it's just filtering that takes place to show the correct records. Since reshaping allows access to recordsets without re-querying the data provider, you can use the following shape command to access the complete set of records for the child:

```
SHAPE rsSales
```

This would give you a recordset of all sales items.

Limitations

Reshaping allows quite a lot of flexibility but there are some limitations to its use:

❑ You cannot APPEND new columns to an existing shaped recordset

❑ You cannot reshape parameterized recordsets

Usage

The actual commands to reshape are no different from those used to create an initial shape. For example, consider the following Visual Basic code:

```
objConn.Open strConn

strShape = "SHAPE {SELECT * FROM titles} as rsTitles" & _
           "APPEND ({SELECT * FROM sales} AS rsSales" & _
           "RELATE title_id TO title_id)"

objRs.Open strShape, objConn

objRs1.Open "SHAPE rsSales " & _
            "COMPUTE rsSales, SUM(rsSales.qty) BY stor_id", objConn

objRs2.Open "SHAPE {select * from publishers} " & _
            "APPEND (rsTitles RELATE pub_id TO pub_id)", objConn
```

Once the original recordset has been opened, the data shape provider caches the shape details and they then become available for use in reshaping, unless the recordset is closed.

Grandchild Aggregates

When using aggregation to produce summary values, you are not limited to just one level, and you can aggregate multiple levels down by including the full object hierarchy. For example, imagine you wanted to list the quantity of books sold, broken down by publisher, store, and book. Something like this:

New Moon Books	208
You Can Combat Computer Stress!	35
Fricative Bookshop	35
Is Anger the Enemy?	108
Eric the Read Books	3
Barnum's	75
News & Brews	10
Doc-U-Mat: Quality Laundry and Books	20
Life Without Fear	25
Doc-U-Mat: Quality Laundry and Books	25
Prolonged Data Deprivation: Four Case Studies	15
Doc-U-Mat: Quality Laundry and Books	15
Emotional Security: A New Algorithm	25
Doc-U-Mat: Quality Laundry and Books	25
Binnet & Hardley	150
Silicon Valley Gastronomic Treats	10
Fricative Bookshop	10
The Gourmet Microwave	40
Doc-U-Mat: Quality Laundry and Books	25
Bookbeat	15
The Psychology of Computer Cooking	
Computer Phobic AND Non-Phobic Individuals...	20
Doc-U-Mat: Quality Laundry and Books	20
Onions, Leeks, and Garlic: Cooking Secrets of ...	40
News & Brews	40
Fifty Years in Buckingham Palace Kitchens	20
News & Brews	20
Sushi, Anyone?	20
News & Brews	20

So, what you need is a structure like this:

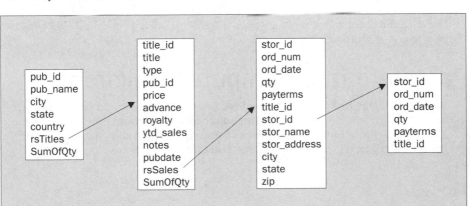

13

Data Shaping

If the quantity sold is only held at the bottom level, then you need to be able to sum this value from the parent, and the grandparent. Here's the SHAPE command:

```
SHAPE {SELECT * FROM publishers}
    APPEND ((SHAPE {SELECT * FROM titles}
        APPEND ({SELECT * FROM sales INNER JOIN
                    stores on sales.stor_id = stores.stor_id}
        RELATE title_id TO title_id) AS rsSales, SUM(rsSales.qty)
AS SumOfQty)
            RELATE pub_id TO pub_id) AS rsTitles,
SUM(rsTitles.rsSales.qty)
                    As SumOfQty
```

The SUM statement at the bottom applies to the parent, so it includes the names for both the child and the grandchild. You can produce the table of data with the following Visual Basic code:

```
objRsPubs.Open strShape, objConn

While Not objRsPubs.EOF
    Debug.Print objRsPubs("pub_name") & "~~~" &
objRsPubs("SumOfQty")
    Set objRsTitles = objRsPubs("rsTitles").Value
    While Not objRsTitles.EOF
        Debug.Print "~" & objRsTitles("title") & _
                    "~~" & objRsTitles("SumOfQty")
        Set objRsStoreSales = objRsTitles("rsSales").Value
        While Not objRsStoreSales.EOF
            Debug.Print "~~" & objRsStoreSales("stor_name") & _
                    "~" & objRsStoreSales("qty")
            objRsStoreSales.MoveNext
        Wend
        objRsTitles.MoveNext
    Wend
    objRsPubs.MoveNext
Wend
```

I've used the tilde symbol (~) to separate the columns being produced – this makes it easy to convert into a Word table.

Parameterized Computed Children

If a SHAPE command has a child based on a parameterized stored procedure, there's no reason why you can't have an intermediate table to perform grouping on certain values in the procedure. For example, imagine you want to show the book titles grouped by book type and by publisher. Something like this:

New Moon Books
    business
        You Can Combat Computer Stress!
    psychology
        Is Anger the Enemy?
        Life Without Fear
        Prolonged Data Deprivation: Four Case Studies
        Emotional Security: A New Algorithm
Binnet & Hardley
    mod_cook
        Silicon Valley Gastronomic Treats
        The Gourmet Microwave
    psychology
        Computer Phobic AND Non-Phobic Individuals: Behavior Variations
    UNDECIDED
        The Psychology of Computer Cooking
Algodata Infosystems
    business
        The Busy Executive's Database Guide
        Cooking with Computers: Surreptitious Balance Sheets

The code used to produce this is similar to the parent/child/grandchild example shown earlier.

Here's the structure that will give us this analysis:

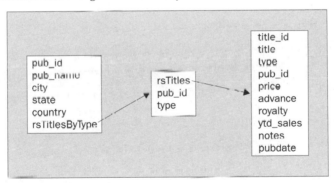

This is easy to do with three SQL commands, but suppose you want to use a parameterized query for the book titles so that you always see the latest data. Here's the SHAPE command:

```
SHAPE {{CALL dbo.usp_PublishersByCountry('?')}}
    APPEND ((SHAPE {{CALL dbo.usp_TitlesByPubID('?')}} AS rsTitles
        COMPUTE rsTitles By pub_id, type)
        RELATE pub_id TO PARAMETER 0) AS rsTitlesByType
```

The advantage of using a COMPUTE statement for the book types is that the COMPUTE is based upon the child. Since the child is a parameterized query it always shows the latest data, therefore so does the COMPUTE. If a new book is added with a new book type this is automatically reflected by the COMPUTE.

13

Data Shaping

Creating New Shapes

The shape language allows you to create shaped recordsets that are not bound to a data provider. This is useful if you want to create a local store of complex, structured data, perhaps to replace collections.

To create a new shape you need to set the Data Provider option in the connection string to none:

```
Provider=MSDataShape; Data Provider=none
```

You can then construct your recordset in the shape command:

```
SHAPE APPEND
    NEW adChar(4) AS pub_id,
    NEW adVarChar(40) AS pub_name,
    NEW adVarChar(20) AS city,
    NEW adChar(2)     AS state,
    NEW adVarChar(30) AS country,
    ((SHAPE APPEND
        NEW adVarChar(6)  AS title_id,
        NEW adVarChar(80) AS title,
        NEW adCurrency    AS price,
        NEW adChar(4)     AS pub_id)
    RELATE pub_id TO pub_id) AS rsTitles
```

You can then open the recordset and add records. Here's an example in Visual Basic:

```
' open the new shape
objRs.Open strShape, "Provider=MSDataShape; Data Provider=none", _
                adOpenStatic, adLockOptimistic

' add some records
With objRs
    .AddNew
    .Fields("pub_id") = "1234"
    .Fields("pub_name") = "Wrox Press"
    .Fields("city") = "Birmingham"
    .Fields("state") = "WM"
    .Fields("country") = "England"
    .Update
End With

' now some children
Set objRsT = objRs("rsTitles").Value
```

```
With objRsT
    .AddNew
    .Fields("title_id") = "2688"
    .Fields("title") = "ADO 2.1 Prog Ref"
    .Fields("price") = 29.99
    .Update
    .AddNew
    .Fields("title_id") = "1266"
    .Fields("title") = "Professional ASP 2.0"
    .Fields("price") = 59.95
    .Update
End With
```

Once created, the shaped recordset behaves exactly like a shaped recordset created from a data provider.

Dynamic Properties

The shape provider now has some new dynamic properties to help with the shape service. These apply to the Recordset and are set using the dynamic Properties collection:

```
objRs.Properties("property_name") = value
```

The Name Property

The Name property is a read-only property that identifies the name of the Recordset in a shape. The recordset name is generally defined by the AS keyword in the shape language – if this is omitted the shape provider will generate a name for you. For example, in the following code fragment there is a parent recordset named rsTitles, and a child recordset named rsSales:

```
SHAPE {SELECT * FROM titles} AS rsTitles
    APPEND ({SELECT * FROM sales} AS rsSales
           RELATE title_id TO title_id)
```

The Unique Reshape Names Property

The Unique Reshape Names property specifies whether or not unique values for the name are generated. For example, a SHAPE command that assigned the same name (using the AS keyword) to two different recordsets can be forced to be unique by setting this property to True.

13

Data Shaping

I thank God I am as honest as any man
living that is an old man and no honester than

Can counsel and speak comfort to that
which they themselves not feel

Much Ado About Nothing.

He wears his faith but as the fashion of his

As merry as the day

He hath indeed better bettered expectation

(Act i. Sc. i.).

He wears his faith but as the fashion of his hat.
(Ibid)

As merry as the day is long.

h indeed better bettered expectation

(Act i. Sc. i.).

(Ibid)

Can counsel and speak comfort to that grief
Which they themselves not feel.

He wears his faith but as the fashion of his hat.
(Ibid)

I was not born under

a rhyming planet

I was not born under a rhyming planet
(Sc. 2

For there was never yet
That could endure the to

merry as the day is long

(Sc. 2)

Can counsel and speak comfort to that grief
Which they themselves not feel.

(Ibid)

He hath indeed better bettered expectation

(Ibid)

I thank God I am as honest as any

living that is an old man and no honest

He wears his faith but as the fashion of his ha
(Ibi

Much Ado About Nothing.

For there was never yet philospher
That could endure the toothache patiently.

(Ibid)

I was not born u

For there was never yet philospher
That could endure the toothache patiently

14

Performance

This chapter looks at one of the most critical issues for all data store programmers – that of **performance**. Microsoft has stated that one of its goals for ADO was to achieve the best performance possible. However, during testing, and through its various versions, the newsgroups have contained several messages regarding poor performance. What we plan to do here is show you whether or not those criticisms were justified.

Most of the performance statistics were generated using a Test Tool, built especially for this purpose in Visual Basic 5. The source code for this tool is available from the Wrox Press web site, at http://www.wrox.com, along with a test Access database, some SQL Scripts for creating the test database in SQL Server, and an Access database for logging the results.

This tool is provided as is, with no warranty of its fitness for purpose. You can use it as you find it, or extend it in your own environment. For obvious reasons, we can't guarantee the same results on your systems. At the end of this chapter you'll see how this tool works, but we won't cover it in depth. Its sole purpose is to run various queries under different conditions, and to time them. Not all of the tests were carried out using this tool, and we created several tools just for testing purposes. Some of these are also available on the web site.

The tests were primarily run on a Dell Dimension Pentium II 450MHz, with 128Mb memory and 8GB EIDE disk, running Windows 2000 Professional. We tested both Access 97 and Access 2000 databases, and these generally gave similar results. Any major differences have been highlighted. SQL Server versions 6.5, 7.0, and 2000 (beta 2) were all tested. I've avoided explicit performance tests between versions 6.5 and 7.0 because these are beyond the scope of this chapter – the intention was not to compare performance of the two versions of SQL Server, but to test ADO. There are some major differences between 6.5, 7.0 and 2000, and these have been highlighted where appropriate.

All tests were run on this server machine, so those involving client cursors don't have the added network lag to contend with. Although this is less realistic, it ensures that only the difference between cursor types (and not the network) is tested. This is important because network traffic can vary widely from situation to situation, and it's unlikely that my machines – all within 10 feet of each other – would ever give any kind of useful indication. It would therefore be wrong for me to say 'these timings take into account network usage', when this is quite clearly not the case. So, when running the tests yourself, make sure you allow for this.

One further thing to note is that ADO and the data stores were not under any stress here. The tests were performed in a single-user environment, and you may experience different results if your server and data store are being used heavily. The tests were also run 10 times and the results averaged, to take account of cached data. The standard deviations were generally very small.

For the majority of tests, the following table was used:

Column	Type	Length
KeyCol	int (IDENTITY)	
Description	varchar	(50)
ForeignKey	int	
TextField	varchar	(10)
CurrencyField	money	
BitField	bit	

There were several copies of this table, all with varying amounts of dummy data. When testing ADO yourself, you should use your own tables and data to get a more accurate picture.

I've tried to explain why some of the tests give the results that they do – although in some cases this is not possible, simply because I don't know what OLE DB and the providers are actually doing underneath. It would be nice to have these details explained, but as an ADO programmer, it's not really necessary. As long as we know which mechanisms to use to give us best performance, and we have a way of testing that, we should be relatively happy.

Cursor Type, Location and Locking

Here are three questions that are often asked, by beginners and experienced users alike:

- ❑ What's the best cursor type to use?
- ❑ Should I use server-side or client-side cursors?
- ❑ What locking scheme should I use?

Like many design questions, the answer is always the same: it depends. The cursor type and location that you choose will not only affect performance, but also the functionality. So, whilst in some cases it's easy to establish a particular cursor type as the fastest, it may not be the type that best suits your particular business needs.

The OLE DB Provider for Jet

The charts below show the results from opening and closing a table, using the OLE DB Provider for Access. The code used for this test is simple:

```
objRs.Open "table_name", objConn
objRs.Close
```

We timed only this fragment of the code, adding the various locking modes and cursor types to the Open command. This was run ten times (that is, we performed the Open/Close combination ten times), and the average time wastaken. We took an average in this way in all of the tests performed, to ensure that the first run didn't distort the results because of data not being cached. However, bear in mind that many applications perform a single table access, and may not 'hit' that table again. This is another reason why you need to perform testing in your own application situations.

Times are given in milliseconds.

Server-Side Cursors

The following figures were produced using server-side cursors, with a table holding 100 rows.

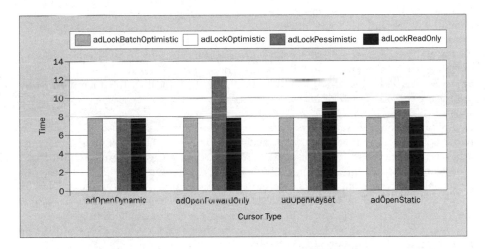

You might wonder why there is so little difference between the cursor types – but recall that, when using server-side cursors, Access only supports keyset cursors (unless you specify a read-only recordset). So if you are locking your recordset, Access will always return a keyset cursor – no matter what cursor type you request.

You might also expect that larger tables would have an impact, but the times are almost exactly the same – even for a table of the same type with 100,000 records! The lack of difference in speed when using larger tables is because, if you are using server-side cursors, only the first batch of data is read into the recordset. Consequently, it doesn't matter how many records there are when you open the table. And that's an important point. This test is essentially just opening and closing the table, without reading any data in.

Performance

14

379

Client-Side Cursors

The following chart shows the speed using client-side cursors, with the test table holding 100 rows.

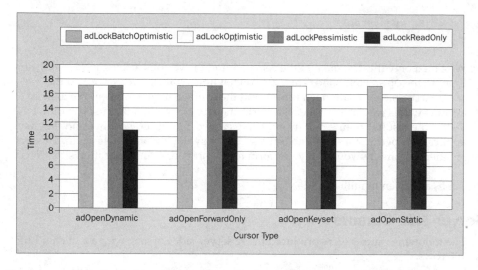

You can see that client-side cursors are much slower than server-side cursors, being generally twice as slow. Relatively speaking, however, cursors with no locking are faster than the other cursor types. Client-side cursors are inherently slower because they actually copy the entire data set (regardless of its size) into a cache on the local machine, using the memory and disk space if necessary. This is why they are named client-side cursors – the cursor facility is located in the central OLE DB handler, rather than being provided by the data store.

Comparing locking cursors, you can see that the read-only cursor is faster than the other two locking types (optimistic and pessimistic) – and between those two there is very little difference. The graphs also suggest that there's little difference between the cursor types. You might wonder at this, but note that when locking is required, the OLE DB Provider for Jet only supports static cursors. Therefore, whatever cursor type you request, you'll always get a static cursor back. In fact, a static cursor is the only cursor type that really makes sense when dealing with client-side cursors. The Errors collection of the Connection object may well have a warning indicating that the cursor type is different from that requested, although this will depend upon the provider.

The reasons for the time differences between read-only and updateable locking should be fairly clear. With read-only cursors, Jet can stream out the data without having to keep track of the records, as it knows that no changes will ever take place. This is obviously going to be faster than trying to keep track of the changes. For updateable cursors, the cursor type has to be changed – but this fact can be ignored, because you can see that for a static cursor, the timings are approximately the same.

Have a look at the same test over a table with 1000 rows:

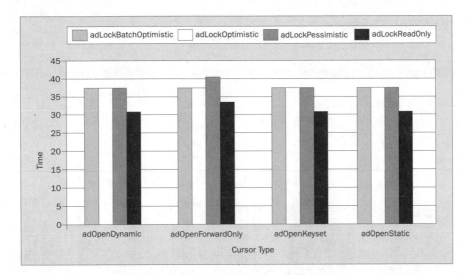

Again, not much difference between the locking types, but the difference in speed between read-only access and read/write access is not as marked as before. The overall times have increased, reflecting that much more data is being pushed to the client, as compared to the server-side cursors, where there was little difference.

With 50000 records, the result looks like this:

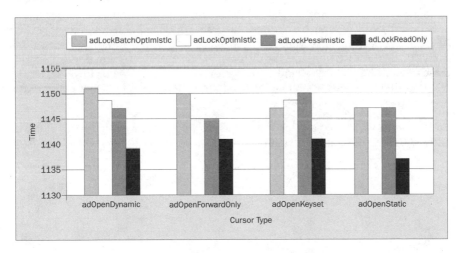

Now we see some more interesting results, with a much greater variation between the various cursor types and locking mechanisms. I've no explanation for this difference, especially since Jet is really only using one cursor type.Again, the average times have increased to reflect the amount of data.

The OLE DB Provider for SQL Server

The same tests for SQL Server show remarkably different results. Again, these are comprised of opening and closing a recordset 10 times, then taking the average figure.

Performance

14

Server-Side Cursors

SQL Server provides full support for server-side cursors.

The following figure shows the results for a table of 100 rows on SQL 7.0 and SQL 2000.

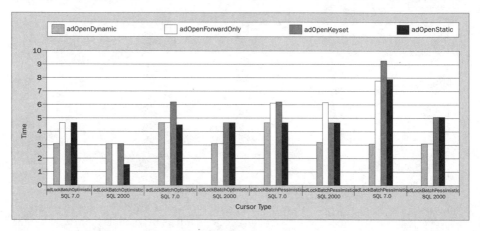

An issue with SQL Server 6.5, (not shown in the graph), is that there was a dramatic improvement in performance, when using dynamic and forward-only cursors, when compared with keyset and static cursors. The reason for this is simple – in SQL 6.5, both keyset and static cursors require a copy of the data to be put into SQL Server's temporary database, (tempdb), before the cursor is created. In fact, a keyset cursor only puts the keys and the first buffer full of data into temporary storage. SQL 7.0 and 2000 don't appear to suffer from this problem, except with read-only cursors, although I've yet to confirm whether this is due to a general improvement in performance, or if these versions handle keyset and static cursors in a different way. However, any relative difference between cursor types on the same version indicates a difference in how the cursor type is handled.

You can see how this has a marked effect as the number of rows increases. For a table with 1000 rows, the change is significant:

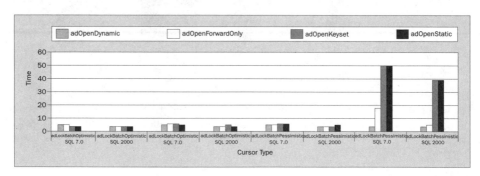

The difference between keyset and static forward-only cursors, and other cursor combinations is now obvious.

Client-Side Cursors

So how does this compare with client-side cursors, given that all the client-side cursor types were slower in Jet? For the initial test of 100 rows we get the following figure:

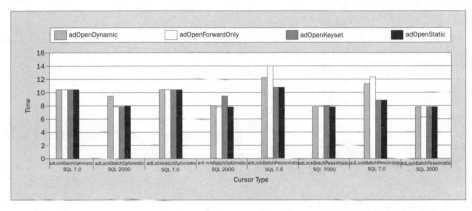

These seem to bear out what we know about client cursors – they are slower because all of the data is read into the client. Overall, the performance is close for all cursor types and lock types, and this remains so as we scale the table up to 50000 rows. On the other hand, the overall speed is slower than server-based dynamic and forward-only cursors (as expected) because all of the data is returned to the client.

If you want to learn more about SQL Server cursor types and how they are used, then by far the best description can be found in Inside Microsoft SQL Server 6.5 *(Microsoft Press, ISBN 1572313315). In fact, this book is full of extremely useful information for the SQL Server developer. A new version for SQL 7.0 (ISBN 0735605173) was released in April 1999.*

The OLE DB Provider for ODBC

For ODBC, the tests show similar results for the cursor types, locations, and locking mechanisms. We'll be contrasting the OLE DB Provider for ODBC against the native driver later in this chapter.

Cursor Summary

Despite the figures you've seen so far, it's not always possible to use the faster method because it may not meet your needs. For example, although server-side cursors are quicker to open, they don't always provide the same functionality that client-side cursors do, and cannot be used if you need to disconnect your recordsets. In the n-tier world of client-server development, you may well be using disconnected recordsets to pass data between the various tiers in your application, so you'll have to use client cursors. If this is the case, then you want to minimize the amount of data being passed around.

Performance

14

With locking, you can see that in most cases read-only mode is faster, as you would expect. Use this to your advantage if you are just providing data browsing capabilities.If you need both browsing and editing in your application, it's worth considering using read-only cursors for browsing, and then opening another recordset with a writable cursor for editing.

You've seen that in some cases the cursor type you get is not necessarily the one you requested – this depends upon the provider, the cursor location, and the locking mechanism used. The following tables describe the cursor type that you receive according to these conditions.

OLE DB Provider for SQL Server

adUseServer (Indexed Table)

Lock type	Cursor type requested			
	Forward-Only	Keyset	Dynamic	Static
Read-Only	Forward-Only	Keyset	Dynamic	Static
Pessimistic	Forward-Only	Keyset	Dynamic	Keyset
Optimistic	Forward-Only	Keyset	Dynamic	Keyset
Batch Optimistic	Forward-Only	Keyset	Dynamic	Keyset

adUseServer (Non-Indexed Table)

Lock type	Cursor type requested			
	Forward-Only	Keyset	Dynamic	Static
Read-Only	Forward-Only	Static	Dynamic	Static
Pessimistic	Forward-Only	Dynamic	Dynamic	Keyset
Optimistic	Forward-Only	Dynamic	Dynamic	Keyset
Batch Optimistic	Forward-Only	Dynamic	Dynamic	Keyset

adUseClient

Lock type	Cursor type requested			
	Forward-Only	Keyset	Dynamic	Static
Read-Only	Static	Static	Static	Static
Pessimistic	Static	Static	Static	Static
Optimistic	Static	Static	Static	Static
Batch Optimistic	Static	Static	Static	Static

OLE DB Provider for Jet

adUseServer

Lock type	Cursor type requested			
	Forward-Only	**Keyset**	**Dynamic**	**Static**
Read-Only	Forward-Only	Keyset	Static	Static
Pessimistic	Keyset	Keyset	Keyset	Keyset
Optimistic	Keyset	Keyset	Keyset	Keyset
Batch Optimistic	Keyset	Keyset	Keyset	Keyset

adUseClient

Lock type	Cursor type requested			
	Forward-Only	**Keyset**	**Dynamic**	**Static**
Read-Only	Static	Static	Static	Static
Pessimistic	Static	Static	Static	Static
Optimistic	Static	Static	Static	Static
Batch Optimistic	Static	Static	Static	Static

OLE DB Provider for ODBC with SQL Server

adUseServer (Indexed Table)

Lock type	Cursor type requested			
	Forward-Only	**Keyset**	**Dynamic**	**Static**
Read-Only	Forward-Only	Keyset	Dynamic	Static
Pessimistic	Forward-Only	Keyset	Dynamic	Keyset
Optimistic	Forward-Only	Keyset	Dynamic	Keyset
Batch Optimistic	Forward-Only	Keyset	Dynamic	Keyset

adUseServer (Non-Indexed Table)

Lock type	Cursor type requested			
	Forward-Only	**Keyset**	**Dynamic**	**Static**
Read-Only	Forward-Only	Static	Dynamic	Static

Performance

14

385

Lock type	Cursor type requested			
	Forward-Only	**Keyset**	**Dynamic**	**Static**
Pessimistic	Forward-Only	Static	Dynamic	Static
Optimistic	Forward-Only	Static	Dynamic	Static
Batch Optimistic	Forward-Only	Static	Dynamic	Static

adUseClient

Lock type	Cursor type requested			
	Forward-Only	**Keyset**	**Dynamic**	**Static**
Read-Only	Static	Static	Static	Static
Pessimistic	Static	Static	Static	Static
Optimistic	Static	Static	Static	Static
Batch Optimistic	Static	Static	Static	Static

OLE DB Provider for ODBC with Access

adUseServer

Lock type	Cursor type requested			
	Forward-Only	**Keyset**	**Dynamic**	**Static**
Read-Only	Forward-Only	Keyset	Keyset	Static
Pessimistic	Forward-Only	Keyset	Keyset	Keyset
Optimistic	Forward-Only	Keyset	Keyset	Keyset
Batch Optimistic	Forward-Only	Keyset	Keyset	Keyset

adUseClient

Lock type	Cursor type requested			
	Forward-Only	**Keyset**	**Dynamic**	**Static**
Read-Only	Static	Static	Static	Static
Pessimistic	Static	Static	Static	Static
Optimistic	Static	Static	Static	Static
Batch Optimistic	Static	Static	Static	Static

Moving Through Records

Since you very rarely just open and close a recordset, we need to look at moving through records, where the cursor type and mode can also have an impact on performance. The time taken to open and close the recordset were not included as part of the timing – only movement through the recordset.

There are two main ways of getting at the data in a recordset. The first is to use MoveNext to move from one end of the recordset to the other, and the second is to use GetRows to read the data into an array. For client-based cursors, of any type and locking mode, the figures were extremely close between using MoveNext and GetRows. This is because the data is already on the client, and in both cases, the client cursor service is fetching the data from its local cache. For server-based cursors, however, there are differences.

GetRows can also be used to fetch a smaller number of rows, and then this operation repeated until the whole recordset is read; although this method, called GetRows(chunked) in the graph, is less common. This method involves fetching data in batches. Consider a table of 1000 rows, on SQL Server 2000 (the figures were very similar for Optimistic, Batch Optimistic and Pessimistic locking modes), as shown below:

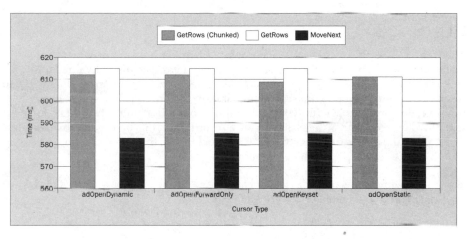

Here you can see that MoveNext is clearly the fastest method, but that using GetRows with small chunks, is faster than trying to retrieve all of the records into an array at once. However, the difference is minor so you may not consider the extra effort involved worthwhile. The interesting figures come when you use a read-only cursor, as shown below. This is the same 1000 rows using SQL Server 2000:

Performance

14

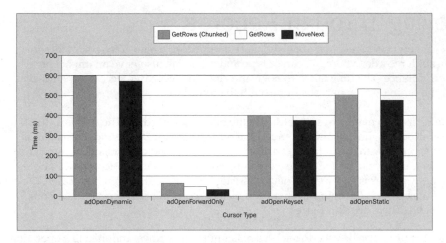

With a forward-only cursor there is a vast improvement in the speed, because using server-based, forward-only cursors makes use of the SQL Server native cursor (firehose), which is much faster than other cursor types. With other providers you're unlikely to see this difference.

Cache Size

The `Recordset` object's `CacheSize` property identifies how many records are fetched in one go and stored in a local cache on the client. The default value for this property is 1, so with a large table you are able to fetch each record individually (if you desire). This could be quite time consuming if moving through the records. For example, imagine a table with 1000 rows. If the `CacheSize` property is equal to 1, then it would require 1000 fetches to create a recordset on this table and move through all 1000 rows. If the `CacheSize` property is equal to 100, the same task would take only 10 fetches (each visit fetching 100 records).

The graph below shows the results of changing the cache size for a client-side read-only cursor on a table of 1000 rows in SQL 2000.

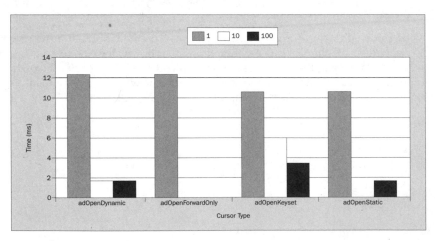

Notice that using a larger cache size is much faster. In some cases there's no difference between a cache size of 10 and 100,so you'll need to experiment. Also notice that there are times when the speed was too fast to be measured! For server-side cursors the results are even more significant:

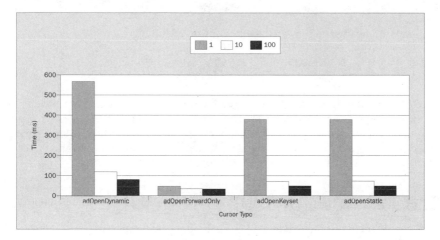

Here you can see that moving from a cache size of 1 to 10 has a dramatic effect, and for some cursor types this can be improved even more by increasing the cache size to 100.

Although you might never fetch 1000 rows directly for processing, the cache size can have a big impact even on small tables. For processing large tables, you are nearly always better off building SQL statements and executing them on the server. Also, the cache size can be affected by the amount of data in the row being fetched. A larger row will result in more data being fetched into the cache, thus using more resources.

Command and Recordset Options

ADO 2.0 introduced a new constant value, adCmdTableDirect, for the CommandTypeEnum constant type. adCmdTableDirect gives us a new option when specifying the command type, by indicating that the provider is to return all rows from the table named in the CommandText property. The documentation states that using this will cause some internal code to work differently, but does it make any performance difference? Under ADO 2.0 and 2.1 it did make a small difference, with the use of adCmdTableDirect being marginally quicker. Under ADO 2.1 the difference between adCmdTable and adCmdTableDirect was negligible under our tests. Under ADO 2.6 with SQL Server 2000, however, there is a difference once again, but only for server cursors, where adCmdTableDirect was *slower* in most cases. (For client cursors the difference was negligible.) This could be due to the test being run on both a beta of ADO 2.6 and SQL Server 2000, which may still have debug code in them. I expect the released versions to show improved performance.

Another option worth testing is the ExecuteOptionEnum constant on command execution, which, when set to adExecuteNoRecords, tells ADO that an action query will not return any records.

Performance

14

389

To test this, the following code was used without the option set:

```
strSQL = "UPDATE tblOneThousand SET TextField = 'abc 123'" & _
         "WHERE KeyField = 587"
Set objRs = objConn.Execute(strSQL, , adCmdText)
```

and compared against code with the extra option included:

```
Set objRs = objConn.Execute(strSQL, , adCmdText + _
                            adExecuteNoRecords)
```

We won't show a graph, but there is a speed improvement by specifying the extra option, although it's not a major improvement. The reason is that without this option, (the default) ADO creates a recordset and then discards it. With the option added, ADO does not create the unused recordset. Thus, the increase in application speed is probably due to ADO not creating and destroying this recordset.

Stored Procedure Or Direct SQL?

Many people often put SQL statements directly into their programs, and there are a couple of reasons why:

- ❑ They feel it keeps together everything required to run the program.
- ❑ They are unsure about stored procedures and the benefits they can bring.

Using stored procedures not only allows you to alter them without affecting your program, but brings the performance advantage of compiled SQL. When you run SQL statements they are parsed by SQL Server, and then executed. The SQL engine has to carry this out every time the statement is used, unless it's been prepared. When you create a stored procedure, the SQL is converted into a compiled form – thus eliminating this step when the procedure is run. In addition, stored procedures are placed into a procedure cache, which is an in-memory store of the compiled SQL – improving performance even more. Of course, if your table statistics change frequently, then the stored execution plan for stored procedures could become out of date. This is another reason why good test data is so important – compiling stored procedures against non-realistic (or empty) data can result in a sub-optimal execution plan being generated.

You can bring the stored procedure benefit to straight SQL text strings by setting the `Prepared` property of the `Command` object before execution – but this is only useful if you intend to run the command several times on the same connection. With `Prepared` set to `True`, a prepared statement is created the first time the command is run; and subsequent runs of the command on the same connection will use the prepared statement. So the first run will be slower, but subsequent runs will be quicker. In ASP, you will not notice any benefit in using prepared statements, because you should always work in a disconnected mode – creating database connections as you require them, which means subsequent runs of the SQL will use a new connection, and will therefore prepare a new statement.

On SQL Server 6.5, prepared statements are compiled into temporary stored procedures. On SQL Server 7 prepared statements are fully supported.

Consider the following SQL statement, using the `pubs` database, to analyze sales by publisher, state, and author:

```
SELECT publishers.pub_name, publishers.state,
       (au_lname + ', ' + au_fname) AS author,
       Sum(sales.qty) AS SumOfqty
FROM (publishers INNER JOIN titles
                    ON publishers.pub_id = titles.pub_id)
   INNER JOIN (authors INNER JOIN titleauthor
                    ON authors.au_id = titleauthor.au_id)
   ON titles.title_id = titleauthor.title_id)
INNER JOIN sales ON titles.title_id = sales.title_id
GROUP BY publishers.pub_name, publishers.state,
         (au_lname + ', ' + au_fname)
```

Executing this statement 10 times on the same connection resulted in the following:

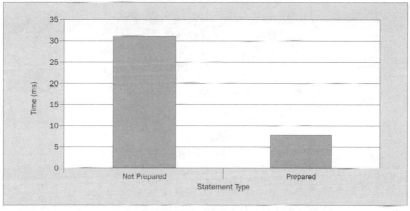

You can clearly see that prepared statements are faster for concurrent executions. Simple SQL statements may yield less impressive performance improvements, as the SQL optimizer will have less to do.

Parameters

When I started using ADO, I had a lot of trouble using parameters, partly because of the data types. I then discovered the `Refresh` method, and I started to use this during development to print out details of what the parameters should be. If you use SQL `Trace` when connecting to SQL Server, you can clearly see that using `Refresh` can have a big overhead as it makes a trip back to the server to get the parameters. However, I did wonder what the speed difference was between the following three methods:

❑   Using direct SQL.

❑   Using the `Parameters` argument of the `Command`'s `Execute` method.

❑   Using the `Parameters` collection.

The following test used the pubs database supplied with SQL Server. The stored procedure contains the following commands:

```
CREATE PROCEDURE usp_SalesTest
     @iQty          int,
     @sPayTerms     varchar(12)
AS
     SELECT    *
     FROM      sales
     WHERE     qty = @iQty
     OR        payterms = @sPayTerms
```

Let's search for 20 for the quantity and Net 60 for the payment terms.

A Command object was created for each of the three tests, giving us three sections of code. For the direct SQL statement used:

```
objCmd.CommandText = "SELECT * FROM sales WHERE qty=20 OR" &_
                     "payterms='Net 60'"
objCmd.CommandType = adCmdText
Set objRs = objCmd.Execute
```

Passing the parameters into the Execute method, I used:

```
objCmd.CommandText = "usp_SalesTest"
objCmd.CommandType = adCmdStoredProc
Set objRs = objCmd.Execute(, Array(20, "Net 60"))
```

To create a Parameters collection I used:

```
objCmd.CommandText = "usp_SalesTest"
objCmd.CommandType = adCmdStoredProc
objCmd.Parameters.Append objCmd.CreateParameter("@iQty", adInteger,
_
                              adParamInput, 8, 20)
objCmd.Parameters.Append objCmd.CreateParameter("@sPayTerms", _
                              adVarChar, adParamInput, 12, "Net
60")
Set objRs = objCmd.Execute
```

Again, these were run 10 times and the average taken, and each set of runs executed three times, closing the connection between runs. The following diagram shows three runs for SQL 7.0 and 2000.

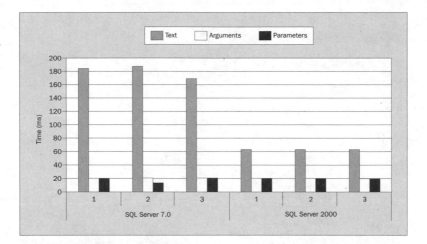

Both 7.0 and 2000 show a marked difference between the use of plain text and stored procedures, but the difference between passing the parameters on the command line, or explicitly declaring `Parameter` objects is negligible. The `Parameter` method has the advantage of making the parameters explicit, and of course you have to use this method if you require output parameters. Many databases don't support the extraction of parameters, so you might have to use explicit parameters – that is create them explicitly with `CreateParameter`.

Connection Pooling

The subject of connection pooling is a constant source of confusion. The documentation states that to free a connection you should set the connection variable to `Nothing`. However, the question has arisen as to whether this clears the connection from the pool of connections, and therefore has a detrimental effect on performance. So, using the `Open`/`Close` method again, using SQL Server, we'll try it with and without clearing the memory, and see if that has an impact. For the first test, the code was as follows:

```
Dim objConn As ADODB.Connection
Set objConn = New ADODB.Connection
strConn = "Provider = . . ."

For intLoop = 1 To 10
    objConn.Open strConn
    objConn.Close
Next
```

And for the second:

```
Dim objConn As ADODB.Connection
Set objConn = New ADODB.Connection
strConn = "Provider = . . ."
```

Performance

14

```
For intLoop = 1 To 10
    objConn.Open strConn
    objConn.Close
    Set objConn = Nothing
Next
```

The figures for ADO 2.0 were as follows:

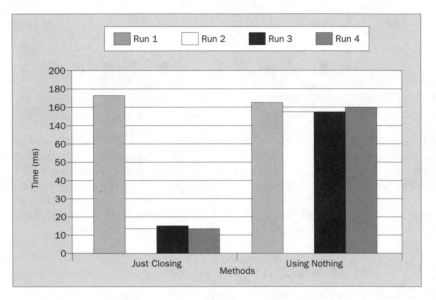

The results show four consecutive runs of the code shown above. The figures on the left clearly show that, after the first time, just closing the connection is considerably faster, because the connection has been pooled. The figures on the right, however, show that setting the `Connection` object variable to `Nothing` produces very similar figures for all four batches.

But does this really answer the question about connection pooling? Setting the object variable to `Nothing` deallocates the COM object, so it could be just the creation of the COM object that is time-consuming. If you run SQL Trace whilst testing this, you'll see that for the first test, only one connection is made. However, for the second test, there are ten connection/disconnections in a row, showing that the connection has been removed from the pool.

In fact, if you put the two pieces of code on two separate command buttons and watch SQL Trace as you press them, you'll see that for the first code, where we just open and close the connection, SQL Trace just shows a connection without a disconnection. Pressing the button again doesn't show another connection because the first is still active and held in the pool. If you don't press a button for 60 seconds you'll see the disconnection. With the second command button, where we set the object variable to `Nothing`, each time you press the button you get both a connection and a disconnection.

In ADO 2.1 and above, you can set the `Connection` object variable to `Nothing` and this will *not* remove the connection from the connection pool. Thus, the test demonstrated on ADO 2.0 above gives a very different conclusion when run against

ADO 2.1 and above – in both parts of the test (that is just closing and setting the object variable to Nothing), the outcome looks very similar to the left-hand section of the graph shown on the previous page. To summarize, in ADO 2.0, if you set the object variable to Nothing, the conection was removed from the pool. From ADO 2.1 onwards, pooling works in all situations.

Performance Summary

The first thing to remember is that these figures only show certain traits, under certain circumstances, so don't rely on them. Perform your own analysis, using your own data and see what results you achieve. You should also make sure that you test your application under circumstances that are similar to those in which it will run – that is, on a well used network, on a server that is heavily used, on a database with multiple users, etc. You can use this chapter as a guideline for some of the criteria to test.

Having said that, there are some key points that we've established from these tests:

❏   When opening recordsets, server-side cursors are generally quicker than client-side cursors, because less data is initially being transferred. However, the fetching of data is then slower, because the data is retrieved from the server, rather than from the local cache.

❏   If you need to use disconnected recordsets, then you'll have to use client-side cursors. In this case, try and keep the amount of data transferred to a minimum, for example, don't do "select *" when you only need a couple of columns.

❏   If using SQL Server 6.5 and server-side cursors; then dynamic or forward-only cursors are more efficient when selecting data. This is because the data is not initially copied into tempdb. For SQL Server 7.0 and 2000, this effect is greatly reduced.

❏   Use the native OLE DB providers, because they are quicker and offer more functionality than the ODBC ones. However, if you are using Oracle you may want to use the OLE DB Provider for ODBC, since it has greater functionality than the OLE DB Provider for Oracle.

❏   Use the correct cursor types. If you're not going to change any data, then use read-only cursors. Don't waste the resources of the data store.

There is also the performance aspect of performing large batch jobs on the server, and only transferring data to the client when required. These are general ways to improve application performance, and should be used in conjunction with any ADO performance enhancements.

The Performance Test Tool

As mentioned at the beginning of this chapter, this tool is intended to help you do your own performance tests. It began its life in the form of a few small routines, used to help decide a few issues, and has grown into the program that is now available from http://www.wrox.com. I considered expanding this into a large test suite, and supplying

Performance

14

it as a fully finished program, but then decided that – as a programmer – this is probably not what you really want. Therefore we've decided to give it away as it stands. Bear in mind that it's a far-from-complete product, has little or no error handling, and has some options that won't work under all conditions. Having said that, it does perform basic tests fairly well.

The opening screen allows you to connect to a data store:

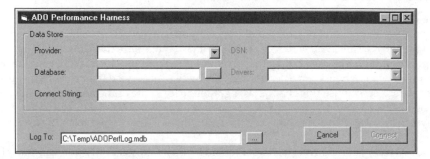

Here you can pick a provider (and, if using ODBC, pick a DSN or a driver). The Connect String box will supply some default values, and you should overwrite these with your specific values before connecting. The Log To box allows you to pick the database to log timings to. Currently this is an Access database, but there's no reason why you couldn't convert the code to use another database.

Once you've connected, you get to the main timing screen:

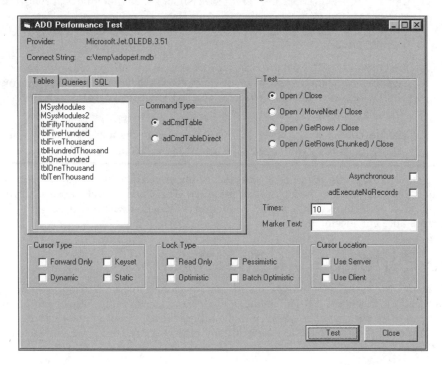

The tab control allows you to select from tables, queries, or your own SQL text. To the right, you pick which test you want to run, but remember that some of these may not be suitable for SQL queries that don't return recordsets. Below this, you can select whether records are to be returned. The asynchronous option isn't implemented, and was added to give you the opportunity to supply this. You can specify the number of times that the test is run, and add some marker text (to be written to the logging database), so that you can identify individual tests. At the bottom of the screen, you can pick the cursor type, lock type and cursor location. In order to run a test, you must select at least one of each – and you can pick more options to allow several tests to be compared.

The logging database just consists of one simple table into which the results are written. The graphs in this chapter were produced by pulling the figures from this table into Excel; it's often easier to appreciate the performance differences in visual form, so you may wish to consider doing the same.

Summary

In this chapter, we've shown you the results of our experimentation with the various options available in ADO 2.6. In particular, we've looked at the performance implications of using different data providers, as well as the often significant differences given by the various cursor types and locking options. To finish, we discussed the VB tool that we used to run the tests with, and encouraged you to download it and use it, or customize it for your own purposes. You can download it from our web site: you'll find the samples page that supports this book at http://www.wrox.com.

With this consideration of the performance implications of ADO 2.6, our discussion of ADO is complete. The appendices that follow this chapter are intended to provide a reference for using ADO 2.6. The documentation Microsoft supply is not quite complete, and wherever possible we have tried to include undocumented features.

Performance

14

I thank God I am as honest as any man
living that is an old man and no honester th

Can counsel and speak comfort to th(

Which they themselves not feel

For there was never yet philospher
That could endure the toothache patiently.

Much Ado About Nothing.

He wears his faith but as the fashion of !

As merry as the day

He hath indeed better bettered expectation

(Act i. Sc. 1).

He wears his faith but as the fashion of his hat.
(Ibid)

As merry as the day is long.

h indeed better bettered expectation

(Act i. Sc. 1).

(Ibid)

an counsel and speak comfort to that grief

Much Ado About Nothing.

Which they themselves not feel.

He wears his faith but as the fashion of his hat.
(Ibid)

I was not born under

a rhyming plane

I was not born under a rhyming plane

sc.

For there was never yet
That could endure the to

merry as the day is long (sc. 2)

Can counsel and speak comfort to that grief

Which they themselves not feel.

(Ibid)

(Ibid)

He hath indeed better bettered expectation

I thank God I am as honest as an

living that is an old man and no honest

He wears his faith but as the fashion of his ha
(Ibi

Much Ado About Nothing.

For there was never yet philospher
That could endure the toothache patiently.

(Ibid)

I was not born u

ADO Object Summary

Microsoft ActiveX Data Objects 2.6 Library Reference

Properties and methods that are new to version 2.6 are shown in **bold** in the first column.

> All properties are read/write unless otherwise stated.

The Objects

The Main Objects	Description
Command	A Command object is a definition of a specific command that you intend to execute against a data source.
Connection	A Connection object represents an open connection to a data store.
Recordset	A Recordset object represents the entire set of records from: a base table; the results of an executed command; or a fabricated recordset. At any given time, the 'current record' of a Recordset object refers to a single record within the recordset.
Record	A Record object represents a single resource (file or directory) made available from a Document Source Provider, or a single row from a singleton query.

The Main Objects	Description
Stream	A Stream object is an implementation of the IStream COM interface, allowing reading and writing to blocks of memory. In conjunction with the OLE DB Provider for Internet Publishing it allows access to the contents of resources (files) made available from a Document Source Provider. It can also be used to accept the output from executed Commands.

The Other Objects	Description
Error	An Error object contains the details of a data access error pertaining to a single operation involving the provider.
Field	A Field object represents a single column of data within a common data type (Recordset or Record).
Parameter	A Parameter object represents a single parameter or argument associated with a Command object based on a parameterized query or stored procedure.
Property	A Property object represents a single dynamic characteristic of an ADO object that is defined by the provider.

The Collections	Description
Errors	The Errors collection contains all of the Error objects created in response to a single failure involving the provider.
Fields	A Fields collection contains all of the Field objects for a Recordset or Record object.
Parameters	A Parameters collection contains all the Parameter objects for a Command object.
Properties	A Properties collection contains all the Property objects for a specific instance of an ADO object.

The Command Object

Methods of the Command Object	Return Type	Description
Cancel		Cancels execution of a pending Execute or Open call.
CreateParameter	Parameter	Creates a new Parameter object.
Execute	Recordset	Executes the query, SQL statement, or stored procedure specified in the CommandText property.

Note that the `CommandStream` and `NamedParameters` properties are new to ADO 2.6.

Properties of the Command Object	Return Type	Description
ActiveConnection	Variant	Indicates to which Connection object the command currently belongs.
CommandStream	Variant	Identifies the Stream object that contains the commands to be issued against a data provider.
CommandText	String	Contains the text of a command to be issued against a data provider.
CommandTimeout	Long	Indicates how long to wait, in seconds, while executing a command before terminating the command and generating an error. Default is 30.
CommandType	CommandType Enum	Indicates the type of command specified by the Command object.
Dialect	String	A Globally Unique IDentifier (GUID) that identifies the command dialect to be used by a particular command.
Name	String	Indicates the name of the Command object
NamedParameters	Boolean	Indicates whether or not the Parameter names are sent to the provider or whether Parameters are identified by their position in the collection.
Prepared	Boolean	Indicates whether or not to save a compiled version of a command before execution.
State	Long	Describes whether the Command object is open or closed. Read-only.

Collections of the Command Object	Return Type	Description
Parameters	Parameters	Contains all of the Parameter objects for a Command object.
Properties	Properties	Contains all of the Property objects for a Command object.

Appendices

The Connection Object

Methods of the Connection Object	Return Type	Description
BeginTrans	Integer	Begins a new transaction.
Cancel		Cancels the execution of a pending, asynchronous Execute or Open operation.
Close		Closes an open connection and any dependent objects.
CommitTrans		Saves any changes and ends the current transaction.
Execute	Recordset	Executes the query, SQL statement, stored procedure, or provider-specific text.
Open		Opens a connection to a data store, so that provider-specific statements (such as SQL statements) can be executed against it.
OpenSchema	Recordset	Obtains database schema information from the provider.
RollbackTrans		Cancels any changes made during the current transaction and ends the transaction.

Properties of the Connection Object	Return Type	Description
Attributes	Long	Indicates one or more characteristics of a Connection object. Default is 0.
CommandTimeout	Long	Indicates how long, in seconds, to wait while executing a command before terminating the command and generating an error. The default is 30.
Connection String	String	Contains the information used to establish a connection to a data source.
Connection Timeout	Long	Indicates how long, in seconds, to wait while establishing a connection before terminating the attempt and generating an error. Default is 15.
CursorLocation	CursorLocation Enum	Sets or returns the location of the cursor engine.
DefaultDatabase	String	Indicates the default database for a Connection object.

Properties of the Connection Object	Return Type	Description
IsolationLevel	Isolation Level Enum	Indicates the level of transaction isolation for a Connection object.
Mode	ConnectMode Enum	Indicates the available permissions for modifying data in a Connection.
Provider	String	Indicates the name of the provider for a Connection object.
State	ObjectState Enum	Describes whether the Connection object is open, closed, or currently executing a statement. Read-only.
Version	String	Indicates the ADO version number. Read-only.

Collections of the Connection Object	Return Type	Description
Errors	Errors	Contains all of the Error objects created in response to a single failure involving the provider.
Properties	Properties	Contains all of the Property objects for a Connection object.

Events of the Connection Object	Description
BeginTrans Complete	Fired after a BeginTrans operation finishes executing.
CommitTrans Complete	Fired after a CommitTrans operation finishes executing.
ConnectComplete	Fired after a connection opens.
Disconnect	Fired after a connection closes.
ExecuteComplete	Fired after a command has finished executing.
InfoMessage	Fired whenever a ConnectionEvent operation completes successfully and additional information is returned by the provider.
RollbackTrans Complete	Fired after a RollbackTrans operation has finished executing.
WillConnect	Fired before a connection starts.
WillExecute	Fired before a pending command executes on the connection.

Appendices

The Error Object

Properties of the Error Object	Return Type	Description
Description	String	A description string associated with the error. Read-only.
HelpContext	Integer	Indicates the ContextID in the help file for the associated error. Read-only.
HelpFile	String	Indicates the name of the help file. Read-only.
NativeError	Long	Indicates the provider–specific error code for the associated error. Read-only.
Number	Long	Indicates the number that uniquely identifies an Error object. Read-only.
Source	String	Indicates the name of the object or application that originally generated the error. Read-only.
SQLState	String	Indicates the SQL state for a given Error object. It is a five–character string that follows the ANSI SQL standard. Read-only.

The Errors Collection

Methods of the Errors Collection	Return Type	Description
Clear		Removes all of the Error objects from the Errors collection.
Refresh		Updates the Error objects with information from the provider.

Properties of the Errors Collection	Return Type	Description
Count	Long	Indicates the number of Error objects in the Errors collection. Read-only.
Item	Error	Allows indexing into the Errors collection to reference a specific Error object. Read-only.

The Field Object

Methods of the Field Object	Return Type	Description
AppendChunk		Appends data to a large or binary Field object (such as an image or text field in SQL Server).
GetChunk	Variant	Returns all or a portion of the contents of a large or binary Field object (such as an image or text field in SQL Server).

Properties of the Field Object	Return Type	Description
ActualSize	Long	Indicates the actual length of a field's value. Read-only.
Attributes	Long	Indicates one or more characteristics of a Field object.
DataFormat	Variant	Identifies the format in which data should be displayed.
DefinedSize	Long	Indicates the defined size of the Field object.
Name	String	Indicates the name of the Field object.
NumericScale	Byte	Indicates the scale of numeric values for the Field object.
OriginalValue	Variant	Indicates the value of a Field object that existed in the record before any changes were made. Read-only.
Precision	Byte	Indicates the degree of precision for numeric values in the Field object. Read-only.
Status	Field Status Enum	Identifies the current state of the field. Read-only.
Type	DataType Enum	Indicates the data type of the Field object.
Underlying Value	Variant	Indicates a Field object's current value in the database. Read-only.
Value	Variant	Indicates the value assigned to the Field object.

Collections of the Field Object	Return Type	Description
Properties	Properties	Contains all of the Property objects for a Field object.

The Fields Collection

Methods of the Fields Collection	Return Type	Description
Append		Appends a Field object to the Fields collection.
CancelUpdate		Cancels any changes made to the Fields collection of a Record object.
Delete		Deletes a Field object from the Fields collection.

Methods of the Fields Collection	Return Type	Description
Refresh		Updates the Field objects in the Fields collection.
Resync		Resynchronizes the values of the Fields collection of a Record object, with values from the data provider.
Update		Confirms any changes made to Field objects in the Fields collection of a Record object.

Properties of the Fields Collection	Return Type	Description
Count	Long	Indicates the number of Field objects in the Fields collection. Read-only.
Item	Field	Allows indexing into the Fields collection to reference a specific Field object. Read-only.

The Parameter Object

Methods of the Parameter Object	Return Type	Description
AppendChunk		Appends data to a large or binary Parameter object (such as an image or text field in SQL Server).

Properties of the Parameter Object	Return Type	Description
Attributes	Long	Indicates one or more characteristics of a Parameter object.
Direction	Parameter Direction Enum	Indicates whether the Parameter object represents an input parameter, an output parameter, or an input/output parameter, or if the parameter is a return value from a statement.
Name	String	Indicates the name of the Parameter object.
NumericScale	Byte	Indicates the scale of numeric values for the Parameter object.
Precision	Byte	Indicates the degree of precision for numeric values in the Parameter object.

Properties of the Parameter Object	Return Type	Description
Size	Long	Indicates the maximum size (in bytes or characters) of a Parameter object.
Type	DataType Enum	Indicates the data type of the Parameter object.
Value	Variant	Indicates the value assigned to the Parameter object.

Collections of the Parameter Object	Return Type	Description
Properties	Properties	Contains all of the Property objects for a Parameter object.

The Parameters Collection

Methods of the Parameters Collection	Return Type	Description
Append		Appends a Parameter object to the Parameters collection.
Delete		Deletes a Parameter object from the Parameters collection.
Refresh		Updates the Parameter objects in the Parameters collection.

Properties of the Parameters Collection	Return Type	Description
Count	Long	Indicates the number of Parameter objects in the Parameters collection. Read-only.
Item	Parameter	Allows indexing into the Parameters collection to reference a specific Parameter object. Read-only.

The Properties Collection

Methods of the Properties Collection	Return Type	Description
Refresh		Updates the Property objects in the Properties collection with the details from the provider.

Appendices

407

A

Properties of the Properties Collection	Return Type	Description
Count	Long	Indicates the number of Property objects in the Properties collection. Read-only.
Item	Property	Allows indexing into the Properties collection to reference a specific Property object. Read-only.

The Property Object

Properties of the Property Object	Return Type	Description
Attributes	Long	Indicates one or more characteristics of a Property object.
Name	String	Indicates the name of the Property object. Read-only.
Type	DataType Enum	Indicates the data type of the Property object.
Value	Variant	Indicates the value assigned to the Property object.

The Record Object

Methods of the Record Object	Return Type	Description
Cancel		Cancels any pending, asynchronous method call.
Close		Closes the currently open Record.
CopyRecord	String	Copies a file, or a directory and its contents, to a new location.
DeleteRecord		Deletes a file, or a directory and its contents.
GetChildren	Recordset	Returns a Recordset containing the child resources of the Record's underlying resource.
MoveRecord	String	Moves a resource and its contents to a new location.
Open		Opens an existing resource, or creates a new resource.

Properties of the Record Object	Return Type	Description
ActiveConnection	Variant	Identifies the connection details for the resource. Can be a connection string or a Connection object.
Mode	Connect ModeEnum	Indicates the permissions used when opening a Record.
ParentURL	String	Identifies the absolute URL of the parent of the current Record.
RecordType	Record TypeEnum	Indicates the type of the record, whether it's a directory, a simple file, or a complex file.
Source	Variant	Identifies the source of the Record. This will either be a URL or a reference to a Recordset object.
State	Object StateEnum	Indicates whether the Record is open, closed, or a statement is currently executing.

Collections of the Record Object	Return Type	Description
Fields	Fields	Contains a Field object for each property of the resource.
Properties		Contains all of the Property objects for the current Record object.

The Recordset Object

Methods of the Recordset Object	Return Type	Description
AddNew		Creates a new record for an updateable Recordset object.
Cancel		Cancels execution of a pending asynchronous Open operation.
CancelBatch		Cancels a pending batch update.
CancelUpdate		Cancels any changes made to the current record, or to a new record, prior to calling the Update method.
Clone	Recordset	Creates a duplicate Recordset object from an existing Recordset object.
Close		Closes the Recordset object and any dependent objects, including clones.

Methods of the Recordset Object	Return Type	Description
CompareBookmarks	Compare Enum	Compares two bookmarks and returns an indication of the relative values.
Delete		Deletes the current record or group of records.
Find		Searches the Recordset for a record that matches the specified criteria.
GetRows	Variant	Retrieves multiple records of a Recordset object into an array.
GetString	String	Returns a Recordset as a string.
Move		Moves the position of the current record in a Recordset.
MoveFirst		Moves the position of the current record to the first record in the Recordset.
MoveLast		Moves the position of the current record to the last record in the Recordset.
MoveNext		Moves the position of the current record to the next record in the Recordset.
MovePrevious		Moves the position of the current record to the previous record in the Recordset.
NextRecordset	Recordset	Clears the current Recordset object and returns the next Recordset by advancing to the next in a series of commands.
Open		Opens a Recordset.
Requery		Updates the data in a Recordset object by re–executing the query on which the object is based.
Resync		Refreshes the data in the Recordset object with the current data from the underlying data store.
Save		Saves the Recordset to a file, a Stream, or any object that supports the standard COM IStream interface (such as the ASP Response object).
Seek		Searches the recordset index to locate a value.
Supports	Boolean	Determines whether a specified Recordset object supports particular functionality.

Methods of the Recordset Object	Return Type	Description
Update		Saves any changes made to the current Recordset object.
UpdateBatch		Writes all pending batch modifications (updates, inserts, and deletes) to the underlying data store.

Properties of the Recordset Object	Return Type	Description
AbsolutePage	PositionEnum	Specifies the page in which the current record resides.
AbsolutePosition	PositionEnum	Specifies the ordinal position of the Recordset object's current record.
ActiveCommand	Object	Indicates the Command object that created the associated Recordset object. Read-only.
ActiveConnection	Variant	Indicates the Connection object to which the Recordset object currently belongs.
BOF	Boolean	Indicates whether the record pointer is pointing before the first record in the Recordset object. Read-only.
Bookmark	Variant	Returns a bookmark that uniquely identifies the current record in the Recordset object, or sets the record pointer to point to the record identified by a valid bookmark.
CacheSize	Long	Indicates the number of records from the Recordset object that are cached locally in memory.
CursorLocation	Cursor LocationEnum	Sets or returns the location of the cursor engine.
CursorType	CursorType Enum	Indicates the type of cursor used in the Recordset object.
DataMember	String	Specifies the name of the data member to be retrieved from the object referenced by the DataSource property.
DataSource	Object	Specifies an object containing data, to be represented by the Recordset object.

Appendices

Properties of the Recordset Object	Return Type	Description
EditMode	EditMode Enum	Indicates the editing status of the current record. Read-only.
EOF	Boolean	Indicates whether the record pointer is pointing beyond the last record in the Recordset object. Read-only.
Filter	Variant	Indicates a filter for data in the Recordset.
Index	String	Identifies the name of the index currently being used.
LockType	LockType Enum	Indicates the type of locks placed on records during editing.
MarshalOptions	Marshal Options Enum	Indicates which records are to be marshaled back to the server, or across thread or process boundaries.
MaxRecords	Long	Indicates the maximum number of records that can be returned to the Recordset object from a query. Default is zero (no limit).
PageCount	Long	Indicates how many pages of data are contained in the Recordset object (and is thus dependent on the values of PageSize and RecordCount). Read-only.
PageSize	Long	Indicates how many records constitute one page in the Recordset.
RecordCount	Long	Indicates the current number of records in the Recordset object. Read-only.
Sort	String	Specifies one or more field names the Recordset is sorted on, and the direction of the sort.
Source	String	Indicates the statement used to populate the data in the Recordset object.
State	Long	Indicates whether the recordset is open, closed, or whether it is executing an asynchronous operation. Read-only.
Status	Integer	Indicates the status of the current record with respect to batch updates or other bulk operations. Read-only.
StayInSync	Boolean	Indicates, in a hierarchical Recordset object, whether the parent row should change when the set of underlying child records changes. Read-only.

Collections of the Recordset Object	Return Type	Description
Fields	Fields	Contains all of the Field objects for the Recordset object.
Properties	Properties	Contains all of the Property objects for the current Recordset object.

Events of the Recordset Object	Description
EndOfRecordset	Fired when there is an attempt to move to a row past the end of the Recordset.
FetchComplete	Fired after a Recordset has been populated with all of the rows from an asynchronous operation.
FetchProgress	Fired periodically during a lengthy asynchronous operation, to report how many rows have currently been retrieved.
FieldChange Complete	Fired after the value of one or more Field objects has been changed.
MoveComplete	Fired after the current position in the Recordset changes.
RecordChange Complete	Fired after one or more records change.
RecordsetChange Complete	Fired after the Recordset has changed.
WillChangeField	Fired before a pending operation changes the value of one or more Field objects.
WillChangeRecord	Fired before one or more rows in the Recordset change.
WillChange Recordset	Fired before a pending operation changes the Recordset.
WillMove	Fired before a pending operation changes the current position in the Recordset.

The Stream Object

Methods of the Stream Object	Return Type	Description
Cancel		Cancels any pending, asynchronous commands.
Close		Closes the current Stream.
CopyTo		Copies a number of characters or bytes into another Stream object.

Appendices

Methods of the Stream Object	Return Type	Description
Flush		Forces the contents of the buffer into the underlying object.
LoadFromFile		Loads the contents of a file into the Stream object.
Open		Opens a Stream object from a URL or a Record object.
Read	Variant	Reads a number of bytes from the Stream.
ReadText	String	Reads a number of characters from the Stream.
SaveToFile		Saves the contents of a Stream to a file.
SetEOS		Sets the position that identifies the end of the stream.
SkipLine		Skips a line when reading in a text stream. Uses the LineSeparator property to identify the end of line character.
Write		Writes binary data to the stream.
WriteText		Writes text data to the stream.

Properties of the Stream Object	Return Type	Description
Charset	String	Indicates the character set to translate the Stream contents into.
EOS	Boolean	Indicates whether or not the end of the Stream has been reached.
LineSeparator	Line Separator Enum	Identifies the binary character that separates lines.
Mode	Connect ModeEnum	Identifies the permissions used when opening the Stream.
Position	Long	Identifies the current position with the Stream.
Size	Long	Indicates, in bytes, the size of the Stream.
State	Object StateEnum	Indicates whether the Stream is open or closed.
Type	Stream TypeEnum	Indicates whether the Stream contains binary or text data.

ADO Method Calls – Quick Reference

Command Object Methods

```
Command.Cancel
Parameter = Command.CreateParameter([Name As String], _
            [Type As DataTypeEnum], _
            [Direction As ParameterDirectionEnum], _
            [Size As Integer], _
            [Value As Variant])
Recordset = Command.Execute([RecordsAffected As Variant], _
            [Parameters As Variant], [Options As Long])
```

Connection Object Methods

```
Long = Connection.BeginTrans
Connection.Cancel
Connection.Close
Connection.CommitTrans
Recordset = Connection.Execute(CommandText As String, _
            [RecordsAffected As Variant], [Options As Long])
Connection.Open([ConnectionString As String], [UserID As String], _
            [Password As String], [Options As Long])
Recordset = Connection.OpenSchema(Schema As SchemaEnum, _
            [Restrictions As Variant], [SchemaID As Variant])
Connection.RollbackTrans
```

Errors Collection Methods

```
Errors.Clear
Errors.Refresh
```

Field Object Methods

```
Field.AppendChunk(Data As Variant)
Variant = Field.GetChunk(Length As Long)
```

Fields Collection Methods

```
Fields.Append(Name As String, Type As DataTypeEnum,
            [DefinedSize As Long], _
            [Attrib As FieldAttributeEnum], _
            [FieldValue As Variant])
Fields.CancelUpdate
Fields.Delete(Index As Variant)
Fields.Refresh
Fields.Resync([ResyncValues As ResyncEnum])
Fields.Update
```

Parameter Object Methods

```
Parameter.AppendChunk(Val As Variant)
```

Appendices

415

A

Parameters Collection Methods

```
Parameters.Append(Object As Object)
Parameters.Delete(Index As Variant)
Parameters.Refresh
```

Properties Collection Methods

```
Properties.Refresh
```

Record Object Methods

```
Record.Cancel
Record.Close
String = Record.CopyRecord([Source As String], _
            [Destination As String], _
            [UserName As String], [Password As String], _
            [Options As CopyRecordOptionsEnum], [Async As Boolean])
Record.DeleteRecord([Source As String], [Async As Boolean])
Recordset = Record.GetChildren
String = Record.MoveRecord([Source As String], _
            [Destination As String], _
            [UserName As String], [Password As String], _
            [Options As MoveRecordOptionsEnum], [Async As Boolean])
Record.Open([Source As Variant], [ActiveConnection As Variant], _
            [Mode As ConnectModeEnum], _
            [CreateOptions As RecordCreateOptionsEnum], _
            [Options as RecordOpenOptionsEnum], _
            [UserName As String], _
            [Password As String])
```

Recordset Object Methods

```
Recordset.AddNew([FieldList As Variant], [Values As Variant])
Recordset.Cancel
Recordset.CancelBatch([AffectRecords As AffectEnum])
Recordset.CancelUpdate
Recordset = Recordset.Clone([LockType As LockTypeEnum])
Recordset.Close
CompareEnum = Recordset.CompareBookmarks(Bookmark1 As Variant, _
            Bookmark2 As Variant)
Recordset.Delete([AffectRecords As AffectEnum])
Recordset.Find(Criteria As String, [SkipRecords As Long], _
            [SearchDirection As SearchDirectionEnum], _
            [Start As Variant])
Variant = Recordset.GetRows([Rows As Long], [Start As Variant], _
            [Fields As Variant])
String = Recordset.GetString(StringFormat As StringFormatEnum, _
            [NumRows As Long], [ColumnDelimeter As String], _
            [RowDelimeter As String], [NullExpr As String])
Recordset.Move(NumRecords As Long, [Start As Variant])
Recordset.MoveFirst
Recordset.MoveLast
```

```
Recordset.MoveNext
Recordset.MovePrevious
Recordset = Recordset.NextRecordset([RecordsAffected As Variant])
Recordset.Open([Source As Variant], _
               [ActiveConnection As Variant], _
               [CursorType As CursorTypeEnum], _
               [LockType As LockTypeEnum], _
               [Options As Long])
Recordset.Requery([Options As Long])
Recordset.Resync([AffectRecords As AffectEnum], _
                 [ResyncValues As ResyncEnum])
Recordset.Save([FileName As String], _
               [PersistFormat As PersistFormatEnum])
Recordset.Seek(KeyValues As Variant, SeekOption As SeekEnum)
Boolean = Recordset.Supports(CursorOptions As CursorOptionEnum)
Recordset.Update([Fields As Variant], [Values As Variant])
Recordset.UpdateBatch([AffectRecords As AffectEnum])
```

Stream Object Methods

```
Stream.Cancel
Stream.Close
Stream.CopyTo(DestStream As Stream, [CharNumber As Long])
Stream.Flush
Stream.LoadFromFile(FileName As String)
Stream.Open([Source As Variant], [Mode As ConnectModeEnum], _
            [Options As StreamOpenOptionsEnum], _
            [UserName As String], _
            [Password As String])
Variant = Stream.Read([NumBytes As Long])
String = Stream.ReadText([NumChars As Long])
Stream.SaveToFile(FileName As String, [Options As SaveOptionsEnum])
Stream.SetEOS
Stream.SkipLine
Stream.Write(Buffer As Variant)
Stream.WriteText(Data As String, [Options As StreamWriteEnum])
```

I thank God I am as honest as any man
living that is an old man and no honester th...

Can counsel and speak comfort to th...
Which they themselves not feel

Much Ado About Nothing.

For there was never yet philospher
That could endure the toothache patiently.

He wears his faith but as the fashion of...

As merry as the day

He hath indeed better bettered expectation

(Act i. Sc. i).

He wears his faith but as the fashion of his hat.
(Ibid)

As merry as the day is long.

th indeed better bettered expectation

(Ibid)

(Act i. Sc. i).

Can counsel and speak comfort to that grief
Which they themselves not feel.

Much Ado About Nothing.

He wears his faith but as the fashion of his hat.
(Ibid)
(Ibid)

I was not born under

I was not born under a rhyming plan
(Sc.
For there was never yet
That could endure the t

a rhyming plane

merry as the day is long
(Sc. 2)

Can counsel and speak comfort to that grief
Which they themselves not feel.
(Ibid)

He hath indeed better bettered expectation
(Ibid)
(Act i. Sc.

I thank God I am as honest as any man
living that is an old man and no hones

He wears his faith but as the fashion of his h
(Ibi

Much Ado About Nothing.

For there was never yet philospher
That could endure the toothache patiently.
(Ibid)

I was not born u

ADO Constants

Standard Constants

The following constants are predefined by ADO. For scripting languages these are included in adovbs.inc or adojava.inc, which can be found in the Program Files\Common Files\System\ado directory. In ASP you can either include these file, or use the METADATA tag:

```
<!-- METADATA TYPE="typelib" FILE="C:\Program Files\Common Files\
System\ado\msado15.dll" -->
```

This should appear on a single line, and you'll have to put the correct path in. Don't worry about the name of the DLL – it's the current version, whatever its name.

In Visual Basic, these constants are included automatically when you reference the ADO library.

AffectEnum

Name	Value	Description
adAffectAll	3	Operation affects all records in the recordset.
adAffectAllChapters	4	Operation affects all child (chapter) records.
adAffectCurrent	1	Operation affects only the current record.
adAffectGroup	2	Operation affects records that satisfy the current Filter property.

BookmarkEnum

Name	Value	Description
adBookmarkCurrent	0	Default. Start at the current record.
adBookmarkFirst	1	Start at the first record.
adBookmarkLast	2	Start at the last record.

CEResyncEnum

Name	Value	Description
adResyncAll	15	Resynchronizes the data for each pending row.
adResyncAuto Increment	1	Resynchronizes the auto-increment values for all successfully inserted rows. This is the default.
adResyncConflicts	2	Resynchronizes all rows for which an update or delete operation failed due to concurrency conflicts.
adResyncInserts	8	Resynchronizes all successfully inserted rows, including the values of their identity columns.
adResyncNone	0	No resynchronization is performed.
adResyncUpdates	4	Resynchronizes all successfully updated rows.

CommandTypeEnum

Name	Value	Description
adCmdFile	256	Indicates that the provider should evaluate CommandText as a previously persisted file.
adCmdStoredProc	4	Indicates that the provider should evaluate CommandText as a stored procedure.
adCmdTable	2	Indicates that the provider should generate a SQL query to return all rows from the table named in CommandText.
adCmdTableDirect	512	Indicates that the provider should return all rows from the table named in CommandText.
adCmdText	1	Indicates that the provider should evaluate CommandText as textual definition of a command, such as a SQL statement.
adCmdUnknown	8	Indicates that the type of command in CommandText unknown.
adCmdUnspecified	-1	The command type is unspecified.

CompareEnum

Name	Value	Description
adCompareEqual	1	The bookmarks are equal.
adCompareGreaterThan	2	The first bookmark is after the second.
adCompareLessThan	0	The first bookmark is before the second.
adCompareNot Comparable	4	The bookmarks cannot be compared.
adCompareNotEqual	3	The bookmarks are not equal and not ordered.

ConnectModeEnum

Name	Value	Description
adModeRead	1	Indicates read-only permissions.
adModeReadWrite	3	Indicates read/write permissions.
adModeRecursive	4194304	Apply permissions recursively.
adModeShareDenyNone	16	Prevents others from opening connection with any permissions.
adModeShareDenyRead	4	Prevents others from opening connection with read permissions.
adModeShareDenyWrite	8	Prevents others from opening connection with write permissions.
adModeShareExclusive	12	Prevents others from opening connection.
adModeUnknown	0	Default. Indicates that the permissions have not yet been set or cannot be determined.
adModeWrite	2	Indicates write-only permissions.

ConnectOptionEnum

Name	Value	Description
adAsyncConnect	16	Open the connection asynchronously.
adConnectUnspecified	-1	The connection mode is unspecified.

ConnectPromptEnum

Name	Value	Description
adPromptAlways	1	Always prompt for connection information.

Appendices

421

A

Name	Value	Description
adPromptComplete	2	Only prompt if not enough information was supplied.
adPromptComplete Required	3	Only prompt if not enough information was supplied, but disable any options not directly applicable to the connection.
adPromptNever	4	Default. Never prompt for connection information.

CopyRecordOptionsEnum

Name	Value	Description
adCopyAllowEmulation	4	Use a download/upload if the copy fails.
adCopyNonRecursive	2	Copy only the current directory, but no children.
adCopyOverWrite	1	Overwrite an existing file or directory.
adCopyUnspecified	-1	The default copy operation is performed. Default.

CursorLocationEnum

Name	Value	Description
adUseClient	3	Use client-side cursors supplied by the local cursor library.
adUseNone	1	No cursor services are used.
adUseServer	2	Default. Uses data provider driver supplied cursors.

CursorOptionEnum

Name	Value	Description
adAddNew	16778240	You can use the AddNew method to add new records.
adApproxPosition	16384	You can read and set the AbsolutePosition and AbsolutePage properties.
adBookmark	8192	You can use the Bookmark property to access specific records.
adDelete	16779264	You can use the Delete method to delete records.

Name	Value	Description
adFind	524288	You can use the Find method to find records.
adHoldRecords	256	You can retrieve more records or change the next retrieve position without committing all pending changes.
adIndex	8388608	You can use the Index property to set the current index.
adMovePrevious	512	You can use the MoveFirst, MovePrevious, Move, and GetRows methods.
adNotify	262144	The recordset supports Notifications.
adResync	131072	You can update the cursor with the data visible in the underlying database with the Resync method.
adSeek	4194304	You can use the Seek method to find records by an index.
adUpdate	16809984	You can use the Update method to modify existing records.
adUpdateBatch	65536	You can use the UpdateBatch or CancelBatch methods to transfer changes to the provider in groups.

CursorTypeEnum

Name	Value	Description
adOpenDynamic	2	Opens a dynamic type cursor.
adOpenForwardOnly	0	Default. Opens a forward-only type cursor.
adOpenKeyset	1	Opens a keyset type cursor.
adOpenStatic	3	Opens a static type cursor.
adOpenUnspecified	-1	Indicates an unspecified value for cursor type.

DataTypeEnum

Name	Value	Description
adArray	8192	An array of data types.
adBigInt	20	An 8-byte signed integer.
adBinary	128	A binary value.
adBoolean	11	A Boolean value.
adBSTR	8	A Null-terminated character string.

Appendices

423

A

Name	Value	Description
adChapter	136	A chapter type, indicating a child recordset.
adChar	129	A String value.
adCurrency	6	A currency value. An 8-byte signed integer scaled by 10,000, with 4 digits to the right of the decimal point.
adDate	7	A Date value. A Double where the whole part is the number of days since December 30 1899, and the fractional part is the fraction of the day.
adDBDate	133	A date value (yyyymmdd).
adDBTime	134	A time value (hhmmss).
adDBTimeStamp	135	A date-time stamp (yyyymmddhhmmss plus a fraction in nanoseconds).
adDecimal	14	An exact numeric value with fixed precision and scale.
adDouble	5	A double-precision floating point value.
adEmpty	0	No value was specified.
adError	10	A 32-bit error code.
adFileTime	64	A DOS/Win32 file time. The number of 100-nanosecond intervals since Jan 1 1601.
adGUID	72	A globally unique identifier.
adIDispatch	9	A pointer to an IDispatch interface on an OLE object.
adInteger	3	A 4-byte signed integer.
adIUnknown	13	A pointer to an IUnknown interface on an OLE object.
adLongVarBinary	205	A long binary value.
adLongVarChar	201	A long String value.
adLongVarWChar	203	A long Null-terminated string value.
adNumeric	131	An exact numeric value with a fixed precision and scale.
adPropVariant	138	A variant that is not equivalent to an Automation variant.
adSingle	4	A single-precision floating point value.
adSmallInt	2	A 2-byte signed integer.
adTinyInt	16	A 1-byte signed integer.
adUnsignedBigInt	21	An 8-byte unsigned integer.
adUnsignedInt	19	A 4-byte unsigned integer.
adUnsignedSmallInt	18	A 2-byte unsigned integer.

Name	Value	Description
adUnsignedTinyInt	17	A 1-byte unsigned integer.
adUserDefined	132	A user-defined variable.
adVarBinary	204	A binary value.
adVarChar	200	A String value.
adVariant	12	An Automation Variant.
adVarNumeric	139	A variable width exact numeric, with a signed scale value.
adVarWChar	202	A Null-terminated Unicode character string.
adWChar	130	A Null-terminated Unicode character string.

EditModeEnum

Name	Value	Description
adEditAdd	2	Indicates that the AddNew method has been invoked and the current record in the buffer is a new record that hasn't been saved to the database.
adEditDelete	4	Indicates that the Delete method has been invoked.
adEditInProgress	1	Indicates that data in the current record has been modified but not saved.
adEditNone	0	Indicates that no editing is in progress.

ErrorValueEnum

Name	Value	Description
adErrBoundToCommand	3707	The application cannot change the ActiveConnection property of a Recordset object with a Command object as its source.
adErrCannotComplete	3732	The server cannot complete the operation.
adErrCantChange Connection	3748	Connection denied, as the characteristics differ from the connection in use.
adErrCantChange Provider	3220	The requested provider is different from the one in use.
adErrCant Convertvalue	3724	The data value cannot be converted. The reason is something other than an overflow or sign mismatch.

Appendices

425

A

Name	Value	Description
adErrCantCreate	3725	Value cannot be set or retrieved. The reason is an unknown data type or insufficient resources.
adErrCatalogNotSet	3747	A valid `ParentCatalog` is required.
adErrColumnNotOnThis Row	3726	The record does not contain this field.
adErrDataConversion	3421	The application is using a value of the wrong type for the current application.
adErrDataOverflow	3721	The value is too large for the field.
adErrDelResOutOfScope	3738	Deleting the requested URL is not allowed as it is outside of the record scope.
adErrDenyNotSupported	3750	Sharing restrictions are not supported by the provider.
adErrDenyTypeNot Supported	3751	The requested sharing restriction is not supported by the provider.
adErrFeatureNot Available	3251	The operation requested by the application is not supported by the provider.
adFieldsUpdateFailed	3749	An update to the `Fields` collection failed. The `Status` property of the `Field` objects will contain more information.
adErrIllegalOperation	3219	The operation requested by the application is not allowed in this context.
adErrIntegrity Violation	3719	Changing the value conflicts with the integrity constraints of the field.
adErrInTransaction	3246	The application cannot explicitly close a `Connection` object while in the middle of a transaction.
adErrInvalidArgument	3001	The application is using arguments that are the wrong type, are out of the acceptable range, or are in conflict with one another.
adErrInvalid Connection	3709	The application requested an operation on an object with a reference to a closed or invalid `Connection` object.
adErrInvalidParamInfo	3708	The application has improperly defined a `Parameter` object.

Name	Value	Description
adErrInvalid Transaction	3714	The coordinating transaction has not started or is invalid.
adErrInvalidURL	3729	The supplied URL is invalid.
adErrItemNotFound	3265	ADO could not find the object in the collection.
adErrNoCurrentRecord	3021	Either BOF or EOF is True, or the current record has been deleted. The operation requested by the application requires a current record.
adErrNotExecuting	3715	The operation is not executing.
adErrNotReentrant	3710	The operation is not reentrant.
adErrObjectClosed	3704	The operation requested by the application is not allowed if the object is closed.
adErrObjectIn Collection	3367	Can't append. Object already in collection.
adErrObjectNotSet	3420	The object referenced by the application no longer points to a valid object.
adErrObjectOpen	3705	The operation requested by the application is not allowed if the object is open.
adErrOpeningFile	3002	The requested file could not be opened.
adErrOperation Cancelled	3712	The operation was cancelled.
adErrOutOfSpace	3734	The provider cannot obtain enough space to complete the operation.
adErrPermissionDenied	3720	Insufficient permissions to complete the operation.
adErrPropConflicting	3742	The property value conflicts with the related property.
adErrPropInvalid Column	3739	This field cannot have the property applied to it.
adErrPropInvalid Option	3740	The property attribute is invalid.
adErrPropInvalidValue	3741	The property value is invalid.
adErrPropNotAll Settable	3743	The property cannot be set, perhaps because it is read-only.
adErrPropNotSet	3744	An optional property value was not set.
adErrPropNotSettable	3745	A read-only property was not set.

Appendices

427

A

Name	Value	Description
adErrPropNotSupported	3746	The property is not supported by the provider.
adErrProviderFailed	3000	The requested operation failed to be performed by the provider.
adErrProviderNotFound	3706	ADO could not find the specified provider.
adErrReadFile	3003	The file could not be read.
adErrResourceExists	3731	The destination URL already exists.
adErrResourceLocked	3730	The resource specified by the URL is locked by another process.
adErrResourceOutOf Scope	3735	The supplied URL is outside the scope of the current record.
adErrSchemaViolation	3722	The value conflicts with the constraints or data type of the field.
adErrSignMismatch	3723	The value is signed and the data type is unsigned.
adErrStillConnecting	3713	The operation is still connecting.
adErrStillExecuting	3711	The operation is still executing.
adTreePermission Denied	3728	Current permissions are not sufficient to access the tree or sub-tree.
adErrUnavailable	3736	The operation failed and the status is unavailable.
adErrUnsafeOperation	3716	The operation is unsafe under these circumstances.
adErrURLDoesNotExist	3727	The URL, or the parent of the destination URL, does not exist.
adErrURLNamedRowDoes NotExist	3737	The record named by this URL does not exist.
adErrVolumeNotFound	3733	The device indicated by the URL cannot be found.
adErrWriteFile	3004	Failed to write to the file.
adWrnSecirutyDialog	3717	This is for internal use only, and should not be used. It's included for completeness.
adWrnSecurityDialog Header	3718	This is for internal use only, and should not be used. It's included for completeness.

EventReasonEnum

Name	Value	Description
adRsnAddNew	1	A new record is to be added.
adRsnClose	9	The object is being closed.
adRsnDelete	2	The record is being deleted.
adRsnFirstChange	11	The record has been changed for the first time.
adRsnMove	10	A Move has been invoked and the current record pointer is being moved.
adRsnMoveFirst	12	A MoveFirst has been invoked and the current record pointer is being moved.
adRsnMoveLast	15	A MoveLast has been invoked and the current record pointer is being moved.
adRsnMoveNext	13	A MoveNext has been invoked and the current record pointer is being moved.
adRsnMovePrevious	14	A MovePrevious has been invoked and the current record pointer is being moved.
adRsnRequery	7	The recordset was requeried.
adRsnResynch	8	The recordset was resynchronized.
adRsnUndoAddNew	5	The addition of a new record has been cancelled.
adRsnUndoDelete	6	The deletion of a record has been cancelled.
adRsnUndoUpdate	4	The update of a record has been cancelled.
adRsnUpdate	3	The record is being updated.

EventStatusEnum

Name	Value	Description
adStatusCancel	4	Request cancellation of the operation that is about to occur.
adStatusCantDeny	3	A Will event cannot request cancellation of the operation about to occur.
adStatusErrorsOccurred	2	The operation completed unsuccessfully, or a Will... event cancelled the operation.
adStatusOK	1	The operation completed successfully.
adStatusUnwantedEvent	5	Events for this operation are no longer required.

ExecuteOptionEnum

Name	Value	Description
adAsyncExecute	16	The operation is executed asynchronously.
adAsyncFetch	32	The records are fetched asynchronously.
adAsyncFetchNon Blocking	64	The records are fetched asynchronously without blocking subsequent operations.
adExecuteNoRecords	128	Indicates CommandText is a command or stored procedure that does not return rows. Always combined with adCmdText or adCmdStoreProc.
adExecuteRecord	2048	Indicates the CommandText property of the command returns a single row, and should be returned as a Record object.
adExecuteStream	1024	Indicates that the results of the command should be returned as a Stream object. The output stream is defined by the Output Stream dynamic property.
adOptionUnspecified	-1	The command is unspecified.

FieldAttributeEnum

Name	Value	Description
adFldCacheDeferred	4096	Indicates that the provider caches field values and that subsequent reads are done from the cache.
adFldFixed	16	Indicates that the field contains fixed-length data.
adFldIsChapter	8192	Indicates that the field contains a chaptered value – that is, a recordset.
adFldIsCollection	262144	Indicates that the field represents a resource made up of other resources, such as a directory.
adFldIsDefaultStream	131072	Indicates that the field contains the default stream for the resource.
adFldIsNullable	32	Indicates that the field accepts Null values.
adFldIsRowURL	65536	The field is a URL representing a resource.

Name	Value	Description
adFldKeyColumn	32768	The field is part of a key column.
adFldLong	128	Indicates that the field is a long binary field, and that the AppendChunk and GetChunk methods can be used.
adFldMayBeNull	64	Indicates that you can read Null values from the field.
adFldMayDefer	2	Indicates that the field is deferred, that is, the field values are not retrieved from the data source with the whole record, but only when you access them.
adFldNegativeScale	16384	The field has a negative scale.
adFldRowID	256	Indicates that the field is some kind of record ID.
adFldRowVersion	512	Indicates that the field is a time or date stamp used to track updates.
adFldUnknownUpdatable	8	Indicates that the provider cannot determine if you can write to the field.
adFldUnspecified	-1	Attributes of the field are unspecified.
adFldUpdatable	4	Indicates that you can write to the field.

FieldEnum

Name	Value	Description
adDefaultStream	-1	When used to index into the Fields collection, returns the default Stream object associated with the Record.
adRecordURL	-2	When used to index into the Fields collection, returns the absolute URL for the current Record.

FieldStatusEnum

Name	Value	Description
adFieldAlreadyExists	26	The field already exists.
adFieldBadStatus	12	An incorrect status value was received by OLE DB from ADO.
adFieldCannotComplete	20	The server of the Source URL could not complete the operation.
adFieldCannotDeleteSource	23	The source could not be deleted after a move operation.
adFieldCantConvertValue	2	The field cannot be set or retrieved without data loss.

Appendices

431

A

Name	Value	Description
adFieldCantCreate	7	The field could not be created due to a provider limitation (for example on the number of fields).
adFieldDataOverflow	6	The provider returned data that overflowed the field data type.
adFieldDefault	13	The default value for the field has been used to set the value.
adFieldDoesNotExist	16	The requested field does not exist.
adFieldIgnore	15	This field was skipped when setting values.
adFieldIntegrity Violation	10	The field is calculated or derived and the value cannot be set.
adFieldInvalidURL	17	The URL is invalid.
adFieldIsNull	3	The provider returned a Null value.
adFieldOK	0	The field was successfully added or deleted.
adFieldOutOfSpace	22	The provider was unable to allocate enough space to complete the operation.
adFieldPendingChange	262144	The value of the field has changed, or the field has been removed and added with another data type. Calling Update will confirm the change.
adFieldPendingDelete	131072	The field has been marked for deletion, but will not be deleted until Update is called.
adFieldPendingInsert	65536	The field is a new field, but will not be added until Update is called.
adFieldPendingUnknown	524288	The field status has been set, but the provider cannot determine why.
adFieldPendingUnknown Delete	1048576	The field status has been set to delete the field, but the provider cannot determine why. The field will be deleted after an Update.
adFieldPermission Denied	9	The field cannot be modified as it is read-only.
adFieldReadOnly	24	The field in the data store is read-only.
adFieldResourceExists	19	A resource at the specified URL already exists.
adFieldResourceLocked	18	The specified resource is locked by another process.

Name	Value	Description
adFieldResourceOutOf Scope	25	The Source or Destination URL is outside the scope of the record.
adFieldSchemaViolation	11	The value conflicts with the schema constraint.
adFieldSignMismatch	5	The provider returned a signed value, but the ADO field type is unsigned.
adFieldTruncated	4	The data was truncated when retrieved from the data store.
adFieldUnavailable	8	The provider could not determine the value from the data source (for example a new record).
adFieldVolumeNotFound	21	The volume of the URL was not found.

FilterGroupEnum

Name	Value	Description
adFilterAffected Records	2	Allows you to view only records affected by the last Delete, Resync, UpdateBatch, or CancelBatch method.
adFilterConflicting Records	5	Allows you to view the records that failed the last batch update attempt.
adFilterFetched Records	3	Allows you to view records in the current cache.
adFilterNone	0	Removes the current filter and restores all records to view.
adFilterPending Records	1	Allows you to view only the records that have changed but have not been sent to the server. Only applicable for batch update mode.
adFilterPredicate	4	Allows you to view records that failed the last batch update attempt.

GetRowsOptionEnum

Name	Value	Description
adGetRowsRest	-1	Retrieves the remainder of the rows in the recordset.

IsolationLevelEnum

Name	Value	Description
adXactBrowse	256	Indicates that from one transaction you can view uncommitted changes in other transactions.

Name	Value	Description
adXactChaos	16	Indicates that you cannot overwrite pending changes from more highly isolated transactions.
adXact CursorStability	4096	Default. Indicates that from one transaction you can view changes in other transactions only after they have been committed.
adXactIsolated	1048576	Indicates that transactions are conducted in isolation from other transactions.
adXact ReadCommitted	4096	Same as adXactCursorStability.
adXactRead Uncommitted	256	Same as adXactBrowse.
adXact RepeatableRead	65536	Indicates that from one transaction you cannot see changes made in other transactions, but that requerying can bring new recordsets.
adXact Serializable	1048576	Same as adXactIsolated.
adXact Unspecified	-1	Indicates that the provider is using a different IsolationLevel than specified, but that the level cannot be identified.

LineSeparatorEnum

Name	Value	Description
adCR	13	The carriage return character.
adCRLF	-1	The carriage return and line feed characters.
adLF	10	The line feed character.

LockTypeEnum

Name	Value	Description
adLockBatch Optimistic	4	Optimistic batch updates.
adLock Optimistic	3	Optimistic locking, record by record. The provider locks records when Update is called.
adLock Pessimistic	2	Pessimistic locking, record by record. The provider locks the record immediately upon editing.
adLockReadOnly	1	Default. Read-only, data cannot be modified.
adLock Unspecified	-1	The clone is created with the same lock type as the original.

MarshalOptionsEnum

Name	Value	Description
adMarshalAll	0	Default. Indicates that all rows are returned to the server.
adMarshalModifiedOnly	1	Indicates that only modified rows are returned to the server.

MoveRecordOptionsEnum

Name	Value	Description
adMoveAllowEmulation	4	Use download, upload, delete operations to simulate the move operation.
adMoveDontUpdate Links	2	Do not update hypertext links of the source record. Updating of links is provider-specific.
adMoveOverWrite	1	Overwrite the destination file or directory, even if it exists.
adMoveUnspecified	-1	Perform the default move operation. Default.

ObjectStateEnum

Name	Value	Description
adStateClosed	0	Default. Indicates that the object is closed.
adStateConnecting	2	Indicates that the object is connecting.
adStateExecuting	4	Indicates that the object is executing a command.
adStateFetching	8	Indicates that the rows of the recordset are being fetched.
adStateOpen	1	Indicates that the object is open.

ParameterAttributesEnum

Name	Value	Description
adParamLong	128	Indicates that the parameter accepts long binary data.
adParamNullable	64	Indicates that the parameter accepts Null values.
adParamSigned	16	Default. Indicates that the parameter accepts signed values.

Appendices

435

A

ParameterDirectionEnum

Name	Value	Description
adParamInput	1	Default. Indicates an input parameter.
adParamInputOutput	3	Indicates both an input and an output parameter.
adParamOutput	2	Indicates an output parameter.
adParamReturnValue	4	Indicates a return value.
adParamUnknown	0	Indicates parameter direction is unknown.

PersistFormatEnum

Name	Value	Description
adPersistADTG	0	Default. Persist data in Advanced Data TableGram format.
adPersistXML	1	Persist data in XML format.

PositionEnum

Name	Value	Description
adPosBOF	-2	The current record pointer is at BOF.
adPosEOF	-3	The current record pointer is at EOF.
adPosUnknown	-1	The Recordset is empty, or the current position is unknown, or the provider does not support the AbsolutePage property.

PropertyAttributesEnum

Name	Value	Description
adPropNot Supported	0	Indicates that the property is not supported by the provider.
adPropOptional	2	Indicates that the user does not need to specify a value for this property before the data source is initialized.
adPropRead	512	Indicates that the user can read the property.
adPropRequired	1	Indicates that the user must specify a value for this property before the data source is initialized.
adPropWrite	1024	Indicates that the user can set the property.

RecordCreateOptionsEnum

Name	Value	Description
adCreateCollection	8192	Create a new collection resource (for example a directory).
adCreateNon Collection	0	Create a new simple resource (for example a file).
adCreateOverwrite	67108864	When added to the other adCreate options, forces any existing file or directory to be overwritten.
adCreateStructDoc	-2147483648	Create a new structured document.
adFailIfNotExists	-1	Generate an error if the source does not exist.
adOpenIfExists	335544322	When added to the other adCreate options (except adCreateOverwrite), forces any existing file or directory to be opened.

RecordOpenOptionsEnum

Name	Value	Description
adDelayFetch Fields	32768	Do not fetch fields until their first access.
adDelayFetch Stream	16384	Do not fetch the default stream until requested.
adOpenAsync	4096	Open the record asynchronously.
adOpenExecute Command	65536	The source of the record is a Command object.
adOpenRecord Unspecified	-1	No specific open options are specified.
adOpenSource	8388608	Open the source of the resource, rather than its processed output (for example an ASP file).

RecordStatusEnum

Name	Value	Description
adRecCanceled	256	The record was not saved because the operation was cancelled.

Name	Value	Description
adRecCantRelease	1024	The new record was not saved because of existing record locks.
adRecConcurrency Violation	2048	The record was not saved because optimistic concurrency was in use.
adRecDBDeleted	262144	The record has already been deleted from the data source.
adRecDeleted	4	The record was deleted.
adRecIntegrityViolation	4096	The record was not saved because the user violated integrity constraints.
adRecInvalid	16	The record was not saved because its bookmark is invalid.
adRecMaxChangesExceeded	8192	The record was not saved because there were too many pending changes.
adRecModified	2	The record was modified.
adRecMultipleChanges	64	The record was not saved because it would have affected multiple records.
adRecNew	1	The record is new.
adRecObjectOpen	16384	The record was not saved because of a conflict with an open storage object.
adRecOK	0	The record was successfully updated.
adRecOutOfMemory	32768	The record was not saved because the computer has run out of memory.
adRecPendingChanges	128	The record was not saved because it refers to a pending insert.
adRecPermissionDenied	65536	The record was not saved because the user has insufficient permissions.
adRecSchemaViolation	131072	The record was not saved because it violates the structure of the underlying database.
adRecUnmodified	8	The record was not modified.

RecordTypeEnum

Name	Value	Description
adCollectionRecord	1	The record represents a collection resource, such as a directory.

Name	Value	Description
adSimpleRecord	0	The record represents a simple resource, such as a text or HTML file.
adStructDoc	2	The record represents a structured document.

ResyncEnum

Name	Value	Description
adResyncAllValues	2	Default. Data is overwritten and pending updates are cancelled.
adResyncUnderlyingValues	1	Data is not overwritten and pending updates are not cancelled.

SaveOptionsEnum

Name	Value	Description
adSaveCreateNotExist	1	Create a new file if one doesn't already exist. Default.
adSaveCreateOverWrite	2	Overwrite the file if it already exists.

SchemaEnum

Name	Value	Description
adSchemaActions	41	Request action information.
adSchemaAsserts	0	Request assert information.
adSchemaCatalogs	1	Request catalog information.
adSchemaCharacterSets	2	Request character set information.
adSchemaCheckConstraints	5	Request check constraint information.
adSchemaCollations	3	Request collation information.
adSchemaColumnPrivileges	13	Request column privilege information.
adSchemaColumns	4	Request column information.
adSchemaColumnsDomainUsage	11	Request column domain usage information.
adSchemaCommands	42	Request command information.
adSchemaConstraintColumnUsage	6	Request column constraint usage information.

Appendices

439

A

Name	Value	Description
adSchemaConstraintTable Usage	7	Request table constraint usage information.
adSchemaCubes	32	For multi-dimensional data, view the Cubes schema.
adSchemaDBInfoKeywords	30	Request the keywords from the provider.
adSchemaDBInfoLiterals	31	Request the literals from the provider.
adSchemaDimensions	33	For multi-dimensional data, view the Dimensions schema.
adSchemaForeignKeys	27	Request foreign key information.
adSchemaFunctions	40	Request function information.
adSchemaHierarchies	34	For multi-dimensional data, view the Hierarchies schema.
adSchemaIndexes	12	Request index information.
adSchemaKeyColumnUsage	8	Request key column usage information.
adSchemaLevels	35	For multi-dimensional data, view the Levels schema.
adSchemaMeasures	36	For multi-dimensional data, view the Measures schema.
adSchemaMembers	38	For multi-dimensional data, view the Members schema.
adSchemaPrimaryKeys	28	Request primary key information.
adSchemaProcedureColumns	29	Request stored procedure column information.
adSchemaProcedure Parameters	26	Request stored procedure parameter information.
adSchemaProcedures	16	Request stored procedure information.
adSchemaProperties	37	For multi-dimensional data, view the Properties schema.
adSchemaProviderSpecific	-1	Request provider-specific information.
adSchemaProviderTypes	22	Request provider type information.
adSchemaReferential Contraints	9	Request referential constraint information.
adSchemaReferential Constraints	9	Request referential constraint information.
adSchemaSchemata	17	Request schema information.
adSchemaSets	43	Request set information.

Name	Value	Description
adSchemaSQLLanguages	18	Request SQL language support information.
adSchemaStatistics	19	Request statistics information.
adSchemaTableConstraints	10	Request table constraint information.
adSchemaTablePrivileges	14	Request table privilege information.
adSchemaTables	20	Request information about the tables.
adSchemaTranslations	21	Request character set translation information.
adSchemaTrustees	39	Request trustee information.
adSchemaUsagePrivileges	15	Request user privilege information.
adSchemaViewColumnUsage	24	Request column usage in views information.
adSchemaViews	23	Request view information.
adSchemaViewTableUsage	25	Request table usage in views information.

Due to a misspelling in the type library, adSchemaReferentialConstraints is included twice – once for the original spelling and once for the corrected spelling.

SearchDirectionEnum

Name	Value	Description
adSearchBackward	-1	Search backward from the current record.
adSearchForward	1	Search forward from the current record.

SeekEnum

Name	Value	Description
adSeekAfter	8	Seek the key just after the match.
adSeekAfterEQ	4	Seek the key equal to or just after the match.
adSeekBefore	32	See the key just before the match.
adSeekBeforeEQ	16	Seek the key equal to or just before the match.
adSeekFirstEQ	1	Seek the first key equal to the match.
adSeekLastEQ	2	Seek the last key equal to the match.

Appendices

A

StreamOpenOptionsEnum

Name	Value	Description
adOpenStream Async	1	Open the stream asynchronously.
adOpenStream FromRecord	4	Use the contents of an already open Record object as the resource to open.
adOpenStream Unspecified	-1	Open the stream with default options. Default.

StreamReadEnum

Name	Value	Description
adReadAll	-1	Read the entire contents of the stream, starting at the current position and ending at the end of the stream. Default.
adReadLine	-2	Read the next line from the stream. Uses the LineSeparator property to determine the end of the line.

StreamTypeEnum

Name	Value	Description
adTypeBinary	1	The stream contains binary data.
adTypeText	2	The stream contains text data. Default.

StreamWriteEnum

Name	Value	Description
adWriteChar	0	Write the text string to the stream.
adWriteLine	1	Write the text string and a line separator (as defined by the LineSeparator property) to the stream.

StringFormatEnum

Name	Value	Description
adClipString	2	Rows are delimited by user-defined values.

XactAttributeEnum

Name	Value	Description
adXactAbort Retaining	262144	The provider will automatically start a new transaction after a RollbackTrans method call.

Name	Value	Description
adXactAsync PhaseOne	524288	Perform an asynchronous commit.
adXactCommit Retaining	131072	The provider will automatically start a new transaction after a CommitTrans method call.
adXactSync PhaseOne	1048576	Performs a synchronous commit.

Miscellaneous Constants

These values are not included in the standard adovbs.inc include file (and are not automatically supplied when using Visual Basic), but can be found in adocon.inc (for ASP) and adocon.bas (for Visual Basic) from the supporting web site.

Many of these may not be necessary for you as an ADO programmer, but they are included here for completeness. They are only really useful as bitmask values for entries in the Properties collection.

DB_COLLATION

Name	Value	Description
DB_COLLATION_ ASC	1	The sort sequence for the column is ascending.
DB_COLLATION_ DESC	2	The sort sequence for the column is descending.

DB_IMP_LEVEL

Name	Value	Description
DB_IMP_LEVEL_ ANONYMOUS	0	The client is anonymous to the server, and the server process cannot obtain identification information about the client and cannot impersonate the client.
DB_IMP_LEVEL_ DELEGATE	3	The process can impersonate the client's security context while acting on behalf of the client. The server process can also make outgoing calls to other servers while acting on behalf of the client.
DB_IMP_LEVEL_ IDENTIFY	1	The server can obtain the client's identity, and can impersonate the client for ACL checking, but cannot access system objects as the client.
DB_IMP_LEVEL_ IMPERSONATE	2	The server process can impersonate the client's security context while acting on behalf of the client. This information is obtained upon connection and not on every call.

Appendices

443

A

DB_MODE

Name	Value	Description
DB_MODE_READ	1	Read-only.
DB_MODE_READWRITE	3	Read/write (equal to DB_MODE_READ + DB_MODE_WRITE).
DB_MODE_SHARE_DENY_NONE	16	Neither read nor write access can be denied to others.
DB_MODE_SHARE_DENY_READ	4	Prevents others from opening in read mode.
DB_MODE_SHARE_DENY_WRITE	8	Prevents others from opening in write mode.
DB_MODE_SHARE_EXCLUSIVE	12	Prevents others from opening in read/write mode (equal to DB_MODE_SHARE_DENY_WRITE + DB_MODE_SHARE_DENY_WRITE).
DB_MODE_WRITE	2	Write-only.

DB_PROT_LEVEL

Name	Value	Description
DB_PROT_LEVEL_CALL	2	Authenticates the source of the data at the beginning of each request from the client to the server.
DB_PROT_LEVEL_CONNECT	1	Authenticates only when the client establishes the connection with the server.
DB_PROT_LEVEL_NONE	0	Performs no authentication of data sent to the server.
DB_PROT_LEVEL_PKT	3	Authenticates that all data received is from the client.
DB_PROT_LEVEL_PKT_INTEGRITY	4	Authenticates that all data received is from the client and that it has not been changed in transit.
DB_PROT_LEVEL_PKT_PRIVACY	5	Authenticates that all data received is from the client, that it has not been changed in transit, and protects the privacy of the data by encrypting it.

DB_PT

Name	Value	Description
DB_PT_FUNCTION	3	Function; there is a returned value.
DB_PT_PROCEDURE	2	Procedure; there is no returned value.
DB_PT_UNKNOWN	1	It is not known whether there is a returned value.

DB_SEARCHABLE

Name	Value	Description
DB_ALL_EXCEPT_ LIKE	3	The data type can be used in a WHERE clause with all comparison operators except LIKE.
DB_LIKE_ONLY	2	The data type can be used in a WHERE clause only with the LIKE predicate.
DB_SEARCHABLE	4	The data type can be used in a WHERE clause with any comparison operator.
DB_UNSEARCHABLE	1	The data type cannot be used in a WHERE clause.

DBCOLUMNDESCFLAG

Name	Value	Description
DBCOLUMNDESCFLAG_ CLSID	8	The CLSID portion of the column description can be changed when altering the column.
DBCOLUMNDESCFLAG_ COLSIZE	16	The column size portion of the column description can be changed when altering the column.
DBCOLUMNDESCFLAG_ DBCID	32	The DBCID portion of the column description can be changed when altering the column.
DBCOLUMNDESCFLAG_ ITYPEINFO	2	The type information portion of the column description can be changed when altering the column.
DBCOLUMNDESCFLAG_ PRECISION	128	The precision portion of the column description can be changed when altering the column.
DBCOLUMNDESCFLAG_ PROPERTIES	4	The property sets portion of the column description can be changed when altering the column.
DBCOLUMNDESCFLAG_ SCALE	256	The numeric scale portion of the column description can be changed when altering the column.
DBCOLUMNDESCFLAG_ TYPENAME	1	The type name portion of the column description can be changed when altering the column.
DBCOLUMNDESCFLAG_ WTYPE	64	The data type portion of the column description can be changed when altering the column.

Appendices

A

DBCOLUMNFLAGS

Name	Value	Description
DBCOLUMNFLAGS_CACHEDEFERRED	4096	Indicates that the value of a deferred column is cached when it is first read.
DBCOLUMNFLAGS_ISCHAPTER	8192	The column contains a Chapter value.
DBCOLUMNFLAGS_ISFIXEDLENGTH	16	All of the data in the column is of a fixed length.
DBCOLUMNFLAGS_ISLONG	128	The column contains a BLOB value that contains long data.
DBCOLUMNFLAGS_ISNULLABLE	32	The column can be set to Null, or the provider cannot determine whether the column can be set to Null.
DBCOLUMNFLAGS_ISROWID	256	The column contains a persistent row identifier.
DBCOLUMNFLAGS_ISROWVER	512	The column contains a timestamp or other row versioning data type.
DBCOLUMNFLAGS_MAYBENULL	64	Nulls can be got from the column.
DBCOLUMNFLAGS_MAYDEFER	2	The column is deferred.
DBCOLUMNFLAGS_WRITE	4	The column may be updated.
DBCOLUMNFLAGS_WRITEUNKNOWN	8	It is not known if the column can be updated.

DBLITERAL

Name	Value	Description
DBLITERAL_INVALID	0	An invalid value.
DBLITERAL_BINARY_LITERAL	1	A binary literal in a text command.
DBLITERAL_CATALOG_NAME	2	A catalog name in a text command.
DBLITERAL_CATALOG_SEPARATOR	3	The character that separates the catalog name from the rest of the identifier in a text command.
DBLITERAL_CHAR_LITERAL	4	A character literal in a text command.

Name	Value	Description
DBLITERAL_COLUMN_ALIAS	5	A column alias in a text command.
DBLITERAL_COLUMN_NAME	6	A column name used in a text command or in a data-definition interface.
DBLITERAL_CORRELATION_NAME	7	A correlation name (table alias) in a text command.
DBLITERAL_CURSOR_NAME	8	A cursor name in a text command.
DBLITERAL_ESCAPE_PERCENT_PREFIX	9	The character used in a LIKE clause to escape the character returned for the DBLITERAL_LIKE_PERCENT literal.
DBLITERAL_ESCAPE_PERCENT_SUFFIX	29	The escape character, if any, used to suffix the character returned for the DBLITERAL_LIKE_PERCENT literal.
DBLITERAL_ESCAPE_UNDERSCORE_PREFIX	10	The character used in a LIKE clause to escape the character returned for the DBLITERAL_LIKE_UNDERSCORE literal.
DBLITERAL_ESCAPE_UNDERSCORE_SUFFIX	30	The escape character, if any, used to suffix the character returned for the DBLITERAL_LIKE_UNDERSCORE literal.
DBLITERAL_INDEX_NAME	11	An index name used in a text command or in a data-definition interface.
DBLITERAL_LIKE_PERCENT	12	The character used in a LIKE clause to match zero or more characters.
DBLITERAL_LIKE_UNDERSCORE	13	The character used in a LIKE clause to match exactly one character.
DBLITERAL_PROCEDURE_NAME	14	A procedure name in a text command.
DBLITERAL_SCHEMA_NAME	16	A schema name in a text command.
DBLITERAL_SCHEMA_SEPARATOR	27	The character that separates the schema name from the rest of the identifier in a text command.

Name	Value	Description
DBLITERAL_TABLE_NAME	17	A table name used in a text command or in a data-definition interface.
DBLITERAL_TEXT_COMMAND	18	A text command, such as a SQL statement.
DBLITERAL_USER_NAME	19	A user name in a text command.
DBLITERAL_VIEW_NAME	20	A view name in a text command.
DBLITERAL_QUOTE_PREFIX	15	The character used in a text command as the opening quote for quoting identifiers that contain special characters.
DBLITERAL_QUOTE_SUFFIX	28	The character used in a text command as the closing quote for quoting identifiers that contain special characters.

DBPARAMTYPE

Name	Value	Description
DBPARAMTYPE_INPUT	1	The parameter is an input parameter.
DBPARAMTYPE_INPUTOUTPUT	2	The parameter is both an input and an output parameter.
DBPARAMTYPE_OUTPUT	3	The parameter is an output parameter.
DBPARAMTYPE_RETURNVALUE	4	The parameter is a return value.

DBPROMPT

Name	Value	Description
DBPROMPT_COMPLETE	2	Prompt the user only if more information is needed.
DBPROMPT_COMPLETEREQUIRED	3	Prompt the user only if more information is required. Do not allow the user to enter optional information.
DBPROMPT_NOPROMPT	4	Do not prompt the user.
DBPROMPT_PROMPT	1	Always prompt the user for initialization information.

DBPROPVAL_AO

Name	Value	Description
DBPROPVAL_AO_RANDOM	2	Columns can be accessed in any order.
DBPROPVAL_AO_SEQUENTIAL	0	All columns must be accessed in sequential order determined by the column ordinal.
DBPROPVAL_AO_SEQUENTIAL STORAGEOBJECTS	1	Columns bound as storage objects can only be accessed in sequential order as determined by the column ordinal.

DBPROPVAL_ASYNCH

Name	Value	Description
DBPROPVAL_ASYNCH_ BACKGROUNDPOPULATION	8	The rowset is populated asynchronously in the background.
DBPROPVAL_ASYNCH_ INITIALIZE	1	Initialization is performed asynchronously.
DBPROPVAL_ASYNCH_ POPULATEONDEMAND	32	The consumer prefers to optimize for getting each individual request for data returned as quickly as possible.
DBPROPVAL_ASYNCH_ PREPOPULATE	16	The consumer prefers to optimize for retrieving all data when the row set is materialized.
DBPROPVAL_ASYNCH_ RANDOMPOPULATION	4	Rowset population is performed asynchronously in a random manner.
DBPROPVAL_ASYNCH_ SEQUENTIALPOPULATION	2	Rowset population is performed asynchronously in a sequential manner.

DBPROPVAL_BG

Name	Value	Description
DBPROPVAL_GB_COLLATE	16	A COLLATE clause can be specified at the end of each grouping column.
DBPROPVAL_GB_CONTAINS_ SELECT	4	The GROUP BY clause must contain all non-aggregated columns in the select list. It can contain columns that are not in the select list.

Appendices

A

Name	Value	Description
`DBPROPVAL_GB_EQUALS_SELECT`	2	The GROUP BY clause must contain all non-aggregated columns in the select list. It cannot contain any other columns.
`DBPROPVAL_GB_NO_RELATION`	8	The columns in the GROUP BY clause and the select list are not related. The meaning on non-grouped, non-aggregated columns in the select list is data source dependent.
`DBPROPVAL_GB_NOT_SUPPORTED`	1	GROUP BY clauses are not supported.

DBPROPVAL_BI

Name	Value	Description
`DBPROPVAL_BI_CROSSROWSET`	1	Bookmark values are valid across all rowsets generated on this table.

DBPROPVAL_BMK

Name	Value	Description
`DBPROPVAL_BMK_KEY`	2	The bookmark type is key.
`DBPROPVAL_BMK_NUMERIC`	1	The bookmark type is numeric.

DBPROPVAL_BO

Name	Value	Description
`DBPROPVAL_BO_NOINDEXUPDATE`	1	The provider is not required to update indexes based on inserts or changes to the rowset. Any indexes need to be re-created following changes made through the rowset.
`DBPROPVAL_BO_NOLOG`	0	The provider is not required to log inserts or changes to the rowset.
`DBPROPVAL_BO_REFINTEGRITY`	2	Referential integrity constraints do not need to be checked or enforced for changes made through the rowset.

DBPROPVAL_BP

Name	Value	Description
DBPROPVAL_BP_NOPARTIAL	2	Fail the bulk operation if there is a single error.
DBPROPVAL_BP_PARTIAL	1	Allow the bulk operation to partially complete, possibly resulting in inconsistent data.

DBPROPVAL_BT

Name	Value	Description
DBPROPVAL_BT_ DEFAULT	0	Use the value defined in the dynamic property Jet OLEDB:Global Bulk Transactions
DBPROPVAL_BT_ NOBULKTRANSACTIONS	1	Bulk operations are not transacted.
DBPROPVAL_BT_ BULKTRANSACTION	2	Bulk operations are transacted.

DBPROPVAL_CB

Name	Value	Description
DBPROPVAL_CB_NON_ NULL	2	The result is the concatenation of the non-Null valued column or columns.
DBPROPVAL_CB_NULL	1	The result is Null valued.

DBPROPVAL_CB

Name	Value	Description
DBPROPVAL_CB_DELETE	1	Aborting a transaction deletes prepared commands.
DBPROPVAL_CB_PRESERVE	2	Aborting a transaction preserves prepared commands.

DBPROPVAL_CD

Name	Value	Description
DBPROPVAL_CD_NOTNULL	1	Columns can be created non-nullable.

Appendices

A

DBPROPVAL_CL

Name	Value	Description
DBPROPVAL_CL_END	2	The catalog name appears at the end of the fully qualified name.
DBPROPVAL_CL_START	1	The catalog name appears at the start of the fully qualified name.

DBPROPVAL_CO

Name	Value	Description
DBPROPVAL_CO_BEGINSWITH	32	Provider supports the BEGINSWITH and NOTBEGINSWITH operators.
DBPROPVAL_CO_ CASEINSENSITIVE	8	Provider supports the CASEINSENSITIVE operator.
DBPROPVAL_CO_ CASESENSITIVE	4	Provider supports the CASESENSITIVE operator.
DBPROPVAL_CO_CONTAINS	16	Provider supports the CONTAINS and NOTCONTAINS operators.
DBPROPVAL_CO_EQUALITY	1	Provider supports the following operators: LT, LE, EQ, GE, GT, NE.
DBPROPVAL_CO_STRING	2	Provider supports the BEGINSWITH operator.

DBPROPVAL_CS

Name	Value	Description
DBPROPVAL_CS_ COMMUNICATIONFAILURE	2	The DSO is unable to communicate with the data store.
DBPROPVAL_CS_ INITIALIZED	1	The DSO is in an initialized state and able to communicate with the data store.
DBPROPVAL_CS_ UNINITIALIZED	0	The DSO is in an uninitialized state.

DBPROPVAL_CU

Name	Value	Description
DBPROPVAL_CU_DML_ STATEMENTS	1	Catalog names are supported in all Data Manipulation Language statements.
DBPROPVAL_CU_INDEX_ DEFINITION	4	Catalog names are supported in all index definition statements.

Name	Value	Description
DBPROPVAL_CU_ PRIVILEGE_ DEFINITION	8	Catalog names are supported in all privilege definition statements.
DBPROPVAL_CU_TABLE_ DEFINITION	2	Catalog names are supported in all table definition statements.

DBPROPVAL_DF

Name	Value	Description
DBPROPVAL_DF_INITIALLY_ DEFERRED	1	The foreign key is initially deferred.
DBPROPVAL_DF_INITIALLY_ IMMEDIATE	2	The foreign key is initially immediate.
DBPROPVAL_DF_NOT_ DEFERRABLE	3	The foreign key is not deferrable.

DBPROPVAL_DL

Name	Value	Description
DBPROPVAL_DL_OLDMODE	0	Mode used in previous versions of the Jet database.
DBPROPVAL_DL_ALCATRAZ	1	Use new method, allowing row level locking.

DBPROPVAL_DST

Name	Value	Description
DBPROPVAL_DST_MDP	2	The provider is a multidimensional provider (MD).
DBPROPVAL_DST_TDP	1	The provider is a tabular data provider (TDP).
DBPROPVAL_DST_TDPANDMDP	3	The provider is both a TDP and a MD provider.
DBPROPVAL_DST_DOCSOURCE	4	The provider is a document source (Internet Publishing Provider).

DBPROPVAL_GU

Name	Value	Description
DBPROPVAL_GU_ NOTSUPPORTED	1	URL suffixes are not supported. This is the only option supported by the Internet Publishing Provider in this version of ADO.
DBPROPVAL_GU_ SUFFIX	2	URL suffixes are generated by the Internet Publishing Provider.

Appendices

453

A

DBPROPVAL_HT

Name	Value	Description
DBPROPVAL_HT_ DIFFERENT_ ATALOGS	1	The provider supports heterogeneous joins between catalogs.
DBPROPVAL_HT_ DIFFERENT_ ROVIDERS	2	The provider supports heterogeneous joins between providers.

DBPROPVAL_IC

Name	Value	Description
DBPROPVAL_IC_LOWER	2	Identifiers in SQL are case insensitive and are stored in lower case in system catalog.
DBPROPVAL_IC_MIXED	8	Identifiers in SQL are case insensitive and are stored in mixed case in system catalog.
DBPROPVAL_IC_ SENSITIVE	4	Identifiers in SQL are case sensitive and are stored in mixed case in system catalog.
DBPROPVAL_IC_UPPER	1	Identifiers in SQL are case insensitive and are stored in upper case in system catalog.

DBPROPVAL_IN

Name	Value	Description
DBPROPVAL_IN_ ALLOWNULL	0	The index allows Null values to be inserted.
DBPROPVAL_IN_ DISALLOW NULL	1	The index does not allow entries where the key columns are Null. An error will be generated if the consumer attempts to insert a Null value into a key column.
DBPROPVAL_IN_ IGNOREANY NULL	4	The index does not insert entries containing Null keys.
DBPROPVAL_IN_ IGNORENULL	2	The index does not insert entries where some column key has a Null value.

DBPROPVAL_IT

Name	Value	Description
DBPROPVAL_IT_BTREE	1	The index is a B+ tree.
DBPROPVAL_IT_ CONTENT	3	The index is a content index.
DBPROPVAL_IT_HASH	2	The index is a hash file using linear or extensible hashing.
DBPROPVAL_IT_OTHER	4	The index is some other type of index.

DBPROPVAL_JCC

Name	Value	Description
DBPROPVAL_JCC_ PASSIVESHUTDOWN	1	New connections to the database are disallowed.
DBPROPVAL_JCC_NORMAL	2	Users are allowed to connect to the database.

DBPROPVAL_LG

Name	Value	Description
DBPROPVAL_LG_PAGE	1	Use page locking.
DBPROPVAL_LG_ALCATRAZ	2	Use row-level locking.

DBPROPVAL_MR

Name	Value	Description
DBPROPVAL_MR_CONCURRENT	2	More than one rowset created by the same multiple results object can exist concurrently.
DBPROPVAL_MR_NOTSUPPORTED	0	Multiple results objects are not supported.
DBPROPVAL_MR_SUPPORTED	1	The provider supports multiple results objects.

DBPROPVAL_NC

Name	Value	Description
DBPROPVAL_NC_END	1	Nulls are sorted at the end of the list, regardless of the sort order.
DBPROPVAL_NC_HIGH	2	Nulls are sorted at the high end of the list.
DBPROPVAL_NC_LOW	4	Nulls are sorted at the low end of the list.
DBPROPVAL_NC_START	8	Nulls are sorted at the start of the list, regardless of the sort order.

DBPROPVAL_NP

Name	Value	Description
DBPROPVAL_NP_ABOUTTODO	2	The consumer will be notified before an action (the Will event).
DBPROPVAL_NP_DIDEVENT	16	The consumer will be notified after an action (the Complete event).
DBPROPVAL_NP_FAILEDTODO	8	The consumer will be notified if an action failed (a Will or Complete event).
DBPROPVAL_NP_OKTODO	1	The consumer will be notified of events.
DBPROPVAL_NP_SYNCHAFTER	4	The consumer will be notified when the rowset is resynchronized.

DBPROPVAL_NT

Name	Value	Description
DBPROPVAL_NT_ MULTIPLEROWS	2	For methods that operate on multiple rows, and generate multi-phased notifications (events), the provider calls OnRowChange once for all rows that succeed and once for all rows that fail.
DBPROPVAL_NT_ SINGLEROW	1	For methods that operate on multiple rows, and generate multi-phased notifications (events), the provider calls OnRowChange separately for each phase for each row.

DBPROPVAL_OA

Name	Value	Description
DBPROPVAL_OA_ ATEXECUTE	2	Output parameter data is available immediately after the Command.Execute returns.
DBPROPVAL_OA_ ATROWRELEASE	4	Output parameter data is available when the rowset is released. For a single rowset operation this is when the rowset is completely released (closed) and for a multiple rowset operation this is when the next rowset if fetched. The consumer's bound memory is in an indeterminate state before the parameter data becomes available.
DBPROPVAL_OA_ NOTSUPPORTED	1	Output parameters are not supported.

DBPROPVAL_OO

Name	Value	Description
DBPROPVAL_OO_ BLOB	1	The provider supports access to BLOBs as structured storage objects.
DBPROPVAL_OO_ DIRECTBIND	16	The provider supports direct binding to BLOBs.
DBPROPVAL_OO_ IPERSIST	2	The provider supports access to OLE objects through OLE.
DDPROPVAL_OO_ SCOPED	8	Row objects implement scoped operations.
DBPROPVAL_OO_ SINGLETON	32	The provider supports singleton selects.

DBPROPVAL_ORS

Name	Value	Description
DBPROPVAL_ORS_ TABLE	0	The provider supports opening tables.
DBPROPVAL_ORS_ INDEX	1	The provider supports opening indexes.
DBPROPVAL_ORS_ INTEGRATEDINDEX	2	The provider supports both the table and index in the same open method.
DBPROPVAL_ORS_ STOREDPROC	4	The provider supports opening rowsets over stored procedures.
DBPROPVAL_ORS_ HISTOGRAM	8	The provider supports opening rowsets over histograms.

Appendices

A

DBPROPVAL_OS

Name	Value	Description
DBPROPVAL_OS_ENABLEALL	-1	All services should be invoked. This is the default.
DBPROPVAL_OS_RESOURCEPOOLING	1	Resources should be pooled.
DBPROPVAL_OS_TXNENLISTMENT	2	Sessions in an MTS environment should automatically be enlisted in a global transaction where required.
DBPROPVAL_OS_CLIENT_CURSOR	4	Disable client cursor.
DBPROPVAL_OS_DISABLEALL	0	All services should be disabled.
DBPROPCAL_OS_AGR_AFTERSESSION	8	Session level aggregation only.

DBPROPVAL_PT

Name	Value	Description
DBPROPVAL_PT_GUID	8	The GUID is used as the persistent ID type.
DBPROPVAL_PT_GUID_NAME	1	The GUID Name is used as the persistent ID type.
DBPROPVAL_PT_GUID_PROPID	2	The GUID Property ID is used as the persistent ID type.
DBPROPVAL_PT_NAME	4	The Name is used as the persistent ID type.
DBPROPVAL_PT_PGUID_NAME	32	The Property GUID name is used as the persistent ID type.
DBPROPVAL_PT_PGUID_PROPID	64	The Property GUID Property ID is used as the persistent ID type.
DBPROPVAL_PT_PROPID	16	The Property ID is used as the persistent ID type.

DBPROPVAL_RD

Name	Value	Description
DBPROPVAL_ RD_RESETALL	-1	The provider should reset all states associated with the data source, with the exception that any open object is not released.

DBPROPVAL_RT

Name	Value	Description
DBPROPVAL_RT_APTMTTHREAD	2	The DSO is apartment threaded.
DBPROPVAL_RT_FREETHREAD	1	The DSO is free threaded.
DBPROPVAL_RT_SINGLETHREAD	4	The DSO is single threaded.

DBPROPVAL_SQ

Name	Value	Description
DBPROPVAL_SQ_COMPARISON	2	All predicates that support subqueries support comparison subqueries.
DBPROPVAL_SQ_CORRELATEDSUBQUERIES	1	All predicates that support subqueries support correlated subqueries.
DBPROPVAL_SQ_EXISTS	4	All predicates that support subqueries support EXISTS subqueries.
DBPROPVAL_SQ_IN	8	All predicates that support subqueries support IN subqueries.
DBPROPVAL_SQ_QUANTIFIED	16	All predicates that support subqueries support quantified subqueries.

DBPROPVAL_SQL

Name	Value	Description
DBPROPVAL_SQL_ANDI89_IEF	8	The provider supports the ANSI SQL89 IEF level.
DBPROPVAL_SQL_ANSI92_ENTRY	16	The provider supports the ANSI SQL92 Entry level.
DBPROPVAL_SQL_ANSI92_FULL	128	The provider supports the ANSI SQL92 Full level.
DBPROPVAL_SQL_ANSI92_INTERMEDIATE	64	The provider supports the ANSI SQL92 Intermediate level.
DBPROPVAL_SQL_CORE	2	The provider supports the ODBC 2.5 Core SQL level.
DBPROPVAL_SQL_ESCAPECLAUSES	256	The provider supports the ODBC escape clauses syntax.
DBPROPVAL_SQL_EXTENDED	4	The provider supports the ODBC 2.5 EXTENDED SQL level.

Appendices

Name	Value	Description
DBPROPVAL_SQL_FIPS_TRANSITIONAL	32	The provider supports the ANSI SQL92 Transitional level.
DBPROPVAL_SQL_MINIMUM	1	The provider supports the ODBC 2.5 EXTENDED SQL level.
DBPROPVAL_SQL_NONE	0	SQL is not supported.
DBPROPVAL_SQL_ODBC_CORE	2	The provider supports the ODBC 2.5 Core SQL level.
DBPROPVAL_SQL_ODBC_EXTENDED	4	The provider supports the ODBC 2.5 EXTENDED SQL level.
DBPROPVAL_SQL_ODBC_MINIMUM	1	The provider supports the ODBC 2.5 EXTENDED SQL level.
DBPROPVAL_SQL_SUBMINIMUM	512	The provider supports the DBGUID_SQL dialect and parses the command text according to SQL rules, but does not support either the minimum ODBC level or the ANSI SQL92 Entry level.

DBPROPVAL_SS

Name	Value	Description
DBPROPVAL_SS_ILOCKBYTES	8	The provider supports IlockBytes.
DBPROPVAL_SS_ISEQUENTIALSTREAM	1	The provider supports IsequentialStream.
DBPROPVAL_SS_ISTORAGE	4	The provider supports Istorage.
DBPROPVAL_SS_ISTREAM	2	The provider supports IStream.

DBPROPVAL_SU

Name	Value	Description
DBPROPVAL_SU_DML_STATEMENTS	1	Schema names are supported in all Data Manipulation Language statements.
DBPROPVAL_SU_INDEX_DEFINITION	4	Schema names are supported in all index definition statements.
DBPROPVAL_SU_PRIIVILEGE_DEFINITION	8	Schema names are supported in all privilege definition statements.
DBPROPVAL_SU_TABLE_DEFINITION	2	Schema names are supported in all table definition statements.

DBPROPVAL_TC

Name	Value	Description
DBPROPVAL_TC_ALL	8	Transactions can contain DDL and DML statements in any order.
DBPROPVAL_TC_DDL_COMMIT	2	Transactions can contain only DML statements. The transaction will be committed if a table or index is modified within a transaction.
DBPROPVAL_TC_DDL_IGNORE	4	Transactions can contain only DML statements. Any attempt to modify a table or index within a transaction is ignored.
DBPROPVAL_TC_DDL_LOCK	16	Transactions can contain both Data Manipulation (DML) and table or index modifications. The table or index will be locked until the transaction completes.
DBPROPVAL_TC_DML	1	Transactions can only contain DML statements. DDL statements within a transaction cause an error.
DBPROPVAL_TC_NONE	0	Transactions are not supported.

DBPROPVAL_TI

Name	Value	Description
DBPROPVAL_TI_ BROWSE	256	Changes made by other transactions are visible before they are committed.
DBPROPVAL_TI_ CHAOS	16	Transactions cannot overwrite pending changes from more highly isolated transactions. This is the default.
DBPROPVAL_TI_ CURSORSTABILITY	4096	Changes made by other transactions are not visible until those transactions are committed.

Name	Value	Description
DBPROPVAL_TI_ ISOLATED	1048576	All concurrent transactions will interact only in ways that produce the same effect as if each transaction were entirely executed one after the other.
DBPROPVAL_TI_ READCOMMITTED	4096	Changes made by other transactions are not visible until those transactions are committed.
DBPROPVAL_TI_ READUNCOMMITTED	256	Changes made by other transactions are visible before they are committed.
DBPROPVAL_TI_ REPEATABLEREAD	65536	Changes made by other transactions are not visible.
DBPROPVAL_TI_ SERIALIZABLE	1048576	All concurrent transactions will interact only in ways that produce the same effect as if all transactions were entirely executed one after the other.

DBPROPVAL_TR

Name	Value	Description
DBPROPVAL_TR_ABORT	16	The transaction preserves its isolation context (it preserves its locks if that is how isolation is implemented) across the retaining abort.
DBPROPVAL_TR_ABORT_DC	8	The transaction may either preserve or dispose of isolation context across a retaining abort.
DBPROPVAL_TR_ABORT_NO	32	The transaction is explicitly not to preserve its isolation across a retaining abort.
DBPROPVAL_TR_BOTH	128	Isolation is preserved across both a retaining commit and a retaining abort.
DBPROPVAL_TR_COMMIT	2	The transaction preserves its isolation context (it preserves its locks if that is how isolation is implemented) across the retaining commit.
DBPROPVAL_TR_COMMIT_DC	1	The transaction may either preserve or dispose of isolation context across a retaining commit.

Name	Value	Description
DBPROPVAL_TR_COMMIT_NO	4	The transaction is explicitly not to preserve its isolation across a retaining commit.
DBPROPVAL_TR_DONTCARE	64	The transaction may either preserve or dispose of isolation context across a retaining commit or abort. This is the default.
DBPROPVAL_TR_NONE	256	Isolation is explicitly not to be retained across either a retaining commit or abort.
DBPROPVAL_TR_OPTIMISTIC	512	Optimistic concurrency control is to be used.

DBPROPVAL_TS

Name	Value	Description
DBPROPVAL_TS_CARDINALITY	1	Column and tuple cardinality information on columns in a statistic are supported.
DBPROPVAL_TS_HISTOGRAM	2	Histogram information on the first column of a statistic is supported.

DBPROPVAL_UP

Name	Value	Description
DBPROPVAL_UP_CHANGE	1	Indicates that SetData is supported.
DBPROPVAL_UP_DELETE	2	Indicates that DeleteRows is supported.
DBPROPVAL_UP_INSERT	4	Indicates that InsertRow is supported.

JET_ENGINETYPE

Name	Value	Description
JET_ENGINETYPE_UNKNOWN	0	The database type is unknown.
JET_ENGINETYPE_JET10	1	Jet 1.0
JET_ENGINETYPE_JET11	2	Jet 1.1
JET_ENGINETYPE_JET2X	3	Jet 2.x
JET_ENGINETYPE_JET3X	4	Jet 3.x
JET_ENGINETYPE_JET4X	5	Jet 4.x

Appendices

A

Name	Value	Description
JET_ENGINETYPE_DBASE3	10	DBase III
JET_ENGINETYPE_DBASE4	11	DBase IV
JET_ENGINETYPE_DBASE5	12	DBase V
JET_ENGINETYPE_EXCEL30	20	Excel 3
JET_ENGINETYPE_EXCEL40	21	Excel 4
JET_ENGINETYPE_EXCEL50	22	Excel 5 (Excel 95)
JET_ENGINETYPE_EXCEL80	23	Excel 8 (Excel 97)
JET_ENGINETYPE_EXCEL90	24	Excel 9 (Excel 2000)
JET_ENGINETYPE_EXCHANGE4	30	Exchange Server
JET_ENGINETYPE_LOTUSWK1	40	Lotus 1
JET_ENGINETYPE_LOTUSWK3	41	Lotus 3
JET_ENGINETYPE_LOTUSWK4	42	Lotus 4
JET_ENGINETYPE_PARADOX3X	50	Paradox 3.x
JET_ENGINETYPE_PARADOX4X	51	Paradox 4.5
JET_ENGINETYPE_PARADOX5X	52	Paradox 5.x
JET_ENGINETYPE_PARADOX7X	53	Paradox 7.x
JET_ENGINETYPE_TEXT1X	60	Text
JET_ENGINETYPE_HTML1X	70	HTML

MD_DIMTYPE

Name	Value	Description
MD_DIMTYPE_MEASURE	2	A measure dimension.
MD_DIMTYPE_OTHER	3	The dimension is neither a time nor a measure dimension.
MD_DIMTYPE_TIME	1	A time dimension.
MD_DIMTYPE_UNKNOWN	0	The provider is unable to classify the dimension.

SQL_FN_NUM

Name	Value	Description
SQL_FN_NUM_ABS	1	The ABS function is supported by the data source.
SQL_FN_NUM_ACOS	2	The ACOS function is supported by the data source.
SQL_FN_NUM_ASIN	4	The ASIN function is supported by the data source.

Name	Value	Description
SQL_FN_NUM_ATAN	8	The ATAN function is supported by the data source.
SQL_FN_NUM_ATAN2	16	The ATAN2 function is supported by the data source.
SQL_FN_NUM_CEILING	32	The CEILING function is supported by the data source.
SQL_FN_NUM_COS	64	The COS function is supported by the data source.
SQL_FN_NUM_COT	128	The COT function is supported by the data source.
SQL_FN_NUM_DEGREES	262144	The DEGREES function is supported by the data source.
SQL_FN_NUM_EXP	256	The EXP function is supported by the data source.
SQL_FN_NUM_FLOOR	512	The FLOOR function is supported by the data source.
SQL_FN_NUM_LOG	1024	The LOG function is supported by the data source.
SQL_FN_NUM_LOG10	524288	The LOG10 function is supported by the data source.
SQL_FN_NUM_MOD	2048	The MOD function is supported by the data source.
SQL_FN_NUM_PI	65536	The PI function is supported by the data source.
SQL_FN_NUM_POWER	1048576	The POWER function is supported by the data source.
SQL_FN_NUM_RADIANS	2097152	The RADIANS function is supported by the data source.
SQL_FN_NUM_RAND	131072	The RAND function is supported by the data source.
SQL_FN_NUM_ROUND	4194304	The ROUND function is supported by the data source.
SQL_FN_NUM_SIGN	4096	The SIGN function is supported by the data source.
SQL_FN_NUM_SIN	8192	The SIN function is supported by the data source.
SQL_FN_NUM_SQRT	10384	The SQRT function is supported by the data source.
SQL_FN_NUM_TAN	32768	The TAN function is supported by the data source.
SQL_FN_NUM_TRUNCATE	8388608	The TRUNCATE function is supported by the data source.

Appendices

SQL_FN_STR

Name	Value	Description
SQL_FN_STR_ASCII	8192	The ASCII function is supported by the data source.
SQL_FN_STR_BIT_LENGTH	524288	The BIT_LENGTH function is supported by the data source.
SQL_FN_STR_CHAR	16384	The CHAR function is supported by the data source.
SQL_FN_STR_CHAR_LENGTH	1048576	The CHAR_LENGTH function is supported by the data source.
SQL_FN_STR_CHARACTER_LENGTH	2097152	The CHARACTER_LENGTH function is supported by the data source.
SQL_FN_STR_CONCAT	1	The CONCAT function is supported by the data source.
SQL_FN_STR_DIFFERENCE	32768	The DIFFERENCE function is supported by the data source.
SQL_FN_STR_INSERT	2	The INSERT function is supported by the data source.
SQL_FN_STR_LCASE	64	The LCASE function is supported by the data source.
SQL_FN_STR_LEFT	4	The LEFT function is supported by the data source.
SQL_FN_STR_LENGTH	16	The LENGTH function is supported by the data source.
SQL_FN_STR_LOCATE	32	The LOCATE function is supported by the data source.
SQL_FN_STR_LOCATE_2	65536	The LOCATE_2 function is supported by the data source.
SQL_FN_STR_LTRIM	8	The LTRIM function is supported by the data source.
SQL_FN_STR_OCTET_LENGTH	4194304	The OCTET_LENGTH function is supported by the data source.
SQL_FN_STR_POSITION	8388608	The POSITION function is supported by the data source.
SQL_FN_STR_REPEAT	128	The REPEAT function is supported by the data source.
SQL_FN_STR_REPLACE	256	The REPLACE function is supported by the data source.
SQL_FN_STR_RIGHT	512	The RIGHT function is supported by the data source.
SQL_FN_STR_RTRIM	1024	The RTRIM function is supported by the data source.

Name	Value	Description
SQL_FN_STR_SOUNDEX	131072	The SOUNDEX function is supported by the data source.
SQL_FN_STR_SPACE	262144	The SPACE function is supported by the data source.
SQL_FN_STR_SUBSTRING	2048	The SUBSTRING function is supported by the data source.
SQL_FN_STR_UCASE	4096	The UCASE function is supported by the data source.

SQL_FN_SYS

Name	Value	Description
SQL_FN_SYS_DBNAME	2	The DBNAME system function is supported.
SQL_FN_SYS_IFNULL	4	The IFNULL system function is supported.
SQL_FN_SYS_USERNAME	1	The USERNAME system function is supported.

SQL_OJ

Name	Value	Description
SQL_OJ_ALL_COMPARISON_OPS	64	The comparison operator in the ON clause can be any of the ODBC comparison operators. If this is not set, only the equals (=) comparison operator can be used in an outer join.
SQL_OJ_FULL	4	Full outer joins are supported.
SQL_OJ_INNER	32	The inner table (the right table in a left outer join or the left table in a right outer join) can also be used in an inner join. This does not apply to full out joins, which do not have an inner table.
SQL_OJ_LEFT	1	Left outer joins are supported.
SQL_OJ_NESTED	8	Nested outer joins are supported.
SQL_OJ_NOT_ORDERED	16	The column names in the ON clause of the outer join do not have to be in the same order as their respective table names in the OUTER JOIN clause.
SQL_OJ_RIGHT	2	Right outer joins are supported.

Appendices

A

SQL_SDF_CURRENT

Name	Value	Description
SQL_SDF_CURRENT_DATE	1	The CURRENT_DATE system function is supported.
SQL_SDF_CURRENT_TIME	2	The CURRENT_TIME system function is supported.
SQL_SDF_CURRENT_TIMESTAMP	4	The CURRENT_TIMESTAMP system function is supported.

SSPROP_CONCUR

Name	Value	Description
SSPROP_CONCUR_LOCK	4	Use row locking to prevent concurrent access.
SSPROP_CONCUR_READ_ONLY	8	The rowset is read-only. Full concurrency is supported.
SSPROP_CONCUR_ROWVER	1	Use row versioning to determining concurrent access violations. The SQL table or tables must contain a timestamp column.
SSPROP_CONCUR_VALUES	2	Use the values of columns in the rowset.

SSPROPVAL_USEPROCFORPREP

Name	Value	Description
SSPROPVAL_ USEPROCFORPRE_OFF	0	A temporary stored procedure is not created when a command is prepared.
SSPROPVAL_ USEPROCFORPRE_ON	1	A temporary stored procedure is created when a command is prepared. Temporary stored procedures are dropped when the session is released.
SSPROPVAL_ USEPROCFORPREP_ON_DROP	2	A temporary stored procedure is created when a command is prepared. The procedure is dropped when the command is unprepared, or a new command text is set, or when all application references to the command are released.

I thank God I am as honest as any man

iving that is an old man and no honester th

Can counsel and speak comfort to th

which they themselves not feel

Much Ado About Nothing.

He wears his faith but as the fashion of !

As merry as the day

He hath indeed better bettered expectation

(Act i. Sc. i.).

He wears his faith but as the fashion of his hat.

(Ibid)

As merry as the day is long.

h indeed better bettered expectation

(Act i. Sc. i.).

(Ibid)

an counsel and speak comfort to that grief

Much Ado About Nothing.

Which they themselves not feel.

He wears his faith but as the fashion of his hat.

(Ibid)

(Ibid)

I was not born under

a rhyming plane

I was not born under a rhyming plane

sc. 2

For there was never yet

That could endure the to

merry as the day is long

(Sc 2)

Can counsel and speak comfort to that grief

Which they themselves not feel.

(Ibid)

He hath indeed better bettered expectation

(Ibid)

I thank God I am as honest as any

(Act. sc. i.

living that is an old man and no honest

He wears his faith but as the fashion of his hat

(Ibid

Much Ado About Nothing.

For there was never yet philospher

That could endure the toothache patiently.

(Ibid)

For there was never yet philospher
That could endure the toothache patiently

themselves not feel.

(Ibid)

I was not born u

ADO Properties Collection

The `Properties` collection deals with dynamic properties that are specific to the provider. All ADO objects have a fixed set of properties (such as `Name`), but since ADO is designed for use with different providers, a way was needed to allow providers to specify their own properties. The `Properties` collection contains these properties, and this appendix deals with which properties are supported by which providers, and what these properties actually do.

Some of the properties refer to `rowsets`. This is just the OLE DB term for `Recordsets`.

Property Usage

As you can see from the tables in this appendix, there are very many properties – however, using them is actually quite simple. You simply index into the `Properties` collection, by using the property name itself. For example, to find out the name the provider gives to procedures you could do this:

```
Print objConn.Properties("Procedure Term")
```

For SQL Server, this returns `stored procedure` and for Access this returns `STORED QUERY`.

You can iterate through the entire set of properties very simply:

```
For Each objProp In objConn.Properties
    Print objProp.Name
    Print objProp.Value
Next
```

This will print out the property names and values.

For those properties that return custom types, you need to identify whether these return a bitmask or a simple value – the property description identifies this, as it says 'one of' or 'one or more of'. In the first case, the property will just return a single value. For example, to find out whether your provider supports output parameters on stored procedures you can query the Output Parameter Availability property. This is defined as returning values of type DBPROPVAL_OA, which are as follows:

Constant	Value
DBPROPVAL_OA_ATEXECUTE	2
DBPROPVAL_OA_ATROWRELEASE	4
DBPROPVAL_OA_NOTSUPPORTED	1

Examining this property when connected to SQL Server gives you a value of 4, indicating that output parameters are available when the recordset is closed. Access, on the other hand, returns a value of 1, indicating that output parameters are not supported.

For those properties that return bitmask, you'll need to use Boolean logic to identify which values are set. For example, to query the provider and examine what features of SQL are supported, you can use the SQL Support property. For Access this returns 512, which corresponds to DBPROPVAL_SQL_SUBMINIMUM, indicating that not even the ANSI SQL92 Entry level SQL facilities are provided. On the other hand, SQL Server returns 283, but there isn't a single value for this, so it must be a combination of values. In fact, it corresponds to the sum of the following:

Constant	Value
DBPROPVAL_SQL_ESCAPECLAUSES	256
DBPROPVAL_SQL_ANSI92_ENTRY	16
DBPROPVAL_SQL_ANDI89_IEF	8
DBPROPVAL_SQL_CORE	2
DBPROPVAL_SQL_MINIMUM	1

In order to see whether a specific value is set, use the Boolean AND operator. For example:

```
lngSQLSupport = oConn.Properties("SQL Support")
If (lngSQLSupport AND DBPROPVAL_SQL_CORE) = DBPROPVAL_SQL_CORE Then
    'core facilities are supported
End If
```

A full description of the constants is given in Appendix B.

Property Support

The following table shows a list of all OLE DB properties, and indicates which of them are supported by three widely used drivers: the Microsoft OLE DB driver for Jet, the Microsoft OLE DB driver for ODBC, and the Microsoft OLE DB driver for SQL Server. Since this list contains dynamic properties, not every property may show up under all circumstances. Other providers may also implement properties not listed in this table.

A tick (✓) indicates that the property is supported, and a blank space indicates it is not supported. Note that support for recordset properties may depend upon the locking type, cursor type and cursor location.

Note. This list doesn't include the `Iproperty` (such as `IRowset`, etc.) properties. Although these are part of the collection they are not particularly useful for the ADO programmer.

For the *Object Type* column, the following applies:

- ❏ RS = Recordset
- ❏ R = Record
- ❏ C = Connection
- ❏ CM = Command
- ❏ F = Field

Property Name	Object Type	ODBC	Jet	SQL	Internet Publishing (IIS5)	MSDataShape	Persist	Remote	Indexing Service	Diretory Services	Exchange	Oracle
Access Order	RS/CM	✓	✓	✓		✓	✓	✓	✓	✓		✓
Accessible Procedures	C	✓										
Accessible Tables	C	✓										
Active Sessions	C	✓	✓	✓	✓				✓	✓	✓	✓
Active Statements	C	✓										
ADSI Flag	C									✓		
Allow Native Variant	C			✓								
Alter Column Support	C		✓	✓								

Property Name	Object Type	ODBC	Jet	SQL	Internet Publishing (IIS5)	MSDataShape	Persist	Remote	Indexing Service	Diretory Services	Exchange	Oracle
Always use content index	RS								✓			
Append-Only Rowset	RS	✓	✓	✓		✓	✓	✓	✓	✓		
Application Name	C			✓								
Asynchable Abort	C	✓	✓	✓							✓	✓
Asynchable Commit	C	✓	✓	✓							✓	✓
Asynchronous Processing	C					✓						
Asynchronous Rowset Processing	RS	✓	✓	✓		✓	✓	✓	✓	✓	✓	
Auto Recalc	RS	✓	✓	✓		✓	✓	✓	✓			
Auto Translate	C			✓								
Autocommit Isolation Levels	C	✓	✓	✓		✓	✓	✓	✓	✓	✓	✓
Background Fetch Size	RS	✓	✓	✓	✓	✓	✓	✓	✓	✓		
Background Thread Priority	RS	✓	✓	✓	✓	✓	✓	✓	✓	✓		
Base Path	CM			✓								
BASECATALOGNAME	F	✓	✓	✓	✓	✓	✓	✓	✓	✓		✓
BASECOLUMNNAME	F	✓	✓	✓	✓	✓	✓	✓	✓	✓		✓
BASESCHEMANAME	F	✓	✓	✓	✓	✓	✓	✓	✓	✓		✓
BASETABLEINSTANCE	F			✓								
BASETABLENAME	F	✓	✓	✓	✓	✓	✓	✓	✓	✓		✓
Batch Size	RS	✓	✓	✓	✓	✓	✓	✓	✓	✓		
Bind Flags	C				✓	✓						
BLOB accessibility on Forward-Only cursor	RS	✓										
Blocking Storage Objects	RS/ CM	✓	✓	✓		✓	✓	✓	✓	✓		✓
Bookmark Information	RS/ CM	✓		✓								
Bookmark Type	RS/ CM	✓	✓	✓		✓	✓	✓	✓	✓	✓	
Bookmarkable	RS/ CM	✓	✓	✓	✓	✓	✓	✓	✓	✓	✓	
Bookmarks Ordered	RS	✓	✓	✓		✓	✓	✓	✓	✓	✓	

Property Name	Object Type	ODBC	Jet	SQL	Internet Publishing (IIS5)	MSDataShape	Persist	Remote	Indexing Service	Diretory Services	Exchange	Oracle
Cache Aggressively	C				✓							
Cache Authentication	C		✓			✓		✓				
Cache Child Rows	RS	✓	✓	✓		✓	✓	✓	✓	✓		
Cache Deferred Columns	RS	✓	✓	✓		✓	✓	✓	✓	✓	✓	✓
CALCULATIONINFO	F	✓	✓	✓		✓	✓	✓	✓	✓		
Catalog Location	C	✓	✓	✓					✓	✓		✓
Catalog Term	C	✓	✓	✓					✓	✓		✓
Catalog Usage	C	✓		✓					✓	✓		✓
Change Inserted Rows	RS/CM	✓	✓	✓		✓	✓	✓			✓	
Chapter	C						✓					
CLSID	F	✓										
COLLATINGSEQUENCE	F	✓	✓									
Column Definition	C	✓	✓	✓					✓			✓
Column Privileges	RS/CM	✓	✓	✓		✓	✓	✓	✓	✓	✓	
Column Set Notification	RS/CM	✓	✓	✓		✓	✓	✓	✓	✓		
Column Writable	RS	✓	✓	✓		✓	✓	✓	✓	✓		
Command Properties	C							✓				
Command Time Out	RS/CM	✓	✓	✓	✓	✓	✓	✓	✓	✓		
Command Type	CM			✓								
COMPFLAGS	F			✓								
COMPUTEMODE	F	✓		✓								
Connect Timeout	C	✓		✓	✓	✓	✓	✓		✓		
Connection Status	C	✓		✓								✓
Content Type	CM			✓								
Current Catalog	C	✓	✓	✓					✓			✓
Current DFMode	C							✓				
Current Language	C			✓								
Cursor Auto Fetch	RS/CM			✓								

Property Name	Object Type	ODBC	Jet	SQL	Internet Publishing (IIS5)	MSDataShape	Persist	Remote	Indexing Service	Diretory Services	Exchange	Oracle
Cursor Engine Version	RS	✓	✓	✓		✓	✓	✓	✓	✓		
Data Provider	C					✓						
Data Source	C	✓	✓	✓	✓	✓		✓	✓	✓	✓	✓
Data Source Name	C	✓	✓	✓					✓	✓	✓	
Data Source Object Threading Model	C	✓	✓	✓		✓		✓	✓	✓	✓	✓
Datasource Type	C				✓						✓	
DATETIMEPRECISION	F	✓		✓								
DBMS Name	C	✓	✓	✓					✓		✓	✓
DBMS Version	C	✓	✓	✓					✓		✓	✓
DEFAULTVALUE	F	✓										
Defer Column	RS/CM	✓	✓	✓		✓	✓	✓	✓	✓	✓	✓
Defer Prepare	CM			✓								
Defer scope and security testing	RS								✓			
Delay Storage Object Updates	RS/CM	✓	✓	✓		✓	✓	✓	✓	✓		
Determine Key Columns For Rowset	RS/CM											✓
DFMode	C							✓				
DOMAINCATALOG	F	✓										
DOMAINNAME	F	✓										
DOMAINSCHEMA	F	✓										
Driver Name	C	✓										
Driver ODBC Version	C	✓										
Driver Version	C	✓										
Enable Fastload	C			✓								
Encrypt Password	C		✓			✓		✓		✓		
Extended Properties	C	✓	✓	✓		✓		✓		✓		✓
Fastload Options	RS/CM			✓								
Fetch Backwards	RS/CM	✓	✓	✓	✓	✓	✓	✓	✓	✓	✓	✓
File Usage	C	✓										

Property Name	Object Type	ODBC	Jet	SQL	Internet Publishing (IIS5)	MSDataShape	Persist	Remote	Indexing Service	Diretory Services	Exchange	Oracle
Filter Operations	RS	✓	✓	✓		✓	✓	✓	✓	✓		
Find Operations	RS	✓	✓	✓		✓	✓	✓	✓	✓		
Force no command preparation when executing a parameterized command	RS	✓										
Force no command reexecution when failure to satisfy all required properties	RS	✓										
Force no parameter rebinding when executing a command	RS	✓										
Force SQL Server Firehose Mode cursor	RS	✓										
Generate a Rowset that can be marshalled	RS	✓										
General Timeout	C	✓		✓								
Generate URL	C				✓							
GROUP BY Support	C	✓	✓	✓					✓			✓
Handler	C							✓				
HASDEFAULT	F	✓										
Heterogeneous Table Support	C	✓	✓	✓					✓			✓
Hidden Columns	RS/CM	✓	✓	✓		✓	✓	✓	✓	✓		✓
Hold Rows	RS/CM	✓	✓	✓	✓	✓	✓	✓	✓	✓	✓	✓
Identifier Case Sensitivity	C	✓	✓	✓								✓
Ignore Cached Data	C				✓							
Immobile Rows	RS/CM	✓	✓	✓		✓	✓	✓	✓	✓	✓	
Impersonation Level	C					✓		✓				
Include SQL_FLOAT, SQL_DOUBLE, and SQL_REAL in QBU WHERE clauses	RS	✓										

A

Property Name	Object Type	ODBC	Jet	SQL	Internet Publishing (IIS5)	MSDataShape	Persist	Remote	Indexing Service	Diretory Services	Exchange	Oracle
Initial Catalog	C	✓		✓		✓		✓				
Initial Fetch Size	RS	✓	✓	✓		✓	✓	✓	✓	✓		
Initial File Name	C			✓								
Integrated Security	C			✓		✓		✓		✓		
Integrity Enhancement Facility	C	✓										
Internet Timeout	C								✓			
ISAUTOINCREMENT	F	✓	✓	✓		✓	✓	✓	✓			✓
ISCASESENSITIVE	F	✓	✓	✓								
Isolation Levels	C	✓	✓	✓						✓	✓	✓
Isolation Retention	C	✓	✓	✓						✓	✓	✓
ISSEARCHABLE	F	✓		✓								
ISUNIQUE	F	✓										
Jet OLEDB:Bulk Transactions	RS		✓									
Jet OLEDB:Compact Reclaimed Space Amount	C		✓									
Jet OLEDB:Compact Without Replica Repair	C		✓									
Jet OLEDB:Connection Control	C		✓									
Jet OLEDB:Create System Database	C		✓									
Jet OLEDB:Database Locking Mode	C		✓									
Jet OLEDB:Database Password	C		✓									
Jet OLEDB:Don't Copy Locale on Compact	C		✓									
Jet OLEDB:Enable Fat Cursors	RS		✓									
Jet OLEDB:Encrypt Database	C		✓									
Jet OLEDB:Engine Type	C		✓									
Jet OLEDB:Exclusive Async Delay	C		✓									

Property Name	Object Type	ODBC	Jet	SQL	Internet Publishing (IIS5)	MSDataShape	Persist	Remote	Indexing Service	Directory Services	Exchange	Oracle
Jet OLEDB:Fat Cursor Cache Size	RS		✓									
Jet OLEDB:Flush Transaction Timeout	C		✓									
Jet OLEDB:Global Bulk Transactions	C		✓									
Jet OLEDB:Global Partial Bulk Ops	C		✓									
Jet OLEDB:Grbit Value	RS		✓									
Jet OLEDB:Implicit Commit Sync	C		✓									
Jet OLEDB:Inconsistent	RS		✓									
Jet OLEDB:Lock Delay	C		✓									
Jet OLEDB:Lock Retry	C		✓									
Jet OLEDB:Locking Granularity	RS		✓									
Jet OLEDB:Max Buffer Size	C		✓									
Jet OLEDB:Max Locks Per File	C		✓									
Jet OLEDB:New Database Password	C		✓									
Jet OLEDB:ODBC Command Time Out	C		✓									
Jet OLEDB:ODBC Parsing	C		✓									
Jet OLEDB:ODBC Pass-Through Statement	RS		✓									
Jet OLEDB:Page Locks to Table Lock	C		✓									
Jet OLEDB:Page Timeout	C		✓									
Jet OLEDB:Partial Bulk Ops	RS		✓									
Jet OLEDB:Pass Through Query Bulk-Op	RS		✓									
Jet OLEDB:Pass Through Query Connect String	RS		✓									

Appendices

A

Property Name	Object Type	ODBC	Jet	SQL	Internet Publishing (IIS5)	MSDataShape	Persist	Remote	Indexing Service	Directory Services	Exchange	Oracle
Jet OLEDB:Recycle Long-Valued Pages	C		✓									
Jet OLEDB:Registry Path	C		✓									
Jet OLEDB:Reset ISAM Stats	C		✓									
Jet OLEDB:Sandbox Mode	C		✓									
Jet OLEDB:SFP	C		✓									
Jet OLEDB:Shared Async Delay	C		✓									
Jet OLEDB:Stored Query	RS		✓									
Jet OLEDB:System database	C		✓									
Jet OLEDB:Transaction Commit Mode	C		✓									
Jet OLEDB:Use Grbit	RS		✓									
Jet OLEDB:User Commit Sync	C		✓									
Jet OLEDB:Validate Rules On Set	RS		✓									
Keep Identity	RS/ CM			✓								
Keep Nulls	RS/ CM			✓								
KEYCOLUMN	F	✓	✓	✓		✓	✓	✓	✓	✓		✓
Like Escape Clause	C	✓										
Literal Bookmarks	RS/ CM	✓	✓	✓		✓	✓	✓	✓	✓	✓	
Literal Row Identity	RS/ CM	✓	✓	✓		✓	✓	✓	✓	✓	✓	✓
Locale Identifier	C	✓	✓	✓	✓	✓		✓	✓	✓	✓	✓
Location	C	✓				✓			✓	✓	✓	
Lock Mode	RS/ CM		✓	✓								
Lock Owner	C				✓							
Maintain Change Status	RS	✓	✓	✓	✓	✓	✓	✓	✓	✓		

Property Name	Object Type	ODBC	Jet	SQL	Internet Publishing (IIS5)	MSDataShape	Persist	Remote	Indexing Service	Diretory Services	Exchange	Oracle
Maintain Property Values	C						✓					
Mapping schema	CM			✓								
Mark For Offline	C				✓							
Mask Password	C		✓			✓		✓				
Max Columns in Group By	C	✓										
Max Columns in Index	C	✓										
Max Columns in Order By	C	✓										
Max Columns in Select	C	✓										
Max Columns in Table	C	✓										
Maximum BLOB Length	RS/ CM			✓								
Maximum Index Size	C	✓	✓	✓								✓
Maximum Open Chapters	C			✓					✓			✓
Maximum Open Rows	RS/ CM	✓	✓	✓		✓	✓	✓	✓	✓	✓	✓
Maximum Pending Rows	RS/ CM	✓	✓	✓		✓	✓	✓	✓	✓		
Maximum Row Size	C	✓	✓	✓					✓	✓	✓	✓
Maximum Row Size Includes BLOB	C	✓	✓	✓								✓
Maximum Rows	RS/ CM	✓	✓	✓		✓	✓	✓	✓	✓	✓	✓
Maximum Tables in SELECT	C	✓	✓	✓					✓			✓
Memory Usage	RS	✓	✓	✓		✓	✓	✓	✓	✓		
Mode	C	✓	✓		✓	✓		✓			✓	✓
Multi-Table Update	C	✓	✓	✓								✓
Multiple Connections	C			✓								
Multiple Parameter Sets	C	✓	✓	✓				✓	✓			✓
Multiple Results	C	✓	✓	✓		✓		✓	✓		✓	✓
Multiple Storage Objects	C	✓	✓	✓					✓		✓	✓
Network Address	C			✓								

Property Name	Object Type	ODBC	Jet	SQL	Internet Publishing (IIS5)	MSDataShape	Persist	Remote	Indexing Service	Diretory Services	Exchange	Oracle
Network Library	C			✓								
Notification Granularity	RS/CM	✓	✓	✓		✓	✓	✓	✓	✓		✓
Notification Phases	RS/CM	✓	✓	✓		✓	✓	✓	✓	✓		✓
Null Collation Order	C	✓	✓	✓					✓			✓
Null Concatenation Behavior	C	✓	✓	✓								✓
Numeric Functions	C	✓										
Objects Transacted	RS/CM	✓	✓	✓		✓	✓	✓	✓	✓		✓
OCTETLENGTH	F	✓		✓								
ODBC Concurrency Type	RS	✓										
ODBC Cursor Type	RS	✓										
OLE DB Services	C	✓								✓		✓
OLE DB Version	C	✓	✓	✓	✓				✓	✓	✓	✓
OLE Object Support	C	✓	✓	✓					✓	✓	✓	✓
OLE Objects	C				✓							
Open Rowset Support	C	✓	✓	✓								
OPTIMIZE	F	✓	✓	✓		✓	✓	✓	✓	✓		
ORDER BY Columns in Select List	C	✓	✓	✓					✓			✓
Others' Changes Visible	RS/CM	✓	✓	✓		✓	✓	✓	✓	✓	✓	✓
Others' Inserts Visible	RS/CM	✓	✓	✓		✓	✓	✓	✓	✓	✓	✓
Outer Join Capabilities	C	✓										
Outer Joins	C	✓										
Output encoding	CM			✓								
Output Parameter Availability	C	✓	✓	✓					✓	✓		✓
Output stream	CM			✓								
Own Changes Visible	RS/CM	✓	✓	✓		✓	✓	✓	✓	✓	✓	✓
Own Inserts Visible	RS/CM	✓	✓	✓		✓	✓	✓	✓	✓	✓	✓

Property Name	Object Type	ODBC	Jet	SQL	Internet Publishing (IIS5)	MSDataShape	Persist	Remote	Indexing Service	Directory Services	Exchange	Oracle
Packet Size	C			✓								
Pass By Ref Accessors	C	✓	✓	✓					✓	✓	✓	✓
Password	C	✓	✓	✓	✓	✓		✓		✓	✓	✓
Persist Encrypted	C					✓						
Persist Format	C						✓					
Persist Schema	C						✓					
Persist Security Info	C	✓		✓		✓		✓				
Persistent ID Type	C	✓	✓	✓					✓	✓	✓	✓
Position on the last row after insert	RS	✓										
Prepare Abort Behavior	C	✓	✓	✓							✓	✓
Prepare Commit Behavior	C	✓	✓	✓							✓	✓
Preserve on Abort	RS/CM	✓	✓	✓		✓	✓	✓	✓	✓	✓	✓
Preserve on Commit	RS/CM	✓	✓	✓		✓	✓	✓	✓	✓	✓	✓
Procedure Term	C	✓	✓	✓								✓
Prompt	C	✓	✓	✓	✓	✓		✓	✓	✓		✓
Protection Level	C					✓		✓				
Protocol Provider	C				✓							
Provider Friendly Name	C	✓	✓	✓				✓	✓	✓		✓
Provider Name	C	✓	✓	✓	✓			✓	✓	✓	✓	✓
Provider Version	C	✓	✓	✓	✓			✓	✓	✓	✓	✓
Query Based Updates/Deletes/Inserts	RS	✓										
Query Restriction	RS								✓			
Quick Restart	RS/CM	✓	✓	✓		✓	✓	✓	✓	✓	✓	✓
Quoted Catalog Names	C			✓								
Quoted Identifier Sensitivity	C	✓		✓								✓
Read-Only Data Source	C	✓	✓	✓					✓	✓	✓	

Property Name	Object Type	ODBC	Jet	SQL	Internet Publishing (IIS5)	MSDataShape	Persist	Remote	Indexing Service	Directory Services	Exchange	Oracle
Reentrant Events	RS/CM	✓	✓	✓		✓	✓	✓	✓	✓	✓	✓
RELATIONCONDITIONS	F	✓	✓	✓		✓	✓	✓	✓	✓		
Remote Provider	C							✓				
Remote Server	C							✓				
Remove Deleted Rows	RS/CM	✓	✓	✓		✓	✓	✓	✓	✓	✓	✓
Report Multiple Changes	RS/CM	✓	✓	✓		✓	✓	✓	✓	✓	✓	
Reshape Name	RS	✓	✓	✓	✓	✓	✓	✓				
Reset Connection	C			✓								
Reset Datasource	C	✓		✓					✓			
Resync Command	RS	✓	✓	✓		✓	✓	✓	✓	✓		
Return Pending Inserts	RS/CM	✓	✓	✓		✓	✓	✓	✓	✓		
Return PROPVARIANTs in variant binding	RS								✓			
Row Delete Notification	RS/CM	✓	✓	✓		✓	✓	✓	✓	✓		
Row First Change Notification	RS/CM	✓	✓	✓		✓	✓	✓	✓	✓		
Row Insert Notification	RS/CM	✓	✓	✓		✓	✓	✓	✓	✓		
Row Privileges	RS/CM	✓	✓	✓		✓	✓	✓	✓	✓	✓	
Row Resynchronization Notification	RS/CM	✓	✓	✓		✓	✓	✓	✓	✓		
Row Threading Model	RS/CM	✓	✓	✓		✓	✓	✓	✓	✓	✓	✓
Row Undo Change Notification	RS/CM	✓	✓	✓		✓	✓	✓	✓	✓		
Row Undo Delete Notification	RS/CM	✓	✓	✓		✓	✓	✓	✓	✓		
Row Undo Insert Notification	RS/CM	✓	✓	✓		✓	✓	✓	✓	✓		
Row Update Notification	RS/CM	✓	✓	✓		✓	✓	✓	✓	✓		
Rowset Conversions on Command	C	✓	✓	✓					✓	✓		✓

Property Name	Object Type	ODBC	Jet	SQL	Internet Publishing (IIS5)	MSDataShape	Persist	Remote	Indexing Service	Diretory Services	Exchange	Oracle
Rowset Fetch Position Change Notification	RS/CM	✓	✓	✓		✓	✓	✓	✓	✓		✓
Rowset Query Status	RS								✓			
Rowset Release Notification	RS/CM	✓	✓	✓	✓	✓	✓	✓	✓	✓		✓
Schema Term	C	✓	✓	✓								✓
Schema Usage	C	✓	✓	✓								✓
Scroll Backwards	RS/CM	✓	✓	✓	✓	✓	✓	✓	✓	✓	✓	✓
Server Cursor	RS/CM	✓	✓	✓	✓	✓	✓	✓	✓	✓	✓	✓
Server Data on Insert	RS/CM		✓	✓								
Server Name	C	✓		✓								
Skip Deleted Bookmarks	RS/CM	✓	✓	✓	✓	✓	✓	✓	✓	✓	✓	
Sort Order Name	C			✓								
SORTID	F			✓								
Special Characters	C	✓										
SQL Content Query Locale String	RS								✓			
SQL Grammar Support	C	✓										
SQL Support	C	✓	✓	✓					✓	✓	✓	✓
Qsqlxmlx.dll Progid	C			✓								
SS Stream Flags	CM			✓								
Stored Procedures	C	✓										
String Functions	C	✓										
Strong Row Identity	RS/CM	✓	✓	✓	✓	✓	✓	✓	✓	✓	✓	✓
Structured Storage	C	✓	✓	✓					✓		✓	✓
Subquery Support	C	✓	✓	✓					✓			✓
System Functions	C	✓										
Table Statistics Support												

Property Name	Object Type	ODBC	Jet	SQL	Internet Publishing (IIS5)	MSDataShape	Persist	Remote	Indexing Service	Directory Services	Exchange	Oracle
Table Term	C	✓	✓	✓							✓	✓
Tag with column collation when possible	C											
TDSCOLLATION	F			✓								
Time/Date Functions	C	✓										
Transact Updates	C							✓				
Transaction DDL	C	✓	✓	✓						✓	✓	✓
Treat As Offline	C				✓							
Unicode Comparison Style	C			✓								
Unicode Locale ID	C			✓								
Unique Catalog	RS	✓	✓	✓		✓	✓	✓	✓	✓		
Unique Reshape Names	C					✓						
Unique Rows	RS/CM	✓	✓	✓		✓	✓	✓	✓	✓		✓
Unique Schema	RS	✓	✓	✓		✓	✓	✓	✓	✓		
Unique Table	RS	✓	✓	✓		✓	✓	✓	✓	✓		
Updatability	RS/CM	✓	✓	✓	✓	✓	✓	✓	✓	✓	✓	
Update Criteria	RS	✓	✓	✓		✓	✓	✓	✓	✓		
Update Resync	RS	✓	✓	✓		✓	✓	✓	✓	✓		
URL Generation	C										✓	
Use Bookmarks	RS/CM	✓	✓	✓	✓	✓	✓	✓	✓	✓	✓	✓
Use Encryption for Data	C			✓								
Use Procedure for Prepare	C			✓								
User ID	C	✓	✓	✓	✓	✓		✓		✓	✓	✓
User Name	C	✓	✓	✓						✓		✓
Window Handle	C	✓	✓	✓	✓	✓		✓	✓	✓		✓
Workstation ID	C			✓								
XML root	CM			✓								
XSL	CM			✓								

Object Properties

This section details the properties by object type, including the enumerated values that they support. These values are not included in the standard adovbs.inc include file (and are not automatically supplied when using Visual Basic), but can be found in adoconvb.inc and adoconjs.inc (for ASP, in VBScript and JScript format) and adocon.bas (for Visual Basic) from the supporting web site.

Some properties in this list are undocumented, and I've had to make an educated guess as to their purpose. I've marked these properties with a # symbol in their description field.

The Connection Object's Properties

Property Name	Description	DataType
Access Permissions	Identifies the permissions used to access the data source. Read/Write.	Connect ModeEnum
Accessible Procedures	Identifies accessible procedures. Read-only.	Boolean
Accessible Tables	Identifies accessible tables. Read-only.	Boolean
Active Sessions	The maximum number of sessions that can exist at the same time. A value of 0 indicates no limit. Read-only.	Long
Active Statements	The maximum number of statements that can exist at the same time. Read only.	Long
Allow Native Variant	For SQL Variant columns, identifies whether or not the data is returned as a SQL Variant, or an OLE DB Variant. The default value is False.	Boolean
Alter Column Support	Identifies which portions of the column can be altered.	DBCOLUMN DESCFLAG
Application Name	Identifies the client application name. Read/Write.	String
Asynchable Abort	Whether transactions can be aborted asynchronously. Read-only.	Boolean
Asynchable Commit	Whether transactions can be committed asynchronously. Read-only.	Boolean
Asynchronous Processing	Specifies the asynchronous processing performed on the rowset. Read/Write.	DBPROPVAL_ ASYNCH
Auto Translate	Indicates whether OEM/ANSI character conversion is used. Read/Write.	Boolean

Appendices

Property Name	Description	DataType
Autocommit Isolation Level	Identifies the transaction isolation level while in auto-commit mode. Read/Write.	`DBPROPVAL_OS`
Bind Flags	Identifies the binding behavior for resources. Allows binding to the results of a resource rather than the resource itself.	`DBBINDURLFLAG`
Cache Aggressively	Identifies whether or not the provider will download and cache all properties of the resource, and its stream.	`Boolean`
Cache Authentication	Whether or not the data source object can cache sensitive authentication information, such as passwords, in an internal cache. Read/Write.	`Boolean`
Catalog Location	The position of the catalog name in a table name in a text command. Returns 1 (`DBPROPVAL_CL_START`) if the catalog is at the start of the name (such as Access with \Temp\Database.mdb), and 2 (`DBPROPVAL_CL_END`) if the catalog is at the end of name (such as Oracle with **ADMIN.EMP@EMPDATA**). Read/Write.	`DBPROPVAL_CL`
Catalog Term	The name the data source uses for a catalog, such as 'catalog' or 'database'. Read/Write.	`String`
Catalog Usage	Specifies how catalog names can be used in text commands. A combination of zero or more of the `DBPROPVAL_CU` constants. Read/Write.	`DBPROPVAL_CU`
Column Definition	Defines the valid clauses for the definition of a column. Read/Write.	`DBPROPVAL_CD`
Command Properties	Indicates the values that will be added to the string of properties by the MSRemote provider.	`String`
Connect Timeout	The amount of time, in seconds, to wait for the initialization to complete. Read/Write.	`Long`
Connection Status	The status of the current connection. Read-only.	`DBPROPVAL_CS`
Current Catalog	The name of the current catalog. Read/Write.	`String`
Current DFMode	Identifies the actual version of the Data Factory on the server. Can be: "21" (the default) for version 2.1 "20" for version 2.0 "15" for version 1.5	`String`

Property Name	Description	DataType
Current Language	Identifies the language used for system messages selection and formatting. The language must be installed on the SQL Server or initialization of the data source fails. Read/Write.	String
Data Provider	For a shaped (hierarchical) recordset, this identifies the provider that supplies the data.	String
Data Source	The name of the data source to connect to. Read/Write.	String
Data Source Name	The name of the data source. Read-only.	String
Data Source Object Threading Model	Specifies the threading models supported by the data source object. Read-only.	DBPROPVAL_RT
Datasource Type	The type of data source.	DBPROPVAL_DST
DBMS Name	The name of the product accessed by the provider. Read-only.	String
DBMS Version	The version of the product accessed by the provider. Read-only.	String
DFMode	Identifies the Data Factory mode. Can be: "21" (the default) for version 2.1 "20" for version 2.0 "15" for version 1.5	String
Driver Name	Identifies the ODBC Driver name. Read-only.	String
Driver ODBC Version	Identifies the ODBC Driver version. Read-only.	String
Driver Version	Identifies the Driver ODBC version. Read-only.	String
Enable Fastload	Indicates whether bulk-copy operations can be used between the SQL Server and the consumer.	Boolean
Encrypt Password	Whether the consumer required that the password be sent to the data source in an encrypted form. Read/Write.	Boolean
Extended Properties	Contains provider-specific, extended connection information. Read/Write.	String
File Usage	Identifies the usage count of the ODBC driver. Read-only.	Long
Generate URL	Identifies the level of support of the Internet Server for generating URL suffixes.	DBPROPVAL_GU

Appendices

489

A

Property Name	Description	DataType
General Timeout	The number of seconds before a request times out. This applies to requests other than the connection opening or a command execution.	Long
GROUP BY Support	The relationship between the columns in a GROUP BY clause and the non-aggregated columns in the select list. Read-only.	DBPROPVAL_ BG
Handler	The name of the server-side customization program, and any parameters the program uses.	String
Heterogeneous Table Support	Specifies whether the provider can join tables from different catalogs or providers. Read-only.	DBPROPVAL_ HT
Identifier Case Sensitivity	How identifiers treats case. Read-only.	DBPROPVAL_ IC
Ignore Cached Data	Identifies whether the provider should ignore any cached data for this resource.	Boolean
Impersonation Level	Identifies the level of client impersonation the server can take while performing actions on behalf of the client.	DB_IMP_ LEVEL
Initial Catalog	The name of the initial, or default, catalog to use when connecting to the data source. If the provider supports changing the catalog for an initialized data source, a different catalog name can be specified in the Current Catalog property. Read/Write.	String
Initial File Name	The primary file name of an attachable database. #	String
Integrated Security	Contains the name of the authentication service used by the server to identify the user. Read/Write.	String
Integrity Enhancement Facility	Indicates whether the data source supports the optional Integrity Enhancement Facility. Read-only.	Boolean
Internet Timeout	The maximum number of milliseconds to wait before generating an error.	Long
Isolation Levels	Identifies the supported transaction isolation levels. Read-only.	DBPROPVAL_ TI
Isolation Retention	Identifies the supported transaction isolation retention levels. Read-only.	DBPROPVAL_ TR

Property Name	Description	DataType
Jet OLEDB:Compact Reclaimed Space Amount	The approximate amount of space that would be reclaimed by a compaction. This is not guaranteed to be exact.	Long
Jet OLEDB:Compact Without Replica Repair	Indicates whether or not to find and repair damaged replicas.	Boolean
Jet OLEDB:Compact Without Relationships	Indicates whether or not to copy relationships to the new database.	Boolean
Jet OLEDB:Connection Control	Identifies the state of the connection, indicating whether other users are allowed to connect to the database or not.	DBPROPVAL_JCC
Jet OLEDB:Create System Database	Indicates whether or not a system database is generated when creating a new data source.	Boolean
Jet OLEDB:Database Locking Mode	Identifies the mode to use when locking the database. The first person to open a database identifies the mode.	DBPROPVAL_DL
Jet OLEDB:Database Password	The database password. Read/Write.	String
Jet OLEDB:Don't Copy Locale on Compact	Indicates that the database sort order should be used when compacting, rather that the locale.	Boolean
Jet OLEDB:Encrypt Database	Indicates whether or not to encrypt the new database.	Boolean
Jet OLEDB:Engine Type	Identifies the version of the database to open, or the version of the database to create.	JET_ENGINE TYPE
Jet OLEDB:Exclusive Async Delay	The maximum time (in milliseconds) that Jet will delay asynchronous writes to disk, when the database is open in exclusive mode.	Long
Jet OLEDB:Flush Transaction Timeout	Amount of time of inactivity before the asynchronous write cache is written to the disk.	Long
Jet OLEDB:Global Bulk Transactions	Identifies whether bulk operations are transacted.	DBPROPVAL_BT
Jet OLEDB:Global Partial Bulk Ops	Identifies whether Bulk operations are allowed with partial values. Read/Write.	DBPROPVAL_BP

Appendices

491

A

Property Name	Description	DataType
Jet OLEDB:Implicit Commit Sync	Indicates whether or not implicit transactions are written synchronously.	Boolean
Jet OLEDB:Lock Delay	The time to wait between lock attempts, in milliseconds.	Long
Jet OLEDB:Lock Retry	The number of attempts made to access a locked page.	Long
Jet OLEDB:Max Buffer Size	The largest amount of memory (in kilobytes) that can be used before it starts flushing changes to disk.	Long
Jet OLEDB:Max Locks Per File	The maximum number of locks that can be placed on a database. This defaults to 9500.	Long
Jet OLEDB:New Database Password	Sets the database password.	String
Jet OLEDB:ODBC Command Time Out	The number of seconds before remote ODBC queries timeout.	Long
Jet OLEDB:ODBC Parsing	Indicates whether or not Jet should attempt parsing of ODBC SQL syntax, or only use native Jet syntax.	Boolean
Jet OLEDB:Page Locks to Table Lock	The number of page locks to apply to a table before escalating the lock to a table lock. 0 means the lock will never be promoted.	Long
Jet OLEDB:Page Timeout	The amount of time (in milliseconds) that is waited before Jet checks to see if the cache is out of date with the database.	Long
Jet OLEDB:Recycle Long-Valued Pages	Indicates whether or not Jet aggressively tries to reclaim BLOB pages when they are freed.	Boolean
Jet OLEDB:Registry Path	The registry key that contains values for the Jet database engine. Read/Write.	String
Jet OLEDB:Reset ISAM Stats	Determines whether or not the ISAM statistics should be reset after the information has been returned.	Boolean
Jet OLEDB:Sandbox Mode	Indicates whether the database is in Sandbox mode. #	Boolean

Property Name	Description	DataType
Jet OLEDB:Shared Async Delay	The maximum time (in milliseconds) to delay asynchronous writes when in multi-user mode.	Long
Jet OLEDB:System database	The path and file name for the workgroup file. Read/Write.	String
Jet OLEDB: Transaction Commit Mode	A value if 1 indicates that the database commits updates immediately, rather than caching them.	Long
Jet OLEDB:User Commit Sync	Indicates whether or not explicit user transactions are written synchronously.	Boolean
Like Escape Clause	Identifies the LIKE escape clause. Read-only.	String
Locale Identifier	The locale ID of preference for the consumer. Read/Write.	Long
Location	The location of the data source to connect to. Typically this will be the server name. Read/Write.	String
Lock Owner	The string to show when you lock a resource and other users attempt to access that resource. Ignored for the WEC protocol, used with FrontPage Server Extensions. Read/Write.	String
Log text and image writes	Identifies whether writes to text and image fields are logged in the transaction log. Read/Write.	Boolean
Maintain Property Values	Indicates whether or not the property values are persisted along with the data when saving a recordset. Defaults to True. #	Boolean
Mark For Offline	Indicates that the URL can be marked for offline use. #	Integer
Mask Password	The consumer requires that the password be sent to the data source in masked form. Read/Write.	Boolean
Max Columns in Group By	Identifies the maximum number of columns in a GROUP BY clause. Read-only.	Long
Max Columns in Index	Identifies the maximum number of columns in an index. Read-only.	Long
Max Columns in Order By	Identifies the maximum number of columns in an ORDER BY clause. Read-only.	Long
Max Columns in Select	Identifies the maximum number of columns in a SELECT statement. Read-only.	Long

Appendices

A

Property Name	Description	DataType
Max Columns in Table	Identifies the maximum number of columns in a table. Read-only.	Long
Maximum Index Size	The maximum number of bytes allowed in the combined columns of an index. This is 0 if there is no specified limit or the limit is unknown. Read-only.	Long
Maximum Open Chapters	The maximum number of chapters that can be open at any one time. If a chapter must be released before a new chapter can be opened, the value is 1. If the provider does not support chapters, the value is 0. Read-only.	Long
Maximum OR Conditions	The maximum number of disjunct conditions that can be supported in a view filter. Multiple conditions of a view filter are joined in a logical OR. Providers that do not support joining multiple conditions return a value of 1, and providers that do not support view filters return a value of 0. Read-only.	Long
Maximum Row Size	The maximum length of a single row in a table. This is 0 if there is no specified limit or the limit is unknown. Read-only.	Long
Maximum Row Size Includes BLOB	Identifies whether Maximum Row Size includes the length for BLOB data. Read-only.	Boolean
Maximum Sort Columns	The maximum number of columns that can be supported in a View Sort. This is 0 if there is no specified limit or the limit is unknown. Read-only.	Long
Maximum Tables in SELECT	The maximum number of tables allowed in the FROM clause of a SELECT statement. This is 0 if there is no specified limit or the limit is unknown. Read-only.	Long
Mode	Specifies the access permissions. Read/Write.	DB_MODE
Multi-Table Update	Identifies whether the provider can update rowsets derived from multiple tables. Read-only.	Boolean
Multiple Connections	Identifies whether the provider silently creates additional connections to support concurrent Command, Connection or Recordset objects. This only applies to providers that have to spawn multiple connections, and not to providers that support multiple connections natively. Read/Write.	Boolean

Property Name	Description	DataType
Multiple Parameter Sets	Identifies whether the provider supports multiple parameter sets. Read-only.	`Boolean`
Multiple Results	Identifies whether the provider supports multiple results objects and what restrictions it places on those objects. Read-only.	`DBPROPVAL_ MR`
Multiple Storage Objects	Identifies whether the provider supports multiple, open storage objects at the same time. Read-only.	`Boolean`
Network Address	Identifies the network address of the SQL Server. Read/Write.	`String`
Network Library	Identifies the name of the Net-Library (DLL) used to communicate with SQL Server. Read/Write.	`String`
Null Collation Order	Identifies where Nulls are sorted in a list. Read-only.	`DBPROPVAL_ NC`
Null Concatenation Behavior	How the data source handles concatenation of Null-valued character data type columns with non-Null valued character data type columns. Read-only.	`DBPROPVAL_ CB`
Numeric Functions	Identifies the numeric functions supported by the ODBC driver and data source. Read-only.	`SQL_FN_NUM`
OLE DB Services	Specifies the OLEDB services to enable. Read/Write.	`DBPROPVAL_ OS`
OLE DB Version	Specifies the version of OLEDB supported by the provider. Read-only.	`String`
OLE Object Support	Specifies the way in which the provider supports access to BLOBs and OLE objects stored in columns. Read only.	`DBPROPVAL_ OO`
OLE Objects	Indicates the level of binding support for OLE Objects.	`DBPROPVAL_ OO`
Open Rowset Support	Indicates the level of support for opening rowsets.	`DBPROPVAL_ ORS`
ORDER BY Columns in Select List	Identifies whether columns in an `ORDER BY` clause must be in the `SELECT` list. Read-only.	`Boolean`
Outer Join Capabilities	Identifies the outer join capabilities of the ODBC data source. Read-only.	`SQL_OJ`
Outer Joins	Identifies whether outer joins are supported or not. Read-only.	`Boolean`

Appendices

495

A

Property Name	Description	DataType
Outer Join Capabilities	Identifies the outer join capabilities of the ODBC data source. Read-only.	SQL_OJ
Output Parameter Availability	Identifies the time at which output parameter values become available. Read-only.	DBPROPVAL_OA
Packet Size	Specifies the network packet size in bytes. It must be between 512 and 32767. The default is 4096. Read/Write.	Long
Pass By Ref Accessors	Whether the provider supports the DBACCESSOR_PASSBYREF flag. Read-only.	Boolean
Password	The password to be used to connect to the data source. Read/Write.	String
Persist Encrypted	Whether or not the consumer requires that the data source object persist sensitive authentication information, such as a password, in encrypted form. Read/Write.	Boolean
Persist Format	Indicates the format for persisting data.	PersistFormatEnum
Persist Schema	Indicates whether or not the schema is persisted along with the data.	Boolean
Persist Security Info	Whether or not the data source object is allowed to persist sensitive authentication information, such as a password, along with other authentication information. Read/Write.	Boolean
Persistent ID Type	Specifies the type of DBID that the provider uses when persisting DBIDs for tables, indexes, and columns. Read-only.	DBPROPVAL_PT
Prepare Abort Behavior	Identifies how aborting a transaction affects prepared commands. Read-only.	DBPROPVAL_CB
Prepare Commit Behavior	Identifies how committing a transaction affects prepared commands. Read-only.	DBPROPVAL_CB
Procedure Term	Specifies the data source providers name for a procedure, such as 'database procedure' or 'stored procedure'. Read-only.	String
Prompt	Specifies whether to prompt the user during initialization. Read/Write.	DBPROMPT
Protection Level	The level of protection of data sent between client and server. This property applies only to network connections other than RPC. Read/Write.	DB_PROT_LEVEL

Property Name	Description	DataType
Protocol Provider	The protocol to use when using the IPP to connect to a resource. This should be WEC to use the FrontPage Web Extender Client protocol, and DAV to use the Web Distributed Authoring and Versioning (WebDAV) protocol.	String
Provider Friendly Name	The friendly name of the provider. Read-only.	String
Provider Name	The filename of the provider. Read-only.	String
Provider Version	The version of the provider. Read-only.	String
Quoted Catalog Names	Indicates whether or not quoted identifiers are allowed for catalog names.	Boolean
Quoted Identifier Sensitivity	Identifies how quoted identifiers treat case. Read-only.	DBPROPVAL_IC
Read-Only Data Source	Whether or not the data source is read-only. Read-only.	Boolean
Remote Provider	The data provider used to supply the data from a remote connection.	String
Remote Server	The name of the server supplying data from a remote connection.	String
Reset Datasource	Specifies the data source state to reset. Write only.	DBPROPVAL_RD
Rowset Conversions on Command	Identifies whether callers can enquire on a command, and about conversions supported by the command. Read only.	Boolean
Schema Term	The name the data source uses for a schema, such as 'schema' or 'owner'. Read-only.	String
Schema Usage	Identifies how schema names can be used in commands. Read-only.	DBPROPVAL_SU
Server Name	The name of the server. Read-only.	String
Sort on Index	Specifies whether the provider supports setting a sort order only for columns contained in an index. Read-only.	Boolean
Sort Order Name	Indicates the sort order to use for data types.	String
Special Characters	Identifies the data store's special characters. Read-only.	String
SQL Grammar Support	Identifies the SQL grammar level supported by the ODBC driver. 0 represents no conformance, 1 indicates Level 1 conformance, and 2 represents Level 2 conformance. Read-only.	Long

Appendices

A

ADO Properties Collection

Property Name	Description	DataType
SQL Support	Identifies the level of support for SQL. Read-only.	`DBPROPVAL_SQL`
SQLOLE execute a `SET TEXTLENGTH`	Identifies whether SQLOLE executes a `SET TEXTLENGTH` before accessing BLOB fields #. Read-only.	`Boolean`
Stored Procedures	Indicates whether stored procedures are available. Read-only.	`Boolean`
String Functions	Identifies the string functions supported by the ODBC driver and data source. Read-only.	`SQL_FN_STR`
Structured Storage	Identifies what interfaces the rowset supports on storage objects. Read-only.	`DBPROPVAL_SS`
Subquery Support	Identifies the predicates in text commands that support sub-queries. Read-only.	`DBPROPVAL_SQ`
System Functions	Identifies the system functions supported by the ODBC Driver and data source. Read-only.	`SQL_FN_SYS`
Table Term	The name the data source uses for a table, such as 'table' or 'file'. Read-only.	`String`
Time/Date Functions	Identifies the time/date functions supported by the ODBC Driver and data source. Read-only.	`SQL_SDF_CURRENT`
Table Statistics Support	Lists the table statistics that are available for a given table.	`DBPROPVAL_TS`
Tag with column collations when possible	If possible, use collation details specified on the columns.	`Boolean`
Transact Updates	Indicates whether or not an `UpdateBatch` method call is performed within a transaction. The default value is `False`.	`Boolean`
Transaction DDL	Indicates whether Data Definition Language (DDL) statements are supported in transactions. Read-only.	`DBPROPVAL_TC`
Treat As Offline	Indicates whether or not the resource should treated as an offline resource.	`Boolean`
Unicode Comparison Style	Determines the sorting options used for Unicode data.	`Long`
Unicode Locale ID	The locale ID to use for Unicode sorting.	`Long`
Unique Reshape Names	Indicates whether or not the value of the `Name` property of a recordset would conflict with an existing name, resulting in a unique name being generated.	`Boolean`

Property Name	Description	DataType
URL Generation	Indicates whether the provider requires data store generated URLs.	DBPROPVAL_GU
Use Encryption for Data	Indicates whether or not the data is encrypted.	Boolean
Use Procedure for Prepare	Indicates whether SQL Server is to use temporary stored procedures for prepared statements. Read/Write.	SSPROPVAL_USE PROCFORPREP
User Authentication mode	Indicates whether Windows NT Authentication is used to access SQL Server. Read/Write.	Boolean
User ID	The User ID to be used when connecting to the data source. Read/Write.	String
User Name	The User Name used in a particular database. Read-only.	String
Window Handle	The window handle to be used if the data source object needs to prompt for additional information. Read/Write.	Long
Workstation ID	Identifies the workstation. Read/Write.	String

The Recordset Object's Properties

Property Name	Description	DataType
Access Order	Indicates the order in which columns must be accessed on the rowset. Read/Write.	DBPROPVAL_AO
Always use content index	Indicates whether or not to use the content index to resolve queries, even if the index is out of date.	Boolean
Append-Only Rowset	A rowset opened with this property will initially contain no rows. Read/Write.	Boolean
Asynchronous Rowset Processing	Identifies the asynchronous processing performed on the rowset. Read/Write.	DBPROPVAL ASYNCH
Auto Recalc	Specifies when the MSDataShape provider updates aggregated and calculated columns. Read/Write.	ADCPROP AUTORECALC ENUM
Background Fetch Size	The number of rows to fetch in each batch, during asynchronous reads.	Long
Background thread Priority	The priority of the background thread for asynchronous actions. Read/Write.	ADCPROP ASYCTHREAD PRIORITY_ENUM

Appendices

499 A

Property Name	Description	DataType
Batch Size	The number of rows in a batch. Read/Write.	`Integer`
BLOB accessibility on Forward-Only cursor	Indicates whether or not BLOB columns can be accessed irrespective of their position in the column list. If True then the BLOB column can be accessed even if it is not the last column. If False then the BLOB column can only be accessed if it the last BLOB column, and any non-BLOB columns after this column will not be accessible. Read/Write.	`Boolean`
Blocking Storage Objects	Indicates whether storage objects might prevent use of other methods on the rowset. Read/Write.	`Boolean`
Bookmark Information	Identifies additional information about bookmarks over the rowset. Read-only.	`DBPROPVAL_BI`
Bookmark Type	Identifies the bookmark type supported by the rowset. Read/Write.	`DBPROPVAL_BMK`
Bookmarkable	Indicates whether bookmarks are supported. Read-only.	`Boolean`
Bookmarks Ordered	Indicates whether boomarks can be compared to determine the relative position of their rows in the rowset. Read/Write.	`Boolean`
Bulk Operations	Identifies optimizations that a provider may take for updates to the rowset. Read-only.	`DBPROPVAL_BO`
Cache Child Rows	Indicates whether child rows in a chaptered recordset are cached, or whether they are re-fetched when the rows are accessed. Read/Write.	`Boolean`
Cache Deferred Columns	Indicates whether the provider caches the value of a deferred column when the consumer first gets a value from that column. Read/Write.	`Boolean`
Change Inserted Rows	Indicates whether the consumer can delete or update newly inserted rows. An inserted row is assumed to be one that has been transmitted to the data source, as opposed to a pending insert row. Read/Write.	`Boolean`
Column Privileges	Indicates whether access rights are restricted on a column-by-column basis. Read-only.	`Boolean`
Column Set Notification	Indicates whether changing a column set is cancelable. Read-only.	`DBPROPVAL_NP`
Column Writable	Indicates whether a particular column is writable. Read/Write.	`Boolean`

Property Name	Description	DataType
Command Time Out	The number of seconds to wait before a command times out. A value of 0 indicates an infinite timeout. Read/Write.	`Long`
Concurrency Control Method	Identifies the method used for concurrency control when using server based cursors. Read/Write.	`SSPROPVAL _CONCUR`
Cursor Engine Version	Identifies the version of the cursor engine. Read-only.	`String`
Defer Column	Indicates whether the data in a column is not fetched until specifically requested. Read/Write.	`Boolean`
Defer scope and security testing	Indicates whether or not the search will defer scope and security testing.	`Boolean`
Delay Storage Object Updates	Indicates whether, when in delayed update mode, if storage objects are also used in delayed update mode. Read/Write.	`Boolean`
Determine Key Columns For Rowset	Determines which of the columns in the recordset are key columns. #	`Boolean`
Fastload Options	Indicates the options to use when in Fastload mode.	`String`
Fetch Backward	Indicates whether a rowset can fetch backwards. Read/Write.	`Boolean`
Filter Operations	Identifies which comparison operations are supported when using Filter on a particular column. Read-only.	`DBPROPVAL _CO`
Find Operations	Identifies which comparison operations are supported when using Find on a particular column. Read-only.	`DBPROPVAL _CO`
FOR BROWSE versioning columns	Indicates that the rowset contains the primary key or a timestamp column. Only applicable with rowsets created with the SQL FOR BROWSE statement. Read/Write.	`Boolean`
Force no command preparation when executing a parameterized command	Identifies whether or not a temporary statement is created for parameterized commands. #. Read/Write.	`Boolean`
Force no command re-execution when failure to satisfy all required properties	Identifies whether or not the command is re-executed if the command properties are invalid. #. Read/Write.	`Boolean`

Appendices

501

A

Property Name	Description	DataType
Force no parameter rebinding when executing a command	Identifies whether or not the command parameters are rebound every time the command is executed. #. Read/Write.	Boolean
Force SQL Server Firehose Mode cursor	Identifies whether or not a forward-only, read-only cursor is always created. #. Read/Write.	Boolean
Generate a Rowset that can be marshaled	Identifies whether or not the ODBC Driver generates a rowset that can be marshaled across process boundaries. Read/Write.	Boolean
Hidden Columns	Indicates the number of hidden columns in the rowset added by the provider to uniquely identify rows.	Long
Hold Rows	Indicates whether the rowset allows the consumer to retrieve more rows or change the next fetch position while holding previously fetched rows with pending changes. Read/Write.	Boolean
Immobile Rows	Indicates whether the rowset will reorder inserted or updated rows. Read/Write.	Boolean
Include SQL_FLOAT, SQL_DOUBLE, and SQL_REAL in QBU where clauses	When using a query-based update, setting this to True will include REAL, FLOAT and DOUBLE numeric types in the WHERE clause, otherwise they will be omitted. Read/Write.	Boolean
Initial Fetch Size	Identifies the initial size of the cache into which records are fetched. Read/Write.	Long
Jet OLEDB:Bulk Transaction	Determines whether bulk operations are transacted.	DBPROPVAL _BT
Jet OLEDB:Enable Fat Cursors	Indicates whether or not Jet caches multiple rows for remote row sources.	Boolean
Jet OLEDB:Fat Cursor Cache Size	The number of rows that should be cached if the dynamic property Jet OLEDB:Enable Fat Cursors is set to True.	Long
Jet OLEDB:Inconsistent	Indicates whether or not inconsistent updates are allowed on queries.	Boolean
Jet OLEDB:Locking Granularity	Identifies the lock mode used to open a table. This only applies if Jet OLEDB:Database Locking Mode is set to DBPROPVAL_DL_ALCATRAZ.	DBPROPVAL _LG

Property Name	Description	DataType
Jet OLEDB:ODBC Pass-Through Statement	Identifies the statement used for a SQL pass-through statement. Read/Write.	`String`
Jet OLEDB:Partial Bulk Ops	Indicates whether on not bulk operations will complete if some of the values fail.	`Boolean`
Jet OLEDB:Pass Through Query Bulk-Op	Indicates whether or not the pass-through query is a bulk operation.	`Boolean`
Jet OLEDB:Pass Through Query Connect String	Identifies the connect string for an ODBC pass through query. Read/Write.	`String`
Jet OLEDB:Stored Query	Indicates whether or not the command should be interpreted as a stored query.	`Boolean`
Jet OLEDB:Validate Rules On Set	Indicates whether Jet validation rules are applied when the value in a column is set (`True`) or when the changes are commited (`False`).	`Boolean`
Keep Identity	Indicates whether or not `IDENTITY` columns should keep the values if supplied by the client during an `INSERT`. #	`Boolean`
Keep Nulls	Indicates whether or not `Null` values supplied by the client should be kept if `DEFAULT` values exist on the columns.	`Boolean`
Literal Bookmarks	Indicates whether bookmarks can be compared literally, that is as a series of bytes. Read/Write.	`Boolean`
Literal Row Identity	Indicates whether the consumer can perform a binary comparison of two row handles to determine whether they point to the same row. Read-only.	`Boolean`
Lock Mode	Identifies the level of locking performed by the rowset. Read/Write.	`DBPROPVAL_LM`
Maintain Change Status	Indicates whether or not to maintain the status of a row if a conflict happens during row updates. #	`Boolean`
Maximum BLOB Length	Identifies the maximum length of a BLOB field. Read-only.	`Long`
Maximum Open Rows	Specifies the maximum number of rows that can be active at the same time. Read/Write.	`Long`

Appendices

A

Property Name	Description	DataType
Maximum Pending Rows	Specifies the maximum number of rows that can have pending changes at the same time. Read/Write.	Long
Maximum Rows	Specifies the maximum number of rows that can be returned in the rowset. This is 0 if there is no limit. Read/Write.	Long
Memory Usage	Specifies the amount of memory that can be used by the rowset. If set to 0 the amount is unlimited. If between 1 and 99 it specifies a percentage of the available virtual memory. If 100 or greater it specifies the number of kilobytes. Read/Write.	Long
Notification Granularity	Identifies when the consumer is notified for methods that operate on multiple rows. Read/Write.	DBPROPVAL _NT
Notification Phases	Identifies the notification phases supported by the provider. Read-only.	DBPROPVAL _NP
Objects Transacted	Indicates whether any object created on the specified column is transacted. Read/Write.	Boolean
ODBC Concurrency Type	Identifies the ODBC concurrency type. Read-only.	Integer
ODBC Cursor Type	Identifies the ODBC cursor type. Read-only.	Integer
Others' Changes Visible	Indicates whether the rowset can see updates and deletes made by someone other that the consumer of the rowset. Read/Write.	Boolean
Others' Inserts Visible	Indicates whether the rowset can see rows inserted by someone other than the consumer of the rowset. Read/Write.	Boolean
Own Changes Visible	Indicates whether the rowset can see its own updates and deletes. Read/Write.	Boolean
Own Inserts Visible	Indicates whether the rowset can see its own inserts. Read/Write.	Boolean
Position on the last row after insert	Identifies whether or not the cursor is placed on the last row after an insert. #. Read-only.	Boolean
Preserve on Abort	Indicates whether, after aborting a transaction, the rowset remains active. Read/Write.	Boolean
Preserve on Commit	Indicates whether after committing a transaction the rowset remains active. Read/Write.	Boolean

Property Name	Description	DataType
Query Based Updates/Deletes/Inserts	Identifies whether or not queries are used for updates, deletes, and inserts. #. Read/Write.	`Boolean`
Quick Restart	Indicates whether `RestartPosition` is relatively quick to execute. Read/Write.	`Boolean`
Query Restriction	Indicates the restriction to use for a query.	`String`
Reentrant Events	Indicates whether the provider supports reentrancy during callbacks. Read-only.	`Boolean`
Remove Deleted Rows	Indicates whether the provider removes rows it detects as having been deleted from the rowset. Read/Write.	`Boolean`
Report Multiple Changes	Indicates whether an update or delete can affect multiple rows and the provider can detect that multiple rows have been updated or deleted. Read-only.	`Boolean`
Reshape Name	Indicates the name of the recordset that can be used in reshaping commands.	`String`
Resync Command	The command string that the `Resync` method will use to refresh data in the Unique Table.	`String`
Return PROPVARIANTs in variant binding	Indicates whether or not to return PROPVARIANTS when binding to variant columns.	`Boolean`
Return Pending Inserts	Indicates whether methods that fetch rows can return pending insert rows. Read-only.	`Boolean`
Row Delete Notification	Indicates whether deleting a row is cancelable. Read-only.	`DBPROPVAL_NP`
Row First Change Notification	Indicates whether changing the first row is cancelable. Read-only.	`DBPROPVAL_NP`
Row Insert Notification	Indicates whether inserting a new row is cancelable. Read-only.	`DBPROPVAL_NP`
Row Privileges	Indicates whether access rights are restricted on a row-by-row basis. Read-only.	`Boolean`
Row Resynchronization Notification	Indicates whether resynchronizing a row is cancelable. Read-only.	`DBPROPVAL_NP`
Row Threading Model	Identifies the threading models supported by the rowset. Read/Write.	`DBPROPVAL_RT`
Row Undo Change Notification	Indicates whether undoing a change is cancelable. Read-only.	`DBPROPVAL_NP`

Appendices

Property Name	Description	DataType
Row Undo Delete Notification	Indicates whether undoing a delete is cancelable. Read-only.	DBPROPVAL _NP
Row Undo Insert Notification	Indicates whether undoing an insert is cancelable. Read-only.	DBPROPVAL _NP
Row Update Notification	Indicates whether updating a row is cancelable. Read-only.	DBPROPVAL _NP
Rowset Fetch Position Change Notification	Indicates whether changing the fetch position is cancelable. Read-only.	DBPROPVAL _NP
Rowset Release Notification	Indicates whether releasing a rowset is cancelable. Read-only.	DBPROPVAL _NP
Scroll Backward	Indicates whether the rowset can scroll backward. Read/Write.	Boolean
Server Cursor	Indicates whether the cursor underlying the rowset (if any) must be materialized on the server. Read/Write.	Boolean
Server Data on Insert	Indicates whether, at the time an insert is transmitted to the server, the provider retrieves data from the server to update the local row cache. Read/Write.	Boolean
Skip Deleted Bookmarks	Indicates whether the rowset allows positioning to continue if a bookmark row was deleted. Read/Write.	Boolean
SQL Content Query Locale String	The locale string to use for queries.	String
Strong Row Identity	Indicates whether the handles of newly inserted rows can be compared. Read-only.	Boolean
Unique Catalog	Specifies the catalog or database name containing the table named in the Unique Table property.	String
Unique Rows	Indicates whether each row is uniquely identified by its column values. Read/Write.	Boolean
Unique Schema	Specifies the schema, or owner of the table named in the Unique Table property.	String
Unique Table	Specifies the name of the base table upon which edits are allowed. This is required when updateable recordsets are created from one-to-many JOIN statements.	String

Property Name	Description	DataType
Updatability	Identifies the supported methods for updating a rowset. Read/Write.	`DBPROPVAL_UP`
Update Criteria	Specifies which fields can be used to detect conflicts during optimistic updates. Read/Write.	`ADCPROP_UPDATE CRITERIA_ENUM`
Update Operation	For chaptered recordsets, identifies the operation to be performed with a requery. Read/Write.	`String`
Update Resync	Specifies whether an implicit `Resync` method is called directly after an `UpdateBatch` method	`CEResyncEnum`
Use Bookmarks	Indicates whether the rowset supports bookmarks. Read/Write.	`Boolean`

The Field Object's Properties

The field properties names are different from the other properties because they are less readable and appear more like the schema column names.

Property Name	Description	DataType
`BASECATALOG NAME`	The name of the catalog. Read-only.	`String`
`BASECOLUMN NAME`	The name of the column. Read-only.	`String`
`BASESCHEMA NAME`	The name of the schema. Read-only.	`String`
`BASETABLE INSTANCE`	The SQL Server 2000 instance of the base table.	`Integer`
`BASETABLE NAME`	The table name. Read-only.	`String`
`CALCULATION INFO`	This is only available of client cursors.	`Binary`
`CLSID`	The class ID of the field.	`GUID`
`COLLATING SEQUENCE`	The locale ID of the sort sequence.	`Long`
`COMPFLAGS`	Compatibility flags for SL Variants.	`Integer`
`COMPUTEMODE`	Indicates the mode of recalculation for computed fields.	`DBCOMPUTEMODE`
`DATETIME PRECISION`	The number of digits in the fraction seconds portion if a datetime column. Read-only.	`Long`

Appendices

A

Property Name	Description	DataType
DEFAULT VALUE	The default value of the field.	Variant
DOMAIN CATALOG	The name of the catalog containing this column's domain.	String
DOMAINNAME	The name of the domain of which this column is a member.	String
DOMAIN SCHEMA	The name of the schema containing this column's domain.	String
HASDEFAULT	Indicates whether or not the field has a default value.	Boolean
ISAUTO INCREMENT	Identifies whether the column is an auto increment column, such as an Access Autonumber or a SQL Server IDENTITY column. Read-only.	Boolean
ISCASE SENSITIVE	Identifies whether the contents of the column are case sensitive. Useful when searching. Read-only.	Boolean
IS SEARCHABLE	Identifies the searchability of the column. Read-only.	DB_ SEARCHABLE
ISUNIQUE	Indicates whether or not the field uniquely identifies the row.	Boolean
KEYCOLUMN	Identifies whether or not the column is a key column, used to uniquely identify the row. Read-only.	Boolean
OCTETLENGTH	The maximum column length in bytes, for character or binary data columns. Read-only.	Long
OPTIMIZE	Identifies whether the column is indexed locally. This is only available of client cursors. Read/Write.	Boolean
RELATION CONDITIONS	Identifies the relationship between fields. This is only available on client cursors. #	Binary
SORTID	The Sort Order ID for the collation of the column.	Integer

The Command Object's Properties

Property Name	Description	DataType
Access Order	Indicates the order in which columns must be accessed on the rowset. Read/Write.	DB PROPVAL_ AO
Base Path	The path where XPATH mapping schema and template files are stored. The default is the current directory. Read/Write.	String

Property Name	Description	DataType
Blocking Storage Objects	Indicates whether storage objects might prevent use of other methods on the rowset. Read/Write.	Boolean
Bookmark Information	Identifies additional information about bookmarks over the rowset. Read-only.	DBPROP VAL_BI
Bookmark Type	Identifies the bookmark type supported by the rowset. Read/Write.	DBPROP VAL_BMK
Bookmarkable	Indicates whether bookmarks are supported. Read-only.	Boolean
Change Inserted Rows	Indicates whether the consumer can delete or update newly inserted rows. An inserted row is assumed to be one that has been transmitted to the data source, as opposed to a pending insert row. Read/Write.	Boolean
Column Privileges	Indicates whether access rights are restricted on a column-by-column basis. Read-only.	Boolean
Column Set Notification	Indicates whether changing a column set is cancelable. Read-only.	DBPROP VAL_NP
Command Time Out	The number of seconds to wait before a command times out. A value of 0 indicates an infinite timeout. Read/Write.	Long
Content type	For URL access to SQL Server 2000, specifies the Content-Type of the returned document.	String
Cursor Auto Fetch	Indicates whether a cursor is automatically fetched. Corresponds to the adExecuteNoRecords option for the Execute method.	Boolean
Defer Column	Indicates whether the data in a column is not fetched until specifically requested. Read/Write.	Boolean
Defer Prepare	Indicates whether or not command parsing is deferred until the statement is prepared.	Boolean
Delay Storage Object Updates	Indicates whether, when in delayed update mode, storage objects are also used in delayed update mode. Read/Write.	Boolean
Determine Key Columns For Rowset	Determines which of the columns in the recordset are key columns. #	Boolean
Fastload Options	Indicates the options to use when in Fastload mode.	String
Fetch Backward	Indicates whether a rowset can fetch backwards. Read/Write.	Boolean

Property Name	Description	DataType
Hidden Columns	Indicates the number of hidden columns in the rowset added by the provider to uniquely identify rows.	Long
Hold Rows	Indicates whether the rowset allows the consumer to retrieve more rows or change the next fetch position while holding previously fetched rows with pending changes. Read/Write.	Boolean
Immobile Rows	Indicates whether the rowset will reorder inserted or updated rows. Read/Write.	Boolean
Keep Identity	Indicates whether or not IDENTITY columns should keep the values if supplied by the client during an INSERT.	Boolean
Keep Nulls	Indicates whether or not Null values supplied by the client should be kept if DEFAULT values exist on the columns.	Boolean
Literal Bookmarks	Indicates whether bookmarks can be compared literally, as a series of bytes. Read/Write.	Boolean
Literal Row Identity	Indicates whether the consumer can perform a binary comparison of two row handles to determine whether they point to the same row. Read-only.	Boolean
Lock Mode	Identifies the level of locking performed by the rowset. Read/Write.	DBPROPVAL _LM
Mapping Schema	The name of the XPATH mapping schema to be used. The path is taken from the Base Path dynamic property.	String
Maximum BLOB Length	Identifies the maximum length of a BLOB field. Read-only.	Long
Maximum Open Rows	Specifies the maximum number of rows that can be active at the same time. Read/Write.	Long
Maximum Pending Rows	Specifies the maximum number of rows that can have pending changes at the same time. Read/Write.	Long
Maximum Rows	Specifies the maximum number of rows that can be returned in the rowset. This is 0 if there is no limit. Read/Write.	Long
Notification Granularity	Identifies when the consumer is notified for methods that operate on multiple rows. Read/Write.	DBPROPVAL _NT
Notification Phases	Identifies the notification phases supported by the provider. Read-only.	DBPROPVAL _NP

Property Name	Description	DataType
Objects Transacted	Indicates whether any object created on the specified column is transacted. Read/Write.	`Boolean`
Others' Changes Visible	Indicates whether the rowset can see updates and deletes made by someone other that the consumer of the rowset. Read/Write.	`Boolean`
Others' Inserts Visible	Indicates whether the rowset can see rows inserted by someone other than the consumer of the rowset. Read/Write.	`Boolean`
Output Encoding	Specifies the encoding to use in the stream returned by the command. The default is UTF8. Read/Write.	`String`
Output Stream	Identifies the `Stream` object (or object supporting the `IStream` interface), into which the results of the command should be stored.	`Stream`
Own Changes Visible	Indicates whether the rowset can see its own updates and deletes. Read/Write.	`Boolean`
Own Inserts Visible	Indicates whether the rowset can see its own inserts. Read/Write.	`Boolean`
Preserve on Abort	Indicates whether, after aborting a transaction, the rowset remains active. Read/Write.	`Boolean`
Preserve on Commit	Indicates whether after committing a transaction the rowset remains active. Read/Write.	`Boolean`
Quick Restart	Indicates whether `RestartPosition` is relatively quick to execute. Read/Write.	`Boolean`
Reentrant Events	Indicates whether the provider supports reentrancy during callbacks. Read-only.	`Boolean`
Remove Deleted Rows	Indicates whether the provider removes rows it detects as having been deleted from the rowset. Read/Write.	`Boolean`
Report Multiple Changes	Indicates whether an update or delete can affect multiple rows and the provider can detect that multiple rows have been updated or deleted. Read-only.	`Boolean`
Return Pending Inserts	Indicates whether methods that fetch rows can return pending insert rows. Read-only.	`Boolean`
Row Delete Notification	Indicates whether deleting a row is cancelable. Read-only.	`DBPROPVAL _NP`
Row First Change Notification	Indicates whether changing the first row is cancelable. Read-only.	`DBPROPVAL _NP`

Property Name	Description	DataType
Row Insert Notification	Indicates whether inserting a new row is cancelable. Read-only.	DBPROPVAL _NP
Row Privileges	Indicates whether access rights are restricted on a row-by-row basis. Read-only.	Boolean
Row Resynchronization Notification	Indicates whether resynchronizing a row is cancelable. Read-only.	DBPROPVAL _NP
Row Threading Model	Identifies the threading models supported by the rowset. Read/Write.	DBPROPVAL _RT
Row Undo Change Notification	Indicates whether undoing a change is cancelable. Read-only.	DBPROPVAL _NP
Row Undo Delete Notification	Indicates whether undoing a delete is cancelable. Read-only.	DBPROPVAL _NP
Row Undo Insert Notification	Indicates whether undoing an insert is cancelable. Read-only.	DBPROPVAL _NP
Row Update Notification	Indicates whether updating a row is cancelable. Read-only.	DBPROPVAL _NP
Rowset Fetch Position Change Notification	Indicates whether changing the fetch position is cancelable. Read-only.	DBPROPVAL _NP
Rowset Release Notification	Indicates whether releasing a rowset is cancelable. Read-only.	DBPROPVAL _NP
Scroll Backward	Indicates whether the rowset can scroll backward. Read/Write.	Boolean
Server Cursor	Indicates whether the cursor underlying the rowset (if any) must be materialized on the server. Read/Write.	Boolean
Server Data on Insert	Indicates whether, at the time an insert is transmitted to the server, the provider retrieves data from the server to update to update the local row cache. Read/Write.	Boolean
Skip Deleted Bookmarks	Indicates whether the rowset allows positioning to continue if a bookmark row was deleted. Read/Write.	Boolean
SS Stream Flags	SQL Server flags for the TDS Stream. #	Integer
Strong Row Identity	Indicates whether the handles of newly inserted rows can be compared. Read-only.	Boolean

Property Name	Description	DataType
Unique Rows	Indicates whether each row is uniquely identified by it's column values. Read/Write.	`Boolean`
Updatability	Identifies the supported methods for updating a rowset. Read/Write.	`DBPROPVAL _UP`
Use Bookmarks	Indicates whether the rowset supports bookmarks. Read/Write.	`Boolean`
XML root	The tag name to wrap the resulting XML in.	`String`
XSL	Specifies an XSL file or URL used to transform the XML. Read/Write.	`String`

I thank God I am as honest as any man
living that is an old man and no honester th...

Can counsel and speak comfort to th...
Which they themselves not feel

For there was never yet philospher
That could endure the toothache patiently.

Much Ado About Nothing.

He wears his faith but as the fashion of ...

As merry as the day

He hath indeed better bettered expectation

(Act i. Sc. 1.).

He wears his faith but as the fashion of his hat.
(Ibid)

As merry as the day is long.

h indeed better bettered expectation

(Act i. Sc. 1.)

(Ibid)

Can counsel and speak comfort to that grief

Which they themselves not feel.

Much Ado About Nothing.

He wears his faith but as the fashion of his hat.
(Ibid)

I was not born under

a rhyming planet

I was not born under a rhyming plan
sc.

For there was never yet
That could endure the to

merry as the day is long

(sc. 2)

Can counsel and speak comfort to that grief

Which they themselves not feel.

(Ibid)

He hath indeed better bettered expectation

(Ibid)

I thank God I am as honest as an...

living that is an old man and no hones...

He wears his faith but as the fashion of his ha...
(Ibi...

Much Ado About Nothing.

For there was never yet philospher
That could endure the toothache patiently.

(Ibid)

I was not born u

D

Schemas

There are two terms that are important when dealing with schemas:

- ❏ A **Catalog** is like a normal paper catalog, but contains a list of schemas. It always contains a schema named INFORMATION_SCHEMA, which is the information schema. When dealing with Microsoft SQL Server and Access, a catalog is a database.

- ❏ A **Schema** is a collection of database objects that are owned (or have been created by) a particular user. Microsoft Access does not have an equivalent to a schema, and so all database objects appear in a single schema.

This appendix details the schema objects that can be accessed using the OpenSchema method of the Connection object.

The table below shows the main providers and the list of schemas supported by them:

Schema	ODBC Access 97	ODBC Access 2000	ODBC SQL 6.5	ODBC SQL 7/2000	OLEDB Access 97	OLEDB Access 2000	OLEDB SQL 6.5	OLEDB SQL 7/2000	OLAP
adSchemaActions									✓
adSchemaAsserts									
adSchemaCatalogs	✓	✓	✓	✓			✓	✓	✓
adSchemaCharacterSets									
adSchemaCheckConstraints					✓	✓			

Schema	ODBC Access 97	ODBC Access 2000	ODBC SQL 6.5	ODBC SQL 7/2000	OLEDB Access 97	OLEDB Access 2000	OLEDB SQL 6.5	OLEDB SQL 7/2000	OLAP
adSchemaCollations									
adSchemaColumnPrivileges			✓	✓			✓	✓	
adSchemaColumns	✓	✓	✓	✓	✓	✓	✓	✓	✓
adSchemaColumnsDomainUsage									
adSchemaCommands									
adSchemaConstraintColumnUsage					✓	✓			
adSchemaConstraintTableUsage									
adSchemaCubes									✓
adSchemaDBInfoKeywords	✓	✓	✓	✓	✓	✓	✓	✓	✓
adSchemaDBInfoLiterals	✓	✓	✓	✓	✓	✓	✓	✓	✓
adSchemaDimensions									✓
adSchemaForeignKeys			✓	✓	✓	✓	✓	✓	
adSchemaFunctions									✓
adSchemaHierarchies									✓
adSchemaIndexes	✓	✓	✓	✓	✓	✓	✓	✓	
adSchemaKeyColumnUsage					✓	✓			
adSchemaLevels									✓
adSchemaMeasures									✓
adSchemaMembers									✓
adSchemaPrimaryKeys			✓	✓	✓	✓	✓	✓	
adSchemaProcedureColumns	✓	✓							
adSchemaProcedureParameters	✓	✓	✓	✓			✓	✓	
adSchemaProcedures	✓	✓	✓	✓	✓	✓	✓	✓	
adSchemaProperties									✓
adSchemaProviderTypes	✓	✓	✓	✓	✓	✓	✓	✓	✓
adSchemaReferentialContraints					✓	✓			
adSchemaSchemata			✓	✓			✓	✓	
adSchemaSets									✓
adSchemaSQLLanguages									
adSchemaStatistics					✓	✓	✓	✓	
adSchemaTableConstraints					✓	✓	✓	✓	
adSchemaTablePrivileges							✓	✓	

Schema	ODBC Access 97	ODBC Access 2000	ODBC SQL 6.5	ODBC SQL 7/2000	OLEDB Access 97	OLEDB Access 2000	OLEDB SQL 6.5	OLEDB SQL 7/2000	OLAP
adSchemaTables	✓	✓	✓	✓	✓	✓	✓	✓	✓
adSchemaTranslations									
adSchemaTrustees									
adSchemaUsagePrivileges									
adSchemaViewColumnUsage									
adSchemaViews					✓	✓			
adSchemaViewTableUsage									

Schema Usage

Using schemas is quite easy, since all you need to do is use the OpenSchema method of the Connection object. For example, to list all of the tables on a particular connection:

```
Set objRec = objConn.OpenSchema (adSchemaTables)
While Not objRec.EOF
   Print objRec("TABLE_NAME")
   objRec.MoveNext
Wend
```

This simply opens a recordset on the tables schema and loops through it, printing each table name. You can use the TABLE_TYPE column to check for system tables:

```
Set objRec = objConn.OpenSchema (adSchemaTables)
While Not objRec.EOF
   If objRec("TABLE_TYPE") <> "SYSTEM TABLE" Then
      Print objRec("TABLE_NAME")
   End If
   objRec.MoveNext
Wend
```

You can use the Restrictions argument of OpenSchema to return only certain rows. This argument accepts an array that matches the column names. For example, to find only the system tables:

```
Set objRec = objConn.OpenSchema (adSchemaTables, _
                     Array (Empty, Empty, Empty, _
   "SYSTEM_TABLE"))
```

Since the type is the fourth column in the recordset, you need to specify empty values for the columns you wish to skip.

For multi-dimensional providers using `adSchemaMembers`, the restrictions can either be the columns in the members schema, or one of the `MDTREEOP` constants, as defined in Appendix L.

When connecting to Microsoft Access, there are some interesting things you should be aware of. If you wish to see the queries, then you might have to use both `adSchemaProcedures` and `adSchemaViews` depending upon the query type. Normal select queries appear as Views, whereas action queries (Update, Delete, etc) and CrossTab queries appear as procedures. This is only for the native Jet provider. For the ODBC provider, Select and CrossTab queries appear as tables with a table type set to `VIEW`.

adSchemaActions

This identifies the actions which are linked to data in the cube.

Column name	Type	Description
CATALOG_NAME	String	The catalog name.
SCHEMA_NAME	String	Schema name, or `Null` if the provider does not support schemas.
CUBE_NAME	String	The name of the cube.
ACTION_NAME	String	The name of the action.
COORDINATE	String	A string identifying the 'coordinate' of the action.
COORDINATE_TYPE	Integer	One of the `MDACTION` constants, as shown in Appendix L.
CAPTION	String	The friendly name of the action.
DESCRIPTION	String	A description of the action.
CONTENT	String	The string containing the action.
APPLICATION	String	The application name.

adSchemaAsserts

This identifies the assertions defined in the catalog.

Column name	Type	Description
CONSTRAINT_CATALOG	String	Catalog name, or `Null` if the provider does not support catalogs.
CONSTRAINT_SCHEMA	String	Schema name, or `Null` if the provider does not support schemas.
CONSTRAINT_NAME	String	Constraint name.
IS_DEFERRABLE	Boolean	`True` if the assertion is deferrable, `False` otherwise.

Column name	Type	Description
INITIALLY_DEFERRED	Boolean	True if the assertion is initially deferred, False otherwise.
DESCRIPTION	String	Description of the assertion.

adSchemaCatalogs

This defines the physical attributes of the catalogs of a database. When using SQL Server the catalogs are the databases within the Server, and for Access the catalogs contain the current database.

Column name	Type	Description
CATALOG_NAME	String	Catalog name.
DESCRIPTION	String	Catalog description.

adSchemaCharacterSets

This identifies the character sets supported by the catalog.

Column name	Type	Description
CHARACTER_SET_CATALOG	String	Catalog name, or Null if the provider does not support catalogs.
CHARACTER_SET_SCHEMA	String	Schema name, or Null if the provider does not support schemas.
CHARACTER_SET_NAME	String	Character set name.
FORM_OF_USE	String	Name of form-of-use of the character set.
NUMBER_OF_CHARACTERS	Big Integer	Number of characters in the character repertoire.
DEFAULT_COLLATE_CATALOG	String	Catalog name containing the default collation, or Null if the provider does not support catalogs or different collations.
DEFAULT_COLLATE_SCHEMA	String	Schema name containing the default collation, or Null if the provider does not support schemas or different collations.
DEFAULT_COLLATE_NAME	String	Default collation name, or Null if the provider does not support different collations.

adSchemaCheckConstraints

This identifies the check constraints available in the catalog. Check constraints identify the valid values allowed for columns.

Column name	Type	Description
CONSTRAINT_CATALOG	String	Catalog name, or Null if the provider does not support catalogs.
CONSTRAINT_SCHEMA	String	Schema name, or Null if the provider does not support schemas.
CONSTRAINT_NAME	String	Constraint name.
CHECK_CLAUSE	String	The WHERE clause specified in the CHECK constraint.
DESCRIPTION	String	Check constraint description.

adSchemaCollations

Collations identify how the catalog sorts data.

Column name	Type	Description
COLLATION_CATALOG	String	Catalog name, or Null if the provider does not support catalogs.
COLLATION_SCHEMA	String	Schema name, or Null if the provider does not support schemas.
COLLATION_NAME	String	Collation name.
CHARACTER_SET_CATALOG	String	Catalog name containing the character set on which the collation is defined, or Null if the provider does not support catalogs or different character sets.
CHARACTER_SET_SCHEMA	String	Schema name containing the character set on which the collation is defined, or Null if the provider does not support schemas or different character sets.
CHARACTER_SET_NAME	String	Character set name on which the collation is defined, or Null if the provider does not support different character sets.
PAD_ATTRIBUTE	String	'NO PAD' if the collation being described has the NO PAD attribute, 'PAD SPACE' if the collation being described has the PAD SPACE attribute. This identifies whether variable length character columns are padded with spaces.

adSchemaColumnPrivileges

This identifies the privileges on table columns for a given user.

Column name	Type	Description
GRANTOR	String	User who granted the privileges on the table in TABLE_NAME.
GRANTEE	String	User name (or "PUBLIC") to whom the privilege has been granted.
TABLE_CATALOG	String	Catalog name in which the table is defined, or Null if the provider does not support catalogs.
TABLE_SCHEMA	String	Schema name in which the table is defined, or Null if the provider does not support schemas.
TABLE_NAME	String	Table name.
COLUMN_NAME	String	Column name.
COLUMN_GUID	GUID	Column GUID.
COLUMN_PROPID	Long	Column property ID.
PRIVILEGE_TYPE	String	Privilege type. One of the following: SELECT, DELETE, INSERT, UPDATE, REFERENCES.
IS_GRANTABLE	Boolean	True if the privilege being described was granted with the WITH GRANT OPTION clause; False if the privilege being described was not granted with the WITH GRANT OPTION clause.

adSchemaColumns

This identifies the columns of tables.

Column name	Type	Description
TABLE_CATALOG	String	Catalog name, or Null if the provider does not support catalogs.
TABLE_SCHEMA	Long	Schema name, or Null if the provider does not support schemas.
TABLE_NAME	String	Table name. This column cannot contain a Null.
COLUMN_NAME	String	The name of the column, or Null if this cannot be determined.
COLUMN_GUID	GUID	Column GUID, or Null for providers that do not use GUIDs to identify columns.

Appendices

Column name	Type	Description
COLUMN_PROPID	Long	Column property ID, or Null for providers that do not associate PROPIDs with columns.
ORDINAL_POSITION	Long	The ordinal of the column, or Null if there is no stable ordinal value for the column. Columns are numbered starting from one.
COLUMN_HASDEFAULT	Boolean	True if column has a default value, False if the column does not have a default value or it is unknown whether the column has a default value.
COLUMN_DEFAULT	String	Default value of the column.
COLUMN_FLAGS	Long	A bitmask that describes column characteristics. The DBCOLUMNFLAGS enumerated type specifies the bits in the bitmask. The values for DBCOLUMNFLAGS can be found in Appendix B. This column cannot contain a Null value.
IS_NULLABLE	Boolean	True if the column might be Nullable, False if the column is known not to be Nullable.
DATA_TYPE	Integer	The column's data type. If the data type of the column varies from row to row, this must be a Variant. This column cannot contain Null. For a list of valid Types, see DataTypeEnum in Appendix B.
TYPE_GUID	GUID	The GUID of the column's data type. Providers that do not use GUIDs to identify data types should return Null in this column.
CHARACTER_MAXIMUM_ LENGTH	Long	The maximum possible length of a value in the column. See below.
CHARACTER_OCTET_LENGTH	Long	Maximum length in octets (bytes) of the column, if the type of the column is character or binary. A value of zero means the column has no maximum length. Null for all other types of columns.
NUMERIC_PRECISION	Integer	If the column's data type is numeric, this is the maximum precision of the column. The precision of columns with a data type of Decimal or Numeric depends on the definition of the column If the column's data type is not numeric, this is Null.

Column name	Type	Description
NUMERIC_SCALE	Integer	If the column's Type is Decimal or Numeric, this is the number of digits to the right of the decimal point. Otherwise, this is Null.
DATETIME_PRECISION	Long	Datetime precision (number of digits in the fractional seconds portion) of the column if the column is a datetime or interval type. If the column's data type is not datetime, this is Null.
CHARACTER_SET_CATALOG	String	Catalog name in which the character set is defined, or Null if the provider does not support catalogs or different character sets.
CHARACTER_SET_SCHEMA	String	Schema name in which the character set is defined, or Null if the provider does not support schemas or different character sets.
CHARACTER_SET_NAME	String	Character set name, or Null if the provider does not support different character sets.
COLLATION_CATALOG	String	Catalog name in which the collation is defined, or Null if the provider does not support catalogs or different collations.
COLLATION_SCHEMA	String	Schema name in which the collation is defined, or Null if the provider does not support schemas or different collations.
COLLATION_NAME	String	Collation name, or Null if the provider does not support different collations.
DOMAIN_CATALOG	String	Catalog name in which the domain is defined, or Null if the provider does not support catalogs or domains.
DOMAIN_SCHEMA	String	Unqualified schema name in which the domain is defined, or Null if the provider does not support schemas or domains.
DOMAIN_NAME	String	Domain name, or Null if the provider does not support domains.
DESCRIPTION	String	Description of the column, or Null if there is no description associated with the column.
SS_DATA_TYPE	Integer	SQL Server data type.
COLUMN_LCID	Integer	The locale ID of the column.
COLUMN_COMPFLAGS	Integer	Column comparison flags.
COLUMN_SORTID	Integer	Column sort order.
COLUMN_TDS COLLATION	Integer	SQL Server collation.

CHARACTER_MAXIMUM_LENGTH will vary depending upon the data type of the column. For character, binary, or bit columns, this is one of the following:

❑ The maximum length of the column in characters, bytes, or bits, respectively, if one is defined. For example, a CHAR(5) column in an SQL table has a maximum length of five.

❑ The maximum length of the data type in characters, bytes, or bits, respectively, if the column does not have a defined length.

❑ Zero if neither the column nor the data type has a defined maximum length.

It will be Null for all other types of columns.

adSchemaColumnsDomainUsage

This identifies the columns that use domains for integrity checking.

Column name	Type	Description
DOMAIN_CATALOG	String	Catalog name, or Null if the provider does not support catalogs.
DOMAIN_SCHEMA	String	Schema name, or Null if the provider does not support schemas.
DOMAIN_NAME	String	View name.
TABLE_CATALOG	String	Catalog name in which the table is defined, or Null if the provider does not support catalogs.
TABLE_SCHEMA	String	Unqualified schema name in which the table is defined, or Null if the provider does not support schemas.
TABLE_NAME	String	Table name.
COLUMN_NAME	String	Column name. This column, together with the COLUMN_GUID and COLUMN_PROPID columns, forms the column ID. One or more of these columns will be Null depending on which elements of the DBID structure the provider uses.
COLUMN_GUID	GUID	Column GUID.
COLUMN_PROPID	Long	Column property ID.

adSchemaConstraintColumnUsage

This identifies the columns used for referential integrity constraints, unique constraints, check constraints, and assertions.

Column name	Type	Description
TABLE_CATALOG	String	Catalog name in which the table is defined, or Null if the provider does not support catalogs.

Column name	Type	Description
TABLE_SCHEMA	String	Schema name in which the table is defined, or Null if the provider does not support schemas.
TABLE_NAME	String	Table name.
COLUMN_NAME	String	Column name.
COLUMN_GUID	GUID	Column GUID.
COLUMN_PROPID	Long	Column property ID.
CONSTRAINT_CATALOG	String	Catalog name, or Null if the provider does not support catalogs.
CONSTRAINT_SCHEMA	String	Schema name, or Null if the provider does not support schemas.
CONSTRAINT_NAME	String	Constraint name.

adSchemaConstraintTableUsage

This identifies the tables used for referential integrity constraints, unique constraints, check constraints, and assertions.

Column name	Type	Description
TABLE_CATALOG	String	Catalog name in which the table is defined, or Null if the provider does not support catalogs.
TABLE_SCHEMA	String	Schema name in which the table is defined, or Null if the provider does not support schemas.
TABLE_NAME	String	Table name.
CONSTRAINT_CATALOG	String	Catalog name, or Null if the provider does not support catalogs.
CONSTRAINT_SCHEMA	String	Schema name, or Null if the provider does not support schemas.
CONSTRAINT_NAME	String	Constraint name.

adSchemaCubes

Identifies the cubes in an OLAP catalog.

Column name	Type	Description
CATALOG_NAME	String	Catalog name in which the table is defined, or Null if the provider does not support catalogs.
SCHEMA_NAME	String	Schema name in which the table is defined, or Null if the provider does not support schemas.

Appendices

525

A

Column name	Type	Description
CUBE_NAME	String	The name of the cube.
CUBE_TYPE	String	Either CUBE to indicate a regular cube, or VIRTUAL CUBE to indicate a virtual cube.
CUBE_GUID	String	The GUID of the cube, or Null if no GUID exists.
CREATED_ON	Date	Date and time cube was created.
LAST_SCHEMA_UPDATE	Date	Date and time schema was last updated.
SCHEMA_UPDATED_BY	String	User ID of person who last updated the schema.
LAST_DATA_UPDATE	Date	Date and time data was last updated.
DATA_UPDATED_BY	String	User ID of person who last updated the data.
Description	String	The cube description.

adSchemaDBInfoKeywords

This identifies a list of provider-specific keywords.

Column name	Type	Description
Keyword	String	The keyword supported by the provider.

adSchemaDBInfoLiterals

This identifies a list of provider-specific literals used in text commands.

Column name	Type	Description
LiteralName	String	The literal name.
LiteralValue	String	The literal value.
InvalidChars	String	Characters which are invalid as part of a literal.
InvalidStarting Chars	String	Characters which the literal cannot start with.
Literal	Integer	The literal type. This can be one of the DBLITERAL constants described in Appendix B.
Supported	Boolean	True if the provider supports the literal.
Maxlen	Integer	Maximum length of the literal name.

adSchemaDimensions

Identifies the dimensions in an OLAP catalog.

Column name	Type	Description
CATALOG_NAME	String	Catalog name in which the table is defined, or Null if the provider does not support catalogs.
SCHEMA_NAME	String	Schema name in which the table is defined, or Null if the provider does not support schemas.
CUBE_NAME	String	The name of the cube to which this dimension belongs.
DIMENSION_NAME	String	The name of the dimension.
DIMENSION_UNIQUE_NAME	String	The fully qualified name of the dimension.
DIMENSION_GUID	GUID	The GUID of the dimension, or Null if no GUID exists.
DIMENSION_CAPTION	String	The name of the dimension.
DIMENSION_ORDINAL	Long	The number of the ordinal. This is zero based.
DIMENSION_TYPE	Integer	The type of the dimension. Can be one of: MD_DIMTYPE_MEASURE, to indicate a measure dimension; MD_DIMTYPE_TIME, to indicate a time dimension; MD_DIMTYPE_OTHER, to indicate neither a measure nor a time dimension; MD_DIM_TYPE_UNKNOWN, to indicate the type is unknown.
DIMENSION_CARDINALITY	Long	The number of members in the dimension. This figure is not guaranteed to be accurate.
DEFAULT_HIERARCHY	String	The default hierarchy for this dimension, or Null if no default exists.
DESCRIPTION	String	The description of the hierarchy.
IS_VIRTUAL	Boolean	True if the dimension is a virtual one, False otherwise.

Appendices

adSchemaForeignKeys

This identifies the foreign key columns, as used in referential integrity checks.

Column name	Type	Description
PK_TABLE_CATALOG	String	Catalog name in which the primary key table is defined, or Null if the provider does not support catalogs.
PK_TABLE_SCHEMA	String	Schema name in which the primary key table is defined, or Null if the provider does not support schemas.
PK_TABLE_NAME	String	Primary key table name.
PK_COLUMN_NAME	String	Primary key column name.
PK_COLUMN_GUID	GUID	Primary key column GUID.
PK_COLUMN_PROPID	Long	Primary key column property ID.
FK_TABLE_CATALOG	String	Catalog name in which the foreign key table is defined, or Null if the provider does not support catalogs.
FK_TABLE_SCHEMA	String	Schema name in which the foreign key table is defined, or Null if the provider does not support schemas.
FK_TABLE_NAME	String	Foreign key table name.
FK_COLUMN_NAME	String	Foreign key column name.
FK_COLUMN_GUID	GUID	Foreign key column GUID.
FK_COLUMN_PROPID	Long	Foreign key column property ID.
ORDINAL	Long	The order of the column in the key. For example, a table might contain several foreign key references to another table. The ordinal starts over for each reference; for example, two references to a three-column key would return 1, 2, 3, 1, 2, 3.
UPDATE_RULE	String	The action if an UPDATE rule was specified. This will be Null only if the provider cannot determine the UPDATE_RULE. In most cases, this implies a default of NO ACTION.
DELETE_RULE	String	The action if a DELETE rule was specified. This will be Null if the provider cannot determine the DELETE_RULE. In most cases, this implies a default of NO ACTION.
FK_NAME	String	Foreign key name, or Null if the provider does not support named foreign key constraints.

Column name	Type	Description
PK_NAME	String	Primary key name, or Null if the provider does not support named primary key constraints.
DEFERRABILITY	Integer	Deferability of the foreign key. Value is one of the DBPROPVAL_DF types, as shown in Appendix B.

For UPDATE_RULE and DELETE_RULE, the value will be one of the following:

❑ CASCADE – A referential action of CASCADE was specified

❑ SET NULL – A referential action of SET NULL was specified

❑ SET DEFAULT – A referential action of SET DEFAULT was specified

❑ NO ACTION – A referential action of NO ACTION was specified

adSchemaFunctions

Identifies all of the supported functions of the OLAP provider.

Column name	Type	Description
FUNCTION_NAME	String	The name of the function.
DESCRIPTION	String	The description of the function.
PARAM_LIST	String	A comma delimited list of parameters, in Visual Basic style (like Age As Integer).
RETURN_TYPE	Integer	The data type of the function return value.
ORIGIN	Integer	The origin of the function (provider-supplied function or user-defined function).
INTERFACE_NAME	String	The name of the interface for a user defined function, or the group name for an MDX function.
LIBRARY_NAME	String	The name of the type library for user-defined functions, or NULL for MDX functions.
DLL_NAME	String	The name of the .dll or .exe implementing the function, or NULL for MDX functions.
HELP_FILE	String	The name of the help file documenting this function, or NULL for MDX functions.
HELP_CONTEXT	Integer	The Help Context ID in the help file for this function.
OBJECT	String	The object to which this function applies (such as a level or dimension).

Appendices

adSchemaHierarchies

Identifies the hierarchies in an OLAP catalog.

Column name	Type	Description
CATALOG_NAME	String	Catalog name in which the table is defined or Null if the provider does not support catalogs.
SCHEMA_NAME	String	Schema name in which the table is defined or Null if the provider does not support schemas.
CUBE_NAME	String	The name of the cube to which this hierarchy belongs.
DIMENSION_UNIQUE_NAME	String	The fully qualified name of the dimension to which this hierarchy belongs.
HIERARCHY_NAME	String	The name of the hierarchy.
HIERARCHY_UNIQUE_NAME	String	The fully qualified name of the hierarchy.
HIERARCHY_GUID	GUID	The GUID of the hierarchy, or Null if no GUID exists.
HIERARCHY_CAPTION	String	The name of the hierarchy.
DIMENSION_TYPE	Integer	The type of the dimension. Can be one of: MD_DIMTYPE_ MEASURE, to indicate a measure dimension; MD_DIMTYPE_TIME, to indicate a time dimension; MD_DIMTYPE_OTHER, to indicate neither a measure nor a time dimension; MD_DIMTYPE_ UNKNOWN, to indicate the type is unknown.
HIERARCHY_CARDINALITY	Long	The number of members in the hierarchy. This figure is not guaranteed to be accurate.
DEFAULT_MEMBER	String	The default level for this hierarchy, or Null if no default exists.
ALL_MEMBER	String	The name of the default member if the first level is All, or Null if the first level is not All.
DESCRIPTION	String	The description of the hierarchy.

adSchemaIndexes

Identifies the list of indexes in the catalog.

Column name	Type	Description
TABLE_CATALOG	String	Catalog name, or Null if the provider does not support catalogs.
TABLE_SCHEMA	String	Unqualified schema name, or Null if the provider does not support schemas.
TABLE_NAME	String	Table name.
INDEX_CATALOG	String	Catalog name, or Null if the provider does not support catalogs.
INDEX_SCHEMA	String	Schema name, or Null if the provider does not support schemas.
INDEX_NAME	String	Index name.
PRIMARY_KEY	Boolean	Whether the index represents the primary key on the table, or Null if this is not known.
UNIQUE	Boolean	Whether index keys must be unique. This will be True if the index keys must be unique, and False if duplicate keys are allowed.
CLUSTERED	Boolean	Whether an index is clustered.
TYPE	Integer	The type of the index. One of the DBPROPVAL_IT constants as shown in Appendix B
FILL_FACTOR	Long	For a B+ tree index, this property represents the storage utilization factor of page nodes during the creation of the index.
INITIAL_SIZE	Long	The total amount of bytes allocated to this structure at creation time.
NULLS	Long	Whether Null keys are allowed. This will be one of the DBPROVAL_IN constants as shown in Appendix B.
SORT_BOOKMARKS	Boolean	How the index treats repeated keys. This will be True if the index sorts repeated keys by bookmark, and False if it doesn't.
AUTO_UPDATE	Boolean	Whether the index is maintained automatically when changes are made to the corresponding base table. This will be True if the index is automatically maintained, and False if it isn't.

Appendices

Column name	Type	Description
NULL_COLLATION	Long	How Nulls are collated in the index. This will be one of the DBPROPVAL_NC constants as shown in Appendix B.
ORDINAL_POSITION	Long	Ordinal position of the column in the index, starting with one.
COLUMN_NAME	String	Column name.
COLUMN_GUID	GUID	Column GUID.
COLUMN_PROPID	Long	Column property ID.
COLLATION	Integer	Identifies the sort order, and will be one of the DB_COLLATION constants as shown in Appendix B.
CARDINALITY	Unsigned Big Integer	Number of unique values in the index.
PAGES	Long	Number of pages used to store the index.
FILTER_CONDITION	String	The WHERE clause identifying the filtering restriction.
INTEGRATED	Boolean	Whether the index is integrated, that is, all base table columns are available from the index. This will be True if the index is integrated, and False if it isn't. Clustered indexes always set this value to True.

adSchemaKeyColumnUsage

This identifies the key columns, and table names, in the catalog.

Column name	Type	Description
CONSTRAINT_CATALOG	String	Catalog name, or Null if the provider does not support catalogs.
CONSTRAINT_SCHEMA	String	Schema name, or Null if the provider does not support schemas.
CONSTRAINT_NAME	String	Constraint name.
TABLE_CATALOG	String	Catalog name in which the table containing the key column is defined, or Null if the provider does not support catalogs.

Column name	Type	Description
TABLE_SCHEMA	String	Schema name in which the table containing the key column is defined, or Null if the provider does not support schemas.
TABLE_NAME	String	Table name containing the key column.
COLUMN_NAME	String	Name of the column participating in the unique, primary, or foreign key.
COLUMN_GUID	GUID	Column GUID.
COLUMN_PROPID	Long	Column property ID.
ORDINAL_POSITION	Long	Ordinal position of the column in the constraint being described.

adSchemaLevels

Identifies the levels in an OLAP catalog.

Column name	Type	Description
CATALOG_NAME	String	Catalog name, or Null if the provider does not support catalogs.
SCHEMA_NAME	String	Schema name, or Null if the provider does not support schemas.
CUBE_NAME	String	The cube name to which the level belongs.
DIMENSION_UNIQUE_ NAME	String	The unique name of the dimension to which the level belongs.
HIERARCHY_UNIQUE_ NAME	String	The unique name of the hierarchy to which the level belongs.
LEVEL_NAME	String	The level name.
LEVEL_UNIQUE_NAME	String	The unique level name.
LEVEL_GUID	String	The GUID of the level, or Null if no GUID exists.
LEVEL_CAPTION	String	The Caption of the level.
LEVEL_NUMBER	String	The index number of the level.
LEVEL_CARDINALITY	Long	The number of members in the level. This figure is not guaranteed to be accurate.
LEVEL_TYPE	Integer	The Type of the level. This can be one of the MDLEVEL_TYPE constants, as described in Appendix L.
DESCRIPTION	String	The description of the level.

adSchemaMeasures

Identifies the measures in an OLAP catalog.

Column name	Type	Description
CATALOG_NAME	String	Catalog name, or Null if the provider does not support catalogs.
SCHEMA_NAME	String	Schema name, or Null if the provider does not support schemas.
CUBE_NAME	String	The cube name to which the measure belongs.
MEASURE_NAME	String	The name of the measure.
MEASURE_UNIQUE_NAME	String	The unique name of the measure.
MEASURE_CAPTION	String	The caption of the measure.
MEASURE_GUID	GUID	The GUID of the measure, or Null if no GUID exists.
MEASURE_AGGEGATOR	Long	The type of aggregation for the measure. This can be one of the MDMEASURE_AGGR constants, as described in Appendix L.
DATA_TYPE	Integer	The data type that most closely matches the OLAP Provider type.
NUMERIC_PRECISION	Integer	The numeric precision of the data type.
NUMERIC_SCALE	Integer	The numeric scale of the data type.
MEASURE_UNITS	String	The unit of measurement for the measure.
DESCRIPTION	String	Description of the measure.
EXPRESSION	String	The expression that the measure is based upon.

adSchemaMembers

Identifies the members in an OLAP catalog.

Column name	Type	Description
CATALOG_NAME	String	Catalog name, or Null if the provider does not support catalogs.
SCHEMA_NAME	String	Schema name, or Null if the provider does not support schemas.
CUBE_NAME	String	The cube name to which the member belongs.
DIMENSION_UNIQUE_ NAME	String	The unique name of the dimension to which the member belongs.

Column name	Type	Description
HIERARCHY_UNIQUE_NAME	String	The unique name of the hierarchy to which the member belongs.
LEVEL_UNIQUE_NAME	String	The unique name of the level to which the member belongs.
LEVEL_NUMBER	Long	The position of the member.
MEMBER_ORDINAL	Long	The ordinal of the member, indicating the sorting rank.
MEMBER_NAME	String	The name of the member.
MEMBER_UNIQUE_NAME	String	The unique name of the member.
MEMBER_TYPE	Integer	The type of the member. Can be one of the MemberTypeEnum constants, as detailed in Appendix L.
MEMBER_GUID	GUID	The GUID of the member, or Null if no GUID exists.
MEMBER_CAPTION	String	The caption of the member.
CHILDREN_CARDINALITY	Long	The number of children that the member contains. This number is not guaranteed to be accurate.
PARENT_LEVEL	Long	The position, or level number, of the member's parent.
PARENT_UNIQUE_NAME	String	The unique name of the member's parent.
PARENT_COUNT	Long	The number of parents that this member has.
DESCRIPTION	String	The description of the member.

adSchemaPrimaryKeys

This identifies the primary keys, and table name, in the catalog.

Column name	Type	Description
TABLE_CATALOG	String	Catalog name in which the table is defined, or Null if the provider does not support catalogs.
TABLE_SCHEMA	String	Schema name in which the table is defined, or Null if the provider does not support schemas.
TABLE_NAME	String	Table name.
COLUMN_NAME	String	Primary key column name.
COLUMN_GUID	GUID	Primary key column GUID.
COLUMN_PROPID	Long	Primary key column property ID.

Appendices

A

Column name	Type	Description
ORDINAL	Long	The order of the column names (and GUIDs and property IDs) in the key.
PK_NAME	String	Primary key name, or Null if the provider does not support primary key constraints.

adSchemaProcedureColumns

This identifies the columns used in procedures.

Column name	Type	Description
PROCEDURE_CATALOG	String	Catalog name, or Null if the provider does not support catalogs.
PROCEDURE_SCHEMA	String	Schema name, or Null if the provider does not support schemas.
PROCEDURE_NAME	String	Table name.
COLUMN_NAME	String	The name of the column, or Null if this cannot be determined. This might not be unique.
COLUMN_GUID	GUID	Column GUID.
COLUMN_PROPID	Long	Column property ID.
ROWSET_NUMBER	Long	Number of the rowset containing the column. This is greater than one only if the procedure returns multiple rowsets.
ORDINAL_POSITION	Long	The ordinal of the column, or Null if there is no stable ordinal value for the column. Columns are numbered starting from one.
IS_NULLABLE	Boolean	Will be True if the column might be Nullable, or False if the column is known not to be Nullable.
DATA_TYPE	Integer	The indicator of the column's data type. For a list of valid types, see DataTypeEnum in Appendix B.
TYPE_GUID	GUID	The GUID of the column's data type.
CHARACTER_MAXIMUM_ LENGTH	Long	The maximum possible length of a value in the column. See below.
CHARACTER_OCTET_ LENGTH	Long	Maximum length in octets (bytes) of the column, if the type of the column is character or binary. A value of zero means the column has no maximum length. Null for all other types of columns.

Column name	Type	Description
NUMERIC_PRECISION	Integer	If the column's data type is numeric, this is the maximum precision of the column. If the column's data type is not numeric, this is Null.
NUMERIC_SCALE	Integer	If the column's type is DBTYPE_DECIMAL or DBTYPE_NUMERIC, this is the number of digits to the right of the decimal point. Otherwise, this is Null.
DESCRIPTION	String	Column description.

CHARACTER_MAXIMUM_LENGTH will vary depending upon the data type of the column. For character, binary, or bit columns, this is one of the following:

❑ The maximum length of the column in characters, bytes, or bits, respectively, if one is defined. For example, a CHAR(5) column in an SQL table has a maximum length of five.

❑ The maximum length of the data type in characters, bytes, or bits, respectively, if the column does not have a defined length.

❑ Zero if neither the column nor the data type has a defined maximum length.

It will be Null for all other types of columns.

adSchemaProcedureParameters

This identifies the parameters of stored procedures.

Column name	Type	Description
PROCEDURE_CATALOG	String	Catalog name, or Null if the provider does not support catalogs.
PROCEDURE_SCHEMA	String	Schema name, or Null if the provider does not support catalogs.
PROCEDURE_NAME	String	Procedure name.
PARAMETER_NAME	String	Parameter name, or Null if the parameter is not named.
ORDINAL_POSITION	Integer	If the parameter is an input, input/output, or output parameter, this is the one-based ordinal position of the parameter in the procedure call. If the parameter is the return value, this is zero.

Appendices

Column name	Type	Description
PARAMETER_TYPE	Integer	The type (direction) of the parameter, which will be one of the DBPARAMTYPE constants, as shown in Appendix B. If the provider cannot determine the parameter type, this is Null.
PARAMETER_HASDEFAULT	Boolean	True if the parameter has a default value, or False if it doesn't or the provider doesn't know whether it has a default value.
PARAMETER_DEFAULT	String	Default value of parameter. A default value of Null is a valid default.
IS_NULLABLE	Boolean	True if the parameter might be Nullable, or False if the parameter is not Nullable.
DATA_TYPE	Integer	The indicator of the parameter's data type. For a list of valid types, see DataTypeEnum in Appendix B.
CHARACTER_MAXIMUM_LENGTH	Long	The maximum possible length of a value in the parameter.
CHARACTER_OCTET_LENGTH	Long	Maximum length in octets (bytes) of the parameter, if the type of the parameter is character or binary. A value of zero means the parameter has no maximum length. Null for all other types of parameters.
NUMERIC_PRECISION	Integer	If the column's data type is numeric, this is the maximum precision of the column. If the column's data type is not numeric, this is Null.
NUMERIC_SCALE	Integer	If the column's type is DBTYPE_DECIMAL or DBTYPE_NUMERIC, this is the number of digits to the right of the decimal point. Otherwise, this is Null.
DESCRIPTION	String	Parameter description.
TYPE_NAME	String	Provider-specific data type name.
LOCAL_TYPE_NAME	String	Localized version of TYPE_NAME, or Null if the data provider does not support a localized name.
SS_DATA_TYPE	Integer	The SQL Server data type.

CHARACTER_MAXIMUM_LENGTH will vary depending upon the data type of the column. For character, binary, or bit columns, this is one of the following:

- The maximum length of the column in characters, bytes, or bits, respectively, if one is defined. For example, a CHAR(5) column in an SQL table has a maximum length of five.

- The maximum length of the data type in characters, bytes, or bits, respectively, if the column does not have a defined length.

- Zero if neither the column nor the data type has a defined maximum length.

It will be Null for all other types of columns.

adSchemaProcedures

This identifies the stored procedures or queries.

Column name	Type	Description
PROCEDURE_CATALOG	String	Catalog name, or Null if the provider does not support catalogs.
PROCEDURE_SCHEMA	String	Schema name, or Null if the provider does not support schemas.
PROCEDURE_NAME	String	Procedure name.
PROCEDURE_TYPE	Integer	Identifies whether there will be a return value or not, and will be one of the DB_PT constants as defined in Appendix B.
PROCEDURE_DEFINITION	String	Procedure definition.
DESCRIPTION	String	Procedures description.
DATE_CREATED	Date/Time	Date when the procedure was created or Null if the provider does not have this information.
DATE_MODIFIED	Date/Time	Date when the procedure definition was last modified or Null if the provider does not have this information.

adSchemaProperties

This identifies the properties for each level of a dimension.

Column name	Type	Description
CATALOG_NAME	String	The name of the catalog to which the property belongs.
SCHEMA_NAME	String	The name of the schema to which the property belongs.
CUBE_NAME	String	The name of the cube to which the property belongs.

Appendices

Column name	Type	Description
DIMENSION_UNIQUE_NAME	String	The unique name of the dimension.
HIERARCHY_UNIQUE_NAME	String	The unique name of the hierarchy.
LEVEL_UNIQUE_NAME	String	The unique name of the level.
MEMBER_UNIQUE_NAME	String	The unique name of the member.
PROPERTY_TYPE	Integer	The type of the property. Can be one of: MDPROP_MEMBER, to indicate the property relates to a member; MDPROP_CELL, to indicate the property relates to a cell.
PROPERTY_NAME	String	The name of the property.
PROPERTY_CAPTION	String	The caption of the property.
DATA_TYPE	Long	The data type of the property. For a list of valid types, see DataTypeEnum in Appendix B.
CHARACTER_MAXIMUM_LENGTH	Long	The maximum possible length of data in the property, or 0 to indicate no defined maximum.
CHARACTER_OCTET_LENGTH	Long	The maximum length in bytes of the property, for character and binary data types, or 0 to indicate no defined maximum.
NUMERIC_PRECISION	Integer	The numeric precision of the data type.
NUMERIC_SCALE	Integer	The numeric scale of the data type.
DESCRIPTION	String	The description of the property.

adSchemaProviderSpecific

The contents returned by this setting are dependent upon the provider, and you should consult the provider-specific information for details regarding them.

adSchemaProviderTypes

This identifies the data types supported by the provider.

Column name	Type	Description
TYPE_NAME	String	Provider-specific data type name.
DATA_TYPE	Integer	The indicator of the data type.

Column name	Type	Description
COLUMN_SIZE	Long	The length of a non-numeric column or parameter refers to either the maximum or the defined length for this type set by the provider. For character data, this is the maximum or defined length in characters. For datetime data types, this is the length of the String representation (assuming the maximum allowed precision of the fractional seconds component). If the data type is numeric, this is the upper bound on the maximum precision of the data type.
LITERAL_PREFIX	String	Character or characters used to prefix a literal of this type in a text command.
LITERAL_SUFFIX	String	Character or characters used to suffix a literal of this type in a text command.
CREATE_PARAMS	String	The creation parameters are specified by the consumer when creating a column of this data type. For example, the SQL data type DECIMAL needs a precision and a scale. In this case, the creation parameters might be the string "precision, scale". In a text command to create a DECIMAL column with a precision of 10 and a scale of 2, the value of the TYPE_NAME column might be DECIMAL() and the complete type specification would be DECIMAL(10,2)
IS_NULLABLE	Boolean	True if the data type is Nullable, False if the data type is not Nullable, and Null if it is not known whether the data type is Nullable.
CASE_SENSITIVE	Boolean	True if the data type is a character type and is case sensitive, or False if the data type is not a character type or is not case sensitive.
SEARCHABLE	Long	Identifies whether the column can be used in WHERE clauses, and will be one of the DB_SEARCHABLE constants as shown in Appendix B.
UNSIGNED_ATTRIBUTE	Boolean	True if the data type is unsigned, False if the data type is signed, or Null if not applicable to data type.
FIXED_PREC_SCALE	Boolean	True if the data type has a fixed precision and scale, or False if the data type does not have a fixed precision and scale.
AUTO_UNIQUE_VALUE	Boolean	True if values of this type can be auto-incrementing, or False if values of this type cannot be auto-incrementing.

Appendices

Column name	Type	Description
LOCAL_TYPE_NAME	String	Localized version of TYPE_NAME, or Null if a localized name is not supported by the data provider.
MINIMUM_SCALE	Integer	The minimum number of digits allowed to the right of the decimal point, for decimal and numeric data types. Otherwise, this is Null.
MAXIMUM_SCALE	Integer	The maximum number of digits allowed to the right of the decimal point, for a decimal and numeric data types. Otherwise, this is Null.
GUID	GUID	The GUID of the type. All types supported by a provider are described in a type library, so each type has a corresponding GUID.
TYPELIB	String	The type library containing the description of this type.
VERSION	String	The version of the type definition. Providers may wish to version type definitions. Different providers may use different version schemes, such as a timestamp or number (integer or float), or Null if not supported.
IS_LONG	Boolean	True if the data type is a BLOB that contains very long data; or False if the data type is a BLOB that does not contain very long data or is not a BLOB. The definition of very long data is provider-specific.
BEST_MATCH	Boolean	True if the data type is the best match between all data types in the data source and the OLEDB data type indicated by the value in the DATA_TYPE column, or False if the data type is not the best match.
IS_FIXEDLENGTH	Boolean	True if columns of this type created by the DDL will be of fixed length. False if columns of this type created by the DDL will be of variable length. If the field is Null, it is not known whether the provider will map this field with a fixed or variable length.

adSchemaReferentialConstraints

This identifies the referential integrity constraints for the catalog.

Column name	Type	Description
CONSTRAINT_CATALOG	String	Catalog name, or Null if the provider does not support catalogs.
CONSTRAINT_SCHEMA	String	Schema name, or Null if the provider does not support schemas.
CONSTRAINT_NAME	String	Constraint name.
UNIQUE_CONSTRAINT_ CATALOG	String	Catalog name in which the unique or primary key constraint is defined, or Null if the provider does not support catalogs.
UNIQUE_CONSTRAINT_ SCHEMA	String	Unqualified schema name in which the unique or primary key constraint is defined, or Null if the provider does not support schemas.
UNIQUE_CONSTRAINT_ NAME	String	Unique or primary key constraint name.
MATCH_OPTION	String	The type of match that was specified.
UPDATE_RULE	String	The action if an UPDATE rule was specified. This will be Null only if the provider cannot determine the UPDATE_RULE. In most cases, this implies a default of NO ACTION.
DELETE_RULE	String	The action if a DELETE rule was specified. This will be Null if the provider cannot determine the DELETE_RULE. In most cases, this implies a default of NO ACTION.
DESCRIPTION	String	Human-readable description of the constraint.

For MATCH_OPTION, the values will be one of:

- ❑ NONE – No match type was specified
- ❑ PARTIAL – A match type of PARTIAL was specified
- ❑ FULL – A match type of FULL was specified

For UPDATE_RULE and DELETE_RULE, the value will be one of the following:

- ❑ CASCADE – A referential action of CASCADE was specified
- ❑ SET NULL – A referential action of SET NULL was specified
- ❑ SET DEFAULT – A referential action of SET DEFAULT was specified
- ❑ NO ACTION – A referential action of NO ACTION was specified

Appendices

adSchemaSchemata

This identifies the schemas that are owned by a particular user.

Column name	Type	Description
CATALOG_NAME	String	Catalog name, or Null if the provider does not support catalogs.
SCHEMA_NAME	String	Unqualified schema name.
SCHEMA_OWNER	String	User that owns the schemas.
DEFAULT_CHARACTER_ SET_CATALOG	String	Catalog name of the default character set for columns and domains in the schemas, or Null if the provider does not support catalogs or different character sets.
DEFAULT_CHARACTER_ SET_SCHEMA	String	Unqualified schema name of the default character set for columns and domains in the schemas, or Null if the provider does not support different character sets.
DEFAULT_CHARACTER_ SET_NAME	String	Default character set name, or Null if the provider does not support different character sets.

adSchemaSets

Identifies the named sets in the schema or catalog.

Column name	Type	Description
CATALOG_NAME	String	Catalog name, or Null if the provider does not support catalogs.
SCHEMA_NAME	String	Schema name, or Null if the provider does not support schemas.
CUBE_NAME	String	Name of the cube to which the set belongs.
SET_NAME	String	The name of the set, as specified by the CREATE SET statement.
SCOPE	Integer	Can be one of: MDSET_ SCOPE _GLOBAL, for global scope; MDSET_SCOPE_SESSION, for session only scope.
DESCRIPTION	String	The description of the set.

adSchemaSQLLanguages

This identifies the conformance levels and other options supported by the catalog.

Column name	Type	Description
SQL_LANGUAGE_SOURCE	String	Should be "ISO 9075" for standard SQL.
SQL_LANGUAGE_YEAR	String	Should be "1992" for ANSI SQL92-compliant SQL.
SQL_LANGUAGE_CONFORMANCE	String	The language conformance level.
SQL_LANGUAGE_INTEGRITY	String	This will be Yes if the optional integrity feature is supported, or No if the optional integrity feature is not supported.
SQL_LANGUAGE_ IMPLEMENTATION	String	Null for "ISO 9075" implementation.
SQL_LANGUAGE_BINDING_ STYLE	String	"DIRECT" for C/C++ callable direct execution of SQL.
SQL_LANGUAGE_ PROGRAMMING_ LANGUAGE	String	Null.

SQL_LANGUAGE_CONFORMANCE will be one of the following values:

❑ ENTRY – for entry level conformance

❑ INTERMEDIATE – for intermediate conformance

❑ FULL – for full conformance

adSchemaStatistics

This identifies the catalog statistics.

Column name	Type	Description
TABLE_CATALOG	String	Catalog name, or Null if the provider does not support catalogs.
TABLE_SCHEMA	String	Schema name, or Null if the provider does not support schemas.
TABLE_NAME	String	Table name.
CARDINALITY	Unsigned Big Integer	Cardinality (number of rows) of the table.

adSchemaTableConstraints

This identifies the referential table constraints.

Column name	Type	Description
CONSTRAINT_CATALOG	String	Catalog name, or Null if the provider does not support catalogs.
CONSTRAINT_SCHEMA	String	Schema name, or Null if the provider does not support schemas.
CONSTRAINT_NAME	String	Constraint name.
TABLE_CATALOG	String	Catalog name in which the table is defined, or Null if the provider does not support catalogs.
TABLE_SCHEMA	String	Unqualified schema name in which the table is defined, or Null if the provider does not support schemas.
TABLE_NAME	String	Table name.
CONSTRAINT_TYPE	String	The constraint type.
IS_DEFERRABLE	Boolean	True if the table constraint is deferrable, or False if the table constraint is not deferrable.
INITIALLY_DEFERRED	Boolean	True if the table constraint is initially deferred, or False if the table constraint is initially immediate.
DESCRIPTION	String	Column description.

CONSTRAINT_TYPE will be one of the following values:

- ❏ UNIQUE – for a unique constraint
- ❏ PRIMARY KEY – for a primary key constraint
- ❏ FOREIGN KEY – for a foreign key constraint
- ❏ CHECK – for a check constraint

adSchemaTablePrivileges

This identifies the user privileges of tables.

Column name	Type	Description
GRANTOR	String	User who granted the privileges on the table in TABLE_NAME.
GRANTEE	String	User name (or "PUBLIC") to whom the privilege has been granted.
TABLE_CATALOG	String	Catalog name in which the table is defined, or Null if the provider does not support catalogs.

Column name	Type	Description
TABLE_SCHEMA	String	Unqualified schema name in which the table is defined, or Null if the provider does not support schemas.
TABLE_NAME	String	Table name.
PRIVILEGE_TYPE	String	Privilege type.
IS_GRANTABLE	Boolean	False if the privilege being described was granted with the WITH GRANT OPTION clause, or True if the privilege being described was not granted with the WITH GRANT OPTION clause.

PRIVILEGE_TYPE will be one of the following values:

- ❏ SELECT – for SELECT privileges
- ❏ DELETE – for DELETE privileges
- ❏ INSERT – for INSERT privileges
- ❏ UPDATE – for UPDATE privileges
- ❏ REFERENCES – for REFERENCE privileges

adSchemaTables

This identifies the tables in a catalog.

Column name	Type	Description
TABLE_CATALOG	String	Catalog name, or Null if the provider does not support catalogs.
TABLE_SCHEMA	String	Schema name, or Null if the provider does not support schemas.
TABLE_NAME	String	Table name. This column cannot contain a Null.
TABLE_TYPE	String	Table type. This column cannot contain a Null.
TABLE_GUID	GUID	GUID that uniquely identifies the table. Providers that do not use GUIDs to identify tables should return Null in this column.
DESCRIPTION	String	Human-readable description of the table, or Null if there is no description associated with the column.
TABLE_PROPID	Long	Property ID of the table. Providers that do not use PROPIDs to identify columns should return Null in this column.

Column name	Type	Description
DATE_CREATED	Date/Time	Date when the table was created or Null if the provider does not have this information.
DATE_MODIFIED	Date/Time	Date when the table definition was last modified or Null if the provider does not have this information.

TABLE_TYPE will be on of the following, or a provider-specific value.

- ❑ ALIAS – the table is an alias
- ❑ TABLE – the table is a normal table
- ❑ SYNONYM – the table is a synonym
- ❑ SYSTEM TABLE – the table is a system table
- ❑ VIEW – the table is a view
- ❑ GLOBAL TEMPORARY – the table is a global, temporary table
- ❑ LOCAL TEMPORARY – the table is a local, temporary table

Provider specific values should be defined in the provider documentation. For example, Access returns PASS-THROUGH for linked tables.

adSchemaTranslations

This identifies character translations that the catalog supports.

Column name	Type	Description
TRANSLATION_CATALOG	String	Catalog name, or Null if the provider does not support catalogs.
TRANSLATION_SCHEMA	String	Schema name, or Null if the provider does not support schemas.
TRANSLATION_NAME	String	Translation name.
SOURCE_CHARACTER_SET_CATALOG	String	Catalog name containing the source character set on which the translation is defined, or Null if the provider does not support catalogs.
SOURCE_CHARACTER_SET_SCHEMA	String	Unqualified schema name containing the source character set on which the translation is defined, or Null if the provider does not support schemas.

Column name	Type	Description
SOURCE_CHARACTER_SET_NAME	String	Source character set name on which the translation is defined.
TARGET_CHARACTER_SET_CATALOG	String	Catalog name containing the target character set on which the translation is defined, or Null if the provider does not support catalogs.
TARGET_CHARACTER_SET_SCHEMA	String	Unqualified schema name containing the target character set on which the translation is defined, or Null if the provider does not support schemas.
TARGET_CHARACTER_SET_NAME	String	Target character set name on which the translation is defined.

adSchemaUsagePrivileges

This identifies the usage privileges that are available to a user.

Column name	Type	Description
GRANTOR	String	User who granted the privileges on the object in OBJECT_NAME.
GRANTEE	String	User name (or "PUBLIC") to whom the privilege has been granted.
OBJECT_CATALOG	String	Catalog name in which the object is defined, or Null if the provider does not support catalogs.
OBJECT_SCHEMA	String	Unqualified schema name in which the object is defined, or Null if the provider does not support schemas.
OBJECT_NAME	String	Object name.
OBJECT_TYPE	String	Object type.
PRIVILEGE_TYPE	String	Privilege type.
IS_GRANTABLE	Boolean	True if the privilege being described was granted with the WITH GRANT OPTION clause, or False if the privilege being described was not granted with the WITH GRANT OPTION clause.

OBJECT_TYPE will be one of the following values:

- ❑ DOMAIN – the object is a domain
- ❑ CHARACTER SET – the object is a character set
- ❑ COLLATION – the object is a collation
- ❑ TRANSLATION – the object is a translation

adSchemaViewColumnUsage

This identifies the columns used in views.

Column name	Type	Description
VIEW_CATALOG	String	Catalog name, or Null if the provider does not support catalogs.
VIEW_SCHEMA	String	Schema name, or Null if the provider does not support schemas.
VIEW_NAME	String	View name.
TABLE_CATALOG	String	Catalog name in which the table is defined, or Null if the provider does not support catalogs.
TABLE_SCHEMA	String	Schema name in which the table is defined, or Null if the provider does not support schemas.
TABLE_NAME	String	Table name.
COLUMN_NAME	String	Column name.
COLUMN_GUID	GUID	Column GUID.
COLUMN_PROPID	Long	Column property ID.

adSchemaViews

This identifies the views in the catalog.

Column name	Type	Description
TABLE_CATALOG	String	Catalog name, or Null if the provider does not support catalogs.
TABLE_SCHEMA	String	Schema name, or Null if the provider does not support schemas.
TABLE_NAME	String	View name.
VIEW_DEFINITION	String	View definition. This is a query expression.
CHECK_OPTION	Boolean	True if local update checking only, or False for cascaded update checking (same as no CHECK OPTION specified on view definition).
IS_UPDATABLE	Boolean	True if the view is updateable, or False if the view is not updateable.
DESCRIPTION	String	View description.
DATE_CREATED	Date/Time	Date when the view was created or Null if the provider does not have this information.
DATE_MODIFIED	Date/Time	Date when the view definition was last modified or Null if the provider does not have this information.

adSchemaViewTableUsage

This identifies the tables used in views.

Column name	Type	Description
VIEW_CATALOG	String	Catalog name, or Null if the provider does not support catalogs.
VIEW_SCHEMA	String	Schema name, or Null if the provider does not support schemas.
VIEW_NAME	String	View name.
TABLE_CATALOG	String	Catalog name in which the table is defined, or Null if the provider does not support catalogs.
TABLE_SCHEMA	String	Schema name in which the table is defined, or Null if the provider does not support schemas.
TABLE_NAME	String	Table name.

Appendices

A

I thank God I am as honest as any man
living that is an old man and no honester th...

Can counsel and speak comfort to th...
which they themselves not feel

Much Ado About Nothing.

He wears his faith but as the fashion of

As merry as the day

He hath indeed better bettered expectation

(Act i. Sc. i.).

He wears his faith but as the fashion of his hat.
(Ibid)

As merry as the day is long.

th indeed better bettered expectation

(Act i. Sc. i.).
(Ibid)

Can counsel and speak comfort to that grief

Much Ado About Nothing.

Which they themselves not feel.

He wears his faith but as the fashion of his hat.
(Ibid)
(Ibid)

I was not born under

a rhyming plane...

I was not born under a rhyming plan...

For there was never yet
That could endure the t...

merry as the day is long

Can counsel and speak comfort to that grief
(Ibid)

Which they themselves not feel.

He hath indeed better bettered expectation

(Act i. Sc. i.).

I thank God I am as honest as any
living that is an old man and no hones...

He wears his faith but as the fashion of his h...
(Ib

Much Ado About Nothing.

For there was never yet philospher
That could endure the toothache patiently.
(Ibid)

For there was never yet philospher
That could endure the toothache patiently.

I was not born u...

online discussion at http://p2p.wrox.com

E

ADO Data Types

You might find the large array of data types supported by ADO confusing, especially since your language or database might not support them all. This appendix details how the DataTypeEnum constants listed in Appendix B map to SQL and Access data types and the data types use in Visual Basic and Visual C++.

ODBC to Access 97

Database Type	ADO Type
Text	adVarChar
Memo	adLongVarChar
Number (Byte)	adUnsignedTinyTnt
Number (Integer)	adSmallInt
Number (Long Integer)	adInteger
Number (Single)	adSingle
Number (Double)	adDouble
Number (Replication ID)	adGUID
Date/Time	adDBTimeStamp
Currency	adCurrency
Long Integer	adInteger
Yes/No	adBoolean
OLE Object	adLongVarBinary
Hyperlink	adLongVarChar

ODBC to Access 2000

Database Type	ADO Type
Text	adVarWChar
Memo	adLongVarWChar
Number (Byte)	adUnsignedTinyInt
Number (Integer)	adSmallInt
Number (Long Integer)	adInteger
Number (Single)	adSingle
Number (Double)	adDouble
Number (Replication ID)	adGUID
Number (Decimal)	adNumeric
Date/Time	adDBTimeStamp
Currency	adCurrency
AutoNumber	adInteger
Yes/No	adBoolean
OLE Object	adLongVarBinary
Hyperlink	adLongVarWChar

ODBC to SQL 6.5

Database Type	ADO Type
binary	adBinary
bit	adBoolean
char	adChar
datetime	adDBTimeStamp
decimal	adNumeric
float	adDouble
image	adLongVarBinary
int	adInteger
money	adCurrency
numeric	adNumeric
real	adSingle
smalldatetime	adDBTimeStamp
smallint	adSmallInt
smallmoney	adCurrency
sysname	adVarChar
text	adLongVarChar
timestamp	adBinary
tinyint	adUnsignedTinyInt
varbinary	adVarBinary
varchar	adVarChar

ODBC to SQL 7.0 / 2000

Database Type	ADO Type
binary	adBinary
bit	adBoolean
char	adChar
datetime	adDBTimeStamp
decimal	adNumeric
float	adDouble
image	adLongVarBinary
int	adInteger
money	adCurrency
nchar	adWChar
ntext	adLongVarWChar
numeric	adNumeric
nvarchar	adVarWChar
real	adSingle
smalldatetime	adDBTimeStamp
smallint	adSmallInt
smallmoney	adCurrency
text	adLongVarChar
timestamp	adBinary
tinyint	adUnsignedTinyInt
uniqueidentifier	adGUID
varbinary	adVarBinary
varchar	adVarChar

Native Jet Provider to Access 97

Database Type	ADO Type
Text	adVarWChar
Memo	adLongVarWChar
Number (Byte)	adUnsignedTinyInt
Number (Integer)	adSmallInt
Number (Long Integer)	adInteger
Number (Single)	adSingle
Number (Double)	adDouble
Number (Replication ID)	adGUID
Date/Time	adDate
Currency	adCurrency
Long Integer	adInteger
Yes/No	adBoolean
OLE Object	adLongVarBinary
Hyperlink	adLongVarWChar

Appendices

A

Native Jet Provider to Access 2000

Database Type	ADO Type
Text	adVarWChar
Memo	adLongVarWChar
Number (Byte)	adUnsignedTinyInt
Number (Integer)	adSmallInt
Number (Long Integer)	adInteger
Number (Single)	adSingle
Number (Double)	adDouble
Number (Replication ID)	adGUID
Number (Decimal)	adNumeric
Date/Time	adDate
Currency	adCurrency
AutoNumber	adInteger
Yes/No	adBoolean
OLE Object	adLongVarBinary
Hyperlink	adLongVarWChar

Native SQL Provider to SQL Server 6.5

Database Type	ADO Type
binary	adBinary
bit	adBoolean
char	adChar
datetime	adDBTimeStamp
decimal	adNumeric
float	adDouble
image	adLongVarBinary
int	adInteger
money	adCurrency
numeric	adNumeric
real	adSingle
smalldatetime	adDBTimeStamp
smallint	adSmallInt
smallmoney	adCurrency
sysname	adVarChar
text	adLongVarChar
timestamp	adBinary
tinyint	adUnsignedTinyInt
varbinary	adVarBinary
varchar	adVarChar

Native SQL Provider to SQL Server 7.0 / 2000

Database Type	ADO Type
binary	adBinary
bit	adBoolean
char	adChar
datetime	adDBTimeStamp
decimal	adNumeric
float	adDouble
image	adLongVarBinary
int	adInteger
money	adCurrency
nchar	adWChar
ntext	adLongVarWChar
numeric	adNumeric
nvarchar	adVarWChar
real	adSingle
smalldatetime	adDBTimeStamp
smallint	adSmallInt
smallmoney	adCurrency
text	adLongVarChar
timestamp	adBinary
tinyint	adUnsignedTinyInt
uniqueidentifier	adGUID
varbinary	adVarBinary
varchar	adVarChar

Language Types

The following table lists the data types you should use in your programming language.

A blank value indicates that the language does not natively support the data type, although there may be support in other libraries, or other data types might be used instead.

Constant	Visual Basic	Visual C++
adBinary	Variant	
adBoolean	Boolean	bool
adChar	String	char[]

Appendices

A

Constant	Visual Basic	Visual C++
adCurrency	Currency	
adDate	Date	
adDBTimeStamp	Variant	
adDouble	Double	double
adGUID		char[]
adInteger	Long	int
adLongVarBinary	Variant	
adLongVarChar	String	
adNumeric		
adSingle	Single	float
adSmallInt	Integer	short
adUnsignedTinyInt	Byte	char
adVarBinary		char[]
adVarChar	String	char[]
adVarWChar	String	char[]

I thank God I am as honest as any man
living that is an old man and no honester th

Can counsel and speak comfort to th
Which they themselves not feel.

Much Ado About Nothing.

He wears his faith but as the fashion of h

As merry as the day

He hath indeed better bettered expectation

(Act i. Sc. i).

He wears his faith but as the fashion of his hat.
(Ibid)

As merry as the day is long.

h indeed better bettered expectation

(Act i. Sc. i).   (Ibid)

an counsel and speak comfort to that grief

Much Ado About Nothing.

Which they themselves not feel.

He wears his faith but as the fashion of his hat.
(Ibid)   (Ibid)

I was not born under

a rhyming plane

I was not born under a rhyming plane
(sc. 2

For there was never yet p
That could endure the too

merry as the day is long

Can counsel and speak comfort to that grief

Which they themselves not feel.
(Ibid)

He hath indeed better bettered expectation

(A

I thank God I am as honest as an

living that is an old man and no honest

He wears his faith but as the fashion of his ha
(Ibic

Much Ado About Nothing.

For there was never yet philospher
That could endure the toothache patiently.
(Ibid)

themselves not feel.

(Ibid)

I was not born u

RDS Object Summary

The Remote Data Service (RDS) provides a set of objects that can be used to allow a client machine to access data remotely over HTTP protocol. This section lists the properties, methods and events for two RDS controls – the **RDS/ADC Data Source Object** (DSO) and the **Tabular Data Control** (TDC). It also lists the properties, methods, events and constants for the DataSpace and DataFactory objects that are used by the RDS/ADC control.

> **All properties are read/write unless otherwise stated.**

The RDS Advanced Data Control (RDS ADC)

The RDS/ADC Data Control is used on the client to provide read/write access to a data store or custom business object on the server. To instantiate the control in a web page, an <OBJECT> tag is used:

```
<OBJECT CLASSID="clsid:BD96C556-65A3-11D0-983A-00C04FC29E33"
        ID="dsoBookList" HEIGHT=0 WIDTH=0>
  <PARAM NAME="Server" VALUE="http://www.yourserver.com">
  <PARAM NAME="Connect" VALUE="DSN=yourdsn;UID=anon;PWD=">
  <PARAM NAME="SQL" VALUE="SELECT * FROM BookList">
</OBJECT>
```

The <PARAM> elements are used to set the properties of the control at design time. They can be changed at run-time using script code. The following tables list the properties, methods, and events for the control.

Properties of the RDS ADC	Return Type	Description
Connect	String	The data store connection string or DSN.
ExecuteOptions	Integer	Specifies if the control will execute asynchronously. Can be one of the adcExecuteOptionEnum constants, as detailed in Appendix G.
FetchOptions	Integer	Specifies if the data will be fetched asynchronously. Can be one of the adcFetchoptionenum constants, as detailed in Appendix G.
FilterColumn	String	Name of the column to filter on.
FilterCriterion	String	The criterion for the filter, can be <, <=, >, >=, =, or <>.
FilterValue	String	The value to match values in FilterColumn with when filtering.
Handler	String	Specifies the server-side security handler to use with the control if not the default.
InternetTimeout	Long	Indicates the timeout (in milliseconds) for the HTTP connection.
ReadyState	Integer	Indicates the state of the control as data is received. Can be one of the adcReadyStateEnum constants, as detailed in Appendix G. Read-only.
Recordset	Object	Provides a reference to the ADO Recordset object in use by the control. Read-only.
Server	String	Specifies the communication protocol and the address of the server to execute the query on.
SortColumn	String	Name of the column to sort on.
SortDirection	Boolean	The sort direction for the column. The default is ascending order (True). Use False for descending order.
SourceRecordset	Object	Can be used to bind the control to a different Recordset object at run time. Write-only.
SQL	String	The SQL statement used to extract the data from the data store.
URL	String	URL to the path of the file.

Methods of the RDS ADC	Description
Cancel	Cancels an asynchronous action such as fetching data.
CancelUpdate	Cancels all changes made to the source recordset.
CreateRecordSet	Creates and returns an empty, disconnected recordset on the client.
MoveFirst	Moves to the first record in a displayed recordset.
MoveLast	Moves to the last record in a displayed recordset.
MoveNext	Moves to the next record in a displayed recordset.
MovePrevious	Moves to the previous record in a displayed recordset.
Refresh	Refreshes the client-side recordset from the data source.
Reset	Updates the local recordset to reflect current filter and sort criteria.
SubmitChanges	Sends changes to the client-side recordset back to the data store.

Methods Syntax

```
datacontrol.Cancel
datacontrol.CancelUpdate
(Set) object = datacontrol.CreateRecordSet(varColumnInfos As Variant)
datacontrol.Recordset.MoveFirst
datacontrol.Recordset.MoveLast
datacontrol.Recordset.MoveNext
datacontrol.Recordset.MovePrevious
datacontrol.Refresh
datacontrol.Reset(refilter As Integer)
datacontrol.SubmitChanges
```

Events of the RDS ADC	Description
onerror	Occurs if an error prevents the data being fetched from the server, or a user action being carried out.
onreadystatechange	Occurs when the value of the ReadyState property changes.

Events Syntax

```
onError(StatusCode, Description, Source, CancelDisplay)
onReadyStateChange()
```

The Tabular Data Control

The Tabular Data Control (TDC) uses a formatted text file that is downloaded to the client and exposed there as an ADO recordset. The control cannot be used to update the server data store. To instantiate the control in a web page, an <OBJECT> tag is used:

```
<OBJECT CLASSID="clsid:333C7BC4-460F-11D0-BC04-0080C7055A83"
        ID="dsoBookList" WIDTH=0 HEIGHT=0>
  <PARAM NAME="DataURL" VALUE="/data/booklist.txt">
  <PARAM NAME="FieldDelim" VALUE=";">
  <PARAM NAME="UseHeader" VALUE="true">
  <PARAM NAME="Sort" VALUE="tCategory; -dReleasedate">
  <PARAM NAME="Filter" VALUE="tCode=16-1*" >
  <PARAM NAME="EscapeChar" VALUE="\">
</OBJECT>
```

The <PARAM> elements are used to set the properties of the control at design time. They can be changed at run-time using script code. The following tables list the properties, methods, and events for the control.

Properties of the TDC	Return Type	Description
AppendData	Boolean	If True, specifies that the Reset method will attempt to append returned data to the existing recordset rather than replacing the recordset. Default value is False.
CaseSensitive	Boolean	Specifies whether string comparisons will be case sensitive. Default is True.
CharSet	String	Specifies the character set for the data. Default is windows-1252 (Western).
DataURL	String	The URL or location of the source text data file.
EscapeChar	String	Single character string that is used to avoid the meaning of the other special characters specified by the FieldDelim, RowDelim, and TextQualifier properties.
FieldDelim	String	Specifies the character in the file that delimits each column (field). Default – if none specified – is a comma. Only a single character may be used.
Filter	String	Specifies the complete filter that will be applied to the data, such as "Name=Jonson". An asterisk acts as a wildcard for any set of characters.
FilterColumn	String	Name of the column to filter on. Not supported in all versions of the TDC.

Properties of the TDC	Return Type	Description
Filter Criterion	String	The criterion for the filter, can be <, <=, >, >=, =, or <>. Not supported in all versions of the TDC.
FilterValue	String	The value to match values in FilterColumn with when filtering. Not supported in all versions of the TDC.
Language	String	Specifies the language of the data file. Default is en-us (US English).
ReadyState	Integer	Indicates the state of the control as data is received. Can be one of the adcReadyStateEnum constants, as detailed in Appendix G. Read-only.
RowDelim	String	Specifies the character in the file that delimits each row (record). Default if not specified is a carriage return. Only a single character may be used.
Sort	String	Specifies the sort order for the data, as a comma-delimited list of column names. Prefix column name with a minus sign (-) for descending order.
SortAscending	Boolean	The sort direction for the column. The default is ascending order (True). Use False for descending order. Not supported in all versions of the TDC.
SortColumn	String	Name of the column to sort on. Not supported in all versions of the TDC.
TextQualifier	String	The character in the data file used to enclose field values. Default is the double-quote (") character.
UseHeader	Boolean	If True, specifies that the first line of the data file is a set of column (field) names and (optionally) the field data type definitions.

Methods of the TDC	Description
Reset	Updates the local recordset to reflect current filter and sort criteria.

Events of the TDC	Description
onreadystatechange	Occurs when the value of the ReadyState property changes.

The RDS DataSpace Object

The `DataSpace` object is responsible for caching the recordset on the client, and connecting it to a data source control. To instantiate the object in a web page, an `<OBJECT>` tag is used:

```
<OBJECT ID="dspDataSpace"
        CLASSID="CLSID:BD96C556-65A3-11D0-983A-00C04FC29E36">
</OBJECT>
```

A `DataSpace` object is also created automatically when a data source object (such as the RDS/ADC) is instantiated. The `DataSpace` object exposes one property and one method:

Properties of the RDS DataSpace Object	Return Type	Description
`InternetTimeout`	`Long`	Indicates the timeout (in milliseconds) for the HTTP connection.

Methods of the RDS Dataspace Object	Description
`CreateObject`	Creates a data factory or custom object of type specified by a class string, at a location specified by the connection (address) parameter.

Methods Syntax

```
variant = dataspace.CreateObject(bstrProgId As String,
                                 bstrConnection As String)
```

For a connection over HTTP, the connection parameter is the URL of the server, while over DCOM the UNC machine name is used. When the `CreateObject` method is used to create in-process objects, the connection should be a `Null` string.

The RDS DataFactory Object

The `DataFactory` object handles transport of the data from server to client and vice versa. It creates a stub and proxy that can communicate over HTTP. To instantiate the object, the `CreateObject` method of an existing `DataSpace` control is used. The class string for the `DataFactory` object is `RDSServer.DataFactory`, and the address of the server on which the object is to be created must also be provided:

```
<OBJECT ID="dspDataSpace"
        CLASSID="CLSID:BD96C556-65A3-11D0-983A-00C04FC29E36">
</OBJECT>
...
<SCRIPT LANGUAGE="JavaScript">
  <myDataFactory = dspDataSpace.CreateObject("RDSServer.DataFactory",
                                    "http://servername.com");
</SCRIPT>
```

A `DataFactory` object is also created automatically when a data source object (such as the RDS ADC) is instantiated. The `DataFactory` object provides four methods:

Methods of the RDS Datafactory Object	Return Type	Description
ConvertToString	String	Converts a recordset into a MIME64-encoded string.
CreateRecordSet	Object	Creates and returns an empty recordset.
Query	Object	Executes a valid SQL string query over a specified connection and returns an ADO recordset object.
SubmitChanges		Marshals the records and submits them to the server for updating the source data store.

Methods Syntax

```
string = datafactory.ConvertToString(recordset As Object)
(Set) recordset = datafactory.CreateRecordSet(varColumnInfos
                                        As Variant)
(Set) recordset = datafactory.Query(bstrConnection As String,
                                bstrQuery As String)
datafactory.SubmitChanges(bstrConnection As String,
                    pRecordset As Object)
```

I thank God I am as honest as any man
living that is an old man and no honester th

Much Ado About Nothing.

For there was never yet philospher
That could endure the toothache patiently.

Can counsel and speak comfort to th
which they themselves not feel

He wears his faith but as the fashion of h

As merry as the day

He hath indeed better bettered expectation

(Act i. Sc. i.).

He wears his faith but as the fashion of his hat.
(Ibid)

As merry as the day is long.

h indeed better bettered expectation

(Act i. Sc. i.).

(Ibid)

Much Ado About Nothing.

an counsel and speak comfort to that grief

Which they themselves not feel.

He wears his faith but as the fashion of his hat.
(Ibid)

(Ibid)

I was not born under

a rhyming plane

I was not born under a rhyming plane
(sc. 2

For there was never yet p
That could endure the too

merry as the day is long

(sc. 2

Can counsel and speak comfort to that grief

(Ibid)

Which they themselves not feel.

He hath indeed better bettered expectation

(Ibid)

I thank God I am as honest as an

living that is an old man and no honest

He wears his faith but as the fashion of his ha
(Ibid

Much Ado About Nothing.

For there was never yet philospher
That could endure the toothache patiently.

(Ibid)

I was not born u

G

RDS Constants

RDS Constants

adcExecuteOptionEnum

Name	Value	Description
adcExecAsync	2	The next Refresh of the recordset is executed asynchronously.
adcExecSync	1	The next Refresh of the recordset is executed synchronously.

adcFetchOptionEnum

Name	Value	Description
adcFetchAsync	3	Records are fetched in the background and control is returned to the application immediately. Attempts to access a record not yet read will cause control to return immediately, and the nearest record to the sought record returned. This indicates that the end of the recordset has been reached, even though there may be more records.
adcFetchBackground	2	The first batch of records is read and control returns to the application. Access to records not in the first batch will cause a wait until the requested record is fetched.
adcFetchUpFront	1	The complete recordset is fetched before control is returned to the application.

adcReadyStateEnum

Name	Value	Description
adcReadyState Complete	4	All rows have been fetched.
adcReadyState Interactive	3	Rows are still being fetched, although some rows are available.
adcReadyStateLoaded	2	The recordset is not available for use as the rows are still being loaded.

ADCPROP_UPDATECRITERIA_ENUM

Name	Value	Description
adCriteriaAllCols	1	Collisions should be detected if there is a change to any column.
adCriteriaKey	0	Collisions should be detected if there is a change to the key column.
adCriteriaTimeStamp	3	Collisions should be detected if a row has been accessed.
adCriteriaUpdCols	2	Collisions should be detected if there is a change to columns being updated.

I thank God I am as honest as any man
living that is an old man and no honester th

Can counsel and speak comfort to th
Which they themselves not feel

Much Ado About Nothing.

He wears his faith but as the fashion of
As merry as the day
He hath indeed better bettered expectation

(Act i. Sc. 1.).

He wears his faith but as the fashion of his hat.
(Ibid)

As merry as the day is long.
th indeed better bettered expectation

(Act i. Sc. 1.) (Ibid)
Much Ado About Nothing.

an counsel and speak comfort to that grief
Which they themselves not feel.

He wears his faith but as the fashion of his hat.
(Ibid)
(Ibid)

I was not born under
a rhyming plane

I was not born under a rhyming plan
sc.

For there was never yet
That could endure the to

merry as the day is long (sc. 2)
Can counsel and speak comfort to that grief
Which they themselves not feel.
(Ibid)
He hath indeed better bettered expectation
(Ibid)
I thank God I am as honest as any
living that is an old man and no honest

He wears his faith but as the fashion of his ha
(Ibi

Much Ado About Nothing.
For there was never yet philospher
That could endure the toothache patiently.
(Ibid)

I was not born u

ADOX Object Summary

This appendix contains details of the Microsoft ActiveX Data Objects 2.5 Extensions for DDL and Security Library.

The ADOX Objects

Name	Description
Catalog	Acts as a parent for the Tables, Groups, Users, Procedures, and Views collections.
Column	An individual Column in a Table, Index, or Key.
Columns	Contains one or more Column objects.
Group	An individual Group account describing data store permissions, and containing a Users collection describing the members of the group.
Groups	Contains one or more Group objects.
Index	An individual index on a Table, containing a Columns collection describing the columns that comprise the index.
Indexes	Contains one or more Index objects.
Key	An individual Key representing a primary or foreign key for a table, and containing a Columns collection to describe the columns that the Key comprises.
Keys	Contains one or more Key objects.
Procedure	Describes a stored procedure, and contains an ADO Command object to obtain the details of the procedure.
Procedures	Contains one or more Procedure objects.
Properties	Contains one or more Property objects.
Property	Describes an individual property of a particular object.
Table	Describes an individual data store table, and contains Columns, Indexes, Keys, and Properties collections.

Name	Description
Tables	Contains one or more `Table` objects.
User	An individual `User` account describing an authorized user of the data store, and containing a `Groups` collection to indicate the groups to which the user belongs.
Users	Contains one or more `User` objects.
View	Describes a virtual table, or a filtered set of records from the data store, and contains an ADO `Command` object to obtain the exact details of the view.
Views	Contains one or more `View` objects.

The Catalog Object

Methods of the Catalog Object	Return Type	Description
Create	Variant	Creates a new catalog, using its argument as a connection string for the catalog.
GetObjectOwner	String	Obtains the name of the user or group that owns a particular catalog object.
SetObjectOwner		Sets the owner for a particular catalog object.

Properties of the Catalog Object	Return Type	Description
ActiveConnection	Object	Sets or returns the ADO `Connection` object or string to which the catalog belongs.

Collections of the Catalog Object	Return Type	Description
Groups	Groups	Contains one or more `Group` objects. Read-only.
Procedures	Procedures	Contains one or more `Procedure` objects. Read-only.
Tables	Tables	Contains one or more `Table` objects. Read-only.
Users	Users	Contains one or more `User` objects. Read-only.
Views	Views	Contains one or more `View` objects. Read-only.

The Column Object

Properties of the Column Object	Return Type	Description
Attributes	Column AttributesEnum	Describes the characteristics of the column.
DefinedSize	Long	Indicates the maximum size for a column.
Name	String	The name of the column.
NumericScale	Byte	The numeric scale of the column. Read-only for existing columns.
ParentCatalog	Catalog	Indicates the Catalog to which the column's parent object belongs.
Precision	Integer	The maximum precision of data in the column. Read-only for existing columns.
RelatedColumn	String	For key columns this indicates the name of the related column in the related table. Read-only for existing columns.
SortOrder	SortOrderEnum	Indicates the order in which the column is sorted. Only applies to columns in an Index.
Type	DataTypeEnum	Identifies the data type of the column. Read-only once the column is appended to a collection.

Collections of the Column Object	Return Type	Description
Properties	Properties	Contains one or more provider specific column properties. Read only

The Columns Collection

Methods of the Columns Collection	Return Type	Description
Append		Appends a Column object to the Columns collection.
Delete		Deletes a Column object from the Columns collection.
Refresh		Updates the Column objects in the Columns collection.

Appendices

A

Properties of the Columns Collection	Return Type	Description
Count	Integer	Indicates the number of Column objects in the Columns collection. Read-only.
Item	Column	Allows indexing into the Columns collection to reference a specific Column object. Read-only.

The Group Object

Methods of the Group Object	Return Type	Description
GetPermissions	Rights Enum	Obtains the permissions on a catalog object for the Group.
SetPermissions		Sets the permissions on a catalog object for the Group.

Properties of the Group Object	Return Type	Description
Name	String	The name of the group.

Collections of the Group Object	Return Type	Description
Users	Users	Contains the User objects that belong to this group. Read-only.
Properties	Properties	Contains a Property object for each provider specific property. Read-only.

The Groups Collection

Methods of the Groups Collection	Return Type	Description
Append		Appends a Group object to the Groups collection.
Delete		Deletes a Group object from the Groups collection.
Refresh		Updates the Group objects in the Groups collection.

Properties of the Groups Collection	Return Type	Description
Count	Integer	Indicates the number of Group objects in the Groups collection. Read-only.
Item	Column	Allows indexing into the Groups collection to reference a specific Group object. Read-only.

The Index Object

Properties of the Index Object	Return Type	Description
Clustered	Boolean	Indicates whether or not the Index is clustered. Read-only on Index objects already appended to a collection.
IndexNulls	Allow Nulls Enum	Indicates whether or not index entries are created for records that have Null values. Read-only on Index objects already appended to a collection.
Name	String	The name of the Index.
PrimaryKey	Boolean	Indicates whether or not the index is the primary key. Read-only on Index objects already appended to a collection.
Unique	Boolean	Indicates whether or not the keys in the Index must be unique. Read-only on Index objects already appended to a collection.

Collections of the Index Object	Return Type	Description
Columns	Columns	Contains one or more Column objects, which make up the Index object. Read-only.
Properties	Properties	Contains provider specific properties for the Index object. Read-only.

The Indexes Collection

Methods of the Indexes Collection	Return Type	Description
Append		Appends an Index object to the Indexes collection.
Delete		Deletes an Index object from the Indexes collection.
Refresh		Updates the Index objects in the Indexes collection.

Properties of the Indexes Collection	Return Type	Description
Count	Integer	Indicates the number of Index objects in the Indexes collection. Read-only.
Item	Column	Allows indexing into the Indexes collection to reference a specific Index object. Read-only.

The Key Object

Properties of the Key Object	Return Type	Description
DeleteRule	RuleEnum	Indicates what happens to the key values when a primary key is deleted. Read-only on Key objects already appended to a collection.
Name	String	The name of the Key.
RelatedTable	String	For foreign keys indicates the name of the foreign table.
Type	KeyType Enum	Specifies the type of the Key. Read-only on Key objects already appended to a collection.
UpdateRule	RuleEnum	Indicates what happens to the key values when a primary key is updated. Read-only on Key objects already appended to a collection.

Collections of the Key Object	Return Type	Description
Columns	Columns	Contains one or more Column objects that make up the Key. Read-only.

The Keys Collection

Methods of the Keys Collection	Return Type	Description
Append		Appends a Key object to the Keys collection.
Delete		Deletes a Key object from the Keys collection.
Refresh		Updates the Key objects in the Keys collection.

Properties of the Keys Collection	Return Type	Description
Count	Integer	Indicates the number of Key objects in the Keys collection. Read only
Item	Column	Allows indexing into the Keys collection to reference a specific Key object. Read only

The Procedure Object

Properties of the Procedure Object	Return Type	Description
Command	Object	Specifies an ADO Command object containing the details of the procedure.
DateCreated	Variant	The date the Procedure was created. Read-only.
DateModified	Variant	The date the Procedure was last modified. Read-only.
Name	String	The name of the Procedure. Read-only.

The Procedures Collection

Methods of the Procedures Collection	Return Type	Description
Append		Appends a Procedure object to the Procedures collection.
Delete		Deletes a Procedure object from the Procedures collection.
Refresh		Updates the Procedure objects in the Procedures collection.

Appendices

A

Properties of the Procedures Collection	Return Type	Description
Count	Integer	Indicates the number of Procedure objects in the Procedures collection. Read-only.
Item	Column	Allows indexing into the Procedures collection to reference a specific Procedure object. Read-only.

The Properties Collection

Methods of the Properties Collection	Return Type	Description
Refresh		Updates the Property objects in the Properties collection.

Properties of the Properties Collection	Return Type	Description
Count	Integer	Indicates the number of Property objects in the Properties collection. Read-only.
Item	Column	Allows indexing into the Properties collection to reference a specific Property object. Read-only.

The Property Object

Properties of the Property Object	Return Type	Description
Attributes	Integer	Indicates one or more characteristics of the Property.
Name	String	The Property Name. Read-only.
Type	Data TypeEnum	The data type of the Property. Read-only.
Value	Variant	The value assigned to the Property.

The Table Object

Properties of the Table Object	Return Type	Description
DateCreated	Variant	The date the Table was created. Read-only.
DateModified	Variant	The date the Table was last modified. Read-only.

580

Properties of the Table Object	Return Type	Description
Name	String	The name of the Table.
ParentCatalog	Catalog	The Catalog to which the Table belongs.
Type	String	Indicates whether the Table is a permanent, temporary, or system table. Read-only.

Collections of the Table Object	Return Type	Description
Columns	Columns	One or more Column objects that make up the Table. Read only.
Indexes	Indexes	Zero or more Index objects that belong to the Table. Read-only.
Keys	Keys	Zero or more Key objects that the Table contains. Read-only
Properties	Properties	One or more Property objects describing provider specific properties. Read-only.

The Tables Collection

Methods of the Tables Collection	Return Type	Description
Append		Appends a Table object to the Tables collection.
Delete		Deletes a Table object from the Tables collection.
Refresh		Updates the Table objects in the Tables collection.

Properties of the Tables Collection	Return Type	Description
Count	Integer	Indicates the number of Table objects in the Tables collection. Read-only.
Item	Column	Allows indexing into the Tables collection to reference a specific Table object. Read-only.

The User Object

Methods of the User Object	Return Type	Description
Change Password		Changes the password for a User.
Get Permissions	Rights Enum	Gets the permissions on a Catalog object for a User.
Set Permissions		Sets the permissions on a Catalog object for a User.

Properties of the User Object	Return Type	Description
Name	String	The user name.

Collections of the User Object	Return Type	Description
Groups	Groups	One or more Group objects, to which the user belongs. Read-only.
Properties	Properties	Contains a Property object for each provider-specific property. Read-only.

The Users Collection

Methods of the Users Collection	Return Type	Description
Append		Appends a User object to the Users collection.
Delete		Deletes a User object from the Users collection.
Refresh		Updates the User objects in the Users collection.

Properties of the Users Collection	Return Type	Description
Count	Integer	Indicates the number of User objects in the Users collection. Read-only.
Item	Column	Allows indexing into the Users collection to reference a specific User object. Read-only.

The View Object

Properties of the View Object	Return Type	Description
Command	Object	Specifies an ADO Command object containing the details of the View.
DateCreated	Variant	The date the View was created. Read-only.
DateModified	Variant	The date the View was last modified. Read-only.
Name	String	The name of the View. Read-only.

The Views Collection

Methods of the Views Collection	Return Type	Description
Append		Appends a View object to the Views collection.
Delete		Deletes a View object from the Views collection.
Refresh		Updates the View objects in the Views collection.

Properties of the Views Collection	Return Type	Description
Count	Integer	Indicates the number of View objects in the Views collection. Read-only.
Item	Column	Allows indexing into the Views collection to reference a specific View object. Read-only.

Method Calls

The Catalog Object

```
Variant = Catalog.Create(ConnectString As String)
String = Catalog.GetObjectOwner(ObjectName As String, _
            ObjectType As ObjectTypeEnum, [ObjectTypeId As Variant])
Catalog.SetObjectOwner(ObjectName As String, _
            ObjectType As ObjectTypeEnum, UserName As String, _
            [ObjectTypeId As Variant])
```

The Columns Collection

```
Columns.Append(Item As Variant, [Type As DataTypeEnum], _
            [DefinedSize As Integer])
Columns.Delete(Item As Variant)
Columns.Refresh
```

Appendices

A

The Group Object

```
RightsEnum = Group.GetPermissions(Name As Variant, _
          ObjectType As ObjectTypeEnum, [ObjectTypeId As Variant])
Group.SetPermissions(Name As Variant, ObjectType As ObjectTypeEnum, _
          Action As ActionEnum, Rights As RightsEnum, _
          [Inherit As InheritTypeEnum], [ObjectTypeId As Variant])
```

The Groups Collection

```
Groups.Append(Item As Variant)
Groups.Delete(Item As Variant)
Groups.Refresh
```

The Indexes Collection

```
Indexes.Append(Item As Variant, [Columns As Variant])
Indexes.Delete(Item As Variant)
Indexes.Refresh
```

The Keys Collection

```
Keys.Append(Item As Variant, [Type As KeyTypeEnum], _
          [Column As Variant], [RelatedTable As String], _
          [RelatedColumn As String])
Keys.Delete(Item As Variant)
Keys.Refresh
```

The Procedures Collection

```
Procedures.Append(Name As String, Command As Object)
Procedures.Delete(Item As Variant)
Procedures.Refresh
```

The Properties Collection

```
Properties.Refresh
```

The Tables Collection

```
Tables.Append(Item As Variant)
Tables.Delete(Item As Variant)
Tables.Refresh
```

The User Object

```
User.ChangePassword(OldPassword As String, NewPassord As String)
RightsEnum = User.GetPermissions(Name As Variant, _
            ObjectType As ObjectTypeEnum, [ObjectTypeId As Variant])
User.SetPermissions(Name As Variant, ObjectType As ObjectTypeEnum, _
            Action As ActionEnum, Rights As RightsEnum, _
            [Inherit As InheritTypeEnum], [ObjectTypeId As Variant])
```

The Users Collection

```
Users.Append(Item As Variant, [Password As String])
Users.Delete(Item As Variant)
Users.Refresh
```

The Views Collection

```
Views.Append(Name As String, Command As Object)
Views.Delete(Item As Variant)
Views.Refresh
```

I thank God I am as honest as any man
living that is an old man and no honester th

Can counsel and speak comfort to th

Much Ado About Nothing.

Which they themselves not feel

He wears his faith but as the fashion of

As merry as the day

He hath indeed better bettered expectation

(Act i. Sc. i.)

He wears his faith but as the fashion of his hat.
(Ibid)

As merry as the day is long.

th indeed better bettered expectation

(Act i. Sc. i.)

(Ibid)

Can counsel and speak comfort to that grief

Which they themselves not feel.

Much Ado About Nothing.

He wears his faith but as the fashion of his hat.
(Ibid)

(Ibid)

I was not born under

a rhyming plane

I was not born under a rhyming plan
(Sc.

For there was never yet
That could endure the t

merry as the day is long

Can counsel and speak comfort to that grief

Which they themselves not feel.

(Ibid)

He hath indeed better bettered expectation

(Ibid)

I thank God I am as honest as an

living that is an old man and no hones

He wears his faith but as the fashion of his ha
(Ibi

themselves not feel.

(Ibid)

Much Ado About Nothing.

For there was never yet philospher
That could endure the toothache patiently.

(Ibid)

I was not born u

ADOX Constants

ActionEnum

Constant Name	Value	Description
adAccessDeny	3	Deny the specific permissions to the Group or User.
adAccessGrant	1	Grant the specific permissions to the Group or User. Other permissions may remain in effect.
adAccessRevoke	4	Revoke any specific access rights to the Group or User.
adAccessSet	2	Set the exact permissions for the Group or User. Other permissions will not remain in effect.

AllowNullsEnum

Constant Name	Value	Description
adIndexNulls Allow	0	Key columns with Null values have index values.
adIndexNulls Disallow	1	Do not allow index entries if the key columns are Null.
adIndexNulls Ignore	2	Null values in key columns are ignored and an index entry is not created.
adIndexNulls IgnoreAny	4	Null values in any part of the key (for multiple columns) are ignored, and an index entry is not created.

ColumnAttributesEnum

Constant Name	Value	Description
adColFixed	1	The column is of a fixed length.
adColNullable	2	The column may contain Null values.

DataTypeEnum

The ADOX data type constants are the same as the ADO data type constants. See the listing for DataTypeEnum in Appendix B.

InheritTypeEnum

Constant Name	Value	Description
adInheritBoth	3	Permissions for the object are inherited by both objects and other containers.
adInherit Containers	2	Permissions for the object are inherited by other containers.
adInheritNone	0	No permissions are inherited.
adInheritNo Propogate	4	The adInheritObjects and adInheritContainers permissions are not propagated to child objects.
adInheritObjects	1	Permissions are only inherited by objects that are not containers.

KeyTypeEnum

Constant Name	Value	Description
adKeyForeign	2	The key is a foreign key.
adKeyPrimary	1	The key is a primary key.
adKeyUnique	3	The key is unique.

ObjectTypeEnum

Constant Name	Value	Description
adPermObjColumn	2	The object is a column.
adPermObjDatabase	3	The object is a database.
adPermObjProcedure	4	The object is a procedure.
adPermObjProvider Specific	-1	The object is of a provider-specific type.
adPermObjTable	1	The object is a table.
adPermObjView	5	The object is a view.

RightsEnum

Constant Name	Value	Description
adRightCreate	16384	The User or Group has permission to create the object.
adRightDelete	65536	The User or Group has permission to delete the object.
adRightDrop	256	The User or Group has permission to drop the object.
adRightExclusive	512	The User or Group has permission to obtain exclusive access to the object.
adRightExecute	536870912	The User or Group has permission to execute the object.
adRightFull	268435456	The User or Group has full permissions on the object.
adRightInsert	32768	The User or Group has permission to insert the object.
adRightMaximum Allowed	33554432	The User or Group has the maximum number of permissions allowed by the provider.
adRightNone	0	The User or Group has no permissions on the object.
adRightRead	-2147483648	The User or Group has permission to read the object.
adRightReadDesign	1024	The User or Group has permission to read the design of the object.
adRightRead Permissions	131072	The User or Group has permission to read the permissions of the object.
adRightReference	8192	The User or Group has permission to reference the object.
adRightUpdate	1073741824	The User or Group has permission to update the object.
adRightWithGrant	4096	The User or Group has permission to grant permissions to other Users or Groups.
adRightWriteDesign	2048	The User or Group has permission to change the design of the object.
adRightWriteOwner	524288	The User or Group has permission to change the owner of the object.
adRightWrite Permissions	262144	The User or Group has permission to change the permissions of the object.

RuleEnum

Constant Name	Value	Description
adRICascade	1	Updates and deletes are cascaded.
adRINone	0	Updates and deletes are not cascaded.
adRISetDefault	3	Set the foreign key to its default value for updates and deletes.
adRISetNull	2	Set the foreign key to Null for updates and deletes.

SortOrderEnum

Constant Name	Value	Description
adSortAscending	1	The key column is in ascending order.
adSortDescending	2	The key column is in descending order.

DBPROPVAL_IN

Constant Name	Value	Description
DBPROPVAL_IN_DISALLOWNULL	1	Keys containing Null values are not allowed. Generates an error if an attempt is made to insert a key that contains Null.
DBPROPVAL_IN_IGNORENULL	2	Keys containing Null values are allowed, but are ignored and not added to the index. No error is generated.
DBPROPVAL_IN_IGNOREANYNULL	4	Keys consisting of multi-columns will allow a Null in any column, but the key is ignored and not added to the index. No error is generated.

DBPROPVAL_IT

Constant Name	Value	Description
DBPROPVAL_IT_BTREE	1	The index is a B+ tree.
DBPROPVAL_IT_CONTENT	3	The index is a content index.
DBPROPVAL_IT_HASH	2	The index is a hash file using linear or extensible hashing.
DBPROPVAL_IT_OTHER	4	The index is some other type of index.

DBPROPVAL_NC

Constant Name	Value	Description
DBPROPVAL_NC_END	1	Null values are collated at the end of the list, irrespective of the collation order.
DBPROPVAL_NC_HIGH	2	Null values are collated at the high end of the list.
DBPROPVAL_NC_LOW	4	Null values are collated at the low end of the list.
DBPROPVAL_NC_START	8	Null values are collated at the start of the list, irrespective of the collation order.

I thank God I am as honest as any man

living that is an old man and no honester th

Can counsel and speak comfort to th

Much Ado About Nothing.

Which they themselves not feel

He wears his faith but as the fashion of h

As merry as the day

He hath indeed better bettered expectation

(Act i. Sc. i).

He wears his faith but as the fashion of his hat.

(Ibid)

As merry as the day is long.

h indeed better bettered expectation

(Act i. Sc. i).

(Ibid)

an counsel and speak comfort to that grief

Which they themselves not feel.

He wears his faith but as the fashion of his hat.

Much Ado About Nothing.

(Ibid)

I was not born under

a rhyming plane

I was not born under a rhyming plane

(sc. 2

For there was never yet

That could endure the too

He wears his faith but as the fashion of his hat.

(Ibid)

merry as the day is long

(sc. 2)

Can counsel and speak comfort to that grie

(Ibid)

Which they themselves not feel.

He hath indeed better bettered expectation

(Ibid)

I thank God I am as honest as any

living that is an old man and no honest

He wears his faith but as the fashion of his ha

Much Ado About Nothing.

For there was never yet philospher

That could endure the toothache patiently.

(Ibid)

For there was never yet philospher

That could endure the toothache patiently.

themselves not feel

(Ibid)

I was not born u

online discussion at http://p2p.wrox.com

ADOX Properties Collection

Property Support

The following table shows a list of all OLE DB properties, and indicates which of them are supported by Microsoft Access and Microsoft SQL Server. The property support is the same whether using the OLE DB Provider for ODBC or the native OLE DB Providers. Since this list contains dynamic properties, not every property may show up under all circumstances. Other providers may also implement properties not listed in this table.

A tick (check) indicates the property is supported, and a blank space indicates it is not supported.

Property Name	Object	Jet	SQL
Auto-Update	Index	✓	
Autoincrement	Column	✓	✓
Clustered	Index	✓	✓
Column Level Collation Name	Column		✓
Default	Column	✓	✓
Description	Column	✓	
Fill Factor	Index	✓	✓
Fixed Length	Column	✓	✓
Increment	Column	✓	
Index Type	Index	✓	
Initial Size	Index	✓	
Jet OLEDB:Allow Zero Length	Column	✓	
Jet OLEDB:AutoGenerate	Column	✓	

Property Name	Object	Jet	SQL
Jet OLEDB:Cache Link Name/Password	Table	✓	
Jet OLEDB:Column Validation Rule	Column	✓	
Jet OLEDB:Column Validation Text	Column	✓	
Jet OLEDB:Compressed UNICODE Strings	Column	✓	
Jet OLEDB:Create Link	Table	✓	
Jet OLEDB:Exclusive Link	Table	✓	
Jet OLEDB:Hyperlink	Column	✓	
Jet OLEDB:IISAM Not Last Column	Column	✓	
Jet OLEDB:Link Datasource	Table	✓	
Jet OLEDB:Link Provider String	Table	✓	
Jet OLEDB:One BLOB per Page	Column	✓	
Jet OLEDB:Remote Table Name	Table	✓	
Jet OLEDB:Table Hidden In Access	Table	✓	
Jet OLEDB:Table Validation Rule	Table	✓	
Jet OLEDB:Table Validation Text	Table	✓	
Null Collation	Index	✓	
Null Keys	Index	✓	
Nullable	Column	✓	✓
Primary Key	Column		✓
Primary Key	Index	✓	✓
Seed	Column	✓	
Sort Bookmarks	Index	✓	
Temporary Index	Index	✓	
Temporary Table	Table	✓	✓
Unique	Column		✓
Unique	Index	✓	✓

The Column Object's Properties

Name	Description	Data Type
Autoincrement	Indicates whether or not the column is autoincrementing.	Boolean
Column Level Collation Name	The collation name in use for the column.	String
Default	Specifies the default value for the column, to be used if no explicit value is supplied.	Variant

Name	Description	Data Type
Description	The column description.	String
Fixed Length	Indicates whether or not the column holds fixed length data.	Boolean
Increment	The value by which autoincrement columns are increased.	Long
Jet OLEDB:Allow Zero Length	Indicates whether or not zero length strings can be inserted into the field.	Boolean
Jet OLEDB:Autogenerate	Indicates whether or not, for a GUID data type, a GUID should be automatically created.	Boolean
Jet OLEDB:Column Validation Rule	The validation rule to apply to column values before allowing the column to be set.	String
Jet OLEDB:Column Validation Text	Errors string to display if changes to a row do not meet the column validation rule.	String
Jet OLEDB:Compressed UNICODE Strings	Indicates whether or not Jet should compress UNICODE strings. Only applicable to Jet 4.0 databases.	Boolean
Jet OLEDB:Hyperlink	Indicates whether or not the column is a hyperlink.	Boolean
Jet OLEDB:IISAM Not Last Column	When creating columns (or a table) for installable IISAMs, this indicates whether or not this is the last column.	Boolean
Jet OLEDB:One BLOB Per Page	Indicates whether or not BLOB columns can share data pages.	Boolean
Nullable	Indicates whether or not the column can contain Null values.	Boolean
Primary Key	Indicates whether or not the column is part of the primary key.	Boolean
Seed	The initial seed value of an autoincrement column.	Long
Unique	Indicates whether or not the column allows unique values.	Boolean

The Index Object's Properties

Property Name	Description	DataType
Auto-Update	Indicates whether or not the index is maintained automatically when changes are made to rows.	Boolean
Clustered	Indicates whether or not the index is clustered.	Boolean
Fill Factor	Identifies the fill-factor of the index. This is the storage use of page-nodes during index creation. It is always 100 for the Jet provider.	Long
Index Type	The type of the index.	DBPROPVAL_IT
Initial Size	The total number of bytes allocated to the index when it is first created.	Long
Null Collation	Specifies how Null values are collated in the index.	DBPROPVAL_NC
Null Keys	Specifies whether key values containing Nulls are allowed.	DBPROPVAL_IN
Primary Key	Indicates whether or not the index represents the primary key on the table.	Boolean
Sort Bookmarks	Indicates whether or not repeated keys are sorted by bookmarks.	Boolean
Temporary Index	Indicates whether or not the index is temporary.	Boolean
Unique	Indicates whether or not index keys must be unique.	Boolean

The Table Object's Properties

Property Name	Description	Data Type
Jet OLEDB:Cache Link Name/Password	Indicates whether or not the authentication information for a linked table should be cached locally in the Jet database.	Boolean
Jet OLEDB:Create Link	Indicates whether or not a link is created to a remote data source when creating a new table.	Boolean
Jet OLEDB:Exclusive Link	Indicates whether or not the remote data source is opened exclusively when creating a link.	Boolean
Jet OLEDB:Link Datasource	The name of the remote data source to link to.	String
Jet OLEDB:Link Provider String	The connection string to the remote provider.	String
Jet OLEDB:Remote Table Name	The name of the remote table in a link.	String
Jet OLEDB:Table Hidden In Access	Indicates whether or not the table is shown in the Access user interface.	Boolean
Jet OLEDB:Table Validation Rule	The validation rule to apply to row values before committing changes to the row.	String
Jet OLEDB:Table Validation Text	Errors string to display if changes to a row do not meet the table validation rule.	String
Temporary Table	Indicates whether or not the table is a temporary table.	Boolean

I thank God I am as honest as any man
living that is an old man and no honester th

Can counsel and speak comfort to the
Which they themselves not feel

Much Ado About Nothing.

He wears his faith but as the fashion of

As merry as the day

He hath indeed better bettered expectation

(Act i. Sc. 1.).

He wears his faith but as the fashion of his hat.
(Ibid)

As merry as the day is long.

h indeed better bettered expectation

(Act i. Sc. 1.).

(Ibid)

an counsel and speak comfort to that grief

Which they themselves not feel.

Much Ado About Nothing.

He wears his faith but as the fashion of his hat.
(Ibid)
(Ibid)

I was not born under

a rhyming plane

I was not born under a rhyming plan
(Sc. 2

For there was never yet
That could endure the to

merry as the day is long (Sc. 2)

Can counsel and speak comfort to that grief

Which they themselves not feel.

(Ibid)

He hath indeed better bettered expectation

(Act i. Sc.)

(Ibid)

I thank God I am as honest as any

living that is an old man and no honest

He wears his faith but as the fashion of his ha
(Ibid

Much Ado About Nothing.

For there was never yet philospher
That could endure the toothache patiently.

(Ibid)

I was not born u

K

ADOMD Object Summary

This appendix contains details of the Microsoft ActiveX Data Objects (Multi-dimensional) 2.6 Library.

The ADOMD Objects

Name	Description
Axes	Contains an Axis object for each axis in the Cellset.
Axis	An Axis of a Cellset, containing members of one or more dimensions.
Catalog	Contains the multi-dimensional schema information.
Cell	The data at an intersection of Axis coordinates.
Cellset	The results of a multi-dimensional query.
CubeDef	A Cube from a multi-dimensional schema, containing related Dimension objects.
CubeDefs	One or more CubeDef objects contained within a Catalog.
Dimension	A dimension of a multi-dimensional cube, containing one or more Hierarchy objects.
Dimensions	One or more Dimension objects, making up the dimensions of a CubeDef.
Hierarchies	One or more Hierarchy objects, representing the ways a Dimension can be aggregated.
Hierarchy	Indicates one way in which aggregation of a Dimension can take place.
Level	Contains the members that make up the Hierarchy.
Levels	Contains one or more Level objects contained within the Hierarchy.
Member	An individual member of the Members collection
Members	A collection of Member objects for the level.
Position	A position in the cellset.
Positions	A collection of Position objects in the cellset.

The Axes Collection

Methods of the Axes Collection	Return Type	Description
Refresh		Refreshes the collection with details from the provider.

Properties of the Axes Collection	Return Type	Description
Count	Long	The number of Axis objects in the collection. Read-only.
Item	Axis	The default property, allowing indexing into the collection. Read-only.

The Axis Object

Properties of the Axis Object	Return Type	Description
DimensionCount	Long	The number of Dimensions on this Axis. Read-only.
Name	String	The name of the Axis. Read only

Collections of the Axis Object	Return Type	Description
Positions	Positions	A collection of Position objects in the Axis. Read-only.
Properties	Properties	A collection of provider-specific properties for the Axis. Read-only.

The Catalog Object

Properties of the Catalog Object	Return Type	Description
ActiveConnection	Object	The ADO Connection object or string, indicating the data provider to which the catalog is attached.
Name	String	The name of the Catalog. Read-only.

Collections of the Catalog Object	Return Type	Description
CubeDefs	CubeDefs	A collection of CubeDef objects available in the catalog. Read-only.

The Cell Object

Properties of the Cell Object	Return Type	Description
FormattedValue	String	The formatted value of the cell.
Ordinal	Long	The unique number identifying a cell. Read-only.
Value	Variant	The value of the cell.

Collections of the Cell Object	Return Type	Description
Positions	Positions	A collection of Position objects available for the cell. Read-only.
Properties	Properties	A collection of provider-specific properties for the cell. Read-only.

The Cellset Object

Methods of the Cellset Object	Return Type	Description
Close		Closes the cellset.
Open		Opens the cellset.

Properties of the Cellset Object	Return Type	Description
Active Connection	Object	The ADO Connection object or string, indicating the data provider to which the catalog is attached.
FilterAxis	Axis	Indicates the filtering information for the cellset. Read-only.
Item	Cell	The default property, which allows indexing into the cellset. Read-only.
Source	Variant	The multi-dimensional query used to generate the cellset.
State	Long	Indicates whether the cellset is open or closed. Read-only.

Collections of the Cellset Object	Return Type	Description
Axes	Axes	A collection of Axis objects in the cellset. Read-only.
Properties	Properties	A collection of provider-specific properties for the cellset. Read-only.

The CubeDef Object

Methods of the CubeDef Object	Return Type	Description
GetSchemaObject	Object	Returns an object from the schema, given the objects name.

Properties of the CubeDef Object	Return Type	Description
Description	String	Text describing the cube. Read-only.
Name	String	The name of the cube. Read-only.

Collections of the CubeDef Object	Return Type	Description
Dimensions	Dimensions	A collection of Dimensions available in the cube. Read-only.
Properties	Properties	A collection of provider-specific properties for the CubeDef. Read-only.

The CubeDefs Collection

Methods of the CubeDefs Collection	Return Type	Description
Refresh		Refreshes the CubeDef objects from the provider.

Properties of the CubeDefs Collection	Return Type	Description
Count	Long	Indicates the number of CubeDef objects in the collection. Read-only.
Item	CubeDef	The default property, which allows indexing into the collection. Read-only.

The Dimension Object

Properties of the Dimension Object	Return Type	Description
Description	String	A description of the dimension. Read-only.
Name	String	The name of the dimension. Read-only.
UniqueName	String	The unique name of the dimension. Read-only.

Collections of the Dimension Object	Return Type	Description
Hierarchies	Hierarchies	A collection of hierarchies available in the dimension. Read-only.
Properties	Properties	A collection of provider-specific properties for the dimension. Read-only.

The Dimensions Collection

Methods of the Dimensions Collection	Return Type	Description
Refresh		Refreshes the Dimensions collection from the provider.

Properties of the Dimensions Collection	Return Type	Description
Count	Long	The number of Dimension objects in the collection. Read-only.
Item	Dimension	The default property, which allows indexing into the collection. Read-only.

The Hierarchies Collection

Methods of the Hierarchies Collection	Return Type	Description
Refresh		Refreshes the Hierarchies collection from the provider.

Properties of the Hierarchies Collection	Return Type	Description
Count	Long	The number of Hierarchy objects in the collection. Read-only.
Item	Hierarchy	The default property, which allows indexing into the collection. Read-only.

The Hierarchy Object

Properties of the Hierarchy Object	Return Type	Description
Description	String	The description of the hierarchy. Read-only.

Properties of the Hierarchy Object	Return Type	Description
Name	String	The name of the hierarchy. Read-only.
UniqueName	String	The unique name of the hierarchy. Read-only.

Collections of the Hierarchy Object	Return Type	Description
Levels	Levels	A collection of levels in the hierarchy. Read-only.
Properties	Properties	A collection of provider specific properties for the hierarchy. Read-only.

The Level Object

Properties of the Level Object	Return Type	Description
Caption	String	The caption of the level. Read-only.
Depth	Integer	How deep in the hierarchy this level is. Read-only.
Description	String	The description of the level. Read-only.
Name	String	The name of the level. Read-only.
UniqueName	String	The unique name of the level. Read-only.

Collections of the Level Object	Return Type	Description
Members	Members	A collection of Member objects available in this level. Read-only.
Properties	Properties	A collection of provider-specific properties for the level. Read-only.

The Levels Collection

Methods of the Levels Collection	Return Type	Description
Refresh		Refreshes the Levels collection from the provider.

Properties of the Levels Collection	Return Type	Description
Count	Long	The number of Level objects in the collection. Read-only.
Item	Level	The default property, which allows indexing into the collection. Read-only.

The Member Object

Properties of the Member Object	Return Type	Description
Caption	String	The caption of the member. Read-only.
ChildCount	Long	The number of children belonging to this member. Read-only.
Description	String	A description of the member. Read-only.
DrilledDown	Boolean	Indicates whether or not this is a leaf node (contains no children). Read-only.
LevelDepth	Long	How deep in the collection this member is. Read-only.
LevelName	String	The name of the Level to which this member belongs. Read-only.
Name	String	The name of the member. Read-only.
Parent	Member	The Member object that is the parent of this member. Read-only.
ParentSameAsPrev	Boolean	Indicates whether the Parent member is the same as the Parent member of the previous member in the collection. Read-only.
Type	Member TypeEnum	The type of the member. Read-only.
UniqueName	String	The unique name of the member. Read-only.

Collections of the Member Object	Return Type	Description
Children	Members	A collection of Member objects that are children of this member. Read-only.
Properties	Properties	A collection of provider specific properties for the member. Read-only.

The Members Collection

Methods of the Members Collection	Return Type	Description
Refresh		Refreshes the Members collection from the provider.

Properties of the Members Collection	Return Type	Description
Count	Long	The number of Member objects in the collection. Read-only.
Item	Member	The default property, which allows indexing into the collection. Read-only.

The Position Object

Properties of the Position Object	Return Type	Description
Ordinal	Long	A unique identifier, indicating the location of the position in the collection. Read-only.

Collections of the Position Object	Return Type	Description
Members	Members	A collection of Member objects in this position. Read-only.

The Positions Collection

Methods of the Positions Collection	Return Type	Description
Refresh		Refreshes the Positions collection from the provider.

Properties of the Positions Collection	Return Type	Description
Count	Long	The number of Position objects in the collection. Read-only.
Item	Position	The default property, which allows indexing into the collection. Read-only.

ADOMD Method Calls

The Axes Collection

```
Axes.Refresh
```

The Cellset Object

```
Cellset.Close
Cellset.Open([DataSource As Variant],
            [ActiveConnection As Variant])
```

The CubeDef Object

```
Set Object = CubeDef.GetSchemaObject(eObjType As
            SchemaObjectTypeEnum, bsUniqueName As String)
```

The CubeDefs Collection

```
CubeDefs.Refresh
```

The Dimensions Collection

```
Dimensions.Refresh
```

The Hierarchies Collection

```
Hierarchies.Refresh
```

The Levels Collection

```
Levels.Refresh
```

The Members Collection

```
Members.Refresh
```

The Positions Collection

```
Positions.Refresh
```

I thank God I am as honest as any man
living that is an old man and no honester t

Can counsel and speak comfort to th
Which they themselves not feel

Much Ado About Nothing.

He wears his faith but as the fashion of

As merry as the day

He hath indeed better bettered expectation

(Act i. Sc. i.).

He wears his faith but as the fashion of his hat.
(Ibid)

As merry as the day is long.

th indeed better bettered expectation

(Act i. Sc. i.).

(Ibid)

Much Ado About Nothing.

Can counsel and speak comfort to that grief
Which they themselves not feel

He wears his faith but as the fashion of his hat.
(Ibid)

I was not born under

a rhyming

I was not born under a rhyming pla

For there was never yet
That could endure the t

merry as the day is long

(Sc. 2)

Can counsel and speak comfort to that grie
Which they themselves not feel.
(Ibid)

He hath indeed better bettered expectatio

I thank God I am as honest as any man
living that is an old man and no hone

He wears his faith but as the fashion of his h
(Ib

For there was never yet philospher
That could endure the toothache patiently.

Much Ado About Nothing.

(Ibid)

I was not born

ADOMD Constants

MemberTypeEnum

Constant Name	Value	Description
adMemberAll	2	The member is the All member, at the top of the members hierarchy.
adMemberFormula	4	The member identifies a formula.
adMemberMeasure	3	The member identifies a measure.
adMemberRegular	1	The member identifies a regular member.
adMemberUnknown	0	The type of member is unknown.

SchemaObjectTypeEnum

Constant Name	Value	Description
adObjectTypeDimension	1	Return a Dimension object from the CubeDef.
adObjectTypeHierarchy	2	Return a Hierarchy object from the CubeDef.
adObjectTypeLevel	3	Return a Level object from the CubeDef.
adObjectTypeMember	4	Return a Member object from the CubeDef.

MDACTION

Constant Name	Value	Description
MDACTION_COORDINATE_CUBE		The COORDINATE column contains the cube name.
MDACTION_COORDINATE_DIMENSION		The COORDINATE column contains a dimension specification.
MDACTION_COORDINATE_LEVEL		The COORDINATE column contains a level specification.
MDACTION_COORDINATE_MEMBER		The COORDINATE column contains a member specification.
MDACTION_COORDINATE_SET		The COORDINATE column contains the name of a set.
MDACTION_COORDINATE_CELL		The COORDINATE column contains a tuple that identifies a single cell.

At the time of writing, values for these were not documented and they weren't included in the header files.

MD_DIMTYPE

Constant Name	Value	Description
MD_DIMTYPE_UNKNOWN	0	The dimension type is unknown.
MD_DIMTYPE_TIME	1	The dimension is a time dimension.
MD_DIMTYPE_MEASURE	2	The dimension is a measure dimension.
MD_DIMTYPE_OTHER	3	The dimension is neither a time nor a measure dimension.

MDLEVEL_TYPE

Constant Name	Value	Description
MDLEVEL_TYPE_REGULAR	0	The level is a regular level.
MDLEVEL_TYPE_ALL	1	The level identifies the top of the hierarchy, or All level.
MDLEVEL_TYPE_CALCULATED	2	The level is a calculated level.
MDLEVEL_TYPE_TIME	4	The level is a time level.
MDLEVEL_TYPE_TIME_YEARS	20	The level is a time level, based on years.
MDLEVEL_TYPE_TIME_HALF_YEAR	36	The level is a time level, based on half-years.
MDLEVEL_TYPE_TIME_QUARTERS	68	The level is a time level, based on quarters.

Constant Name	Value	Description
MDLEVEL_TYPE_TIME_MONTHS	132	The level is a time level, based on months.
MDLEVEL_TYPE_TIME_WEEKS	260	The level is a time level, based on weeks.
MDLEVEL_TYPE_TIME_DAYS	516	The level is a time level, based on days.
MDLEVEL_TYPE_TIME_HOURS	772	The level is a time level, based on hours.
MDLEVEL_TYPE_TIME_MINUTES	1028	The level is a time level, based on minutes.
MDLEVEL_TYPE_TIME_SECONDS	2052	The level is a time level, based on seconds.
MDLEVEL_TYPE_TIME_UNDEFINED	4100	The level type is not defined.
MDLEVEL_TYPE_UNKNOWN	0	The level type is unknown.

MDMEASURE_AGGR

Constant Name	Value	Description
MDMEASURE_AGGR_SUM	1	The aggregate function is SUM.
MDMEASURE_AGGR_COUNT	2	The aggregate function is COUNT.
MDMEASURE_AGGR_MIN	3	The aggregate function is MIN.
MDMEASURE_AGGR_MAX	4	The aggregate function is MAX.
MDMEASURE_AGGR_AVG	5	The aggregate function is AVG.
MDMEASURE_AGGR_VAR	6	The aggregate function is VAR.
MDMEASURE_AGGR_STD	7	The aggregate function is one of SUM, COUNT, MIN, MAX, AVG, VAR, STDEV.
MDMEASURE_AGGR_CALCULATED	127	The aggregate function is derived from formula that is not a standard one.
MDMEASURE_AGGR_UNKNOWN	0	The aggregate function is not known.

MDMEMBER_TYPE

Constant Name	Value	Description
MDMEMBER_TYPE_ALL	1	The member identifies the top of the hierarchy, or All members.
MDMEMBER_TYPE_REGULAR	2	The member is a regular member.
MDMEMBER_TYPE_MEASURE	3	The member is a measure.
MDMEMBER_TYPE_FORMULA	4	The member is a calculated formula.
MDMEMBER_TYPE_UNKNOWN	0	The member type is unknown.

Appendices

611

MDPROPVAL_AU

Constant Name	Value	Description
MDPROPVAL_AU_UNSUPPORTED	0	Updating of aggregated cells is not supported.
MDPROPVAL_AU_UNCHANGED	1	Aggregated cells can be changed, but the cells that make up the aggregation remain unchanged.
MDPROPVAL_AU_UNKNOWN	2	Aggregated cells can be changed, but the cells that make up the aggregation remain undefined.

MDPROPVAL_FS

Constant Name	Value	Description
MDPROPVAL_FS_FULL_SUPPORT	1	The provider supports flattening.
MDPROPVAL_FS_GENERATED_COLUMN	2	The provider supports flattening by using dummy names.
MDPROPVAL_FS_GENERATED_DIMENSION	3	The provider supports flattening by generating one column per dimension.
MDPROPVAL_FS_NO_SUPPORT	4	The provider does not support flattening.

MDPROPVAL_MC

Constant Name	Value	Description
MDPROPVAL_MC_SINGLECASE	1	The provider supports simple case statements.
MDPROPVAL_MC_SEARCHEDCASE	2	The provider supports searched case statements.

MDPROPVAL_MD

Constant Name	Value	Description
MDPROPVAL_MD_BEFORE	2	The BEFORE flag is supported.
MDPROPVAL_MD_AFTER	4	The AFTER flag is supported.
MDPROPVAL_MD_SELF	1	The SELF flag is supported.

MDPROPVAL_MF

Constant Name	Value	Description
MDPROPVAL_MF_WITH_CALCMEMBERS	1	Calculated members are supported by use of the WITH clause.
MDPROPVAL_MF_WITH_NAMEDSETS	2	Named sets are supported by use of the WITH clause.
MDPROPVAL_MF_CREATE_CALCMEMBERS	4	Named calculated members are supported by use of the CREATE clause.
MDPROPVAL_MF_CREATE_NAMEDSETS	8	Named sets are supported by use of the CREATE clause.
MDPROPVAL_MF_SCOPE_SESSION	16	The scope value of SESSION is supported during the creation of named sets and calculated members.
MDPROPVAL_MF_SCOPE_GLOBAL	32	The scope value of GLOBAL is supported during the creation of named sets and calculated members.

MDPROPVAL_MJC

Constant Name	Value	Description
MDPROPVAL_MJC_IMPLICITCUBE	4	An empty FROM clause is supported, and the cube is implicitly resolved.
MDPROPVAL_MJC_SINGLECUBE	1	Only one cube is supported in the FROM clause.
MDPROPVAL_MJC_MULTICUBES	2	More than one cube is supported in the FROM clause.

MDPROPVAL_MMF

Constant Name	Value	Description
MDPROPVAL_MMF_COUSIN	1	The COUSIN function is supported.
MDPROPVAL_MMF_PARALLELPERIOD	2	The PARALLELPERIOD function is supported.
MDPROPVAL_MMF_OPENINGPERIOD	4	The OPENINGPERIOD function is supported.
MDPROPVAL_MMF_CLOSINGPERIOD	8	The CLOSINGPERIOD function is supported.

MDPROPVAL_MNF

Constant Name	Value	Description
MDPROPVAL_MNF_MEDIAN	1	The MEDIAN function is supported.
MDPROPVAL_MNF_VAR	2	The VAR function is supported.
MDPROPVAL_MNF_STDDEV	4	The STDDEV function is supported.
MDPROPVAL_MNF_RANK	8	The RANK function is supported.
MDPROPVAL_MNF_ AGGREGATE	16	The AGGREGATE function is supported.
MDPROPVAL_MNF_ COVARIANCE	32	The COVARIANCE function is supported.
MDPROPVAL_MNF_ CORRELATION	64	The CORRELATION function is supported.
MDPROPVAL_MNF_ LINREGSLOPE	128	The LINREGSLOPE function is supported.
MDPROPVAL_MNF_ LINREGVARIANCE	256	The LINREGVARIANCE function is supported.
MDPROPVAL_MNF_ LINREGR2	512	The LINREGR2 function is supported.
MDPROPVAL_MNF_ LINREGPOINT	1024	The LINREGPOINT function is supported.
MDPROPVAL_MNF_ LINREGINTERCEPT	2048	The LINREGINTERCEPT function is supported.

MDPROPVAL_MO

Constant Name	Value	Description
MDPROPVAL_MO_TUPLE		The tuple. [VALUE] clause can be qualified by a cube name as an argument.

MDPROPVAL_MOQ

Constant Name	Value	Description
MDPROPVAL_MOQ_ DATASOURCE_CUBE	1	Cubes can be qualified by the data source name.
MDPROPVAL_MOQ_ CATALOG_CUBE	2	Cubes can be qualified by the catalog name.
MDPROPVAL_MOQ_ SCHEMA_CUBE	4	Cubes can be qualified by the schema name.
MDPROPVAL_MOQ_CUBE_ DIM	8	Dimensions can be qualified by the cube name.

Constant Name	Value	Description
MDPROPVAL_MOQ_DIM_HIER	16	Hierarchies can be qualified by the dimension name.
MDPROPVAL_MOQ_DIMHIER_LEVEL	32	Levels can be qualified by the schema name, and/or the hierarchy name.
MDPROPVAL_MOQ_LEVEL_MEMBER	64	Members can be qualified by a level name.
MDPROPVAL_MOQ_MEMBER_MEMBER	128	Members can be qualified by their ancestor names.

MDPROPVAL_MS

Constant Name	Value	Description
MDPROPVAL_MS_SINGLETUPLE	2	Only one tuple is supported in the WHERE clause.
MDPROPVAL_MS_MULTIPLETUPLES	1	Multiple tuples are supported in the WHERE clause.

MDPROPVAL_MSC

Constant Name	Value	Description
MDPROPVAL_MSC_LESSTHAN	1	The provider supports the less than operator.
MDPROPVAL_MSC_GREATERTHAN	2	The provider supports the greater than operator.
MDPROPVAL_MSC_LESSTHANEQUAL	4	The provider supports the less than or equal to operator.
MDPROPVAL_MSC_GREATERTHANEQUAL	8	The provider supports the greater than or equal to operator.

MDPROPVAL_MSF

Constant Name	Value	Description
MDPROPVAL_MSF_TOPPERCENT	1	The TOPPERCENT function is supported.
MDPROPVAL_MSF_BOTTOMPERCENT	2	The BOTTOMPERCENT function is supported.
MDPROPVAL_MSF_TOPSUM	4	The TOPSUM function is supported.
MDPROPVAL_MSF_BOTTOMSUM	8	The BOTTOMSUM function is supported.
MDPROPVAL_MSF_DRILLDOWNLEVEL	2048	The DRILLDOWNLEVEL function is supported.

Constant Name	Value	Description
MDPROPVAL_MSF_DRILLDOWNMEMBER	1024	The DRILLDOWNMEMBER function is supported.
MDPROPVAL_MSF_DRILLDOWNMEMBERTOP	4096	The DRILLDOWNMEMBERTOP function is supported.
MDPROPVAL_MSF_DRILLDOWNMEMBERBOTTOM	8192	The DRILLDOWNMEMBERBOTTOM function is supported.
MDPROPVAL_MSF_DRILLDOWNLEVELTOP	16384	The DRILLDOWNLEVELTOP function is supported.
MDPROPVAL_MSF_DRILLDOWNLEVELBOTTOM	32768	The DRILLDOWNLEVELBOTTOM function is supported.
MDPROPVAL_MSF_DRILLUPMEMBER	65536	The DRILLUPMEMBER function is supported.
MDPROPVAL_MSF_DRILLUPLEVEL	131072	The DRILLUPLEVEL function is supported.
MDPROPVAL_MSF_PERIODSTODATE	16	The PERIODSTODATE function is supported.
MDPROPVAL_MSF_LASTPERIODS	32	The LASTPERIODS function is supported.
MDPROPVAL_MSF_YTD	64	The YTD function is supported.
MDPROPVAL_MSF_QTD	128	The QTD function is supported.
MDPROPVAL_MSF_MTD	256	The MTD function is supported.
MDPROPVAL_MSF_WTD	512	The WTD function is supported.

MDPROPVAL_NL

Constant Name	Value	Description
MDPROPVAL_NL_NAMEDLEVELS	1	The provider supports named levels.
MDPROPVAL_NL_NUMBEREDLEVELS	2	The provider supports numbered levels.
MDPROPVAL_NL_SCHEMAONLY	4	The provider supports 'dummy' levels, for display only.

MDPROPVAL_RR

Constant Name	Value	Description
MDPROPVAL_RR_NORANGEROWSET	1	The provider does not support range rowsets.
MDPROPVAL_RR_READONLY	2	The provider supports read-only range rowsets.
MDPROPVAL_RR_UPDATE	4	The provider supports updateable range rowsets.

MDTREEOP

Constant Name	Value	Description
MDTREEOP_ANCESTORS	32	Show only members that are ancestors of the selected member.
MDTREEOP_CHILDREN	1	Show only members that are children of the selected member.
MDTREEOP_SIBLINGS	2	Show only members that are siblings of the selected member.
MDTREEOP_PARENT	4	Show only members that are parents of the selected member.
MDTREEOP_SELF	8	Show the selected member in the list.
MDTREEOP_DESCENDANTS	16	Show only members that are descendants of the selected member.

I thank God I am as honest as any man
living that is an old man and no honester th

Much Ado About Nothing.

He wears his faith but as the fashion of h

As merry as the day

He hath indeed better bettered expectation

(Act i. Sc. i).

He wears his faith but as the fashion of his hat.
(Ibid)

As merry as the day is long.

h indeed better bettered expectation

(Act i. Sc. i). (Ibid)

Can counsel and speak comfort to the
Which they themselves not feel

Much Ado About Nothing.

He wears his faith but as the fashion of his hat.
(Ibid)

I was not born under

a rhyming plane

I was not born under a rhyming plan

merry as the day is long (Sc. 2)

For there was never yet
That could endure the to

Can counsel and speak comfort to that grief

Which they themselves not feel.
(Ibid)

He hath indeed better bettered expectation

I thank God I am as honest as an

living that is an old man and no honest

He wears his faith but as the fashion of his ha
(Ibi

Much Ado About Nothing.   For there was never yet philospher
That could endure the toothache patiently.

(Ibid)

For there was never yet philospher
That could endure the toothache patiently.

was not born u

ADOMD Properties Collection

The following table shows a list of all OLE DB properties for the Microsoft OLAP Provider.

Those descriptions marked with a # indicate undocumented properties, where I've taken a guess at the description.

The Connection Object's Properties

Property Name	Description	Type
Active Sessions	The maximum number of sessions allowable. Zero indicates no limit.	Long
Asynchable Abort	Whether transactions can be aborted asynchronously. Read-only.	Boolean
Asynchable Commit	Whether transactions can be committed asynchronously. Read-only.	Boolean
Asynchronous Initialization	Indicates the asynchronous initialization setting. This can only be DBPROPVAL_ASYNCH_INITIALIZE from the ADO constants.	Long
Auto Synch Period	Identifies the time (in milliseconds) of the synchronization between the client and the server. The default value is 10,000 (10 seconds).	Long
Autocommit Isolation Levels	Indicates the transaction isolation level when in auto-commit mode. Can be one of the DBPROPVAL_TI constants from ADO.	Long
Cache Policy	Reserved for future use.	Long

Property Name	Description	Type
Catalog Location	The position of the catalog name in a table name in a text command. The value can be one of the DBPROPVAL_CL constants from ADO.	Long
Catalog Term	The name the data source uses for a catalog, such as 'catalog' or 'database'. Read/Write.	String
Catalog Usage	Specifies how catalog names can be used in text commands. Can be zero or more of DBPROPVAL_CU constants from ADO.	Long
Client Cache Size	The amount of memory used by the cache on the client. A value of 0 means there is no limit on the client memory that can be used. A value of 1–99 indicates the percentage of virtual memory to use for the cache. A value above 100 indicates the amount in Kb that can be used by the cache.	Long
Column Definition	Defines the valid clauses for the definition of a column. Can be one of the DBPROPVAL_CD constants from ADO.	Long
CompareCase NotSensitive StringFlags	Identifies the type of comparison to perform for case-insensitive strings.	Long
CompareCase Sensitive StringFlags	Identifies the type of comparison to perform for case-sensitive strings.	Long
Connect Timeout	The amount of time, in seconds, to wait for the initialization to complete. Read/Write.	Long
Connection Status	The status of the current connection. Can be one of the DBPROPVAL_CS constants from ADO.	Long
CREATE CUBE	The statement used to create a cube.	String
Current Catalog	The name of the current catalog.	String
Data Source	The name of the data source to connect to.	String
Data Source Name	The name of the data source.	String

Property Name	Description	Type
Data Source Object Threading Model	Specifies the threading models supported by the data source object.	Long
Data Source Type	The type of data source.	Long
DBMS Name	The name of the product accessed by the provider.	String
DBMS Version	The version of the product accessed by the provider.	String
Default Isolation Mode	Identifies whether the isolation mode is 'isolated', or the mode requested by the rowset properties. Isolated mode will be used if this value starts with Y, T or a number other than 0.	String
Default MDX Visual Mode	The default visibility mode of columns.	Integer
Distinct Measures By Key	The key used to obtain distinct measures. #	String
Do Not Apply Commands	The supplied commands are do not apply to this OLAP Provider. #	String
Execution Location	Identifies whether the query is resolved. Values can be: 0, for automatic selection. This is the default; 1, for automatic selection; 2, to execute the query on the client; 3, to execute the query on the server.	Long
Extended Properties	Contains provider-specific, extended connection information.	String
Flattening Support	Indicates the level of support by the provider for flattening.	MDPROPVAL_FS
GROUP BY Support	The relationship between the columns in a GROUP BY clause and the non-aggregated columns in the select list. Can be one of the DBPROPVAL_GB constants from ADO.	Long
Heterogeneous Table Support	Specifies whether the provider can join tables from different catalogs or providers. Can be one of the DBPROPVAL_HT constants from ADO.	Long
Identifier Case Sensitivity	How identifiers treat case sensitivity. Can be one of the DBPROPVAL_IC constants from ADO.	Long

Property Name	Description	Type
Initial Catalog	The name of the initial, or default, catalog to use when connecting to the data source. If the provider supports changing the catalog for an initialized data source, a different catalog name can be specified in the Current Catalog property.	String
INSERTINTO	The statement used for inserting data into a local cube.	String
Integrated Security	Contains the name of the authentication service used by the server to identify the user.	String
Isolation Levels	Identifies the supported transaction isolation levels. Can be one of the DBPROPVAL_TI constants from ADO.	Long
Isolation Retention	Identifies the supported transaction isolation retention levels. Can be one of the DBPROPVAL_TR constants from ADO.	Long
Large Level Threshold	Defines the number of levels a Dimension can have before it is deemed to be a 'large' dimension. A large level Dimension will have the levels sent from the server in increments, rather than all at once.	Long
Locale Identifier	The locale ID of preference for the consumer.	Long
Location	The location of the data source to connect to. Typically this will be the server name.	String
Maximum Index Size	The maximum number of bytes allowed in the combined columns of an index. This is 0 if there is no specified limit or the limit is unknown.	Long
Maximum Row Size	The maximum length of a single row in a table. This is 0 if there is no specified limit or the limit is unknown.	Long
Maximum Row Size Includes BLOB	Identifies whether Maximum Row Size includes the length for BLOB data.	Boolean

Property Name	Description	Type
Maximum Tables in SELECT	The maximum number of tables allowed in the FROM clause of a SELECT statement. This is 0 if there is no specified limit or the limit is unknown.	Long
MDX Calculated Members Extensions	Defines any supported extensions for calculated members. #	Integer
MDX Calculated Members Mode	Reserved for future use.	Integer
MDX DDL Extensions	Defines any DDL extensions supported by the provider.	Long
MDX Unique Name Style	The style used for unique names. Will be one of: 0, same as value 2, but included for compatibility with previous versions. This is the default; 1, to use the key path algorithm [dimension].&[Key1].&[Key2] 2, to use the name path algorithm [dimension].[n1].[n2]. Included for compatibility with SQL Server 7.0; 3, for names that are stable over time. Included for compatibility with SQL Server 2000.	Integer
MDX USE Extensions	Defines the USE extensions supported by the provider, allowing creation of user-defined functions.	Long
Mining Location	The location where data mining takes place. #	String
Mode	Specifies the access permissions. Can be one of the DB_MODE constants from ADO.	Long
Multiple Results	Identifies whether the provider supports multiple results objects and what restrictions it places on those objects.	Long
Multiple Storage Objects	Identifies whether the provider supports multiple, open storage objects at the same time.	Boolean
Multi-Table Update	Identifies whether the provider can update rowsets derived from multiple tables.	Boolean
NULL Collation Order	Identifies where Nulls are sorted in a list.	Long

Property Name	Description	Type
NULL Concatenation Behavior	How the data source handles concatenation of Null-valued character data type columns with non-Null valued character data type columns.	Long
Number of axes in the dataset	Maximum number of axes that the provider supports.	Long
OLE DB for OLAP Version	The version of OLAP in use by the provider.	String
OLE DB Services	Specifies the OLE DB services to enable.	Long
OLE DB Version	Specifies the version of OLE DB supported by the provider.	String
OLE Object Support	Specifies the way on which the provider supports access to BLOBs and OLE objects stored in columns.	Long
ORDER BY Columns in Select List	Identifies whether columns in an ORDER BY clause must be in the SELECT list.	Boolean
Output Parameter Availability	Identifies the time at which output parameter values become available. Can be one of the DBPROPVAL_AO constants in ADO.	Long
Pass By Ref Accessors	Whether the provider supports the DBACCESSOR_PASSBYREF flag.	Boolean
Password	The password to be used to connect to the data source.	String
Perf Cell count	PerfMon cell count. #	Integer
Perf Net count	PerfMon network count. #	Integer
Perf Net Time	PerfMon network time. #	Double
Perf Query count	PerfMon query count. #	Integer
Perf Query time	PerfMon query time. #	Double
Persist Security Info	Whether or not the consumer requires that the data source object persist sensitive authentication information, such as a password, in encrypted form.	Boolean
Persistent ID Type	Specifies the type of DBID that the provider uses when persisting DBIDs for tables, indexes and columns. Can be one of the DBPROPVAL_PT constants in ADO.	Long
Prepare Abort Behavior	Identifies how aborting a transaction affects prepared commands. Can be one of the DBPROPVAL_CB constants in ADO.	Long

Property Name	Description	Type
Prepare Commit Behavior	Identifies how committing a transaction affects prepared commands. Can be one of the DBPROPVAL_CB constants in ADO.	Long
Procedure Term	Specifies the data source provider's name for a procedure, such as 'database procedure' or 'stored procedure'.	String
Prompt	Specifies whether to prompt the user during initialization.	Integer
Provider Friendly Name	The friendly name of the provider.	String
Provider Name	The filename of the provider.	String
Provider Version	The version of the provider.	String
Provider's ability to qualify a cube name	Identifies how object names in a schema can be qualified in an MDX expression.	MDPROPVAL_MOQ
Quoted Identifier Sensitivity	Identifies how quoted identifiers treat case. Can be one of the DBPROPVAL_IC constants from ADO.	Long
Read-Only Session	Reserved for future use.	String
Read-Only Data Source	Whether or not the data source is read-only.	Boolean
Reset Datasource	Specifies the data source state to reset. Can be one of the DBPROPVAL_RD constants from ADO.	Long
Roles	The security roles for the current user.	String
Rowset Conversions on Command	Indicates whether or not callers can enquire about rowset conversions.	Boolean
Schema Usage	Identifies how schema names can be used in commands. Can be one of the DBPROPVAL_SU constants from ADO.	Long
Secured Cell Value	Indicates the return value resulting from the call to a secured cell. Will be one of: 1 if the string '#N/A' is returned; 2, if an error is returned; 3 if Null is returned; 4, if 0 is returned; 5, if the string '#SEC' is returned.	Integer

Property Name	Description	Type
Server Name	The name of the server.	String
SOURCE_DSN	The connection string for the source data store.	String
SOURCE_DSN_ SUFFIX	The suffix to append to the SOURCE_DSN property for a local cube.	String
SQL Compatibility	Identifies the level of compatibility for SQL.	Long
SQL Support	Identifies the level of support for SQL. Can be one of the DBPROPVAL_SQL constants from ADO.	Long
SSPI	Determines the security package that will be used for the session.	String
Structured Storage	Identifies what interfaces the rowset supports on storage objects. Can be one of the DBPROPVAL_SS constants from ADO.	Long
Subquery Support	Identifies the predicates in text commands that support sub-queries. Can be one of the DBPROPVAL_SQ constants from ADO.	Long
Support for cell updates	Indicates whether the provider supports updating of the cells.	MDPROPVAL_ PR
Support for creation of named sets and calculated members	Indicates the level of support for named sets and calculated members.	MDPROPVAL_ MF
Support for MDX case statements	The level of support for case statements.	MDPROPVAL_ MC
Support for named levels	The level of support for named and/or numbered Levels.	MDPROPVAL_ NL
Support for outer reference in an MDX statement	The level of support for outer references.	MDPROPVAL_ MO
Support for query joining multiple cubes	The level of support for joining multiple cubes.	MDPROPVAL_ MJC
Support for querying by property values in an MDX statement	Indicates whether or not the provider supports the query of property statements.	Boolean

Property Name	Description	Type
Support for string comparison operators other than equals and not-equals operators	The level of support for complex string comparison operators.	MDPROPVAL_MSC
Support for updating aggregated cells	The level of support for updating aggregated cells.	MDPROPVAL_AU
Support for various <desc flag> values in the DESCENDANTS function	The level of support for flags when describing descendants.	MDPROPVAL_MD
Support for various member functions	The level of support for functions that act on members.	MDPROPVAL_MMF
Support for various numeric functions	The level of support for numeric functions.	MDPROPVAL_MNF
Support for various set functions	The level of support for set functions.	MDPROPVAL_MSF
Table Term	The name the data source uses for a table, such as 'table' or 'file'.	String
The capabilities of the WHERE clause of an MDX statement	The WHERE clause support for tuples.	MDPROPVAL_MS
Transaction DDL	Indicates whether Data Definition Language (DDL) statements are supported in transactions. Can be one of the DBPROPVAL_TC constants from ADO.	Long
USEEXISTING FILE	When using CREATE CUBE or INSERT INTO, indicates whether an existing local cube file is overwritten. If the value starts with Y, T or a number other than 0, the existing file is used. If the value starts with any other character the existing cube file is overwritten.	String
User ID	The User ID to be used when connecting to the data source.	String
User Name	The User Name used in a particular database.	String
Visual Totals Mode	Determines whether aggregate values reflect the entire aggregation, or only those for a given cellset.	Long

Property Name	Description	Type
Window Handle	The window handle to be used if the data source object needs to prompt for additional information.	Long
Writeback Timeout	The maximum amount of time (in seconds) to wait whilst committing changes back to the server.	Long

The CubeDef Object's Properties

Property Name	Description	Type
CATALOG_NAME	The name of the catalog to which the cube belongs.	String
CREATED_ON	The date the cube was created.	Date/Time
CUBE_GUID	The GUID of the cube.	GUID
CUBE_NAME	The cube name.	String
CUBE_TYPE	Will be CUBE for a standard cube and VIRTUAL CUBE for a virtual cube.	String
DATA_UPDATED_ BY	The ID of the person who last update data in the cube.	String
DESCRIPTION	The cube description.	String
LAST_DATA_ UPDATE	The date the cube data was last updated.	Date/Time
LAST_SCHEMA_ UPDATE	The date the cube schema was last updated.	Date/Time
SCHEMA_NAME	The name of the schema to which this cube belongs.	String
SCHEMA_ UPDATED_BY	The ID of the person who last updated the schema.	String

The Dimension Object's Properties

Property Name	Description	Type
CATALOG_NAME	The name of the Catalog to which this Dimension belongs.	String
CUBE_NAME	The name of the Cube to which this Dimension belongs.	String
EFAULT_ ERARCHY	The unique name of the default Hierarchy for this Dimension.	String

Property Name	Description	Type
DESCRIPTION	The description of the Dimension.	String
DIMENSION CAPTION	The caption of the Dimension.	String
DIMENSION CARDINALITY	The number of members in the Dimension. This figure is not guaranteed to be accurate.	Long
DIMENSION GUID	The GUID of the Dimension, or Null if no GUID exists.	GUID
DIMENSION IS VISIBLE	Indicates whether or not the Dimension is visible.	Boolean
DIMENSION MASTER UNIQUE NAME	The master unique name of the Dimension.	String
DIMENSION NAME	The name of the Dimension.	String
DIMENSION ORDINAL	The number or the ordinal of the Dimension. This is zero based.	Long
DIMENSION TYPE	The type of the Dimension.	MD DIMTYPE
DIMENSION UNIQUE NAME	The unique name of the Dimension.	String
DIMENSION UNIQUE SETTINGS	The unique settings for the Dimension.	Integer
IS READWRITE	Indicates whether or not the Dimension is writeable.	Boolean
IS VIRTUAL	Indicates whether or not the Dimension is a virtual dimension.	Boolean
SCHEMA NAME	The schema name to which this Dimension belongs.	String

The Hierarchy Object's Properties

Property Name	Description	Type
ALL_MEMBER	The name of the default member if the first level is All, or Null if the first level is not All.	String
CATALOG_NAME	Catalog name in which the table is defined or Null if the provider does not support catalogs.	String
CUBE_NAME	The name of the Cube to which this Hierarchy belongs.	String
DEFAULT_ MEMBER	The default Level for this Hierarchy, or Null if no default exists.	String

Property Name	Description	Type
DESCRIPTION	The description of the Hierarchy.	String
DIMENSION_IS_SHARED	Indicates whether or not the dimension is shared.	Boolean
DIMENSION_IS_VISIBLE	Indicates whether or not the dimension is visible.	Boolean
DIMENSION_MASTER_UNIQUE_NAME	The master unique name of the dimension.	String
DIMENSION_TYPE	The type of the dimension.	MD_DIMTYPE
DIMENSION_UNIQUE_NAME	The fully qualified name of the Dimension to which this Hierarchy belongs.	String
DIMENSION_UNIQUE_SETTINGS	The unique settings for the dimension.	Integer
HIERARCHY_CAPTION	The caption of the Hierarchy.	String
HIERARCHY_CARDINALITY	The number of members in the Hierarchy. This figure is not guaranteed to be accurate.	Long
HIERARCHY_GUID	The GUID of the Hierarchy, or Null if no GUID exists.	GUID
HIERARCHY_NAME	The name of the Hierarchy.	String
HIERARCHY_ORDINAL	The ordinal of the hierarchy.	Integer
HIERARCHY_UNIQUE_NAME	The fully qualified name of the Hierarchy.	String
IS_READWRITE	Indicates whether or not the hierarchy is writeable.	Boolean
SCHEMA_NAME	Schema name in which the table is defined or Null if the provider does not support schemas.	String
STRUCTURE	The hierarchy structure in use for the dimension.	Integer

The Level Object's Properties

Property Name	Description	Type
CATALOG_NAME	Catalog name, or Null if the provider does not support catalogs.	String
CUBE_NAME	The Cube name to which the level belongs.	String

Property Name	Description	Type
CUSTOM ROLLUP SETTINGS	The custom settings in use for ROLLUPs.	Integer
DESCRIPTION	The description of the level.	String
DIMENSION_ UNIQUE_NAME	The unique name of the Dimension to which the level belongs.	String
HIERARCHY_ UNIQUE_NAME	The unique name of the Hierarchy to which the level belongs.	String
LEVEL CAPTION	The Caption of the level.	String
LEVEL CARDINALITY	The number of members in the level. This figure is not guaranteed to be accurate.	Long
LEVEL DBTYPE	The database type of the level.	Integer
LEVEL GUID	The GUID of the level, or Null if no GUID exists.	GUID
LEVEL IS VISIBLE	Indicates whether or not the level is visible.	Boolean
LEVEL KEY SQL COLUMN NAME	The SQL column key name details of the level.	String
LEVEL MASTER UNIQUE NAME	The master unique name for the level.	String
LEVEL NAME	The level name.	String
LEVEL NAME SQL COLUMN NAME	The SQL column name from which the level is derived.	String
LEVEL NUMBER	The index number of the level.	Long
LEVEL ORDERING PROPERTY	The ordering details for the level.	String
LEVEL TYPE	The Type of the level.	MDLEVEL TYPE
LEVEL UNIQUE NAME	The unique level name.	String
LEVEL UNIQUE NAME SQL COLUMN NAME	The SQL column name for the unique level name.	String
LEVEL UNIQUE SETTINGS	The unique settings for the level.	Integer
SCHEMA NAME	Schema name, or Null if the provider does not support schemas.	String

The Member Object's Properties

Property Name	Description	Type
EXPRESSION	The expression that underlies a calculated measure.	String

I thank God I am as honest as any man

living that is an old man and no honester th

Can counsel and speak comfort to the

Which they themselves not feel

Much Ado About Nothing.

He wears his faith but as the fashion of h

As merry as the day

He hath indeed better bettered expectation

(Act i. Sc. i.).

He wears his faith but as the fashion of his hat.

(Ibid)

As merry as the day is long.

h indeed better bettered expectation

(Act i. Sc. i.)

(Ibid)

an counsel and speak comfort to that grief

Which they themselves not feel.

Much Ado About Nothing.

He wears his faith but as the fashion of his hat.

(Ibid)

(Ibid)

I was not born under

a rhyming plane

I was not born under a rhyming plane

(sc. 2

For there was never yet p

That could endure the too

merry as the day is long

(sc. 2)

Can counsel and speak comfort to that grief

Which they themselves not feel.

(Ibid)

He hath indeed better bettered expectation

I thank God I am as honest as any

living that is an old man and no honest

He wears his faith but as the fashion of his ha

ich Ado About Nothing.

For there was never yet philospher

That could endure the toothache patiently.

(Ibid)

(Ibic

was not born u

JRO Object Summary

This appendix contains details of the Microsoft Jet and Replication Objects 2.6 Library

JRO Objects

Name	Description
Filter	A Filter that limits replication.
Filters	A collection of Filter objects.
JetEngine	The Jet Database Engine.
Replica	A copy of a replicated database.

The Filter Object

Properties of the Filter Object	Return Type	Description
FilterCriteria	String	The filter criteria, which allow a record to be replicated. Read-only.
FilterType	Filter TypeEnum	The type of the filter. Can be one of the FilterTypeEnum constants, as discussed in Appendix O. Read-only.
TableName	String	The table to which the filter applies. Read-only.

The Filters Collection

Methods of the Filters Collection	Return Type	Description
Append		Adds a new `Filter` object to the collection.
Delete		Removes a `Filter` object from the collection.
Refresh		Refreshes the collection from the design master.

Properties of the Filters Collection	Return Type	Description
Count	Integer	The number of `Filter` objects in the collection. Read-only.
Item	Filter	The default property, which allows indexing into the collection. Read-only.

The JetEngine Object

Methods of the JetEngine Object	Return Type	Description
CompactDatabase		Compacts the requested database.
RefreshCache		Forces the memory cache to write changes to the MDB file, and then refreshes the memory with data from the MDB file.

The Replica Object

Methods of the Replica Object	Return Type	Description
CreateReplica		Creates a new replica of the current, replicable database.
GetObject Replicability	Boolean	Identifies whether or not an object is local or replicable.
MakeReplicable		Make a database replicable.
PopulatePartial		Populates a partial replica with data from the full replica.
SetObject Replicability		Sets whether an object is local or replicable.
Synchronize		Synchronizes two replicable databases.

Properties of the Replica Object	Return Type	Description
Active Connection	Object	An ADO Connection object or string, to which the replica belongs.
Conflict Function	String	The name of the custom function to use for conflict resolution.
Conflict Tables	Recordset	A recordset that contains the tables and conflict tables for each table that had conflicts. Read-only.
DesignMasterId	Variant	The unique identifier of the design master in a replica set.
Priority	Integer	The relative priority of the replica, for use during conflict resolution. Read-only.
ReplicaId	Variant	The unique ID of the replica database in the replica set. Read-only.
ReplicaType	ReplicaType Enum	The type of replica. Can be one of the ReplicaTypeEnum constants, as discussed in Appendix O. Read-only.
RetentionPeriod	Integer	How many days replication histories are kept for.
Visibility	Visibility Enum	Indicates whether the replica is global, local, or anonymous. Can be one of the VisibilityEnum constants, as discussed in Appendix O. Read-only.

Collections of the Replica Object	Return Type	Description
Filters	Filters	A collection of Filter objects, which specify the criteria that records must match to be replicated. Read-only

Method Calls

Filters

```
Filters.Append(TableName As String, FilterType As FilterTypeEnum,
            FilterCriteria As String)
Filters.Delete(Index As Variant)
Filters.Refresh
```

JetEngine

```
JetEngine.CompactDatabase(SourceConnection As String, _
                       Destconnection As String)
JetEngine.RefreshCache(Connection As   )
```

Replica

```
Replica.CreateReplica(replicaName As String, _
                 description As String, _
                 [ReplicaType As ReplicaTypeEnum], _
                 [Visibility As VisibilityEnum], _
                 [Priority As Integer], _
                 [updatability As UpdatabilityEnum])
Boolean = Replica.GetObjectReplicability(objectName As String, _
                              objectType As String)
Replica.MakeReplicable([connectionString As String], _
                 [columnTracking As Boolean])
Replica.PopulatePartial(FullReplica As String)
Replica.SetObjectReplicability(objectName As String, _
                       objectType As String, _
                       replicability As Boolean)
Replica.Synchronize(target As String, syncType As SyncTypeEnum,_
                 [syncMode As SyncModeEnum])
```

I thank God I am as honest as any man living that is an old man and no honester th

Can counsel and speak comfort to th

Much Ado About Nothing.

Which they themselves not feel

He wears his faith but as the fashion of

As merry as the day

He hath indeed better bettered expectation

(Act i. Sc. i.).

He wears his faith but as the fashion of his hat,

(Ibid)

As merry as the day is long.

ch indeed better bettered expectation

(Act i. Sc. i.).

(Ibid)

Can counsel and speak comfort to that grief

Much Ado About Nothing.

Which they themselves not feel.

He wears his faith but as the fashion of his hat.

(Ibid)

(Ibid)

I was not born under

a rhyming planet

I was not born under a rhyming plan

For there was never yet

That could endure the to

merry as the day is long

(Sc.

Can counsel and speak comfort to that grief

Which they themselves not feel.

(Ibid)

He hath indeed better bettered expectation

I thank God I am as honest as any

living that is an old man and no honest

He wears his faith but as the fashion of his ha

(Ibi

ich Ado About Nothing.

For there was never yet philospher
That could endure the toothache patiently.

(Ibid)

was not born

JRO Constants

FilterTypeEnum

Name	Value	Description
jrFilterType Relationship	2	The filter is based upon a relationship.
jrFilterTypeTable	1	The filter is based upon a table. This is the default.

ReplicaTypeEnum

Name	Value	Description
jrRepTypeDesign Master	1	The replica is the design master.
jrRepTypeFull	2	The replica is a full replica.
jrRepTypeNot Replicable	0	The database is not replicable. This is the default.
jrRepTypePartial	3	The replica is a partial replica.

SyncModeEnum

Name	Value	Description
jrSyncModeDirect	2	Use direct synchronization.
jrSyncModeIndirect	1	Use indirect synchronization.
jrSyncModeInternet	3	Use Internet based synchronization.

SyncTypeEnum

Name	Value	Description
jrSyncTypeExport	1	Export changes to the target database.
jrSyncTypeImpExp	3	Import and export changes to and from the target database.
jrSyncTypeImport	2	Import databases from the target database.

UpdatabilityEnum

Name	Value	Description
jrRepUpdFull	0	The replica can be updated.
jrRepUpdReadOnly	2	The replica is read-only.

VisibilityEnum

Name	Value	Description
jrRepVisibilityAnon	4	The replica is anonymous.
jrRepVisibilityGlobal	1	The replica is global.
jrRepVisibilityLocal	2	The replica is local.

I thank God I am as honest as any man
living that is an old man and no honester than

Can counsel and speak comfort to that grief
Which they themselves not feel.

Much Ado About Nothing.

He wears his faith but as the fashion of his hat.

As merry as the day

He hath indeed better bettered expectation

(Act i. Sc. 1).

He wears his faith but as the fashion of his hat.

(Ibid)

As merry as the day is long.

indeed better bettered expectation

(Act i. Sc. 1).

(Ibid)

Much Ado About Nothing.

Can counsel and speak comfort to that grief

Which they themselves not feel.

He wears his faith but as the fashion of his hat.

(Ibid)

I was not born under

a rhyming plane

I was not born under a rhyming plane

(Sc. 2)

For there was never yet

That could endure the to

merry as the day is long

(Sc 2)

Can counsel and speak comfort to that grief

Which they themselves not feel.

(Ibid)

He hath indeed better bettered expectation

(Act i. Sc.

(Ibid)

I thank God I am as honest as any

living that is an old man and no honest

He wears his faith but as the fashion of his hat.

(Ibi

Much Ado About Nothing.

For there was never yet philospher
That could endure the toothache patiently.

(Ibid)

was not born u

ADO Error Codes

The following table lists the standard errors than might get returned from ADO operations.

Constant name	Number	Description
adErrBoundToCommand	3707	The application cannot change the `ActiveConnection` property of a `Recordset` object with a `Command` object as its source.
adErrCannotComplete	3732	The server cannot complete the operation.
adErrCantChange Connection	3748	The connection was refused because the requested connection has different characteristics from the one in use.
adErrCantChange Provider	3220	The supplied provider is different from the one in use.
adErrCantConvert Value	3724	Data cannot be converted for reasons other than an overflow or sign mismatch (such as truncation).
adErrCantCreate	3725	The data value cannot be set, either because the type was not known or because the provider has run out of resources.
adErrCatalogNotSet	3747	The requested operation requires a valid `ParentCatalog`.
adErrColumnNotOn ThisRow	3726	The Record does not contain the requested field.
adErrDataConversion	3421	The application is using a value of the wrong type for the current operation.

Constant name	Number	Description
adErrDataOverflow	3721	The data value is too large for the supplied field.
adErrDelResOutOf Scope	3738	The URL is outside the current Record's scope.
adErrDenyNot Supported	3750	Sharing restrictions are not supported by the provider.
adErrDenyTypeNot Suported	3751	The requested sharing restriction is not supported by the provider.
adErrFeatureNot Available	3251	The operation requested by the application is not supported by the provider.
adErrFieldsUpdate Failed	3749	An update to the Fields collection failed, or a Record or Recordset Update method call failed, due to a problem in one of the fields. The Status property will identify the reason.
adErrIllegal Operation	3219	The operation requested by the application is not allowed in this context.
adErrIntegrity Violation	3719	A data change caused a data integrity conflict.
adErrInTransaction	3246	The application cannot explicitly close a Connection object while in the middle of a transaction.
adErrInvalid Argument	3001	The application is using arguments that are of the wrong type, are out of acceptable range, or are in conflict with one another.
adErrInvalid Connection	3709	The application requested an operation on an object with a reference to a closed or invalid Connection object.
adErrInvalidParam Info	3708	The application has improperly defined a Parameter object.
adErrInvalid Transaction	3714	The coordinating transaction is invalid, or has not started.
adErrInvalidURL	3729	The supplied URL is invalid, and contains invalid characters.
adErrItemNotFound	3265	ADO could not find the object in the collection corresponding to the name or ordinal reference requested by the application.

Constant name	Number	Description
adErrNoCurrent Record	3021	Either BOF or EOF is True, or the current record has been deleted; the operation requested by the application requires a current record.
adErrNotReentrant	3710	Cannot perform this operation while an event is being processed.
adErrObjectClosed	3704	The operation requested by the application is not allowed if the object is closed.
adErrObjectIn Collection	3367	Can't append. The object is already in the collection.
adErrObjectNotSet	3420	The object referenced by the application no longer points to a valid object.
adErrObjectOpen	3705	The operation requested by the application is not allowed if the object is open.
adErrOpeningFile	3002	The requested file could not be opened.
adOperation Cancelled	3712	The user cancelled the operation, with a CancelBatch or CancelUpdate method call.
adErrOutOfSpace	3734	The provider cannot obtain enough space to complete the operation.
adErrPermission Denied	3720	The field cannot be written to because of insufficient permissions.
adErrProp Conflicting	3742	The action cannot be completed due to conflicting properties.
adErrPropInvalid Column	3739	The property references an invalid column.
adErrPropInvalid Option	3740	The property option supplied is invalid.
adErrPropInvalid Value	3741	The property value supplied is invalid.
adErrPropNotAll Settable	3743	The property values supplied cannot all be set.
adErrPropNotSet	3744	The property is not set.
adErrPropNot Settable	3745	The property is read-only.
adErrPropNot Supported	3746	The provider does not support this property.

Constant name	Number	Description
adErrProvider Failed	3000	The provider failed to perform the operation.
adErrProviderNot Found	3706	ADO could not find the specified provider.
adErrReadFile	3003	The supplied file could not be read.
adErrResourceExists	3731	The copy operation cannot complete, because a resource exists at the target location. To overwrite specify adCopyOverwrite.
adErrResourceLocked	3730	The requested resource is locked by another process.
adErrResourceOutOf Scope	3735	Either the source or destination URL is outside the scope of the current Record.
adErrSchema Violation	3722	The data values violate the schema (such as the data type or field constraint).
adErrSignMismatch	3723	Conversion failed due to the provider using an unsigned field, and the supplied value being signed.
adErrStill Connecting	3713	The provider is still connecting (during an asynchronous open).
adErrStilLExecuting	3711	The provider is still executing a previous command (during an asynchronous fetch).
adErrTreePermission Denied	3728	Insufficient privileges to access the tree or sub-tree.
adErrUnavailable	3736	The operation failed and the status is unavailable.
adErrUnsafe Operation	3716	You cannot access data on another domain due to a safety setting on this computer.
adErrUrlDoesNot Exists	3727	The source URL or the parent of the destination does not exist.
adErrURLNamedRow DoesNotExist	3737	The Record named by this URL does not exist.
adErrVolumeNot Found	3733	The storage device in the URL cannot be located.
adErrWriteFile	3004	The write to a file failed.
adWrnSecurityDialog	3717	For internal use only. Included for completeness.
adWrnSecurityDialog Header	3718	For internal use only. Included for completeness.

The following table lists the extended ADO errors and their descriptions:

Error Number	Description
-2147483647	Not implemented.
-2147483646	Ran out of memory.
-2147483645	One or more arguments are invalid.
-2147483644	No such interface supported.
-2147483643	Invalid pointer.
-2147483642	Invalid handle.
-2147483641	Operation aborted.
-2147483640	Unspecified error.
-2147483639	General access denied error.
-2147483638	The data necessary to complete this operation is not yet available.
-2147467263	Not implemented.
-2147467262	No such interface supported.
-2147467261	Invalid pointer.
-2147467260	Operation aborted.
-2147467259	Unspecified error.
-2147467258	Thread local storage failure.
-2147467257	Get shared memory allocator failure.
-2147467256	Get memory allocator failure.
-2147467255	Unable to initialize class cache.
-2147467254	Unable to initialize RPC services.
-2147467253	Cannot set thread local storage channel control.
-2147467252	Could not allocate thread local storage channel control.
-2147467251	The user supplied memory allocator is unacceptable.
-2147467250	The OLE service mutex already exists.
-2147467249	The OLE service file mapping already exists.
-2147467248	Unable to map view of file for OLE service.
-2147467247	Failure attempting to launch OLE service.
-2147467246	There was an attempt to call CoInitialize a second time while single threaded.
-2147467245	A Remote activation was necessary but was not allowed.
-2147467244	A Remote activation was necessary but the server name provided was invalid.
-2147467243	The class is configured to run as a security ID different from the caller.
-2147467242	Use of OLE1 services requiring DDE windows is disabled.

Error Number	Description
-2147467241	A RunAs specification must be <domain name>\<user name> or simply <user name>.
-2147467240	The server process could not be started. The pathname may be incorrect.
-2147467239	The server process could not be started as the configured identity. The pathname may be incorrect or unavailable.
-2147467238	The server process could not be started because the configured identity is incorrect. Check the username and password.
-2147467237	The client is not allowed to launch this server.
-2147467236	The service providing this server could not be started.
-2147467235	This computer was unable to communicate with the computer providing the server.
-2147467234	The server did not respond after being launched.
-2147467233	The registration information for this server is inconsistent or incomplete.
-2147467232	The registration information for this interface is inconsistent or incomplete.
-2147467231	The operation attempted is not supported.
-2147418113	Catastrophic failure.
-2147024891	General access denied error.
-2147024890	Invalid handle.
-2147024882	Ran out of memory.
-2147024809	One or more arguments are invalid.

Listed below are the OLE DB errors and, whilst they might not be relevant for some ADO work, they are included for completeness:

Error Number	Description
-2147217920	Invalid accessor.
-2147217919	Creating another row would have exceeded the total number of active rows supported by the rowset.
-2147217918	Unable to write with a read-only accessor.
-2147217917	Given values violate the database schema.
-2147217916	Invalid row handle.
-2147217915	An object was open.
-2147217914	Invalid chapter.
-2147217913	A literal value in the command could not be converted to the correct type due to a reason other than data overflow.
-2147217912	Invalid binding info.

Error Number	Description
-2147217911	Permission denied.
-2147217910	Specified column does not contain bookmarks or chapters.
-2147217909	Some cost limits were rejected.
-2147217908	No command has been set for the command object.
-2147217907	Unable to find a query plan within the given cost limit.
-2147217906	Invalid bookmark.
-2147217905	Invalid lock mode.
-2147217904	No value given for one or more required parameters.
-2147217903	Invalid column ID.
-2147217902	Invalid ratio.
-2147217901	Invalid value.
-2147217900	The command contained one or more errors.
-2147217899	The executing command cannot be cancelled.
-2147217898	The provider does not support the specified dialect.
-2147217897	A data source with the specified name already exists.
-2147217896	The rowset was built over a live data feed and cannot be restarted.
-2147217895	No key matching the described characteristics could be found within the current range.
-2147217894	Ownership of this tree has been given to the provider.
-2147217893	The provider is unable to determine identity for newly inserted rows.
-2147217892	No non-zero weights specified for any goals supported, so goal was rejected; current goal was not changed.
-2147217891	Requested conversion is not supported.
-2147217890	lRowsOffset would position you past either end of the rowset, regardless of the cRows value specified; cRowsObtained is 0.
-2147217889	Information was requested for a query, and the query was not set.
-2147217888	Provider called a method from IrowsetNotify in the consumer and the method has not yet returned.
-2147217887	Errors occurred.
-2147217886	A non-Null controlling IUnknown was specified and the object being created does not support aggregation.
-2147217885	A given HROW referred to a hard- or soft-deleted row.
-2147217884	The rowset does not support fetching backwards.
-2147217883	All HROWs must be released before new ones can be obtained.
-2147217882	One of the specified storage flags was not supported.

Error Number	Description
-2147217881	Invalid comparison operator.
-2147217880	The specified status flag was neither DBCOLUMNSTATUS_OK nor DBCOLUMNSTATUS_ISNULL.
-2147217879	The rowset cannot scroll backwards.
-2147217878	Invalid region handle.
-2147217877	The specified set of rows was not contiguous to or overlapping the rows in the specified watch region.
-2147217876	A transition from ALL* to MOVE* or EXTEND* was specified.
-2147217875	The specified region is not a proper subregion of the region identified by the given watch region handle.
-2147217874	The provider does not support multi-statement commands.
-2147217873	A specified value violated the integrity constraints for a column or table.
-2147217872	The given type name was unrecognized.
-2147217871	Execution aborted because a resource limit has been reached; no results have been returned.
-2147217870	Cannot clone a Command object whose command tree contains a rowset or rowsets.
-2147217869	Cannot represent the current tree as text.
-2147217868	The specified index already exists.
-2147217867	The specified index does not exist.
-2147217866	The specified index was in use.
-2147217865	The specified table does not exist.
-2147217864	The rowset was using optimistic concurrency and the value of a column has been changed since it was last read.
-2147217863	Errors were detected during the copy.
-2147217862	A specified precision was invalid.
-2147217861	A specified scale was invalid.
-2147217860	Invalid table ID.
-2147217859	A specified type was invalid.
-2147217858	A column ID occurred more than once in the specification.
-2147217857	The specified table already exists.
-2147217856	The specified table was in use.
-2147217855	The specified locale ID was not supported.
-2147217854	The specified record number is invalid.
-2147217853	Although the bookmark was validly formed, no row could be found to match it.
-2147217852	The value of a property was invalid.

Error Number	Description
-2147217851	The rowset was not chaptered.
-2147217850	Invalid accessor.
-2147217849	Invalid storage flags.
-2147217848	By-ref accessors are not supported by this provider.
-2147217847	Null accessors are not supported by this provider.
-2147217846	The command was not prepared.
-2147217845	The specified accessor was not a parameter accessor.
-2147217844	The given accessor was write-only.
-2147217843	Authentication failed.
-2147217842	The change was canceled during notification; no columns are changed.
-2147217841	The rowset was single-chaptered and the chapter was not released.
-2147217840	Invalid source handle.
-2147217839	The provider cannot derive parameter info and SetParameterInfo has not been called.
-2147217838	The data source object is already initialized.
-2147217837	The provider does not support this method.
-2147217836	The number of rows with pending changes has exceeded the set limit.
-2147217835	The specified column did not exist.
-2147217834	There are pending changes on a row with a reference count of zero.
-2147217833	A literal value in the command overflowed the range of the type of the associated column.
-2147217832	The supplied HRESULT was invalid.
-2147217831	The supplied LookupID was invalid.
-2147217830	The supplied DynamicErrorID was invalid.
-2147217829	Unable to get visible data for a newly inserted row that has not yet been updated.
-2147217828	Invalid conversion flag.
-2147217827	The given parameter name was unrecognized.
-2147217826	Multiple storage objects cannot be opened simultaneously.
-2147217825	Cannot open requested filter.
-2147217824	Cannot open requested order.
-2147217823	Invalid tuple.
-2147217822	Invalid coordinate.
-2147217821	Invalid axis for this dataset.
-2147217820	One or more cell ordinals are invalid.

Error Number	Description
-2147217819	Invalid `columnID`.
-2147217817	Command does not have a DBID.
-2147217816	DBID already exists.
-2147217815	Maximum number of sessions supported by the provider already created. Consumer must release one or more currently held sessions before obtaining a new session object.
-2147217814	Invalid trustee value.
-2147217813	Trustee is not for the current data source.
-2147217812	Trustee does not support memberships/collections.
-2147217811	Object is invalid or unknown to the provider.
-2147217810	No owner exists for the object.
-2147217809	Invalid access entry list.
-2147217808	Trustee supplied as owner is invalid or unknown to the provider.
-2147217807	Invalid permission in the access entry list.
-2147217806	Invalid index ID.
-2147217805	Initialization string does not conform to specification.
-2147217804	OLE DB root enumerator did not return any providers that matched any requested `SOURCES_TYPE`.
-2147217803	Initialization string specifies a provider that does not match the currently active provider.
-2147217802	Invalid DBID.
-2147217801	`ConstraintType` is invalid or not supported by the provider.
-2147217800	`ConstraintType` is not `DBCONSTRAINTTYPE_FOREIGNKEY` and `cForeignKeyColumns` is not zero.
-2147217799	Deferability is invalid or the value is not supported by the provider.
-2147217798	`MatchType` is invalid or the value is not supported by the provider.
-2147217782	`UpdateRule` or `DeleteRule` is invalid or the value is not supported by the provider.
-2147217781	`pConstraintID` does not exist in the data source.
-2147217780	Invalid `dwFlags`.
-2147217779	`rguidColumnType` points to a GUID that does not match the object type of this column, or this column was not set.
-2147217778	URL is out of scope.
-2147217776	Provider cannot drop the object.
-2147217775	No source row.

Error Number	Description
-2147217774	OLE DB object represented by this URL is locked by one or more other processes.
-2147217773	Client requested an object type that is valid only for a collection.
-2147217772	Caller requested write access to a read-only object.
-2147217771	Provider does not support asynchronous binding.
-2147217770	Provider cannot connect to server for this object.
-2147217769	Attempt to bind to the object timed out.
-2147217768	Provider cannot create an object at this URL because an object named by this URL already exists.
-2147217767	Constraint already exists.
-2147217766	Provider cannot create an object at this URL because the server is out of physical storage.
-2147217765	Unsafe operation was attempted in safe mode. Provider denied this operation.
265920	Fetching requested number of rows would have exceeded total number of active rows supported by the rowset.
265921	One or more column types are incompatible; conversion errors will occur during copying.
265922	Parameter type information has been overridden by caller.
265923	Skipped bookmark for deleted or non-member row.
265924	Errors found in validating tree.
265925	There are no more rowsets.
265926	Reached start or end of rowset or chapter.
265927	The provider re-executed the command.
265928	Variable data buffer full.
265929	There are no more results.
265930	Server cannot release or downgrade a lock until the end of the transaction.
265931	Specified weight was not supported or exceeded the supported limit and was set to 0 or the supported limit.
265932	Consumer is uninterested in receiving further notification calls for this operation.
265933	Input dialect was ignored and text was returned in different dialect.
265934	Consumer is uninterested in receiving further notification calls for this phase.
265935	Consumer is uninterested in receiving further notification calls for this reason.
265936	Operation is being processed asynchronously.

Error Number	Description
265937	In order to reposition to the start of the rowset, the provider had to re-execute the query; either the order of the columns changed or columns were added to or removed from the rowset.
265938	The method had some errors; errors have been returned in the error array.
265939	Invalid row handle.
265940	A given HROW referred to a hard-deleted row.
265941	The provider was unable to keep track of all the changes; the client must re-fetch the data associated with the watch region using another method.
265942	Execution stopped because a resource limit has been reached; results obtained so far have been returned but execution cannot be resumed.
265943	Method requested a singleton result but multiple rows are selected by the command or rowset. First row is returned.
265944	A lock was upgraded from the value specified.
265945	One or more properties were changed as allowed by provider.
265946	Errors occurred.
265947	A specified parameter was invalid.
265948	Updating this row caused more than one row to be updated in the data source.
265949	Row has no row-specific columns.

I thank God I am as honest as any man
living that is an old man and no honester th

Can counsel and speak comfort to th
Much Ado About Nothing.
which they themselves not feel

He wears his faith but as the fashion of

As merry as the day

He hath indeed better bettered expectation

(Act i. Sc. 1.)

He wears his faith but as the fashion of his hat.
(Ibid)

As merry as the day is long.

better bettered expectation

(Act i. Sc. 1.)

(Ibid)

Can counsel and speak comfort to that grief

Much Ado About Nothing.

Which they themselves not feel.

He wears his faith but as the fashion of his hat.
(Ibid)

I was not born under

I was not born under a rhyming plan
(sc.

a rhyming plane

For there was never yet

That could endure the t

merry as the day is long

(sc.

Can counsel and speak comfort to that grief

(Ibid)

Which they themselves not feel.

He hath indeed better bettered expectation

I thank God I am as honest as an

living that is an old man and no honest

He wears his faith but as the fashion of his ha

Much Ado About Nothing.

For there was never yet philospher
That could endure the toothache patiently.

(Ibid)

For there was never yet philospher
That could endure the toothache patiently.

I was not born u

Support, Errata, and P2P.Wrox.Com

One of the most irritating things about any programming book is when you find that bit of code you've just spent an hour typing simply doesn't work. You check it a hundred times to see if you've set it up correctly and then you notice the spelling mistake in the variable name on the book page. Of course, you can blame the authors for not taking enough care and testing the code, the editors for not doing their job properly, or the proofreaders for not being eagle-eyed enough, but this doesn't get around the fact that mistakes do happen.

We try hard to ensure no mistakes sneak out into the real world, but we can't promise that this book is 100% error free. What we can do is offer the next best thing by providing you with immediate support and feedback from experts who have worked on the book and try to ensure that future editions eliminate these gremlins. We also now commit to supporting you not just while you read the book, but once you start developing applications as well through our online forums where you can put your questions to the authors, reviewers, and fellow industry professionals.

In this appendix we'll look at how to:

- ❏ Enroll in the peer to peer forums at http://p2p.wrox.com
- ❏ Post and check for errata on our main site, http://www.wrox.com
- ❏ e-Mail technical support a query or feedback on our books in general

Between all three support procedures, you should get an answer to your problem in no time flat.

The Online Forums at P2P.Wrox.Com

As yet p2p.wrox.com does not support a list specifically for ADO users. However you can join other mailing lists such as VB or SQL for author and peer support. Our system provides **programmer to programmer™ support** on mailing lists, forums and newsgroups all in addition to our one-to-one email system, which we'll look at in a minute. Be confident that your query is not just being examined by a support professional, but by the many Wrox authors and other industry experts present on our mailing lists.

How to Enrol for Support

Just follow this four-step system:

1. Go to p2p.wrox.com in your favorite browser.
   Here you'll find any current announcements concerning P2P – new lists created, any removed and so on:

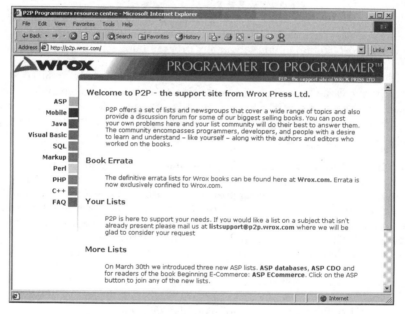

2. Click on the Visual Basic or SQL buttons in the left hand column.

3. Choose the list you want to access.

4. If you are not a member of the list, you can choose to either view the list without joining it or create an account in the list, by hitting the respective buttons.

5. If you wish to join, you'll be presented with a form in which you'll need to fill in your e-mail address, name and a password (of at least 4 characters). Choose how you would like to receive the messages from the list and then hit Save.

6. Congratulations. You're now a member of your chosen mailing list.

Why This System Offers the Best Support

You can choose to join the mailing lists or you can receive them as a weekly digest. If you don't have the time or facility to receive the mailing list, then you can search our online archives. You'll find the ability to search on specific subject areas or keywords. As these lists are moderated, you can be confident of finding good, accurate information quickly. Mails can be edited or moved by the moderator into the correct place, making this a most efficient resource. Junk and spam mail are deleted, and your own e-mail address is protected by the unique Lyris system from web-bots that can automatically hoover up newsgroup mailing list addresses. Any queries about joining or leaving lists or any query about the list should be sent to: danielw@wrox.com.

Checking the Errata Online at www.wrox.com

The following section will take you step by step through the process of posting errata to our web site to get that help. The sections that follow, therefore, are:

- ❏ Wrox Developer's Membership

- ❏ Finding a list of existing errata on the web site

- ❏ Adding your own erratum to the existing list

- ❏ What happens to your erratum once you've posted it (why doesn't it appear immediately)?

There is also a section covering how to e-mail a question for technical support. This comprises:

- ❏ What your e-mail should include

- ❏ What happens to your e-mail once it has been received by us

So that you only need view information relevant to yourself, we ask that you register as a Wrox Developer Member. This is a quick and easy process, which will save you time in the long-run. If you are already a member, just update membership to include this book.

Wrox Developer's Membership

To get your FREE Wrox Developer's Membership click on **Membership** in the top navigation bar of our home site – http://www.wrox.com. This is shown in the following screenshot:

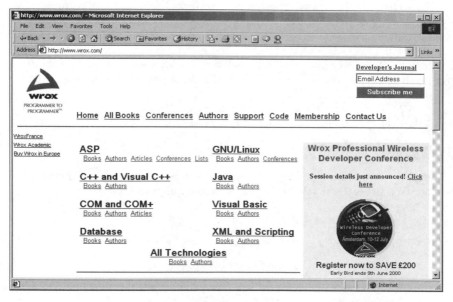

Then, on the next screen (not shown), click on **New User**. This will display a form. Fill in the details on the form and submit the details using the **Register** button at the bottom. Before you can say 'The best read books come in Wrox Red' you will get the following screen:

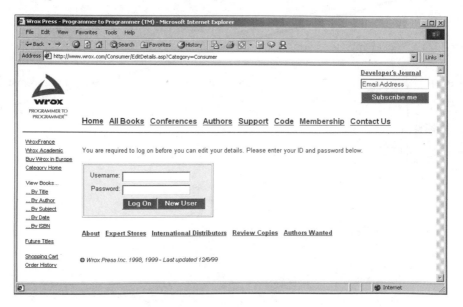

Type in your password once again and click Log On. The following page allows you to change your details if you need to, but now you're logged on, you have access to all the source code downloads and errata for the entire Wrox range of books.

Finding an Erratum on the Web Site

Before you send in a query, you might be able to save time by finding the answer to your problem on our web site – http://www.wrox.com.

Each book we publish has its own page and its own errata sheet. You can get to any book's page by clicking on Support from the top navigation bar.

Halfway down the main support page is a drop down box called Title Support. Simply scroll down the list until you see ADO 2.6 Programmer's Reference. Select it and then hit Errata.

This will take you to the errata page for the book. Select the criteria by which you want to view the errata, and click the Apply criteria button. This will provide you with links to specific errata. For an initial search, you are advised to view the errata by page numbers. If you have looked for an error previously, then you may wish to limit your search using dates. We update these pages daily to ensure that you have the latest information on bugs and errors.

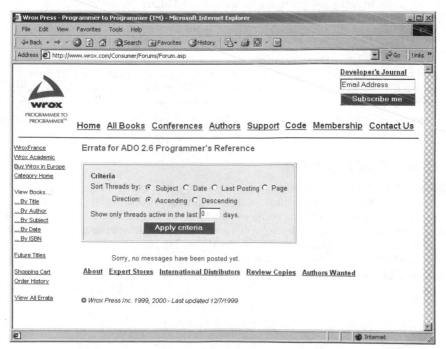

Add an Erratum : e-Mail Support

If you wish to point out an erratum to put up on the website or directly query a problem in the book page with an expert who knows the book in detail then e-mail support@wrox.com, with the title of the book and the last four numbers of the ISBN in the subject field of the e-mail. A typical e-mail should include the following things:

❑ The **name, last four digits of the ISBN** and **page number** of the problem in the Subject field;

❑ Your **name, contact info** and the **problem** in the body of the message.

We won't send you junk mail. We need the details to save your time and ours. If we need to replace a disk or CD we'll be able to get it to you straight away. When you send an e-mail it will go through the following chain of support:

Customer Support

Your message is delivered to one of our customer support staff who are the first people to read it. They have files on most frequently asked questions and will answer anything general immediately. They answer general questions about the book and the web site.

Editorial

Deeper queries are forwarded to the technical editor responsible for that book. They have experience with the programming language or particular product and are able to answer detailed technical questions on the subject. Once an issue has been resolved, the editor can post the errata to the web site.

The Authors

Finally, in the unlikely event that the editor can't answer your problem, they will forward the request to the author. We try to protect the author from any distractions from writing. However, we are quite happy to forward specific requests to them. All Wrox authors help with the support on their books. They'll mail the customer and the editor with their response, and again all readers should benefit.

What We Can't Answer

Obviously with an ever-growing range of books and an ever-changing technology base, there is an increasing volume of data requiring support. While we endeavor to answer all questions about the book, we can't answer bugs in your own programs that you've adapted from our code. So, while you might have loved the chapters on file handling, don't expect too much sympathy if you cripple your company with a routine which deletes the contents of your hard drive. But do tell us if you're especially pleased with the routine you developed with our help.

How to Tell Us Exactly What You Think

We understand that errors can destroy the enjoyment of a book and can cause many wasted and frustrated hours, so we seek to minimize the distress that they can cause.

You might just wish to tell us how much you liked or loathed the book in question. Or you might have ideas about how this whole process could be improved. In which, case you should e-mail feedback@wrox.com. You'll always find a sympathetic ear, no matter what the problem is. Above all you should remember that we do care about what you have to say and we will do our utmost to act upon it.

I thank God I am as honest as any man
living that is an old man and no honester than

Can counsel and speak comfort to the
Which they themselves not feel

Much Ado About Nothing.

He wears his faith but as the fashion of

As merry as the day

He hath indeed better bettered expectation

(Act i. Sc. i.).

He wears his faith but as the fashion of his hat.
(Ibid)

As merry as the day is long.

th indeed better bettered expectation

(Act i. Sc. i.). (Ibid)

Can counsel and speak comfort to that grief
Which they themselves not feel.

Much Ado About Nothing.

He wears his faith but as the fashion of his hat.
(Ibid)

I was not born under

a rhyming plane

I was not born under a rhyming pla

For there was never yet
That could endure the t

merry as the day is long (sc. 2)

Can counsel and speak comfort to that grie
Which they themselves not feel. (Ibid)

(Ibid)

He hath indeed better bettered expectati

I thank God I am as honest as an

living that is an old man and no hones

He wears his faith but as the fashion of his h
(Ib

Much Ado About Nothing.   For there was never yet philospher
That could endure the toothache patiently.
(Ibid)

I was not born u

Index

A Guide to the Index

The index is arranged hierarchically, in alphabetical order, with symbols preceding the letter A. Most second-level entries and many third-level entries also occur as first-level entries. This is to ensure that users will find the information they require however they choose to search for it.

F

G

GetChildren method
Record object, 177
GetChunk method
Field object, 211
getDocument method
XML DSO in IE4, 264
getError method
XML DSO in IE4, 264
GetObjectOwner method
Catalog object, 287
ObjectTypeEnum constants, 288
GetObjectReplicability method
Replica object, 342
GetPermissions method
Group object, 300
ObjectTypeEnum constants, 300
User object, 304
GetRows method
BookmarkEnum constants, 129
Recordset object, 129
getSchema method
XML DSO in IE4, 264
GetSchemaObject method
adObjectTypeEnum constants, 320
CubeDef object, 319
GetString method
Recordset object, 130
getXML method
XML DSO in IE4, 264
Globally Unique IDs
see GUIDs
grandchild aggregates, 370
grandchild recordsets, 361
Group object, ADOX, 44, 300, 576
collections, 303
GetPermissions method, 300
methods, 300
Name property, 302
ParentCatalog property, 303
properties, 302
Properties collection, 303
SetPermissions method, 301
Users collection, 303
Groups collection, ADOX, 44, 576
Append method, 308
Catalog object, 290
User object, 304
GUIDs
DesignMasterId property, 347
ReplicaId property, 347

H

Handler property
RDS data control, 248
HelpContext property
Error object, 203
HelpFile property
Error object, 203
hierarchical recordsets, 355
see also data shaping
reshaping of, 368
limitations, 370
usage, 370
Hierarchies collection, ADOMD, 603
Dimension object, 322
Hierarchy object, ADOMD, 316, 322, 603
collections, 323
Description property, 322
Levels collection, 323
Name property, 322
properties, 322, 629
Properties collection, 323
UniqueName property, 322
HTML
client HTML tags, 240
data binding, 279
formatting data, 281
single record data binding, 281
tabular data binding, 280

I

identity fields, 120
images, 227
ASP and, 235
databases and, 227
fields and, 230
passing images in smaller chunks, 231
retrieving images, 232
retrieving images in smaller chunks, 233
storing images, 230
parameters and, 227
passing images in smaller chunks, 229
retrieving images, 230
storing images, 228
retrieving into a stream, 234
Index object, ADOX, 43, 292, 577
Clustered property, 292
collections, 294
Columns collection, 294
IndexNulls property, 293
Name property, 293
PrimaryKey property, 293
properties, 292, 596
Properties collection, 294
Unique property, 293

I thank God I am as honest as any man living that is an old man and no honester than I.

Much Ado About Nothing.

He wears his faith but as the fashion of his hat.

As merry as the day

He hath indeed better bettered expectation

(Act i. Sc. i.).

He wears his faith but as the fashion of his hat.
(Ibid)

As merry as the day is long.

He hath indeed better bettered expectation

(Act i. Sc. i.).

(Ibid)

Much Ado About Nothing.

Can counsel and speak comfort to that grief
Which they themselves not feel.

He wears his faith but as the fashion of his hat.
(Ibid)

I was not born under a rhyming planet

For there was never yet philospher
That could endure the toothache patiently.

I was not born under a rhyming planet
(Sc. i.)

As merry as the day is long
(Sc 2)

Can counsel and speak comfort to that grief
Which they themselves not feel.
(Ibid)

He hath indeed better bettered expectation
(Ibid)

I thank God I am as honest as any man
living that is an old man and no honester than I.

He wears his faith but as the fashion of his hat.
(Ibid)

Much Ado About Nothing.

For there was never yet philospher
That could endure the toothache patiently.
(Ibid)

I was not born u